P9-DBI-557

WITHDRAWN

rijk

Yda Ea

W Napier

Lieut. General Sir W. Napier, Pinx.ᵗ — F. Halpin, Sculp.ᵗ

Redfield, Publisher, New York

946.06
N162h
v.1

HISTORY

OF THE

WAR IN THE PENINSULA

AND IN THE

SOUTH OF FRANCE

FROM A. D. 1807 TO A. D. 1814

BY MAJOR-GENERAL SIR W. F. P. NAPIER, K.C.B.

COLONEL TWENTY-SEVENTH REGIMENT,
MEMBER OF THE ROYAL SWEDISH ACADEMY OF
MILITARY SCIENCES

IN FIVE VOLUMES

WITH PORTRAITS AND PLANS

VOL. I.

REDFIELD

34 BEEKMAN STREET, NEW-YORK

1856

11-1-57 Richmond 230

CAT Sc 7 57

9-19-57 Richmond

PREFACE.

For six years the Peninsula was devastated by the war of independence. The blood of France, Germany, England, Portugal, and Spain was shed in the contest, and in each of those countries, authors, desirous of recording the sufferings, or celebrating the valor of their countrymen, have written largely touching that fierce struggle. It may, therefore, happen that some will demand, why I should again relate "a thrice-told tale?" I answer, that two men observing the same object, will describe it diversely, following the point of view from which either beholds it ; that which in the eyes of one is a fair prospect, to the other shall appear a barren waste, and yet neither may see aright! Wherefore, truth being the legitimate object of history, I hold it better that she should be sought for by many than by few, lest, for want of seekers, amongst the mists of prejudice, and the false lights of interest, she be lost altogether.

That much injustice has been done, and much justice left undone, by those authors who have hitherto written concerning this war, I can assert from personal knowledge of the facts. That I have been able to remedy this, without falling into similar errors, is more than I will venture to assume ; but I have endeavored to render as impartial an account of the campaigns in the Peninsula, as the feelings which must warp the judgment of a contemporary historian will permit. I was an eye-witness to many of the transactions that I relate ; and a wide acquaintance with military men has enabled me to consult distinguished officers, both French and English, and to correct my own recollections and opinions by their superior knowledge.

Thus assisted, and thus encouraged to undertake the work, I offer it to the world with the less fear, because it contains original documents, which will suffice to give it interest, although it should have no other merit. Many of those documents I owe to the liberality of Marshal Soult, who, disdaining national prejudices, with the confidence of a great mind, placed

121455

them at my disposal, without even a remark to check the freedom of my pen. I take this opportunity to declare that respect which I believe every British officer, who has had the honor to serve against him, feels for his military talents. By those talents the French cause in Spain was long upheld, and after the battle of Salamanca, if his counsel had been followed by the intrusive monarch, the fate of the war might have been changed.

Military operations are so dependent upon accidental circumstances, that, to justify censure, it should always be shown that an unsuccessful general has violated the received maxims and established principles of war. By that rule I have been guided, but, to preserve the narratives unbroken, my own observations are placed at the end of certain transactions of magnitude, where, their real source being known, they will pass for as much as they are worth, and no more: when they are not well supported by argument, I freely surrender them to the judgment of abler men.

Of those transactions, which, commencing with "the secret treaty of Fontainebleau," ended with "the Assembly of Notables" at Bayonne, little is known, except through the exculpatory and contradictory publications of men interested to conceal the truth; and to me it appears, that the passions of the present generation must subside, and the ultimate fate of Spain be known, before that part of the subject can be justly or usefully handled. I have, therefore, related no more of those political affairs than would suffice to introduce the military events that followed: neither have I treated largely of the disjointed and ineffectual operations of the native armies; for I cared not to swell my work with apocryphal matter, and neglected the thousand narrow winding currents of Spanish warfare, to follow that mighty English stream of battle, which burst the barriers of the Pyrenees, and left deep traces of its fury in the soil of France.

The Spaniards have boldly asserted, and the world has believed, that the deliverance of the Peninsula was the work of their hands; this assertion, so contrary to the truth, I combat; it is unjust to the fame of the British General, and injurious to the glory of the British arms. Military virtue is not the growth of a day, nor is there any nation so rich and populous, that, despising it, can rest secure. Now the imbecility of Charles IV., the vileness of Ferdinand, and the corruption of Godoy, were undoubtedly the proximate causes of the calamities that overwhelmed Spain; but the primary cause, that which belongs to history, was the despotism arising from the union of a superstitious court with a sanguinary priesthood; a despotism which, by repressing knowledge and contracting the public mind, sapped the foundation of all military as well as civil virtues, and prepared the way for invasion. No foreign potentate would have attempted to steal into the fortresses of a great kingdom, if the prying eyes, and the thousand clamorous tongues belonging to a free press, had been ready to expose his projects, and a well-disciplined army present to avenge the insult; but Spain, being destitute of both, was first circumvented by the wiles, and then ravaged by the arms of Napoleon. She was deceived and fettered because the public voice was stifled; she was scourged and torn because her military institutions were decayed.

From the moment that an English force took the field, the Spaniards ceased to act as principals in a contest carried on in the heart of their country, and involving their existence as an independent nation. They were self-sufficient, and their pride was wounded by insult; they were superstitious, and their religious feelings were roused to fanatic fury by an all-powerful clergy who feared to lose their own rich endowments; but after the first burst of indignation the cause of independence created little enthusiasm. Horrible barbarities were exercised on all French soldiers thrown by sickness or the fortune of war into the power of the invaded, and a dreadful spirit of personal hatred was kept alive by the exactions and severe retaliations of the invaders, yet no great and general exertion to drive the latter from the soil was made, at least none was sustained with steadfast courage in the field. Manifestoes, decrees, and lofty boasts, like a cloud of canvas covering a rotten hull, made a gallant appearance, when real strength and firmness were nowhere to be found. The Spanish insurrection presented indeed a strange spectacle. Patriotism was seen supporting a vile system of government; a popular assembly working for the restoration of a despotic monarch; the higher classes seeking a foreign master; the lower armed in the cause of bigotry and misrule. The upstart leaders, secretly abhorring freedom, though governing in her name, trembled at the democratic activity they had themselves excited; they called forth all the bad passions of the multitude, and repressed the patriotism that would regenerate as well as save. The country suffered the evils, without enjoying the benefits, of a revolution; for while tumults and assassinations terrified or disgusted the sensible part of the community, a corrupt administration of the resources extinguished patriotism, and neglect ruined the armies. The peasant-soldier, usually flying at the first onset, threw away his arms and returned to his home, or, attracted by the license of the *partidas*, joined the banners of men who, for the most part, originally robbers, were as oppressive to the people as the enemy; and these *guerilla* chiefs would, in their turn, have been as quickly exterminated, had not the French, pressed by Lord Wellington's battalions, been obliged to keep in large masses; this was the secret of Spanish constancy. It was the copious supplies from England, and the valor of the Anglo-Portuguese troops, that supported the war, and it was the gigantic vigor with which the Duke of Wellington resisted the fierceness of France, and sustained the weakness of three inefficient cabinets, that delivered the Peninsula. Faults he committed, and who in war has not ? yet shall his reputation stand upon a sure foundation, a simple majestic structure, that envy cannot undermine, nor the meretricious ornaments of party penegyric deform. The exploits of his army were great in themselves, great in their consequences, abounding with signal examples of heroic courage and devoted zeal. They should neither be disfigured nor forgotten, being worthy of more fame than the world has yet accorded them—worthy also of a better historian.

NOTICE.

Of the manuscript authorities consulted for this history, those marked with the letter S. the author owes to the kindness of Marshal Soult.

For the notes dictated by Napoleon, and the plans of campaign sketched out by King Joseph, he is indebted to his Grace the Duke of Wellington.

The returns of the French army were extracted from the original half-monthly statements presented by Marshal Berthier to the Emperor Napoleon.

Of the other authorities it is unnecessary to say more, than that the author had access to the original papers, with the exception of Dupont's Memoirs, of which a copy only was obtained.

LIST OF PLATES.

TABLE OF CONTENTS.

BOOK I.

CHAPTER I.

CHAPTER II.

CHAPTER III.

CHAPTER IV.

CHAPTER V.

CHAPTER VI.

CHAPTER VII.

CHAPTER VIII.

BOOK II.

CHAPTER I.

CHAPTER II.

CHAPTER III.

CHAPTER IV.

CHAPTER V.

CHAPTER VI.

BOOK II.

CHAPTER I.

CHAPTER II.

CHAPTER III.

BOOK IV.

CHAPTER I.

CHAPTER II.

CHAPTER III.

CHAPTER IV.

CHAPTER V.

CHAPTER VI.

BOOK V.

CHAPTER I.

BOOK VI.

CHAPTER I.

CHAPTER II.

CHAPTER III.

APPENDIX.

APPENDIX

HISTORY

OF THE

PENINSULAR WAR.

BOOK I.

CHAPTER I.

INTRODUCTION.

The hostility of the European aristocracy caused the enthusiasm of republican France to take a military direction, and forced that powerful nation into a course of policy which, however outrageous it might appear, was in reality one of necessity. Up to the treaty of Tilsit, the wars of France were essentially defensive,—for the bloody contest that wasted the continent so many years was not a struggle for pre-eminence between ambitious powers, not a dispute for some accession of territory, nor for the political ascendency of one or other nation, but a deadly conflict to determine whether aristocracy or democracy should predominate, whether equality or privilege should henceforth be the principle of European governments.

The French Revolution was pushed into existence before the hour of its natural birth. The power of the aristocratic principle was too vigorous, and too much identified with that of the monarchical principle, to be successfully resisted by a virtuous democratic effort, much less could it be overthrown by a democracy rioting in innocent blood, and menacing destruction to political and religious establishments the growth of centuries, somewhat decayed, indeed, yet scarcely showing their gray hairs. The first military events of the Revolution, the disaffection of Toulon and Lyons, the civil war of La Vendée, the feeble, although successful resistance made to the Duke of Brunswick's invasion, and the frequent and violent change of rulers whose fall none regretted, were all proofs that the French Revolution, intrinsically too feeble to sustain the physical and moral force pressing it down, was fast sinking, when the wonderful genius of Napoleon, baffling all reasonable calculation, raised and fixed it on the basis of victory, the only one capable of supporting the crude production.

Nevertheless that great man knew the cause he upheld was not sufficiently in unison with the feelings of the age, and his first care was to disarm, or neutralize, monarchical and sacerdotal enmity, by restoring a church establishment, and by becoming a monarch himself. Once a sovereign, his vigorous character, his pursuits, his talents, and the critical nature of the times, inevitably rendered him a despotic one; yet while he sacrificed political liberty, which to the great bulk of mankind has never been more than a pleasing sound, he cherished with the utmost care equality, a sensible good that produces increasing satisfaction as it descends in the scale of society. But this, the real principle of his government and secret of his popularity, made him the people's monarch, not the sovereign of the aristocracy, and hence Mr. Pitt called him " The child and the champion of democracy," a truth as evident as that Mr. Pitt and his successors were the children and the champions of aristocracy; hence, also, the privileged classes of Europe consistently transferred their natural and implacable hatred of the French Revolution to his person,—for they saw that in him innovation had found a protector, that he alone having given pre-eminence to a system so hateful to them, was really what he called himself, " The State."

The treaty of Tilsit, therefore, although it placed Napoleon in a commanding situation with regard to the potentates of Europe, unmasked the real nature of the war, and brought him and England, the respective champions of equality and privilege, into more direct contact; peace could not be between them while both were strong, and all that the French Emperor had hitherto gained only enabled him to choose his future field of battle.

When the catastrophe of Trafalgar forbade him to think of invading England, his fertile genius had conceived the plan of sapping her naval and commercial strength by depriving her of the markets for her manufactured goods—that is, he prohibited the reception of English wares in any part of the continent, and exacted from allies and dependants the most rigid compliance with his orders; but this " continental system," as it was called, became inoperative when French troops were not present to enforce his commands. It was thus in Portugal, where British influence was really paramount, although the terror inspired by the French arms seemed at times to render it doubtful. Fear is, however, momentary, while self-interest is lasting, and Portugal was but an unguarded province of England; from thence, and from Gibraltar, English goods freely passed into Spain. To check this traffic by force was not easy, and otherwise impossible.

Spain stood nearly in the same position with regard to France that Portugal did to England: a warm feeling of friendship for the enemy of Great Britain* was the natural consequence of the unjust seizure of the Spanish frigates in a time of peace. But although this rendered the French cause popular in Spain, and the court of Madrid was from weakness subservient to the French Emperor, nothing could induce the people to refrain from a profitable contraband trade; they would not pay that respect to the wishes of a foreign power which they refused to the regulations of their own government. Neither was the aristocratical enmity to Napoleon asleep in Spain. A proclamation issued by the Prince of Peace previous to the battle of Jena, although hastily recalled when the result of that conflict was known, sufficiently indicated the tenure upon which the friendship of the Spanish court was held.

This state of affairs drew the French Emperor's attention towards the Peninsula, and a chain of remarkable circumstances, which fixed it there, induced him to remove the reigning family and place his brother Joseph on the throne of Spain.† He thought that the people of that country, sick of an effete government, would be quiescent under such a change; and although it should prove otherwise, the confidence he reposed in his own fortune, unrivalled talents, and vast power, made him disregard the consequences, while the cravings of his military and political system, the danger to be apprehended from the vicinity of a Bourbon dynasty, and above all the temptations offered by a miraculous folly which outrun even his desires, urged him to a deed that, well accepted by the people of the Peninsula, would have proved beneficial, but, being enforced contrary to their wishes, was unhallowed either by justice or benevolence.

In an evil hour for his own greatness and the happiness of others, he commenced this fatal project. Founded in violence and executed with fraud, it spread desolation through the fairest portions of the Peninsula, was calamitous to France, destructive to himself; and the conflict between his hardy veterans and the vindictive race he insulted assumed a character of unmitigated ferocity disgraceful to human nature,—for the Spaniards did not fail to defend their

* Monsieur de Champagny's Report, 21st Oct., 1807.
† Napoleon in Las Casas, Vol. II. 4th part.

just cause with hereditary cruelty, while the French army struck a terrible balance of barbarous actions. Napoleon observed with surprise the unexpected energy of the people, and therefore bent his whole force to the attainment of his object, while England, coming to the assistance of the Peninsula, employed all her resources to frustrate his efforts. Thus the two leading nations of the world were brought into contact, at a moment when both were disturbed by angry passions, eager for great events, and possessed of surprising power.

The extent and population of the French Empire, including the Kingdom of Italy, the Confederation of the Rhine, the Swiss Cantons, the Duchy of Warsaw, and the dependent states of Holland and Naples, enabled Bonaparte, through the medium of the conscription, to array an army in number nearly equal to the great host that followed the Persian of old against Greece. Like that multitude, also, his troops were gathered from many nations, but they were trained in a Roman discipline, and ruled by a Carthaginian genius. Count Mathieu Dumas, in a work that, with unrivalled simplicity and elegance, tells the military story of the world for ten years, has shown how vigorous and well-contrived was the organization of Napoleon's army ; the French officers, accustomed to victory, were as bold and enterprising as the troops they led were hardy and resolute, and to this power on land the Emperor joined a formidable marine.* The ships of France were, indeed, chained in her harbors, but her naval strength was only rebuked, not destroyed. Inexhaustible resources for building, vast establishments, a coast line of many thousand miles, and, above all, the creative genius of Napoleon, were fast nursing up a navy, the efficiency of which the war then impending between Great Britain and the United States promised to aid.† Maritime commerce was certainly fainting in France,‡ but her internal and continental traffic was robust, her manufactures were rapidly improving, her debt small, her financial operations conducted on a prudent plan and with exact economy, the supplies were all raised within the year, without any great pressure from taxation, and from a sound metallic currency.§ Thus there seemed no reason to think that Napoleon could fail of bringing any war to a favorable termination. By a happy combination of vigor and flattery, of order, discipline, and moral excitement, admirably adapted to the genius of his people, he had created a power which appeared resistless, and in truth

---

* Exposé de l'Empire, 1807-8-9-13.
† Napoleon's Memoirs, Las Casas, 7th part. Lord Collingwood's letters
‡ Exposé 1808-9. Napoleon, in Las Casas, vol. ii. 4th part.
§ Ibid. 6th part.

would have been so if applied to only one great object at a time ; but this the ambition of the man, or rather the force of circumstances, did not permit.

On the other hand, England, omnipotent at sea, was little regarded as a military power. Her enormous debt was yearly increasing in an accelerated ratio, and this necessary consequence of anticipating the resources of the country and dealing in a factitious currency, was fast eating into the vital strength of the state : for although the merchants and great manufacturers were thriving from the accidental circumstances of the times, the laborers were suffering and degenerating in character; pauperism, and its sure attendant, crime, were spreading over the land, and the population was fast splitting into distinct classes,—the one rich and arbitrary, the other poor and discontented ; the former composed of those who profited, the latter of those who suffered by the war. Of Ireland it is unnecessary to speak ; her wrongs and her misery, peculiar and unparalleled, are too well known, and too little regarded, to call for remark.

This general comparative statement, so favorable to France, would, however, be a false criterion of the relative strength of the belligerents with regard to the approaching struggle in the Peninsula. A cause manifestly unjust is a heavy weight upon the operations of a general; it reconciles men to desertion—it sanctifies want of zeal, and is a pretext for cowardice—it renders hardships more irksome, dangers more obnoxious, and glory less satisfactory to the mind of the soldier. Now, the invasion of the Peninsula, whatever might have been its real origin, was an act of violence on the part of Napoleon repugnant to the feelings of mankind : the French armies were burdened with a sense of its iniquity, the British troops exhilarated by a contrary sentiment. All the continental nations had smarted under the sword of Napoleon, but, with the exception of Prussia, none were crushed ; a common feeling of humiliation, the hope of revenge, and the ready subsidies of England, were bonds of union among their governments stronger than the most solemn treaties. France could only calculate on their fears, England was secure in their self-love.

The hatred to what were called French principles was at this period in full activity. The privileged classes of every country hated Napoleon, because his genius had given stability to the institutions that grew out of the revolution, because his victories had baffled their calculations and shaken their hold of power. As the chief of revolutionary France, he was constrained to continue his career until the final accomplishment of her destiny,—and this necessity, overlooked by the great bulk of mankind, afforded plausible ground for imputing insatiable ambition to the French government and to the French nation, of which ample use was made. Rapacity, insolence, injustice, cruelty, even cowardice, were said to be inseparable from the character of a Frenchman; and, as if such vices were nowhere else to be found, it was more than insinuated that all the enemies of France were inherently virtuous and disinterested. Unhappily, history is but a record of crimes, and it is not wonderful that the arrogance of men, buoyed up by a spring-tide of military glory, should, as well among allies as among vanquished enemies, have produced sufficient disgust to insure a ready belief of any accusation, however false and absurd.

Napoleon was the contriver and the sole support of a political system that required time and victory to consolidate; he was the connecting link between the new interests of mankind, and what of the old were left in a state of vigor; he held them together strongly, but he was no favorite with either, and consequently in danger from both; his power, unsanctified by time, depended not less upon delicate management than upon vigorous exercise; he had to fix the foundations of, as well as to defend, an empire, and he may be said to have been rather peremptory than despotic; there were points of administration with which he durst not meddle even wisely, much less arbitrarily. Customs, prejudices, and the dregs of the revolutionary license interfered to render his policy complicated and difficult, but it was not so with his inveterate adversaries. The delusion of parliamentary representation enabled the English government safely to exercise an unlimited power over the persons and property of the nation, and, through the influence of an active and corrupt press, it exercised nearly the same power over the public mind. The commerce of England, penetrating, as it were, into every house on the face of the globe, supplied a thousand sources of intelligence; the spirit of traffic, which seldom acknowledges the ties of country, was universally on the side of Great Britain, and those twin curses, paper money and public credit—so truly described as "strength in the beginning, but weakness in the end"—were recklessly used by statesmen, whose policy regarded not the interests of posterity. Such were the adventitious causes of England's power, and her natural, legitimate resources were many and great. If any credit is to be given to the census, the increasing population of the United Kingdom amounted at this period to nearly twenty millions, and France reckoned but twenty-seven millions when Frederick the Great declared that, if he were her king, "not a gun should be fired in Europe without his leave."

The French army was undoubtedly very formidable from numbers, discipline, skill, and bravery; but contrary to the general opinion, the British army was inferior to it in none of these points save the first, and in discipline it was superior, because a national army will always bear a sterner code than a mixed force will suffer. Amongst the latter, military crimes may be punished, but moral crimes can hardly be repressed; men will submit to death for a breach of great regulations which they know by experience to be useful, but the constant restraint of petty, though wholesome rules, they will escape from by desertion, or resist by mutiny, when the ties of custom and country are removed; for the disgrace of bad conduct attaches not to them, but to the nation under whose colors they serve. Great indeed is that genius that can keep men of different nations firm to their colors, and preserve a rigid discipline at the same time. Napoleon's military system was, from this cause, inferior to the British, which, if it be purely administered, combines the solidity of the Germans with the rapidity of the French, excluding the mechanical dulness of the one, and the dangerous vivacity of the other; yet, before the campaign of the Peninsula had proved its excellence in every branch of war, the English army was absurdly under-rated in foreign countries, and absolutely despised in its own. It was reasonable to suppose that it did not possess that facility of moving in large bodies which long practice had given to the French, but the individual soldier was most falsely stigmatized as deficient in intelligence and activity, the officers ridiculed, and the idea that a British could cope with a French army, even for a single campaign, considered chimerical.

The English are a people very subject to receive, and to cherish false impressions; proud of their credulity as if it were a virtue, the majority will adopt any fallacy, and cling to it with a tenacity proportioned to its grossness. Thus an ignorant contempt for the British soldiery had been long entertained, before the ill-success of the expeditions in 1794 and 1799 appeared to justify the general prejudice. The true cause of those failures was not traced, and the excellent discipline afterwards introduced and perfected by the Duke of York was despised. England, both at home and abroad, was in 1808 scorned as a military power, when she possessed, without a frontier to swallow up large armies in expensive fortresses, at least two hundred thousand of the best equipped and best disciplined soldiers in the universe,* together with an immense recruiting establishment; and, through the medium of the militia, the power of drawing upon the population without limit. It is true that of this number many were necessarily employed in the defence of the colonies, but enough remained to compose a disposable force greater than that with which Napoleon won the battle of

* See Abstract of the military force of Great Britain in 1808

Austerlitz, and double that with which he conquered Italy.   In all the materials of war the superior ingenuity and skill of the English mechanics were visible, and that intellectual power which distinguishes Great Britain amongst the nations in science, arts, and literature, was not wanting to her generals in the hour of danger.

CHAPTER II.

Dissensions in the Spanish court—Secret treaty and convention of Fontainebleau —Junot's army enters Spain—Dupont's and Moncey's corps enter Spain—Duhesme's corps enters Catalonia—Insurrection of Aranjuez and Madrid—Charles the Fourth abdicates—Ferdinand proclaimed King—Murat marches to Madrid —Refuses to recognize Ferdinand as King—The sword of Francis the First delivered to the French General—Savary arrives at Madrid—Ferdinand goes to Bayonne—The fortresses of St. Sebastian, Figueras, Pampeluna, and Barcelona, treacherously seized by the French—Riot at Toledo 23d of April, Tumult at Madrid 2d May—Charles the Fourth abdicates a second time in favor of Napoleon—Assembly of the Notables at Bayonne—Joseph Bonaparte declared King of Spain—Arrives at Madrid.

For many years antecedent to the French invasion, the royal family of Spain were distracted with domestic quarrels; the son's hand was against his mother, the father's against his son, and the court was a scene of continual broils, under cover of which artful men, as is usual in such cases, pushed their own interest forward, while they seemed to act only for the sake of the party whose cause they espoused.   Charles IV. attributed this unhappy state of his house to the intrigues of his sister-in-law, the Queen of the Two Sicilies;* he himself, a weak and inefficient old man, was governed by his wife, and she again by Don Manuel Godoy,† of whose person, it is said, she was enamored even to folly.   From the rank of a simple gentleman of the royal guards, this person had been raised to the highest dignities, and the title of Prince of the Peace was conferred upon him whose name must be for ever connected with one of the bloodiest wars that fill the page of history.

Ferdinand, Prince of the Asturias, hated this favorite, and the miserable death of his young wife, his own youth, and apparently forlorn condition, created such an interest in his favor, that the people partook of his feelings; thus the disunion of the royal family, extending its effects beyond the precincts of the court, involved the nation in ruin.   Those who know how Spaniards hate

---

* Nellerto. The Anagram of Llorente.
† Vide Doblado's Letters.

will comprehend why Godoy, who, though sensual, was a mild, good-natured man, has been so overloaded with imprecations, as if he, and he alone, had been the cause of the disasters in Spain. It was not so. The canon, Escoíquiz, a subtle politician, who appears to have been the chief of Ferdinand's party,* finding the influence of the Prince of the Peace too strong, looked for support in a powerful quarter, and under his tuition, Ferdinand wrote upon the 11th of October, 1807, to the Emperor Napoleon.† In this letter he complained of the influence which bad men had obtained over his father, prayed for the interference of the "hero destined by Providence," so ran the text, "to save Europe and to support thrones;" asked an alliance by marriage with the Bonaparte family, and finally desired that his communication might be kept secret from his father, lest it should be taken as a proof of disrespect. He received no answer, and fresh matter of quarrel being found by his enemies at home, he was placed in arrest, and upon the 29th of October, Charles denounced him to the Emperor as guilty of treason, and of having projected the assassination of his own mother. Napoleon caught eagerly at this pretext for interfering in the domestic policy of Spain,—and thus the honor and independence of a great people were placed in jeopardy, by the squabbles of two of the most worthless persons.

Some short time before this, Godoy, either instigated by an ambition to found a dynasty, or fearing that the death of the King would expose him to the vengeance of Ferdinand, had made proposals to the French court to concert a plan for the conquest and division of Portugal, promising the assistance of Spain, on condition that a principality for himself should be set apart from the spoil. Such is the turn given by Napoleon to this affair. But the article which provided an indemnification for the King of Etruria, a minor, who had just been obliged to surrender his Italian dominions to France, renders it doubtful if the first offer came from Godoy, and Napoleon eagerly adopted the project if he did not propose it. The advantages were all on his side. Under the pretext of supporting his army in Portugal, he might fill Spain with his troops; the dispute between the father and the son, now referred to his arbitration, placed the golden apples within his reach, and he resolved to gather the fruit if he had not planted the tree.

A secret treaty was immediately concluded at Fontainebleau, between Marshal Duroc on the part of France, and Eugenio Izquerdo on the part of Spain. This treaty, together with a convention dependent on it, was signed the 27th, and ratified by Napoleon on

* Napoleon in Las Casas.
† Nellerto.

the 29th of October, the contracting parties agreeing on the following conditions:

The house of Braganza to be driven forth of Portugal, and that kingdom divided into three portions. The province of Entre Minho e Duero, including the town of Oporto, to be called the kingdom of North Lusitania, and given as an indemnification to the dispossessed sovereign of Etruria.

The Alemtejo and the Algarves to be erected into a principality for Godoy, who, taking the title of Prince of the Algarves, was still to be in some respects dependent upon the Spanish crown.

The central provinces of Estremadura, Beira, and the Tras os Montes, together with the town of Lisbon, to be held in deposit until a general peace, and then to be exchanged under certain conditions for English conquests.

The ultramarine dominions of the exiled family to be equally divided between the contracting parties, and in three years at the longest, the King of Spain to be gratified with the title of Emperor of the two Americas. Thus much for the treaty. The terms of the convention were:

France to employ 25,000 infantry and 3,000 cavalry. Spain 24,000 infantry, 30 guns, and 3,000 cavalry.

The French contingent to be joined at Alcantara by the Spanish cavalry, artillery, and one third of the infantry, and from thence to march to Lisbon. Of the remaining Spanish infantry, 10,000 were to take possession of the Entre Minho e Duero and Oporto, and 6,000 were to invade Estremadura and the Algarves. In the mean time a reserve of 40,000 men was to be assembled at Bayonne, ready to take the field by the 20th of November, if England should interfere, or the Portuguese people resist.

If the King of Spain or any of his family joined the troops, the chief command to be vested in the person so joining, but, with that exception, the French general to be obeyed whenever the armies of the two nations came into contact, and during the march through Spain, the French soldiers were to be fed by that country, and paid by their own government.

The revenues of the conquered provinces to be administered by the general actually in possession, and for the benefit of the nation in whose name the province was held.

Although it is evident that this treaty and convention favored Napoleon's ulterior operations in Spain, by enabling him to mask his views, and introduce large bodies of men into that country without creating much suspicion, it does not follow, as some authors have asserted, that they were contrived by the Emperor for the sole purpose of rendering the Spanish royal family odious to the world, and by this far-fetched expedient, to prevent other nations from taking an interest in their fate, when he should find it convenient to apply the same measure of injustice to his associate, that they had accorded to the family of Braganza. To say nothing of the weakness of such a policy, founded, as it must be, on the error that governments acknowledge the dictates of justice at the expense of their supposed interests, it must be observed that Portugal was intrinsically a great object. History does not speak of the time when the inhabitants of that country were deficient in spirit; the natural obstacles to an invasion had more than once frustrated the efforts of large armies, and the long line of communication between Bayonne and the Portuguese frontier, could only be supported by Spanish co-operation. Add to this, the facility with which England could, and the probability that she would, succor her ancient ally, and the reasonable conclusion is, that Napoleon's first intentions were in accordance with the literal meaning of the treaty of Fontainebleau, his subsequent proceedings being the result of new projects, conceived as the wondrous imbecility of the Spanish Bourbons became manifest.* Again, the convention provided for the organization of a large Spanish force, to be stationed in the north and south of Portugal, that is, in precisely the two places from whence they could most readily march to the assistance of their country, if it was invaded. In fact the division of the Marquis of Solano in the south, and that of General Taranco in the north of Portugal, did, when the Spanish insurrection broke out, (Nov. 1807,) form the strength of the Andalusian and Gallician armies, the former of which gained the victory at Baylen, while the latter contended for it, although ineffectually, at Rio Seco.

The French force, destined to invade Portugal, was already assembled at Bayonne, under the title of the "First army of the Garonne," and actually entered Spain before the treaty was signed. It was commanded by General Junot, a young man of a bold, ambitious disposition, but of greater reputation for military talent than he was able to support; and his soldiers, principally conscripts, were ill fitted to endure the hardships which awaited them. At first by easy marches, and in small divisions, he led his troops through Spain, but the inhabitants, either from a latent fear of what was to follow, or from a dislike of foreigners common to all secluded people, were not friendly.† When the head of the columns reached Salamanca, the General halted, intending to complete the organization of his troops in that rich country, and there to await the most favorable moment for penetrating the sterile frontier which guarded

* Voice from St. Helena, vol. ii.
† Thiebault, Exp. du Portugal.

his destined prey; but political events marched faster than his calculations, and fresh instructions from the Emperor prescribed an immediate advance upon Lisbon; Junot obeyed, and the family of Braganza, at his approach, fled to the Brazils. The series of interesting transactions which attended this invasion will be treated of hereafter; at present, I must return to Spain, now bending to the first gusts of that hurricane, which soon swept over her with destructive violence.

The accusation of treason and intended parricide preferred by Charles IV. against his son Ferdinand, (Dec. 1807,) gave rise to some judicial proceedings, which ended in the submission of the Prince, who, being absolved of the imputed crime, wrote a letter to his father and mother, acknowledging his own fault, but accusing the persons in his confidence of being the instigators of deeds which he himself abhorred.* The intrigues of his advisers, however, continued, and the plans of Napoleon advanced as a necessary consequence of the divisions in the Spanish court.

By the terms of the convention of Fontainebleau, forty thousand men were to be held in reserve at Bayonne; but a greater number were assembled on different points of the frontier, and in the course of December, two corps had entered the Spanish territory, and were quartered in Vittoria, Miranda, Briviesca, and the neighborhood. The one, commanded by General Dupont, was called the second army of observation of the "Gironde." The other, commanded by Marshal Moncey, took the title of the army of observation of the "Côte d'Ocean." In the gross, they amounted to fifty-three thousand men, of which above forty thousand were fit for duty;† and in the course of the month of December, Dupont advanced to Valladolid, while a reinforcement for Junot, four thousand seven hundred in number, took up their quarters at Salamanca. It thus appeared as if the French troops were quietly following the natural line of communication between France and Portugal; but in reality, Dupont and Moncey's positions cut off the capital from all intercourse with the northern provinces, and secured the direct road from Bayonne to Madrid.‡ Small divisions under different pretexts continually reinforced these two bodies, and through the Eastern Pyrenees twelve thousand men, commanded by General Duhesme, penetrated into Catalonia, and established themselves in Barcelona.

In the mean time the dispute betwen the King (March, 1808)

* Nellerto. Historia de la Guerra contra Nap.

† Return of the French army, Appendix. Journal of Dupont's Operations, MSS.

‡ Notes of Napoleon, found in the portfolio of King Joseph at the battle of Vittoria.

and his son, or rather between the Prince of the Peace and the advisers of Ferdinand, was brought to a crisis by insurrections at Aranjuez and Madrid, which took place upon the 17th, 18th, and 19th of March, 1808. The old King, deceived by intrigues, or frightened at the difficulties which surrounded him, had determined, as it is supposed by some, to quit Spain, and take refuge in his American dominions, and preparations were made for a flight to Seville, when the Prince's grooms commenced a tumult, in which the populace of Aranjuez soon joined, and were only pacified by the assurance that no journey was in contemplation.

Upon the 18th, the people of Madrid, following the example of Aranjuez, sacked the house of the obnoxious Manuel Godoy, and upon the 19th, the riots having recommenced at Aranjuez, that minister secreted himself; but his retreat being discovered, he was maltreated, and on the point of being killed, when the soldiers of the royal guard rescued him. Charles IV., terrified by the violent proceedings of his subjects, had abdicated the day before, and this event being proclaimed at Madrid on the 20th, Ferdinand was declared King, to the great joy of the nation at large: little did the people know what they rejoiced at, and time has since taught them that the fable of the frogs demanding a monarch had its meaning.

During these transactions (March, 1808) Murat, Grand Duke of Berg, who had taken the command of all the French troops in Spain, quitted his quarters at Aranda de Duero, passed the Somosierra, and entered Madrid the 23d, with Moncey's corps and a fine body of cavalry; Dupont at the same time, deviating from the road to Portugal, crossed the Duero, and occupied Segovia, the Escurial, and Aranjuez. Ferdinand, who arrived at Madrid on the 24th, was not recognized by Murat as King; nevertheless, at the demand of his powerful guest, he delivered to him the sword of Francis I. with much ceremony. Meanwhile Charles protested to Murat that his abdication had been forced, and also wrote to Napoleon in the same strain. This state of affairs being unexpected by the Emperor, he sent General Savary to conduct his plans, which appear to have been considerably deranged by the vehemence of the people, and the precipitation with which Murat had seized the capital.* But previous to Savary's arrival, Don Carlos, the brother of Ferdinand, departed from Madrid, hoping to meet the Emperor Napoleon, whose presence in that city was confidently expected; and upon the 10th of April, Ferdinand, having first appointed a supreme junta, of which his uncle, Don Antonio, was named president and Murat a member, commenced

* Napoleon in Las Casas.

his own remarkable journey to Bayonne. The true causes of this measure have not yet been developed; perhaps, when they shall be known, some petty personal intrigue may be found to have had a greater influence than the grand machinations attributed to Napoleon, who could not have anticipated, much less have calculated a great political scheme upon such a surprising example of weakness.

The people everywhere manifested their anger at this journey; in Vittoria they cut the traces of Ferdinand's carriage, and at different times several gallant men offered, at the risk of their lives, to carry him off by sea, in defiance of the French troops quartered along the road. Unmoved by their entreaties and zeal, and regardless of the warning contained in a letter that he received at this period from Napoleon, (who, withholding the title of majesty, sharply reproved him for his past conduct, and scarcely expressed a wish to meet him,) Ferdinand continued his progress, and, on the 20th of April, 1808, found himself a prisoner in Bayonne. In the mean time, Charles, under the protection of Murat, resumed his authority, obtained the liberty of Godoy, and quitting Spain, also threw himself, his cause and kingdom, into the Emperor's hands.

These events were in themselves quite enough to urge a more cautious people than the Spaniards into action; but other measures had been pursued, which proved beyond the possibility of a doubt, that the country was destined to be the spoil of the French. The troops of that nation had been admitted, without reserve or precaution, into the different fortresses upon the Spanish frontier, and, taking advantage of this hospitality to forward the views of their chief, they got possession, by various artifices, of the citadels of St. Sebastian in Guipuscoa, of Pampeluna in Navarre, and of the forts of Figueras and Monjuik, and the citadel of Barcelona, in Catalonia. Thus, under the pretence of mediating between the father and the son, in a time of profound peace, a foreign force was suddenly established in the capital, on the communications, and in the principal frontier fortresses; its chief was admitted to a share of the government, and a fiery, proud, and jealous nation was laid prostrate at the feet of a stranger, without a blow being struck, without one warning voice being raised, without a suspicion being excited in sufficient time to guard against those acts upon which all were gazing with stupid amazement.

It is idle to attribute this surprising event to the subtlety of Napoleon's policy, to the depth of his deceit, or to the treachery of Godoy; such a fatal calamity could only be the result of bad government, and the consequent degradation of public feeling. It matters but little to those who wish to derive a lesson from experience, whether it be a Godoy or a Savary that strikes the last bargain of corruption, the silly father or the rebellious son that signs the final act of degradation and infamy. Fortunately, it is easier to oppress the people of all countries, than to destroy their generous feelings; when all patriotism is lost among the upper classes, it may still be found among the lower; in the Peninsula it was not found, but started into life with a fervor and energy that ennobled even the wild and savage form in which it appeared; nor was it the less admirable that it burst forth attended by many evils; the good feeling displayed was the people's own, their cruelty, folly, and perverseness were the effects of a long course of misgovernment.

There are many reasons why Napoleon should have meddled with the interior affairs of Spain; there seems to be no good one for his manner of doing it. The Spanish Bourbons could never have been sincere friends to France while Bonaparte held the sceptre, and the moment that the fear of his power ceased to operate, it was quite certain that their apparent friendship would change to active hostility; the proclamation issued by the Spanish cabinet just before the battle of Jena was evidence of this fact. But if the Bourbons were Napoleon's enemies, it did not follow that the people sympathized with their rulers; his great error was that he looked only to the court, and treated the nation with contempt. Had he, before he openly meddled in their affairs, brought the people into hostile contact with their government,—and how many points would not such a government have offered!—instead of appearing as the treacherous arbitrator in a domestic quarrel, he would have been hailed as the deliverer of a great people.

The journey of Ferdinand, the liberation of Godoy, the flight of Charles, the appointing Murat to be a member of the governing junta, and the movements of the French troops who were advancing from all parts towards Madrid, aroused the indignation of the nation, and tumults and assassinations had taken place in various parts; at Toledo, a serious riot occurred on the 23d of April, the peasants joined the inhabitants of the town, and it was only by the advance of a division of infantry and some cavalry of Dupont's corps, then quartered at Aranjuez, that order was restored.[*] The agitation of the public mind, however, increased; the French troops were all young men, or rather boys, taken from the last conscription, and disciplined after they had entered Spain; their youth and apparent feebleness excited the contempt of the Spaniards, who pride themselves much upon individual prowess, and the swelling indignation at last broke out.

* Journal of Dupont's Operations, MSS.

Upon the 2d of May, a carriage being prepared, as the people supposed, to convey Don Antonio, the uncle of Ferdinand, to France, a crowd collected about it; their language indicated a determination not to permit the last of the royal family to be spirited away, the traces of the carriage were cut, and loud imprecations against the French burst forth on every side; at that moment Colonel La Grange, aide-de-camp to Murat, appeared—he was assailed and maltreated, and in an instant the whole city was in commotion. The French soldiers, expecting no violence, were killed in every street; about four hundred fell, and the hospital was attacked, but the attendants and sick men defended themselves; and meanwhile the alarm having spread to the camp outside the city, the French cavalry galloped in to the assistance of their countrymen by the gate of Alcala, while General Lanfranc, with three thousand infantry, descending from the heights on the northwest quarter, entered the Calle Ancha de Bernardo. As he crossed the end of the street Maravelles, Daois and Velarde, two Spanish officers who were in a state of great excitement, discharged a cannon at the passing troops, and were immediately attacked and killed by some voltigeurs; the column, however, continued its march, releasing, as it advanced, several superior officers, who were in a manner besieged by the populace. The cavalry at the other end of the town, treating the affair as a tumult, and not as an action, made some hundred prisoners, and some men were killed or maimed by the horses; but Marshal Moncey, General Harispe, and Gonzalvo O'Farril restored order.* Nevertheless, after nightfall, the peasantry of the neighborhood, who were armed and in considerable numbers, beset the city gates, and the French guards, firing upon them, killed twenty or thirty, and wounded more.

In the first moment of irritation, Murat ordered all the prisoners to be tried by a military commission, which condemned them to death; but the municipality interfering, represented to that prince the extreme cruelty of visiting this angry ebullition of an injured and insulted people with such severity, whereupon, admitting the weight of their arguments, he forbade any executions on the sentence. Yet it is said that General Grouchy, in whose immediate power the prisoners remained, after exclaiming that his own life had been attempted, that the blood of the French soldiers was not to be spilt with impunity, and that the prisoners, having been condemned by a council of war, ought and should be executed, proceeded to shoot them in the Prado. Forty were thus slain before Murat could cause his orders to be effectually obeyed. The next day some of the Spanish authorities having discovered that

* Memoir of Azanza and O'Farril.

a colonel commanding the imperial guards still retained a number of prisoners in the barracks, applied to have them also released. Murat consented, but it is said by some, although denied by others of greater authority, that the colonel getting intelligence of what was passing, and being enraged at the loss of so many choice soldiers, put forty-five of his captives to death before the order arrived to stay his bloody proceedings.*

Such were nearly the circumstances that attended this celebrated tumult, in which the wild cry of Spanish warfare was first heard; and as many authors, adopting without hesitation all the reports of the day, have represented it, sometimes as a wanton and extensive massacre on the part of the French, sometimes as a barbarous political stroke to impress a dread of their power, I think it necessary to remark—First, that it was commenced by the Spaniards; their fiery tempers, the irritation produced by passing events, and the habits of violence which they had acquired in their late successful insurrection against Godoy, rendered an explosion inevitable. Second, that if the French had secretly stimulated this disposition, and had resolved in cold blood to make a terrible example, they would have prepared some check on the Spanish soldiers of the garrison; they would not have left their own hospital unguarded, still less have arranged the plan so that their loss should far exceed that of the Spaniards; and surely nothing would have induced them to relinquish the profit of such policy after having suffered all the injury! Yet Marshal Moncey and General Harispe were actively engaged in restoring order; and it is certain that, including the peasants shot outside the gates, and the executions afterwards, the whole number of Spaniards slain did not amount to one hundred and twenty persons, while several hundred French fell.† Of the imperial guards seventy men were wounded, and this fact alone would suffice to prove that there was no premeditation on the part of Murat;‡ for if he was base enough to sacrifice his own men with such unconcern, he would not have exposed the select soldiers of the French empire in preference to the conscripts who abounded in his army.

The affair itself was certainly accidental, and not very bloody for the patriots, but policy induced both sides to attribute secret motives, and to exaggerate the slaughter. The Spaniards in the provinces, impressed with an opinion of French atrocity, were thereby excited to insurrection on the one hand; and, on the other, the French, well aware that such an impression could not be effaced

---

* See Gen. Harispe's observations at the end of this work.
† Manifesto of the Council of Castile, page 28.
‡ Surgical Campaigns of Baron Larrey.

by an accurate relation of what did happen, seized the occasion to convey a terrible idea of their own power and severity. It is the part of history to reduce such amplifications. But it is impossible to remain unmoved in recording the gallantry and devotion of a populace that could thus dare to assail the force commanded by Murat, rather than abandon one of their princes; such, however, was the character of the Spaniards throughout this war, they were prone to sudden and rash actions, and though weak in military execution, fierce and confident individually, and they had always an intuitive perception of what was great and noble.

The commotion of the 2d of May was the forerunner of insurrections in every part of Spain, few of which were so honorable to the actors as that of Madrid. Unprincipled villains hailed the opportunity of directing the passions of the multitude, and under the mask of patriotism, turned the unthinking fury of the people against whomever it pleased them to rob or to destroy. Pillage, massacres, assassinations, cruelties of the most revolting kind, were everywhere perpetrated, and the intrinsic goodness of the cause was disfigured by the enormities committed at Cadiz, Seville, Badajos, and other places, but chiefly at Valencia, pre-eminent in barbarity at a moment when all were barbarous! The first burst of popular feeling being thus misdirected, and the energy of the people wasted in assassinations, lassitude and fear succeeded to the insolence of tumult at the approach of real danger; for it is one thing to shine in the work of butchery, and another to establish that discipline which can alone sustain the courage of the multitude in the hour of trial.

To cover the suspicious measure of introducing more troops than the terms of the convention warranted, a variety of reports relative to the ultimate intentions of the French Emperor had been propagated; at one time Gibraltar was to be besieged, and officers were dispatched to examine the Mediterranean coasts of Spain and Barbary; at another, Portugal was to become the theatre of great events; and a mysterious importance was attached to all the movements of the French armies, with a view to deceive a court that fear and sloth disposed to the belief of anything but the truth, and to impose upon a people whose unsuspicious ignorance was at first mistaken for tameness.

In the mean time, active agents were employed to form a French party at the capital; and, as the insurrections of Aranjuez and Madrid discovered the fierceness of the Spanish character, Napoleon enjoined more caution and prudence upon his lieutenant than the latter was disposed to practise. In fact, Murat's precipitation was the cause of hastening the discovery of his master's real views before they were ripe for execution. For Dupont's first division and cavalry had crossed the Duero as early as the 14th of March, and upon the 10th of April had occupied Aranjuez, while his second and third divisions took post at the Escurial and at Segovia, thus encircling the capital, which was soon occupied by Moncey's corps. In was then evident that Murat designed to control the provisional government left by Ferdinand; and the riot at Toledo, although promptly quelled by the interference of the French troops, indicated the state of the public mind, before the explosion at Madrid had placed the parties in a state of direct hostility. Murat seems to have been intrusted with only a half confidence, and as his natural impetuosity urged him to play a rash rather than a timid part, he appeared with the air of a conqueror before a ground of quarrel was laid. His policy was too coarse and open for such difficult affairs, yet he was not entirely without grounds for his proceeding; a letter addressed to him about this time by Napoleon contained these expressions: "*The Duke of Infantado has a party in Madrid; it will attack you; dissipate it, and seize the government.*"

At Bayonne the political events kept pace with those of Madrid. Charles IV. having reclaimed his rights in presence of Napoleon, commanded the infant, Don Antonio, to relinquish the presidency of the governing Junta to Murat, who at the same time received the title of lieutenant-general of the kingdom. This appointment, and the restoration of Charles to the regal dignity, were proclaimed in Madrid, with the acquiescence of the Council of Castile, on the 10th of May; but five days previous to that period the old monarch had again ceded his authority to Napoleon, and Ferdinand and himself were consigned, with large pensions, to the tranquillity of private life. The throne of Spain being thus rendered vacant, the right to fill it was assumed by the French Emperor, in virtue of the cession made by Charles IV., and he desired that a king might be chosen from his own family. After some hesitation, the Council of Castile, in concert with the municipality of Madrid and the governing Junta, declared that their choice had fallen upon Joseph Bonaparte, who was then King of Naples; and Cardinal Bourbon, Primate of Spain, first cousin of Charles IV., and Archbishop of Toledo, not only acceded to this arrangement, but actually wrote to Napoleon a letter testifying his adhesion to the new order of things. As it was easy to foretell the result of the election, the King of Naples was already journeying towards Bayonne, where he arrived on the 7th of June. The principal men of Spain had been previously invited to meet in that town upon the 15th, with a view to obtain their assent to a constitution prepared by Napoleon; and at this meeting, called "The Assembly of Notables," ninety-one Spaniards of eminence appeared. They accepted Joseph as their king, proceeded to discuss the constitution in detail, and after several sittings adopted it, and swore to maintain its provisions. Thus finished the first part of this eventful drama.

The new constitution was calculated to draw forth all the resources of Spain; compared to the old system it was a blessing, and it would have been received as such under different circumstances, but now arms were to decide its fate, for in every province the cry of war had been raised. In Catalonia, in Valencia, in Andalusia, Estremadura, Gallicia, and the Asturias, the people were gathering, and fiercely declaring their determination to resist French intrusion. Nevertheless, Joseph, apparently contented with the acquiescence of the ninety-one notables, and trusting to the powerful support of his brother, crossed the frontier on the 9th of July, and on the 12th arrived at Vittoria. The inhabitants, still remembering the journey to Bayonne, seemed disposed to hinder his entrance; but their opposition did not break out into actual violence, and the next morning he continued his progress by Miranda del Ebro, Breviesca, Burgos, and Buitrago. The 20th of July he entered Madrid, and on the 24th he was proclaimed King of Spain and the Indies, with all the solemnities usual upon such occasions, thus making himself the enemy of eleven millions of people, the object of a nation's hatred! With a strange accent, and from the midst of foreign bands, he called upon a fierce and haughty race to accept of a constitution which they did not understand, and which few of them had ever heard of, his only hope of success resting on the strength of his brother's arms, his claims upon the consent of an imbecile monarch, and the weakness of a few pusillanimous nobles, in contempt of the rights of millions now arming to oppose him. This was the unhallowed part of the enterprise; this it was that rendered his offered constitution odious, covered it with a leprous skin, and drove the noble-minded far from the pollution of its touch!

CHAPTER III.

Council of Castile refuses to take the oath of allegiance—Supreme Junta estab-
lished at Seville—Marquis of Solano murdered at Cadiz, and the Conde d'Agui-
lar at Seville—Intercourse between Castanos and Sir Hew Dalrymple—General
Spencer and Admiral Purvis offer to co-operate with the Spaniards—Admiral
Rossily's squadron surrenders to Morla—General insurrection—Massacre at
Valencia—Horrible murder of Filanghieri.

JOSEPH, being proclaimed King, required the Council of Castile
to take the oath of allegiance prescribed by the constitution; but,
with unexpected boldness, that body, hitherto obsequious, met his
orders with a remonstrance, for war, virtually declared on the 2d
of May, was at this time raging in all parts of the Peninsula, and
the Council was secretly apprised that a great misfortune had befallen the French arms.* It was no longer a question between
Joseph and some reluctant public bodies; it was an awful struggle
between great nations; and how the spirit of insurrection, breaking forth simultaneously in every province, was nourished in each
until it acquired the consistence of regular warfare, I will now
relate.

Just before the tumult of Aranjuez, the Marquis of Solano y
Socoro, commanding the Spanish auxiliary force in the Alemtejo,
had received an order from Godoy to withdraw his division and
post it on the frontier of Andalusia, to cover the projected journey
of Charles IV. Napoleon was aware of this order, but would not
interrupt its execution, wherefore Solano quitted Portugal without
difficulty, and in the latter end of May, observing the general agitation, repaired to his government of Cadiz, in the harbor of which
place five French sail of the line and a frigate, under Admiral Rossily, had just before taken refuge from the English fleet. Seville
was in a great ferment, and Solano, in passing through, was required to put himself at the head of an insurrection in favor of
Ferdinand VII. He refused, and passed on to his own government; but there, also, the people were ripe for a declaration against
the French. A local government was established at Seville,
which, assuming the title of "Supreme Junta of Spain and the
Indies," declared war in form against the intrusive monarch, commanded all men between the ages of sixteen and forty-five to take
arms, called upon the troops of the camp of San Roque to acknowledge their authority, and ordered Solano to attack the French
squadron. That unfortunate man would not acknowledge the

* Memoir of O'Farril, and Azanza.

authority of this self-constituted government, and as he hesitated to commit his country in war against a power whose strength he knew better than he did the temper of his own countrymen, he was murdered. His ability, his courage, his amiable and unblemished character, have never been denied; and yet there is too much reason to believe that the Junta of Seville sent an agent to Cadiz for the express purpose of procuring his assassination. This foul stain upon the cause was enlarged by the perpetration of similar, or worse deeds, in every part of the kingdom. At Seville, the Conde d'Aguilar was dragged from his carriage, and, without even the imputation of guilt, inhumanly butchered; and here again it is said that the mob were instigated by a leading member of the Junta, Count Gusman de Tilly, a man described as "capable of dishonoring a whole nation by his crimes," while his victim was universally admitted to be virtuous and accomplished.

As early as April, General Castaños, then commanding the camp of San Roque, had entered into communication with Sir Hew Dalrymple, the Governor of Gibraltar. He was resolved to seize any opportunity that offered to resist the French, and he appears to have been the first Spaniard who united patriotism with prudent calculation,—readily acknowledging the authority of the Junta of Seville, and stifling the workings of self-interest, with a virtue by no means common to his countrymen at that period. When the insurrection first broke out, Admiral Purvis commanded the British squadron off Cadiz, and, in concert with General Spencer, who happened to be in that part of the world with five thousand men, offered to co-operate with Solano in an attack upon the French ships of war in the harbor. Upon the death of that unfortunate man, this offer was renewed and pressed upon Don Thomas Morla, his successor; but he, for reasons hereafter to be mentioned, refused all assistance, and reduced the hostile ships himself. Castaños, however, united himself closely with the British commanders, and obtained from them supplies of arms, ammunition, and money; and at the instance of Sir Hew Dalrymple the merchants of Gibraltar advanced a loan of forty-two thousand dollars for the service of the Spanish patriots.*

Meanwhile the assassinations at Cadiz and Seville were imitated in every part of Spain; hardly can a town be named in which some innocent and worthy persons were not slain.† Grenada had its murders; Carthagena rivalled Cadiz in ruthless cruelty, and Valencia reeked with blood. Don Miguel de Saavedra, the governor of that city, was killed, not in the first fury of commotion,

* Sir Hew Dalrymple's correspondence.
† Moniteur. Azanza and O'Farril : Nellerto.

which he escaped, but having returned, was deliberately sacrificed. Balthazar Calvo, a canon of the church of San Isido, at Madrid, came down to Valencia, and having collected a band of fanatics, commenced a massacre of the French residents; and this ruthless villain continued his slaughters unchecked until, French victims failing, his raging thirst for murder urged him to menace the Junta, who, with the exception of the English consul, Mr. Tupper, had given way to his previous violence, but now readily found the means to crush his power. The canon, while in the act of braving their authority, was seized by stratagem, and soon afterwards strangled, together with two hundred of his band. The Conde de Serbelloni, Captain-General of the province, then proceeded to organize an army; and the old Count Florida Blanca placed himself at the head of the Murcian insurrection, and his force acted in unison with that of Valencia.

In Catalonia the occupation of Barcelona repressed the popular effervescence, but the feeling was the same, and an insurrection, breaking out at the town of Manresa, soon spread to all the unfettered parts of the province.

In Aragon the arrival of Don Joseph Palafox kindled the fire of patriotism. He had escaped from Bayonne, and his family were greatly esteemed in a country where it was of the noblest among a people absurdly vain of their ancient descent. The Captain-General, fearful of a tumult, ordered Palafox to quit the province, but this circumstance, joined to some appearance of mystery in his escape from Bayonne, increased the passions of the multitude; a crowd surrounded his abode, and forced him to assume the command, the Captain-General was confined, some persons were murdered, and a junta was formed. Palafox was considered by his companions as a man of slender capacity and great vanity, and there is nothing in his exploits to create a doubt of the justness of this opinion; it was not Palafox that upheld the glory of Aragon; it was the spirit of the people, which he had not excited, and could so little direct, that for a long time after the commencement of the first siege, he was kept a sort of prisoner in Zaragoza, his courage and fidelity being distrusted by the population which he is supposed to have ruled.

The example of Aragon aroused the Navarrese, and Logrono became the focus of an insurrection which extended along most of the valleys of that kingdom. In the northern and western provinces, the spirit of independence was equally fierce and as decidedly pronounced, accompanied also by the same excesses. In Badajos the Conde de la Torre del Frenio was butchered by the populace, and his mangled carcass dragged through the streets in triumph.

At Talavera de la Reyna, the corregidor with difficulty escaped a similar fate by a hasty flight; Leon presented a wide, unbroken scene of anarchy, and, generally speaking, in all the great towns violent hands were laid upon those who opposed the people's wishes.

Gallicia seemed to hold back for a moment, but the example of Leon, and the arrival of an agent from the Asturias, where the insurrection was in full force, produced a general movement. A junta was formed, and Filanghieri, the Governor of Coruña, an Italian, was called upon to exercise the functions of royalty by declaring war in form against France. Like every man of sense in Spain he was unwilling to commence a revolution upon such uncertain grounds, and the impatient populace sought his death; he was saved at the moment by the courage of an officer of his staff, yet his horrible fate was only deferred. Being a man of talent and sincerely attached to Spain, he exerted himself to organize the military resources of the province, and no suspicion attached to his conduct; but such was the inherent ferocity of the people and of the time, that the soldiers of the regiment of Navarre seized him at Villa Franca del Bierzo, and, as some say, stuck him full of bayonets, while others assert that they planted their weapons in the ground, and then tossing him on to their points, left him there to struggle, and then disbanded themselves.

The Asturians were the first who proclaimed their indefeasible right of choosing a new government when the old one ceased to afford them protection. They established a local junta, declared war against the French, and dispatched deputies to England to solicit assistance. Meanwhile, although the great towns in Biscay and the Castiles were overawed by fifty thousand bayonets, the peasantry commenced a war, in their own manner, against the stragglers and the sick, and thus a hostile chain surrounding the French army was completed in every link.

This universal and nearly simultaneous effort of the Spanish people was beheld by the rest of Europe with astonishment and admiration: astonishment at the energy thus suddenly put forth by a nation hitherto deemed unnerved and debased; admiration at the devoted courage of an act, which, seen at a distance and its odious parts unknown, appeared with all the ideal beauty of Numantian patriotism. In England the enthusiasm was unbounded; dazzled at first with the splendor of such an agreeable, unlooked-for spectacle, men of all classes gave way to the impulse of a generous sympathy, and forgot, or felt disinclined to analyze, the real causes of this apparently magnanimous exertion. It may, however, be fairly doubted if the disinterested vigor of the Spanish character was the true source of the resistance; it was, in fact, produced by several co-operating causes, many of which were anything but commendable. Constituted as modern states are, with little in their systems of government or education adapted to nourish intense feelings of patriotism, it would be miraculous indeed if such a result was obtained from the pure virtue of a nation, which for two centuries had groaned under the pressure of civil and religious despotism.

The Spanish character, with relation to public affairs, is distinguished by inordinate pride and arrogance. Dilatory and improvident, the individual as well as the mass all possess an absurd confidence that everything is practicable which their heated imaginations suggest; once excited, they can see no difficulty in the execution of a project, and the obstacles they encounter are attributed to treachery; hence the sudden murder of so many virtuous men at the commencement of this commotion. Kind and warm in his attachments, but bitter in his anger, the Spaniard is patient under privations, firm in bodily suffering, prone to sudden passion, vindictive, bloody, remembering insult longer than injury, and cruel in his revenge. With a strong natural perception of what is noble, his promise is lofty, but as he invariably permits his passions to get the mastery of his reason, his performance is mean. In the progress of this war, the tenacity of vengeance peculiar to the nation supplied the want of cool, persevering intrepidity; but it was a poor substitute for that essential quality, and led rather to deeds of craft and cruelty than to daring acts of patriotism. Now the abstraction of the royal family, and the unexpected pretension to the crown, so insultingly put forth by Napoleon, had aroused all the Spanish pride, and the tumults of Madrid and Aranjuez prepared the public mind for a violent movement; the protection afforded by the French to the obnoxious Godoy increased the ferment of popular feeling, because a dearly cherished vengeance was thus frustrated at the moment of its expected accomplishment, and the disappointment excited all that fierceness of anger which with Spaniards is, for the moment, uncontrollable; and then came the tumult of Madrid, which, swollen and distorted, was cast like Cæsar's body before the people to urge them to phrenzy; they arose, not to meet a danger the extent of which they had calculated, and were prepared for the sake of independence to confront, but to gratify the fury of their hearts, and to slake their thirst of blood.

During Godoy's administration the property of the church had been trenched upon, and it was evident, from the example of France and Italy, that under the new system the operation would be repeated; this was a matter that involved the interests, and, of course, stimulated the activity of a multitude of monks and priests, who found no difficulty in persuading an ignorant and bigoted people that the aggressive stranger was also the enemy of religion and accursed of God. With processions, miracles, prophecies, distribution of reliques, and the appointment of saints to the command of the armies, they fanaticized the mass of the patriots, and in every part of the Peninsula the clergy were distinguished for their active zeal; monks and friars were invariably either leaders in the tumults, or at the side of those who were, instigating them to barbarous actions. Bonaparte found the same cause produce similar effects during his early campaigns in Italy; and if the shape of that country had been as favorable for protracted resistance, and a like support had been furnished by Great Britain, the patriots of Spain would have been rivalled by modern Romans.*

The continental system of mercantile exclusion was another spring of this complicated machinery. It threatened to lessen the already decayed commerce of the maritime towns, and the contraband trade, which has always been carried on in Spain to an incredible extent, was certain of destruction; with that trade the fate of one hundred thousand excise and custom-house officers was involved.† It required but a small share of penetration to perceive that a system of armed revenue officers, organized after the French manner and stimulated by a vigorous administration, would quickly put an end to the smuggling, which was, in truth, only a consequence of monopolies and internal restrictions upon the trade of one province with another—vexations abolished by the constitution of Bayonne: hence all the activity and intelligence of the merchants engaged in foreign trade, and all the numbers and lawless violence of the smugglers were enlisted in the cause of the country, swelling the ranks of the insurgent patriots; and hence, also, the readiness of the Gibraltar merchants to advance the loan before spoken of.

The state of civilization in Spain was likewise exactly suited to an insurrection; for if the people had been a little more enlightened they would have joined the French—if very enlightened, the invasion could not have happened at all. But in a country where the comforts of civilized society are less needed and therefore less attended to than in any other part of Europe, where the warmth and dryness of the climate render it no sort of privation, or even inconvenience, to sleep for the greatest part of the year in the open air, and where the universal custom is to go armed, it was not dif-

* Napoleon's Mémoires, Campagne d'Italie, Venise.
† Wellesley's letter to Burrard.

ficult for any energetic man to assemble and keep together large masses of the credulous peasantry. No story could be too gross for their belief, if it agreed with their wishes. "Es verdad, los dicen"— "It is true, they say it"—is the invariable answer of a Spaniard if a doubt be expressed of the truth of an absurd report. Temperate, possessing little furniture, and generally hoarding all the gold he can get, he is less concerned for the loss of his house than the inhabitant of another country would be, and the effort that he makes in relinquishing his abode must not be measured by the scale of an Englishman's exertion in a like case; once engaged in an adventure, the lightness of his spirits and the brilliancy of his sky make it a matter of indifference to the angry peasant whither he wanders.

The evils which had afflicted the country previous to the period of the French interference also tended to prepare the Spaniards for violence, and aided in turning that violence against the intruders. Famine, oppression, poverty, and disease, the loss of commerce, and unequal taxation, had pressed sorely upon them. For such a system the people could not be enthusiastic; but they were taught to believe that Godoy was the sole author of the misery they suffered, that Ferdinand would redress their grievances—and as the French were the protectors of the former and the oppressors of the latter, it was easy to add this bitterness to their natural hatred of the domination of a stranger, and it was so done.*

Such were the principal causes which combined to produce this surprising revolution, from which so many great events flowed, without one man of eminent talent being cast up to control or direct the spirit thus accidentally excited. Nothing more directly shows the heterogeneous nature of the feelings and interests which were brought together than this last fact, which cannot be attributed to a deficiency of natural talent, for the genius of the Spanish people is notoriously ardent, subtle, and vigorous; but there was no common bond of feeling save that of individual hatred to the French, which a great man could lay hold of to influence large masses. Persons of sagacity perceived very early that the Spanish revolution, like a leafy shrub in a violent gale of wind, greatly agitated, but disclosing only slight unconnected stems, afforded no sure hold for the ambition of a master-spirit, if such there were. It was clear that the cause would fail unless supported by England; and then England would direct all, and not suffer her resources to be wielded for the glory of an individual whose views and policy might afterwards thwart her own; nor was it difficult to perceive that the downfall

* Historia de la Guerra contra Napoleon.

of Napoleon, not the regeneration of Spain, was the object of her cabinet.

The explosion of public feeling was fierce in its expression, because political passions will always be vehement at the first moment of their appearance among a people new to civil commotion, and unused to permit their heat to evaporate in public discussions. The result was certainly a wonderful change in the affairs of Europe—it seems yet undecided whether that change has been for the better or for the worse; and in the progress of their struggle the Spaniards certainly developed more cruelty than courage, more violence than intrepidity, more personal hatred of the French than enthusiasm for their own cause. They opened, indeed, a wide field for the exertions of others, they presented a fulcrum upon which a lever was rested that moved the civilized world, but assuredly the presiding genius, the impelling power, came from another quarter; useful accessories they were, but as principals they displayed neither wisdom, spirit, nor skill sufficient to resist the prodigious force by which they were assailed. If they appeared at first heedless of danger, it was not because they were prepared to perish rather than submit, but that they were reckless of provoking a power whose terrors they could not estimate, and in their ignorance despised.

It is, however, not surprising that great expectations were at first formed of the heroism of the Spaniards, and those expectations were greatly augmented by their agreeable qualities. There is not upon the face of the earth a people so attractive in the friendly intercourse of society. Their majestic language, fine persons, and becoming dress, their lively imaginations, the inexpressible beauty of their women, and the air of romance which they throw over every action, and infuse into every feeling, all combine to delude the senses and to impose upon the judgment. As companions, they are incomparably the most agreeable of mankind, but danger and disappointment attend the man who, confiding in their promises and energy, ventures upon a difficult enterprise. "Never do to-day what you can put off until to-morrow," is the favorite proverb in Spain, and rigidly followed.

CHAPTER IV.

New French corps formed in Navarre—Duhesme fixes himself at Barcelona—Importance of that city—Napoleon's military plan and arrangements.

THE commotion of Aranjuez undeceived the French Emperor; he perceived that he was engaged in a delicate enterprise, and that the people he had to deal with were anything but tame and quiescent under insult. Determined, however, to persevere, he pursued his political intrigues, and without relinquishing the hope of a successful termination to the affair by such means, he arranged a profound plan of military operations, and so distributed his forces, that at the moment when Spain was pouring forth her swarthy bands, the masses of the French army were concentrated upon the most important points, and combined in such a manner, that, from their central position, they had the power of overwhelming each separate province, no three of which could act in concert without first beating a French corps. And if any of the Spanish armies succeeded in routing a French force, the remaining corps could unite without difficulty, and retreat without danger. It was the skill of this disposition which enabled seventy thousand men, covering a great extent of country, to brave the simultaneous fury of a whole nation; an army less ably distributed would have been trampled under foot, and lost amidst the tumultuous uproar of eleven millions of people.

In a political point of view the inconvenience which would have arisen from suffering a regular army to take the field, was evident. To have been able to characterize the opposition of the Spanish people as a partial insurrection of peasants, instigated by some evil-disposed persons to act against the wishes of the respectable part of the nation, would have given some color to the absorbing darkness of the invasion. And to have permitted that which was at first an insurrection of peasants, to take the form and consistence of regular armies and methodical warfare, would have been a military error, dangerous in the extreme. Napoleon, who well knew that scientific war is only a wise application of force, laughed at the delusion of those who regarded the want of a regular army as a favorable circumstance, and who hailed the undisciplined peasant as the more certain defender of the country. He knew that a general insurrection can never last long, that it is a military anarchy, and incapable of real strength; he knew that it was the disciplined battalions of Valley Forge, not the volunteers of Lexington, that established American independence; that it was the veterans of Arcole and

Marengo, not the republicans of Valmy, that fixed the fate of the French Revolution. Hence his efforts were directed to hinder the Spaniards from drawing together any great body of regular soldiers, an event that might easily happen, for the gross amount of the organized Spanish force was, in the month of May, about one hundred and twenty-seven thousand men of all arms. Fifteen thousand of these were in Holstein, under the Marquis of Romana, but twenty thousand were already partially concentrated in Portugal, and the remainder, in which were comprised eleven thousand Swiss and thirty thousand militia, were dispersed in various parts of the kingdom, principally in Andalusia. Besides this force, there was a sort of local reserve called the urban militia, much neglected indeed, and more a name than a reality, yet the advantage of such an institution was considerable; men were to be had in abundance, and as the greatest difficulty in a sudden crisis is to prepare the framework of order, it was no small resource to find a plan of service ready, the principle of which was understood by the people.*

The French army in the Peninsula about the same period, although amounting to eighty thousand men, exclusive of those under Junot in Portugal, had not more than seventy thousand capable of active operations; the remainder were sick or in dépôts. The possession of the fortresses, the central position, and the combination of this comparatively small army, gave it great strength, but it had also many points of weakness; it was made up of the conscripts of different nations, French, Swiss, Italians, Poles, and even Portuguese whom Junot had expatriated; and it is a curious fact, that some of the latter remained in Spain until the end of the war. A few of the imperial guards were also employed, and here and there, an old regiment of the line was mixed with the young troops to give them consistence; yet with these exceptions the French army must be considered as a raw levy, fresh from the plough and unacquainted with discipline;† so late even as the month of August, many of the battalions had not completed the first elements of their drill,‡ and if they had not been formed upon good skeletons, the difference between them and the insurgent peasantry would have been very trifling.§ This fact explains, in some measure, the otherwise incomprehensible checks and defeats which the French sustained at the commencement of the contest, and it likewise proves how little of vigor there was in Spanish resistance at the moment of the greatest enthusiasm.

---

* Historia de la Guerra contra Napoleon Bonaparte.
† Napoleon's notes.
‡ Thiebault.
§ Dupont's Journal, MSS.

In the distribution of these troops Napoleon attended principally to the security of Madrid. As the capital, and the centre of all interests, its importance was manifest, and the great line of communication between it and Bayonne was early and constantly covered with troops. But the imprudence with which the Grand Duke of Berg brought up the corps of Moncey and Dupont to the capital, together with his own haughty, impolitic demeanor, drew on the crisis of affairs before the time was ripe, obliged the French monarch to hasten the advance of other troops, and to make a greater display of his force than was consistent with his policy. For Murat's movement, while it threatened the Spaniards and provoked their hostility, isolated the French army, by stripping the line of communication, and the arrival of fresh battalions to remedy this error generated additional anger and suspicion at a very critical period.

It was, however, absolutely necessary to fill the void left by Moncey's advance, and a fresh corps sent into Navarre, being by successive reinforcements increased to twenty-three thousand men, received in June the name of the "army of the Western Pyrenees."* Marshal Bessieres assumed the command, and, on the first appearance of commotion, fixed his headquarters at Burgos, occupied Vittoria, Miranda de Ebro, and other towns, and pushed advanced posts into Leon. This position, while it protected the line from Bayonne to the capital, enabled him to awe the Asturias and Biscay, and also by giving him the command of the valley of the Duero to keep the kingdom of Leon and the province of Segovia in check. The town and castle of Burgos, put into a state of defence, contained his dépôts and became the centre and pivot of his operations, while intermediate posts, and the fortresses, connected him with Bayonne, where a reserve of twenty thousand men was formed under General Drouet, then commanding the eleventh military division of France.

By the convention of Fontainebleau, the Emperor was entitled to send forty thousand men into the northern parts of Spain, and though the right thus acquired was grossly abused, the exercise of it, being expected, created at first but little alarm; it was however different on the eastern frontier. Napoleon had never intimated a wish to pass forces by Catalonia, neither the treaty nor the convention authorized such a measure, nor could the pretence of supporting Junot in Portugal be advanced as a mask;† nevertheless, so early as the 9th of February eleven thousand infantry, sixteen hundred cavalry, and eighteen pieces of artillery, under the command of

* Napoleon's notes.
† St. Cyr.

General Duhesme,* had crossed the frontier at La Jonquera, and marched upon Barcelona, leaving a detachment at the town of Figueras, the strong citadel of which commands the principal pass of the mountains. Arrived at Barcelona, Duhesme prolonged his residence there, under the pretext of waiting for instructions from Madrid relative to a pretended march upon Cadiz;† but his secret orders were to obtain exact information concerning the Catalonian fortresses, dépôts, and magazines,—to ascertain the state of public feeling,—to preserve a rigid discipline,—scrupulously to avoid giving any offence to the Spaniards, and to enter into close communication with Marshal Moncey, at that time commanding the whole of the French army in the north of Spain.

The political affairs were then beginning to indicate serious results, and as soon as the troops in the north were in a condition to execute their orders, Duhesme, whose report had been received, was directed to seize upon the citadel of Barcelona and the fort of Monjuick. The citadel was obtained by stratagem; the fort, one of the strongest in the world, was surrendered by the governor, Alvarez, because that brave and worthy man knew that from a base court he should receive no support. It is said that, stung by the disgrace of his situation, he was at one time ready to spring a mine beneath the French detachments, yet his mind, betraying his spirit, sank under the weight of unexpected events. What a picture of human weakness do these affairs present!—the boldest shrinking from the discharge of their trust like the meanest cowards, the wisest following the march of events, confounded, and without a rule of action! If such a firm man as Alvarez afterwards proved himself to be, could think the disgrace of surrendering his charge at the demand of an insolent and perfidious guest, a smaller misfortune than the anger of a miserable court, what must the state of public feeling have been, and how can those who, like O'Farril and Azanza, served the intruder, be with justice blamed, if, amidst the general stagnation, they could not perceive the elements of a salutary tempest? At the view of such scenes Napoleon might well enlarge his ambitious designs; his fault was not in the projection, but in the rough execution of his plan; another combination would have insured success, and the resistance he encountered only shows that nations, like individuals, are but the creatures of circumstances, at one moment weak, trembling, and submissive, at another proud, haughty, and daring; every novel combination of events has an effect upon public sentiment distinct from, and often at variance with what is called national character.

* Napoleon's notes.
† Duhesme's Instructions, Jan. 28th. Vide St. Cyr.

The treacherous game played at Barcelona was renewed at Figueras, with equal success; the citadel of that place fell into the hands of the detachment left there; a free entrance, and a secure base of operations, was thus established in Catalonia; and when the magazines of Barcelona were filled, Duhesme, whose corps took the name of the "army of the Eastern Pyrenees," concluded that his task was well accomplished. The affair was indeed a momentous one, and Napoleon earnestly looked for its termination before the transactions at Madrid could give an unfavorable impression of his ulterior intentions; for he saw the importance which, under certain circumstances, a war would confer upon Barcelona, which, with its immense population, great riches, good harbor, and strong forts, might be called the key of the south of France or Spain, just as it happened to be in the possession of the one or the other nation. The proximity of Sicily, where a large British force was kept in a state of constant preparation, made it more than probable that an English army would be quickly carried to Barcelona, and a formidable systematic war be established upon the threshold of France; and hence Napoleon, seeing the extent of the danger, obviated it, at the risk of rendering abortive the attempt to create a French party in Madrid. The greater evil of finding an English army at Barcelona left no room for hesitation; thirty or forty thousand British troops occupying an intrenched camp in front of that town, supported by a powerful fleet, and having reserve dépôts in Sicily and the Spanish islands, might have been so wielded as to give ample occupation to a hundred and fifty thousand enemies. Under the protection of such an army, the Spanish levies might have been organized and instructed; and as the actual numbers assembled could have been easily masked, increased, or diminished, and the fleet always ready to co-operate, the south of France, whence the provisions of the enemy must have been drawn, would have been exposed to descents, and all the inconvenience of actual hostilities. The Spanish provinces of Valencia, Murcia, and even Andalusia, being thus covered, the war would have been drawn to a head, and concentrated about Catalonia, the most war-like, rugged, sterile portion of Spain. Duhesme's success put an end to this danger, and the affairs of Barcelona sank into comparative insignificance; nevertheless, that place was carefully watched, the troops were increased to twenty-two thousand men, their General corresponded directly with Napoleon, and Barcelona became the centre of a system distinct from that which held the other corps rolling round Madrid as their point of attraction.

The capital of Spain is situated in a sort of basin, formed by a semi-circular range of mountains, which, under the different denominations of the Sierra de Guadarama, the Carpentanos and the Sierra de Guadalaxara, sweep in one unbroken chain from east to west, touching the Tagus at either end of an arch, of which that river is the chord. All direct communication between Madrid and France, or between the former and the northern provinces of Spain, must therefore necessarily pass over one or other of these Sierras, which are separated from the great range of the Pyrenees by the valley of the Ebro, and from the Biscayan and Asturian mountains by the valley of the Duero.

Now the principal roads which lead from France directly upon Madrid are four.

The first a royal causeway, which, passing the frontier at Iran, runs under St. Sebastian, and through a wild and mountainous country, full of dangerous defiles, to the Ebro. It crosses that river by a stone bridge at Miranda, goes to Burgos, and then turning short to the left, is carried over the Duero at Aranda. Afterwards encountering the Carpentanos and the Sierra de Guadalaxara, it penetrates them by the strong pass of the Somosierra, and descends upon the capital.

The second, which is an inferior road, commences at St. Jean Pied de Port, unites with the first at Pampeluna, runs through Taffalla, crosses the Ebro at Tudela, and enters the basin of Madrid by the eastern range of the Sierra de Guadalaxara, where the declination of the mountains presents a less rugged barrier than the snowy summits of the northern and western part of the chain.

The third threads the Pyrenees by the way of Jaca, passes the Ebro at Zaragoza, and uniting with the second, likewise crosses the Guadalaxara ridge.

The fourth is the great route from Perpignan by Figueras, Gerona, Barcelona, Cervera, Lerida, and Zaragoza, to Madrid.

Thus Zaragoza, which contained fifty thousand inhabitants and was one of the great Spanish magazines for arms, furnished a point of union for two great roads, and was consequently of strategic importance. An army in position there could operate on either bank of the Ebro, intercept the communication between the Eastern and Western Pyrenees, and block three out of the four great routes to Madrid. If the French had occupied it in force, their army in the capital would have been free and unconstrained in its operations, and might have acted with more security against Valencia, and the danger from the united forces of Gallicia and Leon would also have been diminished when the road of Burgos ceased to be the only line of retreat from the capital. Nevertheless, Napoleon neglected Zaragoza at first, because, having no citadel, a small body of troops could not control the inhabitants, and a large force, by creating suspicion too soon, would have prevented the success of the attempts against Pampeluna and Barcelona, objects of still greater importance; neither was the heroic defence afterwards made within a reasonable calculation.

The Grand Duke of Berg and the Duke of Rovigo remained at Madrid, and from that central point appeared to direct the execution of the French Emperor's projects; but he distrusted their judgment, and exacted the most detailed information of every movement and transaction. In the course of June, Murat, who was suffering from illness, quitted Spain, leaving behind him a troubled people and a name for cruelty which was foreign his character. Savary remained the sole representative of the new monarch, and his situation was delicate. He was in the midst of a great commotion, and as upon every side he beheld the violence of insurrection and the fury of an insulted nation, it behoved him to calculate with coolness and to execute with vigor. Each Spanish province had its own junta of government, and they were alike enraged, yet not alike dangerous in their anger. The attention of the Catalonians was completely absorbed by Duhesme's operations, but the soldiers which had composed the Spanish garrisons of Barcelona, Monjuick, and Figueras, quitted their ranks after the seizure of those places, and joined the patriotic standards in Murcia and Valencia; the greatest part belonged to the Spanish and Walloon guards, and they formed a good basis for an army which the riches of the two provinces and the arsenal of Carthagena afforded ample military resources to equip.* The French had, however, nothing to fear from any direct movement of this army against Madrid, as such an operation could only bring on a battle; but if, by a march towards Zaragoza, the Valencians had united with the Aragonese, and then operated against the line of communication with France, the insurrection of Catalonia would have been supported and the point of union for three great provinces fixed. In the power of executing this project lay the sting of the Valencian insurrection, and to besiege Zaragoza and prevent such a junction was the remedy.

The importance of Andalusia was greater. The regular troops which, under the command of the unhappy Solano, had been withdrawn from Portugal, were tolerably disciplined; a large veteran force was assembled at the camp of San Roque, under General Castaños, and the garrisons of Ceuta, Algeziras, Cadiz, Granada and other places, being united, the whole formed a considerable army, while a superb cannon foundry at Seville and the arsenal at Cadiz furnished the means of equipping a train of artillery. An

---

* Cabane's War in Catalonia, 1st Part.

active intercourse was maintained between the patriots and the English, and the Juntas of Granada, Jaen and Cordova, and the army of Estremadura, admitted the supremacy of the Junta of Seville. Thus Andalusia, rich, distant from the capital, and well fenced by the Sierra Morena, afforded the means to establish a systematic war, by drawing together all the scattered elements of resistance in the southern and western provinces of Spain and Portugal.* This danger, pregnant with future consequences, was, however, not immediate; there was no line of offensive moment against the flank or rear of the French army open to the Andalusian patriots, and as a march to the front, against Madrid, would have been tedious and dangerous, the true policy of the Andalusians was palpably defensive.

In Estremadura, neither the activity nor means of the Junta were at first sufficient to excite much attention; but in Leon, Old Castile, and Gallicia, a cloud was gathering that threatened a perilous storm. Don Gregorio Cuesta was Captain-General of the two former kingdoms. Inimical to popular movements, and of a haughty, resolute disposition, he at first checked the insurrection with a rough hand, and thus laid the foundation for quarrels and intrigues, which afterwards impeded the military operations and split the northern provinces into factions; yet finally he joined the side of the patriots. Behind him the kingdom of Gallicia, under the direction of Filanghieri, had prepared a large and efficient force, chiefly composed of the strong and disciplined body of troops which, under the command of Tarranco, had taken possession of Oporto, and after that general's death had returned with Belesta to Gallicia: the garrisons of Ferrol and Coruña, and a number of soldiers flying from the countries occupied by the French, swelled this army; the agents of Great Britain were active to blow the flame of insurrection, and money, arms and clothing were poured into the province through their hands, because Coruña afforded an easy and direct intercourse with England. A strict connection was also maintained between the Gallician and Portuguese patriots, and the facility of establishing the base of a regular systematic war in Gallicia was therefore as great as in Andalusia,—the resources were perhaps greater, on account of the proximity of Great Britain, and the advantage of position at this time was essentially in favor of Gallicia, because, while the sources of her strength were as well covered from the direct line of the French operations, the slightest offensive movement upon her part, by threatening the communications of the French army in Madrid, endangered the safety of any corps marching from the capital against the southern provinces.

* Mr. Stuart's Letters; vide Parliamentary Papers, 1810.

To be prepared against the Gallician forces was, therefore, a matter of pressing importance ; a defeat from that quarter would have been felt in all parts of the army, and no considerable or sustained operation could be undertaken against the other insurgent forces until the strength of Gallicia had been first broken.

Biscay and the Asturias wanted regular troops and fortified towns, and the contracted shape of those provinces placed them completely within the power of the French, who had nothing to fear as long as they could maintain possession of the seaports.

From this sketch it results that Savary, in classing the dangers of his situation, should have rated Gallicia and Leon in the first, Zaragoza in the second, Andalusia in the third, and Valencia in the fourth rank, and by that scale he should have regulated his operations. It was thus Napoleon looked at the affair, but the Duke of Rovigo, wavering in his opinions, neglected or misunderstood the spirit of his instructions, lost the control of the operations, and sunk amidst the confusion which he had himself created.

Nearly fifty thousand French and eighty guns were disposable for offensive operations in the beginning of June; collected into one mass, such an army was more than sufficient to crush any or all of the insurgent armies combined, but it was necessary to divide it, and to assail several points at the same time. In doing this, the safety of each minor body depended upon the stability of the central point from whence it emanated, and again the security of that centre depended upon the strength of its communications with France; in other words, Bayonne was the base of operations against Madrid, and Madrid in turn became the base of operations against Valencia, Murcia, and Andalusia. To combine all the movements of a vast plan, which would embrace the operations against Catalonia, Aragon, Biscay, the Asturias, Gallicia, Leon, Castile, Andalusia, Murcia, and Valencia, in such a simple manner as that the corps of the army working upon one principle might mutually support and strengthen each other, and at the same time preserve their communication with France, was the great problem to be solved. Napoleon felt that it required a master mind, and from Bayonne he put all the different armed masses in motion himself, and with the greatest caution; for it is a mistaken notion, although one very generally entertained, that he plunged headlong into the contest, without foresight, as having to do with adversaries he despised.

In his instructions to the Duke of Rovigo, he says: "*In a war of this sort it is necessary to act with patience, coolness, and upon calculation.*" "*In civil wars it is the important points only which should be guarded—we must not go to all places;*" and he inculcates the doctrine, that to spread the troops over the country without the

power of uniting upon emergency, would be a dangerous display
of activity. The principle upon which he proceeded may be illustrated by the comparison of a closed hand thrust forward and the
fingers afterwards extended : as long as the solid part of the member was securely fixed and guarded, the return of the smaller
portions of it and their flexible movement was feasible and without
great peril; whereas a wound given to the hand or arm, not only
endangered that part, but paralyzed the action of the whole limb.
Hence all the care and attention with which his troops were arranged along the road to Burgos; hence all the measures of precaution already described, such as the seizure of the fortresses and
the formation of the reserves at Bayonne.

The insurrection having commenced, Bessieres was ordered to
put Burgos into a state of defence,—to detach a division of four or
five thousand men, under General Lefebre Desnouettes, against
Zaragoza,—to keep down the insurgents of Biscay, Asturias, and
Old Castile,—and to observe the army assembling in Gallicia; he
was likewise enjoined to occupy and watch with jealous care the
port of Santander and the coast towns. A reinforcement of nine
thousand men was also prepared for Duhesme, which, it was supposed, would enable him to tranquillize Catalonia, and co-operate
with a division marching from Madrid against Valencia. The reserve under General Drouet was nourished by drafts from the
interior; it supplied Bessieres with reinforcements, and afforded a
detachment of four thousand men to watch the openings of the
valleys of the Pyrenees, especially towards the Castle of Jaca, then
in possession of the Spanish insurgents.* A smaller reserve was
established at Perpignan, another body watched the openings of the
eastern frontier; and all the generals commanding corps, or even
detachments, were directed to correspond daily with General Drouet.

The security of the rear being thus provided for, the main body
at Madrid commenced offensive operations. Marshal Moncey was
directed, with part of his corps, upon Cuenca, to intercept the march
of the Valencian army upon Zaragoza;† General Dupont, with ten
thousand men, marched towards Cadiz, and the remainder of his
and Moncey's troops being kept in reserve, were distributed in various parts of La Mancha and the neighborhood of Madrid. Napoleon likewise directed that Segovia should be occupied and put
in a state of defence; that Gobert's division of Moncey's corps
should co-operate with Bessieres on the side of Valladolid, and that
movable columns should scour the country in rear of the acting
bodies, uniting again at stated times, upon points of secondary

* Napoleon's notes.
† Journal of Moncey's Operations, MSS.

interest.* Thus linking his operations together, Napoleon hoped, by grasping as it were the ganglia of the insurrection, to paralyze its force, and reduce it to a few convulsive motions, which would soon subside; the execution of his plan failed in the feeble hands of his lieutenants, but it was well conceived, embraced every probable immediate chance of war, and even provided for the uncertain contingency of an English army landing upon the flank or rear of his corps, at either extremity of the Pyrenean frontier.

Military men would do well to reflect upon the prudence which the French Emperor displayed upon this occasion. Not all his experience, his power, his fortune, nor the contempt which he felt for the prowess of his adversaries, could induce him to relax in his precautions; every chance was considered, and every measure calculated with as much care and circumspection as if the most redoubtable enemy was opposed to him. The conqueror of Europe was as fearful of making false movements before an army of peasants as if Frederick the Great had been in his front—and yet he failed! Such is the uncertainty of war!

CHAPTER V.

First operations of Marshal Bessieres—Spaniards defeated at Cabeçon, at Segovia, at Logrono, at Torquemada—French take Santander—Lefebre Desnouettes defeats the Spaniards on the Ebro, on the Huecha, on the Xalon—First siege of Zaragoza—Observations.

As all the insurrections of the Spanish provinces took place nearly at the same period, the operations of the French divisions were nearly simultaneous; I shall, therefore, narrate their proceedings separately, classing them by the effect each produced upon the stability of the intrusive government of Madrid.

OPERATIONS OF MARSHAL BESSIERES.

This officer had scarcely fixed his quarters at Burgos when a general movement of revolt took place.† On his right, the Bishop of Santander excited the inhabitants of the diocese to take arms.‡ In his rear, a mechanic assembled some thousand armed peasants at the town of Logrono. In front, five thousand men took possession of the Spanish artillery dépôt at Segovia, and an equal num-

* Napoleon's notes.
† Moniteur.
‡ Victoires et Conquêtes des Français.

ber assembling at Palencia, advanced to the town of Torquemada, while General Cuesta, with some regular troops and a body of organized peasantry, took post on the Pisuerga at Cabeçon.

Bessieres immediately divided his disposable force, which was not more than twelve thousand men, into several columns, and traversing the country in all directions, disarmed the towns and interrupted the combinations of the insurgents, while a division of Dupont's corps, under General Frere, marched from the side of Madrid to aid his efforts. General Verdier attacked Logrono on the 6th of June, dispersed the peasantry, and put the leaders to death after the action. General Lasalle, departing from Burgos with a brigade of light cavalry, passed the Pisuerga, fell upon the Spaniards at Torquemada on the 7th, broke them, and pursuing with a merciless sword, burnt that town, and entered Palencia on the 8th. Meanwhile Frere defeated the Spanish force at Segovia, taking thirty pieces of artillery; and General Merle, marching through the country lying between the Pisuerga and the Duero with a division of infantry, joined Lasalle at Duenas on the 12th; from thence they proceeded to Cabeçon, where Cuesta accepting battle, he was overthrown with much slaughter, the loss of his artillery, and several thousand muskets.

The flat country being thus subdued, Lasalle's cavalry remained to keep it under, while Merle, marching northward, commenced operations, in concert with General Ducos, against the province of Santander. On the 20th, the latter General drove the Spaniards from the pass of Soncillo; on the 21st, he forced the pass of Venta de Escudo, and descending the valley of the river Pas, approached Santander; on the 22d, Merle, after some resistance, penetrating by Lantueno, followed the course of the Besaya to Torre La Vega, then turning to his right, entered Santander on the 23d. Ducos arrived at the same time, the town submitted, and the Bishop fled, with the greatest part of the clergy. The authorities of Segovia, Valladolid, Palencia and Santander were then compelled to send deputies to take the oath of allegiance to Joseph. By these operations the above-named provinces were completely disarmed, and so awed by the activity of Bessieres that no further insurrections took place; his cavalry raised contributions and collected provisions without the least difficulty. Frere's division then returned to Toledo, and from thence marched to San Clemente, on the borders of Murcia.

While Bessieres thus broke the northern insurrections, the march of General Lefebre Desnouettes against the province of Aragon brought on the first siege of Zaragoza. To that place had flocked from the most distant parts soldiers, flying from Madrid and Pam-

peluna, the engineers of the school of Alcala, and all the retired
officers in Aragon.* With their assistance Palafox's forces were
rapidly organized, and numerous battalions were posted on the
roads leading to Navarre. The Baron de Versage, an officer of
the Walloon guards, occupied Calatayud with a regiment composed
of students, and made a levy there to protect the powder mills of
Villa Felice, and to keep a communication with Soria and Siguenza.
The arsenal of Zaragoza supplied the patriots with arms; the people of Tudela broke their bridge on the Ebro, and Palafox reinforced them with five hundred fusileers.

It was in this situation of affairs Lefebre commenced his march
from Pampeluna on the 7th of June, at the head of three or four
thousand infantry, some field batteries, and a regiment of Polish
cavalry.† On the 9th he forced the passage of the Ebro, put the
leaders of the insurrection to death after the action, and then continued his movement by the right bank to the Mallen.‡ On the
Huecha, Palafox, with ten thousand infantry, two hundred dragoons, and eight pieces of artillery, disputed the passage, but on the
13th he was overthrown. The 14th the French reached the Xalon,
where another combat and another victory carried Lefebre across
that river. The 15th he was on the Huerba, in front of the heroic
city.

FIRST SIEGE OF ZARAGOZA.

Zaragoza contained fifty thousand inhabitants. Situated on the
right bank of the Ebro, it was connected with a suburb on the opposite side by a handsome stone bridge. Its immediate vicinity
was flat, and on the side of the suburb low and marshy. The small
river Huerba, running through a deep cleft, cut the plain on the
right bank, and taking its course close to the walls, fell into the
Ebro nearly opposite to the mouth of the Gallego, which, descending from the mountains on the opposite side, also cut the plain on
the left bank. The convent of St. Joseph, built on the right of
the Huerba, covered a bridge over that torrent, and at the distance
of cannon-shot a step of land commenced, which, gradually rising,
terminated at eighteen hundred yards from the convent, in a hill
called the Monte Torrero. On this hill, which commanded all the
plain, and overlooked the town, several storehouses, built for the
use of the canal, were intrenched, and occupied by twelve hundred
men, and the canal itself, a noble work, furnished water carriage
without a single lock from Tudela to Zaragoza.§

* Cavallero.
† S. Journal of Lefebre's Operations, MSS.
‡ Moniteur. Victoires et Conquêtes des Français. Cavallero.
§ Cavallero. Siege of Zaragoza.

The city, surrounded by a low brick wall, presented no regular defences, and possessed very few guns in a serviceable state ; but the houses were strongly constructed, and for the most part of two stories, each story vaulted, so as to be nearly fire-proof. Every house had its garrison, and the massive convents, rising like castles around the circuit and inside the place, were crowded with armed men. Such was Zaragoza when Lefebre Desnouettes appeared before it, his previous movements having cut the direct communication with Calatayud, and obliged the Baron Versage to retire to Belchite with his volunteers and fresh levies.

Palafox had occupied the olive groves and houses on the step of land between the convent of St. Joseph and Monte Torrero, but his men, cowed by their previous defeats, were easily driven from thence on the 16th.* The town was then closely invested on the right bank of the Ebro, and so great was the terror of the Spaniards, that some of the French, penetrating without difficulty into the street of St. Engracia, were like to have taken the city.† Palafox, accompanied by his brother Francisco, an aid-de-camp, and one hundred dragoons, endeavored, under pretence of seeking succor, to go forth on the side of the suburb at the moment when the French were entering on the side of Engracia ; but the plebeian leaders, suspicious of his intentions, would not suffer him to depart without a guard of infantry, commanded by *Tio*, or goodman Jorge. It was this person and *Tio* Marin who by their energy contributed most to the defence of the city in the first siege ; but for them Palafox, who has gathered the honors, would have fled at one gate while the enemy was pressing in at another,—and Zaragoza was then on the verge of destruction, for the streets were filled with clamor, the troops making little resistance, and all things in confusion. But the French, either fearful of an ambuscade or ignorant of their advantages, suddenly retired, and then the people, as if inspired, changed from the extreme of terror to that of courage, suddenly fell to casting up defences, piercing loop-holes in the walls of the houses, and constructing ramparts with sand-bags,— working with such vigor that, under the direction of their engineers, in twenty-four hours they put the place in a condition to withstand an assault. Whereupon Lefebre, confining his operations to the right bank of the Ebro, established posts close to the gates, and waited for reinforcements.

Meanwhile Palafox, crossing the Ebro at Pina, joined Versage at Belchite, and having collected seven or eight thousand men, and four pieces of artillery, gained the Xalon in rear of the French.

* S. Journal of Lefebre's Operations, MSS.
† Cavallero.

From thence he proposed to advance through Epila and relieve Zaragoza by a battle, but his officers, amazed at this project, resisted his authority, and would have retired upon Valencia.* Nevertheless, ignorant of war, and probably awed by Tio Jorge, he expressed his determination to fight, saying, with an imposing air, "that those who feared might retire." Touched with shame, all agreed to follow him to Epila, but two French regiments, detached by Lefebre, met him on the march, and the Spaniards, unable to form any order of battle, were, notwithstanding their superior numbers, defeated with the loss of three thousand men. Palafox, who did not display that firmness in danger which his speech promised, must have fled early, for he reached Calatayud in the night, although many of his troops arrived there unbroken the next morning. After this disaster, leaving Versage at Calatayud, to make fresh levies, the Spanish chief repaired, with all the beaten troops that he could collect, to Belchite, and from thence regained Zaragoza on the 2d of July.

Meanwhile Lefebre had taken the Monte Torrero by assault, and on the 29th of June was joined by General Verdier with a division of infantry and a large battering train; and being then twelve thousand strong, attacked the convents of St. Joseph and the Capuchins, the very day that Palafox returned. A first assault on St. Joseph's failed, but the second succeeded, and the Capuchins, after some fighting, was set fire to by the Spaniards and abandoned. All this time the suburb was left open and free for the besieged; and Napoleon, who blamed this mode of attack, sent orders to throw a bridge across the Ebro—to press the siege on the left bank—and to profit of the previous success, by raising a breaching battery in the convent of St. Joseph.† A bridge was accordingly constructed at St. Lambert, two hundred yards above the town, and two attacks were carried on at the same time. A change also took place in the command, for hitherto the French troops employed in the siege formed a part of Marshal Bessieres' corps, but the Emperor now directed Lefebre to rejoin that Marshal with a brigade, and then constituting the ten thousand men who remained with Verdier a separate corps, gave him the command.

Verdier continued to press the siege as closely as his numbers would permit, but around him the insurgents were rapidly organizing small armies, and threatened to inclose him in his camp, wherefore he sent detachments against them;‡ and it is singular that, with so few men, while daily fighting with the besieged, he

* Cavallero.
† S. Journal of Lefebre's Operations, MSS.
‡ Napoleon's Notes.

3*

should have been able to scour the country, and put down the insurrection, as far as Lerida, Barbastro, Tudela, Jacca and Calatayud, without any assistance save what the garrison of Pampeluna could give him from the side of Navarre. In one of these expeditions the powder-mills of Villa Felice, thirty miles distant, were destroyed, and the Baron Versage was defeated, and forced to retire with his division towards Valencia.*

During the course of July, Verdier made several assaults on the gate of El Carmen and the Portillo, but he was repulsed in all, and the besieged having been reinforced by the regiment of Estremadura, composed of eight hundred old soldiers, made a sally with two thousand men to retake the Monte Torrero; they were, however, beaten, with the loss of their commander, and regular approaches were then commenced by the French against the quarter of St. Engracia and the castle of Aljaferia. The 2d of August, the besieged were again reinforced by two hundred men of the Spanish guards and volunteers of Aragon, who brought some artillery with them, but the French also were strengthened by two old regiments of the line, which increased their numbers to fifteen thousand men; and on the 3d of August the breaching batteries opened against St. Engracia and Aljaferia; the mortars threw shells at the same time, and a Spanish magazine of powder blowing up in the Cosso, a public walk formed on the line of the ancient Moorish ramparts, destroyed several houses, and killed many of the defenders. The place was then summoned, but as Palafox rejected all offers, a breach in the convent of St. Engracia was stormed on the 4th. The French penetrated to the Cosso, and a confused and terrible scene ensued, for while some Spaniards defended the houses and some drew up in the streets, others fled by the suburb to the country, where the cavalry fell upon them.† Cries of treason, the sure signals for assassinations, were everywhere heard, and all seemed lost, when a column of the assailants, seeking a way to the bridge over the Ebro, got entangled in the Arco de Cineja, a long crooked street, and being attacked in that situation, were driven back to the Cosso; others began to plunder, and the Zaragozans, recovering courage, fought with desparation, and finally set fire to the convent of Francisco: at the close of day the French were in possession of one side of the Cosso, and the Spaniards of the other. A hideous and revolting spectacle was exhibited during this action, for the public hospital being set on fire, the madmen confined there issued forth among the combatants, muttering, shouting, singing, and moping, each according to the

* Cavallero.
† Ibid.

character of his disorder, while drivelling idiots mixed their un-meaning cries with the shouts of contending soldiers.*

The Spaniards now perceived that, with courage, the town might still be defended, and from that day the fighting was mur-derous and constant; one party endeavoring to take, the other to defend the houses. In this warfare, where skill was nearly useless, Verdier's force was too weak to make a rapid progress, and events disastrous to the French arms taking place in other parts of Spain, he received, about the 10th, orders from the King to raise the siege, and retire to Logrono. Of this operation I shall speak in due time.†

OBSERVATIONS.

1. Mere professional skill and enterprise do not constitute a great general. Lefebre Desnouettes, by his activity and boldness, with a tithe of their numbers, defeated the insurgents of Aragon in several actions, and scoured the open country; but the same Lefebre, wanting the higher qualities of a general, failed miserably where that intuitive sagacity which reads passing events aright, was required. There were thousands in the French army who could have done as well as he, probably not three who could have reduced Zaragoza; and yet it is manifest that Zaragoza owed her safety to accident, and that the desperate resistance of the inhabit-ants was more the result of chance than of any peculiar virtue.

2. The feeble defence made at Mallen, at the Xalon, at the Monte Torrero, at Epila; the terror of the besieged on the 16th, when the French penetrated into the town; the flight of Palafox under the pretence of seeking succor; nay, the very assault which in such a wonderful manner called forth the energy of the Zarago-zans, and failed only because the French troops plundered, and, by missing the road to the bridge, missed that to victory, proves that the fate of the city was determined by accident, in more than one of those nice conjunctures, which men of genius know how to seize, but others leave to the decision of fortune. However, it must be acknowledged that Lefebre and Verdier, especially the latter, displayed both vigor and talent; for it was no mean exploit to quell the insurrections to a distance of fifty miles on every side, at the same time investing double their own numbers, and pushing the attack with such ardor as to reduce to extremity a city so defended.

3. The current romantic tales, of women rallying the troops and leading them forward at the most dangerous periods of this siege,

* Cavallero.
† S. Journal of Lefebre's Operations, MSS.

I have not touched upon, and may perhaps be allowed to doubt; yet it is not unlikely that, when suddenly environed with horrors, the delicate sensitiveness of women, driving them to a kind of phrenzy, might produce actions above the heroism of men—and in patient suffering their superior fortitude is acknowledged by all nations; wherefore I neither wholly believe, nor will deny their exploits at Zaragoza, merely remarking that for a long time afterwards Spain swarmed with heroines from that city, clothed in half uniforms, and loaded wtth weapons.

4. The two circumstances that principally contributed to the success of the defence were, the bad discipline of the French soldiers and the system of terror which was established by the Spanish leaders, whoever those leaders were. Few soldiers can be restrained from plunder when a town is taken by assault, yet there is no period when the chances of war are so sudden and so decisive, none where the moral responsibility of a general is so great. Will military regulations alone secure the necessary discipline at such a moment? The French army are not deficient in a stern code, and the English army, taken all together, is probably the best regulated of modern times; but here it is seen that Lefebre failed to take Zaragoza in default of discipline, and in the course of this work it will appear that no wild horde of Tartars ever fell with more license upon their rich effeminate neighbors than did the English troops upon the Spanish towns taken by storm. The inference to be drawn is, that national institutions only will produce that moral discipline necessary to make a soldier capable of fulfilling his whole duty; yet the late Lord Melville was not ashamed to declare in Parliament that the worst men make the best soldiers, and this odious, narrow-minded, unworthy maxim had its admirers. That a system of terror was at Zaragoza successfully employed to protract the defence, is undoubted. The commandant of Monte Torrero, ostensibly for suffering himself to be defeated, but according to some for the gratification of private malice, was tried and put to death. A general of artillery was in a more summary manner killed without any trial, and the chief engineer, a man of skill and undaunted courage, was arbitrarily imprisoned. The slightest word, or even gesture of discontent, was punished with instant death.* A stern band of priests and plebeian leaders, in whose hands Palafox was a tool, ruled with such furious energy that resistance to the enemy was less dangerous than disobedience to their orders: suspicion was the warrant of death; and this system, once begun, ceased not until the town was taken in the second siege.

* Cavallero.

CHAPTER VI.

Operations in Catalonia—General Swartz marches against the town of Manresa, and General Chabran against Tarragona—French defeated at Bruch—Chabran recalled,—Burns Arbos—Marches against Bruch—Retreats—Duhesme assaults Gerona—Is repulsed with loss—Action on the Llobregat—General insurrection of Catalonia—Figueras blockaded—General Reille relieves it—First siege of Gerona—The Marquis of Palacios arrives in Catalonia with the Spanish troops from the Balearic isles, declared Captain-General under St. Narcissus, re-establishes the line of the Llobregat—The Count of Caldagues forces the French lines at Gerona—Duhesme raises the siege and returns to Barcelona—Observations—Moncey marches against Valencia, defeats the Spaniards at Pajaso, at the Siete Aguas, and at Quarte—Attacks Valencia, is repulsed, marches into Murcia—Forces the passage of the Xucar, defeats Serbelloni at San Felippe, arrives at San Clemente—Insurrection at Cuença quelled by General Caulincourt—Observations.

WHEN Barcelona fell into the power of the French, the Spanish garrison amounted to nearly four thousand men, wherefore Duhesme, daily fearing a riot in the city, connived at their escape in parties, and even sent the regiment of Estremadura entire to Lerida;[*] but, strange to relate, the gates were shut against it! and thus discarded by both parties, it made its way into Zaragoza during the siege of that place. Many thousand citizens also fled from Barcelona and joined the patriotic standards in the neighboring provinces.

After the first ebullition at Manresa, the insurrection of Catalonia lingered awhile, yet the Junta of Gerona continued to excite the people to take arms, and it was manifest that a general commotion approached.[†] This was a serious affair, for there were in the beginning of June, including those who came out of Barcelona, five thousand veteran troops in the province, and in the Balearic islands above ten thousand. Sicily contained an English army, and English fleets covered the Mediterranean.[‡] Moreover, by the constitution of Catalonia, the whole of the male population fit for war are obliged to assemble at certain points of each district, with arms and provisions, whenever the alarum bell, called the *somaten*, is heard to ring, hence the name of *somatenes;* and these warlike peasants, either from tradition or experience, are well acquainted with the military value of their mountain holds.

Hostilities soon commenced. Duhesme, following his instructions, detached General Chabran, with five thousand two hundred men, to secure Tarragona and Tortosa, to incorporate the Swiss

---

[*] Cabanes, 1st Part.
[†] Napoleon's Notes.
[‡] Cabanes, 1st Part.

regiment of Wimpfen with his own troops, and to aid Marshal Moncey in an attack on Valencia. At the same time General Swartz, having more than three thousand Swiss, Germans and Italians under his command, was detached by the way of Martorel and Montserrat to Manresa.* His orders were to raise contributions, to put down the insurrection, to destroy the powder mills at the last town, to get possession of Lerida, to incorporate all the Swiss troops found there in his own brigade, to place five hundred men in the citadel, and finally to penetrate into Aragon and co-operate with Lefebre against Zaragoza.

These two columns quitted Barcelona the 3d and the 4th of June, but a heavy rain induced Swartz to halt the 5th at Martorel; the 6th he resumed his march, without any military precautions, although the object of his expedition was known, and, the somaten ringing out among the hills, the peasants of eight districts were assembled in arms.† These men having taken a resolution to defend the pass of Bruch, the most active of the Manresa and Igualada districts, assisted by a few old soldiers, immediately repaired there, and when Swartz came on in a careless manner, opened a heavy but distant fire from the rocks. Some confusion arose, but the Catalans were soon beaten from their fastness, and pursued for four or five miles along the main road to Casa Mansana, where a cross road leads to Manresa; here one part broke away, while the others continued their flight to Igualada.

Swartz, a man evidently destitute of talent, halted at the very moment when his success was complete, and the Catalans, seeing his hesitation, first rallied in the rear of Casa Mansana, then returned to the attack, and finally drove the advanced guard back upon the main body. The French General now became alarmed, formed a square, and retired hastily towards Esparraguéra, followed and flanked by clouds of somatenes, whose courage and numbers increased every moment. At Esparraguéra, which was a long single street, the inhabitants had prepared an ambush; but Swartz, who arrived at twilight, getting intelligence of their design, passed to the right and left of the houses, and continuing his flight, reached Martorel the 7th. He lost a gun and many men by this inglorious expedition, from which he returned in such disorder, and with his soldiers so discouraged, that Duhesme thought it necessary to recall Chabran from Tarragona. That General, although the country westward of the Llobregat is rugged and difficult for an army, had reached Tarragona on the 8th, without encountering an enemy; but when he attempted to return, the line of his march was inter-

* St. Cyr. Victoirés et Conquêtes des Français. Foy. Cabanes.
† Ibid.

cepted by the insurgents, who took post at Vendrill, Arbos and Villa Franca, and spread themselves along the banks of the Llobregat. As he approached Vendrill, the somatenes fell back to Arbos, and were defeated there; whereupon the French set fire to the town and proceeded to Villa França. Here the excesses so common at this time among the Spaniards were not spared; the governor, an old man, and several of his friends, had been murdered, and the perpetrators of these crimes, as might be expected, made little or no defence against the enemy. Meanwhile General Lechi moved out of Barcelona, and acting in concert with Swartz's brigade, which had reached Martorel, cleared the banks of the Llobregat, and formed a junction at San Felice with Chabran on the 11th. The latter, after a day's rest, then marched with his own and Swartz's brigade on Manresa, to repair the former disgrace, and he arrived at Bruch the 14th; but the somatenes, assisted by some regular troops with artillery, were again there, and Chabran, more timid even than Swartz, finding that in a partial skirmish he made no impression, took the extraordinary resolution of retreating, or rather flying from those gallant peasants, who pursued him with scoffs and a galling fire back to the very walls of Barcelona.

These successes spurred on the insurrection. Gerona, Rosas, Hostalrich, and Tarragona prepared for defence. The somatenes of the Ampurdan obliged the French commandant to quit the town of Figueras and shut himself up with three hundred men in the citadel, while others, gathering between the Ter and the Besos, intercepted all communication between France and Barcelona. In this predicament, Duhesme resolved to make a sudden attempt on Gerona, with six thousand of his best troops and eight pieces of artillery; but as the fortress of Hostalrich stood in the direct road, he followed the coast line, and employed a French privateer then in the harbor to attend his march. The somatenes soon got intelligence of his designs: one multitude took possession of the heights of Moncada, which are six miles from Barcelona, and overhang the road to Hostalrich; another multitude was posted on the ridge of Mongat, which, at the same distance from Barcelona, abuts on the sea; and these last were protected on the left by an intrenched castle with a battery of fifteen guns, and on the right were slightly connected with the people at Moncada. The 17th, Duhesme, after some false movements, defeated them, and a detachment from Barcelona dispersed those at Moncada the same day; the 18th, the town of Mattaro was taken and plundered, the somatenes were again defeated at the pass of St. Pol, and at nine o'clock in the morning of the 20th, the French appeared before Gerona.

This town, built on the right bank of the Ter, is cut in two by the

Oña. To the eastward it is confined by strong rocky hills, whose points filling the space between the Oña and the Ter, overlook the town at different distances. Fort Mont Jouy, a regular fortification, crowned the nearest hill or table land, at five hundred yards' distance; three other forts, namely, that of the Constable, that of Queen Ann, and that of Capuchins, all connected by a ditch and rampart, formed one irregular outwork a thousand yards in length, and commanding all the ridge to the south-east. The summit of this ridge is five, eight, and twelve hundred yards from Gerona, and sixteen hundred from Fort Mont Juoy, and is separated from the latter by the narrow valley and stream of the Gallegan.

South-west, between the left of the Oña and Ter, the country is comparatively flat, but full of hollows and clefts close to the town, and the body of the place on that side was defended by a ditch and five regular bastions, connected by a wall with towers. To the west the city was covered by the Ter, and on the east fortified by a long wall with towers, having an irregular bastion at each extremity, and some small detached works placed at the opening of the valley of Gallegan. Three hundred of the regiment of Ultonia and some artillery-men composed the garrison of Gerona; they were assisted by volunteers and by the citizens, and the somatenes also assembled on the left of the Ter to defend the passage of that river.

Duhesme, after provoking some cannon-shot from the forts, occupied the village of St. Eugenia, in the plain, and making a feint as if to pass the Ter by the bridge of Salt, engaged the somatenes in a useless skirmish. Great part of the day was spent by him in preparing ladders for the attack; at five o'clock in the evening the French artillery opened from the heights of Palau, and then a column crossing the Oña passed between the outworks and the town, threw out a detachment to keep the garrison of the former in check, and assaulted the gate of El Carmen.* This attempt failed completely, and with great loss to the assailants. Two hours after, another column advancing by the left of the Oña assaulted the bastion of Santa Clara, but with so little arrangement or discipline, that the storming party had only three or four ladders;† and although by favor of the hollows they reached the walls unperceived, and the Neapolitan Colonel Ambrosio and the engineer Lafaille actually gained the top of the ramparts, the confusion amongst the assailants was such that no success was obtained. Duhesme tried negotiation on the following day, yet dreading a

* St. Cyr.
† Lafaille.

longer absence from Barcelona, broke up on the 22d, and returned by forced marches, leaving Chabran with some troops in Mattaro as he passed. During his absence the victorious somatenes of Bruch had descended the Llobregat, rallied those of the lower country, and getting artillery from Tarragona and other fortresses, planted batteries at the different passages of the river, and intrenched a line from San Boy to Martorel. Regular officers now took the command of the peasants. Colonel Milans assembled a body at Granollers; Don Juan Claros put himself at the head of the peasants of the Ampurdan; Colonel Baget took the command of those at Bruch.

Chabran, after a few days' rest at Mattaro, made a foraging excursion through the district of El Valles, but Milans, who held the valley of the Congosta, encountered him near Granollers, and both sides claimed the victory; Chabran, however, retired to Barcelona, and Milans remained on the banks of the Besos. The 30th, Duhesme caused the somatenes on the Llobregat to be attacked, sent Lechi to menace those at the bridge of Molinos del Rey, and the brigades of Bessieres and Goullus to cross at San Boy; the latter, having surprised a battery at that point, turned the whole line, and Lechi then crossing the river by the bridge of Molinos, ascended the left bank, took all the artillery, burnt several villages, and put the insurgents to flight. They however rallied again at Bruch and Igualada, and returning the 6th of July, infested the immediate vicinity of Barcelona, taking possession of all the hills between San Boy and Moncada, and connecting their operations with Colonel Milans. Other parties collected between the Besos and the Ter, and the line of insurrection was extended to the Ampurdan; Juan Claros occupied the flat country about Rosas, and the French garrison of Figueras having burnt the town, were blocked up in the Fort of San Fernando by two thousand somatenes of the Pyrenees; a nest of Spanish privateers was formed in Palamos Bay, and two English frigates, the Impérieuse and the Cambrian, watched the coast from Rosas to Barcelona. A supreme junta was now established at Lerida, and opened an intercourse with Aragon, Valencia, Seville, Gibraltar, and the Balearic islands; it also decreed that forty tercios, or regiments of one thousand men, to be selected from the somatenes, should be paid and organized as regular troops, and that forty others should be kept in reserve, but without pay.

This state of affairs being made known to Napoleon through the medium of the movable columns watching the valleys of the eastern Pyrenees, he ordered General Reille, then commanding the reserve at Perpignan, to take the first soldiers at hand and march to the relief of Figueras; after which, his force being increased by drafts from the interior of France to nine thousand, he was to assault Rosas and besiege Gerona; and the Emperor imagined that the fall of the latter place would induce the surrender of Lerida, and would so tranquillize Catatonia, that five thousand men might again be detached towards Valencia. On receiving this order, Reille, with two battalions of Tuscan recruits, conducted a convoy safely to Figueras and raised a blockake, but not without difficulty, for his troops were greatly terrified, and could scarcely be kept to their colors.* He however relieved the place the 10th of July, and the same day, Duhesme, who had been preparing for a second attack on Gerona, quitted Barcelona with six thousand infantry, some cavalry, a battering train of twenty-two pieces, and a great number of country carriages to transport his ammunition and stores, leaving Lechi in the city with five thousand men. Meanwhile Reille, having victualled Figueras and received a part of his reinforcements, proceeded to invest Rosas; but he had scarcely appeared before it when Juan Claros raised the country in his rear, and Captain Otway, of the Montague, landing with some marines, joined the migueletes, whereupon the French retired with a loss of two hundred men.†

Duhesme pursued his march by the coast, but the somatenes broke up the road in his front, Milans hung on his left, and Lord Cochrane, with the Impérieuse frigate and some Spanish vessels, cannonaded his right. Thus incommoded, he halted five days in front of Arenas de Mar, and then dividing his force, sent one part across the mountains by Villagorguin, and another by San Isicle. The first column made an attempt on Hostalrich, and failed; the second, beating Milans, dispersed the somatenes of the Tordera; and finally, Duhesme united his forces before Gerona, but he lost many carriages on his march. The 23d he passed the Ter, and dispersed the migueletes that guarded the left bank. The 24th General Reille, coming from Figueras with six thousand men, took post at Puente Mayor, and the town was invested, from that point, by the heights of San Miguel to the Monte Livio; from Monte Livio by the plain to the bridge of Salt; and from thence along the left bank of the Ter to Sarria. The garrison, consisting of five hundred migueletes and four hundred of the regiment of Ultonia, was reinforced on the 25th by thirteen hundred of the regiment of Barcelona, who entered the town with two guns; the defences were in bad repair, but the people were resolute.

In the night of the 27th, a French column passed the valley of the

* Foy's History.
† Lord Collingwood's despatch, Aug. 27. Foy's History.

Galligan, gained the table land of Mont Jouy, and of three towers, which the Spaniards abandoned in a panic. This advantage so elated Duhesme, that he resolved, without consulting his engineer, to break ground on that side ;* but at this period a great change in the affairs of Catalonia had taken place.† The insurrection, hitherto confined to the exertions of the unorganized somatenes, was now consolidated by a treaty between Lord Collingwood, who commanded the British navy in the Mediterranean, and the Marquis of Palacios, who was Captain-General of the Balearic isles ; thus the Spanish fleet and the troops in Minorca, Majorca, and Ivica, became disposable for the service of the patriots.‡ Palacios immediately sent thirteen hundred men to the port of San Felice di Quixols to reinforce the garrison of Gerona, and these men entered that city, as we have seen, on the 25th, while Palacios himself disembarked four thousand others, together with thirty-seven pieces of artillery, at Tarragona, an event which excited universal joy, and produced a surprising eagerness to fight the French. The Supreme Junta immediately repaired to that town, declared Palacios their President, and created him Commander-in-Chief, subject, however, to their tutelar saint, Narcissus, who was appointed generalissimo of the forces by sea and land, the ensigns of authority being, with due solemnity, placed on his coffin.

The first object with Palacios was to re-establish the line of the Llobregat. To effect this, the Count of Caldagues, with eighteen hundred men and four guns, marched from Tarragona in two columns, the one moving by the coast way to San Boy, and the other by the royal road, through Villafranca and Ordal. Caldagues, in passing by the bridge of Molino del Rey, established a post there, and then ascending the left bank, fixed his quarters at Martorel, where Colonel Baget joined him with three thousand migueletes of the new levy. Now the Llobregat runs within a few miles of Barcelona, but as the right bank is much the steepest, the lateral communications easier, and as the heights command a distinct view of everything passing on the opposite side, the line taken by Caldagues was strong, for the country in his rear was rough with defiles, and very fitting for a retreat after the loss of a battle.

General Lechi, thus hemmed in on the west, was also hampered on the north, because the mountains filling the space between the Llobregat and the Besos approach in tongues as near as two and three miles from Barcelona, and the somatenes of the Manresa and Valls districts occupying them, skirmished daily with the French

* St. Cyr. Campaign in Catalonia.
† Cabanes' History.
‡ St. Cyr. Cabanes' History, 2d Part.

outposts. And beyond the Besos, which bounds Barcelona on the eastward, a lofty continuous ridge, extending to Hostalrich, runs parallel to and at the distance of two or three miles from the sea-coast, separating the main from the marine roads, and sending its shoots down to the water's edge; this ridge also swarmed with somatenes, who cut off all communication with Duhesme, and lay in leaguer round the castle of Mongat, in which were eighty or ninety French. The Cambrian and the Impérieuse frigates blockaded the harbor of Barcelona itself; and, on the 31st, Lord Cochrane having brought his vessel alongside of Mongat, landed his marines, and in concert with the somatenes, took it, blew up the works, and rolled the rocks and ruins down in such a manner as to destroy the road.* Thus, at the very moment that Duhesme commenced the siege of Gerona, he was cut off from his own base of operations, and the communication between Figueras and General Reille's division was equally insecure; for the latter's convoys were attacked the 28th of July and the 3d of August; and so fiercely on the 6th, that a Neapolitan battalion was surrounded, and lost one hundred and fifty men.†

Palacios, whose forces increased daily, now wished to make an effort in favor of Gerona, and with this view sent the Count of Caldagues, at the head of three or four thousand men, part miguel-etes, part regulars, to interrupt the progress of the siege, intending to follow himself with greater forces. Caldagues marched by Tar-rasa, Sabadell, Granollers, and San Celoni, and reached Hostalrich the morning of the 10th, where his force was increased to five thousand men and four guns. The 13th he entered Llagostera, and the 14th Castellar, a small place situated behind the ridges that overlook Gerona, and only five miles from the French camps. Here Juan Claros, with two thousand five hundred migueletes, mixed with some Walloon and Spanish guards from Rosas, met him, as did also Milans with eight hundred somatenes. A commu-nication with the Junta of Gerona was then opened. Fort Mont Jouy was upon the point of surrendering; but the French, who were ignorant of Caldagues' approach, had, contrary to good dis-cipline, heaped their forces in the plain between the left of the Oña and the Ter, but only kept a slender guard on the hills, while a single battalion protected the batteries raised against Mont Jouy. Being an enterprising man, the Spanish general resolved to make an immediate effort for the relief of the place, and, after a careful observation, sent, on the 16th, several columns against the weak part of the besiegers' line; the garrison sallied forth at the same

* Lord Collingwood's despatches.
† St. Cyr.

time from Mont Jouy, and the French guards being taken between two fires, were quickly overpowered, and driven first to the Puente Mayor, and finally over the Ter. The Catalans re-formed on the hills, expecting to be attacked; but Duhesme and Reille remained quiet until dark, and then breaking up the siege, fled, the one to Figueras, the other to Barcelona, leaving both artillery and stores behind.

Duhesme at first wished to retreat by the coast, but at Callella he learned that the road was cut, that an English frigate was ready to rake his columns, and that the somatenes were on all the heights; wherefore, destroying his ammunition, he threw his artillery over the rocks, and, taking to the mountains, forced a passage through the somatenes to Mongat, where Lechi met him and covered the retreat to Barcelona.

OBSERVATION 1st.—Three great communications pierce the Pyrenean frontier of Catalonia, leading directly upon Barcelona.

The first, or Puycerda road, penetrates between the sources of the Segre and the Ter.

The second, or Campredon road, between the sources of the Ter and the Fluvia.

The third, or Figueras road, between the sources of the Muga and the sea-coast.

The first and second unite at Vicque; the second and third are connected by a transverse road running from Olot, by Castle Follit, to Gerona; the third, also dividing near the latter town, leads with one branch through Hostalrich, and with the other follows the line of the coast. After the union of the first and second at Vicque, a single route pursues the stream of the Besos to Barcelona, thus turning the Muga, the Fluvia, the Ter, the Tordera, Besos, and an infinity of minor streams, which, in their rapid course to the Mediterranean, furrow all the country between the eastern Pyrenees and Barcelona. The third, which is the direct and best communication between Perpignan and the capital of Catalonia, crosses all the above-named rivers, and their deep channels and sudden floods offer serious obstacles to the march of an army.

All these roads, with the exception of that from Olot to Gerona, are separated by craggy mountain ridges scarcely to be passed by troops; and the two first, leading through wild and savage districts, are incommoded by defiles, and protected by a number of old castles and walled places, more or less capable of resistance. The third, passing through many rich and flourishing places, is however completely blocked, to an invader, by the strong fortresses of Figueras and Rosas on the Muga, of Gerona on the Ter, and Hostalrich on the Tordera. Palamos and other castles likewise impede the coast road, which is moreover skirted by rocky mountains, and exposed for many leagues to the fire of a fleet. Such is Catalonia, eastward and northward of Barcelona.

On the west, at five or six miles distance, the Llobregat cuts it off from a rough and lofty tract, through which the Cardena, the Noga, the Foix, Gaya, Anguera, and Francoli rivers, breaking down deep channels, descend in nearly parallel lines to the coast, and the spaces between are gorged with mountains, and studded with fortified places which command all the main roads.

So few and contracted are the plains and fertile valleys, that Catalonia may, with the exception of the rich parts about Lerida and the Urgel, be described as a huge mass of rocks and torrents, incapable of supplying subsistence even for the inhabitants, whose prosperity depends entirely upon manufactures and commerce. Barcelona, the richest and most populous city in Spain, is the heart of the province; and who masters it, if he can hold it, may suck the strength of Catalonia away. But a French army, without a commanding fleet to assist, can scarcely take or keep Barcelona; the troops must be supplied by regular convoys from France, the fortresses on the line of communication must be taken and provisioned, and the active intelligent population of the country must be beaten from the rivers, pursued into their fortresses, and warred down by exertions which none but the best troops are capable of: for the Catalans are robust, numerous, and brave enough after their own manner.

Observation 2d.—It follows, from this exposition, that Duhesme evinced a surprising want of forethought and military sagacity, in neglecting to secure Gerona, Hostalrich, and Tarragona, with garrisons, when his troops were received into those places. It was this negligence that rendered the timid operations of Swartz and Chabran capital errors; it was this that enabled some poor, injured, indignant peasants to kindle a mighty war, and in a very few weeks obliged Napoleon to send thirty thousand men to the relief of Barcelona.

Observation 3d.—Duhesme was experienced in battles, and his energy and resources of mind have been praised by a great authority;[*] but undoubtedly an absence of prudent calculation and arrangement, a total neglect of military discipline, marked all his operations in Catalonia. Witness his mode of attack on Gerona—the deficiency of ladders, and the confusion of the assaults;[†] witness also his raising of the second siege, and absolute flight from

* Napoleon.
† St. Cyr.

Caldagues, whose rash enterprise, although crowned with success, should have caused his own destruction. In those affairs it is certain Duhesme displayed neither talent nor vigor; but in the severities he exercised at the sacking of Mattaró, in the burning of villages, which he executed to the extreme verge of, if not beyond, what the harshest laws of war will justify, an odious energy was apparent ;* and as the ardor of the somatenes was rather increased than repressed by these rigorous proceedings, his conduct may be deemed as impolitic as it was barbarous. It is however to be remembered that Duhesme has not wanted defenders, who, asserting that he was humane and just, accuse Lechi, his equal in rank, of being the author of the severities exercised at Barcelona.†

OBSERVATION 4th.—In Catalonia all the inherent cruelty of the Spaniards was as grossly displayed as in any other province of Spain. The Catalans were likewise vain and superstitious. But their courage was higher, their patriotism purer, and their efforts more sustained; the somatenes were bold and active in battle, the population of the towns firm, and some of the juntas apparently disinterested. The praise merited and bestowed upon the people of Zaragoza is great, yet Gerona more justly claims the admiration of mankind. For the Aragonese troops were by Lefebre driven from the open country in crowds to their capital, and little was wanted to induce them to surrender at once; it was not until the last hour that, gathering courage from despair, the people of Zaragoza put forth all their energy, whereas those of Gerona, although attacked by a greater force, and possessing fewer means of defence, without any internal system of terror to counterbalance their fear of the enemy, manfully and successfully resisted from the first. The people of Zaragoza rallied at their hearthstones, those of Gerona stood firm at the porch. But, quitting these matters, I must now, following the order I have marked out, proceed to relate the occurrences in Valencia.

OPERATIONS OF MARSHAL MONCEY.

The execution of Calvo and his followers changed the horrid aspect of the Valencian insurrection; the spirit of murder was checked, and the patriotic energy assumed a nobler appearance. Murcia and Valencia were united as one province, and towards the end of June nearly thirty thousand men, armed and provided with artillery, attested the resources of these rich provinces, and the activity of their chiefs. The Valencians then conceived the plan of marching to the assistance of the Aragonese; but Napoleon had

* Napoleon's Notes.   St. Cyr.   Cabanes.
† Lafaille.

already prescribed the measures which were to render such a movement abortive.

An order dated the 30th of May had directed Moncey to move with a column of ten thousand men upon Cuença; from that point he was to watch the country comprised between the lower Ebro and Carthagena, and he was empowered to act against the city of Valencia if he judged it fitting to do so. The position of Cuença was advantageous; a short movement from thence to the left would place Moncey's troops upon the direct line between Valencia and Zaragoza, and enable him to intercept all communication between those towns;* and a few marches to the right would place him upon the junction of the roads leading from Carthagena and Valencia to Madrid. If he thought it essential to attack Valencia, the division of General Chabran was to co-operate from the side of Catalonia, by which combination the operations of Lefebre Desnouettes at Zaragoza, and those of Duhesme in Catalonia, were covered from the Valencians; and at the same time the flank of the French army at Madrid was protected on the side of Murcia.

The 6th of June Moncey marched from Aranjuez by Santa Cruz, Tarancon, Carascoso, and Villa del Osma, and reached Cuença the 11th. Here receiving information of the rapid progress of the insurrection, of the state of the Valencian army, and of the projected movement to relieve Zaragoza, he resolved to make an attempt against the city of Valencia.† In this view, supposing General Chabran to be at Tortosa, he ordered him to march upon Castellon de la Plana, a town situated at some distance eastward of the river Guadalaviar, proposing himself to clear the country westward of that river; and he fixed the 25th of June as the latest period at which the two columns were to communicate in the immediate vicinity of Valencia.

Halting from the 11th to the 16th at Cuença, he marched the 17th to Tortola, the 18th to Buenaches, the 19th to Matilla, the 20th to Minglanilla, and the 21st to Pesquiera; but from Buenaches to Pesquiera no inhabitants were to be seen, the villages were deserted, and either from fear or hatred, every living person fled before his footsteps. At length a Swiss regiment, some of the Spanish guards, and a body of armed peasantry, made a stand at the bridge of Pajaso, upon the river Cabriel, and the manner in which the country had been forsaken, the gloomy and desolate marches, and the sudden appearance of an armed force ready to dispute this important pass, prognosticated a desperate conflict; yet the event belied the omens,—scarcely any resistance was made.

* S. Journal of Moncey's Operations, MSS.
† Ibid.

Moncey, having informed General Chabran of this success, appointed the 27th and 28th for a junction under the walls of Valencia. The next day he took a position at Otiel;* but hearing that the defeated patriots had rallied, and, reinforced to the number of ten or twelve thousand, were intrenching themselves upon his left, he quitted the direct line of march to attack them in their post of Cabrillas, which was somewhat in advance of the Siete Aguas. The Spanish position was of extraordinary strength; the flanks rested upon steep rocky mountains, and the only approach to the front was through a long narrow defile, formed by high scarped rocks, whose tops, inaccessible from the French side, were covered with the armed peasantry of the neighborhood. As a direct assault upon such a position could not succeed, and General Harispe was directed to turn it by the right, while the cavalry and artillery occupied the attention of the Spaniards in front, that general soon overcame the obstacles of ground, reached the Spanish troops, and defeated them, with the loss of all their cannon, ammunition and baggage, and also of the Swiss regiment, which came over to the victors. This action happened on the 24th; it freed Moncey's left flank, and he resumed his march by the direct road to Valencia, where he arrived the 27th. The ancient walls remained, all the approaches were commanded by works hastily repaired or newly raised, the citadel was in a state of defence, and the population were willing to fight.

A city containing eighty thousand people actuated by violent passions cannot be easily overcome; and Valencia, built upon low ground, and encircled with numerous canals and cuts, made for the purposes of irrigation, had its deep ditches filled with water, so that no approach could be made except against the gates. An assault seemed hopeless, but it is said that the Marshal had corrupted a smuggler, who promised to betray the city during the heat of the assault, and it is probable that some secret understanding of that kind induced him to make an attempt which would otherwise have been rash and unmilitary.

Don Joseph Caro, a brother to the Marquis of Romana, was with four thousand men intrenched behind the canal of the Guadalaviar, five miles in advance of the city gates; and as the village of Quarte, and some thickly planted mulberry trees, helped to render this post very strong, Moncey, who attacked it upon the 27th, met with a vigorous resistance. Caro was, however, beaten and chased into the city, with the loss of some cannon, and on the 28th the French drove in the outposts, and occupied all the principal avenues of the town. Enthusiastic as the Valencians were while

* S. Journal of Moncey's Operations, MSS.

the enemy was at a distance, Moncey's appearance filled them with terror, and it is possible that a vigorous assault might have succeeded at the first moment of consternation ; yet the favorable opportunity, if it really existed, quickly passed away. Padre Rico, a friar distinguished by his resolution, traversed the streets with a cross in one hand and a sword in the other, arousing the sinking spirit and exciting the fanaticism of the multitude. The fear of retaliation for the massacre of the French residents, and the certainty that Moncey's troops were few, powerfully seconded his efforts ; and as it is usual for undisciplined masses to pass suddenly from one extreme to another, fear was soon succeeded by enthusiasm.

After disposing his field-pieces at the most favorable points, Moncey, while the impression of Caro's defeat was fresh, summoned the governor. The latter answered, "that he would defend the city," and the French fire then opened; but the heavy guns of the Spaniards soon overpowered it. A warm skirmish about the houses of the suburbs and at the gates ensued, and the Valencians fought so well, that when the night fell, no impression had been made on the defences ; the assailants were repulsed with loss at every point, and the situation of the French Marshal became delicate. The persons sent to seek Chabran could gain no intelligence of that general's movements ; the secret connexions of the town, if any there were, had failed ; the ammunition was nearly expended, and the army was encumbered with seven or eight hundred wounded men, and among them the general of engineers. Moncey, swayed by these circumstances, relinquished his attack, and the 29th fell back to Quarte.

When it is considered that in a great city only a small number of persons can estimate justly the immense advantages of their situation and the comparative weakness of the enemy, it must be confessed that the spirit displayed by the Valencians upon this occasion was very great. Unfortunately it ended here ; nothing worthy of such an energetic commencement was afterwards performed, although very considerable armies were either raised or maintained in the province.

At Quarte, the French ascertained that the Captain-General, Serbelloni, was marching upon Almanza to intercept the communication with Chieva and Buñol, whereupon Moncey resolved to relinquish the line of Cuença, and attack him before he could quit the kingdom of Murcia.* This vigorous resolution he executed with great celerity; for, directing the head of his column towards Torrente, he continued his march until night, halting a short distance from that town, and by a forced march the next day reached

* Journal of Moncey.

Alcira, only one league from the river Xucar. From his bivouac at that place he dispatched advice to General Chabran of this change of affairs, and meanwhile Serbelloni, surprised in the midst of his movement, and disconcerted in his calculations by the decision and rapidity of Moncey, took up a position to defend the passage of the Xucar. The line of that river is strong, and offers many advantageous points of resistance, but the Spaniards imprudently occupied both banks, and in this exposed situation they were attacked on the morning of the 1st of July. The division on the French side of the river was overthrown, the passage forced without loss of time, and Serbelloni retired to the heights of San Felice, which covered the main road leading from Alcira to Almanza, hoping to secure the defiles in front of the latter town before the enemy could arrive there. But Moncey was again too quick for him; leaving San Felice to his left, he continued his march on another route, and by a strenuous exertion seized the gorge of the defiles near Almanza late in the night of the 2d, and when the Spanish troops approached his position, he dispersed them at day-break on the 3d, and captured some of their guns. The road being now open, Moncey entered Almanza, and then marched by Bonete and Chinchilla to Albacete, where he got intelligence that Frere's division, which he expected to find at San Clemente, was gone to Requeña.

To understand this movement of Frere, it must be known, that, when Dupont and Moncey marched against Andalusia and Valencia, two divisions were retained by Savary to scour the country near Madrid, and to connect the operations of the main bodies; but they were ill-managed. General Gobert, who, following Napoleon's orders, should have been at Valladolid, reinforced Dupont; and General Frere was sent to Requeña to reinforce Moncey, when he should have been at San Clemente, a central point from whence he could gave gained the road of Seville, that of Valencia and Cuença, or that of Carthagena. Meanwhile the people of the Cuença district having suddenly overpowered a detachment left there by Moncey, Savary ordered Frere to move from San Clemente to Requeña, and sent Caulaincourt from Taracon to quell the insurgents, which was effected with great slaughter on the 3d of July; and the town of Cuença was pillaged. Hence when Frere, who quitted San Clemente on the 26th, reached Requeña, he found the country quiet, heard of Caulaincourt's success, and discovered that Moncey, having crossed the Xucar, was on the road to San Clemente. Then retracing his steps, he returned to the latter place with troops sickly, wearied, and exhausted by these long useless marches in the heat of summer.

Moncey now re-organized his forces, and was preparing artillery and other means for a second attempt against Valencia, when he was interrupted by Savary, who, alarmed at the advance of Cuesta and Blake, recalled Frere towards Madrid. The Marshal, extremely offended that the Duke of Rovigo, inflated with momentary power, should treat him with so little ceremony, then abandoned San Clemente, and returned by the way of Ocaña to the capital.*

OBSERVATIONS.

1. The result of Marshal Moncey's campaign was published by the Spaniards, as a great and decisive failure, and produced extravagant hopes of final success ; a happy illusion, if the chiefs had not partaken of it, and pursued their wild course of mutual flattery and exaggeration, without reflecting that in truth there was nothing very satisfactory in the prospect of affairs. Moncey's operation was in the nature of a movable column, the object of which was to prevent the junction of the Valencian army with the Aragonese ; the attempt upon the town of Valencia was, therefore, a simple experiment, which, successful, would have produced great effects— failing, was of trifling consequence in a military point of view. Valencia was not the essential object of the expedition, and the fate of the general campaign depended upon the armies in Old Castile.

2. It was consoling that a rich and flourishing town had not fallen into the power of the enemy ; but at the same time, a want of real nerve in the Spanish insurrection was visible. The kingdoms of Murcia and Valencia acted in concert, and contained two of the richest sea-port towns in the Peninsula ; their united force amounted to thirty thousand organized troops, exclusive of the armed peasants in various districts, and the populace of Valencia were deeply committed by the massacre of the French residents. Here then, if in any place, a strenuous resistance was to be expected ; nevertheless, Marshal Moncey, whose whole force was, at first, only eight thousand French, and never exceeded ten thousand men, continued marching and fighting without cessation for a month, forced two of the strongest mountain passes in the world, crossed several large and difficult rivers, and carried the war into the streets of Valencia. Disappointed of assistance from Catalonia, he yet extricated himself from a difficult situation, defeated his opponents in five actions, killed and wounded a number of them equal in amount to the whole of his own force, and made a circuit of above three hundred miles through a hostile and populous country, without having sustained any serious loss, without any

* Foy's History.

desertion from the Spanish battalions incorporated with his own, and what was of more importance, having those battalions much increased by desertions from the enemy. In short, the great object of the expedition had been attained, the plan of relieving Zaragoza was entirely frustrated, and the organization of an efficient Spanish force retarded. But Moncey could hardly have expected to succeed against the town of Valencia; for, to use Napoleon's words, "*a city with eighty thousand inhabitants, barricadoed streets, and artillery placed at the gates, cannot be* TAKEN BY THE COLLAR."

3. General Frere's useless march to Requeña was very hurtful to the French, and the Duke of Rovigo was rated by the Emperor for his want of judgment upon the occasion. "It was a folly," the latter writes, "to dream of reinforcing Moncey, because, if that Marshal failed in taking the city by a sudden assault, it became an affair of artillery, and twenty thousand men, more or less, would not enable him to succeed."—"Frere could do nothing at Valencia, but he could do a great deal at San Clemente; because from that post he could support either Madrid or General Dupont."

4. Moncey was slightly blamed by the Emperor for not halting within a day's march of Valencia, in order to break the spirit of the people, and make them feel the weight of the war; but this opinion was probably formed upon an imperfect knowledge of the local details. The Marshal's line of operations from Cuença was infested by insurgent bands, his ammunition was nearly exhausted, he could hear nothing of Chabran's division, the whole force of Murcia was collecting upon his flank and rear, the country behind him was favorable for his adversaries, and his army was encumbered by a number of wounded men; it was surely prudent, under such circumstances, to open his communications again with Madrid as quickly as possible.

By some authors, the repulse at Valencia has been classed with the inglorious defeat of Dupont at Baylen, but there was a wide difference between the events, the generals, and the results. Moncey, although an old man, was vigorous, active, and decided, and the check he received produced little effect. Dupont was irresolute, slow, and incapable, if not worse, as I shall hereafter show; but before describing his campaign, I must narrate the operations of the Gallician army.

CHAPTER VII.

Second operations of Bessieres—Blake's and Cuesta's armies unite at Benevente
—Generals disagree—Battle of Rio Seco—Bessieres' endeavor to corrupt the
Spanish Generals fails—Bessieres marches to invade Gallicia, is recalled, and
falls back to Burgos—Observations.

OPERATIONS OF BESSIERES AGAINST BLAKE AND CUESTA.

WHILE Bessieres' movable columns, ranging over the Asturian
and Biscayan mountains, dispersed the insurgent patriots of those
provinces, Cuesta, undismayed by his defeat at Cabezon, collected
another army at Benevente, and prepared to advance again towards
Burgos; and he was supported by the Gallician army, which Filanghieri had organized without difficulty, because the abundant
supplies poured in from England were beginning to be felt, and
patriotism is never more efficacious than when supported by large
sums of money. Taranco's soldiers, joined to the garrisons of Ferrol and Coruña, had been reinforced with new levies to twenty-five
thousand men, and being well equipped, and provided with a considerable train of artillery, were assembled at Manzanal, a strong
post in the mountains, twelve miles behind Astorga.

The situation of that city offered great advantages to the Spaniards, for the old Moorish walls which surrounded it were complete,
and susceptible of being strengthened, so as to require a regular
siege; but a siege could not be undertaken by a small force, while
the army of Gallicia was intrenched at Manzanal, and while Cuesta
remained at Benevente; neither could Bessieres, with any prudence, attack the Gallicians at Manzanal while Cuesta was at Benevente, and while Astorga contained a strong garrison. Filanghieri, who appears to have had some notion of its value, had commenced forming an intrenched camp in the mountains; but being
slain by his soldiers, Joachim Blake succeeded to the command, and
probably fearing a similar fate, if the army remained stationary, left
one division at Manzanal, and with the remainder marched towards
Benevente to unite with Cuesta.

Bessieres immediately collected his scattered columns at Palencia,
and his plan, founded upon instructions from Bayonne, was to make
a rapid movement against Cuesta, in the hope of beating him, while
Blake was still behind Leon; then wheeling to the right, to drive
the Gallicians back to the mountains, to overrun the flat country
with his numerous cavalry, to open a communication with Portugal, and after receiving certain reinforcements, preparing for him,

to subdue Gallicia, or assist Junot, as might seem most fitting at the time.*

At this period the King was on his journey to Madrid, and the military system of Napoleon was brought to its first great crisis; for unless Bessieres was successful, there could be no sure footing for the French in the capital; and as Madrid was the base of Moncey's and Dupont's operations, the farther prosecution of their plans depended upon the result of the approaching struggle in the plains of Leon. Napoleon, foreseeing this crisis, had directed Savary to occupy Segovia, to send General Gobert's division to Valladolid, and to hold Vedel's and Frere's, the one in La Mancha, a few marches from the capital, and the other at San Clemente, a central point connecting Moncey, Dupont, and Madrid. But Savary, unable to estimate justly the relative importance of the different operations, sent Vedel and Gobert into Andalusia to reinforce Dupont, when he should rather have recalled the latter to the northern side of the Sierra Morena; he caused Frere, as we have seen, to quit San Clemente, and march by Requeña against Valencia, at the moment when Moncey was retiring from that city through Murcia to San Clemente; thus he dispersed and harassed his reserves by long marches to the south without any definite object, when the essential interests were at stake in the north. Now, struck with fear at the approach of Cuesta and Blake, whose armies he had hitherto disregarded, he precipitately recalled Frere, Vedel, Gobert, and even Dupont, to Madrid; too late to take part with Bessieres in the coming battle, but exactly timed to frustrate Moncey's projects, and, as we shall hereafter find, to insure the ruin of Dupont. In this manner, steering his vessel against every wind that blew, he could not fail of storms.

Greatly was Napoleon discontented with these errors; he relied, and with reason, on the ability of Bessieres for a remedy, but to Savary he sent the following instructions, dated the 13th of July:

"The French affairs in Spain would be in an excellent state, if Gobert's division had marched upon Valladolid, and Frere's had occupied San Clemente, with a movable column, three or four marches upon the route of General Dupont. Gobert having been directed upon Dupont, Frere being with Moncey, harassed and enfeebled by marches and countermarches, the position of the French army is become less advantageous.

"Marshal Bessieres is this day at Medina del Rio Seco with fifteen thousand men, infantry, cavalry, and artillery; the 15th or 16th he will attack Benevente, open a communication with Portu-

---

* Journal of Bessieres' Operations, MSS. Napoleon's Notes.

gal, drive the rebels into Gallicia, and seize upon Leon. If his operations succeed thus, and in a brilliant manner, the position of the French army will again be as good as it was.

"If General Cuesta retires from Benevente without fighting, he will move by Zamora and Salamanca to gain Avila and Segovia, certain that then Bessieres cannot pursue him, as, in that case, he would be menaced by the army of Gallicia, whose advanced guard is at Leon. The general who commands at Madrid must then be able to assemble six or seven thousand men and march upon Cuesta; the citadel of Segovia must be occupied by three or four hundred convalescents, with some guns and six weeks' biscuit. It was a great fault not to have occupied this citadel when the major-general ordered it; of all the possible positions, Segovia is the most dangerous for the army—the capital of a province, and situated between two routes, it deprives the army of all its communications; and the enemy once posted in the citadel, the French army cannot dislodge him. Three or four hundred convalescents, a good commandant, and a squad of artillery, will render the castle of Segovia impregnable for some time, and will insure to the army the important position of Segovia.

"If General Cuesta throws himself into Gallicia without fighting or suffering a defeat, the position of the army will become better; of course it will be still better if he does so, after having suffered a defeat.

"If Marshal Bessieres faces Cuesta at Benevente without attacking him, or if he is repulsed by him, his object will always be to cover Burgos, and to hold the enemy in check as long as possible; he could, perhaps, be reinforced with the three thousand troops of the line which accompany the King, but then there would be no room for hesitation. If Bessieres retires without a battle, he must be reinforced instantly with six thousand men. If he retreats after a battle wherein he has suffered great loss, it will be necessary to make great dispositions—to recall Frere, Gobert, Caulaincourt, and Vedel, by forced marches to Madrid; to withdraw Dupont into the Sierra Morena, or even bring him nearer to Madrid (keeping him always, however, seven or eight marches off), then to crush Cuesta and all the Gallician army, while Dupont will serve as an advanced guard to hold the army of Andalusia in check."

However, before Bessieres could collect his troops, Blake effected a junction with Cuesta, at Benevente, and three plans were open to those generals.

1. To remove into the mountains, and take a position covering Gallicia.

2. To maintain the head of the Gallician army in advance of

Astorga, while Cuesta, with his Castilians, pushing by forced marches through Salamanca and Avila, reached Segovia.

3. To advance farther into the plains, and try the fate of a battle.

This last was rash, seeing that Bessieres was well provided with horsemen, and that the Spaniards had scarcely any; but Cuesta, assuming the chief command, adopted it. He left a division at Benevente to protect his stores, and advanced, much against Blake's wishes, with twenty-five thousand regular infantry, a few hundred cavalry, and from twenty to thirty pieces of artillery, in the direction of Palencia. His march, as we have seen, dismayed Savary. To use Napoleon's expressions, he who had been "*hitherto acting as if the army of Gallicia was not in existence*," now acted "*as if Bessieres was already beaten;*" but that Marshal, firm and experienced, rather than risk an action of such importance with insufficient means, withdrew even the garrison from the important post of Santander, and having quickly collected fifteen thousand men and thirty pieces of artillery at Palencia, moved forward on the 12th of July to the encounter.

His line of battle consisted of two divisions of infantry, one of light cavalry, and twenty-four guns; his reserve was formed of four battalions and some horse grenadiers of the Imperial Guards, with six pieces of artillery. On the 13th he halted at Ampudia and Torre de Mormojon, but advancing on the 14th in two columns, he drove in an advanced guard of one hundred and fifty Spanish cavalry, and arrived about nine o'clock in front of Rio Seco, where Cuesta's army was drawn up like some heavy domestic animal, awaiting the spring of an active wild beast.*

BATTLE OF RIO SECO.

The first line of the Spaniards, with all the heavy guns, were posted along the edge of a step of land which had an abrupt fall towards the French. The second line, composed of the best troops, augmented but not strengthened by some eighteen thousand armed peasants, was displayed at a great distance behind the first, and the town of Rio Seco was in rear of the centre. Bessieres was at first startled at their numbers, and doubted if he should attack; but soon perceiving the vice of Cuesta's disposition, he ordered General Lasalle to make a feint against the front with the light cavalry, while he himself, marching obliquely to the right, outstretched the left of the Spaniards, and suddenly thrust Merle's and Mouton's divisions and the Imperial Guards, horse and foot, between the lines, and

* S. Journal of Bessieres' Operations.

threw the first into confusion. At that moment Lasalle charged furiously, the Spanish front went down at once, and fifteen hundred dead bodies strewed the field.*

The victor's ranks were disordered, and Cuesta made a gallant effort to retrieve the day; for, supported by the fire of all his remaining artillery, he advanced with his second line upon the French, and his right wing falling on boldly, took six guns; but his left hung back, and the flank of the right was thus exposed. Bessieres, with great readiness, immediately charged on this naked flank with Merle's division and the horse grenadiers, while the fourteenth provisionary regiment made head against the front. A fierce short struggle ensued, and the Spaniards were overborne, broken and dispersed. Meanwhile the first line rallied in the town of Rio Seco, but being a second time defeated by Mouton's division, fled over the plains, pursued by the light cavalry and suffering severely in their flight.†

Five or six thousand Spaniards were killed and wounded on the field, twelve hundred prisoners, eighteen guns, and a great store of ammunition, remained in the hands of the French, and the vanquished sought safety in all directions, chiefly on the side of Benevente.‡ Blake and Cuesta separated in wrath with each other: the former made for the mountains of Gallicia, and the latter towards Leon, while the division left at Benevente dispersed. The French, who had lost fifty killed and three hundred wounded, remained at Rio Seco all the 15th, and the 16th advanced to Benevente, where they found many thousand English muskets and vast quantities of ammunition, clothing and provisions. The communication with Portugal was now open, and Bessieres at first resolved to give his hand to Junot, but hearing that the fugitives were likely to rally on the side of Leon, he pursued them by the road of Villafere. On his march, learning that Cuesta was gone to Mayorga, he turned aside to that place, and on the 22d captured there another great collection of stores; for the Spanish general, with the usual improvidence of his nation, had established all his magazines in the open towns of the flat country.

After this, Bessieres entered the city of Leon and remained there until the 29th, during which time he received the submission of the municipality, and prepared to carry the war into Gallicia. Meanwhile the Junta of Castile and Leon, whose power had hitherto been restrained by Cuesta, retired to Puente-Ferrada, assumed supreme authority, and the quarrel between the generals having

* S. Journal of Bessieres' Operations.
† Ibid.
‡ Mr. Stuart's Papers.

become rancorous, they sided with Blake. This appeared to Bessieres a favorable occasion to tamper with the fidelity of the chiefs. He therefore sent his prisoners back, argued the hopeless state of the insurrection, offered the viceroyalty of Mexico to Cuesta, and promised military ranks and honors to Blake; but as neither would listen to him, he had reached Puente Orbigo the 31st, intending to break into Gallicia, when he was suddenly recalled to protect the King; for Dupont had surrendered with a whole army in Andalusia. The victory of Rio Seco was rendered useless, the court was in consternation, and Bessieres immediately returned to Mayorga, where he took a defensive position.

OBSERVATIONS.

1. As Blake was overruled by Cuesta, he is not responsible for the errors of this short campaign; but the faults were gross on both sides, and it seems difficult to decide whether Savary or Cuesta made the greatest number. If Savary had sent Gobert's division tn Valladolid, Bessieres would have had twenty-two thousand men and forty pieces of artillery in the field; a force not at all too great, when it is considered that the fate of three French armies depended upon a battle to which the Spaniards might have brought at least double the number. On the other hand, Cuesta, having determined upon an offensive movement, disregarded the powerful cavalry of his enemy, and chose a field of battle precisely in the country where that arm would have the greatest advantage; when he should have brought every man to bear upon the quarter which he did attack, he displayed his ignorance of the art of war by fighting the battle of Rio Seco with twenty-five thousand men only, leaving ten thousand disciplined troops in the rear, to guard positions which could not be approached until he himself was first beaten. Neither was the time well chosen for his advance: had he waited a few days, the port of Santander would have been attacked by eight English frigates, and a detachment of Spanish troops under the command of General du Ponte; an enterprise that would have distracted and weakened Bessieres, but which was relinquished in consequence of the battle of Rio Seco.

2. Once united to Blake, Cuesta's real base of operations was Gallicia, and he should have kept all his stores within the mountains, and not have heaped them up in the open towns of the flat country, exposed to the marauding parties of the enemy; or covered, as at Benevente, by strong detachments, which weakened his troops in the field, and confined him to a particular line of operations in the plain.

3. The activity and good sense of Marshal Bessieres overbalanced the errors of Savary, and the victory of Rio Seco was of infinite importance, because, as we have seen, a defeat in that quarter would have shaken the French military system to its centre; it would also have obliged the King, then on his journey to Madrid, to halt at Vittoria until the distant divisions of the army were recalled to the capital, and a powerful effort made to crush the victorious enemy. Napoleon's observations are full of strong expressions of discontent at the imprudence of his lieutenant. *"A check given to Dupont,"* he says, *"would have a slight effect, but a wound received by Bessieres would give a locked jaw to the whole army. Not an inhabitant of Madrid, not a peasant of the valleys that does not feel that the affairs of Spain are involved in the affairs of Bessieres; how unfortunate, then, that in such a great event you have wilfully given the enemy twenty chances against yourself."* When he heard of the victory, he exclaimed that it was the battle of Almanza, and that Bessieres had saved Spain. The prospect was indeed very promising; the King had arrived in Madrid, bringing with him the veteran brigade of General Rey and some French guards, and all fears upon the side of Leon being allayed, the affairs of Andalusia alone remained of doubtful issue; for Zaragoza, hard pushed by Verdier, was upon the point of destruction, in despite of the noble courage of the besieged.* Nor did the subjugation of Andalusia appear in reason a hard task, seeing that Moncey was then at San Clemente, and from that point threatened Valencia, without losing the power of succoring Dupont, while Frere's and Caulaincourt's troops were disposable for any operation. In fine, the French army possessed the centre, the Spaniards were dispersed upon a variety of points on the circumference without any connection with each other, they were in force only upon the side of Andulasia, and the great combinations of the French Emperor were upon the point of being crowned with success, when a sudden catastrophe overturned his able calculations, and raised the sinking hopes of Spain.

It was the campaign in Andalusia which produced such important effects, and it offers one of the most interesting and curious examples recorded by history of the vicissitudes of war; disorder, unaccompanied by superior valor, triumphed over discipline; inexperienced officers were successful against practised generals, and a fortuitous combination of circumstances enabled the Spaniards, without any skill, to defeat in one day an immense plan, wisely arranged, embracing a variety of interests, and until that moment happily conducted in all its parts. This blow, which felled Joseph

* Napoleon's Notes.

from his throne, marked the French army with a dishonorable scar, the more conspicuous because it was the only one of its numerous wounds that misbecame it.

CHAPTER VIII.

Dupont marches against Andalusia, forces the bridge of Alcolea, takes Cordoba —Alarm at Seville—Castaños arrives, forms a new army—Dupont retreats to Andujar, attacks the town of Jaen—Vedel forces the pass of Despeñas Perros, arrives at Baylen—Spanish army arrives on the Guadalquiver—General Gobert defeated and killed—Generals Vedel and Darfour retire to Carolina—General Reding takes possession of Baylen—Dupont retires from Andujar—Battle of Baylen—Dupont's capitulation, eighteen thousand French troops lay down their arms—Observations—Joseph holds a council of war, resolves to abandon Madrid—Impolicy of so doing.

OPERATIONS IN ANDALUSIA.

Dupont was ordered to march against Cadiz with a force composed of the Spanish-Swiss regiments of Preux and Reding—Barbou's division of French infantry; Fresia's division of cavalry—a marine battalion of the imperial guards, and eighteen pieces of artillery.* Three thousand infantry, five hundred cavalry, and ten guns, were to join him at Seville, from the army of Portugal; three other Swiss regiments were in Andalusia, and it was expected that both they and the troops at San Roque would join the French army.

In the latter end of May he traversed La Mancha, entered the Sierra Morena by the pass of Despeñas Perros, and proceeded by Carolina and Baylen to Andujar, where he arrived the 2d of June. There he was informed that a supreme junta of government was established at Seville, that minor juntas ruled in Granada, Jaen, and Cordoba; that war was formally declared against the French, that the whole of Andalusia was in arms, and the Swiss regiments ranged under the Spanish banners; lastly, that General Avril, commanding the detachment expected from Portugal, had halted at Tavora, and was preparing to return to Lisbon.

Alarmed by this intelligence, Dupont wrote to Murat and Savary to demand reinforcements, and in the mean time closed up the rear of his columns, and established a hospital in Andujar. The 6th he crossed the Guadalquiver and continued his march towards Cordoba, following the left bank of the river. But two leagues

---

* Journal of Dupont's Operations, MSS.

from that ancient city the road re-crossed the Guadalquiver by a long stone bridge, at the farthest end of which stood the village of Alcolea; and when the French general arrived there at day-break on the 7th, his progress was opposed by the Spanish General Echevaria, who had fortified the head of the bridge, placed twelve guns in battery on the right bank, and was prepared to dispute the passage with a force composed of three thousand regulars, supported by ten thousand new levies and smugglers. Besides these troops, a small reserve was left in a camp close to Cordoba, and a cloud of armed peasants, from the side of Jaen, hovered on the hills behind the French, ready to fall on the rear when they should attack the bridge.

Dupont having observed this disposition, placed the cavalry, the Swiss regiments, and the marine battalion in reserve, facing the hills, and with the division of Barbou stormed the head of the bridge. The Spaniards there, making a feeble resistance, were driven across the river, and their whole line immediately fled to the camp at Cordoba. The multitude on the hills descended during the battle, but were beaten back by the cavalry, with loss; and the French general then, leaving the marine battalion at Alcolea to se-cure the bridge, marched with the rest of his forces to complete the victory. At his approach the Spaniards took refuge in the town, and opened a fire of musketry from the walls, whereupon the French, bursting the gates with their field-pieces, broke in, and after a short and confused fight Echevaria's men fled along the Se-ville road, pursued by the cavalry. As the inhabitants took no part in the contest, and received the French without any signs of aversion, the first disorders attendant on the action were soon sup-pressed, the town was protected from pillage, and Dupont, fixing his quarters there, sent patroles as far as Ecija without finding an enemy.

In Seville the news of this disaster, and the arrival of the fugi-tives, struck such a terror that the Junta were only prevented from retiring to Cadiz by their dread of the populace; they even enter-tained thoughts of abandoning Spain altogether and flying to South America.* Castaños, who a few days before had been declared Captain-General of the armies, and was at this time in march with seven thousand troops of the line from San Roque, repaired to Se-ville the 9th, and after a short conference with the Junta, proceeded to take the command of Echevaria's forces. The greater part of these were re-assembled at Carmona, but in such confusion, and so moody, that Castaños returned immediately. Having persuaded the president, Saavedra, to accompany him, he fixed his head-

* Nellerto.

quarters at Utrera, where he gathered two or three thousand regulars from the nearest garrisons, directed all the new levies to repair to him, and hastened the march of his own men from San Roque.* He also pressed General Spencer to disembark and take up a position with the British forces at Xeres; but that officer, for reasons hereafter to be mentioned, sailed to Ayamonte,—a circumstance which augmented the general distrust of the English prevailing at the time, and secretly fomented by Morla and by several members of the Junta.

Andalusia was lost if Dupont had advanced. His inactivity saved it. Instead of pushing his victory, he wrote to Savary for reinforcements, and to General Avril, desiring that he would without delay come to his assistance, remaining himself meanwhile in Cordoba, overwhelmed with imaginary dangers and difficulties. For although Castaños had in a few days collected at Carmona and Utrera seven or eight thousand regulars and above fifty thousand new levies, and although Dupont's desponding letters were intercepted and brought to him, such was the condition of affairs, that, resigning all thoughts of making a stand, he had, under the pretence of completing the defences of Cadiz, embarked the heavy artillery and stores at Seville, resolving, if Dupont should advance, to burn the timbers and harness of his field artillery and retreat to Cadiz. Nevertheless, he continued the organization of his forces, filled up the old regiments with new levies, and formed fresh battalions; in which he was assisted by two foreigners—the Marquis de Coupigny, a crafty French emigrant, of some experience in war, and Reding, a Swiss, a bold, enterprising, honest man, but without judgment, and of very moderate talents as an officer.

Castaños wished to adopt a defensive plan, to make Cadiz his place of arms, and to form an intrenched camp, where he hoped to be joined by ten or twelve thousand British troops, and in security to organize and discipline a large army; but, in reality, he had merely the name and the troubles of a commander-in-chief, without the power.† Morla was his enemy, and the Junta, containing men determined to use their authority for their own emolument and the gratification of private enmity, were jealous lest Castaños should control their proceedings. They thwarted him, humored the caprice and insolence of the populace, and meddled with affairs foreign to the matter in hand. But as the numbers at Utrera increased, the general confidence augmented, and a retreat was no longer contemplated. Plans were laid to surround Dupont in Cordoba, and one detachment of peasants, commanded by regular

† Sir Hew Dalrymple's Papers.
* Ibid.

officers, was sent to occupy the passes of the Sierra Morena leading into Estremadura; another detachment marched from Granada, accompanied by a regiment of the line, to seize Carolina and cut off the communication with La Mancha; a third, under Colonel Valderaños, proposed to attack the French in Cordoba without any assistance: and this eagerness for action was increased by a knowledge of the situation of affairs in Portugal, and by rumors exaggerating the strength of Filanghieri and Cuesta. It was believed that the latter had advanced to Valladolid, and had offered Murat the option of abiding an attack or retiring immediately to France by stated marches, and that, alarmed at Cuesta's power, the Grand Duke was fortifying the Retiro. These reports, so congenial to the wishes and vanity of the Andalusians, caused the defensive plan proposed by Castaños to be rejected; and when Dupont's despatches, magnifying his own danger, and pressing in the most urgent manner for reinforcements, were again intercepted and brought to headquarters, it was resolved to attack Cordoba immediately.

Dupont's fears outstripped the Spaniard's impatience. After ten days of inactivity, by which he lost the immediate fruit of his victory at Alcolea, the lead in an offensive campaign, and all the imposing moral force of the French reputation in arms, he resolved to fall back to Andujar, because Savary would not promise any succor save what Moncey, after subduing Valencia, could give by the circuitous route of Murcia.* This retreat was commenced the 17th of June, and the French were followed as far as Carpio by the advanced guard of the Andalusians, under General Coupigny.†

Along the line of march, and in the town of Andujar, where he arrived the evening of the 18th, Dupont found terrible proofs of Spanish ferocity; his stragglers had been assassinated, and his hospital taken; the sick, the medical attendants, the couriers, the staff officers, in fine, all who had the misfortune to be weaker than the insurgents, were butchered, with circumstances of extraordinary barbarity, and upwards of four hundred men had perished in this miserable manner since the fight of Alcolea.‡ The fate of Colonel Frené was horrible. He had been sent on a mission to Portugal, previous to the breaking out of hostilities, and was on his return, travelling in the ordinary mode, without arms, attached to no army, engaged in no operations of war; but being recognized as a Frenchman, he was seized, mutilated, and then being placed, living, between two planks, was sawed in two.

* Journal of Dupont's Operations.
† Napoleon's Notes.
‡ Whittingham. Journal of Dupont. Foy's History. Victoires et Conquêtes.

At Andujar the French General collected provisions, and prepared to maintain himself until he should be reinforced; yet wishing to punish the city of Jaen, from whence the bands had come to murder his sick, he sent Captain Baste, a naval officer, with a battalion of infantry and some cavalry, to accomplish that object. The soldiers, inflamed by the barbarity of their enemies, inflicted a severe measure of retaliation, because it is the nature of cruelty to reproduce itself in war; and for this reason, although the virtue of clemency is to all persons becoming, it is peculiarly so to an officer, the want of it leading to so many and such great evils. Meanwhile the Andalusian army remained quiet, and Dupont, who knew that General Vedel, with a division of infantry, and escorting a large convoy for the army, was marching through La Mancha, sent Captain Baste with a second detachment to clear the pass of Despeñas Perros, which was now occupied by insurgents and smugglers from Granada to the number of three thousand. This pass was of incredible strength, and the Spaniards had artillery, and were partially intrenched; however their commander, a colonel of the line, deserted to the enemy, and before Baste could arrive, Vedel had forced his way to Carolina, where he left a detachment, and then descended to Baylen, a small town sixteen miles from Andujar. But other insurgents came from Granada to Jaen, and would have moved on Despeñas Perros and Carolina, by the Linhares road; wherefore Vedel sent General Cassagne against them, Jaen was again taken, and the Granadans were driven back with slaughter; but the French, who lost two hundred men, returned on the 5th to Baylen without the provisions, to obtain which had been one object of the expedition.

Notwithstanding these successes, and that Vedel, besides his own division, brought reinforcements for Barbou's division and the cavalry, Dupont's fears increased. His position at Andujar covered the main road from Seville to Carolina; but eight miles lower down the river, it could be turned by the bridge of Marmolexo; sixteen miles higher up by the roads leading from Jaen to the ferry of Mengibar and Baylen; and beyond that line by roads from Jaen and Granada to Uzeda, Linhares, and the passes of El Rey and Despeñas Perros. The dryness of the season had rendered the Guadalquivir fordable in many places; the regular force under Castaños was daily increasing in strength; the population around was actively hostile, and the young French soldiers were drooping under privations and the heat of the climate: six hundred were in hospital, and the whole were discouraged.* It is in such situations that the worth of a veteran is found; in battle the ardor of youth

* Dupont's Journal. Foy's History.

often appears to shame the cool indifference of the old soldier, but when the strife is between the malice of fortune and fortitude, between human endurance and accumulating hardships, the veteran becomes truly formidable, when the young soldier resigns himself to despair.

After the actions at Jaen, Vedel posted General Ligier Bellair's brigade at the ferry of Mengibar, with a post beyond the river, but on the 13th this post was driven across the Guadalquivir, and on the 15th Gobert, who should have been at Rio Seco with Bessières, arrived at Baylen with a division of infantry and some cuirassiers. Vedel then advanced to Mengibar, and it was full time, seeing that the whole Spanish army was on the opposite bank of the river.* For when Dupont's retreat from Cordoba had frustrated the plan of the Spaniards to surround him, Castaños would have returned to his old project of a rigorous defensive system, but the Junta, although at first they acquiesced, were unsettled in their policy, and getting intelligence of Vedel's march, had ordered Castaños to attack Dupont at Andujar before the reinforcements could arrive.†

The Spanish General had twenty-five thousand regular infantry, two thousand cavalry, and a very heavy train of artillery. Large bodies of armed peasantry, commanded by officers of the line, attended this army, and the numbers varied from day to day, but the whole multitude that advanced towards the Guadalquivir could not have been less than fifty thousand men; hence the intelligence that Vedel had actually arrived did not much allay the general fierceness. Castaños, however, was less sanguine than the rest, and learning that Spencer had again returned to Cadiz with his division, he once more requested him to land and advance to Xeres, to afford a point of retreat in the event of a disaster, and the English General consented to disembark, but refused to advance farther than Port St. Mary.‡

From the 1st of July the Spanish army occupied a position extending from Carpio to Porcuñas, and the 11th, a council of war being held, it was resolved that Reding's division should cross the Guadalquivir at the ferry of Mengibar, and gain Baylen;§ that Coupigny should cross at Villa Nueva, and support Reding; and that Castaños, with the other two divisions, advancing to the heights of Argonilla, should attack Andujar in front, while Reding and Coupigny should descend from Baylen and attack it in the rear: some detachments of light troops under Colonel Cruz were also or-

* Vedel's Précis of Operations.
† Whittingham's Correspondence, MSS.
‡ Ibid.
§ Ibid.

Explanatory Sketch
of the
BATTLE OF BAYLEN

Vol. 1. Plate
Face Page 8

Spanish Army 16.th July
French   Do   Do
Spanish   Do   19.even.g
French   Do   Do

Bridge of Marmolexo

Porcuña

8 Miles

Heights of Arjonilla

Gen.l Castaños

Col.l Cruz
Gen.l Dupont 400 men

ANDUJAR
Gen.l Castaños

16 Miles

Villa
Nueva

Gen.l Coupigny

18 Miles

Gen.l La Peñas Div.n

R. Piedras

Gen.l Reading

Jaen

Mengibar

Gen.l Reding

Ferry of Mengibar

Gen.l Gobert

Baylen

Gen.l Vedel

Gen.l Vedels Div.n

Guaroman

8 Miles

Guadalquivir R.

Linares

Baeza

Ubeda

dered to pass the Guadalquivir by Marmolexo, and to seize the passes leading through the Morena to Estremadura. The 13th, Reding, with the first division, and three or four thousand peasantry, marched towards Mengibar, and, as I have said, drove the French post over the Guadalquivir, while Coupigny, with the second division, took the road of Villa Nueva.* The 15th, Castaños crowned the heights of Argonilla, in front of Andujar, with two divisions of infantry, and a multitude of irregular troops; Coupigny skirmished with the French picquets at Villa Nueva, and Reding attacked Ligier Bellair, but when Vedel came up retired.† When Dupont saw the heights of Argonilla covered with enemies, he sent to Vedel for succor, broke the bridge of Marmolexo, occupied an old tower on the bridge of Andujar, and detached cavalry parties to watch the fords above and below the town. The 15th Castaños cannonaded the bridge of Andujar, while Colonel Cruz, with four thousand men, crossed the river near Marmolexo. The 16th he attacked, and Cruz fell upon the French rear, but was chased into the hills by a single battalion, and about two o'clock Vedel, who had marched all night, arrived, which put an end to the action.‡

During these events, Reding passed the Guadalquivir at Mengibar, and drove Ligier Bellair before him. Gobert arrived and renewed the action, but fell mortally wounded, and General Dufour succeeded him. The French then returned to Baylen—Reding to Mengibar; and Dufour, finding the Spanirds did not push their success, rashly credited a rumor that they were in march by Linhares, and therefore retreated to Carolina. Meanwhile Dupont, hearing, on the evening of the 16th, that Mengibar had been forced, sent Vedel again to Baylen, but with instructions so vague that he was induced to follow Dufour on the 17th; whereupon Reding, who, strange to say, had remained tranquil at Mengibar, being now reinforced by Coupigny, seized Baylen in the night, and throwing out a detachment on the side of Carolina, took a position facing Andujar with about twenty thousand men, including a multitude of peasants.

The armies were thus interlaced in a singular manner—Dupont between Reding and Castaños, Reding between Dupont and Vedel; and the affair became one of time: yet Castaños remained tranquil in his camp, and Dupont, although he knew on the 17th of Vedel's march to Carolina, did not quit Andujar until the night of the 18th. His movement was unobserved by Castaños, and at daybreak he

* Whittingham's Correspondence, MSS.
† Dupont's Journal. Foy.
‡ Vedel's Précis.

reached the Tiedras—a torrent with rugged banks, only two miles from Reding's position, which was strong, well shaded with olive trees, and intersected by deep ravines. Dupont, hoping that Vedel would return, immediately passed the Tiedras, and leaving Barbou with a few battalions on that stream, to check Castaños if he should arrive during the action, fell on, yet feebly and with few troops; for his march had been unmilitary, and his best soldiers were employed guarding the baggage, which was enormous, and mixed with the columns. For some time the French appeared to gain ground, but, fatigued by their night's work and unable to force the principal points, they became discouraged. The Swiss then went over to the Spaniards, and about twelve o'clock, after losing two thousand men, killed and wounded, Dupont proposed an armistice with a view to a convention, which Reding, hard pressed, willingly granted.

Vedel had quitted Carolina at five in the morning of the 19th. The sound of battle became distinct as he advanced, yet he halted at Guaroman, two leagues from Baylen, and remained there until three o'clock, to refresh his men and to ascertain if any enemy was at Linhares.* When the firing had entirely ceased, he resumed his march, and coming upon the rear of Reding, attacked, and, after some fighting, captured two guns and made fifteen hundred prisoners.† An aide-de-camp of Dupont's then brought him an order to cease the attack, whereupon he awaited the result of this singular crisis.

Castaños, who did not discover Dupont's march until eight hours after the latter's departure from Andujar, had sent La Peña's division in pursuit, but remained himself in that town.‡ La Peña reached the Tiedras about five o'clock, and soon after, one Villoutreys passed his posts, going to ask Castaños' consent to the terms accepted by Reding; and on the 20th, Generals Marescot and Chabert likewise passed to Andujar, being empowered by Dupont to conclude a convention.§ They demanded permission for the French army to retire peaceably upon Madrid; and Castaños was ready to grant this, but Savary's letter, written just before the battle of Rio Seco, to recall Dupont, was intercepted, and brought at this moment to the Spanish head-quarters. The aspect of affairs immediately changed, and a convention was no longer in question. Dupont's troops were required to lay down their arms and become prisoners of war, on condition of being sent by sea to France; and

* Foy.
† Journal of Dupont's Operations, MSS.
‡ Whittingham's Correspondence, MSS.
§ Ibid.

Vedel's division was to surrender, and be sent to France likewise, but not as prisoners of war. Without hesitation these terms were accepted.

Meanwhile Vedel had proposed to Dupont to make a joint attack upon Reding, and General Privé gave a like counsel; but the French General refused, and sent Vedel orders to give up his prisoners and retreat to Carolina.* Castaños menaced Dupont with death if Vedel did not return; and the latter, on receiving his commander's orders to that effect, did come back to Baylen the 22d, and surrendered. Thus above eighteen thousand French soldiers laid down their arms, before a raw army incapable of resisting half that number led by an able man. Nor did this end the disgraceful transaction; for Villoutreys, as if to show how far fear and folly combined will carry men, passed the Morena with a Spanish escort, and gathering up the detachments left by Dupont in La Mancha, even to within a short distance of Toledo, sent them to Andujar as prisoners under the convention. Nay, he even informed Castaños how to capture two French battalions that had been left to guard the passes into La Mancha; and these unheard-of proceedings were quietly submitted to by men belonging to that army which for fifteen years had been the terror of Europe—a proof how much the character of soldiers depends upon their immediate chief.

This capitulation, shameful in itself, was shamefully broken. The French troops, instead of being sent to France, were maltreated, and numbers of them murdered in cold blood, especially at Lebrixa, where above eighty officers were massacred in the most cowardly manner. Armed only with their swords, they kept the assassins for some time at bay, and gathering in a company, upon an open space in the town, endeavored to save their lives; but a fire from the neighboring houses was kept up until the last of those unfortunate gentlemen fell. No distinction was made between Dupont's and Vedel's troops, and all who survived the march to Cadiz, after being exposed to every species of indignity, were cast into the hulks at Cadiz, whence a few hundreds escaped, two years afterwards, by cutting the cables of their prison-ship, and drifting in a storm upon a lee shore: the remainder, transported to the desert island of Cabrera, perished by lingering torments in such numbers, that few remained alive at the termination of the war. Dupont himself was permitted to return to France, and to take with him all the generals; and it is curious that General Privé, who had remonstrated strongly against the capitulation, and had pressed Dupont on the field to force a passage through Reding's army, was the only one left behind.†

* Vedel's Précis of Operations.   † Victoires et Conquêtes.

Don Thomas Morla, after a vain attempt to involve Lord Collingwood and Sir Hew Dalrymple in the transaction, formally defended the conduct of the Junta in breaking the capitulation, and soon afterwards betrayed his own country, with the readiness that might be expected from his shameless conduct on this occasion.

OBSERVATIONS.

1. The gross amount of Dupont's corps when it first entered Spain was about twenty-four thousand men, with three thousand five hundred horses; of these twenty-one thousand were fit for duty.* It was afterwards strengthened by a provisionary regiment of cuirassiers, a marine battalion of the guard, and the two Swiss regiments of Preux and Reding. It could not therefore have been less than twenty-four thousand fighting men when Dupont arrived in Andalusia; and as the whole of Vedel's and the greatest part of Gobert's division had joined before the capitulation, and as eighteen thousand men laid down their arms at Baylen, Dupont must have lost, by wounds, desertion, and deaths in hospital or the field, above five thousand men.

2. The order which directed his corps upon Cadiz was despatched from Bayonne before the Spanish insurrection broke out; it was therefore strange that Dupont should have persevered in his march, when he found affairs in such a different state from that contemplated by Napoleon at the time the instructions for this expedition were framed. If the Emperor considered it necessary to reinforce the division, which marched under Dupont's own command, with a detachment from the army in Portugal, before the insurrection broke out, it was evident that he never could have intended that that General should blindly follow the letter of his orders when a great and unexpected resistance was opposed to him, and that the detachment from Portugal was unable to effect a junction. The march to Cordoba was therefore an error; and it was a great error, because Dupont confesses in his memoir he advanced under the conviction that his force was too weak to obtain success, and consequently, having no object, his operations could only lead to a waste of lives.

3. At Cordoba, Dupont remained in a state of torpor for ten days. This was the second error of a series which led to his ruin; he should either have followed up his victory and attacked Seville in the first moment of consternation, or he should have retired to Andujar while he might do so without the appearance of being compelled to it. If he had followed the first plan, the city would inevitably have fallen before him, and thus time would have been

* Return of the French Army.

gained for the arrival of the second and third divisions of his corps. It may be objected that ten thousand men dared not penetrate so far into a hostile country; but at Alcolea Dupont boasts of having defeated forty thousand men, without any loss to himself: from such armies, then, he had nothing to fear, and the very fact of his having pushed his small force between the multitudes he defeated upon the 7th, proves that ha despised them.* " He retired from Cordoba," he says in his memoir, " because to fight a battle when victory can be of no use is against all discretion;" but to make no use of a victory when it is gained comes to the same thing, and he should never have moved from Andujar unless with the determination of taking Seville. These errors were, however, redeemable. The position behind the Guadalquivir, the checks given to the patriots at Jaen after the arrival of Vedel at Carolina upon the 27th, above all, the opportune junction of Gobert at the moment when Castaños and Reding appeared in front of the French line, proved that it was not fortune, but common sense that deserted Dupont. The Spanish forces, divided, and extended from Argonilla to Mengibar, were exposed to be beaten in detail; but as their adversary was indulgent to them, their false movements were successful, and, amidst the mass of greater errors on both sides, appeared like acts of wisdom.

4. At Mengibar a variety of roads branch off, leading to Jaen, to Linhares, to Baylen and other places. From Andujar, a road nearly parallel to the Guadalquivir runs to the ferry of Mengibar, and forms the base of a triangle, of which Baylen may be taken as the apex. The distance of this latter town from the ferry is about six miles, from the ferry to Andujar is about eighteen, and from the latter to Baylen the distance may be sixteen miles. Fifteen miles above Baylen the town of Carolina, situated in the gorge of the Sierra Morena, was the point of communication with La Mancha and the line of retreat for the French in the event of a defeat; hence Baylen, not Andujar, was the pivot of operations. The French force was inferior in number to that under Castaños; yet Dupont spread his divisions upon several points, and the natural results followed. The Spaniards, although the most unwieldy body, took the lead and became the assailants; the French divisions were worn out by useless marches; the orders of their chief were mistaken or disobeyed; one position being forced, another was of necessity abandoned; confusion ensued; and finally Dupont says he surrendered with *eighteen thousand* men, because his fighting force was reduced to *two thousand*.† Such an avowal saves the

* Dupont's Journal of Operations.
† Dupont's Journal, MSS.

honor of his soldiers, but destroys his own reputation as a general. The first question to ask is, what became of the remainder? Why had he so few, when ten thousand of his army never fired a shot? It must be confessed that Dupont, unless a worse explanation can be given of his conduct, was incapable to the last degree. But this worse explanation has been given. His own officers, as well as the Spaniards, assert that his baggage was filled with plunder, and that he surrendered to save it!

5. There were two plans, either of which promised a reasonable chance of success under the circumstances in which the French army was placed on the 14th. 1st. To abandon Andujar, send all the incumbrances into La Mancha, secure the passes, unite the fighting men at Carolina, and fall in one mass upon the first corps of Spaniards that advanced. The result of such an attack could hardly have been doubtful; but if, contrary to all probability, the Spaniards had been successful, the retreat was open and safe. 2dly. To secure Carolina by a detachment, and placing small bodies in observation at Andujar and the ferry of Mengibar, to unite the army on the 15th at Baylen, and in that central position await the enemy. If the two corps of the Spanish army had presented themselves simultaneously upon both roads, the position was strong for battle and the retreat open; if one approached before the other, each might have been encountered and crushed separately. Dupont had a force more than sufficient for this object, and fortune was not against him.

6. On the Spanish side, the direction in which Reding marched was good, but it should have been followed by the whole army. The heights of Argonilla would have screened the march of Castaños, and a few troops with some heavy guns left in front of the bridge of Andujar would have sufficed to occupy Dupont's attention. If the latter General had attacked Castaños upon the morning of the 16th, when Vedel's division arrived from Baylen, the twelve thousand men thus united by accident would easily have overthrown the two Spanish divisions in front of Andujar; and Reding, if he had lost an hour in retreating to Jaen, might have been taken in flank by the victorious troops, and in front by Gobert, and so destroyed. Instead of availing himself of this opening, the French General sent Vedel back to Baylen, followed himself two days after, and, being encountered by Reding, vainly hoped that the divisions which with so much pains he had dispersed would reunite to relieve him from his desperate situation.

7. In the action Dupont clung tenaciously to the miserable system of dividing his troops, when his only chance of safety was to force Reding before Castaños could arrive upon the Tiedras. It

was a wretched misapplication of rules to have a reserve watching that torrent, and to fight a formal battle with a first and second line and half-a-dozen puny columns of attack. An energetic officer would have formed his troops in a dense mass and broken at once through the opposing force upon the weakest point: there are few armies so good that such an assault would not open a passage through them. Seven thousand infantry, with cavalry and artillery, is a powerful column of attack, and the Spanish line could not have withstood it for a moment. The battle should have been one of half an hour; Dupont, by his ridiculous evolutions, made it one of ten hours, and yet so badly did the patriots fight, that in all that time not a single prisoner or gun fell into their hands,—and the fact of Reding's entering at all into a convention proves his fears for the final result. It is truly astonishing that Dupont, who from his rank must have been well acquainted with Napoleon's Italian campaigns, should have caught so little of the spirit of his master. And then the capitulation of Vedel, after his retreat was actually effected! Vedel, who might have given battle and disputed the victory by himself, without any great imprudence! Joseph called Dupont's capitulation a "*defection*."

8. Castaños, although active in preparation, discovered but little talent in the field; his movements were slow, uncertain, and generally false. The attempt to turn the French position at Andujar by detaching four thousand men across the river, was ill conceived and badly supported; it was of that class of combinations to which the separate march of Reding's corps belonged. To the latter General the chief honor of the victory is due; yet, if Vedel had returned from Carolina upon the 19th, with the rapidity which the occasion required, Reding would have repented taking post at Baylen. It was undoubtedly a daring step; but instead of remaining at that place, he should have descended instantly upon the rear of Dupont, leaving a corps of observation to delay the march of Vedel. Time not being taken into his calculation, Reding acted like a bold, but rash and unskilful officer. Fortune, however, favored his temerity, and with her assistance war is but child's play.

Intelligence of the capitulation of Baylen was secretly spread among the Spaniards in Madrid as early as the 23d or 24th of July; but the French, although alarmed by rumors of some great disaster, were unable to acquire any distinct information, until the King sent two divisions into La Mancha to open the communication; these troops having reached Madrilejos, one hundred and twenty miles from Baylen, met Villoutreys with his Spanish escort collecting prisoners, and apparently intending to proceed in his dis-

graceful task to the very gates of Madrid;* the extent of the disaster thus became known, and the divisions retraced their steps.
Joseph then called a council of war, and it was proposed to unite
all the French forces, place a small garrison in the Retiro, and fall
upon the Spanish armies in succession as they advanced towards the
capital. But a dislike to the war was prevalent amongst the higher
ranks of the French army, the injustice of it was too glaring;
hence the reasons for a retreat, which might perchance induce Napoleon to desist, being listened to with more complacency than this
proposal, it was resolved to abandon Madrid and retire behind the
Ebro. The operation commenced on the 1st of August. The
King marched by the Somosierra, and Bessières, posted at Mayorga, covered the movement until the court reached Burgos, and
then fell back himself; in a short time the French were all behind
the Ebro, the siege of Zaragoza was raised, and the triumphant
cry of the Spaniards was heard throughout Europe.

This retreat was undoubtedly hasty and ill-considered; whether
as a military or political measure it was unwise. Bessières, with
seventeen thousand victorious troops, and forty pieces of artillery,
paralyzed the northern provinces; the Spanish army of Andalusia
was too distant from that of Valencia to concert a combined movement, and if they had formed a junction, their united force could
not have exceeded forty thousand fighting men, ill provided, and
commanded by jealous independent chiefs. Now the King, without
weakening Bessières' corps too much, could have collected twenty
thousand infantry, five thousand cavalry, and eighty pieces of artillery; the battle of Rio Seco shows what such an army could have
effected, and every motive of prudence and of honor called for
some daring action to wipe off the ignominy of Baylen.

Let it be conceded that Joseph could not have maintained himself in Madrid; the line of the Duero was then the true position
for the French army. Taking Aranda as a centre, and occupying
the Somosierra, Segovia, Valladolid, Palencia, Burgos, and Soria
on the circumference, two ordinary marches would have carried the
King to the succor of any part of his position, and the northern
provinces would thus have been separated from the southern. Then
Blake dared not have made a flank march to the Guadarama, Castaños dared not have remained in the basin of Madrid, and the
siege of Zaragoza might have been continued; because from Aranda
to Zaragoza the distance is not greater than from Valencia, or from
Madrid, and from Soria it is only three marches; wherefore the
King could have succored Verdier if the Valencians attacked
him, and it was impossible for Castaños to have arrived at Zaragoza

* Foy's History.

under a month. Now by taking up the line of the Ebro, Napoleon's plan of separating the provinces, and confining each to its own exertions, was frustrated, and Joseph virtually resigned the throne; for, however doubtful the prudence of opposing the French might have been considered before the retreat, it became imperative upon all Spaniards to aid the energy of the multitude when that energy was proved to be efficient.

In this manner Napoleon's first effort against Spain was frustrated. Yet he had miscalculated neither the difficulties, nor the means to overcome them; for although Bessières was the only general who perfectly succeeded in his operations, the plan of the Emperor was so well combined, that it required the destruction of a whole army to shake it at all. Even when the King, by committing the great fault of abandoning Madrid and raising the siege of Zaragoza, had given the utmost force to Dupont's catastrophe, it was only the political position of the French which was shaken; their military hold of the country was scarcely loosened, and the Spaniards were unable to follow up their victory. But there was another operation, too great indeed for Joseph, yet such a one as in Napoleon's hands would have fixed the fate of the Peninsula. The King might have directed the troops before Zaragoza, and the detachments upon the communication with France, to have assembled round Pampeluna, while he, uniting with Bessières, made, not a retreat, but a march with forty thousand men into Portugal. He would have arrived about the period of the battle of Vimiero, and the English would have been overwhelmed; a demonstration against Seville or Cadiz would then have sufficed to keep the Spanish armies from gathering on the Ebro, and three months later, Napoleon was on that river with two hundred thousand men!

The moral effect of the battle of Baylen was surprising; it was one of those minor events which, insignificant in themselves, are the cause of great changes in the affairs of nations. The defeat of Rio Seco, the preparations of Moncey for a second attack on Valencia, the miserable plight of Zaragoza, the desponding view taken of affairs by the ablest men of Spain, and, above all, the disgust and terror excited among the patriots by the excesses of the populace, weighed heavy on the Spanish cause. One victory more, and probably the moral as well as the physical force of Spain would have been crushed; but the battle of Baylen, opening as it were a new crater for the Spanish fire, all their pride, and vanity, and arrogance burst forth, the glory of past ages seemed to be renewed, every man conceived himself a second Cid, and perceived in the surrender of Dupont, not the deliverance of Spain, but the immediate conquest of France. "We are much obliged to our good friends the English," was a common phrase among them when conversing with the officers of Sir John Moore's army; "we thank them for their good-will, and we shall escort them through France to Calais; the journey will be pleasanter than a long voyage; we shall not give them the trouble of fighting the French, but will be pleased at having them spectators of our victories." This absurd confidence might have led to great things if it had been supported by wisdom, activity, or valor; but it was "a voice, and nothing more."

BOOK II.

〰〰〰

CHAPTER I.

The Asturian deputies received with enthusiasm in England—Ministers precipitate—Imprudent choice of agents—Junot marches to Alcantara, joined by the Spanish contingent, enters Portugal, arrives at Abrantes, pushes on to Lisbon—Prince Regent emigrates to the Brazils; reflections on that transaction—Dangerous position of the French army—Portuguese Council of Regency—Spanish contingent well received—General Taranco dies at Oporto; is succeeded by the French General Quesnel—Solano's troops retire to Badajos—Junot takes possession of the Alemtejo and the Algarves; exacts a forced loan; is created Duke of Abrantes; suppresses the Council of Regency; sends the flower of the Portuguese army to France—Napoleon demands a ransom from Portugal—People unable to pay it—Police of Lisbon—Junot's military position; his character; political position—People discontented—Prophetic eggs—Sebastianists—The capture of Rossily's squadron known at Lisbon—Pope's nuncio takes refuge on board the English fleet—Alarm of the French.

THE uninterrupted success that, for so many years, attended the arms of Napoleon, gave him a moral influence doubling his actual force. Exciting at once terror, admiration, and hatred, he absorbed the whole attention of an astonished world, and, openly or secretly, all men acknowledged the power of his genius; the continent bowed before him, and in England an increasing number of absurd and virulent libels on his person and character indicated the growth of secret fear. Hence, his proceedings against the Peninsula were viewed, at first, with anxiety, rather than with the hope of arresting their progress; yet when the full extent of the injustice became manifest, the public mind was vehemently excited; a sentiment of some extraordinary change being about to take place in the affairs of the world, prevailed among all classes of society; and when the Spanish people rose against the man that all feared, the admiration which energy and courage exact, even from the base and timid, became enthusiastic in a nation conscious of the same virtues.

No factious feelings interfered to check this enthusiasm. The party in power, anxious to pursue a warlike system, necessary to their own political existence, saw with joy that the stamp of justice and high feeling would, for the first time, be affixed to their policy. The party out of power having always derided the impotence of the ancient dynasties, and asserted that regular armies alone were insufficient means of defence, could not consistently refuse their approbation to a struggle originating with, and carried on entirely by the Spanish multitude. The people at large exulted that the superiority of plebeian virtue and patriotism was acknowledged.

The arrival of the Asturian deputies was, therefore, universally hailed as an auspicious event; their wishes were forestalled, their suggestions were attended to with eagerness, their demands were readily complied with; nay, the riches of England were so profusely tendered to them by the ministers, that it can scarcely be doubted the after arrogance and extravagance of the Spaniards arose from the manner in which their first applications were met. There is a way of conferring a favor that appears like accepting one, and this secret being discovered by the English cabinet, the Spaniards soon demanded as a right, what they had at first solicited as a boon. In politics it is a grievous fault to be too generous; gratitude, in state affairs, is unknown, and as the appearance of disinterested kindness never deceives, it should never be assumed.

The capture of the Spanish frigates had placed Great Britain and Spain in a state of hostility without a declaration of war; the invasion of Napoleon produced a friendly alliance between those countries without a declaration of peace; for the cessation of hostilities was not ploclaimed until long after succors had been sent to the juntas. The ministers seemed, by their precipitate measures, to be more afraid of losing the assistance of the Spaniards, than prepared to take the lead in a contest which could only be supported by the power and riches of Great Britain. Instead of adopting a simple and decisive policy towards Spain—instead of sending a statesman of high rank and acknowledged capacity to sustain the insurrection, and to establish the influence of England by a judicious application of money and other supplies—the ministers employed a number of obscure men in various parts of the Peninsula, who, without any experience of public affairs, were empowered to distribute succors of all kinds at their own discretion. Instead of sifting carefully the information obtained from such agents, and consulting distinguished military and naval officers in the arrangement of some comprehensive plan of operations, which, being well understood by those who were to execute it, might be supported vigorously, the ministers formed crude projects, parcelled out their forces in small expeditions without any definite object, altered their plans with every idle report, and changed their commanders as lightly as their plans.

Entering into formal relations with every knot of Spanish politicians that assumed the title of a supreme junta, the government dealt, with unsparing hands, enormous supplies at the demand of those self-elected authorities; they made no conditions, took no assurance that the succors should be justly applied; and with affected earnestness disclaimed all intention of interfering with the internal arrangements of the Spaniards, when the ablest men in Spain expected and wished for such an interference to repress the folly and violence of their countrymen, and when England was entitled, both in policy and justice, not only to interfere, but to direct the councils of the insurgents.* The latter had solicited and obtained her assistance, the cause was become common to both nations; and for the welfare of both, a prudent, just, and vigorous interference on the part of the most powerful and enlightened, was necessary to prevent that cause from being ruined by a few ignorant and conceited men, accidentally invested with authority.

The numbers and injudicious choice of military agents were also the source of infinite mischief. Selected, as it would appear, principally because of their acquaintance with the Spanish language, few of those agents had any knowledge of war beyond the ordinary duties of a regiment, and there was no concert among them, for there was no controlling power vested in any; each did that which seemed good to him.† Readily affecting to consult men whose inexperience rendered them amenable, and whose friendship could supply the means of advancing their own interest in a disorganized state of society, the Spanish generals received the agents with a flattering and confidential politeness, that diverted the attention of the latter from the true objects of their mission. Instead of ascertaining the real numbers and efficiency of the armies, they adopted the inflated language and extravagant opinions of the chiefs with whom they lived; and their reports gave birth to most erroneous notions of the relative strength and situation of the contending forces in the Peninsula. Some exceptions there were, but the ministers seemed to be better pleased with the sanguine than with the cautious, and made their own wishes the measure of their judgments. Accordingly, enthusiasm, numbers, courage, and talent were gratuitously found for every occasion, but money, arms, and clothing were demanded incessantly, and supplied with profusion; the arms were, however, generally left in their cases to rot, or to fall into the hands of the enemy; the clothing seldom reached the soldier's back; and the money, in all instances misapplied, was in some embezzled by the authorities into whose hands it fell, in others employed to create disunion, and to forward the private

* Mr. Stuart's Letters. Lord W. Bentinck's ditto.
† Vide Instructions for Sir Tho. Dyer, &c. Parliamentary Papers, 1809.

views of the juntas, at the expense of the public welfare : it is a
curious fact, that from the beginning to the end of the war, an
English musket was rarely to be seen in the hands of a Spanish
soldier.   But it is time to quit this subject, and to trace the progress of Junot's invasion of Portugal, by which the whole circle of
operations in the Peninsula will be completed, and the reader can
then take a general view of the situation of all parties, at the moment when Sir Arthur Wellesley, disembarking at the Mondego,
commenced those campaigns which furnished the subject of this
history.

INVASION OF PORTUGAL BY JUNOT.

Peremptory orders had obliged Junot to commence operations at
an unfavorable time of year, before his preparations were completed, when the roads were nearly impracticable, and while some
of his troops were still in the rear of Salamanca.*   Hence his march
from that town to Alcantara, where he effected his junction in the
latter end of November, 1807, with the part of the Spanish force
that was to act under his immediate orders, was very disastrous,
and nearly disorganized his inexperienced army.   The succors he
expected to receive at Alcantara were not furnished, and the repugnance of the Spanish authorities to aid him was the cause of so
much embarrassment, that his chief officers doubted the propriety
of continuing operations under the accumulating difficulties of his
situation ; but Junot's firmness was unabated.   He knew that no
English force had landed at Lisbon ; and as the cowardice of the
Portuguese court was notorious, he without hesitation undertook
one of those hardy enterprises which astound the mind by their
success, and leave the historian in doubt if he should praise the
happy daring, or stigmatize the rashness of the deed.

Without money, without transport, without ammunition sufficient
for a general action, and with an auxiliary force of Spaniards by no
means well disposed to aid him, Junot, at the head of a raw army,
penetrated the mountains of Portugal on the most dangerous and
difficult line by which that country can be invaded.   He was ignorant of what was passing in the interior, he knew not if he was to
be opposed, nor what means were prepared to resist him, but trusting to the inertness of the Portuguese government, to the rapidity
of his own movements, and to the renown of the French arms,
he made his way through Lower Beira, and suddenly appeared
in the town of Abrantes, a fearful and unexpected guest.   There
he obtained the first information of the true state of affairs.   Lisbon
was tranquil, and the Portuguese fleet was ready to sail, but the

* Thiebault.

court still remained on shore.   On hearing this, Junot, animated by
the prospect of seizing the Prince Regent, pressed forward, and
reached Lisbon in time to see the fleet, having the royal family on
board, clearing the mouth of the Tagus.   One vessel dragged astern
within reach of a battery ; the French General himself fired a gun
at her, and on his return to Lisbon, meeting some Portuguese troops,
he resolutely commanded them to form an escort for his person, and
thus attended, passed through the streets of the capital.   Nature
alone had opposed the progress of the invaders, yet such were the
hardships endured, that of a column which numbered twenty-five
thousand at Alcantara, two thousand tired grenadiers only entered
Lisbon with their General ; fatigue, and want, and tempests had
scattered the remainder along two hundred miles of rugged mountains, inhabited by a warlike and ferocious peasantry, well acquainted with the strength of their fastnesses, and proud of the many
successful defences made by their forefathers against former enemies.   Lisbon itself contained three hundred thousand inhabitants,
and fourteen thousand regular troops were collected there ; a powerful British fleet was at the mouth of the harbor, and the commander, Sir Sidney Smith, had urged the court to resist, offering to
land his seamen and marines to aid in the defence of the town, but
his offers were declined ; and the people, disgusted with the pusillanimous conduct of their rulers, and confounded by the strangeness
of the scene, evinced no desire to impede the march of events.
Thus three weak battalions sufficed to impose a foreign yoke upon
this great capital, and illustrated the truth of Napoleon's maxim,—
that in war the moral is to the physical force as three parts to one.

The Prince Regent, after having, at the desire of the French
government, expelled the British factory, sent the British minister
plenipotentiary away from his court, sequestered British property,
and shut the ports of Portugal against British merchants ; after
having degraded himself and his nation by performing every submissive act which France could devise to insult his weakness, was
still reluctant to forego the base tenure by which he hoped to hold
his crown.   Alternately swayed by fear and indolence, a miserable
example of helpless folly, he lingered until the reception of a Moniteur which, dated the 13th of November, announced, in startling
terms, that the "*house of Braganza had ceased to reign.*"   Lord
Strangford, the British plenipotentiary whose efforts to make the
royal family emigrate had entirely failed, was then on board the
squadron, with the intention of returning to England ; but Sir
Sidney Smith, seizing the favorable moment, threatened to bombard
Lisbon if the Prince Regent hesitated any longer ; and thus urged
on both sides, the latter embarked with his whole court, and sailed

for the Brazils on the 29th of November, a few hours' before Junot arrived.

Lord Strangford's despatch, relating this event, although dated the 29th of November, on board the Hibernia, was written the 19th December, in London, and was so worded as to create a notion that his exertions during the 27th and 28th had caused the emigration, a notion quite contrary to the fact. For the Prince Regent of Portugal, yielding to the united pressure of the Admiral's menaces and the annunciation in the Moniteur, had embarked on the 27th, before Lord Strangford reached Lisbon; and actually sailed on the 29th, without having had an interview whith that nobleman, who consequently had no opportunity to advance or retard the event in question. Nevertheless, Lord Strangford received the red riband, and Sir Sidney Smith was neglected.

This celebrated emigration was beneficial to the Brazils in the highest degree, and of vast importance to England in two ways, for it insured great commercial advantages, and it threw Portugal completely into her power in the approaching conflict; but it was disgraceful to the Prince, insulting to the brave people he aban-doned, and impolitic, inasmuch as it obliged men to inquire how far subjects were bound to a monarch who deserted them in their need; how far the nation could belong to a man who did not belong to the nation? It has been observed by political economists, that where a gold and paper currency circulate together, if the paper be depre-ciated it will drag down the gold with it, and deteriorate the whole mass; but after a time, the metal revolts from this unnatural state, and asserts its own intrinsic superiority: so a privileged class, corrupted by power and luxury, drags down the national character. Yet there is a point when the people, like the gold, no longer suffering such a degradation, will separate themselves with violence from the vices of their effeminate rulers, and until that time arrives, a nation may appear to be sunk in hopeless lethargy, when it is really capable of great and noble exertions; and thus it was with the Portuguese who were at this time unjustly despised by enemies, and mistrusted by friends.

The invading army, in pursuance of the convention of Fontaine-bleau, was divided into three corps.* The central one, composed of the French troops and a Spanish division under General Caraffa, had penetrated by the two roads which from Alcantara lead, the one by Pedragoa, the other by Sobreira Formosa; but at Abrantes, Caraffa's division had separated from the French and took possession of Thomar, and meantime the right, under General Taranco, marching from Gallicia, had established itself at Oporto, while the

* Thiebault. Foy.

Marquis of Solano, with the left, entered the Alemtejo, and fixed his quarters at Setuval. The Spanish troops did not suffer on their route : but such had been the distress of the French army, that three weeks afterwards it could only muster ten thousand men under arms, and the privations encountered on this march led to excesses, which first produced that rancorous spirit of mutual hatred, so remarkable between the French and Portuguese. Young soldiers always attribute their sufferings to the ill-will of the inhabitants, it is difficult to make them understand that a poor peasantry have nothing to spare ; old soldiers, on the contrary, blame nobody, but know how to extract subsistence, and in most cases without exciting enmity.

Junot passed the month of December in collecting his army, securing the great military points about Lisbon, and in preparations to supplant the power of a Council of Regency, to whom the Prince at his departure had delegated the sovereign authority. As long as the French troops were scattered on the line of march and the fortresses held by Portuguese garrisons, it would have been dangerous to provoke the enmity, or to excite the activity of this Council, hence the members were treated with studious respect ; yet they were of the same leaven as the court they emanated from, and the quick resolute proceedings of Junot soon deprived them of any importance conferred by the critical situation of affairs during the first three weeks.

The Spanish auxiliary forces were well received in the north and in the Alemtejo, and as General Taranco died soon after his arrival at Oporto, the French General Quesnel was sent to command that province. Junot had meanwhile taken possession of Elvas, and detached General Maurin to the Algarves, with sixteen hundred men ; and when Solano was ordered by his court to withdraw from Portugal, nine French battalions and the cavalry, under the command of Kellermann, took possession of the Alemtejo, and occupied the fortress of Setuval.* At the same time Caraffa's division, being replaced at Thomar by a French force, was distributed in small bodies at a considerable distance from each other on both sides of the Tagus, immediately round Lisbon.† As the provisions of the treaty of Fontainebleau were unknown to the Portuguese, the Spanish troops met with a better reception than the French, and the treaty itself was disregarded by Junot, whose conduct plainly discovered that he considered Portugal to be a possession entirely belonging to France. For when all the stragglers were come up, and the army recovered from its fatigues, and

* Return of the French Army.
† Foy.

when a reinforcement of five thousand men had reached Salamanca, on its march to Lisbon, the French General assumed the chief authority.* Commencing by a forced loan of two hundred thousand pounds, he interfered with the different departments of state, and put Frenchmen into all the lucrative offices, while his promises and protestations of amity became loud and frequent in proportion to his encroachments.†

At, last being by Napoleon created Duke of Abrantes, he threw off all disguise, suppressed the Council of Regency, seized the reins of government, and while he established many useful regulations, made the nation sensibly alive to the fact that he was a despotic conqueror. The flag and the arms of Portugal were replaced by those of France; eight thousand men were selected and sent from the kingdom under the command of the Marquis d'Alorna and Gomez Frere, two noblemen of the greatest reputation for military talent among the native officers; five thousand more were attached to the French army, and the rest were disbanded. An extraordinary contribution of four millions sterling, decreed by Napoleon, was then demanded under the curious title of a ransom for the state, but this sum was exorbitant, and Junot prevailed on the Emperor to reduce it one half.‡ He likewise, on his own authority, accepted the forced loan, the confiscated English merchandise, the church plate, and the royal property, in part payment; yet the people were still unable to raise the whole amount, for the court had before taken the greatest part of the church plate and bullion of the kingdom, and had also drawn large sums of money from the people, under the pretext of defending the country; and with this treasure they departed, leaving the public functionaries, the army, private creditors, and even domestic servants, unpaid.

But, although great discontent and misery prevailed, the tranquillity of Lisbon, during the first month after the arrival of the French, was remarkable; no disturbance took place, and the populace were completely controlled by the activity of a police, first established under the Prince Regent's government by the Count de Novion, a French emigrant, and continued by Junot on an extended scale. No capital city in Europe suffers so much as Lisbon from the want of good police regulations, and the French General conferred an unmixed benefit on the inhabitants by giving more effect to Novion's plans; yet, so deeply rooted is the prejudice in favor of ancient customs, that no act gave the Portuguese more offence than the having the streets cleansed, and the wild dogs, who

* Foy,
† Thiebault,
‡ Foy,

infested them by thousands, killed. A French sergeant, distinguished by his zeal in destroying those disgusting and dangerous animals, was in revenge assassinated.

In the course of March and April, Junot's military system was completed.* The arsenal of Lisbon, one of the finest establishments in Europe, contained all kinds of naval and military stores in abundance, and ten thousand workmen excellent in every branch of business appertaining to war; hence the artillery, the carriages, the ammunition, with all the minor equipments of the army, were soon renewed and put in the best possible condition, and the hulks of two line-of-battle ships, three frigates, and seven lighter vessels of war, were refitted, armed, and moored across the river to defend the entrance, and to awe the town. The army itself, perfectly recovered from its fatigues, reinforced, and better disciplined, was grown confident in its chief from the success of the invasion, and being well fed and clothed, was become a fine body of robust men, capable of any exertion. It was re-organized in three divisions of infantry, and one of cavalry. General La Borde commanded the first, General Loison the second, General Travot the third, General Margaron the fourth, and General Taviel directed the artillery. General Kellermann commanded in the Alemtejo, General Quesnel in Oporto, General Maurin in the Algarves, and Junot himself in Lisbon.

The fortresses of Faro in Algarves, of Almeida, of Elvas, La Lippe, St. Lucie, Setuval, Palmela, and those between Lisbon and the mouth of the Tagus, of Ericia and Peniche, were furnished with French garrisons; Estremos, Aldea-Gallegos, Santarem, and Abrantes were occupied, and put in such a state of defence as their decayed ramparts would permit.

The whole army, including the French workmen and marines attached to it, amounted to above fifty thousand men, of which above forty-four thousand were fit for duty;† that is to say, fifteen thousand five hundred Spaniards, five thousand Portuguese, and twenty-four thousand four hundred French.

Of the latter, 1000 were in Elvas and La Lippe,
     1000 in Almeida,
     1000 in Peniche,
     1600 in the Algarves,
     2892 in Setuval,
     750 in Abrantes,
     450 cavalry were kept in Valencia d'Alcantara,
      in Spanish Estremadura,
   and 350 distributed in the proportion of fifteen men

* Thiebault.   † Return of the French Army.

to a post, guarded the lines of communication which were established from Lisbon to Elvas, and from Almeida to Coimbra. Above fifteen thousand men remained disposable.

Lisbon, containing all the civil, military, naval, and greatest part of the commercial establishments, the only fine harbor, two-eighths of the population, and two-thirds of the riches of the whole kingdom, formed a centre which was secured by the main body of the French, while on the circumference a number of strong posts gave support to the operations of their movable columns. The garrison in Peniche secured the only harbor between the Tagus and the Mondego, in which a large disembarkation of English troops could take place; the little port of Figueras, held by a small garrison, blocked the mouth of the latter river; the division at Thomar secured all the great lines of communication to the north-east, and in conjunction with the garrison of Abrantes commanded both sides of the Zezere. From Abrantes to Estremos and Elvas, and to Setuval, the lines of communication were short, and through an open country, suitable for the operations of the cavalry, which was all quartered on the south bank of the Tagus. Thus, without breaking up the mass of the army, the harbors were sealed against the English; a great and rich tract was inclosed by posts, and rendered so pervious to the troops, that any insurrection could be reached by a few marches, and immediately crushed; the connection between the right and left banks of the Tagus at Lisbon was secured, and the entrance to the port defended by the vessels of war which had been refitted and armed. A light squadron was also prepared to communicate with South America, and nine Russian line-of-battle ships and a frigate, under the command of Admiral Siniavin, which had taken refuge some time before from the English fleet, were of necessity engaged in the defence of the harbor, forming an unwilling, but not an unimportant auxiliary force.

These military arrangements were Junot's own, and suitable enough if his army had been unconnected with any other; but they clashed with the general views of Napoleon, who regarded the force in Portugal only as a division of troops to be rendered subservient to the general scheme of subjecting the Peninsula; wherefore, in the month of May he ordered that General Avril, with three thousand infantry, five hundred cavalry, and ten guns, should co-operate with Dupont in Andalusia; and that General Loison, with four thousand infantry, should proceed to Almeida, and from thence co-operate with Bessières in the event of an insurrection taking place in Spain. General Thiebault complains of this order as injurious to Junot, ill combined, and the result of a foolish vanity that prompted the Emperor to direct all the armies himself; yet it would be difficult to show that the arrangement was faulty. Avril's division, if he had not halted at Tavora, for which there was no reason, would have insured the capture of Seville; and if Dupont's defeat had not rendered the victory of Rio Seco useless, Loison's division would have been eminently useful in controlling the country behind Bessières, in case the latter invaded Gallicia; moreover, it was well placed to intercept the communication between the Castilian and the Estremaduran armies. The Emperor's combinations, if they had been fully executed, would have brought seventy thousand men to bear on the defence of Portugal.

Such was the military attitude of the French in May, but their political situation was far from being so favorable. Junot's natural capacity, though considerable, was neither enlarged by study nor strengthened by mental discipline.* Of intemperate habits, indolent in business, prompt and brave in action, quick to give offence yet ready to forget an injury, he was at one moment a great man, the next below mediocrity, and at all times unsuited to the task of conciliating and governing a people like the Portuguese, who, with passions as sudden and vehement as his own, retain a sense of injury or insult with incredible tenacity. He had many difficulties to encounter, and his duty towards France was in some instances incompatible with good policy towards Portugal; yet he was not without resources for establishing a strong French interest, if he had possessed the ability and disposition to soothe a nation that, without having suffered a defeat, was suddenly bowed to a foreign yoke.

But the pride and the poverty of the Portuguese, and the influence of ancient usages, interfered with Junot's policy. The monks, and most of the nobility, were inimical to it, and all the activity of the expelled British factory, and the secret warfare of spies and writers in the pay of England, were directed to undermine his plans, and to render him and his nation odious. On the other hand, he was in possession of the government and of the capital, he had a fine army, he could offer novelty, so dear to the multitude, and he had the name and the fame of Napoleon to assist him. The promises of power are always believed by the many, and there were abundance of grievances to remedy, and wrongs to redress, in Portugal. Among the best educated men, especially at the universities, there existed a strong feeling against the Braganza family, and such an earnest desire for reformed institutions, that steps were actually taken to have Prince Eugene declared King of Portugal;† nor was this spirit extinguished at a much later date.

* Napoleon, in Las Casas. Foy.
† Foy

With these materials and the military vanity of the Portuguese to work upon, Junot might have established a powerful French interest; under an active government, the people would not long have regretted the loss of an independence that had no wholesome breathing amidst the corrupt stagnation of the old system. But the arrogance of a conqueror, and the necessities of an army, which was to be subsisted and paid by an impoverished people, soon gave rise to all kinds of oppression; private abuses followed close upon the heels of public rapacity, and insolence left its sting to rankle in the wounds of the injured. The malignant humors broke out in quarrels and assassinations, and the severe punishments that ensued, many of them unjust and barbarous in the highest degree, created rage, not terror, for the nation had not tried its strength in battle, and would not believe that it was weak. Meanwhile the ports being rigorously blockaded by the English fleet, and the troubles in Spain having interrupted the commerce in grain, by which Portugal had been usually supplied from that country, the unhappy people suffered under the triple pressure of famine, war-contributions, and a foreign yoke.* With all external aliment thus cut off, and a hungry army gnawing at its vitals, the nation could not remain tranquil; yet the first five months of Junot's government was, with the exception of a slight tumult at Lisbon, when the arms of Portugal were taken down, undisturbed by commotion. Nevertheless the whole country was ripe for a general insurrection.

The harvest proved abundant, and Junot hailed the prospect of returning plenty as a relief from his principal difficulty; but as one danger disappeared, another presented itself. The Spanish insurrection excited the hopes of the Portuguese, and agents from the neighboring juntas communicated secretly with the Spanish generals in Portugal; the capture of the French fleet in Cadiz became known, assassinations multiplied, the Pope's nuncio fled on board the English fleet, and all things tended to an explosion. The English agents were, of course, actively engaged in promoting this spirit, and the appearance of two English fleets at different points of the coast, having troops on board, produced great alarm among the French, and augmented the impatient fierceness of the Portuguese.

Among the various ways in which the people discovered their hatred of the invaders, one was very characteristic: an egg being, by a chemical process, marked with certain letters, was exhibited in a church, and the letters were interpreted to indicate the speedy coming of Don Sebastian, King of Portugal, who, like Arthur of

* Thiebault.

romantic memory, is supposed to be hidden in a secret island, waiting for the destined period to re-appear and restore his country to her ancient glory. The trick was turned against the contrivers; other eggs prophesied in the most unpatriotic manner, yet the belief of the Sebastianists lost nothing of its zeal; many people, and those not of the most uneducated classes, were often observed upon the highest points of the hills, casting earnest looks towards the ocean, in the hope of descrying the island in which their long-lost hero is detained.

CHAPTER II.

The Spanish General Bellesta seizes General Quesnel and retires to Gallicia—Insurrection at Oporto—Junot disarms and confines the Spanish soldiers near Lisbon—General Avril's column returns to Estremos—General Loison marches from Almeida against Oporto; is attacked at Mezam Frias; crosses the Douro; attacked at Castro d'Airo; recalled to Lisbon—French driven out of the Algarves—The fort of Figueras taken—Abrantes and Elvas threatened—Setuval in commotion—General Spencer appears off the Tagus—Junot's plan—Insurrection at Villa Viciosa suppressed—Colonel Maransin takes Beja with great slaughter of the patriots—The insurgents advance from Leiria, fall back—Action at Leiria—Loison arrives at Abrantes—Observations on his march—French army concentrated—The Portuguese General Leite, aided by a Spanish corps, takes post at Evora—Loison crosses the Tagus; defeats Leite's advanced guard at Montemor—Battle of Evora—Town taken and pillaged—Unfriendly conduct of the Spaniards—Loison reaches Elvas; collects provisions; is recalled by Junot—Observations.

THE first serious blow was struck at Oporto. The news of what had taken place all over Spain was known there in June, and General Bellesta, the chief Spanish officer, immediately took an honorable and resolute part. He made the French General Quesnel, with his staff, prisoners; after which, calling together the Portuguese authorities, he declared that they were free to act as they judged most fitting for their own interests, and then marched to Gallicia with his army and captives. The opinions of the leading men at Oporto were divided upon the great question of resistance, but, after some vicissitudes, the boldest side was successful; the insurrection, although at one moment quelled by the French party, was finally established in Oporto, and soon extended along the banks of the Douro and the Minho, and to those parts of Beira which lie between the Mondego and the sea-coast.

Junot being informed of this event, perceived that no time was to be lost in disarming the Spanish regiments quartered in the neighborhood of Lisbon, which was not an easy operation. Caraffa's division was above six thousand men, and without employing the garrisons of the citadel and forts of Lisbon, it was difficult to collect an equal force of French; the suspicions of the Spanish regiments had been already excited, they were reluctant to obey the French generals, and one, quartered at Alcacer do Sal, had actually resisted the orders of the General-in-Chief himself.* To avoid a tumult was also a great object, because in Lisbon fifteen thousand Gallicians were ordinarily engaged as porters and water-carriers, and if a popular movement had been excited, these men would naturally have assisted their countrymen. Notwithstanding these difficulties, Junot, in the night of that day upon which he received the information of Bellesta's defection, arranged all his measures, and the next day the Spanish troops, being under various pretexts assembled in such numbers and in such places that resistance was useless, were disarmed, and placed on board the hulks in the Tagus, with the exception of eight hundred of the regiment of Murcia and three hundred of that of Valencia, who escaped. Thus, in the course of twenty-four hours, and with very little bloodshed, Junot, by his promptness and dexterity, averted a very serious danger.

Although this stroke produced considerable effect, it did not prevent the insurrection from becoming general; all couriers and officers carrying orders or commanding small posts of communications were suddenly cut off. Junot, reduced by a single blow from fifty to twenty-eight thousand men, found himself isolated, and dependent upon his individual resources and the courage of his soldiers for the maintenance of his conquest, and even for the preservation of his army. The Russian squadron, indeed, contained six thousand seamen and marines; but while they consumed a great quantity of provisions, it was evident from certain symptoms that they could not be depended upon as useful allies, except in the case of an English fleet attempting to force the entrance of the river. In this situation the Duke of Abrantes would have seized Badajoz, but was deterred by the assembling of an Estremaduran army, then under the command of General Galuzzo. However, Avril's column, having failed to join Dupont, returned to Estremos; and it is probable that Junot never intended that it should do otherwise.

Meanwhile Loison, then in Upper Beira, was ordered to march upon Oporto.† He had reached Almeida on the 5th of June, one day previous to Bellesta's defection, and on the 12th, when he read the order, partly by menace, partly by persuasion, got possession of Fort Conception, a strong but ill-placed Spanish work on that

* Thiebeult.
† Ibid.

frontier. He first attempted to penetrate the Entre-Minho e Douro by Amarante, but as his division was weak, and as it was possible that Bellesta might return and fall upon his flank, he advanced timidly. At Mezam Frias he was opposed, and his baggage was at the same time menaced by other insurgents; whereupon he fell back to Villa Real, and after a trifling skirmish at that place, crossed the Douro at Lamego, and marched to Castro d'Airo, where he turned and defeated the armed peasants of the mountains, who had particularly harassed his flanks. From Castro d'Airo he moved upon Coimbra, whence he dislodged a body of insurgents and was about to scour the country, when he received one of twenty-five despatches—the rest had been intercepted—sent by Junot to recall him to Lisbon. He immediately united his columns, placed his sick and weakly men in Almeida, raised the garrison up to twelve hundred and fifty men, and then, having ruined the defences of Fort Conception, commenced his march to Lisbon, by the way of Guarda.

But while these events were passing in the Beira an insurrection also broke out in the Algarves, where General Maurin commanded. It began near Faro, and Maurin himself, lying sick in that town, was made prisoner. Some Portuguese troops attached to the French force then joined the insurgents, the Spaniards from Andalusia prepared to cross the Guadiana, and General Spencer appeared off Ayamonte with five thousand British troops. The French Colonel Maransin, who had succeeded Maurin, immediately retired to Hertola, leaving his baggage, military chest, and above a hundred prisoners, besides killed and wounded, in the hands of the patriots, who, finding that Spencer would not land, did not pursue beyond the Algarve mountains.

The circle of insurrection was now fast closing round Junot. Emissaries from Oporto excited the people to rise as far as Coimbra, where a French post was overpowered, and a junta was formed, whose efforts spread the flame to Condeixa, Pombal, and Leira. A student named Zagalo, mixing boldness with address, obliged a Portuguese officer and a hundred men to surrender the fort of Figueras, at the mouth of the Mondego; Abrantes was threatened by the insurgents of the valley of the Zezere, and the Spaniards, under Galuzzo, crossing the Guadiana at Juramenha, occupied that place and Campo Mayor. Thus a great, although confused body of men, menaced Kellermann at Elvas; yet, supported by the strength of the town and Fort La Lippe, he easily maintained himself. Avril remained unmolested at Estremos, and Evora, held by a small garrison, was tranquil; but the neighborhood of Setuval was in commotion, the populace of Lisbon was un-

* Thiebault.

quiet; and at this critical moment General Spencer, who had quitted Ayamonte, and whose force report magnified to ten thousand men, appeared at the mouth of the Tagus.*

Junot held a council of war, and after hearing the opinions of the principal general officers, decided on the following plan: 1. To collect the sick in such hospitals as could be protected by the ships of war. 2. To secure the Spanish prisoners by mooring the hulks in which they were confined as far as possible from the city. 3. To arm and provision the forts of Lisbon and remove the powder from the magazines to the ships. 4. To abandon all other fortresses in Portugal, with the exception of Setuval, Almeida, Elvas and Peniche, and to concentrate the army in Lisbon. In the event of bad fortune, the Duke of Abrantes determined to defend the capital as long as he was able, and then crossing the Tagus, move upon Elvas, and from thence retreat to Madrid, Valladolid, or Segovia, as he might find it expedient. This well conceived plan was not executed: the first alarm soon died away, Spencer returned to Cadiz, and when the insurrection was grappled with it proved to be more noisy than dangerous.

Kellermann, having recalled Maransin from Mertola, was preparing to march on Lisbon, when the inhabitants of the town of Villa Viciosa rose on a company of French troops and drove them into an old castle; yet when Avril came from Estremos to their succor the Portuguese fled, and a very few were killed in the pursuit. The town of Beja followed the example of Villa Viciosa, but Colonel Maransin, who was ready to retire from Mertola, marched in that direction with such rapidity that he passed over forty miles in eighteen hours, and falling suddenly upon the patriots, defeated them with considerable slaughter, and pillaged the place. He had eighty men killed or wounded, and General Thiebault writes that an obstinate combat took place in the streets. But the Portuguese never made head for a moment against a strong body during the whole course of the insurrection; how, indeed, was it possible for a collection of miserable peasants, armed with scythes, pitchforks, a few old fowling pieces, and a little bad powder, under the command of some ignorant countryman or fanatic friar, to maintain a battle against an efficient and active corps of French soldiers? For there is this essential difference to be observed in judging between the Spanish and Portuguese insurrections: the Spaniards had many great and strong towns free from the presence of the French, and large provinces in which to collect and train forces at a distance from the invaders, while in Portugal the naked peasants were forced to go to battle the instant even of assembling. The loss which

* Thiebault.

Maransin sustained must have arisen from the stragglers, who in a consecutive march of forty miles would have been numerous, having been cut off and killed by the peasantry.

This blow quieted the Alemtejo for the moment; and Kellermann, having cleared the neighborhood of Elvas of all Spanish parties, placed a commandant in La Lippe, concentrated the detachments under Maransin and Avril, and proceeded himself towards Lisbon, where the Duke of Abrantes was in great perplexity. The intercepting of his couriers and isolated officers, being followed by the detection of all his spies, had exposed him without remedy to every report which the fears of his army or the ingenuity of the people could give birth to; and there are few nations that can pretend to vie with the Portuguese and Spaniards in the fabrication of plausible reports. Among those current, the captivity of Loison was one; but as nothing was certainly known, except that the insurgents from the valley of the Mondego were marching towards Lisbon, General Margaron was ordered to disperse them, and if possible to open a communication with General Loison. He advanced with three thousand men and six pieces of artillery to Leiria, whither the patriots had retired in disorder when they heard of his approach. The greater part dispersed at once; but those who remained were attacked on the 5th of July, and a scene similar to that of Beja ensued;* the French boasted of victory, the insurgents called it massacre and pillage. In a combat with armed peasantry, it is difficult to know where the fighting ceases and the massacre begins; men dressed in peasants' clothes are observed firing and moving about without order from place to place—when do they cease to be enemies? They are more dangerous when single than together; they can hide their muskets in an instant and appear peaceable; the soldier passes, and is immediately shot from behind.

The example at Leiria did not, however, deter the people of Thomar from declaring against the French, and the neighborhood of Alcobaça rose at the same time. Margaron was thus placed between two new insurrections at the moment he had quelled one; English fleets, with troops on board, were said to be hovering off the coast, and as the most alarming reports relative to Loison were corroborated, his safety was despaired of, when, suddenly, authentic intelligence of his arrival at Abrantes revived the spirits of the general-in-chief and the army.

After arranging all things necessary for the security of Almeida, he had quitted that town the 2d of July, at the head of three thousand four hundred and fifty men, and arrived at Abrantes upon the 8th; having in seven days passed through Guarda, Attalaya, Sar-

* Thiebault. Accursio de Nèves.

sedas, Corteja, and Sardoval. During this rapid march he dispersed several bodies of insurgents that were assembled on the line of his route, especially at Guarda and Attalaya, and it has been said that twelve hundred bodies were stretched upon the field of battle near the first town ; but twelve hundred slain would give five thousand wounded, that is to say, six thousand two hundred killed and wounded by a corps of three thousand four hundred and fifty men in half an hour ! and this without cavalry or artillery, and among fastnesses that vie in ruggedness with any in the world ! The truth is, that the peasants, terrified by the reports that Loison himself spread to favor his march, fled on all sides, and if two hundred and fifty Portuguese were killed and wounded during the whole passage, it was the utmost. The distance from Almeida to Abrantes is more than a hundred and eighty miles ; the greatest part is a mountain pathway rather than a road, and the French were obliged to gather their provisions from the country as they passed : to forage, to fight several actions, to pursue active peasants well acquainted with the country so closely as to destroy them by thousands, and to march a hundred and eighty miles over bad roads, and all in seven days, is impossible.

The whole French army was now concentrated. But though Kellermann had quelled the insurrection at Alcobaça, and that of Thomar was quieted, the insurgents from Oporto were gathering strength at Coimbra, and the last of the native soldiers deserted the French colors ; the Spanish troops at Badajos, strengthened by a body of Portuguese fugitives, and commanded by one Moretti, were also preparing to enter the Alemtejo, and that province was again in commotion ;* for the English Admiral had opened a communication with the insurgents on the side of Setuval, and the patriots were assembled in considerable numbers at Alcacer do Sal.

In this dilemma Junot resolved to leave the northern people quiet for a while, and attack the Alemtejo, because that was his line of retreat upon Spain ; from thence only he could provision the capital, and there also his cavalry could act with the most effect. Accordingly, Loison, with seven thousand infantry, twelve hundred cavalry, and eight pieces of artillery, crossed the Tagus the 25th of July, and marched by Os Pegoens, Vendanovas, and Montemor. At the latter place he defeated an advanced guard, which fled to Evora, where the Portuguese General Leite had assembled the mass of the insurgents, and, assisted by three or four thousand Spanish troops under Moretti, had taken a position to cover the town. When Loison discovered them, he directed Margaron and Solignac to turn their flanks, and fell upon their centre himself.

* Ibid. Parliamentary Papers, 1809.

The battle was short, for the Spanish auxiliaries performed no service, and the Portuguese soon took to flight; but there was a great and confused concourse, a strong cavalry was let loose upon the fugitives, and many, being cut off from the main body, were driven into the town, which had been deserted by the principal inhabitants; there, urged by despair, they endeavored to defend the walls and the streets for a few moments, but were soon overpowered, the greater part slain, and the houses pillaged. The French lost two or three hundred men, and the number of the Portuguese and Spaniards that fell was very considerable;* disputes also arose between them, and the latter ravaged the country in their retreat with more violence than the French.

Loison, after resting two days at Evora, proceeded to Elvas, and drove away the numerous Spanish parties which had again infested the neighborhood of that fortress, and were become obnoxious alike to Portuguese and French. He then scoured the country round, and was accumulating provisions to form magazines at Elvas, when he was suddenly interrupted by a despatch from the Duke of Abrantes, recalling him to the right bank of the Tagus, for the British army, so long expected, had, at last, descended upon the coast, and manly warfare reared its honest front amidst the desolating scenes of insurrection.

OBSERVATIONS.

1. Loison's expedition to the Alemtejo was an operation of military police, rather than a campaign. Junot wished to repress the spirit of insurrection by sudden and severe examples, and hence the actions of his lieutenant were of necessity harsh; but they have been represented as a series of massacres and cruelties of the most revolting nature, and Loison disseminated such stories to increase the terror which it was the object of his expedition to create. The credulity of the nation that produced the Sebastianists was not easily shocked; the Portuguese eagerly listened to tales so derogatory to their enemies, and so congenial to their own revengeful dispositions; but the anecdotes of French barbarity current for two years after the convention of Cintra were notoriously false, and the same stories being related by persons remote from each other is no argument of their truth. The report that Loison was captured, on his march from Almeida, reached Junot through fifty different channels; there were men to declare that they had beheld him bound with cords;† others to tell how he had been entrapped; some named the places he had been carried through in triumph, and his

* Thiebault.
† Ibid.

habitual and characteristic expressions were quoted; the story was complete, and the parts were consistent, yet the whole was not only false, but the rumor had not even the slightest foundation of truth.

2. The Portuguese accounts of the events of this period are angry amplifications of every real or pretended act of French barbarity and injustice; the crimes of individuals are made matter of accusation against the whole army. The French accounts are more plausible, yet scarcely more safe as authorities, seeing that they are written by men who, being for the most part actors in the scenes they describe, are naturally concerned to defend their own characters; their military vanity also has had its share in disguising the simple facts of the insurrection; for, willing to enhance the merit of the troops, they have exaggerated the number of the insurgents, the obstinacy of the combats, and the loss of the patriots. English party writers, greedily fixing upon such relations, have changed the name of battle into massacre; and thus prejudice, conceit, and clamor have combined to violate the decorum of history, and to perpetuate error.

3. It would, however, be an egregious mistake to suppose that, because the French were not monsters, there existed no cause for the acrimony with which their conduct has been assailed. The Duke of Abrantes, although not cruel, nor personally obnoxious to the Portuguese, was a sensual and violent person, and his habits were expensive. Such a man is always rapacious; and as the character of the chief influences the manners of those under his command, it may be safely assumed that his vices were aped by many of his followers.* Now the virtuous General Travot was esteemed and his person respected, even in the midst of tumult, by the Portuguese, while Loison was scarcely safe from their vengeance when surrounded by his troops. The execrations poured forth at the mere mention of "the bloody Maneta," as, from the loss of his hand, he was called, proves that he must have committed many heinous acts; and Kellermann appears to have been as justly stigmatized for rapacity as Loison was for violence.

4. It has been made a charge against the French generals, that they repressed the hostility of the Portuguese and Spanish peasants by military executions; but, in doing so, they only followed the custom of war, and they are not justly liable to reproof, save where they may have carried their punishments to excess, and displayed a wanton spirit of cruelty. All armies have an undoubted right to protect themselves when engaged in hostilities. An insurrection of armed peasants is a military anarchy; and men in such circum-

* Napoleon in Las Casas.

stances cannot be restrained within the bounds of civilized warfare. They will murder stragglers, torture prisoners, destroy hospitals, poison wells, and break down all the usages that soften the enmities of modern nations; they wear no badge of an enemy, and their devices cannot, therefore, be guarded against in the ordinary mode; their war is one of extermination, and it must be repressed by terrible examples, or the civilized customs of modern warfare must be discarded, and the devastating system of the ancients revived. The usage of refusing quarter to an armed peasantry, and burning their villages, however unjust and barbarous it may appear at first view, is founded upon a principle of necessity, and is in reality a vigorous infliction of a partial evil, to prevent universal calamity; but, however justifiable it may be in theory, no wise man will hastily resort to it, and no good man will carry it to any extent.

CHAPTER III.

Political and military retrospect—Mr. Fox's conduct contrasted with that of his successors—General Spencer sent to the Mediterranean—Sir John Moore withdrawn from thence; arrives in England; sent to Sweden—Spencer arrives at Gibraltar—Ceuta, the object of his expedition—Spanish insurrection diverts his attention to Cadiz; wishes to occupy that city—Spaniards averse to it—Prudent conduct of Sir Hew Dalrymple and Lord Collingwood—Spencer sails to Ayamonte; returns to Cadiz; sails to the mouth of the Tagus; returns to Cadiz—Prince Leopold of Sicily and the Duke of Orleans arrive at Gibraltar—Curious intrigue—Army assembled at Cork by the Whig administration, with a view to permanent conquest in South America, the only disposable British force—Sir A. Wellesley takes the command—Contradictory instructions of the ministers—Sir John Moore returns from Sweden; ordered to Portugal—Sir Hew Dalrymple appointed commander of the forces—Confused arrangements made by the ministers.

THE subjugation of Portugal was neither a recent nor a secret project of Napoleon's. In 1806, Mr. Fox, penetrating this design, had sent Lord Rosslyn, Lord St. Vincent, and General Simcoe, on a politico-military mission to Lisbon, instructing them to warn the court that a French army destined to invade Portugal was assembling at Bayonne, and to offer the assistance of a British force to meet the attack.* The cabinet of Lisbon affected to disbelieve the information, Mr. Fox died during the negotiation, and as the war with Prussia diverted Napoleon's attention to more important objects, he withdrew his troops from Bayonne. The Tory administration, which soon after overturned the Grenville party, thought no further

---

* Parliamentary Papers, 1809.

of this affair, or at least did not evince as much foresight and ready zeal as its predecessors. They, indeed, sent Sir Sidney Smith with a squadron to Lisbon, but their views seem to have been confined to the emigration of the royal family, and they intrusted the conduct of the negotiation to Lord Strangford, a young man of no solid influence or experience.

But the Russian squadron, under Admiral Siniavin, suddenly entered the Tagus, and this unexpected event produced in the British cabinet an activity which the danger of Portugal had not been able to excite. It was supposed that, as Russia and England were in a state of hostility, the presence of the Russian ships would intimidate the Prince Regent, and prevent him from passing to the Brazils; wherefore Sir Charles Cotton, an admiral of higher rank than Sir Sidney Smith, was sent out with instructions to force the entrance of the Tagus, and attack Siniavin.* General Spencer, then upon the point of sailing with five thousand men upon a secret expedition, was ordered to touch at Lisbon, and ten thousand men, under Sir John Moore, were withdrawn from Sicily to aid this enterprise;† but before the instructions for the commanders were even written, the Prince Regent was on his voyage to the Brazils, and Junot ruled in Lisbon. When Sir John Moore arrived at Gibraltar, he could hear nothing of Sir Sidney Smith, nor of General Spencer, and proceeded to England, which he reached the 31st of December, 1807. From thence, after a detention of four months on ship-board, he was despatched upon that well-known and eminently foolish expedition to Sweden, which ended in such an extraordinary manner,‡ and which seems from the first to have had no other object than the factious one of keeping an excellent general and a superb division of troops at a distance from the only country where their services were really required.

Meanwhile General Spencer's armament, long baffled by contrary winds, and once forced back to port, was finally dispersed in a storm, and a part arrived at Gibraltar, by single ships, the latter end of January, 1808. Sir Hew Dalrymple, the governor of that fortress, hearing, on the 5th of February, that a French fleet had just passed the Strait and run up the Mediterranean, became alarmed for Sicily, and caused the first comers to proceed to that island on the 11th; but Spencer himself, whose instructions included an attack on Ceuta, did not arrive at Gibraltar until the 10th of March, when the deficiency in his armament was supplied by a draft from the garrison, and a council was held to arrange the

* Parliamentary Papers, 1809.
† Sir John Moore's Journal, MSS.
‡ Ibid.

plan of attack on Ceuta. The operation was however finally judged impracticable.

The objects of Spencer's expedition were manifold: he was to co-operate with Moore against the Russian fleet in the Tagus, he was to take the French fleet at Cadiz, he was to assault Ceuta, and he was to make an attempt on the Spanish fleet at Port Mahon! But the wind which brought Moore to Lisbon blowed Spencer from that port, and a consultation with Admiral Purvis convinced him that the French fleet in Cadiz was invulnerable to his force, Ceuta was too strong, and it only remained to sail to Port Mahon, when the Spanish insurrection breaking out, drew him back to Cadiz with altered views. In the relation of Dupont's campaign, I have already touched upon Spencer's proceedings at Cadiz; but in this place it is necessary to give a more detailed sketch of those occurrences, which fortunately brought him to the coast of Portugal at the moment when Sir Arthur Wellesley was commencing the campaign of Vimiero.

When the French first entered Spain, General Castaños commanded the Spanish troops at San Roque: In that situation he was an object of interest to Napoleon, who sent two French officers privately to sound his disposition. Castaños, who had secretly resolved to oppose the designs of the Emperor, thought those officers were coming to arrest him, and at first determined to kill them and fly to Gibraltar; but on discovering his mistake treated them civilly, and prosecuted his original plans.* Through the medium of one Viali, a merchant of Gibraltar, he opened a communication with Sir Hew Dalrymple, and the latter, who had been closely watching the progress of events, encouraged him in his views, and not only promised assistance, but recommended several important measures, such as the immediate seizure of the French squadron in Cadiz, the security of the Spanish fleet at Minorca, and a speedy communication with South America. However, before Castaños could mature his plans, the insurrection took place at Seville, and he acknowledged the authority of the Junta.

Meanwhile Solano arrived at Cadiz, and General Spencer, in conjunction with Admiral Purvis, pressed him to attack the French squadron, offering to assist if he would admit the English troops into the town. Solano, whose mind was not made up to resist the invaders, expressed great displeasure at this proposal to occupy Cadiz, and refused to treat at all with the British; an event not unexpected by Sir Hew, for he knew that most of the Spaniards were mistrustful of the object of Spencer's expedition, and the offer was made without his concurrence. Thus a double intercourse was

* Sir Hew Dalrymple's Correspondence, MS.

carried on between the British and Spanish authorities—the one friendly and confidential between Sir Hew and Castaños, the other of a character proper to increase the suspicions of the Spaniards; and when it is considered that Spain and England were nominally at war,—that the English commanders were acting without the authority of their government,—that the troops which it was proposed to introduce into Cadiz were in that part of the world for the express purpose of attacking Ceuta, and had already taken the island of Perexil, close to that fortress,—little surprise can be excited by Solano's conduct. When he was killed, and Morla had succeeded to the command, Spencer and Purvis renewed their offers; but Morla also declined their assistance, and having himself forced the French squadron to surrender by a succession of such ill-directed attacks that some doubt was entertained of his wish to succeed, he commenced a series of low intrigues calculated to secure his own personal safety, while he held himself ready to betray his country if the French should prove the strongest.

After the reduction of the enemy's ships, the people were inclined to admit the English troops, but the local Junta, swayed by Morla's representations, were averse to it;* and he, while confirming this disposition, secretly urged Spencer to persevere in his offer, saying that he looked entirely to the British force for the future defence of Cadiz. Thus dealing, he passed with the people for an active patriot, yet made no preparations for resistance, and by his double falsehood preserved a fair appearance both with the Junta and the English General. With these affairs Sir Hew Dalrymple did not meddle; he early discovered that Morla was an enemy of Castaños, and having more confidence in the latter, carried on the intercourse at first established between them, without reference to the transactions at Cadiz. He also supplied the Spanish General with arms, and two thousand barrels of powder, and placing one English officer near him as a military correspondent, sent another in the capacity of political agent to the Supreme Junta at Seville.

When Castaños was appointed commander-in-chief of the Andalusian army, and had rallied Echevaria's troops, he asked for the co-operation of the British force, and offered no objection to their entering Cadiz, but he preferred having them landed at Almeria to march to Xeres. General Spencer confined his offers to the occupation of Cadiz, and when Morla pretended that to fit out the Spanish fleet was an object of immediate importance, Colonel Sir George Smith, an officer employed by General Spencer to conduct the negotiations, promised, on his own authority, money to pay the Spanish seamen, who were then in a state of

* Sir Hew Dalrymple's Correspondence, MS.

mutiny. However, Lord Collingwood and Sir Hew Dalrymple refused to fulfil this promise, and the approach of Dupont causing Morla to wish Spencer's troops away, he persuaded that General to sail to Ayamonte, under the pretence of preventing Avril's division from crossing the Guadiana, although he knew well that the latter had no intention of doing so. The effect produced upon Colonel Maransin by the appearance of the British force off Ayamonte has been already noticed. General Thiebault says that Spencer might have struck an important blow at that period against the French; but the British troops were unprovided with any equipment for a campaign, and to have thrown five thousand infantry, without cavalry and without a single place of arms, into the midst of an enemy who occupied all the fortresses, and who could bring twenty thousand men into the field, would have been imprudent to the greatest degree. General Spencer, who had by this time been rejoined by his detachment from Sicily, only made a demonstration of landing, and having thus materially aided the insurrection, returned to Cadiz, from whence he was almost immediately summoned to Lisbon, to execute a new project, which proved to be both ill-considered and fruitless.

Sir Charles Cotton, being unable to force the entrance of the Tagus without troops, had blockaded that post with the utmost rigor, expecting to force the Russian squadron to capitulate for want of provisions. This scheme, which originated with Lord Strangford, never had the least chance of success, and only augmented the privations and misery of the wretched inhabitants.* Junot, therefore, had recourse to various expedients to abate the rigor of the blockade with regard to them, and among others employed a Portuguese named Sataro to make proposals to the English Admiral. This man, who at first pretended that he came without the privity of the French, led Sir Charles to believe that only four thousand French troops remained in Lisbon, and under that erroneous impression, the latter desired General Spencer might join him for the purpose of attacking the enemy while they were so weak. Spencer, by the advice of Sir Hew Dalrymple and Lord Collingwood, obeyed the summons, but on his arrival was led to doubt the correctness of the Admiral's information;† instead of four thousand, it appeared that there could not be less than fifteen thousand French in or near Lisbon, and the attack was of course relinquished.‡ Spencer returned to Cadiz: Castaños again pressed him to co-operate with the Spanish forces, and he so far consented

* Mr. Canning to Lord Castlereagh, 28th Dec., 1807.
† Sir Hew Dalrymple's Correspondence.
‡ Parliamentary Papers, 1809.

as to disembark them at the port of St. Mary, and even agreed to send a detachment to Xeres; yet, deceived by Morla, who still gave him hopes of finally occupying Cadiz, he resolved to keep the greater part close to that city.*

At this period the insurrection of Andalusia attracted all the intriguing adventurers in the Mediterranean towards Gibraltar and Seville, and the confusion of Agramant's camp would have been rivalled, if the prudent firmness of Sir Hew Dalrymple had not checked the first efforts of those political pests. Among the perplexing follies of the moment, one deserves particular notice, on account of some curious circumstances that attended it, the full explanation of which I must, however, leave to other historians, who may, perhaps, find in that and the like affairs a key to that absurd policy which in Sicily so long sacrificed the welfare of two nations to the whims and follies of a profligate court. The introduction of the salique law had long been a favorite object with the Bourbons of Spain; but it had never been promulgated with the formalities necessary to give it validity, and the nation was averse to change the ancient rule of succession. This law was, however, now secretly revived by some of the Junta of Seville, who wished to offer the regency to the Prince of Sicily, because, Ferdinand and his brother dying without sons, the regent would then succeed, to the prejudice of the Princess Carlotta of Portugal. With this object in view, the Chevalier Robertoni, a Sicilian agent, appeared early at Gibraltar, and from thence, as if under the auspices of England, attempted to forward the views of his court, until Sir Hew Dalrymple, being accidentally informed that the British cabinet disapproved of the object of his mission, sent him away.†

Meanwhile Castaños, deceived by some person engaged in the intrigue, was inclined to support the pretensions of the Sicilian Prince to the regency, and proposed to make use of Sir Hew Dalrymple's name to give weight to his opinions,—a circumstance which would have created great jealousy in Spain, if Sir Hew had not promptly refused his sanction. The affair then seemed to droop for a moment; but in the middle of July an English man-of-war suddenly appeared at Gibraltar, having on board Prince Leopold of Sicily, a complete court establishment of chamberlains with their keys and ushers with their white wands;‡ and the Duke of Orleans, who attended his brother-in-law the Prince, making no secret of his intention to negotiate for the regency of Spain, openly demanded that he should be received into Gibraltar. Sir Hew, fore-

* Sir Hew Dalrymple's Correspondence.
† Ibid.
‡ Ibid.

seeing all the mischief of this proceeding, promptly refused to permit the Prince or any of his attendants to land, and the captain of the ship, whose orders were merely to carry him to Gibraltar, refused to take him back to Sicily. Finally, to relieve his Royal Highness from this awkward situation, Sir Hew consented to receive him as a guest, provided that he divested himself of his public character, and that the Duke of Orleans departed instantly from the fortress.

Sir William Drummond, British envoy at Palermo, Mr. Viali, and the Duke of Orleans were the ostensible contrivers of this notable scheme, by which, if it had succeeded, a small party in a local junta would have appointed a regency for Spain, paved the way for altering the laws of succession in that country, established their own sway over the other juntas, and created interminable jealousy between England, Portugal and Spain. With whom the plan originated does not very clearly appear. Sir William Drummond's representations induced Sir Alexander Ball to provide the ship of war, nominally for the conveyance of the Duke of Orleans, in reality for Prince Leopold, with whose intended voyage Sir Alexander does not appear to have been made acquainted. That the Prince should have desired to be regent of Spain was natural, but that he should have been conveyed to Gibraltar in a British ship of the line, when the English government disapproved of his pretensions, was really curious. Sir William Drummond could scarcely have proceeded such lengths in an affair of so great consequence without secret instructions from some member of his own government; yet Lord Castlereagh expressed unqualified approbation of Sir Hew's decisive conduct upon the occasion! Did the ministers act at this period without any confidential communication with each other? or was Lord Castlereagh's policy secretly and designedly thwarted by one of his colleagues? But it is time to quit this digression and turn to

THE PROCEEDINGS IN PORTUGAL.

The Bishop of Oporto, being placed at the head of the insurrectional junta of that town, claimed the assistance of England. "We hope," said he, "for an aid of three hundred thousand cruzado novas; of arms and accoutrements complete, and of cloth for forty thousand infantry and for eight thousand cavalry; three thousand barrels of cannon powder, some cargoes of salt fish, and other provisions, and an auxiliary body of six thousand men, at least, including some cavalry." This extravagant demand would lead to the supposition that an immense force had been assembled by the prelate, yet he could never at any time have put five thousand organized men in motion against the French, and had probably not even thought of any feasible or rational mode of employing the succors he demanded. The times were, however, favorable for extravagant demands, and his were not rejected by the English ministers, who sent agents to Oporto and other parts, with power to grant supplies. The improvident system adopted for Spain being thus extended to Portugal, produced precisely the same effects,—that is, cavils, intrigues, waste, insubordination, inordinate vanity and ambition, among the ignorant upstart men of the day. More than half a year had now elapsed since Napoleon first poured his forces into the Peninsula, every moment of that time was marked by some extraordinary event, and one month had passed since a general and terrible explosion, shaking the unsteady structure of diplomacy to pieces, had left a clear space for the shock of arms; yet the British cabinet was still unacquainted with the real state of public feeling in the Peninsula and with the Spanish character, and although possessing a disposable army of at least eighty thousand excellent troops, was totally unsettled in its plans, and unprepared for any vigorous effort.* Agents were indeed despatched to every accessible province, the public treasure was scattered with heedless profusion, and the din of preparation was heard in every department; but the bustle of confusion is easily mistaken for the activity of business, and time, removing the veil of official mystery covering those transactions, has exposed all their dull and meagre features. It is now clear that the treasure was squandered without judgment and the troops dispersed without meaning. Ten thousand exiled to Sweden proved the truth of Oxenstiern's address to his son; as many more idly kept in Sicily were degraded into the guards of a vicious court. Gibraltar was unnecessarily filled with fighting men, and General Spencer, with five thousand excellent soldiers, was doomed to wander between Ceuta, Lisbon, and Cadiz, seeking, like the knight of La Mancha, for a foe to combat.

A considerable force remained in England, but it was not ready for service, when the minister resolved to send an expedition to the Peninsula, and nine thousand men collected at Cork formed the only disposable army for immediate operations. The Grey and Grenville administration, so remarkable for unfortunate military enterprises, had assembled this handful of men with a view to permanent conquests in South America! upon what principle of policy it is not necessary to inquire, but such undoubtedly was the intention of that administration, perhaps in imitation of the Roman Senate, who sent troops to Spain when Hannibal was at the gates of the city. The Tory administration, relinquishing this scheme of

* Parl. Pap. Lord Castlereagh to Sir A. Wellesley, 21st June.

conquest, directed Sir Arthur Wellesley to inform General Miranda, the military adventurer of the day, not only that he must cease to expect assistance, but that all attempts to separate the colonies of Spain from the parent state would be discouraged by the English government; thus the troops assembled at Cork became available, and Sir Arthur Wellesley being appointed to command them, sailed on the 12th of July, to commence that long and bloody contest in the Peninsula which he was destined to terminate in such a glorious manner.

Two small divisions were soon after ordered to assemble for embarkation at Ramsgate and Harwich, under the command of Generals Anstruther and Acland, yet a considerable time elapsed before they were ready to sail, and a singular uncertainty in the views of the ministers at this period subjected all the military operations to perpetual and mischievous changes.* General Spencer, supposed to be at Gibraltar, was directed to repair to Cadiz, and there await Sir Arthur's orders, and the latter was permitted to sail under the impression that Spencer was actually subject to his command;† other instructions empowered Spencer, at his own discretion, to commence operations in the south, without reference to Sir Arthur Wellesley's proceedings;‡ Admiral Purvis, who, after Lord Collingwood's arrival, had no separate command, was also authorized to undertake any enterprise in that quarter, and even to control the operations of Sir Arthur Wellesley by calling for the aid of his troops, that General being enjoined to "pay all due obedience to any such requisition !§ Yet Sir Arthur himself was informed, that "the accounts from Cadiz were bad;" that "no disposition to move either there or in the neighborhood of Gibraltar was visible;" and that "the Cabinet were unwilling he should go far to the southward, whilst the spirit of exertion appeared to reside more to the northward." Again, the Admiral, Sir Charles Cotton, was informed that Sir Arthur Wellesley was to co-operate with him in a descent at the mouth of the Tagus, but Sir Arthur himself had no definite object given for his own operations, although his instructions pointed to Portugal. Thus in fact no one officer, naval or military, knew exactly what his powers were, with the exception of Admiral Purvis, who, being only second in command for his own service, was really authorized to control all the operations of the land forces, provided he directed them to that quarter which had been declared unfavorable for any operations at all! These inconsistent orders

* Parliamentary Papers, 1808.
† Ibid.
‡ Lord Castlereagh to Sir A. Wellesley, 30th June.
§ Ibid. Ld. Castlereagh to Gen. Spencer, 28th and 30th June. Do. to Adm. Purvis, 28th June.

were calculated to create confusion and prevent all vigor of action, but more egregious conduct followed.

In recommending Portugal as the fittest field of action, the ministers were chiefly guided by the advice of the Asturian deputies. Yet having received Sir Hew Dalrymple's despatches to a late date, their own information must have been more recent and more extensive than any that they could obtain from those deputies, who had left Spain at the commencement of the insurrection, who were ill-informed of what was passing in their own province, utterly ignorant of the state of any other part of the Peninsula, and under any circumstances incapable of judging rightly in such momentous affairs.* But though Sir Arthur Wellesley's instructions were vague and confined with respect to military operations, he was expressly told that the intention of the government was to enable Portugal and Spain to throw off the French yoke, and ample directions were given to him as to his future political conduct in the Peninsula. He was informed how to demean himself in any disputes that might arise between the two insurgent nations, how to act with relation to the settlement of the supreme authority during the interregnum. He was directed to facilitate communications between the colonies and the mother country, and to offer his good offices to arrange any differences between them. The terms upon which Great Britain would acquiesce in any negotiation between Spain and France were imparted to him, and finally he was empowered to recommend the establishment of a paper system in the Peninsula, as a good mode of raising money, and attaching the holders of it to the national cause : the Spaniards were not, however, sufficiently civilized to adopt this recommendation, and barbarously preferred gold to credit, at a time when no man's life, or faith, or wealth, or power, was worth a week's purchase.

Sir Hew Dalrymple was also commanded to furnish Sir Arthur with every information that might be of use in the operations; and when the tenor of these instructions, and the great Indian reputation enjoyed by Sir Arthur Wellesley are considered, it is not possible to doubt that he was first chosen as the fittest man to conduct the armies of England at this important conjuncture.† Yet scarcely had he sailed when he was superseded, not for a man whose fame and experience might have justified such a change, but by an extraordinary arrangement, which can hardly be attributed to mere vacillation of purpose, he was reduced to the fourth rank in that army, for the future governance of which he had fifteen days before received the most extended instructions. Sir Hew Dalrymple

* Parl. Pap. Ld. Castlereagh to Sir A. Wellesley, 30th June.
† Parl. Pap. Ld. Castlereagh to Sir H. Dalrymple, 28th June.

was now appointed to the chief command, and Sir John Moore, who had suddenly and unexpectedly returned from the Baltic, having by his firmness and address saved himself and his troops from the madness of the Swedish monarch, was, with marked disrespect, directed to place himself under the orders of Sir Harry Burrard, and proceed to Portugal. Thus two men comparatively unknown and unused to the command of armies, superseded the only generals in the British service whose talents and experience were indisputable. The secret springs of this proceeding are not so deep as to baffle investigation ; but that task scarcely belongs to the general historian, who does enough when he exposes the effects of envy, treachery, and base cunning, without tracing those vices home to their possessors.

Notwithstanding these changes in the command, the uncertainty of the ministers' plans continued. The same day that Sir Hew Dalrymple was appointed to be commander-in-chief, a despatch, containing the following project of campaign, was sent to Sir Arthur Wellesley :‡ "The motives which have induced the sending so large a force to that quarter (the coast of Portugal), are, 1st, to provide effectually for an attack upon the Tagus ; and, 2dly, to have such an additional force disposable beyond what may be indispensably requisite for that operation, as may admit of a detachment being made to the southward, either with a view to secure Cadiz, if it should be threatened by the French force under General Dupont, or to co-operate with the Spanish troops in reducing that corps, if circumstances should favor such an operation, or any other that may be concerted. His Majesty is pleased to direct that the *attack upon the Tagus should be considered as the first object to be attended to ;* and as the whole force of which a statement is inclosed, when assembled, will amount to not less than thirty thousand, *it is considered that both services may be provided for amply.* The precise distribution, as between Portugal and Andalusia, both as to time and proportion of force, must depend upon circumstances, to be judged of on the spot ; and should it be deemed advisable to fulfil the assurance which Lieutenant General Sir Hew Dalrymple appears to have given to the Supreme Junta of Seville, under the authority of my despatch of (no date), that it was the intention of His Majesty to employ a corps of ten thousand men to co-operate with the Spaniards in that quarter, a corps of this magnitude may, I should hope, be detached without prejudice to the main operation against the Tagus, and may be reinforced, according to circumstances, after the Tagus has been secured. But if, previous to the arrival of the force under orders from England, Cadiz should be

* Parl. Pap. Ld. Castlereagh to Sir A. Wellesley, 15th July.

seriously threatened, it must rest with the senior officer of the Tagus at his discretion to detach, upon receiving a requisition to that
effect, such an amount of force as may place that important place
out of the reach of immediate danger, *even though it should for the
time suspend operations against the Tagus.*"

The inconsistent folly of this despatch is apparent, but the occupation of Cadiz was a favorite project with the Cabinet, which was
not discouraged by Spencer's unsuccessful effort to gain admittance,
nor by the representations of Sir Hew Dalrymple, who had grounds
to believe that the attempt would bring down the army under Castaños to oppose it by force. Neither did the minister consider that,
in a political view, such a measure, pressed as a preliminary, would
give a handle for misrepresentation, and that, in a military view,
the burden of Cadiz would clog operations in Portugal. Adopting
all projects, and weighing none, they displayed the most incredible
confusion of ideas; for the plan of sending ten thousand men to
Seville was said to be in pursuance of a promise made by Sir Hew
Dalrymple to the Junta, whereas the despatch of that General,
quoted as authority for this promise of help, contained nothing of
the kind, and was even written *before any junta existed!*

In England, at this period, personal enmity to Napoleon, and
violent party prejudices, had so disturbed the judgments of men
relative to that monarch, that any information speaking of strength
or success for him was regarded with suspicion even by the ministers, who, as commonly happens in such cases, becoming the dupes
of their own practices, listened with complacency to all those tales
of mutiny among his troops, disaffection of his generals, and insurrections in France, which the cunning or folly of their agents
transmitted to them. Hence sprung such projects as the one above,
the false calculations of which may be exposed by a short comparative statement. The whole English force was not much above
thirty thousand men, distributed off Cadiz, off the coast of Portugal,
on the eastern parts of England, and in the Channel. The French
in Spain and Portugal were about a hundred and twenty thousand
men, and they possessed all the Portuguese, and most of the Spanish fortresses. The English army had no reserve, no fixed plan,
and it was to be divided, and to act upon a double line of operations.
The French had a strong reserve at Bayonne, and the grand French
army of four hundred thousand veterans was untouched, and ready
to succor the troops in the Peninsula if they required it.

Happily, this visionary plan was in no particular followed by the
generals intrusted with the conduct of it. A variety of causes
combined to prevent the execution. The catastrophe of Baylen
marred the great combinations of the French Emperor, fortune

drew the scattered divisions of the English army together, and the decisive vigor of Sir Arthur Wellesley, sweeping away these cob-web projects, obtained all the success that the bad arrangements of the ministers would permit. In the next chapter, resuming the thread of the history, I shall relate the proceedings of the first British campaign in the Peninsula. But I judged it necessary to make an exposition of the previous preparations and plans of the Cabinet, lest the reader's attention, not being fully awakened to the difficulties cast in the way of the English generals, by the incapacity of the government, should, with hasty censure, or niggard praise, do the former injustice; for, as a noble forest hides many noisome swamps and evil things, so the Duke of Wellington's actions have covered the innumerable errors of the ministers.

CHAPTER IV.

Sir A. Wellesley quits his troops and proceeds to Coruña—Junta refuse assistance in men, but ask for and obtain money—Sir Arthur goes to Oporto; arranges a plan with the Bishop; proceeds to the Tagus; rejoins his troops; joined by Spencer; disembarks at the Mondego; has an interview with General Freire d'Andrada; marches to Leiria—Portuguese insurrection weak—Junot's position and dispositons—Laborde marches to Alcobaça, Loison to Abrantes—General Freire separates from the British—Junot quits Lisbon with the reserve—Laborde takes post at Roriça—Action of Roriça—Laborde retreats to Montechique—Sir A. Wellesley marches to Vimiero—Junot concentrates his army at Torres Vedras.

A FEW days after sailing from Cork, Sir Arthur Wellesley, quitting the fleet, repaired in a frigate to Coruña, where he arrived the 20th of July, and immediately held a conference with the Gallician Junta, by whom he was informed of the battle of Rio Seco.* The account was glossed over in the Spanish manner, and the issue of that contest had caused no change of policy, if policy that may be called, which was but a desire to obtain money and to avoid personal inconvenience. The aid of troops was rejected, but arms and gold were demanded, and while the conference went on, the last was supplied, for an English frigate entered the harbor with two hundred thousand pounds. The Junta recommended that the British should be employed in the north of Portugal, promised to aid them by sending a Spanish division to Oporto, and supported their recommendation with an incorrect statement of the number of men, Spanish and Portuguese, who, they asserted, were in arms near that

* Sir A. Wellesley's Narrative. Court of Inquiry.

city. They gave also a still more inaccurate estimate of the forces under Junot, and in this manner persuaded Sir Arthur not to land in their province: yet, at the moment they were rejecting the assistance of the British troops, the whole kingdom of Gallicia was lying at the mercy of Marshal Bessières, and there were neither men nor means to impede the progress of his victorious army.

Mr. Charles Stuart, appointed envóy to the Gallician Junta, had arrived with Sir Arthur Wellesley at Coruña, and quickly penetrating the flimsy veil of Spanish enthusiasm, informed his government of the true state of affairs; but his despatches were unheeded, while the inflated reports of the subordinate civil and military agents were blazoned forth, and taken as sure guides. Meanwhile Sir Arthur proceeded to Oporto, where he found Colonel Browne, an active, intelligent officer, employed to distribute succors. From his reports it appears that no Spanish troops were in the north of Portugal, and that all the Portuguese force was upon the Mondego, to the south of which river the insurrection had already spread. A French division of eight thousand men was supposed to be in their front, and some great disaster was to be expected, for, to use Colonel Browne's words, " with every good will in the people, their exertions were so short-lived, and with so little combination, that there was no hope of their being able to resist the advances of the enemy;*" in fact, only five thousand regulars and militia, half armed, and associated with ten or twelve thousand peasants without any arms, were in the field at all. A large army was, however, made out upon paper by the Bishop of Oporto, who, having assembled his civil and military coadjutors in council, proposed various plans of operation for the allied forces, none of which Sir Arthur was inclined to adopt;† but after some discussion it was finally arranged that the prelate and the paper army should look to the defence of the Tras os Montes against Bessières, and that the five thousand soldiers on the Mondego should co-operate with the British forces.

This being settled, Sir Arthur Wellesley hastened to consult with Sir Charles Cotton relative to the descent at the mouth of the Tagus, which had so long haunted the imaginations of the ministers. The strength of the French, the bar of the river, the disposition of the forts, and the difficulty of landing in the immediate neighborhood, occasioned by the heavy surf playing upon all the undefended creeks and bays, convinced him that such an enterprise was unadvisable, if not impracticable. There remained a choice of landing to the north of Lisbon at such a distance as to avoid the danger of a disputed disembarkation; or of proceeding to the

* Parliamentary Papers, 1809.
† Sir A. Wellesley's Narrative. Court of Inquiry.

southward to join General Spencer, and commence operations in that quarter against Dupont.* Sir Arthur Wellesley decided against the latter, which promised no good result while Junot held Portugal and Bessières hung on the northern frontier; for he foresaw that the jealousy of the Spaniards, evinced by their frequent refusal to admit English troops into Cadiz, would assuredly bring on a tedious negotiation, and waste the season of action before the army could obtain a place of arms; or that the campaign must be commenced without any secure base of operations.† Nothing was then known of the Spanish troops, except that they were inexperienced, and without good aid from them it would have been idle with fourteen thousand men to take the field against twenty thousand, strongly posted in the Sierra Morena, and communicating freely with the main body of the French army. A momentary advance was useless; and if the campaign was protracted, the line of operations, running nearly parallel to the frontier of Portugal, would have required a covering army on the Guadiana to watch the movements of Junot.

The double line of operations, proposed by Lord Castlereagh, was contrary to all military principle, and as Spencer's despatches announced that his division was at St. Mary's, near Cadiz, and disengaged from any connection with the Spaniards—a fortunate circumstance, scarcely to have been expected—Sir Arthur sent him orders to sail to the mouth of the Mondego, whither he himself also repaired, to join the fleet having his own army on board.

Off the Mondego he received the despatches announcing Sir Hew Dalrymple's appointment and the sailing of Sir John Moore's troops, but this mortifying intelligence did not relax his activity; he directed fast-sailing vessels to look out for Anstruther's armament, and conduct it to the Mondego, and having heard of Dupont's capitulation, resolved, without waiting for General Spencer's arrival, to disembark his own troops and commence the campaign—a determination that marked the cool decisive vigor of his character. He was, indeed, sure that, in consequence of Dupont's defeat, Bessières would not enter Portugal; yet his information led him to estimate Junot's own force at sixteen to eighteen thousand men—a number, indeed, below the truth, yet sufficient to make the hardiest general pause before he disembarked with only nine thousand men, and without any certainty that his fleet could remain even for a day in that dangerous offing :‡ another man, also, was coming to profit from any success that might be obtained, and a failure would have

---

* Sir. A. Wellesley's Narrative. Court of Inquiry.
† Sir H. Dalrymple's and Lord Collingwood's Correspondence.
‡ Sir A. Wellesley's Narrative. Court of Inquiry.

ruined his own reputation in the estimation of the English public, always ready to deride the skill of an Indian general.

It was difficult to find a good point of disembarkation. The coast of Portugal, from the Minho to the Tagus, presents, with few exceptions, a rugged and dangerous shore; all the harbors formed by the rivers have bars, that render most of them difficult of access even for boats; with the slightest breeze from the sea-board, a terrible surf breaks along the whole line of coast, forbidding all approach; and when the south wind, which commonly prevails from August to the winter months, blows, a more dangerous shore is not to be found in any part of the world.

The small peninsula of Peniché, about seventy miles northward of the Lisbon Rock, alone offered a safe and accessible bay, perfectly adapted for a disembarkation; but the anchorage was completely within range of the fort, which contained a hundred guns and a garrison of a thousand men. The next best place was the Mondego river, and as the little fort of Figueras, taken, as I have before related, by the student Zagalo, and now occupied by English marines, secured a free entrance, Sir Arthur commenced landing his troops there on the 1st of August. The weather was calm, yet the operation was so difficult, that it was not completed before the 5th, and at that moment, by singular good fortune, General Spencer arrived; he had not received Sir Arthur's orders, but with great promptitude had sailed for the Tagus the moment Dupont surrendered, and by Sir Charles Cotton had been directed to Mondego.* The united forces, however, only amounted to twelve thousand three hundred men, because a veteran battalion, being destined for Gibraltar, was left on board the ships.

When the army was on shore, the British General repaired to Montemor Velho, to confer with Don Bernardin Freire d'Andrada, the Portuguese commander-in-chief, who proposed that the troops of the two nations should relinquish all communication with the coast, and throwing themselves into the heart of Beira, commence an offensive campaign. He promised ample stores of provisions, but Sir Arthur, having already discovered the weakness of the insurrection, placed no reliance on those promises; wherefore furnishing Freire with five thousand stand of arms and ammunition, he refused to separate from his ships, and seeing clearly that the insurgents were unable to give any real assistance, resolved to act with reference to the probability of their deserting him in danger. The Portuguese General, disappointed at this refusal, reluctantly consented to join the British army, yet pressed Sir Arthur to hasten to Leiria, lest a large magazine filled, as he affirmed, with

* Sir A. Wellesley's Narrative. Court of Inquiry.

provisions for the use of the British army, should fall into the enemy's hands. After this the two generals separated, and the necessary preparations being completed, the advanced guard of the English army quitted the bank of the Mondego on the 9th, taking the road to Leiria, and the 10th, Sir Arthur Wellesley followed with the main body.

His plan embraced three principal objects :

1. To hold on by the sea-coast, as well for the sake of his supplies as to avoid the drain upon his army, which the protection of magazines on shore would occasion, and also to cover the disembarkation of the reinforcements expected from England.

2. To keep his troops in a mass, that he might strike an important blow.

3. To strike that blow as near Lisbon as possible, that the affairs of Portugal might be quickly brought to a crisis.

He possessed very good military surveys of the ground in the immediate neighborhood of Lisbon, and he was anxious to carry on his operations in a part of the country where he could avail himself of this resource ;[*] but the utter inexperience of his commissariat staff, and the want of cavalry, rendered his movements slow, and obliged him to be extremely circumspect ; especially as the insurrection, although a generous, was a feeble effort, and its prolongation rather the result of terror than of hope. The blow had been hastily struck in the moment of suffering, and the patriots, conscious of weakness, trembled when they reflected on their own temerity. Bernardin Freire had received arms and equipments complete for five thousand soldiers, yet his army at Leiria did not exceed six thousand men of all arms fit for action, and besides this force there were, in all the provinces north of the Tagus, only three thousand infantry, under the command of the Marquis of Valladeres, half of whom were Spaniards :[†] hence it appears that nothing could be more insignificant than the insurrection, nothing more absurd than the lofty style adopted by the Junta of Oporto in their communications with the British ministers.

Upon the other side, Junot, who had received information of the English descent in the Mondego as early as the 2d, was extremely embarrassed by the distance of his principal force, and the hostile disposition of the inhabitants of Lisbon.[‡] He also was acquainted with the disaster of Dupont, and exaggerated notions of the essential strength of the Portuguese insurgents were generated in his own mind, and in the minds of his principal officers. The patriots

* Sir A. Wellesley's Narrative. Court of Inquiry.
† Proceedings of the Court of Inquiry.
‡ Thiebault.

of the Alemtejo and Algarves, assisted by some Spaniards, and animated by manifestoes and promises assiduously promulgated from
the English fleet, had once more assembled at Alcacer do Sal, from
whence they threatened the garrisons of St. Ubes, and the French
posts on the south bank of the Tagus, immediately opposite to Lisbon. That capital was very unquiet. The anticipation of coming
freedom was apparent in the wrathful looks and stubborn manners
of the populace, and superstition was at work to increase the hatred
and the hopes of the multitude. It was at this time the prophetic
eggs, denouncing death to the French and deliverance to the Portuguese, appeared. But less equivocal indications of approaching
danger were to be drawn from the hesitations of Junot, who, wavering between his fear of an insurrection in Lisbon and his desire to
check the immediate progress of the British army, gave certain
proof of an intellect yielding to the pressure of events.

Loison, having seven or eight thousand men, was now in the
neighborhood of Estremos ; two thousand five hundred men were
in the fortresses of Elvas and Almeida, a few hundred were at
Abrantes, a thousand in Santarem, and the same number in Peniché. General Thomierés, with one brigade, was in the vicinity
of Alcobaça, and the rest of the army was quartered at Lisbon and
on a circuit round, including both sides of the river. The Tagus
itself was guarded on the north bank by the forts of Cascaes, St.
Antonio, St. Julian's, Belem, and the citadel, between which smaller
works kept up a continual line of offence against ships entering by
the northern passage of the harbor. On the southern bank, Fort
Bugio, built upon a low sandy point, crossed its fire with St. Julian's in the defence of the entrance. Upon the heights of Almada
or Palmela stood the fort of Palmela, and St. Ubes and Traffaria
completed the posts occupied by the French on that side.* The
communication between the north and south banks was kept up by
the refitted Portuguese ships of war, by the Russian squadron, and
by the innumerable boats, most of them very fine and large, with
which the Tagus is covered.

Such was the situation of the army on the 3d, when Junot ordered Loison to march by Portalegre and Abrantes, and from
thence effect a junction with General Laborde, who, with three
thousand infantry, five or six hundred cavalry, and five pieces of
artillery, quitted Lisbon upon the 6th, and proceeded by Villa
Franca, Rio Mayor, and Candeiros ; being charged to observe the
movements of the British, and to cover the march of Loison, with
whom he expected to form a junction at Leiria. Junot himself
remained in Lisbon, thinking to control the inhabitants by his pres-

* Thiebault.

ence.* He embarked all the powder from the magazines, took additional precautions to guard his Spanish prisoners, and put the citadel and forts into a state of siege; but disquieted by the patriots assembled at Alcacer do Sal, he sent General Kellermann with a movable column to disperse them, directing him to scour the country between that place and Setuval, to withdraw the garrison from the latter, to abandon all the French posts on the south of the Tagus except Palmela, and to collect the whole force in one mass on the heights of Almada, where an intrenched camp had been already commenced. But Kellermann had scarcely departed, when two English regiments, the one from Madeira, the other from Gibraltar, arriving off the bar of Lisbon, distracted anew the attention of the French, and increased the turbulence of the populace; and in this state of perplexity the Duke of Abrantes lingered until the 15th, when the progress of Sir Arthur Wellesley forced him to assume the command of the army in the field.

Loison entered Abrantes the 9th, and the same day Laborde arrived at Candeiros, from which point he could with facility either move upon Alcobaça and Leiria, or form a junction with Loison upon the side of Santarem. The 10th, Loison halted at Abrantes, and Laborde moved to Alcobaça, where he was joined by Thomières and the garrison of Peniché. Hence the armies on both sides were now in a state of attraction towards each other indicating an approaching shock; and while the news of Bessières' victory at Rio Seco produced a short-lived exultation in the French camp, intelligence of Joseph's flight from Madrid reached the British army, and increased its confidence of victory.

Sir Arthur's advanced guard entered Leiria, and was there joined by Bernardin Freire and the Portuguese army, which immediately seized the magazine without making any distribution to the British troops, the main body of which only arrived on the 11th; but the whole marched in advance upon the 12th.† Laborde had employed the 11th and 12th seeking for a position in the vicinity of Batalha, and finding the ground too extensive for his force, fell back in the night of the 12th to Obidos, a town with a Moorish castle built on a gentle eminence in the middle of a valley.‡ Occupying this place with his piquets, he placed a small detachment at the windmill of Brilos, three miles in front, and retired the 14th to Roriça, a village six miles to the southward, situated at the intersection of the roads leading to Torres Vedras, Montechique, and Alcoentre, and overlooking the whole valley of Obidos. This posi-

* Thiebault.
† Proceedings of the Court of Inquiry.
‡ Thiebault.

tion enabled him to preserve his communication with Loison open;
but as it uncovered Peniché, the fourth Swiss regiment, with the
exception of the flank companies, was sent to re-garrison that important point, and at the same time three hundred men were detached to the right, by Bombarral, Cadaval, and Segura, to obtain
intelligence of Loison.

That General, by a demonstration on the side of Thomar the
11th, had ascertained that Leiria was in the hands of the British,
and fell back the same day upon Torres Novas, then following the
course of the Tagus, he arrived at Santarem upon the 13th, but in
such an exhausted state that he was unable to renew his march
until the 15th. Sir Arthur Wellesley's first movement had thus
cut the line of communication between Loison and Laborde, caused
a loss of several forced marches to the former, and obliged the latter to risk an action with more than twice his own numbers. But
as the hostile troops approached each other, the Portuguese chiefs
became alarmed; for, notwithstanding the confident language of
their public manifestoes and the bombastic style of their conversation,
an internal conviction that a French army was invincible pervaded
all ranks of the patriots. The leaders, aware of their own deficiency, and incredulous of the courage of the English soldiers,
dreaded the being committed in a decisive contest, because a defeat
would deprive them of all hope to make terms with the victors;
whereas by keeping five or six thousand men together, they could
at any time secure themselves by a capitulation. The Junta of
Oporto, also, who were already aiming at supreme authority, foresaw that, in the event of a successful battle, it would be more advantageous for their particular views to be provided with an army
untouched and entirely disconnected with a foreign general; and
Freire, being well instructed in the secret designs of this party,
resolved not to advance a step beyond Leiria. However, to cover
his real motives, he required the British commander to supply him
with provisions, choosing to forget the magazine which he had just
appropriated to himself, and as readily forgetting the formal promises
of the Bishop of Oporto, who had undertaken to feed the English
army.

This extraordinary demand, that an auxiliary army, just disembarked, should nourish the native soldiers, instead of being itself
fed by the people, was met by Sir Arthur Wellesley with a strong
remonstrance. He easily penetrated the secret motive which
caused it, yet feeling that it was important to have a respectable
Portuguese force acting in conjunction with his own, he first ap-
pealed to the honor and patriotism of Freire, warmly admonishing
him that he was going to forfeit all pretension to either by permit-

ting the British army to fight without his assistance. This argument had no effect upon Don Bernardin, and he parried the imputation against his spirit and zeal by pretending that his intention
was to operate independently on the line of the Tagus; hence,
after some further discussion, Sir Arthur, changing his tone of rebuke to one of conciliation, recommended to him not to risk his
troops by an isolated march, but to keep in the rear of the British,
and wait for the result of the first battle. This advice was agreeable to Freire, and at the solicitation of Colonel Trant, a military
agent, he consented to leave fourteen hundred infantry and two
hundred and fifty cavalry under the immediate command of the
English General. But the defection of the native force was a serious evil; it shed an injurious moral influence, and deprived Sir
Arthur of the aid of troops whose means of gaining intelligence and
whose local knowledge might have compensated for his want of
cavalry. Nevertheless, continuing his own march, his advanced
guard entered Caldas the 15th, on which day also Junot reluctantly quitted Lisbon, with a reserve composed of two thousand infantry, six hundred cavalry, and ten pieces of artillery, carrying
with him his grand parc of ammunition and a military chest containing forty thousand pounds.

General Travot was left at Lisbon, with above seven thousand
men, of which number two battalions were formed of stragglers and
convalescents.* He held both sides of the Tagus, and Palmela,
the Bugio fort, and the heights of Almada were occupied by two
thousand men, to protect the shipping from the insurgents of the
Alemtejo, who, under the orders of the Monteiro Mor, were again
gathering at Setuval; a thousand were on board the vessels of war,
to guard the Spanish prisoners and the spare powder; two thousand four hundred were in the citadel and supporting the police; a
thousand were distributed in the forts of Belem, St. Julian's, Cascaes, and Ericeia, which last is situated to the northward of the
Rock of Lisbon, and commands a small harbor a few miles west of
Mafra; finally, a thousand were at Santarem, protecting a large
dépôt of stores. Thus, if the garrisons of Elvas, Peniché and Almeida be included, nearly one-half of the French army was, by
Junot's combinations, rendered inactive, and those in the field were
divided into three parts, without any certain point of junction in
advance, yet each too weak singly to sustain an action. The Duke
of Abrantes seems to have reigned long enough in Portugal to forget that he was merely the chief of an advanced corps, whose safety
depended upon activity and concentration.

The French reserve was transported to Villa Franca by water,

* Thiebault.

from whence it was to march to Otta; but the rope ferry-boat of
Saccavem being removed by the natives, it cost twenty-four hours
to throw a bridge across the creek at that place, and on the 17th,
when the troops were on their march, Junot hastily recalled them
to Villa Franca, because of a report that the English had landed
near the capital.   This rumor proving false, the reserve resumed
the road to Otta, under the command of General Thiebault, and
Junot himself pushed forward to Alcoentre, where he found Loison,
and assumed the personal direction of that General's division.
Meanwhile Sir Arthur Wellesley was pressing Laborde.   The 25th
he had caused the post at Brilos to be attacked, and the piquets to
be driven out of Obidos; but two companies of the 95th and two
of the 5th battalion, 60th, after gaining the windmill without loss,
pursued the retiring enemy with such inconsiderate eagerness that,
at the distance of three miles from their support, they were out-
flanked by two superior bodies of French, and were only saved
by the opportune advance of General Spencer.*   Two officers and
twenty-seven men were killed and wounded in this slight affair,
which gave a salutary check to the rashness, without lowering the
confidence of the troops, and on the 16th Laborde's position was
examined.

The main road from Obidos passed through a valley, which was
closed to the southward by some high table land, on which stood
the village of Roriça, and the French, being posted on a small
plain immediately in front of that place, overlooked all the country
as far as Obidos.   All the favorable points of defence in front, and
on the nearest hills, at each side, were occupied by small detachments, and one mile in the rear a steep ridge, extending about
three-quarters of a mile east and west, and consequently parallel to
the French position, offered a second line of great strength.   The
main road led by a steep defile over this ridge, which was called
the height of Zambugeira, or Columbeira.   Beyond it very lofty
mountains, stretching from the sea-coast to the Tagus, like a wall,
filled all the space between that river and the ocean, down to the
Rock of Lisbon ; and the valley leading from Obidos to Roriça was
bounded on the left by a succession of ridges, rising like steps, until
they were lost in the great mass of the Sierra de Baragueda, itself
a shoot from the Monte Junto.

Laborde's situation was truly embarrassing: Loison was still at
Alcoentre, and the reserve at Villa Franca, that is, one or two
marches distant from Roriça; hence if he retired upon Torres
Vedras his communication with Loison would be lost, and to fall
back on Montechique was to expose the line of Torres Vedras and

* Sir A. Wellesley's despatch.

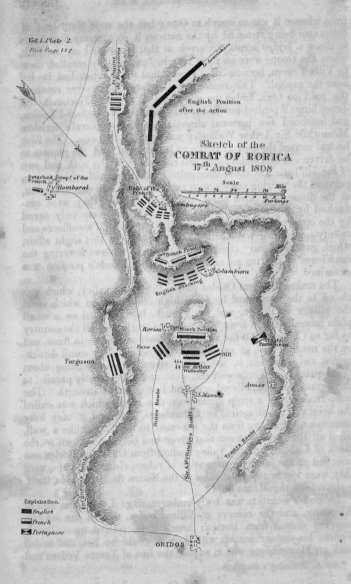

to Rowinham

to Quinta
dr Bugagliera

English Position
after the Action

Sketch of the
COMBAT OF RORICA
17th August 1808

Scale

Mile

Furlones

Detached Comp.y of the
French.
Bombaral

Rals of the
French.

Zambugeira

2nd French Position

Columbeira

English Attacking

Roriça   1st French Position

Pane   Hill

Crants
Portuguese

Ferguson

Sir Arthur
Wellesley

Amias

Fane's Route

Sir A.Wellesley's Route

Trants Route

S.Mamed

Ferguson's Route

Explanation.
English
French
Portuguese

OBIDOS

Mafra; to march upon Alcoentre and unite with Loison was to leave open the shortest road to Lisbon, and remain at Roriça was to fight three times his own force. Nevertheless, encouraged by the local advantages of his position, and justly confident in his own talents, Laborde resolved to abide his enemy's assault, in the feeble hope that Loison might arrive during the action.

COMBAT OF RORICA.

Early in the morning of the 17th, thirteen thousand four hundred and eighty infantry, four hundred and seventy cavalry, and eighteen guns issued from Obidos, and soon afterwards broke into three distinct columns of battle.

The left, commanded by General Ferguson, was composed of his own and Bowes' brigade of infantry, reinforced by two hundred and fifty riflemen, forty cavalry, and six guns, forming a total of four thousand nine hundred combatants. He marched by the crests of the hills adjoining the Sierra de Baragueda, being destined to turn the right flank of Laborde's position, and to oppose the efforts of Loison, if that General, who was supposed to be at Rio Mayor, should appear during the action.

The right, under Colonel Trant, composed of a thousand Portuguese infantry, and fifty horse of the same nation, moved by the village of St. Amias, with the intention of turning the left flank of the French.

The centre, nine thousand in number, with twelve guns, was commanded by Sir Arthur in person, and marched straight against the enemy by the village of Mahmed. It was composed of Generals Hill's, Nightingale's, Catlin Crawfurd's, and Fane's brigades of British infantry, four hundred cavalry, two hundred and fifty of which were Portuguese, and there were four hundred light troops of the same nation.

As this column advanced, Fane's brigade, extending to its left, drove back the French skirmishers, and connected the march of Ferguson's division with the centre. When the latter approached the elevated plain upon which Laborde was posted, General Hill, who moved upon the right of the main road, being supported by the cavalry and covered by the fire of his light troops, pushed forward rapidly to the attack; on his left, General Nightingale displayed a line of infantry, preceded by the fire of nine guns, and Crawfurd's brigade, with the remaining pieces of artillery, formed a reserve. At this moment, Fane's riflemen crowned the nearest hills on the right flank of the French, the Portuguese troops showed the head of a column beyond St. Amias, upon the enemy's left, and General Ferguson was seen descending from the higher grounds in the rear of Fane. Laborde's position appeared desperate; yet with the coolness and dexterity of a practised warrior, he evaded the danger, and, covered by his excellent cavalry, fell back rapidly to the heights of Zambugeira, and a fresh disposition of the English became indispensable to dislodge him from that formidable post.

Colonel Trant now continued his march to turn the left of the new field of battle; Ferguson and Fane were united, and directed through the mountains to outflank the French right; Hill and Nightingale advanced against the front, which was of singular strength, and only to be approached by narrow paths, winding through deep ravines. A swarm of skirmishers starting forward, soon plunged into the passes, and spreading to the right and left, won their way among the rocks and tangled evergreens that overspread the steep ascent; with still greater difficulty the supporting columns followed, their formation being disordered in the confined and rugged passes, and while the hollows echoed with a continued roll of musketry, the shouts of the advancing troops were loudly answered by the enemy, while the curling smoke, breaking out from the side of the mountain, marked the progress of the assailants, and showed how stoutly the defence was maintained.

Laborde, watching anxiously for the arrival of Loison, gradually slackened his hold on the left, but clung tenaciously to the right in the hope of yet effecting a junction with that General, and the ardor of the 9th and 29th regiments, who led the attack, favored this skilful conduct. It was intended that those battalions should take the right-hand path of two leading up the same hollow, and thus have come in upon Laborde's flank in conjunction with Trant's column; but as the left path led more directly to the enemy, the 29th followed it, the 9th being close behind, and both regiments advanced so vigorously as to reach the plain above long before the flank movements of Trant and Ferguson could shake the credit of the position. The right of the 29th arrived first at the top, under a heavy fire, and ere it could form, Colonel Lake was killed, and some French companies coming in on the flank, gallantly broke through, carrying with them a major and fifty or sixty other prisoners. The head of the regiment, thus pressed, fell back and rallied on the left wing, below the brow of the hill, and being there joined by the 9th, whose Colonel, Stewart, also fell in this bitter fight, the whole pushed forward, and regained the dangerous footing above. Laborde, who brought every arm into action at the proper time and place, endeavored to destroy these regiments before they could be succored, and failing in that, he yet gained time to rally his left wing upon his centre and right; but the 5th regiment, following the right-hand path, soon arrived, the English gathered thickly on the heights, and Ferguson, who had at first taken an erroneous direction towards the centre, recovered the true line, and was rapidly passing the right flank of the position. The French General commenced a retreat by alternate masses, protecting his movements by vigorous charges of cavalry, and at the village of Zambugeira he attempted another stand; but the English bore on him too heavily, and thus disputing the ground, he fell back to the Quinta de Bugagliera, where he halted until his detachments on the side of Segura rejoined him. After this, taking to the narrow pass of Runa, he marched all night to gain the position of Montechique, leaving three guns on the field of battle, and the road to Torres Vedras open to the victors.*

The loss of the French was six hundred killed and wounded, among the latter Laborde himself; and the British also suffered considerably, for two lieutenant-colonels and nearly five hundred men were killed, taken, or wounded, and as not more than four thusand men were actually engaged, this hard-fought action was very honorable to both sides.

The firing ceased a little after four o'clock, when Sir Arthur, getting intelligence that Loison's division was at Bombaral, only five miles distant, took up a position for the night in an oblique line to that which he had just forced, his left resting upon a height near the field of battle, and his right covering the road to Lourinham. Believing that Loison and Laborde had effected their junction at the Quinta de Bugagliera, and that both were retiring to Montechique, the English General resolved to march the next morning to Torres Vedras, by which he would have secured an entrance into the mountains. But before night-fall he was informed that General Anstruther's and General Acland's divisions, accompanied by a large fleet of store ships, were off the coast, the dangerous nature of which rendered it necessary to provide for their safety by a quick disembarkation; he therefore changed his plans, and resolved to seek for some convenient post, that, being in advance of his present position, would likewise enable him to cover the landing of these reinforcements. The vigor of Laborde's defence had also an influence upon this occasion, for before an enemy so bold and skilful, no precaution could be neglected with impunity.†

* Thiebault.
† Sir A. Wellesley's Evidence. Court of Inquiry.

CHAPTER V.

Portuguese take Abrantes—Generals Acland and Anstruther land and join the
British army at Vimiero—Sir Harry Burrard arrives—Battle of Vimiero—Junot
defeated—Sir Hew Dalrymple arrives—Armistice ; terms of it—Junot returns
to Lisbon ; negotiates for a convention—Sir John Moore's troops land—State
of the public mind in Lisbon—The Russian Admiral negotiates separately—
Convention concluded—The Russian fleet surrenders upon terms—Conduct of
the people at Lisbon—The Monteiro Mor requires Sir Charles Cotton to interrupt the execution of the convention—Sir John Hope appointed commandant
of Lisbon ; represses all disorders—Disputes between the French and English
commissioners—Reflections thereupon

WHILE the combat of Roriça was fighting, some Portuguese
insurgents attacked Abrantes, and the garrison, being ill commanded,
gave way and was destroyed ; thus nothing remained for Junot but
a battle, and as Sir Arthur marched to Lourinham on the 18th,
the French General quitted Cercal with Loison's division, and
keeping the east side of the Baragueda ridge, crossed the line of
Laborde's retreat, and pushed for Torres Vedras, which he reached
in the evening of the same day. The 19th he was joined by Laborde, and the 20th by his reserve, when he re-organized his army,
and prepared for a decisive action. Meanwhile Wellesley took a
position at Vimiero, a village near the sea-coast, and from thence sent
a detachment to cover the march of General Anstruther's brigade,
which had, with great difficulty and some loss, been landed on the
morning of the 18th on an open sandy beach called the bay of Maceira. The 20th the French cavalry, scouring the neighboring
country, carried off some of the women from the rear of the English camp, and hemmed the army round so closely, that no information of Junot's position could be obtained ; but in the night General Acland's brigade was disembarked, by which the army was
increased to sixteen thousand fighting men, with eighteen pieces of
artillery, exclusive of Trant's Portuguese, and of two British regiments, under General Beresford, which were with the fleet at the
mouth of the Tagus. Thus the principal mass of the English army
was irrevocably engaged in the operations against Junot, while the
ministers were still so intent upon Cadiz, that they had sent Anstruther out with an appointment as governor of that city !

Estimating the whole French army at eighteen thousand men,
Sir Arthur Wellesley judged that, after providing for the security
of Lisbon, Junot could not bring more than fourteen thousand into
the field ; he designed, therefore, not only to strike the first blow,
but to follow it up so as to prevent the enemy from rallying and
renewing the campaign upon the frontier. In this view he had,

before quitting the Mondego, written to Sir Harry Burrard an exact statement of his own proceedings and intentions, and recommended that Sir John Moore, with his division, should disembark at the Mondego, and march without delay to Santarem, by which he would protect the left of the army, block the line of the Tagus, and at the same time threaten the French communication between Lisbon and Elvas. And without danger, because Junot would be forced to defend Lisbon against the coast army; or if, relinquishing the capital, he endeavored to make way to Almeida by Santarem, the ground there was so strong that Sir John Moore might easily maintain it against him. Moreover, the Marquis of Valladeras commanded three thousand men at Guarda, and General Freire, with five thousand men, was at Leiria, and might be persuaded to support the British at Santarem.

From Vimiero to Torres Vedras was about nine miles, and although the number and activity of the French cavalry completely shrouded Junot's position, it was known to be strong, and very difficult of approach, by reason of a long defile through which the army must penetrate in order to reach the crest of the mountain; there was, however, a road leading between the sea-coast and Torres Vedras, which, turning the latter, opened a way to Mafra. Sir Arthur possessed very exact military surveys of the country through which that road led, and he projected, by a forced march on the 21st, to turn the position of Torres Vedras, and to gain Mafra with a strong advanced guard, while the main body, seizing some advantageous heights, a few miles short of that town, would be in a position to intercept the French line of march to Montechique.* The army was therefore re-organized during the 20th in eight brigades of infantry and four weak squadrons of cavalry, and every preparation was made for the next day's enterprise; but at that critical period of the campaign the ministerial arrangements, which provided three commanders-in-chief, began to work. Sir Harry Burrard arrived in a frigate off the bay of Maceira, and Sir Arthur, thus checked in the midst of his operations on the eve of a decisive battle, repaired on board the frigate, to make a report of the situation of affairs, and to renew his former recommendation relative to the disposal of Sir John Moore's troops. Burrard, who had previously resolved to bring the latter down to Maceira, condemned this project, and forbade any offensive movement until the whole army should be concentrated, whereupon Sir Arthur returned to his camp.

The ground occupied by the army, although very extensive, and not very clearly defined as a position, was by no means weak.

* Sir A. Wellesley's Evidence. Court of Inquiry.

The village of Vimiero, situated in a valley, through which the little river of Maceira flows, contained the parc and commissariat stores. The cavalry and the Portuguese were on a small plain close behind the village, and immediately in its front a rugged isolated height, with a flat top, commanded all the ground to the southward and eastward for a considerable distance. Upon this height Fane's and Anstruther's brigades of infantry, with six guns, were posted; the left of Anstruther's occupied a churchyard which blocked a road leading over the extremity of the height of the village; the right of Fane's rested on the edge of the other extremity of the hill, the base of which was washed by the Maceira.

A mountain, that commenced at the coast, swept in a half circle close behind the right of the hill upon which these brigades were posted, and commanded, at rather long artillery range, all its upper surface. Eight guns, and the first, second, third, fourth, and eighth brigades of infantry, occupied this mountain, which was terminated on the left by a deep ravine that divided it from another strong and narrow range of heights over which the road from Vimiero to Lourinham passed; the right of these last heights also overtopped the hill in front of the village, but the left, bending suddenly backward, after the form of a crook, returned to the coast, and ended in a lofty cliff. There was no water upon this last named ridge, wherefore only the 40th regiment and some piquets were placed there. The troops being thus posted, on the night of the 20th, about twelve o'clock, Sir Arthur was aroused by a German officer of dragoons, who galloped into the camp, and with some consternation reported that Junot, at the head of twenty thousand men, was coming on to the attack, and distant but one hour's march. Undisturbed by this inflated report, he merely sent out patrols, warned the piquets to be on the alert, and before daybreak had his troops, following the British custom, under arms; but the sun rose and no enemy appeared. However, at seven o'clock a cloud of dust was observed beyond the nearest hills, and at eight o'clock an advanced guard of horse was seen to crown the heights to the southward, sending forward scouts on every side. Scarcely had this body been discovered, when a force of infantry, preceded by other cavalry, was descried moving along the road from Torres Vedras to Lourinham, and threatening the left of the British position; column after column followed in order of battle, and it soon became evident that the French were coming to fight, but that the right wing of the English was not their object.

The second, third, fourth, and eighth brigades were immediately directed to cross the valley behind the village, and to take post on the heights before mentioned as being occupied by the piquets only;

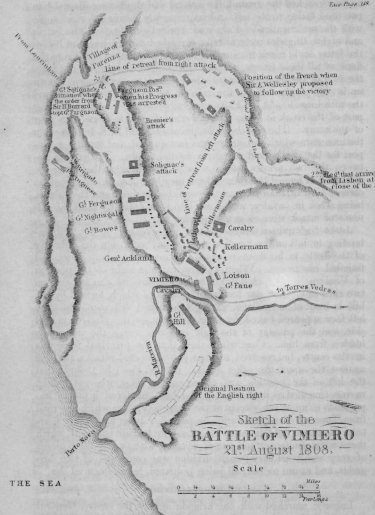

From Leurinham

Village of
Parenza

Line of retreat from right attack

Position of the French when
Sir A. Wellesley proposed
to follow up the victory

G.! Solignac's
Situation where
the order from
Sir H Burrard
stopt G.! Furguson

Furguson Pos.n
when his Progress
was arrested

Bremer's
attack

Road to Torres Vedras

2.nd Reg.t that arriv
from Lisbon at
close of the

1.st brigade
Portuguese

Solignac's
attack

G.! Ferguson

G.! Nightingale

G.! Bowes

Line of retreat from left attack

Kellermann

Cavalry

Kellermann

Gen.l Ackland

VIMIERO

Cavalry

G.! Hill

R. Maceira

Loison
G.! Fane

to Torres Vedras

Original Position
of the English right

THE SEA

Sketch of the
BATTLE OF VIMIERO
21.st August 1808,

Scale

Miles
0   ¼   ½   ¾   1   1¼   1½   3¾   2
2   4   6   8   10   12   1⅘   16
Furlongs

Porto Nova

as they reached the ground, the second and third were disposed in two lines facing to the left, and consequently forming a right angle with the prolongation of Fane and Anstruther's front. The fourth and eighth brigades were to have furnished a third line, but before the latter could reach the summit the battle commenced. From the flank of all these troops, a line of skirmishers was thrown out upon the face of the descent towards the enemy, the cavalry was drawn up in the plain a little to the right of the village of Vimiero, and the fifth brigade and the Portuguese were detached to the returning part of the crook to cover the extreme left, and to protect the rear of the army. The first brigade, under General Hill, remained on the mountain which the others had just quitted, and formed a support for the centre and a reserve for the whole. The ground between the two armies was so wooded and broken, that after the French had passed the ridge where they had been first descried, no correct view of their movements could be obtained, and the British, being weak in cavalry, were forced to wait patiently until the columns of attack were close upon them.

Junot had quitted Torres Vedras the evening of the 20th, intending to fall on the English army at daybreak, but the difficulty of the defile in his front retarded his march for many hours, and fatigued his troops. When he first came in sight of the position of Vimiero, the British order of battle appeared to him as being on two sides of an irregular triangle, the apex of which, formed by the hill in front of the village, was well furnished with men, while the left face appeared naked, for he could only see the piquets on that side, and the passage of the four brigades across the valley was hidden from him. Concluding, then, that the principal force was in the centre, he resolved to form two connected attacks, the one against the apex, the other against the left face; he thought that the left of the position was an accessible ridge, whereas a deep ravine, trenched as it were along the base, rendered it utterly impervious to an attack, except at the extremity, over which the road from Torres Vedras to Lourinham passed. Junot had nearly fourteen thousand fighting men, organized in four divisions, of which three were of infantry and one of cavalry, with twenty-three pieces of very small artillery; each division was composed of two brigades, and at ten o'clock, all being prepared, he commenced the

BATTLE OF VIMIERO.

Laborde marched with one brigade against the centre, General Brennier led another against the left, and Loison's brigades followed in the same order at a short distance.[*]   Kellermann, with a

* Thiebault. Foy.

reserve composed of grenadiers, moved in one body behind Loison, and the cavalry under Margaron, about thirteen hundred in number, was divided, part being on the right of Brennier, part in the rear of the reserve. The artillery, distributed among the columns, opened its fire wherever the ground was favorable. It was designed that Laborde's and Brennier's attacks should be simultaneous, but the latter, coming unexpectedly upon the ravine before mentioned as protecting the English left, got entangled among the rocks and water-courses, and thus Laborde alone engaged Fane and Anstruther under a heavy and destructive fire of artillery, which played on his front and flank; for the eighth brigade being then in the act of mounting the heights where the left was posted, observing the advance of the French columns against the centre, halted, and opened a battery against their right.*

Junot, perceiving this failure in his combinations, ordered Loison to support Laborde's attack with one brigade of his division, and directed General Solignac, with the other, to turn the ravine in which Brennier was entangled, and to fall upon the extremity of the English line. General Fane seeing Loison's advance, and having a discretionary power to use the reserve artillery, immediately directed Colonel Robe to bring it into action, and thus formed with the divisional guns a most powerful battery in opposition. Meanwhile, Loison and Laborde formed a principal and two secondary columns of attack, one of which advanced against Fane's brigade, while the other endeavored to penetrate by a road which passed between the ravine and the church on the extreme left of Anstruther; but the main column, headed by Laborde in person, and preceded by a multitude of light troops, mounted the face of the hill with great fury and loud cries. The English skirmishers were forced in upon the lines in a moment, and the French masses arrived at the summit, yet shattered by the terrible fire of Robe's artillery, and breathless from their exertions; and in this state, first receiving a discharge of musketry from the fiftieth regiment at the distance of half-pistol shot, they were vigorously charged in front and flank, and overthrown. At the same time the remainder of Fane's brigade repulsed the minor attack, and Colonel Taylor, with the very few horsemen he commanded, passing out by the right, rode fiercely among the confused and retreating troops, and scattered them with great execution; but then Margaron's cavalry came suddenly down upon Taylor, who was there slain, and the half of his feeble squadron cut to pieces.

Kellermann took advantage of this check to throw one half of his reserve into a pine wood flanking the line of retreat, and the other

* Sir A. Wellesley's despatch.

half he had before sent to reinforce the attack on the church. The forty-third regiment were engaged in a hot skirmish amongst some vineyards, when these French grenadiers arrived, at a brisk pace, and beat back the advanced companies; but to avoid the artillery which ransacked their left, they dipped a little into the ravine, and were taken on the other flank by the guns of the eighth and fourth brigades. Then, when the narrowness of the way and the sweep of the round shot was disordering the French ranks, the forty-third, rallying in one mass, came furiously down upon the head of the column, and, after a short, desperate fight, drove it back in confusion, but the regiment suffered very severely.

The French were now discomfited in the centre, the woods and hollows were filled with their wounded and straggling men, and seven guns were lost. They retired up the edge of the ravine, in a direction almost parallel to the British line, leaving the road from Vimiero to Torres Vedras open to their opponents. Sir Arthur Wellesley, however, strictly forbade any pursuit at that moment, partly because the grenadiers in the pine wood flanked the line of the French retreat, and partly because Margaron's horsemen, riding stiffly between the two armies, were not to be lightly meddled with. Meanwhile, Brennier being still hampered in the ravine, General Solignac passed along the crest of the ridge above and came upon General Ferguson's brigade, which was posted at the left of the English position; but where the French expected to find a weak flank, they encountered a front of battle, on a depth of three lines, protected by steep declivities on either side,—a powerful artillery swept away their foremost ranks, and on their right the fifth brigade and the Portuguese were seen marching by a distant ridge towards the Lourinham road, threatening the rear.

Ferguson, instantly taking the lead, bore down upon the enemy. The ridge widened as the English advanced, the regiments of the second line running up in succession, increased the front and constantly filled the ground, and the French, falling fast under the fire, drew back, fighting, until they reached the declivity of the ridge. Their cavalry made several efforts to check the advancing troops, but the latter were too compact to be disturbed by these attempts. Solignac himself was carried from the field severely wounded, and his retiring column, continually out-flanked on the left, was cut off from the line of retreat and thrown into the low ground about the village of Perenza, where six guns were captured. General Ferguson, leaving the 82d and 71st regiments to guard those pieces, was continuing to press the disordered columns, when Brennier, having at last cleared the ravine, came suddenly in upon those two battalions and retook the artillery. But his success was only momentary. The surprised troops rallied upon higher ground, poured in a heavy fire of musketry, and with a shout returning to the charge, overthrew him and recovered the guns. Brennier himself was wounded and made prisoner, and Ferguson having thus completely separated the French brigades from each other, would have forced the greatest part of Solignac's to surrender, if an unexpected order had not obliged him to halt. The discomfited troops then re-formed, under the protection of their cavalry, with admirable quickness, and making an orderly retreat, were soon united to the broken brigades which were falling back from the attack on the centre.

Brennier, who the moment he was taken was brought to Sir Arthur Wellesley, eagerly demanded if the reserve under Kellermann had yet charged? Sir Arthur, ascertaining from other prisoners that it had, was then satisfied that all the enemy's attacks were exhausted, that no considerable body of fresh troops could be hidden among the woods and hollows in his front, and that the battle was won. It was only twelve o'clock; thirteen guns had been taken; the fourth and eighth brigades had suffered very little; the Portuguese, the fifth and the first brigades had not fired a shot; and the latter was two miles nearer to Torres Vedras than any part of the French army, which was moreover in great confusion. The relative numbers before the action were considerably in favor of the English: the result of the action had increased that disparity. A portion of the army had defeated the enemy when entire; a portion, then, could effectually follow up the victory. Sir Arthur therefore resolved with the five brigades on the left to press Junot closely, hoping to drive him over the Sierra da Baragueda and force him upon the Tagus, while Hill, Anstruther and Fane, seizing the defile of Torres Vedras, should push on to Montechique, and cut him off from Lisbon.

If this able and decisive operation had been executed, Junot would probably have lost all his artillery and several thousand stragglers, and then, buffeted and turned at every point, would have been glad to seek safety under the guns of Almeida or Elvas; and even that he could only have accomplished because Sir John Moore's troops were not landed in the Mondego. But Sir Harry Burrard, who was present during the action, although partly from delicacy, and partly from approving of Sir Arthur's arrangements, he had not hitherto interfered, now assumed the chief command. From him the order which arrested Ferguson in his victorious career had emanated, and by him further offensive operations were forbidden, for he resolved to wait in the position of Vimiero until the arrival of Sir John Moore. The Adjutant-General Clinton, and Colonel Murray, the quartermaster-general, supported Sir Harry's views, and Sir Arthur's earnest representations could not alter their determination.

Burrard's decision was certainly erroneous, yet error is common in an art which at best is but a choice of difficulties; the circumstances of the moment were imposing enough to sway most generals. The French had failed in the attacks, yet they rallied with surprising quickness under the protection of a strong and gallant cavalry.* Sir Harry knew that his own artillery carriages were so shaken as to be scarcely fit for service; the draft horses were few and bad, and the commissariat parc on the plain was in the greatest confusion, for the hired Portuguese carmen were making off with their carriages in all directions; the English cavalry was totally destroyed, and finally, General Spencer had discovered a line of fresh troops on the ridge behind that occupied by the French army. Weighing all these things in his mind, with the caution natural to age, Burrard was reluctant to hazard the fortune of the day upon what he deemed a perilous throw. Thus the Duke of Abrantes, who had displayed all that reckless courage to which he originally owed his elevation, was enabled by this unexpected cessation of the battle to re-form his broken infantry. Twelve hundred fresh troops joined him at the close of the contest, and then, covered by his cavalry, he retreated with order and celerity until he regained the command of the pass of Torres Vedras, so that when the day closed the relative position of the two armies was the same as on the evening before.

One general, thirteen guns, and several hundred prisoners fell into the hands of the victors, and the total loss of the French was estimated at three thousand men—an exaggeration, no doubt, but it was certainly above two thousand, for their closed columns had been exposed for more than half an hour to sweeping discharges of grape and musketry, and the dead lay thickly together. General Thiebault, indeed, reduces the number to eighteen hundred, and asserts that the whole amount of the French army did not much exceed twelve thousand men, from which number he deducts nearly three thousand for the sick, the stragglers, and all those other petty drains which form the torment of a general-in-chief. But when it is considered that this army was composed of men selected and organized in provisionary battalions expressly for the occasion;† that one half had only been in the field for a fortnight, and that the whole had enjoyed a two days' rest at Torres Vedras, it is evident that the number of absentees bears too great a proportion to the

* Proceedings of the Court of Inquiry.
† Thiebault.

combatants. A French order of battle found upon the field gave a total of fourteen thousand men present under arms, of which thirteen hundred were cavalry; and this amount agrees too closely with other estimates, and with the observations made at the time, to leave any reasonable doubt of its authenticity or correctness.

The arrangements made by Sir Harry Burrard did not remain in force a long time. Early on the morning of the 22d, Sir Hew Dalrymple disembarked and assumed the chief command. Thus, in the short space of twenty-four hours, during which a battle was fought, the army fell successively into the hands of three men, who, coming from the ocean, with different views, habits, and information, had not any previous opportunity of communing even by letter, so as to arrange a common plan of operations; and they were now brought together at a critical moment, when it was more than probable they must all disagree, and that the public service must suffer from that want of vigor which is inherent to divided councils. For when Sir Hew Dalrymple was appointed to the command, Sir Arthur Wellesley was privately recommended to him, by the minister, as a person who should be employed with more than usual confidence; and this unequivocal hint was backed up with too much force by the previous reputation and recent exploits of the latter, not to produce some want of cordiality.* Sir Arthur could not do otherwise than take the lead in discussing affairs of which he had more than laid the foundation; and Sir Hew would have forfeited all claims to independence in his command, if he had not exercised the right of judging for himself between the conflicting opinions of his predecessors.

After receiving information upon the most important points, and taking a hasty view of the situation of the army—although the wounded were still upon the ground, and the wains of the commissariat were employed in removing them—Sir Hew decided to advance upon the 23d, and gave orders to that effect.† Nevertheless, he entirely agreed in opinion with Sir Harry Burrard, that the operation was a perilous one, which it required the concentration of all his troops, and the application of all his means, to bring to a good conclusion; and for this reason he did not rescind the order directing Sir John Moore to fall down to Maceira. This last measure was disapproved of by Sir Arthur, who observed that the provisions on shore would not supply more than eight or nine days' consumption for the troops already at Vimiero; that the country would be unable to furnish any assistance, and that the fleet could not be calculated upon as a resource, because the first of the gales

* Proceedings of the Court of Inquiry.
† Sir H. Dalrymple's Narrative. Court of Inquiry.

common at that season of the year would certainly send it away from the coast, if it did not destroy a great portion of it. Sir Hew thought the evil of having the army separated would be greater than the chance of distress from such events. His position was certainly difficult. The Bishop of Oporto had failed in his promise of assisting the troops with draft cattle—as, indeed, he did in all his promises;* the artillery and commissariat were badly supplied with mules and horses; the cavalry was a nullity, and the enemy was, with the exception of his immediate loss in killed and wounded, suffering nothing from his defeat, which, we have seen, did not deprive him of a single position necessary to his defence. While weighing this state of affairs, he was informed that General Kellermann, escorted by a strong body of cavalry, was at the outposts and demanded an interview. For Junot, after regaining Torres Vedras, had occupied Mafra, and was preparing to fight again, when he received intelligence that Lisbon was on the point of insurrection;† wherefore, sending forward a false account of the action, he followed it up with a reinforcement for the garrison, and called a council of war to advise measures with respect to the English. It is an old and sound remark that "a council of war never fights," and Kellermann's mission was the result of the above consultation.

That General, being conducted to the quarters of the commander-in-chief, demanded a cessation of arms, and proposed the groundwork of a convention under which Junot offered to evacuate Portugal without further resistance. Nothing could be more opportune than this proposition, and Sir Hew Dalrymple readily accepted of it, as an advantage which would accrue without any drawback to the general cause of the Peninsula. He knew, from a plan of operations sketched by the chief of the French engineers, Colonel Vincent, and taken by the Portuguese, that Junot possessed several strong positions in front of Lisbon, and that a retreat, either upon Almeida or across the river upon Elvas, was not only within the contemplation of that General, but considered in this report as a matter of course, and perfectly easy of execution. Hence the proposed convention was an unexpected advantage, offered in a moment of difficulty, and the only subject of consideration was the nature of the articles proposed by Kellermann as a basis for the treaty. Sir Hew, being necessarily ignorant of many details, had recourse to Sir A. Wellesley for information, and the latter, taking an enlarged view of the question in all its bearings, coincided as to the sound policy of agreeing to a convention, by which a strong French army would be quietly got out of a country that it had

* Proceedings of the Court of Inquiry.
† Thiebault.

complete military possession of;* and by which not only a great moral effect in favor of the general cause would be produced, but an actual gain made, both of men and time, for the further prosecution of the war in Spain. By the convention, he observed,

1. That a kingdom would be liberated, with all its fortresses, arsenals, &c., and that the excited population of the Peninsula might then be pushed forward in the career of opposition to France, under the most favorable circumstances.

2. That the Spanish army of Estremadura, which contained the most efficient body of cavalry in the Peninsula, could be reinforced with the four or five thousand Spanish soldiers who were prisoners on board the vessels in the Tagus; and would be enabled to unite with the other patriot armies at a critical period, when every addition of force must tend to increase the confidence and forward the impulse which the victory of Baylen and the flight of Joseph had given to the Spaniards. Finally, that the sacrifice of lives to be expected in carrying the French positions in Portugal, all the difficulties of reducing the fortresses, and the danger of losing a communication with the fleet, would be avoided by this measure, the result of which would be as complete as the most sanguine could expect from the long course of uncertain and unhealthy operations which must follow a rejection of the proposal.† But, while admitting the utility of the measure itself, he differed with the commander-in-chief as to the mode of proceeding, and a long discussion, in which Sir H. Burrard took a part, followed the opening of Kellermann's mission. Sir Arthur's first objection was, that, in point of form, Kellermann was merely entitled to negotiate a cessation of hostilities. Sir Hew Dalrymple judged that, as the good policy and the utility of the convention were recognized, it would be unwise to drive the French to the wall on a point of ceremony, and therefore accepted the proposition. The basis of a definitive treaty was then arranged, subject to the final approbation of Sir Charles Cotton, without whose concurrence it was not to be binding.

Articles 1st and 2d declared the fact of the armistice, and provided for the mode of future proceedings.

Article 3d indicated the river Sisandre as the line of demarcation between the two armies. The position of Torres Vedras to be occupied by neither.

Article 4th. Sir Hew Dalrymple engaged to have the Portuguese included in the armistice, and their boundary line was to extend from Leiria to Thomar.

Article 5th declared, that the French were not to be considered

* Proceedings of the Court of Inquiry.
† Ibid.

as prisoners of war, and that themselves and their property, public and private, were, without any detainer, to be transported to France. To this article Sir Arthur objected, as affording a cover for the abstraction of Portuguese property, whereupon Kellermann said, that it was to be taken in its fair sense of property justly obtained, and upon this assurance it was admitted.

Article 6th provided for the protection of individuals. It guaranteed from political persecution all French residents, all subjects of powers in alliance with France, and all Portuguese who had served the invaders, or become obnoxious for their attachment to them.

Article 7th stipulated for the neutrality of the port of Lisbon as far as the Russian fleet was concerned. At first Kellermann proposed to have the Russian fleet guaranteed from capture, with leave to return to the Baltic, but this was peremptorily refused; indeed, the whole proceeding was designed to entangle the Russians in the French negotiation, that, in case the armistice should be broken, the former might be forced into a co-operation with the latter.

Sir Arthur strenuously opposed this article; he argued, 1. That the interests of the two nations were not blended, and that they stood in different relations towards the British army. 2. That it was an important object to keep them separate, and that the French General, if pressed, would leave the Russians to their fate. 3. That as the British operations had not been so rapid and decisive as to enable them to capture the fleet before the question of neutrality could be agitated, the right of the Russians to such protection was undoubted; and in the present circumstances it was desirable to grant it, because independent of the chances of their final capture, they would be prevented from returning to the Baltic, which in fact constituted their only point of interest when disengaged from the French; but that, viewed as allies of the latter, they became of great weight. Lastly, that it was an affair which concerned the Portuguese, Russians, and British, but with which the French could have no right to interfere. Sir Hew, finding that the discussion of this question became lengthened, and considering that Sir Charles Cotton alone could finally decide, admitted the article merely as a form, without acquiescing in the propriety of it.

Article 8th provided, that all guns of French calibre, and the horses of the cavalry, were to be transported to France.

Article 9th stipulated, that forty-eight hours' notice should be given of the rupture of the armistice.

To this article also Sir Arthur objected; he considered it unnecessary for the interests of the British army, and favorable to the

French; because, if hostilities recommenced, the latter would have forty-eight hours to make arrangements for their defence, for the passage of the Tagus, and for the co-operation of the Russian fleet. Upon the other hand, Sir Hew thought it was an absolute advantage to gain time for the preparations of the British army, and for the arrival of Sir John Moore's reinforcements.

By an additional article it was provided, that all the fortresses held by the French, which had not capitulated before the 25th of August, should be given up to the British; and the basis of a convention being thus arranged, General Kellermann returned to his chief, and Colonel George Murray was ordered to carry the proposed articles to the English Admiral.

Previous to his landing, Sir Hew had received none of the letters addressed to him by Sir Arthur Wellesley, he had met with no person during his voyage from whom he could obtain authentic information of the state of affairs, and his time being at first occupied by the negotiations with Kellermann, he was uninformed of many details of importance. Now, the day after Kellermann's departure, Don Bernardin Freire Andrada, the Portuguese commander-in-chief, came to remonstrate against the armistice just concluded; but, from the circumstance before mentioned, it so happened that Sir Hew was utterly ignorant of the existence of Don Bernardin and his army, at the time the armistice was discussed, and it was therefore difficult for him to manage this interview with propriety, because Andrada had some plausible, although no real, ground of complaint. His remonstrances were, however, merely intended for the commencement of an intrigue, to which I shall hereafter revert.

Colonel Murray soon reached the fleet, and presented the articles of convention to Sir Charles Cotton, but the latter refused to concur therein, declaring that he would himself conduct a separate treaty for the Russian ships. With this answer Colonel Murray returned on the 24th, having first, in reply to a question put by the French officer who accompanied him on board the Hibernia, declared that nothing had passed between him and Sir Charles Cotton which ought to preclude further negotiation. Sir Hew Dalrymple was now urged by Sir Arthur Wellesley to give notice, without further explanation, that hostilities would recommence, leaving it to Junot to renew propositions, if he chose to do so, separately from the Russians.* Sir Hew, however, felt himself in honor bound by Colonel Murray's observation to the French officer, and would not take advantage of the occasion; he likewise felt disinclined to relinquish a negotiation which, from certain circumstances, he deemed upon the point of being crowned with success. He therefore des-

* Proceedings of the Court of Inquiry.

patched Colonel Murray to Lisbon, with directions to inform Junot of the Admiral's objection, and to give notice of the consequent rupture of the armistice, Murray himself being provided, however, with full powers to enter into and conclude a definitive treaty upon a fresh basis. The army was, at the same time, pushed forward to Ramalhal, and Sir J. Moore's troops were landed at Maceira Bay, but the order to repair to that place did not reach them until several regiments had been disembarked in the Mondego;* the reshipping of these, together with contrary winds, had caused a delay of four days, and at Maceira great difficulty and some loss was sustained in getting on shore, an operation only effected by five days of incessant exertion on the part of the navy ; the boats were constantly swamped by the surf, and such was its fury that not more than thirty remained fit for service at the conclusion.

On the 27th, information was received from Colonel Murray that a fresh treaty was in agitation upon an admissible basis ; and the next day the army took a new position, a part occupying Torres Vedras, and the remainder being placed in the rear of that town. Meanwhile, in Lisbon, the agitation of the public mind was excessively great ; hope and fear were magnified by the obscurity of affairs, and the contradictory news which was spread by the French, and by those who held communication with the country, had increased the anxious feeling of joy or grief almost to phrenzy. Junot made every effort to engage Admiral Siniavin in the negotiation, and the necessity by which the latter was forced to put his ships in a hostile and guarded attitude, contributed powerfully to control the populace, and give strength to an opinion industriously spread, that he would make common cause with the French. Nevertheless Siniavin had no intention of this kind, and very early gave notice that he would treat separately ; wherefore the French, being thus left to themselves, had no resource but their own dexterity, and brought all the ordinary machinery of diplomatic subtlety into play. Among other schemes, Junot opened a separate communication with Sir Hew Dalrymple at the moment when Colonel Murray, invested with full powers, was engaged in daily conferences with Kellermann ; and the difficulty of coming to a conclusion was much increased by the natural sources of suspicion and jealousy incident to such a singular transaction, where two foreign nations were seen bargaining, and one of them honestly bargaining, for the goods and interests of a third, yet scarcely hinting even at the existence of the latter. The French being the weakest, were most subtle, and to protect the vital questions advanced extravagant claims ; on the other hand, the Portuguese leaders, no longer fearing a defeat, pro-

* Proceedings of the Court of Inquiry.

tested against the convention, passed the line of demarcation, attacked the French patrols, and menaced an attack from the side of
Santarem.   This movement, and the breach of faith in attacking
the patrols, were promptly and distinctly disavowed by Sir Hew;
yet they kept suspicion awake, and the mutual misunderstandings
arose at last to such a height, that Junot, seeming for a moment to
recover all his natural energy, threatened to burn the public establishments, and make his retreat good at the expense of the city;
a menace which nothing could have prevented him from executing.
Finally, however, a definitive treaty was concluded at Lisbon on
the 30th, and soon afterwards ratified in form.

This celebrated convention, improperly called " of Cintra," consisted of twenty-two original, and three supplementary articles, upon
the expediency of many of which Sir Arthur Wellesley and the
commander-in-chief disagreed; but as their disagreement had
reference to the details and not to the general principle, the historical importance is not sufficient to call for remark.   An informality
on the part of Junot caused some delay in the ratification of the
instrument; the British army marched notwithstanding to take up
the position near Lisbon, assigned to it by the 11th article of the
treaty, and on the march, Sir Hew Dalrymple met two Russian
officers, who were charged to open a separate negotiation for the
Russian squadron; he, however, refused to receive their credentials,
and referred them to Sir Charles Cotton.   Thus baffled in an
attempt to carry on a double treaty, for a naval one was already
commenced, Siniavin, whose conduct appears to have been weak,
was forced to come to a conclusion with the English Admiral.   At
first he claimed the protection of a neutral port, but as singly he
possessed none of that weight which circumstances had given him
before the convention with Junot, his claim was answered by an
intimation that a British flag was flying on the forts at the mouth
of the Tagus; and this was true, for the third and forty-second
regiments, under the command of Major-General Beresford, having
landed and taken possession of them, in virtue of the convention,
the British colors were improperly hoisted instead of the Portuguese.   Foiled again by this proceeding, the justice of which is
somewhat doubtful, Siniavin finally agreed to surrender upon the
following terms:

1. The Russian ships, with their sails, stores, &c., were to be
held by England, as a deposit, until six months after the conclusion
of a peace between the two governments of the contracting parties.

2. The Admiral, officers, and seamen, without any restriction as
to their future services, were to be transported to Russia at the
expense of the British government.

But two additional articles were, subsequently to the ratification of the original treaty, proposed by the Russians, and assented to by the English Admiral. The first stipulated that the imperial flag should be displayed, even in the British harbors, as long as the Russian Admiral remained on board. The second provided that the ships themselves and their stores should be delivered again at the appointed time, in the same state as when surrendered. The rights of the Portuguese were not referred to, but Sir Charles Cotton was justified by his instructions, which authorized him to make prize of the Russian fleet.* Siniavin thus suffered all the inconvenience of hostilities, and the shame of striking his colors, without having violated in any manner the relations of amity in which his nation stood with regard to Portugal. On the other hand, for the sake of a few old and decaying ships, the British government made an injudicious display of contempt for the independence of their ally, because, with singular inconsistency, they permitted the officers and crews, the real strength of the squadron, to return to the Baltic, although scarcely a year had elapsed since the national character was defiled in that quarter, to suppress a navy inimical to Great Britain. This inconsistency belonged wholly to the ministers; for the two original articles of the treaty only were confirmed by them, and they were copied from the Admiralty instructions delivered to Sir Charles Cotton four months previous to the transaction.† Yet that officer, by the very men who had framed those instructions, was, with matchless effrontery, rebuked for having adopted a new principle of maritime surrender!

On the 2d of September head-quarters were established at Oyeras; the right of the army occupied the forts at the mouth of the river, the left rested upon the heights of Bellas. The French army concentrated in Lisbon posted their piquets and guards as if in front of an enemy, and at night the sentries fired upon whoever approached their posts; the police disbanded of their own accord, and the city became a scene of turbulence, anarchy, and crime.‡ Notwithstanding the presence of their enemies, the inhabitants of the capital testified their joy, and evinced their vengeful feelings in a remarkable manner; they refused to sell any provisions, or to deal in any manner with the French; they sung songs of triumph in their hearing, and in their sight fabricated thousands of small lamps for the avowed purpose of illuminating the streets at their

---

* Parl. Pap. 1809.
† Ibid. Admiralty Instructions to Sir C. Cotton, 16th April, 1808. Mr. Wellesley Pole to Sir C. Cotton, 17th Sept. 1808.
‡ Thiebault.

departure; the doors of many of the houses occupied by the troops were marked in one night; men were observed bearing in their hats lists of Portuguese or Frenchmen designed for slaughter, and the quarters of Loison were threatened with a serious attack. Yet amidst all this disorder and violence, General Travot, and some others of the French army, fearlessly and safely traversed the streets, unguarded save by the reputation of their just and liberal conduct when in power, a fact extremely honorable to the Portuguese, and conclusive of the misconduct of Loison.* Junot himself was menaced by an assassin, but he treated the affair with magnanimity, and in general he was respected, although in a far less degree than Travot.

The dread of an explosion, which would have compromised at once the safety of his army and of the city, induced the French General to hasten the period when an English division was to occupy the citadel and take charge of the public tranquillity. Meanwhile emissaries from the Junta of Oporto fomented the disposition of the populace to commit themselves by an attack upon the French, the convention was reprobated, and endeavors were fruitlessly made to turn the tide of indignation even against the English, as abettors of the invaders. The judge of the people, an energetic, but turbulent fellow, issued an inflammatory address in which, calling for a suspension of the treaty, he designated the French as robbers and insulters of religion. The Monteiro Mor, who commanded a rabble of peasantry, which he dignified with the title of an army, took possession of the south bank of the Tagus, and from his quarters issued a protest against the convention, the execution of which he had the audacity to call upon Sir Charles Cotton to interrupt; the latter sent his communications to Sir Hew Dalrymple, who treated them with the contemptuous indignation they merited.

Sir John Hope being appointed English commandant of Lisbon, took possession of the castle of Belem on the 10th, and of the citadel the 12th, and, by his firm and vigorous conduct, reduced the effervescence of the public mind, and repressed the disorders which had arisen to a height that gave opportunity for the commission of any villainy. The Duke of Abrantes, with his staff, embarked the 13th. The first division of his army sailed the 15th; it was followed by the second and third divisions, and on the 30th, all the French, except the garrisons of Elvas and Almeida, were out of Portugal.

But the execution of the convention had not been carried on thus far without much trouble and contestation. Lord Proby, the English commissioner appointed to carry the articles of the treaty

* Thiebault.

into effect, was joined by Major-General Beresford on the 5th, and their united labors were scarcely sufficient to meet the exigencies of a task, in the prosecution of which disputes hourly arose. Anger, the cupidity of individuals, and opportunity, combined to push the French beyond the bounds of honor and decency, and several gross attempts were made to appropriate property which no interpretation of the stipulations could give a color to; amongst the most odious were the abstraction of manuscripts and rare specimens of natural history from the National Museum, and the invasion of the deposito publico, or funds of money awaiting legal decision for their final appropriation. These dishonest attempts were met and checked with a strong hand, and at last a committee, consisting of an individual of each of the three nations, was appointed by the commissioners on both sides. Their office was to receive reclamations, to investigate them, and to do justice by seizing upon all contraband baggage embarked by the French—a measure attended with excellent effect. It must, however, be observed that the loud complaints and violence of the Portuguese, and the machinations of the Bishop of Oporto, seem to have excited the suspicions of the British, and influenced their acts more than the real facts warranted; for the national character of the Portuguese was not then understood, nor the extent to which they supplied the place of true reports by the fabrication of false ones, generally known.

Party writers have not been wanting since to exaggerate the grounds of complaint. The English have imputed fraud and evasions of the most dishonorable kind to the French, and the latter have retorted by accusations of gratuitous insult, and breach of faith, inasmuch as their soldiers, when on board the British ships, were treated with cruelty in order to induce them to desert. It would be too much to affirm that all the error was on one side, but it does appear reasonable and consonant to justice to decide that as the French were originally aggressors and acting for their own interest, and that the British were interfering for the protection of the Portuguese, an indecorous zeal on the part of the latter, if not commendable, was certainly more excusable than in their opponents. Upon the ground of its being impossible for Junot to know what was doing in his name, the British commissioners acquitted him of any personal impropriety of conduct, and his public orders, which denounced severe punishments for such malpractices, corroborated this testimony; yet Kellermann, in his communications with Sir Hew Dalrymple, did not scruple to insinuate matters to the Duke's disadvantage.*   But, amidst all these

* Sir Hew Dalrymple's Narrative.   Court of Inquiry.

conflicting accusations, the British commander's personal good faith and scupulous adherence to justice has never been called in question.

To define the exact extent to which each party should have pushed their claims is not an easy task, yet an impartial investigator would begin by carefully separating the original rights of the French from those rights which they acquired by the convention; and much of the subsequent clamor in England against the authors of that treaty sprung from the error of confounding these essentially distinct grounds of argument. Conquest being the sole foundation of the first, defeat, if complete, extinguished them; if incomplete, nullified a part only. Now the issue of the appeal to arms not having been answerable to the justice of the cause, an agreement ensued, by which a part was sacrificed for the sake of the remainder, and upon the terms of that agreement the whole question of right hinges. If the French were not prisoners of war, it follows that they had not forfeited their claims founded on the right of conquest, but they were willing to exchange an insecure tenure of the whole for a secure tenure of a part. The difficulty consisted in defining exactly what was conceded, and what should be recovered from them. With respect to the latter, the restitution of plunder acquired anterior to the convention was clearly out of the question; if officially obtained, it was part of the rights bargained for—if individually, to what tribunal could the innumerable claims which would follow such an article be referred? Abstract notions of right in such matters are misplaced. If an army surrenders at discretion, the victors may say with Brennus, "Woe to the vanquished;" but a convention implies some weakness, and must be weighed in the scales of prudence, not in those of justice.

CHAPTER VI.

The Bishop and Junta of Oporto aim at the supreme power; wish to establish the seat of government at Oporto; their intrigues; strange proceedings of General Decken; reflections thereupon—Clamor raised against the convention in England and in Portugal; soon ceases in Portugal—The Spanish General Galluzo refuses to acknowledge the convention; invests Fort La Lippe; his proceedings absurd and unjustifiable—Sir John Hope marches against him; he alters his conduct—Garrison of La Lippe; march to Lisbon; embarked—Garrison of Almeida; march to Oporto; attacked and plundered by the Portuguese—Sir Hew Dalrymple and Sir Harry Burrard recalled to England—Vile conduct of the daily press—Violence of public feeling—Convention, improperly called, of Cintra—Observations—On the action of Roriça—On the battle of Vimiero—On the convention.

THE interview that took place at Vimiero between Don Bernardin Freire d'Andrada and Sir Hew Dalrymple has been already noticed as the commencement of an intrigue of some consequence. The Portuguese chief objected at the time to the armistice concluded with Kellermann, ostensibly upon general grounds, but really, as it appeared to Sir Hew, because the Bishop and Junta of Oporto were not named in the instrument. At the desire of Freire, one Ayres Pinto de Souza was received at the English head-quarters as the protector of Portuguese interests during the subsequent negotiation, and he was soon apprised that a treaty for a definitive convention was on foot, himself and his General being invited to state their views and wishes before any further steps were taken. Neither of them took any notice of this invitation, but when the treaty was concluded clamored loudly against it. The British army was, they said, an auxiliary force, and should only act as such; nevertheless, it had assumed the right of treating with the French for Portuguese interests, and a convention had been concluded which protected the enemy from the punishment due to his rapine and cruelty; it was more favorable than the strength of the relative parties warranted, and no notice had been taken of the Portuguese government, or of the native army in the Alemtejo; men who were obnoxious to their countrymen for having aided the invaders, were protected from a just vengeance; finally, the fortresses were bargained for as acquisitions appertaining to the British army—a circumstance which must inevitably excite great jealousy both in Portugal and Spain, and injure the general cause by affording an opportunity for the French emissaries to create disunion among the allied nations. They dwelt also upon the importance of the native forces, the strength of the insurrection, and insinuated that separate operations were likely to be carried on notwithstanding the treaty.

Noble words often cover pitiful deeds: this remonstrance, apparently springing from the feelings of a patriot whose heart was ulcerated by the wrongs his country had sustained, was but a cloak for a miserable interested intrigue. The Bishop of Oporto, a meddling ambitious priest, had early conceived the project of placing himself at the head of the insurrectional authorities, and transferring the seat of government from Lisbon to Oporto. He was aware that he should encounter great opposition, and he hoped that by inveigling the English General to countenance these pretensions, he might, with the aid of Freire's force, and his own influence, succeed in the object of his wishes. With this view he wrote a letter to Sir Charles Cotton dated the fourth of August, in which was inclosed, as the letter describes it, "The form of government with which they, the Junta of Oporto, meant to govern Portugal when the city of Lisbon should be free from the French;" and this letter, together with its inclosure, being transmitted to Sir Arthur Wellesley, he placed them among other public documents in the hands of Sir Hew Dalrymple when the latter first landed at Maceira. In the document itself it was declared that "The body of government had taken the glorious resolution of restoring the Portuguese monarchy in all its extent, and of recovering the crown of Portugal for its lawful sovereign Don Juan VI., their prince." But this "glorious resolution" was burthened with many forms and restrictions; and although the Junta professed the intention of re-establishing a regency, they declared, "that if this new regency should be interrupted by a new invasion of the French, or by *any other thing*, the Junta would immediately take the government on itself, and exercise the authority and jurisdiction which it had done ever since its institution."

Thus prepared for some cabal, Sir Hew Dalrymple was at no loss for an answer to Freire's remonstrance. He observed, that if the government of Portugal had not been mentioned in the treaty, neither had that of England, nor that of France. The convention was purely military, and for the present concerned only the commanders in the field. With regard to the occupation of the fortresses, and the fact of the British army being an auxiliary force, the first was merely a measure of military precaution absolutely necessary, and the latter was in no way rendered doubtful by any act which had been committed; he, Sir Hew, was instructed by his government to assist in restoring the Prince Regent of Portugal to his lawful rights, without any secret or interested motives; finally, the Portuguese General had been invited to assist in the negotiations, and if he had not done so, the blame rested with himself. To this Sir Hew might have justly added, that the conduct of Freire in withdrawing his troops at the most critical moment of the campaign, by no means entitled him to assume a high tone towards those whom he had so disgracefully deserted in the hour of danger.

The Portuguese General was silenced by this plain and decided answer; yet the English General was quickly convinced that the Bishop and his coadjutors, however incapable of conducting great affairs, were experienced plotters. In his first interview with Andrada, Sir Hew Dalrymple had taken occasion to observe, that "no government lawfully representing the Prince Regent actually existed in Portugal;" in fact, a Junta, calling itself independent, was likewise established in Algarvé, and the members of the regency legally invested by the Prince with supreme authority were dispersed, and part of them in the power of the French. This observation, so adverse to the prelate's views, was transmitted to him by Freire, together with a copy of the armistice; and he was well aware that a definitive convention, differing materially from the armistice, was upon the point of being concluded, the refusal of Sir Charles Cotton to concur in the latter having rendered it null and void. Nevertheless, preserving silence on that point, the Bishop forwarded the copy of the armistice to the Chevalier Da Souza, Portuguese minister in London, accompanied by a letter filled with invectives and misrepresentations of its provisions; the Chevalier placed this letter, with its inclosures, in the hands of Mr. Canning, the English Secretary of State for foreign affairs, and at the same time delivering to him an official note, in which, adopting the style of the prelate and Junta, he spoke of them as the representatives of his sovereign, and the possessors of the supreme power in Portugal.

Nor were the efforts of the party confined to formal communications with the ministers: the daily press teemed with invectives against the English General's conduct; ex-parte statements, founded on the provisions of an armistice that was never concluded, being thus palmed upon a public, always hasty in judging of such matters, a prejudice against the convention was raised before either the terms of, or the events which led to it, were known. For Sir Hew, forgetting the ordinary forms of official intercourse, had neglected to transmit information to his government until fifteen days after the commencement of the treaty, and the ministers, unable to contradict or explain any of Souza's assertions, were thus placed in a mortifying situation, by which their minds were irritated and disposed to take a prejudiced view of the real treaty. Meanwhile the Bishop pretended to know nothing of the convention, hence the silence of Freire during the negotiation; but that once concluded, a clamor was, by the party, raised in Portugal, similar to what had already been excited in England: thus both nations appeared to be equally indignant at the conduct of the General, when, in fact, his proceedings were unknown to either.

It would appear that the Bishop had other than Portuguese coadjutors. The Baron Von Decken, a Hanoverian officer, was appointed one of the military agents at Oporto; he was subject to Sir Hew Dalrymple's orders, but as his mission was of a detached nature, he was also to communicate directly with the Secretary of State in England. Von Decken arrived at Oporto upon the 17th August, and the same evening, in concert with the Bishop, concocted a project admirably adapted to forward the views of the latter: they agreed that the prelate was the fittest person to be at the head of the government, and that as he could not or pretended he could not quit Oporto, the seat of government ought to be transferred to that city.

Two obstacles to this arrangement were foreseen: first, the Prince Regent at his departure had nominated a regency, and left full instructions for the filling up of vacancies arising from death or other causes; secondly, the people of Lisbon and of the southern provinces would certainly resist any plan for changing the seat of government; hence, to obviate these difficulties, Von Decken wrote largely in commendation of the proposed arrangement, vilifying the conduct of the regency, and urging Sir Hew not only to give his sanction to the ambitious project, but to employ the British troops in controlling the people of Lisbon, should they attempt to frustrate the Bishop's plans. To conciliate the members of the regency, it was proposed to admit a portion of them into the new government, and Francisco Noronha, Francisco de Cunha, the Monteiro Mor, and the principal Castro, were named as being the only men who were faithful to their sovereign. Now the last had accepted the office of Minister of Worship under the French, and was consequently unfaithful; but he was the half-brother of the Bishop, Castro being legitimately born. Under the pretext of sparing the feelings of the people of Lisbon, it was further proposed to appoint a Portuguese commandant, subject to the British governor, yet with a native force under his orders, to conduct all matters of police, and the Bishop took the occasion to recommend a particular general for that office. Finally, civil dissension and all its attendant evils were foretold as the consequences of rejecting this plan.

Sir Hew Dalrymple's answer was peremptory and decisive. He reprimanded General Von Decken, and at once put an end to the Bishop's hopes of support from the English army. This second repulse—for Sir Hew's answer did not reach Oporto until after Freire's report had arrived there—completed the mortification of the prelate and his Junta, and they set no bounds to their violence. Efforts were made to stimulate the populace of Lisbon to attack both French and English, in the hope that the terrible scene which must have ensued would effectually prevent the re-establishment of the old regency, and at the same time render the transfer of the seat of government to Oporto an easy task. Hence the outrageous conduct of the Monteiro Mor and of the judge of the people, and the former's insolent letter calling upon Sir Charles Cotton to interrupt the execution of the convention.

The 3d September, Sir Hew Dalrymple received instructions from home relative to the formation of a new regency which were completely at variance with the plan arranged between the Bishop and General Von Decken, yet no difficulty attended the execution; and here, as in the case of Prince Leopold, we are arrested by the singularity of the transaction. General Charles Stewart, brother of Lord Castlereagh, was the bearer of Von Decken's first letter. He would not knowingly have lent himself to an intrigue subversive of his brother's views, as explained in the official instructions sent to Sir Hew; neither is it likely that Von Decken should plunge into such a delicate and important affair in one hour after his arrival at Oporto, if he had not been secretly authorized by some member of the English Cabinet: are we then to seek for a clue to these mysteries in that shameful Machiavelian policy that soon afterwards forced Lord Castlereagh to defend his public measures by a duel?

But the usual fate of plans laid by men more cunning than wise attended the Bishop of Oporto's projects. He was successful for a moment in rendering the convention of Cintra odious to the Portuguese, yet the great mass of the people soon acknowledged with gratitude the services rendered them by the English, rejoicing at the fulfilment of a treaty which freed their country at once from the invaders. And well might they rejoice, when they beheld above twenty-five thousand bold and skilful soldiers reluctantly quitting the strongholds of the kingdom, and to the last maintaining the haughty air of an army unsubdued, and capable on the slightest provocation of resorting once more to the decision of battle. The Portuguese people were contented, but the Spanish General Galluzzo appears to have favored the views of the Oporto faction. Detachments of his troops and Portuguese refugees, principally from the northern provinces, and commanded by a Spaniard, were acting in conjunction with the insurgents of the Alemtejo. Many disputes had arisen between the two nations, as I have already related; for the Spaniards treated Portugal as a conquered country, denied the authority of the Portuguese General Leite, who was not of the Bishop's party, and insulted him personally; they even seized his military chest at Campo Mayor, and in all things acted with the utmost violence and rapacity.

Galluzzo himself was required by his own government to join the Spanish armies concentrating on the Ebro; but instead of obeying, he collected his forces near Elvas, and when he heard of the convention concluded at Lisbon, invested Fort La Lippe, and refused to permit the execution of the treaty relative to that impregnable fortress. Colonel Girod de Novillard commanded the French garrison, and, profiting from its situation, had compelled the inhabitants of Elvas to shut their gates also against the Spaniards, and to supply the fort daily with provisions. Galluzzo's proceedings were therefore manifestly absurd in a military point of view, for his attacks were confined to a trifling bombardment of La Lippe from an immense distance, and the utmost damage sustained, or likely to be sustained by that fortress, was the knocking away the cornices and chimneys of the governor's house, every other part being protected by bomb proofs of the finest masonry.

Through Lord Burghersh, who had been appointed to communicate with the Spanish troops in Portugal, Galluzzo was, early in September, officially informed of the articles of the convention, and that the troops of his nation confined on board the hulks at Lisbon were by that treaty released, and would be clothed, armed, and sent to Catalonia. Sir Hew Dalrymple also wrote to the Spanish General on the 5th of September, to repeat this intelligence, and to request that his detachment might be withdrawn from the Alemtejo, where they were living at the expense of the people. Galluzzo, however, took no notice of either communication, pretending that he had opened his fire against La Lippe before the date of the convention, and that no third party had a right to interfere; he declared he would grant no terms to the garrison, nor permit any but Portuguese to enter the fort. Yet at this moment the Spanish armies on the Ebro were languishing for cavalry, which he alone possessed; and his efforts were so despised by Girod that the latter made no secret of his intention, if the fate of the French army at Lisbon should render such a step advisable, to blow up the works and march openly through the midst of Galluzzo's troops.

Colonel Ross being finally detached with the 20th regiment to receive the fort from Colonel Girod, and to escort the garrison to Lisbon under the terms of the convention, sent a flag of truce, and Major Colborne, who carried it, was also furnished with an autograph letter from Kellermann. He was received with civility, but

Girod refused to surrender his post without more complete proof of the authenticity of the treaty, and with the view of acquiring that he proposed that a French officer should proceed to Lisbon to verify the information. He did not affect to disbelieve Colborne's information, but he would not surrender his charge while the slightest doubt capable of being removed was attached to the transaction; and so acting he did well, and like a good soldier. General D'Arcy, who commanded the Spanish investing force, was persuaded to grant a truce for six days, to give time for the journey of the officers appointed to go to Lisbon, but on their return it was not without great difficulty and delay that they were permitted to communicate with Colonel Girod, and no argument could prevail upon the obstinate Galluzzo to relinquish the siege. After a warm intercourse of letters, Sir Hew Dalrymple ordered Sir John Hope to advance to Estremos with a considerable body of troops, to give weight to his remonstrances, and, if pushed to extremity, even to force the Spaniard to desist from his unwarrantable pretensions; for it must be observed that Galluzzo was not only putting aside the convention, by which he profited himself, but violating the independence of the Portuguese, who desired his absence from their territory. He was likewise setting at nought the authority of his own government; for the army of Estremadura pretended to act under the orders of the Junta of Seville, and Laguna, an accredited agent of that Junta, was at the moment receiving from Sir Hew Dalrymple the Spanish prisoners liberated by the effect of the convention, together with money and arms to prepare them for immediate service in Catalonia, whither they were to be transported in British vessels. One more effort was however made to persuade the intractable Galluzzo to submit to reason, before recourse was had to violent measures, which must have produced infinite evil. Colonel Graham repaired upon the 25th of September to Badajos, and his arguments, backed up by the approach of the powerful division under Hope, were finally successful.

Colonel Girod evacuated the forts, and his garrison proceeded to Lisbon, attended by the 52d regiment as an escort; the rival troops agreed very well together, striving to outdo each other by the vigor and the military order of their marches, but the Swiss and French soldiers did not accord, and many of the latter wished to desert. At Lisbon the whole were immediately embarked, and the transports being detained for some time in the river, Major de Bosset, an officer of the Chasseurs Britanniques, contrived to persuade near a thousand of the men to desert, who were afterwards received into the British service.* Girod complained of this as a

* Appendix to Colonel De Bosset's Parga, p. 134.   Thiebault.

breach of the convention, and it must be confessed that it was an equivocal act, yet one common to all armies, and if done simply by persuasion very excusable.

Almeida surrendered without any delay, and the garrison being marched to Oporto, were proceeding to embark, when the populace rose and would have slain them if great exertions had not been made by the British officers to prevent such a disgraceful breach of faith. The escort, although weak, was resolute to sustain the honor of their nation, and would have fired upon the multitude if the circumstances had become desperate; yet several of the French soldiers were assassinated, and, in spite of every effort, the baggage was landed, and the whole plundered, the excuse being, that church plate was to be found amongst it; an accusation easily made, difficult to be disproved to the satisfaction of a violent mob, and likely enough to be true.

This tumult gives scope for reflection upon the facility with which men adapt themselves to circumstances, and regulate their most furious passions by the scale of self-interest. In Oporto, the suffering, in consequence of the invasion, was trifling compared to the misery endured in Lisbon, yet the inhabitants of the former were much more outrageous in their anger. In Lisbon, the very persons who had inflicted the worst evils upon the people were daily exposed, more or less, to violence, yet suffered none; while in Oporto, it was with extreme difficulty that men, until that moment unseen of the multitude, were rescued from their frantic revenge. In both cases fear regulated the degree of hatred shown, and we may conclude from hence, that national insurrections, however spontaneous and vehement, if the result of hatred only, will never successfully resist an organized force, unless the mechanical courage of discipline be grafted upon the first enthusiasm.

While the vexatious correspondence with Galluzzo was going on, Sir Hew Dalrymple renewed his intercourse with Castaños, and prepared to prosecute the war in Spain. The Spanish prisoners, about four thousand in number, were sent to Catalonia, and the British army was cantoned principally in the Alemtejo along the road to Badajos; some officers were despatched to examine the roads through Beira with a view to a movement on that line, and General Anstruther was directed to repair to the fortress of Almeida, for the purpose of regulating everything which might concern the passage of the army, if it should be found necessary to enter Spain by that route. Lord William Bentinck was also despatched to Madrid, having instructions to communicate with the Spanish generals and with the central Junta, and to arrange with them the best line of march, the mode of providing magazines, and the plan of campaign. But in the midst of these affairs, and before the garrison of Elvas arrived at Lisbon, Sir Hew Dalrymple was called home to answer for his conduct relative to the convention; the command then devolved upon Sir Harry Burrard, and he, after holding it a short time, also returned to England, there to abide the fury of the most outrageous and disgraceful public clamor that was ever excited by the falsehoods of venal political writers.

The editors of the daily press, adopting all the misrepresentations of the Portuguese minister, and concluding that the silence of government was the consequence of its dissatisfaction at the convention, broke forth with such a torrent of rabid malevolence, that all feelings of right and justice were overborne, and the voice of truth entirely stifled by their obstreperous cry. Many of the public papers were printed with mourning lines around the text which related to Portuguese affairs, all called for punishment, and some even talked of death to the guilty, before it was possible to know if any crime had been committed; the infamy of the convention was the universal subject of conversation, a general madness seemed to have seized all classes, and, like the Athenians after the sea-fight of Arginusæ, the English people, if their laws would have permitted the exploit, would have condemned their victorious generals to death.

A court was assembled at Chelsea to inquire into the transactions relating to the armistice and the definitive convention. Sir Arthur Wellesley, Sir Harry Burrard, Sir Hew Dalrymple, and the principal generals engaged at Vimiero, were called before it; a minute investigation of all the circumstances took place, and a detailed report was made, at the end of which it was stated that no further judicial measures seemed to be called for. This was not satisfactory to the government, and the members of the court were required to state, individually, whether they approved or disapproved of the armistice and convention. It then appeared, that four approved and three disapproved of the convention, and among the latter the Earl of Moira distinguished himself by a labored criticism, which, however, left the pith of the question entirely untouched. The proceedings of the board were dispassionate and impartial, but the report was not luminous; a circumstance to be regretted, because the rank and reputation of the members were sufficiently great to secure them from the revenge of party, and no set of men were ever more favorably placed for giving a severe and just rebuke to popular injustice.

Thus ended the last act of the celebrated convention of Cintra, the very name of which will always be a signal record of the ignorant and ridiculous vehemence of the public feelings; for the armistice, the negotiations, the convention itself, and the execution of its provisions, were all commenced, conducted and concluded at the distance of thirty miles from Cintra, with which place they had not the slightest connection, political, military, or local. Yet Lord Byron has gravely sung, that the convention was signed in the Marquis of Marialva's house at Cintra; and the author of the " Diary of an Invalid," improving upon the poet's discovery, detected the stains of ink spilt by Junot upon the occasion !

OBSERVATIONS.

1. General Thiebault says, that the scattered state of the French army in the beginning of August rendered its situation desperate, and that the slowness of Sir Arthur Wellesley saved it. Others again have accused the latter of rashness and temerity. Neither of these censures appears to be well founded. It is true that Junot's army was disseminated; yet, to beat an army in detail, a general must be perfectly acquainted with the country he is to act in, well informed of his adversary's movements, and rapid in his own. Now rapidity in war depends as much upon the experience of the troops as upon the energy of the chief; but the English army was raw, the staff and commissariat mere novices, the artillery scantily and badly horsed, few baggage or draft animals were to be obtained in the country, and there were only a hundred and eighty cavalry mounted. Such impediments are not to be removed in a moment, and therein lies the difference betwixt theory and practice—between criticism and execution.

2. To disembark the army without waiting for the reinforcements, was a bold yet not a rash measure. Sir Arthur Wellesley knew that the French troops were very much scattered, although he was not aware of the exact situation of each division, and, from the Bishop of Oporto's promises, he had reason to expect good assistance from the Portuguese, who would have been discouraged if he had not landed at once. Weighing these circumstances, he was justified in disembarking his troops, and the event proved that he was right; he had full time to prepare his army, his marches were methodical, and he was superior in numbers to his enemy in each battle; his plans were characterized by a due mixture of enterprise and caution, well adapted to his own force, and yet capable of being enlarged without inconvenience when the reinforcement should arrive.

3. In the action of Roriça there was a great deal to admire, and some grounds for animadversion. The movement against Laborde's first position was well conceived and executed, but the subsequent attack against the heights of Zambugeira was undoubtedly

faulty, as the march of Ferguson's and Trant's divisions would have dislodged Laborde from that strong ridge without any attack on the front. It is said that such was Sir Arthur's project, and that some mistake in the orders caused General Ferguson to alter the direction of his march from the flank to the centre. This, if true, does not excuse the error, because the commander-in-chief, being present at the attack in front, might have restrained it until Ferguson had recovered the right direction. It is more probable that Sir Arthur did not expect any very vigorous resistance—that, wishing to press the French in their retreat, he pushed on the action too fast; and Laborde, who was unquestionably no ordinary general, made the most of both time and circumstances.

4. Towards the close of the day, when the French had decidedly taken to the mountains, the line of Loison's march was in the power of the English General. If he had sent two thousand men in pursuit of Laborde, left one thousand to protect the field of battle, and with the remaining ten thousand marched against Loison, whose advanced guard could not have been far off, it is probable that the latter would have been surprised and totally defeated; at all events he could only have saved himself by a hasty retreat, which would have broken Junot's combinations and scattered his army in all directions. Sir Arthur Wellesley, however, marched to Lourinham, to cover the immediate landing of his reinforcement and stores; and this was prudent, because a southwest wind would in one night have sent half the fleet on shore in a surf unequalled for fury. Such indeed was the difficulty of a disembarkation, that a detachment from the garrison of Peniché would have sufficed to frustrate it. The existence of a French reserve, estimated by report at four thousand men, was known, its situation was unknown, and it might have been on the coast line; hence great danger to Anstruther, if he attempted a landing without being covered, greater still if he remained at sea. The reasons then for the march to Lourinham were cogent, and, perhaps, outweighed the advantages of attacking Loison; yet it seems to have been an error not to have occupied Torres Vedras on the 18th; the disembarkation of Anstruther's force would have been equally secured, while the junction of the French army, and the consequent battle of Vimiero, would have been prevented.

5. It is an agreeable task to render a just tribute of applause to the conduct of a gallant although unsuccessful enemy; and there is no danger of incurring the imputation of ostentatious liberality, in asserting that Laborde's operations were exquisite specimens of the art of war. The free and confident manner in which he felt for his enemy—the occupation of Brilos, Obidos and Roriça in succession,

by which he delayed the final moment of battle and gained time for Loison—the judgment and nice calculation with which he maintained the position of Roriça—the obstinacy with which he defended the heights of Zambugeira, were all proofs of a consummate knowledge of war, and a facility of command rarely attained.

6. Sir Arthur Wellesley estimated Laborde's numbers at six thousand men, and his estimation was corroborated by the information gained from a wounded French officer during the action. It is possible that at Alcobaça there might have been so many, but I have thought it safer to rate them at five thousand, for the following reasons:—First, it is at all times very difficult to judge of an enemy's force by the eye, and it is nearly impossible to do so correctly when he is skilfully posted, and, as in the present case, desirous of appearing stronger than he really was; secondly, the six hundred men sent on the 14th to Peniché, and three companies employed on the 16th and 17th to keep open the communication with Loison by Bombaral, Cadaval, and Segura, must be deducted; thirdly, Laborde himself, after the convention, positively denied that he had so many as six thousand.* General Thiebault indeed says that only one thousand nine hundred were present under arms; but this assertion is certainly inaccurate, and even injurious to the credit of Laborde, because it casts ridicule upon his really glorious deed of arms. It is surprising that a well-informed and able writer should disfigure an excellent work by such trifling.

7. Vimicro was merely a short combat, yet it led to important results, because Junot was unable to comprehend the advantages of his situation. Profitable lessons may however be drawn from every occurrence in war, and Vimiero is not deficient in good subjects for military speculation. To many officers the position of the British appeared weak from its extent, and dangerous from its proximity to the sea, into which the army must have been driven if defeated. The last objection is well founded, and suggests the reflection that it is unsafe to neglect the principles of the art even for a moment. The ground having been occupied merely as a temporary post, without any view to fighting a battle, the line of retreat by Lourinham was, for the sake of a trifling convenience, left uncovered a few hours. The accidental arrival of Sir Harry Burrard arrested the advance movement projected by Sir Arthur Wellesley for the 21st, and in the mean time Junot took the lead; and had he been successful upon the left, there would have been no retreat for the British army. But the extent of the position at Vimiero, although considerable for a small army, was no cause of weakness, because the line of communication from the right to the

* Sir A. Wellesley's Narrative. Court of Inquiry.

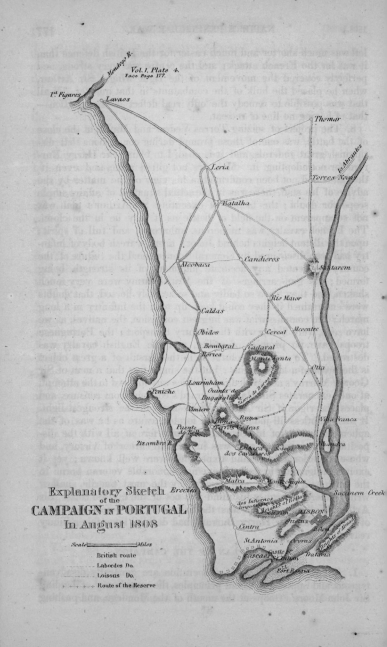

Vol. I. Plate 4.
Face Page 177.

Mondego R.
Pt Figueras
Lavaos
Thomar
Leria
To Abrantes
Torres Novas
Batalha
Candieros
Santarem
Alcobaca
Rio Major
Caldas
Obidos
Mecente
Cercal
Bombaral
Roriça
Cadaval
Monte Funta
Otta
Lourinham
Sierra de Baragueda
Quinta de
Buggabelha
Peniche
Vimiero
Villa Franca
Runa
Alhandra
Torres Vedras
Zizambra R.
Puente
do Rol
Ereira
dos Cavaleiros
Mafra
Montachique
Saccanem Creek
Erected Fort
dos Infernes
Importable Fort of Bellam
Heights of Bellam
LISBON
Cintra
St Antonia
Sacavem
Belen
Heights of Almada
Queluz
Cruz
Cascaes
Castle of
St Julian
Traffaria
Fort Bugio

Explanatory Sketch
of the
CAMPAIGN in PORTUGAL
In August 1808

Scale —————— Miles

————— British route
--------- Labordes Do.
········· Loisons Do.
–·–·–·– Route of the Reserve

left was much shorter and much easier for the British defence than it was for the French attack; and the centre was very strong, and perfectly covered the movement of the right wing. Sir Arthur, when he placed the bulk of the combatants in that quarter, did all that was possible to remedy the only real defect in his position—that of having no line of retreat.

8. The project of seizing Torres Vedras and Mafra, at the close of the battle, was one of those prompt daring conceptions that distinguish great generals, and it is absurd to blame Sir Harry Burrard for not adopting it. Men are not gifted alike, and even if the latter had not been confirmed in his view of the matter by the advice of his staff, there was in the actual situation of affairs ample scope for doubt; the facility of executing Sir Arthur's plan was not so apparent on the field of battle as it may be in the closet. The French cavalry was numerous, unharmed, and full of spirit; upon the distant heights behind Junot's army, a fresh body of infantry had been discovered by General Spencer, and the nature of the country prevented any accurate judgment of its strength being formed; the gun-carriages of the British army were very much shaken, and they were so badly and so scantily horsed, that doubts were entertained if they could keep up with the infantry in a long march; the commissariat was in great confusion, the natives, as we have seen, were flying with the country transport; the Portuguese troops gave no promise of utility, and the English cavalry was destroyed. To overcome obstacles in the pursuit of a great object is the proof of a lofty genius; but the single fact that a man of Sir George Murray's acknowledged abilities was opposed to the attempt, at once exonerates Sir Harry Burrard's conduct from censure, and places the vigor of Sir Arthur Wellesley's in the strongest light. It was doubtless ill-judged of the former, aware as he was of the ephemeral nature of his command, to interfere at all with the dispositions of a general who was in the full career of victory, and whose superior talents and experience were well known; yet it excites indignation to find a brave and honorable veteran borne to the earth as a criminal, and assailed by the most puerile, shallow writers, merely because his mind was not of the highest class. Sir Arthur Wellesley himself was the first to declare before the Court of Inquiry that Sir Harry Burrard had decided upon fair military reasons.

GENERAL PLAN OF THE CAMPAIGN.

1. Although double lines of operation are generally disadvantageous and opposed to sound principles, the expediency of landing Sir John Moore's troops at the mouth of the Mondego, and pushing

them forward to Santarem, was unquestionable; unless the probable consequences of such a movement are taken into consideration, Sir Arthur Wellesley's foresight cannot be justly appreciated.

Lisbon, situated near the end of the tongue of land lying between
the sea-coast and the Tagus, is defended to the northward by vast
mountains, that, rising in successive and nearly parallel ranges, end
abruptly in a line extending from Torres Vedras to Alhandra on
the Tagus; and as these ridges can only be passed at certain points
by an army, the intersections of the different roads form so many
strong positions. Moreover, the great mass of the Monte Junto,
which appears to lead perpendicularly on to the centre of the first
ridge, but stops short at a few miles distance, sends a rugged shoot,
called the Sierra de Barragueda, in a slanting direction towards
Torres Vedras, from which it is only divided by a deep defile.

From this conformation it results, that an army marching from
the Mondego to Lisbon must either pass behind the Monte Junto,
and follow the line of the Tagus, or keeping the western side of
that mountain, come upon the position of Torres Vedras.

If Sir Arthur Wellesley had adopted the first line of operations,
his subsistence must have been drawn by convoys from the Mondego; the enemy's numerous cavalry would then have cut his communications, and in that state he would have had to retreat, or to
force the positions of Alhandra, Alverca, and finally the heights of
Bellas, a strong position the right flank of which was covered by
the creek of Saccavem, and the left flank by the impassable Sierra
dos Infiernos. On the other line, Torres Vedras was to be carried,
and then Mafra or Montechique, following the direction of Junot's
retreat. If Mafra was forced, and it could not well be turned, a
line of march, by Cassim and Quelus, upon Lisbon, would have been
open to the victors; but that route, besides being longer than the
road through Montechique and Loures, would, while it led the
English army equally away from the fleet, have entangled it among
the fortresses of Ereceira, St. Antonio, Cascaes, St. Julian's, and
Belem. Again, supposing the position of Montechique to be
stormed, the heights of Bellas offered a third line of defence; and
lastly, the citadel and forts of Lisbon itself would have sufficed to
cover the passage of the river, and a retreat upon Elvas would
have been secure.

Thus it is certain, that difficulties of the most serious nature
awaited the English army while acting on a single line of operations,
and the double line proposed by Sir Arthur was strictly scientific.
For if Sir John Moore, disembarking at the Mondego, had marched
first to Santarem and then to Saccavem, he would have turned the

positions of Torres Vedras and Montechique; and Sir Arthur, on the other side, would have turned the heights of Bellas by the road of Quelus, and Junot's central situation could not have availed him, because the distance between the British corps would be more than a day's march, and their near approach to Lisbon would have caused an insurrection of the populace. The Duke of Abrantes must then either have abandoned that capital and fallen vigorously upon Sir John Moore, with a view to overwhelm him and gain Almeida or Elvas, or he must have concentrated his forces, and been prepared to cross the Tagus if he lost a battle in front of Lisbon. In the first case, the strength of the country afforded Moore every facility for a successful resistance, and Sir Arthur's corps would have quickly arrived upon the rear of the French. In the second case, Junot would have had to fight superior numbers, with an inveterate populace in his rear, and if, fearing the result of such an encounter, he had crossed the Tagus, and pushed for Elvas, Sir John Moore's division could likewise have crossed the river, and harassed the French in their retreat. The above reasoning being correct, it follows that to re-embark Sir John Moore's army after it had landed at the Mondego, and to bring it down to Maceira bay, was an error which, no convention intervening, might have proved fatal to the success of the campaign; and this error was rendered more important by the danger incurred from the passage, for, as the transports were not sea-worthy, the greatest part would have perished had a gale of wind come on from the south-west.*

2. Sir Arthur Wellesley's project of seizing Mafra by a rapid march on the morning of the 21st, was exceedingly bold; its successful execution would have obliged Junot to make a hurried retreat by Enxara dos Cavalleiros to Montechique, at the risk of being attacked in flank during his march; if he had moved by the longer route of Ruña and Sobral, it is scarcely to be doubted that the British army would have reached Lisbon before him. But was it possible so to deceive an enemy, inured to warfare, as to gain ten miles in a march of sixteen? was it possible to evade the vigilance of an experienced general, who, being posted only nine miles off, possessed a formidable cavalry, the efforts of which could neither be checked nor interrupted by the small escort of horse in the British camp? was it, in fine, possible to avoid a defeat, during a flank march, along a road crossed and interrupted by a river, and several deep gullies which formed the beds of mountain torrents? These are questions which naturally occur to every military man. The sticklers for a rigid adherence to system would probably decide in the negative; Sir Arthur Wellesley was, however, not only prepared

* Captain Pulteney, Malcolm's evidence. Court of Inquiry.

to try at the time, but he afterwards deliberately affirmed that, under certain circumstances of ground, an operation of that kind would succeed. To investigate such questions is the best study for an officer.

A night march is the most obvious mode of effecting such an enterprise, but not always the best in circumstances where expedition is required; great generals have usually preferred the daytime, trusting to their own skill in deceiving the enemy, while their army made a forced march to gain the object in view: thus Turenne, at Landsberg, was successful against the Archduke Leopold in broad day-light, and Cæsar in a more remarkable manner overreached Afranius and Petrieus, near Lerida. Nor were the circumstances at Vimiero unfavorable to Sir Arthur Wellesley. He might have pushed a select corps of light troops, his cavalry, the marines of the fleet, the Portuguese auxiliaries, and a few field pieces, to the entrance of the defile of Torres Vedras before daybreak, with orders to engage the French outposts briskly, and to make demonstrations as for a general attack. There is no doubt that such a movement, if skilfully conducted, would have completely occupied the enemy's attention, while the main body of the army, marching in great coats, and hiding the glitter of their arms, might have profited from the woods and hollows through which the by-road to Mafra led, and gained such a start as would have insured the success of the enterprise.

Let us, however, take a view of the other side. Let us suppose that Junot, instructed by his spies and patrols, or divining the intention of the British General, held the masking division in check with a small force, and carrying the remainder of his army by the Puente de Roll, or some other cross road, and there were several, against the flank of the English, had fallen upon the latter while in march, hemmed in, as they would be, between the sea and the mountains, and entangled among hollows and torrents. What then would have been the result? History answers, by pointing to Condé and the battle of Senef. It must, however, be confessed, that it could be no ordinary general that conceived such a project, and notwithstanding the small numbers of the opposing armies, success would have ranked Sir Arthur high among the eminent commanders of the world, if he had never performed any other exploit. "The statue of Hercules, cast by Lysippus, although only a foot high, expressed," says Pliny, "the muscles and bones of the hero more grandly than the colossal figures of other artists."

3. So many circumstances combine to sway the judgment of an officer in the field which do not afterwards appear of weight, that caution should always be the motto of those who censure the con-

duct of an unfortunate commander; nevertheless, the Duke of Abrantes' faults, during this campaign, were too glaring to be mistaken. He lingered too long at Lisbon; he was undecided in his plans; he divided his army unnecessarily; he discovered no skill on the field of battle. When the English army was landed, affairs were brought to a crisis, and Junot had only two points to consider: Could the French forces under his command defend Portugal without assistance, and if not, how were its operations to be made most available for furthering Napoleon's general plans against the Peninsula? The first point could not be ascertained until a battle with Sir Arthur had been tried; the second evidently required that Junot should keep his army concentrated, preserve the power of retreating into Spain, and endeavor to engage the British troops in the sieges of Elvas and Almeida. If the two plans had been incompatible, the last was certainly preferable to the chance of battle in a country universally hostile. But the two plans were not incompatible.

The pivot of Junot's movements was Lisbon; he had therefore to consider how he might best fall upon and overthrow the English army, without resigning the capital to the Portuguese insurgents during the operation. He could not hope to accomplish the first effectually without using the great mass of his forces, nor to avoid the last except by skilful management, and the utmost rapidity. Now the citadel and forts about Lisbon were sufficiently strong to enable a small part of the French army to control the populace, and to resist the insurgents of the Alemtejo for a few days. The Russian Admiral, although not hostile to the Portuguese, or favorable to the French, was forced, by his fear of the English, to preserve a guarded attitude, and in point of fact, did materially contribute to awe the multitude, who could not but look upon him as an enemy. The Portuguese ships of war which had been fitted out by Junot were floating fortresses requiring scarcely any garrisons, yet efficient instruments to control the city, without ceasing to be receptacles for the Spanish prisoners, and safe dépôts for powder and arms, which might otherwise have fallen into the power of the populace. Wherefore, instead of delaying so long in the capital, instead of troubling himself about the assemblage of Alcacer do Sal, instead of detaching Laborde with a weak division to cover the march of Loison, Junot should have taken the most vigorous resolutions in respect to Lisbon, the moment he heard of the English descent. He should have abandoned the left bank of the Tagus, with the exception of Palmela and the Bugio, which was necessary to the safety of his shipping; he should have seized upon the principal families of the capital, as hostages for the good behavior of the rest; he should have threatened, and been prepared, to bombard the city if refractory; then, leaving nothing more than the mere garrisons of the citadel, forts, and ships behind him, have proceeded, not to Leiria, which was too near the enemy to be a secure point of junction with Loison, but to Santarem, where both corps might have been united without danger and without fatigue. General Thomières, in the mean time, putting a small garrison in Peniché, could have watched the movement of the British General, and thus from eighteen to twenty thousand men would have been assembled at Santarem by the 13th at farthest, and from thence, one march would have brought the whole to Batalha, near which place the lot of battle might have been drawn without trembling. If it proved unfavorable to the French, the ulterior object of renewing the campaign on the frontier was in no manner compromised. The number of large boats that Lisbon can always furnish would have sufficed to transport the beaten army over the Tagus from Santarem in a few hours, especially if the stores had been embarked before Junot moved towards Batalha; and the French army, once in the Alemtejo, with a good garrison in Abrantes, could not have been followed until the forts at the mouth of the Tagus were reduced, and the fleet sheltered in the river. Thus, long before the British could have appeared in force in the Alemtejo, the fortress of Elvas would have been provisioned from the magazines collected by Loison after the battle of Evora, and the campaign could have been easily prolonged until the great French army, coming from Germany, crushed all opposition.

The above is not a theory broached after the event. That Junot would attempt something of the kind, was the data upon which the English General formed his plans, and the intercepted memoir of Colonel Vincent treated such an operation as a matter of course. Junot's threats during the negotiation prove that he was not ignorant of his own resources, but his mind was depressed, and his desponding mood was palpable to those around him; it is a curious fact, that Sattaro, the Portuguese agent, who for some purpose or other was in the British camp, told Sir Arthur Wellesley before the battle of Vimiero, that Junot would willingly evacuate Portugal upon terms.

4. When the French, being fourteen thousand in number, occupied Torres Vedras, that position was nearly impregnable; but though seventeen thousand British could scarcely have carried it by force, they might have turned it in a single march by the coast road, and Junot neither placed a detachment on that side, nor kept a vigilant watch by his patrols; hence, if Sir Arthur Wellesley's intended movement had not been arrested by orders from Burrard,

it must have succeeded, because Junot was entangled in the defiles of Torres Vedras from six o'clock in the evening of the 20th, until late in the morning of the 21st.* The two armies would thus have changed camps in the space of a few hours, without firing a shot; Junot would have lost Lisbon, and have been placed in the most ridiculous situation.

5. In the battle, the Duke of Abrantes showed great courage, but no talent. His army was inferior in numbers, yet he formed two separate attacks—an evident error, that enabled Sir Arthur to beat him in detail without difficulty. He was the less excusable because the comparatively easy nature of the ground over which the road from Torres Vedras to Lourinham led, and the manner in which the English army was heaped to the right when the position first opened to the view, plainly indicated the true line of attack. Junot should, with all his forces concentrated for one effort, have fallen in upon the left of his opponent's position; if victorious, the sea would have swallowed those who escaped his sword—if repulsed, his retreat was open, and his loss could not have been so great in a well-conducted single effort, as it was in the ill-digested, unconnected attacks that took place.

6. The rapidity with which the French soldiers rallied and recovered their order after such a severe check was admirable, but their habitual method of attacking in column cannot be praised; against the Austrians, Russians, and Prussians it may have been successful, but against the British it must always fail, because the English infantry is sufficiently firm, intelligent, and well disciplined to wait calmly in lines for the adverse masses, and sufficiently bold to close upon them with the bayonet. The column is undoubtedly excellent for all movements short of the actual charge, but as the Macedonian phalanx was unable to resist the open formation of the Roman legion, so will the close column be unequal to sustain the fire and charge of a good line, aided by artillery. The natural repugnance of men to trample on their own dead and wounded, the cries and groans of the latter, and the whistling of the cannon-shots as they tear open the ranks, produce the greatest disorder, especially in the centre of attacking columns, which, blinded by smoke, unsteadfast of footing, and bewildered by words of command coming from a multitude of officers crowded together, can neither see what is taking place, nor make any effort to advance or retreat without increasing the confusion; hence no example of courage can be useful, no moral effect can be produced by the spirit of individuals, except upon the head, which is often firm and even victorious at the moment when the rear is flying in terror. Never-

* Thiebault.

theless, well-managed columns are the very soul of military operations; in them is the victory, and in them also is safety to be found after a defeat; the secret consists in knowing when and where to extend the front.

ARMISTICE.—CONVENTION.

1. It is surprising that Junot, having regained Torres Vedras, occupied Mafra, and obtained an armistice, did not profit by the terms of the latter to prepare for crossing the Tagus and establishing the war on the frontiers. Kellermann ascertained during his negotiation, that Sir John Moore was not arrived; it was clear that until he did arrive, the position of Montechique could neither be attacked nor turned, and there was nothing in the armistice itself, nor in the war in which it had been agreed to, which rendered it dishonorable to take such an advantage. The opening thus left for Junot to gain time was Sir Arthur Wellesley's principal objection to the preliminary treaty.

2. With regard to the convention, although some of its provisions were objectionable in point of form, and others imprudently worded, yet taken as a whole it was a transaction fraught with prudence and wisdom. Let it be examined upon fair military and political grounds, let it even be supposed for the sake of argument that Sir Arthur, unimpeded by Sir Harry Burrard, had pursued his own plan, and that Junot, cut off from Lisbon and the half of his forces, had been driven up the Tagus—he was still master of flying to Almeida or Elvas, the thousand men left in Santarem would have joined him in the Alemtejo or fallen down to the capital, and what then would have been the advantages that could render the convention undesirable? The British army, exclusive of Moore's division, had neither provisions, nor means of transporting provisions for more than ten days, and the fleet was the only resource when that supply should be exhausted; but a gale from any point between south and north-west would have driven the ships away or cast them on a lee-shore. It was therefore indispensable first to secure the mouth of the Tagus, for the safety of the fleet; and this could only be done by occupying Cascaes, Bugio, and St. Julian's, the last of which would alone have required ten days, open trenches, and a battering train, which must have been dragged by men over the mountains, for the artillery horses were scarcely able to draw the field guns, and no country animals were to be found.* In the mean time, the French troops in Lisbon, upon the heights of Almada, and in the men-of-war, retiring tranquilly through the Alemtejo, would have united with Junot, or, if he had fallen back

* Proceedings of the Court of Inquiry.

upon Almeida, they could have retired upon Elvas and La Lippe. In this argument the Russians have not been considered, but whatever his secret wishes might have been, Siniavin must have surrendered his squadron in a disgraceful manner, or joined the French with his six thousand men; and it may here be observed, that even after the arrival of Sir John Moore, only twenty-five thousand British infantry were fit for duty.

Let it now be supposed that the forts were taken, the English fleet in the river, the resources of Lisbon organized, the battering guns and ammunition necessary for the siege of Elvas transported to Abrantes by water; seventy miles of land remained to traverse, and then three months of arduous operations in the sickly season, and in the most pestilent of situations, would have been the certain consequences of any attempt to reduce that fortress. Did the difficulty end there? No! Almeida remained, and in the then state of the roads of Portugal, and taking into consideration only the certain and foreseen obstacles, it is not too much to say that six months more would have been wasted before the country would have been entirely freed from the invaders; but long before that period Napoleon's eagles would have soared over Lisbon again! The conclusion is inevitable: the convention was a great and solid advantage for the allies, a blunder on the part of the French.

With the momentary exception of Junot's threat to burn Lisbon if his terms were not complied with, we look in vain for any traces of that vigor which urged the march from Alcantara. We are astonished to perceive the man, who, in the teeth of an English fleet, in contempt of fourteen thousand Portuguese troops, and regardless of a population of three hundred thousand souls, dared, with a few hundred tired grenadiers, to seize upon Lisbon, so changed in half a year, so sunk in energy, that, with twenty-five thousand good soldiers, he declined a manly effort, and resorted to a convention to save an army which was really in very little danger. But such and so variable is the human mind, a momentary slave of every attraction, yet ultimately true to self-interest. When Junot entered Portugal, power, honors, fame, even a throne was within his view; when he proposed the convention, the gorgeous apparition was gone; toil and danger were at hand, fame flitted at a distance, and he easily persuaded himself that prudence and vigor could not be yoked together. A saying attributed to Napoleon perfectly describes the convention in a few words: "I was going to send Junot before a council of war, when, fortunately, the English tried their generals, and saved me the pain of punishing an old friend!"

BOOK III.

~~~~~~~

CHAPTER I.

Comparison between the Portuguese and Spanish people—The general opinion of French weakness and Spanish strength and energy, fallacious—Contracted policy of the English Cabinet—Account of the civil and military agents employed—Many of them act without judgment—Mischievous effects thereof—Operations of the Spanish armies, after the battle of Baylen—Murcian army arrives at Madrid—Valencian army marches to the relief of Zaragoza—General Verdier raises the siege—Castaños enters Madrid—Contumacious conduct of Galluzzo—Disputes between Blake and Cuesta—Dilatory conduct of the Spaniards—Sagacious observation of Napoleon—Insurrection at Bilboa ; quelled by General Merlin—French corps approaches Zaragoza—Palafox alarmed, threatens the Council of Castile—Council of war held at Madrid—Plan of operations—Castaños unable to march from want of money—Bad conduct of the Junta of Seville—Vigorous conduct of Major Cox—Want of arms—Extravagant project to procure them.

THE convention of Cintra, followed by the establishment of a regency at Lisbon, disconcerted the plans of the Bishop and Junta of Oporto, and Portugal was restored to a state of comparative tranquillity ; for the Portuguese people, being of a simple character, when they found their country relieved from the presence of a French army, readily acknowledged the benefit derived from the convention, and refused to listen to the pernicious counsels of the factious prelate and his mischievous coadjutors. Thus terminated what may be called the convulsive struggle of the Peninsular war. Up to that period a remarkable similarity of feeling and mode of acting betrayed the common origin of the Spanish and Portuguese people ; a wild impatience of foreign aggression, extravagant pride, vain boasting, and a passionate reckless resentment, were common to both ; but there the likeness ceased, and the finer marks of national character which had been impressed upon them by their different positions in the political world, became distinctly visible.

Spain, holding, from time immemorial, a high rank among the great powers, and more often an oppressor than oppressed, haughtily rejected all advice. Unconscious of her actual weakness and ignorance, and remembering only her former dignity, she ridiculously assumed an attitude which would scarcely have suited her in the days of Charles V. ; whereas Portugal, always fearing the ambition of a powerful neighbor, and relying for safety as much upon her alliances as upon her own intrinsic strength, was from habit inclined to prudent calculation, and readily submitted to the direction of England. The turbulence of the first led to defeat and disaster; the docility and patience of the second were productive of the most beneficial results.

The difference between these nations was, however, not immediately perceptible. At the period of the convention the Portuguese were despised, while a splendid triumph was anticipated for the Spaniards. It was affirmed and believed, that from every quarter enthusiastic multitudes of the latter were pressing forward to complete the destruction of a baffled and dispirited enemy; the vigor, the courage, the unmatched spring of Spanish patriotism, was in every man's mouth; Napoleon's power and energy seemed weak in opposition. Few persons doubted the truth of such tales, and yet nothing could be more unsound, more eminently fallacious, than the generally entertained opinion of French weakness and of Spanish strength. The resources of the former were unbounded, almost untouched; those of the latter were too slender even to support the weight of victory; in Spain the whole structure of society was shaken to pieces by the violence of an effort which merely awakened the slumbering strength of France. Foresight, promptitude, arrangement, marked the proceedings of Napoleon, but with the Spaniards the counsels of prudence were punished as treason, and personal interests, everywhere springing up with incredible force, wrestled against the public good. At a distance the insurrection appeared of towering proportions and mighty strength, when, in truth, it was a fantastic object, stained with blood, and tottering from weakness. The helping hand of England alone was stretched forth for its support; all other assistance was denied, for the continental powers, although nourishing secret hopes of profit from the struggle, with calculating policy, turned coldly from the patriots' cause. The English Cabinet was indeed sanguine, and resolute to act, yet the ministers, while anticipating success in a preposterous manner, displayed little industry, and less judgment, in their preparations for the struggle; nor does it appear that the real freedom of the Peninsula was much considered in their councils. They contemplated this astonishing insurrection as a mere military opening through which Napoleon might be assailed, and they neglected, or rather feared, to look towards the great moral consequences of such a stupendous event—consequences which were, indeed, above their reach of policy: they were neither able nor willing to seize such a singularly propitious occasion for conferring a benefit upon mankind.

It is, however, certain, that this opportunity for restoring the civil strength of a long degraded people, by a direct recurrence to first principles, was such as had seldom been granted to a sinking nation. Enthusiasm was aroused without the withering curse of faction; the multitude were ready to follow whoever chose to lead; the weight of ancient authority was, by a violent external shock, thrown off, the ruling power fell from the hands of the few, and was caught by the many, without the latter having thereby incurred the odium of rebellion, or excited the malice of mortified grandeur. There was nothing to deter the cautious, for there was nothing to pull down; the foundation of the social structure was already laid bare, and all the materials were at hand for building a noble monument of human genius and virtue, the architect alone was wanting; no anxiety to ameliorate the moral or physical condition of the people in the Peninsula was evinced by the ruling men of England, and if any existed amongst those of Spain, it evaporated in puerile abstract speculations. Napoleon, indeed, offered the blessing of regeneration in exchange for submission, but in that revolting form, accompanied by the evils of war, it was rejected, and amidst the clamorous pursuit of national independence, the independence of man was trampled under foot. The mass of the Spanish nation, blinded by personal hatred, thought only of revenge; the leaders, arrogant and incapable, neither sought nor wished for any higher motive of action: without unity of design, devoid of arrangement, their policy was mean and personal, their military efforts were abortive, and a rude, unscientific warfare disclosed at once the barbarous violence of the Spanish character, and the utter decay of Spanish institutions.

After Joseph's retreat from Madrid, the insurrection of Spain may be said to have ceased; from that period it became a war between France and the Peninsula; the fate of the latter was intrusted to organized bodies of men, and as the first excitement subsided, and danger seemed to recede, all the meaner passions resumed their empire. Hence the transactions of the memorable period which intervened between the battles of Baylen and Coruña were exceedingly confused, and the history of them must necessarily partake somewhat of that confusion. The establishment of a central Supreme Junta, the caprices of the Spanish generals, and their interminable disputes, the proceedings of the French army before the arrival of the Emperor, the operations of the grand army after his arrival, and the campaign of the British auxiliary force, form so many distinct actions, connected indeed by one great catastrophe, yet each attended by a number of minor circumstances of no great historical importance taken separately, but when combined, showing the extent and complicated nature of the disease which destroyed the energy of Spain. For the advantage of clearness, therefore, it will be necessary to sacrifice chronological order; and as frequent reference must be made to the proceedings of a class of men whose interference had a decided, and in many cases a very disastrous influence upon the affairs of that period, I shall first give a brief account of the English agents, under which denomination both civil and military men were employed, yet the distinction was rather nominal than real, as, generally speaking, each person assumed the right of acting in both capacities.

The envoy, Mr. Charles Stuart, was the chief of the civil agents; the persons subordinate to him were, Mr. Hunter, Mr. Duff, and others, consuls and vice-consuls.

Mr. Stuart sailed with Sir A. Wellesley, and was left at Coruña when that officer touched there, previous to the operations in Portugal.

Mr. Hunter was stationed at Gihon in the Asturias.

Mr. Duff proceeded to Cadiz, and the others in like manner were employed at different ports. They were all empowered to distribute money, arms, succors of clothing and ammunition, and the want of system and forethought in the cabinet was palpable from the injudicious zeal of these inferior agents, each of whom conceived himself competent to direct the whole of the political and military transactions. Mr. Stuart was even put to some trouble in establishing his right to control their proceedings.

The military agents were of two classes—those sent from England by the government, and those employed by the generals abroad.

Sir Thomas Dyer, assisted by Major Roche and Captain Patrick, proceeded to the Asturias. The last officer remained at Oviedo, near the Junta of that province; Major Roche went to the headquarters of Cuesta; Sir Thomas Dyer, after collecting some information, returned to England.

Colonel Charles Doyle, having organized the Spanish prisoners at Portsmouth, sailed with them to Coruña. He was accompanied by Captain Carrol and Captain Kennedy, and during the passage a singular instance of turbulent impatience occurred; the prisoners, who had been released, armed, and clothed by England, and who had been as enthusiastic in their expressions of patriotism as the most sanguine could desire, mutinied, seized the transports, carried them into different ports of the Peninsula, disembarked, and proceeded each to his own home.

Colonel Browne was despatched to Oporto, and Major Green to Catalonia.

Those employed by the generals commanding armies were Captain Whittingham, who was placed by Sir Hew Dalrymple near General Castaños; he accompanied the head-quarters of the Andalusian army until the battle of Tudela put an end to his functions. Major Coxe, appointed also by Sir Hew Dalrymple, remained near the Junta of Seville, where his talents and prudent conduct were of great service; it would have been fortunate if all the persons employed as agents had acted with as much judgment and discretion.

All the above-named gentlemen were in full activity previous to the commencement of the campaign in Portugal; but when the convention of Cintra opened a way for operations in Spain, Sir Hew Dalrymple sent Lord William Bentinck to Madrid, that he might arrange a plan of co-operation with the Spanish generals, and transmit exact intelligence of the state of affairs. Such a mission was become indispensable. Up to the period of Lord William's arrival in Madrid, the military intelligence received was very unsatisfactory. The letters from the armies contained abundance of common-place expressions relative to the enthusiasm and patriotism visible in Spain; vast plans were said to be under consideration, some in progress of execution, and complete success was confidently predicted; but by some fatality, every project proved abortive or disastrous, without lowering the confidence of the prognosticators, or checking the mania for grand operations, which seemed to be the disease of the moment.

The English Ministers confirmed the appointment of Lord William Bentinck, and at the same time reorganized the system of the military agents, by marking out certain districts, and appointing a general officer to superintend each. Thus, Major-General Broderick was sent to Gallicia; Major-General Leith, with a large staff, proceeded to the Asturias; Major-General Sontag went to Portugal. At the same time, Sir Robert Wilson, being furnished with arms, ammunition, and clothing for organizing three or four thousand men levied by the Bishop of Oporto, took with him a large regimental staff, and a number of Portuguese refugees, and succeeded in forming a partisan corps, afterwards known as the Lusitanian legion.* Brigadier-General Decken, also a German, being first destined for Spain, was countermanded at sea and directed to Oporto, where he arrived on the 17th of August, and immediately commenced that curious intrigue which has been already mentioned in the campaign of Vimiero. The scope of General Leith's mission was wide; Biscay, Castile, Leon, and even Catalonia, were placed under his superintendence, and he appears to have had instructions

* Sir Hew Dalrymple's Papers, MS.

to prepare the way for the disembarkation of an English army on the coast of Biscay.

When Sir John Moore assumed the command of the army, he sent Colonel Graham to reside at the Spanish head-quarters on the Ebro, and directed Lord William Bentinck to remain at Madrid to forward the arrangement for commencing the campaign.   Lord William found in Mr. Stuart an able coadjutor, and in the letters of these two gentlemen, and the correspondence of Major Coxe, then at Seville, is to be found the history of the evils which at this period afflicted unhappy Spain, and ruined her noble cause.   But the power of distributing supplies, and the independent nature of their appointments, gave to the military agents immediately employed by the minister an extraordinary influence, which was very injudiciously exercised.   They forgot the real objects of their mission, and in many cases took a leading part in affairs with which it was not politic in them to have meddled at all.

Thus, Colonel Doyle having left Captain Kennedy at Coruña, and placed Captain Carrol at the head-quarters of Blake's army, repaired in person to Madrid, where he was received with marked attention, obtained the rank of a general officer in the Spanish service for himself, that of Lieutenant-Colonel for Captains Carrol and Kennedy, and from his letters it would appear that he had a large share in conducting many important measures, such as the arrangement of a general plan of operations, and the formation of a central and supreme government.   He seems to have attached himself principally to the Duke of Infantado, a young man of moderate capacity, but with a strong predilection for those pretty intrigues which constituted the policy of the Spanish court.*   Captain Whittingham likewise gained the confidence of Castaños to such a degree, that he was employed by him to inspect the different Spanish corps on the Ebro early in September, and to report upon their state of efficiency previous to entering upon the execution of the plan laid down for the campaign.†   But notwithstanding the favorable position in which these officers stood, it does not appear that either of them obtained any clear idea of the relative strength of the contending forces; their opinions, invariably and even extravgantly sanguine, were never borne out by the result.

The Spaniards were not slow to perceive the advantages of encouraging the vanity of inexperienced men who had the control of enormous supplies; and while all outward demonstrations of respect and confidence were by them lavished upon subordinate functionaries, especially upon those who had accepted of rank in their

* Sir John Moore's Correspondence, MS.
† Whittingham's Correspondence, MS.

service, the most strenuous exertions of Lord William Bentinck and Mr. Stuart were insufficient to procure the adoption of a single beneficial measure,* or even to establish the ordinary intercourse of official business. The leading Spaniards wished to obtain a medium through which to create a false impression of the state of affairs, and thus to secure supplies and succors from England, without being fettered in the application of them; the subordinate agents answered this purpose, and, satisfied with their docility, the generals were far from encouraging the residence of more than one British agent at their head-quarters. Captain Birch, an intelligent engineer officer, writing from Blake's camp, says, "General Broderick is expected here; but I have understood that the appearance of a British general at these head-quarters, to accompany the army, might give jealousy.† General Blake is not communicative, yet Captain Carrol appears to be on the best footing with him and his officers; and Captain Carrol tells me that he informs him of more than he does any of his generals." Soon after this, General Broderick did arrive, and complained, that "General Blake's reserve was such that he could only get answers to the most direct and particular questions, but by no means candid and explicit replies to general inquiries."‡

No object could be more perfectly accomplished; nothing could be more widely different than Spanish affairs, judged of by the tenor of the military agents' reports, and Spanish affairs when brought to the test of battle; yet the fault did not attach so much to the agents as to the ministers who selected them. It was difficult for inexperienced men to avoid the snare. Living with the chiefs of armies actually in the field, being in habits of daily intercourse with them, holding rank in the same service, and dependent upon their politeness for every convenience, the agent was in a manner forced to see as the general saw, and to report as he wished; a simple spy would have been far more efficacious!

Sir John Moore, perceiving the evil tendency of such a system, recalled all those officers who were under his immediate control, and strongly recommended to ministers that only one channel of communication should exist between the Spanish authorities and the British army. He was convinced of the necessity of this measure, by observing that each of the military agents considered the events passing under his own peculiar cognizance as the only occurrences of importance. Some of those officers treated Sir Hew Dalrymple and himself as persons commanding an auxiliary force

---

* Mr. Stuart's Letters, MS.   Lord W. Bentinck's ditto.
† Sir John Moore's Correspondence, MS.
‡ Letter to Mr. Stuart, MS., Sept. 13.

which was to be moved, divided, and applied at the requisition of every inferior agent, and all the military stores of the British empire as placed at their disposal. Mr. Hunter demanded English cavalry and horse artillery to act with the Spaniards in the Asturian plains, and infantry to garrison their seaport towns. Sir Thomas Dyer was convinced that the horsemen and guns should have been at Rio Seco, in Leon, and that with the aid of two thousand British cavalry and twenty pieces of artillery, the Spaniards would in six weeks have all the French troops "in a state of siege." General Leith says, "Whatever may be the plan of operations and whatever the result, I beg leave, in the strongest manner, to recommend to your consideration the great advantage of ordering all the disposable force, of horse or car artillery, mounted on horses or mules of the country, without a moment's delay, to move on Palencia, where the column or columns will receive such intelligence as may enable them to give the most effectual co-operation."* Captain Whittingham at the same period, after mentioning the wish of General Castaños that some British cavalry should join him, writes, "I cannot quit this subject without once more repeating, that the efforts of the cavalry will decide the fate of the campaign. Should it be possible for your excellency to send one thousand or fifteen hundred horse, the advantages that would result are incalculable." And while these pressing recommendations came the one from Oviedo, the other from Tudela, Colonel Doyle, writing from Madrid, thus expresses himself : " Certain it is, that if your army were here, the French would evacuate Spain before you got within a week's march of them ; indeed, even the light cavalry and two thousand light troops sent on cars, to keep up with the cavalry, to show our friends the nature of outpost duty, would, I think, decide the question."—" A respectable corps of British troops, landed in Catalonia, would so impose, that I have no doubt of the good effects." This last proposition relative to Catalonia was a favorite plan of all the leading men at Madrid ; so certain were they of success on the Ebro, that, finding no British force was likely to be granted, they withdrew eight or nine thousand men from the army near Tudela, and directed them upon Lerida.

Thus much I have thought it necessary to relate about the agents, and now quitting that subject, I shall narrate

THE OPERATIONS OF THE SPANISH ARMIES IMMEDIATELY AFTER THE BATTLE OF BAYLEN.

When that victory caused Joseph to abandon Madrid, the patriotic troops, guided by the caprice of the generals, moved in a

* Sir John Moore's Papers, MS.

variety of directions, without any fixed object in view, and without
the slightest concert; all persons seemed to imagine that the war
was at an end, and that rejoicing and triumph alone ought to occupy
the minds of good Spaniards.

The Murcian and Valencian army separated. General Llamas,
with twelve thousand infantry and a few cavalry, took the road to
Madrid, and arrived there before any of the other generals. St.
Marc, a Fleming by birth, with greater propriety, carried the Valencians to the relief of Zaragoza. On the road he joined his forces
with those of the Baron de Versage, and the united troops, amounting to sixteen thousand, entered Zaragoza on the 15th, one day
after Verdier and Lefebre had broken up the siege and retired to
Tudela, leaving their heavy guns and many stores behind them;
they were pursued by the Valencians and Aragonese, but on the
19th their cavalry turned and defeated the Spanish advanced
guard. On the 20th Lefebre abandoned Tudela, and took a position at Milagro. On the 21st, St. Marc and Versage occupied
Tudela, and the peasantry of the valleys, encouraged by the approach of a regular army, and by the successful defence of Zaragoza,
assembled on the left flank of the French, and threatened their
communications. Meanwhile Palafox gave himself up to festivity
and rejoicing, and did not begin to repair the defences of Zaragoza
until the end of the month; he also assumed supreme authority,
and in various ways discovered inordinate and foolish presumption,
decreeing, among other acts, that no Aragonese should be liable to
the punishment of death for any crime.*

The army of Andalusia was the most efficient body of men in
arms throughout Spain; it contained thirty thousand regular troops,
provided with a good train of artillery and flushed with recent
victory; yet it was constrained to remain idle by the Junta of
Seville, who detained it to secure a supremacy over the other
juntas of Andalusia, and even brought back a part to assist at an
ostentatious triumph in that city.† It was not until a full month
after the capitulation of Dupont, that Castaños made his entry into
the capital at the head of a single division of seven thousand men;
another of the same force was left at Toledo, and the rest of his
army quartered at Puerto del Rey, St. Helena, and Carolina, in the
Sierra Morena.‡

Of the Estremaduran army the infantry was at first composed
only of new levies, but it was afterwards strengthened by some
battalions of the Walloon and Royal Guards, and supplied by Sir

* Cavallero.
† Coxe's Correspondence, MSS.
‡ Whittingham's Correspondence, MSS.

Hew Dalrymple with every needful equipment. Following the terms of a treaty between the Juntas of Badajoz and Seville, the cavalry, four thousand strong, was to be given to Castaños, but, Cuesta excepted, no other general had any horsemen. This cavalry was useless in Estremadura, yet orders and entreaties, and the interference of Sir Hew Dalrymple, alike failed to make Galluzzo send it either to the capital or to Blake; nor would he, as we have seen, desist from his pretended siege of La Lippe, although it delayed the evacuation of Portugal. Meanwhile the Spanish captives, released by the convention of Cintra, were clothed, armed, and sent to Catalonia in British transports, which also carried ten thousand muskets, with ammunition, for the Catalans.*

It has been before stated that one thousand five hundred Spaniards, commanded by the Marquis of Valladeras, co-operated with the Portuguese during the campaign of Vimiero; they never penetrated beyond Guarda, and being destitute of money, were reduced to great distress, for they could not subsist where they were, nor yet march away: Sir Hew, by a timely advance of ten thousand dollars, relieved them, and Valladeras joined Blake, when, after the defeat of Rio Seco, that General had separated from Cuesta and sheltered himself from the pursuit of Bessières in the mountains behind Astorga.† Blake's reserve division had not been engaged in that battle, and the resources of the province, aided by the succors from England, were sufficient to place him again at the head of thirty thousand infantry.‡ Hence, when Bessières retired after the defeat of Baylen, Blake occupied Leon, Astorga, and the pass of Manzanal; and as he dared not enter the plains without cavalry, the Junta of Castile and Leon, then at Ponteferrada, ordered Cuesta, who had one thousand dragoons at Arevalo, to transfer them to the Gallician army. Instead of obeying, the arbitrary old man, exasperated by his defeat and his quarrel with Blake, retired to Salamanca, collected and armed ten thousand peasants, annulled the proceedings of the Junta, and menaced the members with punishment for resisting his authority as Captain-General.§ On the other hand, Blake protected them, and while the generals disputed, three thousand French cavalry, descending the Douro, scoured the plains, and raised contributions in face of both their armies.

Finally, Blake, finding the obstinacy of Cuesta invincible, quitted his cantonments early in September, and skirting the plains on the

* Sir H. Dalyrmple's Papers, MSS.
† Ibid.
‡ Doyle's Letters.
§ Mr. Stuart's Correspondence.

north-east, carried his army by forced marches to the Mantana St. Ander, a rugged district dividing Biscay from the Asturias. The Junta of the latter province had received enormous and very timely succors from England, but made no exertions answerable to the amount of assistance granted, or to the strength and importance of the district; eighteen thousand men were said to be in arms, but only ten thousand were promised to Blake, and but eight thousand joined his army.*

In Catalonia the war was conducted by both sides without much connection or dependence on the movements of the main armies, and at this period it had little influence on the general plan of campaign. Thus it appears that one month after the capitulation of Dupont, only nineteen thousand infantry, without cavalry, and those under the command of more than one general, were collected at Madrid; that only sixteen thousand men were in line upon the Ebro, and that the remainder of the Spanish armies, exclusive of that in Catalonia, computed at eleven thousand men, were many days' march from the enemy, and from each other; that the chiefs, at discord with their respective juntas, and at variance among themselves, were inactive, or, as in the case of Galluzzo, doing mischief.

These feeble and dilatory operations of the armies were partly owing to the inaptitude of the generals, but the principal causes were the unbounded vanity, arrogance, and selfishness of the local governments, among whom the Juntas of Gallicia and Seville were remarkable for their ambition. The time which should have been passed in concerting measures for pushing the victory of Baylen, was spent by them in devising schemes to insure the permanency of their own power, and the money and resources, both of England and Spain, were applied to further this pernicious object; in every part of the country a spirit of interested violence prevailed, the ardor of patriotism was chilled, and the exertions of sensible men were rendered nugatory, or served as a signal for their own destruction.

The argument to be drawn from this state of affairs is conclusive against the policy of Joseph's retreat. Without drafting a man from the garrisons of Pampeluna and St. Sebastian—without interfering with the movable columns employed on the communications of Biscay and Navarre—that monarch drew together about fifty thousand good troops, in twenty days after he had abandoned his capital. At the head of such a force, or even of two thirds of it, he might have bid defiance to the inactive, half-organized, and scattered Spanish armies; and it was so necessary to have maintained

* Capt. Carrol's Letters.

himself in Madrid, that scarcely any disproportion of numbers should have induced him to abandon it without an effort; but the disaster of Dupont had created in Joseph's mind a respect for Spanish prowess, while from his sagacious brother it only drew the following observation: " *The whole of the Spanish forces are not capable of beating twenty-five thousand French in a reasonable position.*" The error of abandoning the capital would, if the Spaniards had been capable of pursuing any general plan of action, have been fatal; but the stone of Cadmus had been cast among them, and the Juntas, turning upon one another in hate, forgot the common enemy.

Ferdinand was now again proclaimed King of Spain, and the pomp and rejoicing attendant on this event put an end to all business, except that of intrigue. Castaños assumed the title of Captain-General of Madrid—a step which seems to have been taken by him, partly to forward his being appointed generalissimo, and partly with a view to emancipate himself from the injurious control of the Seville Junta; for, although the authority of the captains-general had been superseded in most of the provinces by the juntas, it was not universally the case. He expected, and with reason, to be appointed generalissimo of the Spanish armies, but he was of an indolent disposition, and it was manifest that until a central and supreme government was established, such a salutary measure would not be adopted. In the mean time, the Council of Castile, although not generally popular with the people, and hated by the juntas, was accepted as the provisional head of the state in the capital; yet its authority was merely nominal, and the necessity of showing some front to the enemy seems to have been the only link of connection between the Spanish armies.

The evil consequences flowing from this want of unity were soon felt. Scarcely had the French quitted Madrid, when the people of Biscay prepared to rise; and such an event, prudently conducted and well supported, would have been of incalculable advantage; but the nicest arrangement and the utmost prudence were necessary to insure success—for the Biscayans had neither arms nor ammunition, the French were close to them, and the nearest Spanish force was the feeble Asturian levy. A previous junction of Blake's army with the latter was indispensable: that once effected and due preparation made, the insurrection of Biscay, protected by forty thousand regular troops and supplied from the seaboard with money and stores, would have forced the French to abandon the Ebro or to fight a battle, which Blake might have risked, provided that the Andalusian, Murcian, Valencian, and Aragonese troops, assembling about Tudela, were prepared to move at the same time against the left flank of the enemy. In every point of view it was an event pregnant with important consequences, and the impatience of the Biscayans should have been restrained rather than encouraged; yet the Duke of Infantado, Colonel Doyle, and others, at Madrid, made strenuous efforts to hasten the explosion; and the crude manner in which they conducted this serious affair is exposed in the following extracts from Colonel Doyle's despatches :

"I proposed to General Blake that he should send officers to Biscay to stir up the people there, and into the Asturias to beg that, of their 15,000 men, 8,000 might be pushed into Biscay to Bilbao, to assist the people, who were all ready and only waited for arms and ammunition, for both of which I wrote to Mr. Hunter at Gihon, and learned from him that he had sent a large supply of both, and some money to Bilbao, where already 14,000 men had enrolled themselves. The remainder of the Asturians I begged might instantly occupy the passes from Castile into the Asturias and Biscay, that is to say, from Reynosa in the direction of Bilbao." Some days after, he says, "My measures in Biscay and Asturias have perfectly succeeded; the reinforcements of arms, ammunition and men (5,000 stand of arms and ammunition in proportion), have reached Bilbao in safety, and the Asturias have taken possession of the passes I pointed out, so that we are all safe in that part of the world."

In this fancied state of security affairs remained until the 16th of August; Blake was still in the mountains of Gallicia, but the English succors arrived in the port of Bilbao, and the explosion took place. General Merlin, with three thousand grenadiers, immediately came down on the unfortunate Biscayans, Bilbao was taken, and, to use the gloomy expression of King Joseph, "the fire of insurrection was quenched with the blood of twelve hundred men." Fortunately the stores were not landed, and the vessels escaped from the river. Thus, at a blow, one of the principal resources which Blake had a right to calculate upon in his future operations was destroyed; and although the number admitted by the Spaniards to have fallen was less than the above quotation implies, the spirit of resistance was severely checked, and the evil was unmixed and deplorable. This unfortunate event, however, created little or no sensation beyond the immediate scene of the catastrophe; triumphs and rejoicings occupied the people of Madrid and Zaragoza, and it is difficult to say how long the war would have been neglected, if Palafox had not been roused by the reappearance of a French corps, which retook Tudela, and pushed on to the vicinity of Zaragoza itself.

This movement took place immediately after the expedition

against Bilbao; it was intended to suppress the insurrection of the valleys, and to clear the left flank of the French army. Palafox, thus roughly aroused, wrote intemperately to the Council of Castile, ordering that all the troops in the capital should be forwarded to the Ebro, and menacing the members personally for the delay which had already occurred.* Being a young man without any weight of character, and his remonstrances founded only upon his own danger, and not supported by any general plan or clear view of affairs, the presumptuous tone of his letters gave general offence: he chiefly aimed at Castaños, who was not under his command; and, moreover, the Junta of Seville refused to pay, or to subsist the Andalusian army, if it moved beyond the capital before a central government should be established. But the same Junta resorted to every kind of intrigue to retard, if not entirely to prevent the execution of the latter measure. It was, however, necessary to do something, and a council of all the generals commanding armies was held at Madrid on the 5th of September.† Castaños, Llamas, Cuesta, the Duke of Infantado, and some others, assembled. Blake gave his proxy to the Duke; Palafox was represented by a colonel of his own staff.‡ Cuesta proposed that a commander-in-chief should be appointed; the others were too jealous to adopt this proposal, yet they agreed to pursue the following plan of operations:

Llamas, with the Murcians, to occupy Taranzona, Agreda, and Borja. La Peña, with the two divisions of Andalusia already in the capital, to march by Soria, and take possession of Logroña and Najera. The other divisions of that army to follow in due time, and when La Peña should be established in Logroña, Llamas was to advance to Cascante, Corella, and Calahorra.

This united force was to be called the army of the centre, and once securely fixed in its positions, Palafox, under whose command St. Marc's division acted, was to push forward to Sanguessa by the left bank of the Ebro, and thus turn the enemy on the Aragon river. In the mean time it was hoped that Blake would arrive at Palencia, and form his junction with the Asturians, and Cuesta promised to march upon Burgo del Osma, to fill up the space between Blake and the army of the centre. The head of La Peña's column was to be at Soria on the 15th of September, and the Junta confidently expected that this vicious plan, in which every sound military principle was violated, and the enemy's troops considered with regard to position as a fixed immovable mass, would cause the total destruction of the French army; the only fear entertained

* Whittingham's Correspondence, MS.
† Ibid.
‡ Mr. Stuart's Letters. Parliamentary Papers.

was, that a hasty flight into France would save it from Spanish vengeance ! And Captain Whittingham, echoing the sentiments of the Spanish generals with reference to this plan, writes, " As far as my poor judgment leads me, I am satisfied that if the French persist in maintaining their present position, we shall, in less than six weeks, have a second edition of the battle of Baylen !"

But to enable La Peña and Llamas to march, pecuniary aid was requisite; there was a difficulty in raising money at Madrid, and the maritime provinces intercepted all the English supplies. In this dilemma, Colonel Doyle drew bills upon the English treasury, and upon the government at Seville, making the latter payable out of two millions of dollars just transmitted to the Junta through Mr. Duff.* It is probable that such an unprincipled body would have dishonored the bills, if, just before they were presented, Major Coxe had not remonstrated strongly upon the destitute condition of the army, and his representations, although at first haughtily and evasively received, became effectual when the Junta discovered that a plot against their lives, supposed to have been concocted at Madrid, was on the eve of execution : in fact, they had become hateful from their domineering insolence and selfishness, and the public feeling was strongly against them. Alarmed for the consequences, they sent off 200,000 dollars to Madrid, and published a manifesto, in which they inserted a letter purporting to be from themselves to Castaños, dated on the 8th, and giving him full powers to act as he judged fitting for the public good. Their objects were to pacify the people, and to save their own dignity by appearing to have acted voluntarily; but Castaños published the letter in Madrid with its true date of the 11th, and then it became manifest, that to Major Coxe's remonstrance, and not to any sense of duty, this change of conduct was due.

Doyle's bills having been negotiated, the troops in the capital were put in motion, and 40,000 fresh levies were enrolled, yet the foresight and activity of Napoleon in disarming the country had been so effectual, that only 3,200 firelocks could be procured. A curious expedient then presented itself to the imagination of the Duke of Infantado and other leading persons in Madrid : Colonel Doyle, at their desire, wrote to Sir Hew Dalrymple, in the name of the Supreme Council, to request that *the firelocks of Junot's army, and the arms of the Portuguese people*, might be forwarded to the frontier, and from thence carried by post to the capital. And this novel proposition was made at a time when England had already transmitted to Spain 160,000 muskets, a supply considerably exceeding the whole number of men organized throughout the coun-

* Sir Hew Dalrymple's Correspondence. Doyle's Letters. Coxe's do.

try. Fifty thousand of these arms had been sent to Seville, where the Junta shut them up in the arsenals, and left the armies defenceless; for to neglect or misuse real resources, and to fasten with avidity upon the most extravagant projects, is peculiarly Spanish.* No other people could have thought of asking for a neighboring nation's arms at such a conjecture. No other than Spanish rulers could have imagined the absurdity of supplying their levies, momentarily expecting to fight upon the Ebro, with the arms of a French army still unconquered in Portugal. But this project was only one among many proofs afforded at the time, that Cervantes was as profound an observer as he was a witty reprover of the extravagance of his countrymen.

CHAPTER II.

Internal political transactions—Factions in Gallicia, Asturias, Leon, and Castile— Flagitious conduct of the Junta of Seville—Mr. Stuart endeavors to establish a northern Cortes—Activity of the Council of Castile; proposes a supreme government agreeable to the public—Local Juntas become generally odious— Cortes meet at Lugo; declare for a central and supreme government—Deputies appointed—Clamors of the Gallician Junta and Bishop of Orense—Increasing influence of the Council of Castile—Underhanded proceedings of the Junta of Seville, disconcerted by the quickness of the Baily Valdez—Character of Cuesta; he denies the legality of the northern Cortes, abandons the line of military operations, returns to Segovia, arrests the Baily Valdez and other deputies from Lugo—Central and supreme government established at Aranjuez—Popular feeling in favor of the Central Junta; vain and interested proceedings of that body; its timidity, inactivity, and folly; refuses to name a generalissimo—Foreign relations—Mr. Canning leaves Mr. Stuart without any instructions for three months—Mr. Frere appointed envoy extraordinary, &c.

INTERNAL POLITICAL TRANSACTIONS.

WITH the military affairs, thus mismanaged, the civil and political transactions proceeded step by step, and in the same crooked path. Short as the period was between the first breaking forth of the insurrection, and the arrival of Mr. Stuart at Coruña, it was sufficient to create disunion of the worst kind.* The Juntas of Leon, of the Asturias, and of Gallicia, were at open discord, and those provinces were again split into parties, hating each other with as much virulence as if they had been of a hundred years' growth. The money and other supplies sent by the English ministers were considered, by the authorities into whose hands they fell, as a pe-

* Parliamentary Papers, 1810.
† Mr. Stuart's Letters. Parliamentary Papers.

culiar donation to themselves, and appropriated accordingly. The
Junta of one province would not assist another with arms when
there was a surplus, nor permit their troops to march against the
enemy beyond the precincts of the particular province in which
they were first organized.* The ruling power was in the hands
of the provincial nobility and gentry, men of narrow contracted
views, unused to business, proud, arrogant—as extreme ignorance
suddenly clothed with authority will always be—and generally disposed to employ their newly acquired power in providing for their
relations and dependants at the expense of the common cause,
which with them was quite subordinate to the local interests of
their own particular province. A jealousy of their neighbors regulated the proceedings of all the Juntas, and the means they resorted to for increasing their own, or depressing a rival government's influence, were equally characterized by absurdity and want
of principle.

The Junta of Gallicia did their utmost to isolate that province,
as if with a view to a final separation from Spain and a connection
with Portugal. They complained, as of an injury, that the army
of Estremadura had obeyed the orders of the Junta of Seville, yet
they formed an independent alliance with the Junta of Oporto, and
sent troops, as we have seen, under Valladeras, to aid the war in
Portugal ;† but, at the same time, they refused to unite in any
common measure of defence with the provinces of Castile,
until a formal treaty of alliance between them was negotiated,
signed, and ratified; and their selfishness and incapacity created
so much disgust in their own district, that plots were formed to
overthrow their authority. The Bishop of Orense and the Archbishop of St. Jago were their decided enemies. The last-named
prelate, an intriguing man, secretly endeavored to draw Blake,
with the army, into his views, and even wrote to him to desire
that he would lead the troops against the government of Coruña ;‡
the Junta having intercepted the letters, arrested the Archbishop,
yet their own stability and personal safety were still so insecure,
that many persons applied to Mr. Stuart to aid in changing the form
of government by force. The Asturians were even worse ; they
refused to assist Blake when his army was suffering, although the
stores required by him, and supplied by England, were rotting in
the harbors where they were first landed ; money also, sent out
in the Pluto frigate for the use of Leon, was detained at Gihon, and
Leon itself never raised a single soldier for the cause. Thus, only

---

* Mr. Stuart's Letters.   Parliamentary Papers.
† Mr. Stuart's Letters, MS.
‡ Ibid

two months after the first burst of the insurrection, corruption, intrigue, and faction, even to the verge of civil war, were raging in the northern parts of Spain.

Like passions being at work in the south, the same consequences followed. The Junta of Seville, still less scrupulous than that of Gallicia, made no secret of their ambitious views. They stifled all local publications, and even suppressed the public address of Florida Blanca, who, as President of the Murcian Junta, had recommended the formation of a supreme central government; they wasted their time in vain and frivolous disputes, and, neglecting every concern of real importance, sacrificed the general welfare to views of private advantage and interest. They made promotions in the army without regard to public opinion or merit; they overlaid all real patriotism, and bestowed on their own creatures places of emolument, to the patronage of which they had not a legal right; they even usurped the royal prerogative of appointing canons in the church, and their cupidity equalled their ambition. They intercepted, as I have already related, the pecuniary supplies necessary to enable the army to act, and they complained that La Mancha and Madrid, in whose defence they said "*their* troops were sacrificing themselves," did not subsist and supply the force with Castaños.* Under the pretence of forming a nucleus for disciplining thirty thousand levies as a reserve, they retained five battalions at Seville, and, having by this draft weakened the army in the field, they neglected the rest, and never raised a man. The canonries filled up by them had been vacant for several years, and the salaries attached to those offices had been appropriated to the public service; the Junta now applied the money to their own and their creatures' emolument, and at one period they appeared to have contemplated an open partition of the funds received from England among themselves. Against this flagitious Junta also, the public indignation was rife. A plot was formed to assassinate the members; the municipal authorities remonstrated with them, the Archbishop of Toledo protested against their conduct, the Junta of Granada refused to acknowledge their supremacy;† and yet so great was their arrogance, so unprincipled their ambition, that the decided and resolute opposition of Castaños alone prevented them from commencing a civil war, by marching the victorious army of Baylen against the refractory Granadans. Such was the real state of Spain, and such the patriotism of the Juntas, who were at this time filling Europe with the sound of their own praise.

In the northern parts, Mr. Stuart endeavored to reduce the chaos

* Sir H. Dalrymple's Papers. Coxe's Correspondence.
† Ibid.

of folly and wickedness to some degree of order, and to produce that unity of design and action, without which it was impossible to resist the mighty adversary that threatened the independence of the Peninsula. He judged that to abate the conflicting passions of the moment, a supreme authority, upon which the influence of Great Britain could be brought to bear with full force, was indispensable ; and that to convoke the ancient Cortes of the realm was the most certain and natural method of drawing the strength and energy of the nation into one compact mass ; but there Napoleon again interfered, for by an able distribution of the French forces, all direct communication between the northern and southern provinces was intercepted. Bessières, Dupont, and Moncey at that time occupied a circle round Madrid, and would have prevented the local governments of the north from uniting with those of the south, if they had been inclined to do so.

A union of deputies from the nearest provinces, to be called the northern Cortes, then suggested itself to Mr. Stuart as a preliminary step, which would insure the convocation of a general assembly when such a measure should become practicable ; accordingly he strenuously urged its adoption, but his efforts, at first, produced no good results.[*] It was in vain that he represented the danger of remaining in a state of anarchy, when so many violent passions were excited, and such an enemy was in the heart of the country. It was in vain that he pointed out the difficulties that the want of a supreme authority fastened on the intercourse with the British Cabinet, which could not enter into separate relations with every provincial junta. The Spaniards, finding that the supplies were not withheld, that their reputation for patriotism was not lowered in England by actions which little merited praise ; finding, in short, that the English Cabinet was weak enough to gorge their cupidity, flatter their vanity, and respect their folly, assented to all Mr. Stuart's reasoning, but forwarded none of his propositions, and continued to nourish the disorders that were destroying the common cause.

The jarring interests which agitated the northern provinces were not even subdued by the near approach of danger; the result of the battle of Rio Seco rather inflamed than allayed the violence of party feeling, and if Bessières had not been checked by the disaster of Dupont, he would have encountered few obstacles in establishing Joseph's authority in Gallicia and Old Castile. For the enthusiasm of those provinces never rose to a great pitch, and as Bessières was prepared to use address as well as force, he would have found support amongst the factions, and the reinforcements continually arriving from France would have enabled him to maintain his acquisition. The ability of the Emperor's dispositions would then have been apparent; for while Bessières held Gallicia, and Dupont hung on the southern frontier of Portugal with twenty-five thousand men, Junot could have securely concentrated his army in the neighborhood of Lisbon, and have rendered an English disembarkation on the coast nearly impracticable.

Napoleon's combinations were overturned by the disgraceful capitulation of Baylen, and when Joseph evacuated Madrid a fresh impulse was given to the spirit of the people; but, unfortunately for Spain, as a wider scope for ambition was obtained, the workings of self-interest increased, fresh parties sprung up, and new follies and greater absurdities stifled the virtue of the country, and produced irremediable confusion, ending in ruin. The fact of Dupont's capitulation was made known to the Council of Castile before King Joseph was informed of it, and the Council, foreseeing all the consequences of such an event, immediately refused, as I have already related, to promulgate officially his accession to the throne. The King permitted this act of disobedience to pass without much notice, for he was naturally averse to violence, and neither he nor his brother Napoleon did at any period of the contest for Spain constrain a Spaniard to accept or retain office under the intrusive government.* Joseph went further. Before he abandoned Madrid, he released his ministers from their voluntary oath of allegiance to himself, leaving them free to choose their party once more. Don Pedro Cevallos and the Marquis of Pinuelo seized the occasion to change with, what appeared to them, changing fortune; the five others remained steadfast, preferring an ameliorated government, under a foreign prince, to what they believed to be a hopeless struggle, but which, if successful, they knew must end in a degrading native despotism; perhaps, also, a little swayed by their dislike to England, and by the impossibility of obtaining that influence among their countrymen, which, under other circumstances, their talents and characters would have insured.

The boldness of the Council of Castile was not publicly chastised by the intruding monarch, yet secretly he punished the members by a dexterous stroke of policy. General Grouchy wrote to Castaños, saying, that as circumstances required the presence of the French troops in another quarter, he invited the Spanish General to take immediate possession of Madrid, for the preservation of public tranquillity. This was construed to mean the entire evacuation of Spain, and a report so congenial to the vanity and indolence of the Spaniards was greedily received; it contributed to the sub-

* Azanza and O'Farril, Memoirs.

sequent supineness of the nation in preparing for its defence, and
Joseph, by appealing to Castaños, and affecting to treat the Council
of Castile as a body who had lost all influence with the nation, gave
a handle to its enemies, which the latter failed not to lay hold of.
The Juntas dreaded that the influence of the Council would destroy
their own. That of Gallicia would not even communicate with
them, but affirmed that, individually, the members were attached
to the French, and that, collectively, they had been the most active
instrument of the usurper's government. The Junta of Seville
endeavored not only to destroy the authority of the existing members, but to annul the body as an acknowledged tribunal of the
state.* This proscribed Council, however, was not wanting to itself:
the individuals composing it did not hesitate to seize the reins of
government the moment the French had departed; and the prudence with which they preserved tranquillity in the capital, preventing all re-action, while it proves that they were not without
merit, forms a striking contrast to the conduct of the provincial
Juntas, under whose savage sway every kind of excess was committed, and even encouraged.

Aware of the hostility they had to encounter, the members of the
Council lost no time in forming a party to support themselves. Don
Arias Mon y Velarde, dean or president for the time being, wrote
a circular letter to the local Juntas, pointing out the necessity of
establishing a central and supreme power, and proposing that deputies from each province, or nation, as they were sometimes called,
should repair to Madrid, and there concert with the Council the best
mode of carrying such a measure into effect. If this proposal had
been adopted, all power would inevitably have fallen into the hands
of the proposers. Confessedly the first public body in the state,
and well acquainted with the forms of business, the Council must
necessarily have had a preponderating influence in the assembly of
delegates; and it appeared so reasonable that it should take the
lead, when an efficient authority was required to direct the violence
of the people in a useful channel, before the moment of safety was
passed, that all the Juntas trembled at the prospect of losing their
misused power. The minor ones submitted, and agreed to send
deputies; the stronger and more ambitious felt that subtlety would
avail more than open opposition to the project.

The Council followed up this blow by the publication of a manifesto, containing an accurate detail of the events of the revolution,
defending the part taken by its members, and claiming a renewal
of the confidence formerly reposed in them by the nation. This important state paper was so ably written, that a large party, espe-

* Sir Hew Dalrymple's Papers. Coxe's Correspondence.

cially at Valladolid, was immediately formed in favor of its authors, and the Junta of Seville were so sensible of the increasing influence of the Council, that they intercepted a copy of this manifesto, addressed to Sir Hew Dalrymple, and strictly suppressed all writings favorable to the formation of a supreme central authority, nothing they dreaded more.* But it was no longer possible to resist the current, which had set strongly in favor of such a measure; the Juntas, however they might oppose its progress, could not openly deny the propriety of it, and in every province, individuals of talent and consideration called for a change in the Hydra polity which oppressed the country, and was inefficient against the enemy.† Every British functionary, civil or military, in communication with the Spaniards, also urged the necessity of concentrating the executive power.

All the provincial Juntas were become universally odious;‡ some of the generals alone, who had suddenly risen to command under their rule, were favorable to them. Palafox was independent, as a captain-general, whose power was confirmed by success; Castaños openly declared that he would no longer serve under their control; Cuesta was prepared to put them down by force, and to re-establish the royal audienzas and the authority of the captains-general according to the old practice. In this state of affairs, the retreat of Bessières' army having freed the communication with the southern parts, removed all excuse for procrastination, and the Juntas of Gallicia, Castile, Leon, and the Asturias, giving way to the unceasing remonstrances of Mr. Stuart, at his instance agreed to meet in cortes, at Lugo; Gallicia, however, first insisted upon a formal ratification of that treaty with Castile which has been already mentioned.

When the moment of assembling arrived, the Asturians, without assigning any reason, refused to fulfil the engagement they had entered into, and the three remaining Juntas held the session without them. The Bishop of Orense, and the Junta of Gallicia, were prepared to assert the supremacy of that province over the others. But the Baily Valdez of Castile, an able and disinterested man, being chosen president of the convocation, proposed on the first day of assembly, that deputies should be appointed to represent the three provinces in a Supreme Junta, to be assembled in some central place, for the purpose of convoking the ancient Cortes of the whole kingdom, according to the old forms, and of settling the administration of the interior, and the future succession to the

---

* Mr. Stuart's Correspondence.   Coxe's Correspondence.
† Mr. Stuart's Correspondence.
‡ Ibid.

throne. This proposition was immediately carried by the superior number of the Castilians and Leonese, although the Bishop of Orense protested against it, and the Gallician members strongly opposed an arrangement by which their province was placed on the same footing as others; a glaring injustice, they urged, when the numbers of the Gallician army were taken into consideration, for the local feeling of ambition was uppermost, and the general cause disregarded. The other party answered, with great force, that the Gallician army was paid, armed, and clothed by England, and fed by Castile and Leon.

Meanwhile the influence of the Council of Castile greatly increased, and the Junta of Seville, quickened by fear, took the lead in directing what they could not prevent;* the convocation of the Cortes they knew would be fatal to their own existence. Wherefore, in a public letter, addressed to the Junta of Gallicia, dated one day previous to the circular of Don Arias Mon, but evidently written after the receipt of the latter, they opposed the assembling of the Cortes, on the ground that it was "the prerogative of the King to convoke that body; and if it was called together by any other authority, the provinces would not obey;" "there would be no unanimity." The futility of this argument is apparent; the question was not one of form, but of expediency. If the nation was in favor of such a step, and after facts proved that the people were not opposed to it, the same necessity which constituted the right of the Junta to declare war against the French, another prerogative of the monarch, would have sufficed to legalize the convocation of the national assembly. But their sole object was to preserve their own power. They maintained that the juntas, being chosen by the nation, were the only legitimate depositaries of authority, that to members of their own bodies only could any of that authority be delegated; then adopting the suggestion contained in the letter of Arias Mon, they proposed that two deputies from each supreme junta should repair, not to Madrid, but to Ciudad Real, or Almagro, and at the moment of meeting be in fact constituted governors-general of the kingdom, and as such obeyed; nevertheless, the local governments were, with due subordination to the Central Junta, to retain and exercise in their own provinces all the authority with which they had already invested themselves. Thus they had only to choose subservient deputies, and their power would be more firmly fixed than before; and this arrangement would, doubtless, have been adopted by the Junta of Gallicia, had not the rapidity with which Valdez carried his proposition prevented that cause of discord from being added to

* Mr. Stuart's Correspondence.

the numerous disputes which already distracted the northern provinces.

Mr. Stuart proceeded to Madrid, and wherever he passed found the same violence of local party feeling, the same disgust at the conduct of the oligarchical governments. Pride, vanity, corruption, and improvidence were everywhere obtrusively visible. The dispute between Blake and Cuesta, which was raging at the period of the battle of Rio Seco, a period when division was most hurtful to the military operations, was now allayed between the generals; yet their political partisans waged war with more bitterness than ever, as if with the intent to do the greatest possible mischief, by continuing the feud among the civil branches of the government, when union was most desirable in that quarter. The seeds of division had taken deep root.* On the one side was the Bailey Valdez, deputy to the Supreme Junta; on the other Cuesta, a man not to be offended with impunity when he had power to punish, for he was haughty and incredibly obstinate. He had been President of the Council of Castile, and he was Captain-General of Castile and Leon when the insurrection first broke out; but disliking all revolutionary movements, although as inimical to a foreign domination as any of his countrymen, he endeavored to repress the public effervescence, and to maintain the tranquillity of the country at the risk of losing his life as a traitor.

Cuesta was an honest man, insomuch as the Spanish and French interests being put in competition, he would aid the former; yet, between his country's cause and his own passions, he was not honest. He disliked, and with reason, the sway of the local juntas, and, with consistency of opinion, wished to preserve the authority of the captains-general and the royal audienzas, both of which had been overturned by the establishment of those petty governments. But, sullen and ferocious in his temper, he supported his opinion with an authority and severity which had no guide save his own will; and he was prepared, if an opportunity offered, to exercise military influence over the supreme, as well as over the subordinate juntas. He had himself appointed one for Leon and Castile, as a sort of council, subordinate to the authority of the captain-general; yet, after the battle of Rio Seco, the members fled to Ponteferrada, assumed the supreme authority, and, putting themselves under the protection of his enemy Blake, disregarded Cuesta's orders, and commanded him, their superior, to deliver up his cavalry to the former General. Upon this he annulled all their proceedings at Ponteferrada, and now asserting that the election of Valdez and his colleagues was void, as being contrary to the existing laws, directed

* Mr. Stuart's Correspondence.

new juntas to be assembled in a manner- more conformable to existing usages, and a fresh election to be made.

His mandates were disregarded ; Valdez and the other deputies proceeded in defiance of them towards the place appointed for the assembly of the central and supreme government. Cuesta, in return, without hesitation, abandoned the operations of the campaign, which, in the council of war held at Madrid, he had promised to aid, and falling back to Segovia with twelve thousand men, seized the deputies, and shut up Valdez a close prisoner in the tower of that place, declaring his intention to try him by a military tribunal for disobedience. And such was the disorder of the times, that he was not without plausible arguments to justify this act of stubborn violence, for the original election of members to form the Junta of Castile and Leon had been anything but legal ; several districts had been omitted altogether in the representations of those kingdoms, many deputies had been chosen by the city of Leon alone, and Valdez was named president, although neither a native nor a proprietor, and for those reasons ineligible to be a deputy at all : the kingdom of Leon also had appointed representatives for those districts in Castile which were under the domination of the French, and when the enemy retired, the Castilians in vain demanded a more equitable arrangement.

However, amidst all this confusion and violence, the plan of uniting to form a central government gained ground all over the kingdom. Seville, Catalonia, Aragon, Murcia, Valencia, and Asturias appointed their deputies, and although fresh disputes relative to the place of assembly arose, after some time it was agreed to meet at Aranjuez. This royal residence was chosen contrary to the wishes of many, and notably against the opinion of Jovellanos, an eloquent person, and of great reputation for integrity, but of a pertinacious temper, unsuitable to the times : he urged, that the capital was the meetest spot, and he was answered, that the turbulent disposition of the inhabitants of Madrid would impede the formation of a government, and that the same objection would exist against the choice of any other large town. It is extraordinary that such an argument should be held in Spain at a moment when the people were, in all the official and public papers, represented as perfectly enthusiastic and united in one common sacred pursuit, and in the British Parliament were denominated the "universal Spanish nation !"

To seek thus for protection in a corner, instead of manfully and confidently identifying themselves with the people, and courting publicity, augured ill for the intentions of the deputies, nor was the augury belied by the event. The Junta of Seville, who had so

bitterly reviled the Council of Castile, for having partially submitted to the usurper, had, notwithstanding, chosen for their own
deputies Don Vincent Hore, a known creature of the Prince of
Peace, and the Count de Tilly Guzman, who was under the stigma
of a judical sentence for robbery.* Hore declined the appointment, but Tilly, braving the public disgust, repaired to Aranjuez,
and his place as resident with the head-quarters of the Andalusian
army was filled up by Miñiano, another member of the Junta, who
received an enormous salary for performing the mischievous duties
of that office. The instructions given by the different provinces to
the deputies were to confine their deliberations and votes to such
subjects as they should, from time to time, receive directions from
their constituents to treat of, and Seville again took the lead in this
fraudulent policy; and when public indignation, and the remonstrances of some right-minded persons, obliged the Juntas of that
town and of Valencia to rescind these instructions, both substituted
secret orders of the same tenor. In short, the greater part of the
deputies were the mere tools of the Juntas, agents watching over
the interests of their employers, and, conscious of demerit, anxious
to hide themselves from the just indignation of the public until they
had consolidated their power; hence the dislike to large towns, and
the intrigues for fixing the government at Aranjuez. Count Florida
Blanca, a man in the last stage of decrepitude, was chosen first
president in rotation for three months, and all idea of forming an
independent executive was abandoned; for when Jovellanos proposed
to establish a regency selected from their own body, his plan was
rejected on the ground that the members were not authorized to
delegate their powers even to one another: it was palpable that the
Juntas had merely appeared to comply with the public wish for a
central government, but were determined not to part with one iota
of their own real power.

The first act of authority executed by the assembly, was a necessary assertion of its own dignity, which had been violated in the
case of Valdez. Cuesta, who was personally unpopular, and feared
by the central, as well as by the provincial Juntas, was summoned
to release his captive, and to repair to Aranjuez, that cognizance
might be taken of his proceedings; he was at the same time
denounced by the Juntas of Castile and Leon as a traitor, and
exposed to great danger of popular commotion. At first, he
haughtily repelled the interference of Castaños and Florida Blanca,
yet finally he was forced to bend, and after a sharp correspondence
with Mr. Stuart, whose influence was usefully employed to strengthen
the central government, he released his prisoner, and quitting the

* Coxe's Correspondence.

command of the army, appeared at Aranjuez.* No formal proceedings were had upon the case, but after much mutual recrimination, Valdez was admitted to the exercise of his functions, and the old General was detained at the seat of government, a kind of state prisoner at large, until, for the misfortune of his country, he was, by subsequent events, once more placed at the head of an army. About this time Lord William Bentinck joined Mr. Stuart at Madrid. Perfectly coinciding in opinions, they labored earnestly to give a favorable turn to affairs, by directing the attention of the Central Junta to the necessity of military preparations, and active exertion for defence; but the picture of discord, folly, and improvidence exhibited in the provinces, was here displayed in more glaring colors. The lesser tribunals being called upon to acknowledge the authority of the assembled deputies, readily obeyed, and the Council of Castile, reluctant to submit, yet too weak to resist, endeavored to make terms, but was forced to an unconditional submission. A good management of the revenue, a single chief for the army, and, above all, the total suppression of the provincial juntas, were the three next objects of public anxiety.† With respect to the army, no doubt was at first entertained that Castaños would be appointed commander-in-chief; his services entitled him to the office, and his general moderation and conciliating manners fitted him for it at a time when so much jealousy was to be soothed, and so many interests to be reconciled. The past expenditure of the money received from England was also a subject of great importance, and it was loudly required that an account of its disbursement should be demanded of the local juntas, and a surrender of the residue instantly enforced.

These just expectations lasted but a short time. Scarcely were the deputies assembled, when every prospect of a vigorous administration was blasted.‡ Dividing themselves into sections, answering in number to the departments of state under the old King, they appointed a secretary not chosen from their own body to each, and declared all and every one of these sections supreme and independent, having equal authority.

Florida Blanca informed Mr. Stuart and Lord William Bentinck that Castaños would be named generalissimo, and the two last named were even directed to confer upon the plan of campaign for the British troops, then marching from Portugal to the assistance of the Spaniards. The necessity of having a single chief at the head of the armies was imperious, and acknowledged by every individual,

---

* Mr. Stuart's Correspondence. Colonel Graham's ditto.
† Mr. Stuart's Correspondence.
‡ Ibid.

military or civil; yet such was the force of jealousy, and so stubborn were the tools of the different juntas, that in despite of the exertions of Mr. Stuart and Lord William Bentinck, and the influence of the British Cabinet, the generals were all confirmed in their separate and independent commands. The old and miserable system of the Dutch deputies in Marlborough's time, and of the commissaries of the Convention during the French revolution, was partially revived; and the English government were totally disregarded, at a time when it had supplied Spain with two hundred thousand muskets, clothing, ammunition of all kinds, in proportion, and sixteen millions of dollars.* Such ample succors, if rightly managed, ought to have secured unlimited influence; but as the benefits came through one set of persons, and the demands through another, the first were taken as of right, the last unheeded, and thus the resources of Great Britain were wasted without materially improving the condition of Spain. The armies were destitute, the central government was without credit, and notwithstanding the ample subsidies, had contracted a large debt; yet with an insolence of tone appertaining rather to conquerors dictating terms, than to grateful allies demanding further assistance, they required from England an instant gift of ten millions of dollars, and stores to an amount that would have sufficed a well-governed army for many years.

The provisional juntas were still permitted to retain their power within their own districts, and the greatest timidity marked all the proceedings of the central government in relation to those obnoxious bodies. Attentive, however, to their own interests, the members of the Supreme Junta decreed, 1st, that their persons should be inviolable; 2d, that the president should have the title of Highness, with a salary of 25,000 crowns a year; 3d, that each of the deputies, taking the title of Excellency, should have a yearly salary of 5000 crowns; lastly, that the collective body should be addressed by the title of Majesty.† Thinking that they were then sufficiently confirmed in power to venture upon a public entry into Madrid, they made preparations to insure a favorable reception from the populace; that is, they resolved to declare a general amnesty, to lower the duties on tobacco, and to fling large sums among the people during the procession; and in the midst of all this pomp and vanity, the presence of the enemy on the soil was scarcely remembered, and the details of business were totally neglected.‡ This last was a prominent evil, which extended to the lowest branches

* Mr. Canning's Instructions to Mr. Duff, MS.
† Mr. Stuart's Correspondence. Lord W. Bentinck's ditto.
‡ Lord W. Bentinck's Correspondence.

of administration. Self-interest, indeed, produced abundance of activity, but every department, almost every man, seemed struck with torpor when the public welfare was at stake—and, withal, an astonishing presumption was common to the highest and the lowest.

To supply the place of a generalissimo, a council or board of general officers was projected, on whose reports the Junta proposed to regulate the military operations. Castaños was destined to be president, but some difficulty arising relative to the appointment of the other members, the execution of the plan was deferred, with the characteristic remark, " that when the enemy was driven across the frontier, Castaños would have leisure to take his seat."* The idea of a defeat, the possibility of failure, never entered their minds; the government, evincing neither apprehension, nor activity, nor foresight, were contented if the people believed the daily falsehoods they promulgated relative to the enemy; and the people, equally presumptuous, were content to be so deceived: in fine, all the symptoms of a ruined cause were already visible to discerning eyes. The armies neglected even to nakedness ; the soldiers' constancy under privations cruelly abused; disunion, cupidity, incapacity, in the higher orders; the patriotic ardor visibly abating among the lower classes; the rulers grasping, improvident, boasting; the enemy powerful, the people insubordinate, the fighting men without arms or bread ; as a whole, and in all its parts, the government unfitted for its task; the system, cumbrous and ostentatious, was, to use the comprehensive words of Mr. Stuart, " neither calculated to inspire courage nor to increase enthusiasm."

The truth of this picture will be recognized by men who are yet living, and whose exertions were as incessant as unavailing to remedy those evils at the time; it will be recognized by the friends of a great man, who fell a victim to the folly and base intrigues of the day; it will be recognized by that general and army who, winning their own unaided way through Spain, found that to trust Spaniards in war was to lean against a broken reed. To others it may appear exaggerated, for without having seen, it is difficult to believe the extent of a disorder that paralyzed the enthusiasm of a whole people.

EXTERNAL POLITICAL RELATIONS OF SPAIN.

At first these were of necessity confined to England, Sicily, and Portugal; the rest of the Old World was either subject to Bonaparte or directly under his influence, but in the New World it was different. The Brazils, after the emigration of the royal family of

* Lord W. Bentinck's Correspondence.

Braganza, became important under every point of view, and relations were established between the Junta and that court, that afterwards, under the Cortes, created considerable interest, and threatened serious embarrassments to the operations of the Duke of Wellington. The ultra-marine possessions of Spain were also, of course, a matter of great anxiety to both sides, and Napoleon's activity balanced the natural preponderance of the mother country. The slowness of the local juntas, or rather their want of capacity to conduct such an affair, gave the enemy a great advantage, and it was only owing to the exertions of Mr. Stuart in the north, and of Sir Hew Dalrymple and Lord Collingwood in the south, that, after the insurrection broke out, vessels were despatched to South America to confirm the colonists in their adherence to Spain, and to arrange the mode of securing the resources of those great possessions for the parent state.* The hold which Spain retained over her colonies was, however, very slight; her harsh restrictive system had long before weakened the attachment of the South Americans, and the expedition of Miranda, although unsuccessful, had kindled a fire which could not be extinguished; it was apparent to all able statesmen, that Spain must relinquish her arbitrary mode of governing, or relinquish the colonies altogether; the insurrection at home only rendered this more certain. Every argument, every public manifesto put forth in Europe, to animate the Spaniards against foreign aggression, told against them in America; yet for a time the latter transmitted the produce of the mines, and many of the natives served in the Spanish armies.

Napoleon, notwithstanding his activity, and the offers which he made of the viceroyalty of Mexico to Cuesta, Castaños, Blake, and probably to others residing in that country, failed to create a French party of any consequence; for the Americans were unwilling to plunge into civil strife for a less object than their own independence. The arrogance and injustice of Old Spain, however, increased, rather than diminished, under the sway of the insurrectional government; and at last, as it is well known, a general rebellion of the South American States established the independence of the fairest portion of the globe, and proved how little the abstract love of freedom influenced the resistance of the old country to Napoleon.

The Spanish intercourse with the English court, which had been hitherto carried on through the medium of the deputies who first arrived in London to claim assistance, was now placed upon a regular footing. The deputies themselves, at the desire of Mr. Canning, were recalled, Admiral Apodaca was appointed Minister Plenipotentiary at St. James's, and Mr. John Hookham Frere was accred-

* Mr. Stuart's Correspondence, MS.   Sir Hew Dalrymple.

ited, with the same diplomatic rank, near the Central Junta. Mr. Stuart, whose knowledge of the state of the country, whose acquaintance with the character of the leading persons, and whose able and energetic exertions had so much contributed to the formation of a central government, was superseded by this injudicious appointment; and thus the great political machine, with every wheel in violent action, was, at the most critical moment, left without any controlling power or guiding influence. For Mr. Stuart, who, on his own responsibility, had quitted Coruña, and repaired to Madrid, and had remitted the most exact and important information of what was passing, remained for three months without receiving a single line from Mr. Canning, approving or disapproving of his proceedings, or giving him instructions how to act at this important crisis: a strange remissness, indicating the bewildered state of the ministers, who slowly and with difficulty followed, when they should have been prepared to lead. Their tardy, abortive measures demonstrated how wide the space between a sophist and a statesman, and how dangerous to a nation is that public feeling, which, insatiable of words, disregards the actions of men, esteeming more the interested eloquence and wit of an orator like Demades, than the simple integrity, sound judgment, and great exploits of a general like Phocion.

Such were the preparations made by Spain, in September and October, to meet the exigencies of a period replete with danger and difficulty. It would be instructive to contrast the exertions of the "enthusiastic" Spaniards during these three months of their insurrection, with the efforts of "discontented France" in the hundred days of Napoleon's second reign. The Juntas were, however, not devoid of ambition, for before the battle of Baylen, that of Seville was occupied with a project of annexing the Algarves to Spain, and the treaty of Fontainebleau was far from being considered as a dead letter

CHAPTER III.

Political position of Napoleon; he resolves to crush the Spaniards; his energy
and activity; marches his armies from every part of Europe towards Spain;
his oration to his soldiers—Conference at Erfurth—Negotiations for peace—
Petulant conduct of Mr. Canning—160,000 conscripts enrolled in France—
Power of that country—Napoleon's speech to the Senate—He repairs to Bayonne—Remissness of the English Cabinet—Sir John Moore appointed to lead
an army into Spain; sends his artillery by the Madrid road, and marches himself by Almeida—the Central Junta impatient for the arrival of the English
army—Sir David Baird arrives at Coruña; is refused permission to disembark
his troops—Mr. Frere and the Marquis of Romana arrive at Coruña; account of
the latter's escape from the Danish Isles—Central Junta resolved not to appoint
a generalissimo—Gloomy aspect of affairs.

NAPOLEON, surprised and chagrined at the disgrace which, for
the first time, his armies had sustained, was yet nothing dismayed
by a resistance which he had early contemplated as not improba-
ble.* With a piercing glance he had observed the efforts of Spain,
calculated the power of foreign influence in keeping alive the spirit
of resistance, and assigning a just value to the succors which England could afford, foresaw the danger which might accrue, if he
suffered an insurrection of peasants, which had already dishonored
the glory of his arms, to attain the consistency of regular government, to league with powerful nations, and to become disciplined
troops. To defeat the raw levies which the Spaniards had hitherto opposed to his soldiers was an easy matter, but it was necessary to crush them to atoms, that a dread of his invincible power
might still pervade the world, and the secret influence of his genius
remain unabated. The constitution of Bayonne would, he was
aware, weigh heavy in the scale against those chaotic governments,
neither monarchical, nor popular, nor aristocratic, nor federal, which
the Spanish revolution was throwing up; but before the benefit of
that could be felt by the many, before he could draw any advantages from his moral resources, it was necessary to develop all his
military strength.

The moment was critical and dangerous. He was surrounded
by enemies whose pride he had wounded, but whose means of
offence he had not destroyed; if he bent his forces against the
Peninsula, England might again excite the continent to arms, and
Russia and Austria, once more banding together, might raise Prussia and renew the eternal coalitions. The designs of Austria, although covered by the usual artifices of that cunning, rapacious
court, were not so hidden but that, earlier or later, a war with her

* Letter to Murat. Las Casas.

was to be expected as a certain event, and the inhabitants of Prussia, subdued and oppressed, could not be supposed tranquil. The secret societies that, under the name of Tugenbunde, Gymnasiasts, and other denominations, have since been persecuted by those who were then glad to avail themselves of such assistance, were just beginning to disclose their force and plans.* A Baron de Nostiz, Stein the Prussian Councillor of State, Generals Sharnhost and Gneizenau, and Colonel Schill, appear to have been the principal contrivers and patrons of these societies, so characteristic of Germans, who, regular and plodding even to a proverb in their actions, possess the most extravagant imaginations of any people on the face of the earth. But whatever the ulterior views of these associations may have been, at this period they were universally inimical to the French; their intent was to drive the latter over the Rhine, and they were a source of peril to the Emperor, the more to be feared, as the extent of their influence could not be immediately ascertained. Russia, little injured by her losses, was more powerful perhaps from her defeats, because more enlightened as to the cause of them. Napoleon felt that it would tax all his means to repel the hostility of such a great empire, and that, consequently, his Spanish operations must be confined in a manner unsuitable to the fame of his arms. With a long-sighted policy, he had, however, prepared the means of obviating this danger, by what has been called the conference at Erfurth, whither he now repaired to meet the Czar, confiding in the resources of his genius for securing the friendship of that monarch.

At this period, it may be truly said, that Napoleon supported the weight of the world; every movement of his produced a political convulsion; yet so sure, so confident was he of his intellectual superiority, that he sought but to gain one step, and doubted not to overcome all resistance, and preserve his ascendency; time was to him victory—if he gained the one, the other followed: hence, sudden and prompt in execution, he made one of those gigantic efforts which have stamped this age with the greatness of antiquity. His armies were scattered over Europe; in Italy, in Dalmatia, on the Rhine, the Danube, the Elbe, in Prussia, Denmark, Poland, his legions were to be found; over that vast extent, above five hundred thousand disciplined men maintained the supremacy of France. From those bands he drew the Imperial Guards, the select soldiers of the warlike nation he governed, the terror of the other continental troops; these, and the veterans of Jena, of Austerlitz, of Friedland, reduced in number, but of confirmed hardihood, were marched towards Spain; a host of cavalry, unequalled for enterprise and

* Baron Fain's Campaign, 1813.

knowledge of war, were also directed against that devoted land, and a long train of gallant soldiers followed, until two hundred thousand men, accustomed to battle, had penetrated the gloomy fastnesses of the western Pyrenees, while forty thousand of inferior reputation, drawn from the interior of France, from Naples, from Tuscany, and from Piedmont, assembled on the eastern ridges of those gigantic hills. The march of this multitude was incessant, and as the troops passed the capital, Napoleon, neglectful of nothing which could excite their courage and swell their military pride, addressed to them one of his nervous orations. In the tranquillity of peace it may seem inflated, but on the eve of battle it is thus a general should speak.

"Soldiers! after triumphing on the banks of the Vistula and the Danube, with rapid steps you have passed through Germany. This day, without a moment of repose, I command you to traverse France. Soldiers! I have need of you! The hideous presence of the leopard contaminates the peninsula of Spain and Portugal. In terror he must fly before you. Let us bear our triumphal eagles to the Pillars of Hercules! there also we have injuries to avenge. Soldiers! you have surpassed the renown of modern armies, but have you yet equalled the glory of those Romans who, in one and the same campaign, were victorious upon the Rhine and the Euphrates, in Illyria and upon the Tagus? A long peace, a lasting prosperity, shall be the reward of your labors; but a real Frenchman could not, ought not to rest until the seas are free and open to all. Soldiers! all that you have done, all that you will do, for the happiness of the French people, and for my glory, shall be eternal in my heart!"

Thus saying, he sent his army towards the frontiers of Spain, and himself hastened to meet the Emperor Alexander at Erfurth. Their conference, conducted upon the footing of intimate friendship, produced a treaty of alliance offensive and defensive, and the fate of Spain was by the one, with calm indifference, abandoned to the injustice of the other; but the accession of strength which this treaty, and the manifest personal partiality of Alexander, gave to the French Emperor, inspired him, perhaps, with the idea that the English Cabinet would, if a fair occasion offered, gladly enter into negotiations for a general peace.

The two Emperors wrote a joint letter to the King of England. "The circumstances of Europe had," they said, "brought them together; their first thought was to yield to the wish and the wants of every people, and to seek in a speedy pacification the most efficacious remedy for the miseries which oppressed all nations. The long and bloody war which had torn the continent was at an end, without the possibility of being renewed. If many changes had taken place in Europe, if many states had been overthrown, the cause was to be found in the state of agitation and misery in which the stagnation of maritime commerce had placed the greatest nations; still greater changes might yet take place, and all of them contrary to the policy of the English nation. Peace, then, was at once the interest of the people of the continent, as it was the interest of the people of Great Britain. We entreat your Majesty," they concluded, "we unite to entreat your Majesty to listen to the voice of humanity, to silence that of the passions; to seek with the intention of arriving at that object; to conciliate all interests, and thus, preserving all powers which exist, insure the happiness of Europe and of this generation, at the head of which Providence has placed us."

To this joint letter Mr. Canning replied by two letters addressed to the French and Russian ministers, accompanied by an official note. In that addressed to the Russian, he observed that, "however desirous the King might be to reply personally to the Emperor, he was prevented by the unusual mode of communication adopted, which had deprived it of a private and personal character. It was impossible to pay that mark of respect to the Emperor without at the same time acknowledging titles which he had never acknowledged. The proposition for peace would be communicated to Sweden, and to the existing government of Spain. It was necessary that his Majesty should receive an immediate assurance that France acknowledged the government of Spain as a party to the negotiation. That such was the intention of the Emperor could not be doubted, when the lively interest manifested by his Imperial Majesty for the welfare and dignity of the Spanish monarchy was recollected. No other assurance was wanted that the Emperor could not have been induced to sanction by his concurrence or approbation usurpations, the principles of which were not less unjust than their example was dangerous to all legitimate sovereigns."

The letter addressed to Mons. de Champagny, Duke of Cadore, merely demanded that Sweden and Spain should be admitted as parties to the negotiation. The official note commenced by stating the King's desire for peace, on terms consistent with his honor, his fidelity to his engagements, and the permanent repose of Europe. "The miserable condition of the continent, the convulsions it had experienced, and those with which it was threatened, were not imputable to his Majesty. If the cause of so much misery was to be ound in the stagnation of commercial intercourse, although his Majesty could *not be expected to hear with unqualified regret* that the system devised for the destruction of the commerce of his subjects had recoiled upon its authors or its instruments, yet, as it was neither the disposition of his Majesty, nor in the character of the people over whom he reigned, to rejoice in the privations and unhappiness even of the nations which were combined against him, he anxiously desired the termination of the sufferings of the continent." The note then, after stating that the progress of the war had imposed new obligations upon Great Britain, claimed for Sicily, for Portugal, for Sweden, and for Spain, a participation in the negotiations. "Treaties," it stated, "existed with the three first, which bound them and England in peace and war. With Spain, indeed, no formal instrument had yet been executed, but the ties of honor were to the King of England as strong as the most solemn treaties, wherefore it was assumed that the Central Junta, or government of Spain, was understood to be a party to any negotiation in which his Majesty was invited to engage."

The reply of Russia was peremptory. The claims of the sovereigns, allies of Great Britain, she would readily admit; but the insurgents of Spain Russia would not acknowledge as an independent power. The Russians—and England, it was said, could recollect one particular instance—had always been true to this principle; moreover, the Emperor had acknowledged Joseph Bonaparte as King of Spain, and was united to the French Emperor for peace and for war; he was resolved not to separate his interests from those of Napoleon. After some further arguments touching the question, the reply concluded by offering to treat upon the basis of the "uti possidetis," and the respective power of the belligerent parties, or upon *any basis*, for the conclusion of an honorable, just, and equal peace.

The insulting tone of Mr. Canning's communication produced an insulting reply from Mons. de Champagny, which also finished by proposing the "uti possidetis" as a basis for a treaty, and expressing a hope that, without losing sight of the inevitable results of the force of states, it would be remembered that between great powers there could be no solid peace but that which was equal and honorable for both parties. Upon the receipt of these replies, the English minister broke off the negotiations, and all chance of peace vanished; but previous to the conclusion of this remarkable correspondence, Napoleon had returned to Paris.

What his real views in proposing to treat were, it is difficult to determine. He could not have expected that Great Britain would relinquish the cause of Spain; he must therefore have been prepared to make some arrangement upon that head, unless the whole proceeding was an artifice to sow distrust among his enemies. The

English ministers asserted that it was so; but what enemies were they among whom he could create this uneasy feeling? Sweden, Sicily, Portugal? The notion as applied to them was absurd; it is more probable that he was sincere. He said so at St. Helena; and the peculiar circumstances of the period at which the conferences of Erfurth took place warrant a belief in that assertion.* The menacing aspect of Austria, the recent loss of Portugal, the hitherto successful insurrection of Spain, the secret societies of Germany, the desire of consolidating the Polish dominions, and placing while he might a barrier to the power of Russia on that side, the breach which the events of the Peninsula made in his continental system of excluding British goods, and the commercial distresses of Europe, were cogent reasons for a peace; they might well cause him to be suspicious of the future, and render him anxious for an excuse to abandon an unjust contest, in which he could not fail to suffer much, and to risk more than he could gain. In securing the alliance of Russia he only disentangled a part of the Gordian knot of politics; to cut the remainder with his sword was, at this conjuncture, a task which even he might have been doubtful of. The fact that his armies were marching upon Spain proves nothing to the contrary of this supposition. Time was to him of the utmost consequence. His negotiations proving abortive, it would have been too late to have reinforced his troops on the Ebro, and the event evinced the prudence of his measures in that respect.

The refusal to admit the Spaniards as a party to the conferences for peace is scarcely more conclusive; to have done that would have been to resign the weapon in his hands before he entered the lists. That England could not abandon the Spaniards is unquestionable, but that was not the necessary consequence of continuing the negotiations. There was a bar put to the admission of a Spanish diplomatist, but no bar was thereby put to the discussion of Spanish interests; the correspondence of the English minister would not of necessity have compromised Spanish independence, it need not have relaxed in the slightest degree the measures of hostility, nor retarded the succors preparing for the patriots. And when we consider the great power of Napoleon's arms, the subtlety and force of his genius, the good fortune which had hitherto attended his progress in war, the vast additional strength which the alliance of Russia conferred at the moment; and when, to oppose all this, we contrast the scanty means of Spain, and the confusion into which she was plunged, it does appear as if her welfare would have been better consulted by an appeal to negotiation rather than to

* O'Meara. Voice from St. Helena, vol. ii.

battle.   It is true that Austria was arming, yet Austria had been so often conquered, was so sure to abandon the cause of the patriots, and every other cause, when pressed, so certain to sacrifice every consideration of honor or faith to the suggestions of self-interest, that the independence of Spain, through the medium of war, could only be regarded as the object of uncertain hope; a prize to be gained, if gained at all, by wading through torrents of blood, and sustaining every misery that famine and the fury of devastating armies could inflict.   To avoid, if possible, such dreadful evils by negotiation was worth trial, and the force of justice, when urged by the minister of a great nation, would have been difficult to withstand; no power, no ambition, can resist it and be safe.

But such an enlarged mode of proceeding was not in accord with the shifts and subterfuges that characterized the policy of the day, when it was thought wise to degrade the dignity of such a correspondence by a ridiculous denial of Napoleon's titles; and praiseworthy to render a state paper, in which such serious interests were discussed, offensive and mean, by miserable sarcasm, evincing the pride of an author rather than the gravity of a statesman.   There is sound ground also for believing that hope, derived from a silly intrigue carried on through the Princess of Tour and Taxis, with Talleyrand and some others, who were even then ready to betray Napoleon, was the real cause of the negotiation having been broken off by Mr. Canning.   Mr. Whitbread declared in the House of Commons, that he saw no reason for refusing to treat with France at that period, and although public clamor afterwards induced him to explain away this expression, he needed not to be ashamed of it; for if the opinion of Cicero, that an unfair peace is preferable to the justest war, was ever worthy of attention, it was so at this period, when the success of Spain was doubtful, her misery certain, her salvation only to be obtained through the baptism of blood!

Upon the 18th of October Napoleon returned to Paris, secure of the present friendship and alliance of Russia, but uncertain of the moment when the stimulus of English subsidies would quicken the hostility of Austria into life; yet, if his peril was great, his preparations to meet it were likewise enormous.   He called out two conscriptions.   The first, taken from the classes of 1806, 7, 8, and 9, afforded eighty thousand men arrived at maturity; these were destined to replace the veterans directed against Spain.   The second, taken from the class of 1810, also produced eighty thousand, which were disposed of as reserves in the dépôts of France.*   The French troops left in Germany were then concentrated on the side of Austria; Denmark was evacuated, and one hundred thousand sol-

* Imperial Decree, 11th Sept., 1808.

diers were withdrawn from the Prussian states. The army of Italy was powerfully reinforced and placed under the command of Prince Eugene, who was assisted by Marshal Massena. Murat also, who had succeeded Joseph in the kingdom of Naples, was directed to assemble a Neapolitan army on the shores of Calabria, and to threaten Sicily. In short, no measures that prudence could suggest were neglected by this wonderful man, to whom the time required by Austria for the mere preparation of a campaign seemed sufficient for the subjection of the whole Peninsula.

The session of the legislative body was opened on the 24th of October; the Emperor, in his speech from the throne, after giving a concise sketch of the political situation of Europe, touched upon Spain. "In a few days I go," said he, "to put myself at the head of my armies, and, with the aid of God, to crown the King of Spain in Madrid! to plant my eagles on the towers of Lisbon!" Then departing from Paris he repaired to Bayonne, but the labors of his ministers continued; their speeches and reports, more elaborately explicit than usual, exposed the vast resources of France, and were well calculated to impress upon the minds of men the danger of provoking the enmity of such a powerful nation. From those documents it appeared that the expenses of the year, including the interest of the national debt, were under thirty millions sterling, and completely covered by the existing taxes, drawn from a metallic currency;* that no fresh burthens would be laid upon the nation; that numerous public works were in progress; that internal trade, and the commerce carried on by land were flourishing, and nearly one million of men were in arms!

The readiness with which Mr. Canning broke off the negotiation of Erfurth, and defied this stupendous power, would lead to the supposition that on the side of Spain at least he was prepared to encounter it with some chance of success; yet no trace of a matured plan is to be found in the instructions to the generals commanding in Portugal previous to the 25th of September, nor was the project then adopted one which discovered any adequate knowledge of the force of the enemy, or of the state of affairs: indeed the conduct of the Cabinet relative to the Peninsula was scarcely superior to that of the Central Junta itself. Several vague projects, or rather speculations, were communicated to the generals in Portugal, but in none of them was the strength of the enemy alluded to, in none was there a settled plan of operations visible! it was evident that the prodigious activity of the Emperor was not taken into consideration, and that a strange delusion relative to his power, or to his intentions, existed among the English ministers.

* Exposé de l'Empire, 1809.

It was the 6th of October before a despatch, containing the first determinate plan of campaign, arrived at Lisbon.* Thirty thousand infantry and five thousand cavalry were to be employed in the north of Spain, of which ten thousand were to be embarked at the English ports, and the remainder to be composed of regiments drafted from the army then in Portugal. Sir John Moore was appointed to command the whole, and he was authorized, at his own discretion, to effect a junction by a voyage round the coast, or by a march through the interior. He chose the latter, 1, because a voyage at that season of the year would have been tedious and precarious; 2, because the intention of Sir Hew Dalrymple had been to enter Spain by Almeida, and the few arrangements which that General had power to make were made with a view to such a march; 3, because he was informed that the province of Gallicia would be scarcely able to equip the force coming from England, under the command of Sir David Baird. But Moore was directed to take the field immediately, to fix upon some place, either in Gallicia or on the borders of Leon, for concentrating the whole army, and the specific plan of operations was to be concerted afterwards with the Spanish generals! This was a light and idle proceeding, promising no good result, for the Ebro was to be the theatre of war, and the head of the great French host coming from Germany was already in the passes of the Pyrenees; the local difficulties impeding the English General's progress were also abundant, and of a nature to make that which was ill begun, end worse, and that which was well arranged, fail. To be first in the field is a great and decided advantage, yet here the plan of operations was not even arranged when the enemy's first blows were descending.

Sir John Moore had much to execute, and with little help.† He was to organize an army of raw soldiers, and in a poor and unsettled country, just relieved from the pressure of a harsh and griping enemy; he was to procure the transport necessary for his stores, ammunition, and even for the conveyance of the officers' baggage. Assisted by an experienced staff, such obstacles do not very much impede a good general; but here, few of the subordinate officers had served a campaign, and every branch of the administration, civil and military, was composed of men, zealous and willing indeed, yet new to a service where no energy can prevent the effects of inexperience from being severely felt. The roads through Portugal were very bad, and the rainy season, so baleful to an army, was upon the point of setting in; time pressed sorely when it was essential to be quick, and gold, which turneth the

* Lord Castlereagh's Despatch.   Parliamentary Papers.
† Sir John Moore's Papers.

10*

wheels of war, was wanting. And this, at all times a great evil, was the more grievously felt at the moment, inasmuch as the Portuguese, accustomed to fraud on the part of their own government and to forced contributions by the French, could not readily be persuaded that an army of foreigners, paying with promises alone, might be trusted. Nor was this natural suspicion allayed by observing that, while the General and his troops were thus kept without money, all the subordinate agents dispersed throughout the country were amply supplied. Sir David Baird, who, with his portion of troops, was to land at Coruña, and to equip in a country already exhausted by Blake's army, was likewise encompassed with difficulties; for from Coruña to the nearest point where he could effect a junction with the forces marching from Lisbon, was two hundred miles; and he also was without money.

No general-in-chief was appointed to command the Spanish armies, nor was Sir John Moore referred, by the English ministers, to any person with whom he could communicate at all—much less concert a plan of operations for the allied forces. He was unacquainted with the views of the Spanish government, and he was alike uninformed of the numbers, composition, and situation of the armies with whom he was to act and those with whom he was to contend. Twenty-five thousand pounds in his military chest, and his own genius, constituted his resources for a campaign, which was to lead him far from the coast and all its means of supply. He was first to unite the scattered portions of his forces by a winter march of three hundred miles; another three hundred were to be passed before he reached the Ebro; there he was to concert a plan of operations with generals acting each independent of the other, their corps reaching from the northern sea-coast to Zaragoza, themselves jealous and quarrelsome, their men insubordinate, differing in customs, discipline, language, and religion from the English, and despising all foreigners; and all this was to be accomplished in time to defeat an enemy who was already in the field, accustomed to great movements, and conducted by the most rapid and decided of men. It must be acknowledged that the ministers' views were equally vast and inconsiderate, and their miscalculations are the more remarkable, as there was not wanting a man, in the highest military situation, to condemn their plan at the time, and to propose a better.

The Duke of York, in a formal minute, drawn up for the information of the government, observed that the Spanish armies, being unconnected and occupying a great extent of ground, were weak; that the French being concentrated, and certain of reinforcement, were strong; that there could be no question of the relative value of Spanish and French soldiers, and that, consequently, the allies might be beaten before the British could arrive at the scene of action; the latter would then unaided have to meet the French army, and it was essential to provide a sufficient number of troops to meet such an emergency. That number he judged should not be less than sixty thousand men, and by a detailed statement he proved that such a number could have been furnished without detriment to any other service, but his advice was unheeded.

At this period, also, the effects of that incredible folly and weakness, which marked all the proceedings of the Central Junta, were felt throughout Spain. In any other country, the conduct of the government would have been attributed to insanity. So apathetic with respect to the enemy as to be contemptible, so active in pursuit of self-interest as to become hateful; continually devising how to render itself at once despotic and popular, how to excite enthusiasm and check freedom of expression; how to enjoy the luxury of power without its labor, how to acquire great reputation without trouble, how to be indolent and victorious at the same moment.* Fear prevented the members from removing to Madrid after every preparation had been made for a public entrance into that capital. They passed decrees repressing the liberty of the press on the ground of the deceptions practised upon the public, yet themselves never hesitated to deceive the British agents, the generals, the government, and their own countrymen, by the most flagitious falsehoods upon every subject, whether of greater or less importance. They hedged their own dignity round with ridiculous and misplaced forms, opposed to the vital principle of an insurrectional government, devoted their attention to abstract speculations, recalled the exiled Jesuits, and inundated the country with long and labored state papers, while the pressing business of the moment was left uncared for. Every application on the part of Lord William Bentinck and Mr. Stuart, even for an order to expedite a common courier, was met by difficulties and delays, and it was necessary to have recourse to the most painful solicitations to obtain the slightest attention; nor did that mode always succeed.

Sir John Moore strenuously grappled with the difficulties besetting him, and well knowing the value of time in military transactions, urged forward the preparations with all possible activity. He was very desirous that troops who had a journey of six hundred miles to make previous to meeting the enemy, should not, at the commencement, be overwhelmed by the torrents of rain, which, in Portugal, descend at this period with such violence as to destroy the shoes, ammunition, and accoutrements of a soldier, and render

* Mr. Stuart's Letters, MS.

him almost unfit for service. The Spanish generals recommended that the line of march should be conducted by Almeida, Ciudad Rodrigo, Salamanca, Valladolid, and Burgos; and that the magazines for the campaign should be formed at one of the latter towns. This coincided with the previous preparations, and the army was therefore organized in three columns, two of which were directed upon Almeida, by the routes of Coimbra and Guarda, while the third, comprising the artillery, the cavalry, and the regiments quartered in the Alemtejo, was destined to move by Alcantara, upon Ciudad Rodrigo. Almeida itself was chosen for a place of arms, and all the reserve stores and provisions were forwarded there, as time and circumstances would permit; but the want of money, the unsettled state of the country, and the inexperience of the commissariat, rendered it difficult to procure the means of transport even for the light baggage of the regiments, although the quantity of the latter was reduced so much as to create discontent. One Sataro, the same person who has been already mentioned as an agent of Junot's in the negotiation with Sir Charles Cotton, engaged to supply the army, but dishonestly failing in his contract, so embarrassed the operations, that the General resigned all hope of being able to move with more than the light baggage, the ammunition necessary for immediate use, and a scanty supply of medicines; the formation of the magazines at Almeida was also retarded, and the future subsistence of the troops was thus thrown upon a raw commissariat, unprovided with money. The General, however, relying upon its increasing experience, and upon the activity of Lord William Bentinck and Mr. Stuart, did not delay his march, and he sent agents to Madrid and other places to make contracts, and to raise money; for such was the policy of the ministers, that they supplied the Spaniards with gold, and left the English army to get it back in loans.

Many of the regiments were actually in movement when an unexpected difficulty forced the commander-in-chief to make a fresh disposition of the troops. The state of the Portuguese roads north of the Tagus was unknown, but the native officers and the people had alike declared that they were impracticable for artillery; the opinion of Colonel Lopez, a military commissary sent by the Spanish government to facilitate the march of the British, coincided with this information; and the report of Captain Delancey, one of the most intelligent and enterprising of those officers of the Quartermaster-General's department, who were employed to examine the lines of route, corroborated the general opinion. Junot had indeed, with infinite pains, carried his guns along these roads, but his carriages had been broken and the batteries rendered unserviceable by the operation ; wherefore Moore reluctantly determined to send his artillery and cavalry by the south bank of the Tagus to Talavera de la Reyna, from whence they might gain Naval Carneiro, the Escurial, the pass of the Guadarama mountains, Espinar, Arevalo, and Salamanca. He would have marched the whole army by the same route, if this disagreeable intelligence respecting the northern roads had been obtained earlier ; but when the arrangements were all made for the supplies to go to Almeida, and when most of the regiments were actually in movement towards that town, it was too late to alter their destination.

This separation of the artillery, although it violated a great military principle, which prescribes that the point of concentration for an army should be beyond the reach of the enemy, was here a matter of apparent necessity ; and no danger was apprehended from the offensive operations of an adversary represented to be incapable of maintaining his own line of defence. Valladolid and Burgos were considered by the Spaniards as safe places for the English magazines ; Moore shared so much of the universal confidence in the Spanish enthusiasm and courage, as to suppose that Salamanca would not be an insecure point of concentration for his columns, while covered by such numerous patriotic armies as were said to be on the Ebro. One brigade of six-pounders he retained with the head-quarters, but the remainder of his artillery, consisting of twenty-four pieces, the cavalry, amounting to a thousand troopers, the great parc of the army, containing many hundred carriages and escorted by three thousand infantry, he sent by the road of Talavera, under the command of Sir John Hope, an officer qualified by his talents, firmness, and zeal, to conduct the most important enterprises.

The rest of the army marched in three columns, the first by Alcantara and Coria, the second by Abrantes, the third by Coimbra, all having Ciudad Rodrigo as the point of direction ; and with such energy did the General overcome all obstacles, that the whole of the troops were in movement, and head-quarters quitted Lisbon the 26th of October, just twenty days after the receipt of the despatch which appointed him to the chief command ; a surprising diligence, but rendered necessary by the pressure of circumstances. " The army," to use his own words, " ran the risk of finding itself in front of the enemy with no more ammunition than the men carried in their pouches: but had I waited," he adds, " until everything was forwarded, the troops would not have been in Spain until the spring, and I trust that the enemy will not find out our wants as soon as they will feel the effects of what we have."

The Spaniards, however, who expected " everybody to fly, except themselves," thought him slow, and were impatient, and from every quarter indeed letters arrived, pressing him to advance. Lord William Bentinck and Mr. Stuart, witnesses of the sluggish incapacity of the Spanish government, judged that such a support was absolutely necessary to sustain the reeling strength of Spain. The Central Junta was awakened for a moment. Hitherto, as a mask for its ignorance, it had treated the French power with contempt, and the Spanish generals and the people echoed the sentiments of the government; but now, a letter addressed by the Governor of Bayonne to General Jourdan, stating that sixty thousand infantry and seven thousand cavalry would reinforce the French armies between the 16th of October and the 16th of November, was intercepted, and made the Junta feel that a crisis for which it was unprepared was approaching; then with the folly usually attendant on improvidence, these men, who had been so slow themselves, required that others should be supernaturally quick as danger pressed.

In the mean time Sir David Baird's forces arrived at Coruña. Lord William Bentinck had given intimation of their approach, and the Central Junta had repeatedly assured him that every necessary order was given, and that every facility would be afforded, for their disembarkation and supply. This was untrue; no measures of any kind had been taken, no instructions issued, no preparations made; the Junta of Coruña disliked the personal trouble of a disembarkation in that port, and in the hope that Baird would be driven to another, refused him permission to land, until a communication was had with Aranjuez;* yet fifteen days elapsed before an answer could be obtained from a government who were daily pestering Sir John Moore with complaints of the tardiness of his march.

Sir David Baird came without money; Sir John could only give him £8000, a sum which might have been mistaken for a private loan, if the fact of its being public property were not expressly mentioned;† yet at this time Mr. Frere, the plenipotentiary, arrived at Coruña, with two millions of dollars, intended for the use of the Spaniards; and while such large sums, contrary to the earnest recommendations of Mr. Stuart and Major Coxe, were lavished in that quarter, the penury of the English General obliged him to borrow the funds in Mr. Frere's hands. Thus assisted, the troops were put in motion, but wanting all the equipments essential to an amy, they were forced to march by half battalions, conveying their scanty stores on country cars, hired

* Captain Kennedy's Letter. Parl. Pap.
† Sir John Moore to Lord Castlereagh, 27th Oct.

from day to day; nor was that meagre assistance obtained but at great expense, and by compliance with a vulgar mercenary spirit predominant among the authorities of Gallicia. The Junta frequently promised to procure the carriages, but did not; the commissaries, pushed to the wall by the delay, offered an exorbitant remuneration; the cars were then forthcoming, and the procrastination of the government proved to be a concerted plan to defraud the military chest. In fine, the local rulers were unfriendly, crafty, fraudulent, the peasantry suspicious, fearful, rude, disinclined toward strangers, and indifferent to public affairs; a few shots only were required to render theirs a hostile instead of a friendly greeting.

With Mr. Frere came a fleet, conveying a Spanish force, under the Marquis of Romana. When the insurrection first broke forth, that nobleman commanded fourteen or fifteen thousand troops, who were serving with the French armies, and how to recover this disciplined body of men from the enemy was a subject of early anxiety with the Junta of Seville.* Castaños, in his first intercourse with Sir Hew Dalrymple, signified his wish that the British government should adopt some mode of apprising Romana that Spain was in arms, and should endeavor to extricate him and his army from the toils of the enemy; and finally a gentleman named M'Kenzie was employed by the English ministers to conduct the enterprise. The Spanish troops were quartered in Holstein, Sleswig, Jutland, and the islands of Funen, Zealand, and Langeland. Mr. M'Kenzie, through the medium of one Robertson, a Catholic priest, opened a communication with Romana, and as neither the General nor the soldiers he commanded hesitated, a judicious plan was concerted. Sir Richard Keats, with a squadron detached from the Baltic fleet, suddenly appeared off Nyborg, in the island of Funen, and a majority of the Spanish regiments quartered in Sleswig immediately seized all the craft in the different harbors of that coast, and pushed across the channel to Funen; Romana, with the assistance of Keats, had already seized the port and castle of Nyborg without opposition, save from a small Danish ship of war that was moored across the mouth of the harbor, and from thence the Spaniards passed to Langeland, where they embarked, above nine thousand strong, on board the English fleet commanded by Sir James Saumarez. The rest of the troops either remained in Sleswig or were disarmed by the Danish force in Zealand. This enterprise was conducted with prudent activity, and the unhesitating patriotism of the Spanish soldiers was very honorable, but the danger was slight to all but Mr. Robertson. Romana, after touching at Eng-

* Sir Hew Dalrymple's Correspondence.

land, repaired to Coruña; his troops did not, however, land at that port, but at Santander, where they were equipped from the English stores, and proceeded by divisions to join Blake's army in Biscay.

Among the various subjects calling for Sir John Moore's attention, there was none of greater interest than the appointment of a generalissimo to the Spanish armies. Impressed with the imminent danger of procrastination or uncertainty in such a matter, he desired Lord William Bentinck and Mr. Stuart to urge the central government with all their force upon that head; to Lord Castlereagh he represented the injury that must accrue to the cause, if the measure was delayed; and he proposed to go himself to Madrid, with a view of adding weight to these representations. Subsequent events frustrated this intention, and there seems no reason to imagine that his personal remonstrances would have influenced a government described by Mr. Stuart, after a thorough experience of its qualities, as "never having made a single exertion for the public good, neither rewarding merit nor punishing guilt," and being for all useful purposes "absolutely null." The Junta's dislike to a single military chief was not an error of the head, and reason is of little avail against the suggestions of self-interest.

The march of the British troops was as rapid as the previous preparations had been; but General Anstruther had, unadvisedly, halted the leading column in Almeida, and when Moore reached that town on the 8th of November, he found the whole of the infantry assembled there, instead of being on the road to Salamanca. The condition of the men was, however, superb, and their discipline exemplary; on that side all was well, yet from the obstacles encountered by Sir David Baird, and the change of direction in the artillery, it was evident that no considerable force could be brought into action before the end of the month. Meanwhile, the Spaniards were hastening events. Despatches from Lord William Bentinck announced that the enemy remained stationary on the Ebro, although reinforced by ten thousand men; that Castaños was about to cross that river at Tudela; and that the army of Aragon was moving by Sor upon Roncevalles, with a view to gain the rear of the French, while Castaños assailed their left flank. Moore, judging that such movements would bring on a battle, the success of which must be very doubtful, became uneasy for his own artillery. His concern was increased by observing that the guns might have kept with the other columns; "and if anything adverse happens, I have not," he wrote to General Hope, "necessity to plead; the road we are now travelling, that by Villa Velha and Guarda, is practicable for artillery; the brigade under

Wilmot has already reached Guarda, and, as far as I have already seen, the road presents few obstacles, and those easily surmounted. This knowledge was, however, only acquired by our own officers: when the brigade was at Castello Branco, it was not certain if it could proceed." He now desired Hope no longer to trust any reports, but seek a shorter line, by Placentia, across the mountains to Salamanca.

Up to this period, all reports from the agents, all information from the government at home, all communications public and private, coincided upon one subject. *The Spaniards were an enthusiastic, a heroic people, a nation of unparalleled energy! their armies were brave, they were numerous, they were confident! one hundred and eighty thousand men were actually in line of battle, extending from the sea-coast of Biscay to Zaragoza; the French, reduced to a fourth of this number, cooped up in a corner, were shrinking from an encounter; they were deserted by the Emperor, they were trembling, they were spiritless!* Nevertheless, the General was somewhat distrustful; he perceived the elements of disaster in the divided commands, and the lengthened lines of the Spaniards, and early in October he had predicted the mischief that such a system would produce. "As long as the French remain upon the defensive," he observed, "it will not be so much felt, but the moment an attack is made, some great calamity must ensue." However, he was not without faith in the multitude and energy of the patriots, when he considered the greatness of their cause.

Castaños was at this time pointed out by the Central Junta as the person with whom to concert a plan of campaign, and Sir John Moore, concluding that it was a preliminary step towards making that officer generalissimo, wrote to him in a conciliatory style, well calculated to insure a cordial co-operation. It was an encouraging event; the English General believed it to be the commencement of a better system, and looked forward with more hope to the opening of the war. But this favorable state soon changed; far from being created chief of all, Castaños was superseded in the command he already held, the whole folly of the Spanish character broke forth, and confusion and distress followed. At that moment also clouds arose in a quarter which had hitherto been all sunshine; the military agents, as the crisis approached, lowered their sanguine tone, and no longer dwelt upon the enthusiasm of the armies; they admitted that the confidence of the troops was sinking, and that even in numbers they were inferior to the French. In truth, it was full time to change their note, for the real state of affairs could no longer be concealed; a great catastrophe was at hand; but what of wildness in their projects, or skill in the enemy's, what of ignorance, vanity, and presumption in the generals, what of fear among the soldiers, and what of fortune in the events, combined to hasten the ruin of the Spaniards, and how that ruin was effected, I, quitting the English army for a time, will now relate.

CHAPTER IV.

Movements of the Spanish generals on the Ebro; their absurd confidence, their want of system and concert—General opinion that the French are weak—Real strength of the King—Marshal Ney and General Jourdan join the army—Military errors of the King exposed by Napoleon, who instructs him how to make war—Joseph proposes six plans of operation—Operations thereupon.

In the preceding chapters I have exposed the weakness, the folly, the improvidence of Spain, and shown how the bad passions and sordid views of her leaders were encouraged by the unwise prodigality of England. I have dissected the full boast and meagre preparations of the governments in both countries, laying bare the bones and sinews of the insurrection, and by comparing their loose and feeble structure with the strongly knitted frame and large proportions of the enemy, prepared the reader for the inevitable issue of a conflict between such ill-matched champions. In the present book, I shall recount the sudden and terrible manner in which the Spanish armies were overthrown, during the tempestuous progress of the French Emperor. Yet, previous to relating these disasters, I must revert to the period immediately following the retreat of King Joseph, and trace those early operations of the French and Spanish forces, which, like a jesting prologue to a deep tragedy, unworthily ushered in the great catastrophe.

CAMPAIGN OF THE FRENCH AND SPANISH ARMIES BEFORE THE ARRIVAL OF THE EMPEROR.

After General Cuesta was removed from the command, and the Junta of Seville had been forced by Major Coxe to disgorge so much of the English subsidy as sufficed for the immediate relief of the troops in Madrid, all the Spanish armies closed upon the Ebro.

General Blake, reinforced by eight thousand Asturians, established his base of operations at Reynosa, opened a communication with the English vessels off the port of Santander, and directed his views towards Biscay.*

The Castilian army, conducted by General Pignatelli, resumed its march upon Burgo del Osma and Logroño.

The two divisions of the Andalusian troops under La Peña, and the Murcian division of General Llamas, advanced to Taranzona and Tudela.†

Palafox, with the Aragonese and Valencian divisions of St. Marc, operated from the side of Zaragoza.‡

The Conde de Belvedere, a weak youth, not twenty years of age, marched with fifteen thousand Estremadurans upon Logroño, as forming part of Castaños' army, but soon received another destination.§

Between all these armies there was neither concert nor connection; their movements were regulated by some partial view of affairs, or by silly caprices of the generals, who were ignorant of each other's plans, and little solicitous to combine operations. The weak characters of many of the chiefs, the inexperience of all, and this total want of system, opened a field for intriguing men, and invited unqualified persons to interfere in the direction of affairs: thus we find Colonel Doyle making a journey to Zaragoza, and priding himself upon having prevailed with Palafox to detach seven thousand men to Sanguessa. Captain Whittingham, without any knowledge of Doyle's interference, earnestly dissuading the Spaniards from such an enterprise. The first affirming that the movement would "turn the enemy's left flank, threaten his rear, and have the appearance of cutting off his retreat." The second arguing that, Sanguessa being seventy miles from Zaragoza, and only a few leagues from Pampeluna, the detachment would itself be cut off. Doyle judged that, drawing the French from Caparosa and Milagro, it would expose those points to Llamas and La Peña; that it would force the enemy to recall the reinforcements said to be marching against Blake, enable that General to form a junction with the Asturians, and then, with the forty thousand men thus collected, possess himself of the Pyrenees; and if the French army, estimated at thirty-five thousand men, did not fly, cut it off from France, or, by moving on Miranda, sweep clear Biscay and Castile. Palafox, pleased with this plan, sent Whittingham to inform Llamas and La Peña that O'Neil would, with six thousand men, march on the 15th of September to Sanguessa.

* General Broderick's Corrrespondence.
† Captain Whittingham.
‡ Colonel Doyle.
§ Castaños' Vindication.

Those generals disapproved of the movement as dangerous, premature, and at variance with the plan arranged in the council of war held at Madrid; but Palafox, regardless of their opinion, persisted.* O'Neil accordingly occupied Sanguessa, drew the attention of the enemy, and was immediately driven across the Alagon river.

In this manner all their projects, characterized by a profound ignorance of war, were lightly adopted and as lightly abandoned, or ended in disasters; yet victory was more confidently anticipated than if consummate skill had presided over the arrangements; and this vainglorious feeling, extending to the military agents, was by them propagated in England, where the foreboasting was nearly as loud, and as absurd, as in the Peninsula. The delusion was universal; even Lord William Bentinck and Mr. Stuart, deceived by the curious consistency of the Spanish falsehoods, doubted if the French army was able to maintain its position, and believed that the Spaniards had obtained a moral ascendency in the field.†

Drunk with vanity and folly, and despising the "remnants" of the French army on the Ebro, which they estimated at from thirty-five to forty thousand men, the Spanish government proposed that the British army should be directed upon Catalonia; and when they found that this proposal was not acceded to, they withdrew ten thousand men from the Murcian division, and sent them to the neighborhood of Lerida. The innate pride and arrogance of the Spaniards were also nourished by the timid and false operations of King Joseph. Twenty days after the evacuation of Madrid, that monarch was at the head of above fifty thousand fighting men, exclusive of eight thousand employed to maintain the communications, and to furnish the garrisons of Pampeluna, Tolosa, Irun, St. Sebastian and Bilbao; exclusive also of the Catalonian army, which was seventeen thousand strong, and distinct from his command. A strong reserve assembled at Bayonne, under General Drouet, supplied reinforcements, and was itself supported by drafts from the interior of France; six thousand men, forming movable columns, watched the openings of the Pyrenees, from St. John Pied de Port to Roussillon, and guarded the frontier against Spanish incursions; and a second reserve, composed of Neapolitans, Tuscans, and Piedmontese, was commenced at Belgarde, with a view of supporting Duhesme in Catalonia. How the King quelled the nascent insurrection at Bilbao, and how he dispersed the insurgents of the valleys in Aragon, I have already related; but after those operations, the French army made no movement. It was re-organized, and divided

* Whittingham's Correspondence.
† Lord W. Bentinck's Correspondence, MS. Doyle's Correspondence, MS.

into three grand divisions and a reserve. Bessières retained the command of the right wing, Moncey assumed that of the left, and Ney, arriving from Paris, took charge of the centre; the reserve, chiefly composed of detachments from the imperial guard, remained near the person of the King, and the old republican General Jourdan, a man whose day of glory belonged to another era, re-appeared upon the military stage, and filled the office of Major-General to the army.

With such a force, and so assisted, there was nothing in Spain, turn which way he would, capable of opposing King Joseph's march. But the incongruity of a camp with a court is always productive of indecision and of error; the truncheon does not fit every hand, and the French army soon felt the inconvenience of having at its head a monarch who was not a warrior. Joseph remained on the defensive, without understandning the force of the maxim, "*that offensive movements are the foundation of a good defence;*" he held Bilbao, and, contrary to the advice of the generals who conducted the operations on his left, abandoned Tudela, to choose for his field of battle Milagro, a small town situated near the confluence of the Arga and Aragon with the Ebro.* While Bessières held Burgos in force, his cavalry commanded the valley of the Duero, menaced Palencia and Valladolid, and, scouring the plains, kept Blake and Cuesta in check; instead of reinforcing a post so advantageous, the King relinquished Burgos as a point beyond his line of defence, and Bessières' troops were posted in successive divisions behind it, as far as Puente Lara on the Ebro. Ney's force then lined that river down to Logroño, the reserve was quartered behind Miranda, and Trevino, a small obscure place, was chosen as the point of battle, for the right and centre.†

In this disadvantageous situation the army, with some trifling changes, remained from the middle of August until late in September, during which time the artillery and carriages of transport were repaired, magazines were collected, the cavalry remounted, and the preparations made for an active campaign when the reinforcements should arrive from Germany. But the line of resistance thus offered to the Spaniards evinced a degree of timidity which the relative strength of the armies by no means justified; the left of the French evidently leaned towards the great communication with France, and seemed to refuse the support of Pampeluna; Tudela was abandoned, and Burgos resigned to the enterprise of the Spaniards; all this indicated fear, a disposition to retreat if the enemy advanced. The King complained with what extreme difficulty he

* Napoleon's notes.
† S. Journal of the King's operations, MS.

obtained intelligence, yet he neglected by forward movements to feel for his adversaries; wandering as it were in the dark, he gave a loose to his imagination, and conjuring up a phantom of Spanish strength, which had no real existence, anxiously waited for the development of their power, while they were exposing their weakness by a succession of the most egregious blunders.

Joseph's errors did not escape the animadversion of his brother, whose sagacity enabled him, although at a distance, to detect, through the glare of the insurrection, all its inefficiency; he dreaded the moral effect produced by its momentary success, and was preparing to crush the rising hopes of his enemies; but despising the Spaniards as soldiers, Joseph's retreat, and subsequent position, displeased him, and he desired his brother to check the exultation of the patriots, by acting upon a bold and well-considered plan, of which he sent him the outline. His notes, dictated upon the occasion, are replete with genius, and evince his absolute mastery of the art of war. "It was too late," he said, "to discuss the question whether Madrid should have been retained or abandoned; idle to consider, if a position, covering the siege of Zaragoza, might not have been formed; useless to examine, if the line of the Duero was not better than that of the Ebro for the French army. The line of the Ebro was actually taken, and it must be kept; to advance from that river without a fixed object would create indecision, this would bring the troops back again, and produce an injurious moral effect. But why abandon Tudela, why relinquish Burgos? Those towns were of note, and of reputation; the possession of them gave a moral influence, and moral force constituted two-thirds of the strength of armies. Tudela and Burgos had also a relative importance; the first, possessing a strong bridge, was on the communication of Pampeluna and Madrid, it commanded the canal of Zaragoza, it was the capital of a province. When the army resumed offensive operations, their first enterprise would be the siege of Zaragoza; from that town to Tudela, the land carriage was three days, but the water carriage was only fourteen hours, wherefore to have the besieging artillery and stores at Tudela, was the same as to have them at Zaragoza; if the Spaniards got possession of the former, all Navarre would be in a state of insurrection, and Pampeluna exposed. Tudela then was of vast importance, but Milagro was of none; it was an obscure place, without a bridge, and commanding no communication; in short, it was without interest, defending nothing! led to nothing! A river," said this great commander, "though it should be as large as the Vistula, and as rapid as the Danube at its mouth, is nothing, unless there are good points of passage, and a head quick to take the offensive; the Ebro, as a defence, was less than nothing, a mere line of demarcation! and Milagro was useless. The enemy might neglect it, be at Estella, and from thence gain Tolosa, before any preparation could be made to receive him; he might come from Soria, from Logroño, or from Zaragoza.

"Again, Burgos was the capital of a province, the centre of many communications, a town of great fame, and of relative value to the French army; to occupy it in force, and offensively, would threaten Palencia, Valladolid, Aranda, and even Madrid. It is necessary," observed the Emperor, "to have made war a long time to conceive this; it is necessary to have made a number of offensive enterprises, to know how much the smallest event, or even indication, encourages or discourages, and decides the adoption of one enterprise instead of another." "In short, if the enemy occupies Burgos, Logroño, and Tudela, the French army will be in a pitiful position. It is not known if he has left Madrid; it is not known what has become of the Gallician army, and there is reason to suspect that it may have been directed upon Portugal; in such a state, to take up, instead of a bold, menacing, and honorable position like Burgos, a confined, shameful one like Trevino, is to say to the enemy, You have nothing to fear, go elswhere, we have made our dispositions to go farther: or we have chosen our ground to fight, come there, without fear of being disturbed. But what will the French General do if the enemy marches the next day upon Burgos? Will he let the citadel of that town be taken by six thousand insurgents? if the French have left a garrison in the castle, how can four or five hundred men retire in such a vast plain? and, from that time, all is gone; if the enemy masters the citadel, it cannot be retaken. If, on the contrary, we should guard the citadel, we must give battle to the enemy, because it cannot hold out more than three days, and if we are to fight a battle, why should Bessières abandon the ground where we wish to fight?

"These dispositions appear badly considered, and when the enemy shall march, our troops will meet with such an insult as will demoralize them if there are only insurgents or light troops advancing against them. If fifteen thousand insurgents enter Burgos, retrench themselves in the town, and occupy the castle, it will be necessary to calculate a march of several days to enable us to post ourselves there, and to retake the town, which cannot be done without some inconvenience; and if, during this time, the real attack is upon Logroño or Pampeluna, we shall have made countermarches without use, which will have fatigued the army. If we hold it with cavalry only, is it not to say we do not intend stopping, and to invite the enemy to come there? It is the first time that an army has quitted all its offensive positions to take up a bad defensive line, and to affect to choose its field of battle, when the thousand and one combinations which might take place, and the distance of the enemy, did not leave a probability of being able to foresee if the battle would take place at Tudela, between Tudela and Pampeluna, between Soria and the Ebro, or between Burgos and Miranda." Then followed an observation which may be studied with advantage by those authors who, unacquainted with the simplest rudiments of military science, censure the conduct of generals, and are pleased, from some obscure nook, to point out their errors to the world; authors who, profoundly ignorant of the numbers, situation, and resources of the opposing armies, pretend, nevertheless, to detail with great accuracy the right method of executing the most difficult and delicate operations of war. As the rebuke of Turenne, who frankly acknowledged to Louvois that he could pass the Rhine at a particular spot, if the latter's finger were a bridge, has been lost upon such men, perhaps the more recent opinion of Napoleon may be disregarded. "But it is not permitted," says that consummate general, "*it is not permitted, at the distance of three hundred leagues, and without even a state of the situation of the army, to direct what should be done.*"

After having thus protected himself from the charge of presumption, the Emperor proceeded to recommend certain dispositions for the defence of the Ebro. The Spaniards, he said, were not to be feared in the field; twenty-five thousand French in a good position would suffice to beat all their armies united, and this opinion he deduced from the events of Dupont's campaign, of which he gave a short analysis. "Let Tudela," he said, "be retrenched if possible; at all events it should be occupied in force, and offensively towards Zaragoza. Let the General commanding there, collect provisions on all sides, secure the boats, with a view to future operations when the reinforcements should arrive, and maintain his communication with Logroño by the right bank if he can, but certainly by the left; let his corps be considered as one of observation. If a body of insurgents only approach, he may fight them, or keep them constantly on the defensive by his movements against their line or against Zaragoza; if regular troops attack him, and he is forced across the Ebro, let him then operate about Pampeluna until the general-in-chief has made his dispositions for the main body; in this manner no prompt movement upon Estella and Tolosa can take place, and the corps of observation will have amply fulfilled its task.

"Let Marshal Bessières, with all his corps united, and reinforced by the light cavalry of the army, encamp in the wood near Burgos;

let the citadel be well occupied, the hospital, the dépôts, and all encumbrances sent over the Ebro; let him keep in a condition to act, be under arms every day at three o'clock in the morning, and remain until the return of his patrols: he should also send parties to a great extent, as far as two days' march. Let the corps of the centre be placed at Miranda and Briviesca, and all the encumbrances be likewise sent across the Ebro behind Vittoria; this corps should be under arms every morning, and send patrols by the road of Soria, and wherever the enemy may be expected: and it must not be lost sight of, that these two corps, being to be united, they should be connected as little as possible with Logroño, and consider the left wing as a corps detached, having a line of operations upon Pampeluna, and a separate part to act. Tudela is preserved as a post contiguous to the line. Be well on the defensive," he continues; "in short, make war! that is to say, get information from the alcaldes, the curates, the posts, the chiefs of convents, and the principal proprietors; you will then be perfectly informed. The patrols should always be directed upon the side of Soria, and of Burgos, upon Palencia, and upon the side of Aranda; they could thus form three posts of interception, and send three reports of men arrested; these men should be treated well, and dismissed after they had given the information desired of them. Let the enemy then come, and we can unite all our forces, hide our marches from him, and fall upon his flank at the moment he is meditating an offensive movement."

With regard to the minor details, the Emperor thus expressed himself: "Soria is not, I believe, more than two short marches from the actual position of the army, and that town has constantly acted against us; an expedition sent there to disarm it, to take thirty of the principal people as hostages, and to obtain provisions, would have a good effect. It would be useful to occupy Santander; it will be of advantage to move by the direct road of Bilbao to Santander. It will be necessary to occupy and disarm Biscay and Navarre, and every Spaniard taken in arms there should be shot.[*] The manufactories of arms at Placentia should be watched, to hinder them from working for the rebels. The port of Pancorbo should be armed and fortified with great activity, ovens and magazines of provisions and ammunition should be placed there; situated nearly half way between Madrid and Bayonne, it is an intermediate post for the army, and a point of support for troops operating towards Gallicia. The interest of the enemy," he resumes, "is to mask his forces; by hiding the true point of attack, he operates in such a

---

[*] Navarre and Biscay being within the French line of defence, the inhabitants were, according to the civilians, *de facto* French subjects.

manner, that the blow he means to strike is never indicated in a
positive way, and the opposing general can only guess it by a well-
matured knowledge of his own position, and of the mode in which
he makes his offensive system act, to protect his defensive system.
We have no accounts of what the enemy is about; it is said that
no news can be obtained, as if this case was extraordinary in an
army, as if spies were common; they must do in Spain as they do
in other places. Send parties out. Let them carry off, sometimes
the priest, sometimes the alcalde, the chief of a convent, the master
of the post or his deputy, and, above all, the letters. Put these
persons under arrest until they speak; question them twice each
day, or keep them as hostages; charge them to send foot messen-
gers, and to get news. When we know how to take measures of
vigor and force, it is easy to get intelligence. All the posts, all the
letters must be intercepted; the single motive of procuring intelligence will be sufficient to authorize a detachment of four or five
thousand men, who will go into a great town, will take the letters
from the post, will seize the richest citizens, their letters, papers,
gazettes, &c. It is beyond doubt, that even in the French lines,
the inhabitants are all informed of what passes; of course, out of
that line they know more; what, then, should prevent you from
seizing the principal men? Let them be sent back again without
being ill-treated. It is a fact that when we are not in a desert, but
in a peopled country, if the general is not well instructed, it is
because he is ignorant of his trade. The services which the
inhabitants render to an enemy's general are never given from
affection, nor even to get money; the truest method to obtain
them is by safeguards and protections to preserve their lives, their
goods, their towns, or their monasteries!"

Joseph, although by no means a dull man, seems to have had no
portion of his brother's martial genius. The operations recommended by the latter did not appear to the King to be applicable to
the state of affairs; he did not adopt them, but proposed others, in
discussing which he thus defended the policy of his retreat from
Madrid: "When the *defection* of twenty-two thousand men (Dupont's) caused the King to quit the capital, the disposable troops
remaining were divided in three corps, namely, his own, Marshal
Bessières', and General Verdier's, then besieging Zaragoza; but
these bodies were spread over a hundred leagues of ground, and
with the last the King had little or no cennection. His first movement was to unite the two former at Burgos, afterwards to enter
into communication with the third, and then the line of defence on
the Ebro was adopted; an operation, said the King, dictated by
sound reason—because when the events of Andalusia foreboded a

regular and serious war, prudence did not permit three corps, the strongest of which was only eighteen thousand men, to separate to a greater distance than six days' march, in the midst of eleven millions of people in a state of hostility. But fifty thousand French could defend with success a line of sixty leagues, and could guard the two grand communications of Burgos and Tudela, against enemies who had not up to that period been able to carry to either point above twenty-five thousand men. In this mode fifteen thousand French could be united upon either of those roads."

Joseph was dissatisfied with Napoleon's plans, and preferred his own. The disposable troops at his command, exclusive of those at Bilbao, were fifty thousand, which he distributed as follows: The right wing occupied Burgos, Pancorbo, and Puente Lara. The centre was posted between Haro and Logroño. The left extended from Logroño to Tudela, and the latter town was not occupied. He contended that this arrangement, at once offensive and defensive, might be advantageously continued if the great army, directed upon Spain, arrived in September, since it tended to refit the army already there, and menaced the enemy; but that it could not be prolonged until November, because in three months the Spaniards must make a great progress, and would very soon be in a state to take the offensive, with grand organized corps obedient to a central administration, which would have time to form in Madrid. Everything announced, he said, that the month of October was one of those decisive epochs which gave, to the party who knew how to profit from it, the priority of movements and success, the progress of which it was difficult to calculate.

In this view of affairs, the merits of six projects were discussed by the King.

First project. To remain in the actual position. This was declared to be unsustainable, because the enemy could attack the left with forty thousand, the centre with forty thousand, the right with as many. Tudela and Navarre, as far as Logroño, required twenty-five thousand men to defend them. Burgos could not be defended but by an army in a state to resist the united forces of Blake and Cuesta, which would amount to eighty thousand men; it was doubtful if the twenty thousand bayonets which could be opposed to them, could completely beat them; if they did not, the French would be harassed by the insurgents of three provinces—Biscay, Navarre, and Guipuscoa would interpose between the left wing and France.

Second project. To carry the centre and reserve by Tudela, towards Zaragoza or Albazan. United with the left, they would amount to thirty thousand men, who might seek for, and, doubtless, would defeat the enemy, if he was met with on that side. In the mean time, the right wing, leaving garrisons in the citadel of Burgos and the fort of Pancorbo, could occupy the enemy, and watch any movements in the Montaña Santander, or disembarkations that might take place at the ports. But this task was considered difficult, because Pancorbo was not the only defile accessible to artillery; three leagues from thence another road led upon Miranda, and there was a third passage over the point of the chain which stretched between Haro and Miranda.

Third project. To leave the defence of Navarre to the left wing, to carry the centre, the reserve, and the right wing to Burgos, and to beat the enemy before he could unite; an easy task, as the French would be thirty thousand strong. Meanwhile, Moncey would keep the Spaniards in check on the side of Tudela, or, if unable to do that, he was to march up the Ebro, by Logroño and Briviesca, and join the main body: the communication with France would be thus lost, but the army might maintain itself until the arrival of the Emperor. A modification of this project was, that Moncey, retiring to the intrenched camp of Pampeluna, should there await either the arrival of the Emperor, or the result of the operations towards Burgos.

Fourth project. To pass the Ebro in retreat, and to endeavor to tempt the enemy to fight in the plain between that river and Vittoria.

Fifth project. To retire, supporting the left upon Pampeluna, the right upon Montdragon.

Sixth project. To leave garrisons, with the means of six weeks' defence, in Pampeluna, St. Sebastian, Pancorbo, and Burgos. To unite the rest of the army, march against the enemy, attack him wherever he was found, and then wait, either near Madrid or in that country into which the pursuit of the Spaniards or the facility of living should draw the army. This plan relinquished the communications with France entirely, but it was said that the grand army could easily open them again; the troops, already in Spain, would be sufficiently strong to defy all the efforts of the enemy, to disconcert all his projects, and to wait in a noble attitude the general impulse which would be given by the arrival of the Emperor.

Of all these projects, the last was the favorite with the King, who strongly recommended it, and asserted that if it was followed, affairs would be more prosperous when the Emperor arrived than could be expected from any other plan. Marshal Ney and General Jourdan approved of it, but it would appear that Napoleon had other views, and too little confidence in his brother's military judgment to intrust so great a matter to his guidance.

OBSERVATIONS.

1. It is undoubted that there must always be some sympathy of genius in the man who is to execute another's conception in military affairs. Without that species of harmony between their minds, the thousand accidental occurrences and minor combinations which must happen contrary to expectation, will inevitably embarrass the executor to such a degree, that he will be unable to see the most obvious advantages; and in striving to unite the plan he has received with his own views, he will adopt neither, but steering an unsteady, reeling course between both, will fail of success. The reason of this appears to be, that a strong, and, if the term may be used, inveterate attention must be fixed upon certain great principles of action in war, to enable a general to disregard the minor events and inconveniences which cross his purpose : minor they are to the great object, but in themselves sufficient to break down the firmness and self-possession of any but extraordinary men.

2. The original memoir from which Joseph's projects have been extracted, is so blotted and interlined, that it would be unfair to consider it as a mature production. The great error which pervades it, is the conjectured data upon which he founds his plans, and the little real information which he appears to have had relative to the Spanish forces, views, or interior policy. His plans were based upon the notion that the Central Junta would be able and provident, the Spaniards united, the armies strong and well guided; none of which was true. Again, he estimated Cuesta and Blake's armies at eighty thousand, and considered them as one body; but they were never united at all, and if they had, they would scarcely have amounted to sixty thousand. The bold idea of throwing himself into the interior came too late; he should have thought of that before he quitted Madrid, or at least before the central government was established at that capital. His operations might have been successful against the miserable armies opposed to him, but against good and movable troops they would not, as the Emperor's admirable notes prove. The first project, wanting those offensive combinations discussed by Napoleon, was open to all his objections, as being timid and incomplete. The second was crude and ill-considered; for, according to the King's estimate of the Spanish force, thirty thousand men on each wing might oppose the heads of his columns, while sixty thousand could still have been united at Logroño. These might pass the Ebro, excite insurrection in Navarre, Guipuscoa, and Biscay, seize Tolosa and Miranda, and fall upon the rear of the French army, which, thus cut in two and its communications intercepted, would have been extremely embar-

rassed. The third was not better judged. Burgos, as an offensive post, protecting the line of defence, was very valuable, and to unite a large force there was so far prudent; but if the Spaniards retired and refused battle with their left, while the centre and right operated by Logroño and Sanguessa, what would have been the result? The French right must, without any definite object, either have continued to advance, or remained stationary without communication, or returned to fight a battle for those very positions which they had just quitted. The fourth depended entirely upon accident, and is not worth argument. The fifth was an undisguised retreat. The sixth was not applicable to the actual situation of affairs; the King's force was no longer an independent body—it was become the advanced guard of the great army, marching under Napoleon. It was absurd, therefore, to contemplate a decisive movement, without having first matured a plan suitable to the whole mass that was to be engaged in the execution: in short, to permit an advanced guard to determine the operations of the main body, was to reverse the order of military affairs, and to trust to accident instead of design. It is curious, that while Joseph was proposing this irruption into Spain, the Spaniards and the military agents of Great Britain were trembling lest he should escape their power by a precipitate flight. " *War is not a conjectural art !*"

CHAPTER V.

Position and strength of the French and Spanish armies—Blake moves from Reynosa to the Upper Ebro; sends a division to Bilbao; French retire from that town—Ney quits his position near Logroño, and takes Bilbao—The armies of the centre and right approach the Ebro and the Aragon—Various evolutions—Blake attacks and takes Bilbao—Head of the grand French army arrives in Spain—The Castilians join the army of the centre—The Asturians join Blake—Apathy of the Central Junta—Castaños joins the army; holds a conference with Palafox; their dangerous position; arrange a plan of operations—The Spaniards cross the Ebro—The King orders a general attack—Skirmish at Sanguessa, at Logroño, and Lerim—The Spaniards driven back over the Ebro—Logroño taken—Colonel Cruz, with a Spanish battalion, surrenders at Lerim—Francisco Palafox, the military deputy, arrives at Alfaro; his exceeding folly and presumption; controls and insults Castaños—Force of the French army increases hourly; how composed and disposed—Blake ascends the valley of Durango—Battle of Zornosa—French retake Bilbao—Combat at Valmaceda—Observations.

THE Emperor overruled the offensive project of the King, and the latter was forced to distribute the centre and right wing in a manner more consonant to the spirit of Napoleon's instructions;

Explanatory Sketch
of the
FRENCH & SPANISH POSITIONS
26th Octor 1808

Spanish troops
French Do.

R. Ebro
Puent Laro Vittoria to Tolosa
Miranda
del Ebro
Trevino

Pancorbo

Haro

Briviesca
Briones S. Vicente
Divn 2nd Corps Guardia
Ney's Corps

to Burgos

Castillian Divn
Logroña

Sierra de Nalda
Mendavia 3rd Corps
Moncey Estella
Grimarests Divn
Lodosa Sesma
Caparr Lerin
Lapenas Divn Miranda
Calahora Andosilla
Arga R.
3rd Corps Falces
Moncey
Peralta
Centraenigo Milagro Tafalla
Alfaro Olite
Caparosa 3RD Corps Zidasco R.
Valtierra 3rd Corps
12 Miles Moncey
to Taranzona Tudela Sanguessa
40 Miles to Sanguessa Aragon R. O. Niels Divn
to Zaragoza Ebro R.
to Zaragoza Sos
Sadava to Zaragoza

but he still neglected to occupy Tudela, and covered his left wing by the Aragon river.

The 18th of September, the French army was posted in the following manner :—*

	Under Arms.	
Right wing....Marshal Bessières......	15,595	Three divisions of infantry in front of Pancorbo, at Briviesca, Santa Maria, and Cuba ; light cavalry behind Burgos.
Centre.........Marshal Ney.........	13,756	Logroño, Nalda, and Najera.
Left wing......Marshal Moncey.......	16,636	Milagro, Lodosa, Caparosa, and Alfaro ; the garrison of Pampeluna was also under Moncey's command.

Reserve of the King.		
General Saligny...5,413		
Imperial guard.		Miranda, Haro, and Puente Lara.
General Dorsenne.2,423		
Total........——7,833		

Garrisons............................	6,004	Pampeluna.
General Monthion....................	1,500	Bilbao.
General La Grange....................	6,979	Composed of small garrisons and movable columns, guarding the communications of Biscay, Alava, and Guipuscoa.

Grand reserve.		
Movable columns......... 1,984		Bayonne, and watching the valleys of the Pyrenees opening into Navarre.
Stationary...............20,005		
Total, commanded by General Drouet............	21,989	

Total 98,289 present under arms, exclusive of the troops in Catalonia ; and when the communications were secured, the fortresses garrisoned and the fort of Pancorbo armed, there remained above fifty thousand sabres and bayonets disposable on a line of battle extending from Bilbao to Alfaro.

To oppose this formidable force the Spanish troops were divided into three principal masses, denominaded the armies of the right, centre, and left.

	Infantry.	Cavalry.	Guns.	First Line.		
The first, composed of the divisions of St. Marc and O'Neil, numbered about..............	17,500	500	24	Men. 75,400	Guns. 86	
The second, composed of the divisions of Lapeña, Llamas, and Caro....................	26,000	1,300	36			
The third, consisting entirely of Gallicians, about..................................	30,000	100	26			
In the second line the Castilians were at Segovia......................................	12,000	—	—	Second Line.		
The Estremadurans at Talavera	13,000	—	—	57,000		
Two Andalusian divisions were in La Mancha	14,000	—	—			
And the Asturians (posted at Llanes) were called..................................	18,000	—	—			

This estimate, founded upon a number of contemporary returns and other documents, proves the monstrous exaggerations put forth at this time to deceive the Spanish people and the English government. The Spaniards pretended that above one hundred and forty thousand men in arms were threatening the French positions on

* Journal of the King's operations, MS.

the Ebro, whereas less than seventy-six thousand were in line of battle, and those exceedingly ill-armed and provided. The right, under Palafox, held the country between Zaragoza and Sanguessa, on the Aragon river; the centre, under Castaños, occupied Borja, Taranzona, and Agreda; the left, under Blake, was posted at Reynosa, near the sources of the Ebro. The relative position of the French and Spanish armies was also very disadvantageous to the latter. From the right to the left of their line, that is, from Reynosa to Zaragoza, was twice the distance between Bayonne and Vittoria, and the roads more difficult; the reserve under Drouet was consequently in closer military communication with King Joseph's army than the Spanish wings were with one another.

The patriots were acting without concert upon double external lines of operation, and against an enemy far superior in quickness, knowledge, and organization, and even in numbers.

The French were superior in cavalry, and the base of their operations rested on three great fortresses,—Bayonne, St. Sebastian, and Pampeluna; they could in three days carry the centre and the reserve to either flank, and unite thirty thousand combatants without drawing a man from their garrisons.

The Spaniards held but one fortress, Zaragoza, and being divided in corps, under different generals of equal authority, they could execute no combined movement with rapidity or precision, nor under any circumstances could they unite more than 40,000 men at a given point.

In this situation of affairs, General Blake, his army organized in six divisions, each five thousand strong, broke up from Reynosa on the 17th of September.* One division advanced on the side of Burgos, to cover the march of the main body, which, threading the valley of Villarcayo, turned the right of Marshal Bessières, and reached the Ebro; two divisions occupied Traspaderna and Frias, and established a post at Oña, on the right bank of that river; a third division took a position at Medina; a fourth held the town of Erran and the sierra of that name; a fifth halted in the town of Villarcayo, to preserve the communication with Reynosa; and at the same time 8000 Asturians, under General Acevedo, quitted the camp at Llanes, and advanced to Santander.

General Broderick arrived in the Spanish camp, Blake importuned him for money, and obtained it; but treated him otherwise with great coldness, and withheld all information relative to the movements of the army. English vessels hovering on the coast were prepared to supply the Biscayans with arms and ammunition, and Blake thinking himself in a situation to revive the insurrection

* Correspondence of Captain Carrol. Ibid. General Broderick.

in that province, and to extend it to Guipuscoa, detached his fourth division, and five guns, under the command of the Marquis of Portazgo, to attack General Monthion at Bilbao.* The King, getting knowledge of the march of this division, ordered a brigade from his right wing to fall on its flank by the valley of Orduña, and caused General Merlin to reinforce Monthion by the valley of Durango, while Bessières aided these dispositions with a demonstration on the side of Frias. The combination was made too late, Portazgo was already master of Bilbao.† Monthion had retired on the 20th to Durango, and Bessières fell back with his corps to Miranda, Haro, and Puente Lara, having first injured the defences of Burgos.

The King then took post with the reserve at Vittoria, and Ney, immediately abandoning his position on the Ebro, carried his whole force, by a rapid march, to Bilbao, where he arrived on the evening of the 26th; at the same time, General Merle's division executed a combined movement from Miranda upon Osma and Barbaceña. Portazgo, being thus overmatched, occupied the heights above Bilbao, until nightfall, and then retreated to Valmaceda, where he found the third division, for Blake had changed his position, and now occupied Frias with his right, Quincoes with his centre, and Valmaceda with his left; all the Spanish artillery was in the town of Villarcayo, guarded by a division; and in this situation, holding the passes of the mountains, Blake awaited the arrival of the Asturians, who were marching by the valley of Villarcayo. Thus the second effort to raise Biscay failed of success.‡

In the mean time, O'Neil, following Colonel Doyle's plan before mentioned, entered Sanguessa, and was beaten out of it again, with the loss of two guns. However, the Castilian army approached the Ebro by the road of Soria; General La Peña occupied Logroño, Nalda, and Najera;§ Llamas and Caro occupied Corella, Cascante, and Calahorra, and O'Neil took post in the mountains, on the left bank of the Aragon, facing Sanguessa. The peasantry of the valleys assembled in considerable numbers, the country between Zaragoza and the Aragon river appeared to be filled with troops, and Moncey, withdrawing from the Ebro, took a position, with his left flank at the pass of Sanguessa, his centre at Falces, and his right at Estella. Ney also, leaving Merlin with three thousand men at Bilbao, returned to the Ebro, but finding that Logroño was occupied in force by the Spaniards, halted at Guardia on the 5th of October, and remained in observation.‖

* Correspondence of General Leith.
† Journal of the King's Operations, MS.
‡ Correspondence of General Leith.
§ Journal of the King's Operations, MS.
‖ Ibid.

11*

On the 4th, the King and Bessières, at the head of Mouton's and Merle's divisions, quitted Miranda, and advanced along the road of Osma, with the intention of feeling for Blake on the side of Frias and Medina ; the Spaniards were then in force at Valmaceda, but Joseph, deceived by false information, imagined that they were again in march towards Bilbao, and therefore pushed on to Lodio, with the intention of attacking Blake during the movement; at Lodio he ascertained the truth, and being uneasy about Moncey, returned the 7th to Murquia, where he left Merle to protect the rear of the troops at Bilbao, and then proceeded to Miranda with the division of Mouton. On the 12th, Blake, still intent upon the insurrection of Biscay, placed a division at Orduña, and attacked Bilbao with eighteen thousand men.* Merlin retired fighting up the valley of Durango as far as Zornosa, but being joined there by General Verdier, with six battalions, turned and checked the pursuit. At this time, however, the leading columns of the great French army were passing the Spanish frontier; Laval's division advanced to Durango ; Sebastiani, with six thousand men, relieved Merle at Murquia, who repaired to Miranda ; Verdier returned to Vittoria, and Lefebre, Duke of Dantzic, assumed the command of the three divisions posted at Durango.

On the Spanish side, the Marquis of Romana's division had disembarked on the 9th at Santander, and the infantry, eight thousand strong, completely equipped and provided from the English stores, proceeded, by slow marches, to join Blake. The Asturians had halted at Villarcayo, but the Estremaduran army, under the Conde de Belvedere, was put in motion, and the Castilian forces arrived upon the Ebro ; the first and third divisions of the Andalusian army were on the march from La Mancha, and Castaños, quitting Madrid, proceeded towards Tudela. All things announced the approach of a great crisis, yet such was the apathy of the Supreme Junta, that the best friends of Spain hoped for a defeat, as the only mode of exciting sufficient energy in the government to save the state, and by some it was thought that even that sharp remedy would be insufficient. A momentary excitement was, however, caused by the intercepted letter to Jourdan before spoken of; the troops in the second line were ordered to proceed to the Ebro by forced marches ; letters were written, pressing for the advance of the British army, and Castaños was enjoined to drive the enemy, without delay, beyond the frontier. But this sudden fury of action ended with those orders. Sir David Baird's corps was detained in the transports at Coruña, waiting for permission to land ; no assistance was afforded to Sir John Moore ; and although the subsidies already

* Journal of the King's Operations.

paid by England amounted to ten millions of dollars,* and that Madrid was rich, and willing to contribute to the exigencies of the moment, the Central Junta, while complaining of the want of money, would not be at the trouble of collecting patriotic gifts, and left the armies "to all the horrors of famine, nakedness, and misery."† The natural consequence of such folly and wickedness ensued ; the people ceased to be enthusiastic, and the soldiers deserted in crowds.

The conduct of the generals was not less extraordinary. Blake had voluntarily commenced the campaign without magazines, and without any plan, except that of raising the provinces of Biscay and Guipuscoa. With the usual blind confidence of a Spaniard, he pressed forward, ignorant of the force or situation of his adversaries, never dreaming of a defeat; and so little experienced in the detail of command, that he calculated upon the ordinary quantity of provisions contained in an English frigate, which cruised off the coast, as a resource for his army, if the country should fail to supply him with subsistence ;‡ his artillery had only seventy rounds for each gun, his men were without great-coats, many without shoes, and the snow was beginning to fall in the mountains.§   That he was able to make any impression is a proof that King Joseph possessed little military talent; the French, from the habitude of war, were, indeed, able to baffle Blake without difficulty, but the strategic importance of the valley of Orduña they did not appreciate, or he would have been destroyed. The lesson given by Napoleon, when he defeated Wurmser in the valley of Brenta, might have been repeated, under more favorable circumstances, at Orduña and Durango.

But if genius was asleep with the French, it was dead with the Spaniards. As long as Blake remained between Frias and Valmaceda, his position was tolerably secure from an attack; because the Montaña Santander is exceedingly rugged, and the line of retreat by Villarcayo was open; nevertheless, he was cooped up in a corner, and ill placed for offensive movements, which were the only operations he thought of. Instead of occupying Burgos, and repairing the citadel, he descended on Bilbao with the bulk of his army, thereby discovering his total ignorance of war; for several great valleys, the upper parts of which were possessed by the French, met near that town, and it was untenable. The flank of his army was always exposed to an attack from the side of Orduña, and his line of retreat was in the power of Bessières. To protect his flank and rear, Blake detached largely, but that weakened the

* Parliamentary Papers.
† Vindication of Castaños.
‡ General Broderick's Letter.   Parl. Pap.
§ Birch's Letters to Leith, MS.

main body without obviating the danger; nor did he make amends for his bad dispositions by diligence; for his movements were slow, his attacks without vigor, and his whole conduct displayed temerity without decision, rashness without enterprise.

The armies of the centre and right were not better conducted. Castaños having quitted Madrid on the 8th of October, arrived at Tudela on the 17th, and on the 20th held a conference with Palafox at Zaragoza. The aggregate of their forces did not much exceed forty-five thousand men, of which from two to three thousand were cavalry, and sixty pieces of artillery followed the divisions, which were posted in the following manner:—

ARMY OF THE CENTRE,—27,000.

General Pignatelli, with ten thousand Castilian infantry, one thousand five hundred cavalry, and fourteen guns, at Logroño.

General Grimarest, with the second division of Andalusia, five thousand men, at Lodosa.

General La Peña, with the fourth division, five thousand infantry, at Calahorra.

The parc of artillery, and a division of infantry, four thousand, at Centruenigo.

The remainder at Tudela and the neighboring villages.

ARMY OF ARAGON,—18,000.

O'Neil, with seven thousand five hundred men, held Sor, Lumbar, and Sanguessa.

Thirty miles in the rear, St. Marc occupied Exca with five thousand five hundred men.

Palafox, with five thousand men, remained in Zaragoza.

The Ebro rolled between these two corps, but viewed as one army, their front lines occupied two sides of an irregular triangle, of which Tudela was the apex, Sanguessa and Logroño the extremities of the base. From the latter points, the rivers Ebro and Aragon, which meet at Milagro, describe, in their double course, an arc, the convex of which was opposed to the Spaniards. The streams of the Ega, the Arga, and the Zidasco rivers, descending from the Pyrenees in parallel courses, cut the chord of this arc at nearly equal distances, and fall, the first two into the Ebro, the last into the Aragon, and all the roads leading from Pampeluna to the Ebro follow the course of those torrents.

Marshal Moncey's right was at Estella on the Ega; his centre held Falces and Tafalla on the Arga and the Zidasco; his left was in front of Sanguessa on the Aragon; the bridges of Olite and

Peralta were secured by advanced parties, and Caparosa, where there was another bridge, was occupied in force. In this situation he could operate freely between the torrents which intersected his line. He commanded all the roads leading to the Ebro, and he could, from Caparosa, at any moment, issue forth against the centre of the Spanish armies. Now from Tudela to Sanguessa is fifty miles, from Tudela to Logroño sixty miles, but from Tudela to Caparosa is only twelve miles of good road; wherefore, the extremities of the Spanish line were above one hundred miles, or six days' march from each other, while a single day would have sufficed to unite the French within two hours' march of the centre. The weakness of the Spaniards' position is apparent.

If Palafox, crossing the Aragon at Sanguessa, advanced towards Pampeluna, Moncey would be on his left flank and rear; if he turned against Moncey, the garrison of Pampeluna would fall upon his right; if Castaños, to favor the attack of Palafox, crossed the Ebro at Logroño, Ney, being posted at Guardia, was ready to take him in flank; if the two wings endeavored to unite, their line of march was liable to be intercepted at Tudela by Moncey, and the rear of Castaños be attacked by Ney, who could pass the Ebro at Logroño or Lodosa. If they remained stationary, they might easily be beaten in detail.

Any other than Spanish generals would have been filled with apprehension on such an occasion; but Palafox and Castaños, heedless of their own danger, tranquilly proceeded to arrange a plan of offensive operations singularly absurd.* They agreed that the army of the centre, leaving a division at Lodosa and another at Calahorra, should make a flank march to the right, and take a position along the Aragon, the left to be at Tudela, the right at Sanguessa; that is, with less than twenty thousand men to occupy fifty miles of country close to a powerful and concentrated enemy. In the mean time, Palafox, with the Aragonese, crossing the river at Sanguessa, was to extend in an oblique line to Roncesvalles, covering the valleys of Talay, Escay, and Roncal with his centre, and reinforcing his army by the armed inhabitants, who were ready to flock to his standard.† Blake was invited to co-operate, in combination, by Guipuscoa, so as to pass in the rear of the whole French army, unite with Palafox, and thus cut off the enemy's retreat into France, and intercept his reinforcements at the same time.

Castaños returned to Tudela on the 23d, and proceeded to Logroño on the 25th, the grand movement being to commence on

---

* Sir John Moore's Papers.   Colonel Graham's Correspondence.
† Ibid.   Colonel Doyle's Correspondence.

the 27th. But on the 21st, Grimarest had pushed forward strong detachments across the Ebro to Mendavia, Andosilla, Sesma, and Carcur, and one over the Ega to Lerim; the Castilian outposts occupied Viana on the left bank of the Ebro; the Aragonese divisions were already closing upon Sanguessa, and a multitude of peasants crowded to the same place in the hope of obtaining arms and ammunition. Moncey, deceived by this concourse of persons, estimated the force in Sanguessa at twenty thousand, when, in fact, it was only eight thousand regular troops; and his report, and the simultaneous movement of the Spaniards on both extremities, made the King apprehend a triple attack from Logroño, Lodosa, and Sanguessa. He immediately reinforced Ney with Merlin's division from Bessières' corps, and directed him to clear the left bank of the Ebro, while Bonnet's division, also taken from Bessières, descended the right bank from Haro to Briones.* A division of Moncey's corps, stationed at Estella, received orders to follow the course of the Ega, and second Ney's operations; and a part of the garrison of Pampeluna, posted at Montreal and Salinas, was commanded to advance upon Nardues, and make a demonstration against Sanguessa.

When Castaños arrived at Logroño these operations were in full activity. Ney had, on the 24th, driven back the Castilian outposts, crowned the height opposite that town on the 25th, and was cannonading the Spaniards' position. On the 26th, he renewed his fire briskly until twelve o'clock, at which time Castaños, after giving Pignatelli strict orders to defend his post unless he was turned by a force descending the right bank of the Ebro, proceeded himself to Lodosa and Calahorra.† Meanwhile the French from Estella, falling down the Ega, drove the Spanish parties out of Mendavia, Andosilla, Carcur, and Sesma; and Grimarest retired from Lodosa to La Torre with such precipitation, that he left Colonel Cruz, a valuable officer, with a light battalion, and some volunteers at Lerim, where he was taken after a creditable resistance.‡

Pignatelli, regardless of Castaños' orders, retired from Logroño, and abandoned all his guns at the foot of the Sierra de Nalda, only a few miles from the enemy; then crossing the mountains, he gained Centruenigo in such disorder, that his men continued to arrive for twenty-four hours consecutively. On the right, O'Neil skirmished with the garrison of Pampeluna, and lost six men killed and eight wounded, but in the Spanish fashion, announced

---

* Journal of the King's Operations, MS.
† Whittingham's Correspondence, MS.
‡ Colonel Graham's Correspondence, MS.

that, after a hard action of many hours, the enemy was completely overthrown. On the 27th, Merlin's division rejoined Bessières at Miranda, and Bonnet, retiring from Briones, took post in front of Pancorbo. Castaños, incensed at the ill conduct of the Castilians, dismissed Pignatelli and incorporated his troops with the Andalusian division; fifteen hundred men of the latter, being sent back to Nalda under the Conde de Cartoajal, recovered the lost guns, and brought them safe to Centruenigo.

Dissensions followed these reverses. Palafox arrogantly censured Castaños, and a cabal, of which General Coupigny appears to have been the principal mover, was formed against the latter. The Junta, exasperated that Castaños had not already driven the enemy beyond the frontier, encouraged his traducers, and circulated slanderous accusations themselves, as if his inaction alone had enabled the French to remain in Spain; they sent Francisco Palafox, brother of the Captain-General, and a member of the Supreme Junta, to head-quarters, avowedly to facilitate, but really to control the military operations, and he arrived at Alfaro on the 29th, accompanied by Coupigny, and the Conde de Montijo, a turbulent factious man, shallow and vain, but designing and unprincipled. Castaños waited upon this representative of the government, and laid before him the denuded state of the army;* the Captain-General, Palafox, also came up from Zaragoza, and a council of war was held at Tudela, on the 5th of November. The rough manner in which the Spaniards had just been driven from the left bank of the Ebro made no impression on the council, which persisted in the grand project of getting in the rear of the French, although it was known that sixty thousand fresh men had joined the latter. Deeming it, however, fitting that Blake should act the first, it was resolved to await his time, and, as an intermediate operation, it was agreed that the army of the centre, leaving six thousand men at Calahorra, and a garrison at Tudela, should cross the Ebro and attack Caparosa:† French parties had, however, pushed as far as Valtierra, and in the skirmishes which ensued, the conduct of the Castilian battalions was discreditable.‡ Joseph Palafox then returned to Zaragoza, and the deputy separated himself from Castaños.

The loss sustained by desertion and the previous combats was considerable, but some Murcian levies, and a part of the first and third Andalusian divisions, joined the army of the centre, which now mustered twenty-six thousand infantry, and nearly three thousand

---

* Castaños' Vindication.
† Colonel Graham's Correspondence, MS.
‡ Whittingham's Correspondence, MS.

cavalry under arms, with fifty or sixty pieces of artillery. The position of the army extended from Calahorra, by Haro, to Tudela.
La Peña held the first town with five thousand men; Grimarest
and Caro commanded eight thousand at the second; head-quarters,
with thirteen thousand five hundred men, were fixed in the last;
Cartoajal remained with eleven hundred in the Sierra de Nalda,
and eight hundred were posted at Ansejo.* From these points, in
pursuance of the plan arranged, the troops were actually in movement to cross the Ebro, when despatches from Blake announced that
he had met with some disaster on the 31st, the extent of which he
did not communicate.

This news arrested the attack, and the preposterous transactions
that ensued resembled the freaks of Caligula rather than the operations of real war. First, it was arranged that the army should
abandon Tudela, and take a position in two lines, the extremities
of the one to rest on Calahorra and Amedo, the second to extend
from Alfaro to Fitero, and the deputy ordered O'Neil, with the army
of Aragon, to occupy the latter of these lines forthwith;† O'Neil,
however, refused to stir without instructions from the Captain-
General. This was on the 9th; on the 10th the plan was changed.
Castaños fixed his head-quarters at Centruenigo, and the deputy
proposed that O'Neil should descend the right bank of the Aragon
river, and attack Caparosa in the rear; that the troops in Tudela
should attack it in front; and that a division should make a demonstration of passing the Ebro in boats, opposite to Milagro, in order
to favor this attack. Castaños assented, and on the 12th a division
assembled opposite Milagro, while La Peña, with two divisions,
marched against Caparosa; suddenly, the whimsical deputy sent
them orders to repair to Lodosa, forty miles higher up the Ebro, to
attack the bridge at that place, while Grimarest, crossing in the
boats at Calahorra, should ascend the left bank of the Ebro, and
take it in rear. La Peña and Villarcayo, confounded by this change,
wrote to Castaños for an explanation, and this was the first intimation that the latter, who was lying sick at Centruenigo, received of
the altered dispositions.‡ He directed his lieutenants to obey; but
being provoked beyond endurance, wrote sharply to the Junta, demanding to know who was to command the army; and after all this
insolence and vaporing, no operation took place: Francisco Palafox,
declaring that his intention was merely to make a demonstration,
ordered the troops to their quarters, and then, without assigning

* Whittingham's Correspondence, MS.
† Graham's Correspondence, MS.
‡ Castaños' Vindication.

any reason, deprived La Peña of his command, and appointed Cartoajal in his place.[*]

It was at this time that Sir John Moore's letter arrived, but Castaños, no longer master of his own operations, could ill concert a plan of campaign with the general of another army; he could not even tell what troops were to be at his nominal disposal! for the Estremaduran force, originally destined for his command, was now directed by the Junta upon Burgos, and the remainder of his first and third division was detained in Madrid. His enemies, especially Montijo, were active in spreading reports to his disadvantage, the deserters scattered over the country declared that all the generals were traitors, and the people of the towns and villages, deceived by the Central Junta and excited by false rumors, respected neither justice nor government, and committed the most scandalous excesses.[†] Blake's situation was not more prosperous. The road from Bayonne to Vittoria was encumbered with the advancing columns of the great French army.

An imperial decree, issued early in September, incorporated the troops already in Spain with the grand army then marching from Germany, and the united forces were to compose eight divisions, called "Corps d'Armée," an institution analogous to the Roman legion; because each "Corps d'Armée," although adapted for action as a component part of a large army, was also provided with light cavalry, a parc, and train of artillery, engineers, sappers and miners, and a complete civil administration, to enable it to take the field as an independent force. The imperial guards and the heavy cavalry of the army were, however, not included in this arrangement; the first had a constitution of their own, and at this time all the heavy cavalry, and all the artillery, not attached to the "Corps d'Armée," were formed into a large reserve. As the columns arrived in Spain, they were united to the troops already there, and the whole was disposed conformably to the new organization.

Marshal Victor, Duke of Belluno, commanded the First Corps.
Marshal Bessières, Duke of Istria,   "   Second Corps.
Marshal Moncey, Duke of Cornegliano,   "   Third Corps.
Marshal Lefebre, Duke of Dantzic,   "   Fourth Corps.
Marshal Mortier, Duke of Treviso,   "   Fifth Corps.
Marshal Ney, Duke of Elchingen,   "   Sixth Corps.
General St. Cyr,   "   Seventh Corps.
General Junot, Duke of Abrantes,   "   Eighth Corps.

The seventh corps was appropriated to Catalonia, but the remainder were, in the latter end of October, assembled or assembling in Navarre and Biscay. General Merlin, with a division, held

* Graham's Correspondence, MS.
† Vindication of Castaños.

Zornosa, and observed Blake, who remained tranquilly at Bilbao. Two divisions of the fourth corps occupied Durango and the neighboring villages. One division and the light cavalry of the first corps was at Vittoria, a second division of the same corps guarded the bridge of Murguia on the river Bayas, and commanded the entrance to the valley of Orduña.* Haro, Puente, Lara Miranda, and Pancorbo were maintained by the infantry of the King's body guard and the second corps; and the light cavalry of the latter covered the plains close up to Briviesca. The reinforcements were daily crowding up to Vittoria, and the King, restrained by the Emperor's orders to a rigorous system of defence, occupied himself with the arrangements attendant upon such an immense accumulation of force, and left Blake in quiet possession of Bilbao. The latter mistook this apparent inactivity for timidity; he was aware that reinforcements, in number equal to his whole army, had joined the enemy, yet, with wonderful rashness, resolved to press forward, and readily agreed to attempt a junction with Palafox, in the rear of the French position.

At this time Romana's infantry were approaching Bilbao, and the Estremadurans were in march for Burgos; but the country was nearly exhausted of provisions, both armies felt the scarcity, desertion prevailed among the Spaniards, and the Biscayans, twice abandoned, were fearful of a third insurrection. Prudence dictated a retreat towards Burgos, but Blake resolved to advance. First he posted General Acevedo with the Asturians and the second division at Orduña; then he left a battalion at Miravalles, to preserve the communication with Bilbao;† finally he marched himself, on the 24th, at the head of seventeen thousand fighting men, divided in three columns, to attack Zornosa. The right column ascended the valley of Durango by Galdacano, the centre by Larabezua, the left by Rigoytia; and General Acevedo penetrated through the mountains of Gorbea by Ozoco and Villaro, with a view to seize Manares and St. Antonia d'Urquitiola. It was intended by this operation to cut the communication between Miranda on the Ebro, and the town of Durango, and thus to intercept the retreat of Marshal Ney, and oblige him to surrender with sixteen thousand men;‡ for Blake was utterly ignorant of his adversary's position, and imagined that he had only two corps to deal with. He believed that the King, with one, was in his front at Durango and Mont Dragon, and that Ney, with the other, was at Miranda; but, in fact, the latter was at that moment attacking Pignatelli at Logroño.

---

* Journal of the King's Operations, MS.
† Carrol's Correspondence.
‡ Broderick's Correspondence.

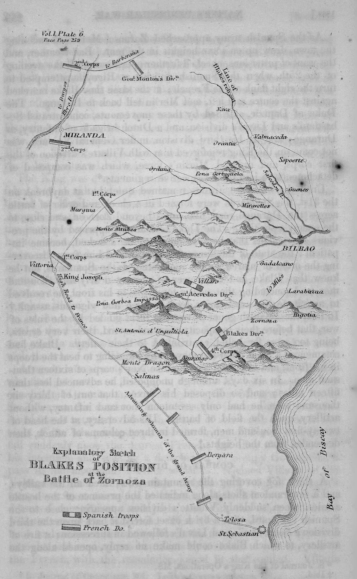

Vol. I. Plate 6.
Face Page 259

Explanatory Sketch
OF
BLAKE'S POSITION
at the
Battle of Zornoza

Spanish troops
French Do.

(map labels:) 2nd Corps to Barberaña; Gen.l Monton's Div.n; Line of Blakes retreat; Ebro R.; to Burgos; MIRANDA; 2nd Corps; Naia; Valmaceda; Orantia; Sopoerte; Orduña; Pena Gorbagnela; Guenes; Salcedon R.; 1st Corps; Maryuia; Miravelles; Monte Altubes; 1st Corps; BILBAO; Vittoria; King Joseph; Badalcano; 10 Miles; Villaro; Larabizua; Pena Gorbea Impassable; Gen.l Acevedos Div.n; Rigotia; High Road to France; Zornoza; St.t Antonio d'Urguitiela; Blakes Div.n; 4th Corps; Monte Dragon; Durango; Salinas; Advancing columns of the Grand Army; Bergara; Bay of Biscay; Tolosa; St. Sebastian

As the Spanish army approached Zornosa, Merlin, abandoning the town, drew up on some heights in the rear. Bad weather, and the want of provisions, checked further operations until the evening of the 25th, when the Spanish division at Rigoytia attempted to turn the right flank of the French ; at the same time Blake marched against the centre and left, and Merlin fell back to Durango. The Duke of Dantzic, alarmed by these movements, concentrated Sebastiani's and Laval's division, and a Dutch brigade of infantry, at Durango ; and as his third division, under General Valence, was not come up, the King reinforced him with Villatte's division of the first corps, and ordered Merlin's force, which was composed of detachments, to join their respective regiments.*

Until the 30th the armies remained quiet, but at daybreak on the 31st, the Spaniards were formed in a checkered order of battle across the Durango road, five miles beyond Zornosa, and close to the enemy's position. The Duke of Dantzic, apprised by the previous movements that he was going to be attacked, became impatient ; the state of the atmosphere prevented him from discovering the order of march, or the real force of the Spaniards, but he knew that Blake had the power of uniting nearly fifty thousand men, and concluding that such a force was in his front, he resolved to anticipate his adversaries by a sudden and vigorous assault.†

In fact, the Spanish generals were so little guided by the rules of war, that before their incapacity was understood, their very errors, being too gross for belief, contributed to their safety. Blake had commenced a great offensive movement, intending to beat the troops in his front, and to cut off and capture Ney's corps of sixteen thousand men. In six days, although unopposed, he advanced less than fifteen miles ; and so disposed his forces, that out of thirty-six thousand men, he had only seventeen thousand infantry, without artillery, upon the field of battle. His adversary, at the head of twenty-five thousand men, formed in three columns of attack, then descended from the heights.‡

COMBAT OF DURANGO.

A thick fog covering the mountain sides, filled all the valleys, and a few random shots alone indicated the presence of the hostile armies, when suddenly Villatte's division appearing close to the Spanish vanguard, with a brisk onset forced it back upon the third division ; Sebastiani's and Laval's followed in succession ; a fire of artillery, to which Blake could make no reply, opened along the

* S. Journal of the King's Operations, MS.
† Ibid.
‡ Carrol's Correspondence.

road, the day cleared, and the Spanish army, heaped in confused masses, was, notwithstanding the example of personal courage given by Blake, and the natural strength of the country, driven from one position to another. At mid-day it was beyond Zornosa, and at three o'clock in full flight for Bilbao, which place it gained, in a state of great confusion, during the night; but the next day Blake crossed the Salcedon, and took a position at Nava.* The Duke of Dantzic pursued as far as Gueñes, and then leaving General Villatte, with seven thousand men, to observe the enemy, returned to Bilbao. Twelve vessels, laden with English stores, were in the river, but contrived to escape.

The King was displeased with the precipitancy of Marshal Lefebre, but to aid him ordered the division of the first corps stationed at Murguia to descend the valley of Orduña, as far as Amurio; at the same time, Mouton's division was detached from the second corps towards Barbareña, from whence it was, according to circumstances, either to join the troops in the valley of Orduña, or to watch Medina and Quincoes, and press Blake in his retreat, if he retired by Villarcayo. The French were ignorant of the situation of General Acevedo, but the day of the action at Zornosa that General was at Villaro, from whence he endeavored to rejoin Blake, by marching to Valmaceda; he reached Miravalles, in the valley of Orduña, on the 3d, at the moment when the head of the French troops coming from Murguia appeared in sight, and after a slight skirmish, the latter, thinking they had to deal with the whole of Blake's army, retired to Orduña.

Acevedo immediately pushed for the Salcedon river, and Villatte, who first got notice of his march, dividing his own troops, posted one half at Orantia, on the road leading from Miravalles to Nava, the other on the road to Valmaceda, thus intercepting the Spaniards' line of retreat.† Blake, informed of Acevedo's danger, in the night of the 4th, promptly passed the bridge of Nava, meaning to fall suddenly upon the nearest French; but they were aware of his intention, and sending a detachment to occupy Gordujuela, a pass in the mountains leading to Bilbao, rejoined Villatte on the Valmaceda road. Five Spanish divisions and some of Romana's troops were now assembled at Orantia. Blake left two in reserve, detached one against Gordujuela, and with the other two drove Villatte across the Salcedon. That General rallied on the left bank and renewed the action, but at this moment Acevedo appeared in sight, and sending two battalions by a circuit to gain the rear of the French, with the remainder joined in the combat. Villatte

---

* S. Journal of Operations, MS.   Leith's Correspondence, MS.
† S. Journal of Operations, MS.   Captain Carrol.

then retired fighting, and encountering the two battalions in his retreat, broke through them, and reached Gueñes, yet with considerable loss of men, and he also left one gun and part of his baggage in the hands of the Spaniards. Thus ended a series of operations and combats, which had lasted for eleven days.

OBSERVATIONS.

1. The Duke of Dantzic's attack at Durango was founded upon false data; it was inconsistent with the general plan of the campaign, hasty, ill-combined, and feebly followed up; and it was an unpardonable fault to leave Villatte without support, close to an army that had met with no signal defeat, and that was five times his strength. The march of Victor's division was too easily checked at Miravalles, and for five days General Acevedo, with at least eight thousand men, wandered unmolested in the midst of the French columns, and finally escaped without any extraordinary effort.

2. General Blake's dispositions, with the exception of his night march from Nava to Orantia, will, if studied, afford useful lessons in an inverse sense. From the 24th of October to the 4th of November, he omitted no error that the circumstances rendered it possible to commit; and then, as if ashamed of the single judicious movement that occurred, he would not profit by it. When Romana's infantry had partly arrived, and the remainder were in the vicinity of Nava, the whole Spanish army was, contrary to all reasonable expectation, concentrated; above thirty thousand fighting men were united in one mass, harassed, but not much discouraged, and the Conde de Belvedere, with twelve thousand infantry, twelve hundred cavalry, and thirty pieces of artillery, was close to Burgos. If Blake had been at all acquainted with the principles of his art, he would then have taken advantage of Villatte's retreat, to march by Espinosa and Villarcayo to the upper Ebro; from thence he could have gained Burgos, brought up the artillery from Reynosa, and uniting Belvedere's troops to his own, have opened a communication with the English army. In that position, with a plentiful country behind him, his retreat open, and his army provided with cavalry, he might have commenced a regular system of operations; but with incredible obstinacy and want of judgment, he now determined to attack Bilbao again, and to renew the ridiculous attempt to surround the French army and unite with Palafox at the foot of the Pyrenees.

Such were the commanders, the armies, the rulers, upon whose exertions the British Cabinet relied for the security of Sir John Moore's troops, during their double march from Lisbon and Coruña! It was in such a state of affairs that the English ministers, anticipating the speedy and complete destruction of the French forces in Spain, were sounding the trumpet for an immediate invasion of France! Of France, defended by a million of veteran soldiers, and governed by the mightiest genius of two thousand years! As if the vast military power of that warlike nation had suddenly become extinct, as if Baylen were a second Zama, and Hannibal flying to Adrumetum instead of passing the Iberus!* But Napoleon, with an execution more rapid than other men's thoughts, was already at Vittoria, and his hovering eagles cast a gloomy shadow over Spain.

* Lord W. Bentinck's Correspondence.

BOOK IV.

CHAPTER I.

Napoleon arrives at Bayonne—Blake advances toward Bilbao—The Count Belvedere arrives at Burgos—The first and fourth corps advance—Combat of Gueñes—Blake retreats—Napoleon at Vittoria; his plan—Soult takes the command of the second corps—Battle of Gamonal—Burgos taken—Battle of Espinosa—Flight from Reynosa—Soult overruns the Montaña de Santander, and scours Leon—Napoleon fixes his head-quarters at Burgos, changes his front, lets 10,000 loose cavalry upon Castile and Leon—Marshals Lasnes and Ney directed against Castaños—Folly of the Central Junta—General St. Juan occupies the pass of the Somosierra—Folly of the Generals on the Ebro—Battle of Tudela.

AFTER the opening of the legislative sessions, the Emperor repaired to Bayonne. He arrived there on the 3d of November. It was his intention that the presumption of the Spanish generals should be encouraged by a strict defensive system until the moment when the blow he was prepared to strike should fall with the greatest effect; hence the precipitate attack at Zornosa displeased him; nor was he satisfied with the subsequent measures of the King, for he thought that Mouton's division would be endangered between the army of Blake and that of the Conde de Belvedere.* To prevent any accident, he judged it necessary that Bessières should advance with the whole of the second corps to Burgos; that Marshal Victor should march by Amurio to Valmaceda, and that Marshal Lefebre should immediately renew his attack on that position from the side of Bilbao. Thus, at the very moment when Blake was leading his harassed and starving troops back to Bilbao, two corps, amounting to fifty thousand men, were in full march to meet him, and a third, having already turned his right flank, was on his rear.

The Spanish General advanced from Valmaceda on the 7th, and thinking that only fifteen hundred men were in Gueñes, prepared to surround them.† Two divisions, making a circuit to the left, passed through Abellana and Sopoerte, with a view to gain the bridge of Sodupe, in the rear of Gueñes, while two other divisions

---

* S. Journal of the King's Operations, MS.
† Captain Carrol's Correspondence.

attacked that position in front; the remainder of the army followed at some distance, but the advanced guard of the 4th corps was in Gueñes, and after an action of two hours, the Spaniards were thrown into such confusion that night alone saved them from a total rout. The same day, one of their flanking divisions was encountered and beaten near Sopoerte, and the retreat of the other being intercepted on the side of Abellana, it was forced to make for Portagalete on the sea-coast, and from thence to Santander.* Blake, whose eyes were now opening to the peril of his situation, resolved to retire upon Espinosa de los Monteros, a mountain position, two marches distant, where he designed to rest his troops, and draw supplies from his magazines at Reynosa. Falling back to Valmaceda in the night, he gained Nava the next day, and on the 9th was at Espinosa. The late division of Romana's infantry joined him on the march, and, with exception of the men cut off at Abellana, the whole army was concentrated on strong ground commanding the intersection of the roads from Santander, Villarcayo, and Reynosa.

Napoleon, accompanied by the Dukes of Dalmatia and Montebello, quitted Bayonne the morning of the 8th, and reached Vittoria in the evening. He was met by the civil and military chiefs at the gates of the town, but refusing to go to the house prepared for his reception, jumped off his horse, entered the first small inn that he observed, and calling for his maps, and a report of the situation of the armies on both sides, proceeded to arrange the plan of his campaign.

The first and fourth corps, after uniting at Valmaceda, had separated again at Nava on the 9th. Victor was therefore pursuing the track of Blake, and Lefebre was marching upon Villarcayo by Medina. The second corps was concentrating at Briviesca. The third corps occupied Tafalla, Peraltes, Caparosa, and Estrella. The sixth corps, the guard, and the reserve, were distributed from Vittoria to Miranda, and a division, under the command of General La Grange, was at Guardia, connecting the positions of the third and sixth corps. The fifth corps was still behind the frontier, and the eighth, composed of the troops removed from Portugal by the convention of Cintra, was marching from the French sea-ports, where it had disembarked.

On the Spanish side, the Conde de Belvedere was at Burgos; Castaños and Palafox, unknowing of their danger, were planning to cut off the French army, and Blake was flying to Espinosa. The English army was scattered from Coruña to Talavera de la Reyna. On these facts, and in two hours, the Emperor had arranged his plans.

* General Leith's Correspondence.

Moncey was directed to leave a division in front of Pampeluna, in observation of the Spaniards on the Aragon, to concentrate the remainder of the third corps at Lodosa, and remain on the defensive until further orders. La Grange was reinforced by Colbert's brigade of light cavalry from the sixth corps, and directed upon Logroño. The first and fourth corps were to press Blake without intermission; the sixth to march towards Arando de Duero. The Duke of Dalmatia, appointed to command the second corps, was ordered to fall headlong upon the Conde de Belvedere, and the Emperor, with the imperial guards and the reserve, followed the movement of the second corps.*

These instructions being issued, the enormous mass of the French army was put in motion with a celerity that marked the vigor of Napoleon's command. Marshal Soult departed on the instant for Briviesca, arrived at day-break on the 9th, received the second corps from Bessières, and in a few hours was in full march for the terrace of Monasterio, which overlooks the plains of Burgos; headquarters were established there, during the night, and Franceschi's light cavalry took the road of Zalducño to Arlanzon, with orders to cross the river of that name, to descend the left bank, cut the communication with Madrid, and prevent the Spaniards rallying at the convent of the Chartreuse, if defeated near Burgos.

At four o'clock on the morning of the 10th, Soult was again in march from Monasterio, and at six o'clock General Lassalle's cavalry reached Villa Fria. The Conde de Belvedere, being informed of their approach, posted the Spanish army at Gamonal, and taking four thousand infantry, eight guns, and the whole of his cavalry, fell upon Lassalle. The latter skirmished for a while, and then, following his orders, retired slowly to Rio Bena, but at eight o'clock the French infantry, which had advanced by two roads, was reunited at this town, and immediately pushed forward on Villa Fria. Belvedere was driven back upon Gamonal, and the Spanish army was discovered in line of battle. The right was in a wood, leaving a clear space of some extent unoccupied between it and the river Arlanzon; the left was posted in the walled park of Vellimer; thirty pieces of artillery covered the front, and seven or eight thousand armed peasants were arrayed on the heights, immediately behind the regular troops; these latter amounted to eleven thousand one hundred and fifty infantry, and eleven hundred and fifty cavalry. This was the best army at that time in Spain; it was composed of the Walloon and Spanish guards, the regiments of Mayorca, Zafra, and Valencia de Alcantara;† the hussars of Va-

* S. Marshal Soult's operations, MS.
† S. Journal of operations, MS.

lencia, the royal carbineers, and some volunteers of good families ; it was completely equipped, and armed principally from the English stores, yet its resistance was even more feeble than that made by the half-famished peasants of Blake's force.

BATTLE OF GAMONAL.

Lassalle, with the light cavalry, leading down upon the Spanish right, filled the plain between the river and the wood, and at the same moment the Spanish artillery opened along the whole of the line ; then the French infantry, formed in columns of regiments, arrived, and Mouton's division, composed of old soldiers, broke at once into the wood at a charging pace. General Bonnet followed closely, but so rapid and effectual was the assault of Mouton's veterans that the Spaniards fled in disorder before Bonnet's troops could fire a shot ; their left wing, although not attacked, followed the example of the right, and the whole mass, victors and vanquished, rushed into the town of Burgos with extraordinary violence and uproar. Bessières, who retained the command of all the heavy cavalry, passed at full gallop toward the Madrid road, where it crosses the Arlanzon, sabring the fugitives, and taking all the guns which had escaped Mouton, while, on the other side of the river, Franceschi was seen cutting in pieces some Catalonian light troops stationed there, and barring all hopes of flight. Never was a defeat more instantaneous, or more complete. Two thousand five hundred Spaniards were killed ; twenty guns, thirty ammunition wagons, six pairs of colors, and nine hundred men were taken on the field ; four thousand muskets were found unbroken, and the fugitives dispersed far and wide. Belvedere himself escaped to Lerma, where he arrived in the evening of the day on which the battle was fought, and meeting some battalions, principally composed of volunteers, on their march to join his army, retired with them to Aranda de Duero during the night ; but first, with true Spanish exaggeration, wrote a despatch, in which he asserted that the French, repulsed in two desperate attacks, had, after thirteen hours' hard fighting, succeeded in a third.

All the ammunition and stores of the defeated army were captured in Burgos ; and the indefatigable Soult, who was still upon the post-horse which he had mounted at Briviesca, who had travelled from Bayonne to Burgos, taken the latter town, and gained a decisive victory, all within the space of fifty hours, now detached one column in pursuit on the side of Lerma, another towards Palencia and Valladolid, and marched himself with a third, on the very day of the battle, towards Reynosa, where he hoped to intercept Blake's

line of retreat to the plains of Leon.*   This last-mentioned General had reached Espinosa, as we have seen, on the evening of the
9th, with six divisions, including Romana's infantry, who also
dragged with them six guns of small calibre; but the separation of
the fourth division at Abellana, the deserters, and the losses sustained in battle, had reduced his army below twenty-five thousand
fighting men; and the parc of ammunition and artillery, guarded
by two thousand infantry, were behind Reynosa, at Aguilar del
Campo, on the road to Leon; yet his position was strong, and he
hoped to remain in it for some days unmolested.   His left wing,
composed of the Asturians and the first division, occupied some
heights which covered the road of Santander; the centre, consisting of the third division, and the reserve, formed a line across the
road of Reynosa, which leads through Espinosa directly to the
rear; the second division was established on a commanding height,
a little on the right hand of the town; Romana's infantry were
posted in a wood, two miles in advance of the right, and the vanguard, with six guns, formed a reserve behind the centre of the
position.†

BATTLE OF ESPINOSA.

On the 10th, the Duke of Belluno came up, and at two o'clock
in the afternoon, the head of a French column, driving back
Romana's infantry, seized the wood, but the Spaniards, reinforced
by the third division, renewed the combat; a second column then
opened its fire upon the Spanish centre, thus weakened by the
advance of the third division, and at the same time some light
troops ascending the heights on the left, menaced that wing of
Blake's army.   Meanwhile the contest on the right was maintained
with vigor, and the Spaniards, supported by the fire of the six
guns in their centre, even appeared to be gaining ground, when the
night closed and put an end to the action, leaving the French in
possession of the wood, and of a ridge of hills, which, at the distance of a cannon shot, run parallel to the centre of the position.

The Generals S. Roman and Riquielmé were mortally wounded
on the Spanish side, and at daylight the next morning Victor, who
had relieved his left with fresh troops during the night, renewed
the attack.   General Maison, throwing out a cloud of skirmishers
along the front of the Spanish centre and left wing, under cover of
their fire, passed rapidly to his own right, and fell upon the Asturians and the first division.   Blake, observing this movement,
detached a column of grenadiers to reinforce the latter, and advanced in person with three regiments from the centre, to take

* Carrol's Correspondence.
† Ibid.

Maison in flank during his march; but it was too late. Three Asturian generals fell at the first fire, and the troops of that kingdom fled without waiting for the enemy: they were soon followed by the first division, and Maison, continuing his course without a check, intercepted the line of retreat by Santander, and also that by the town of Espinosa. In the mean time, the French troops posted on the parallel ridge before spoken of, attacked the centre, and when the division in the wood also advanced against the right, the whole Spanish army gave way in terrible confusion, crowding heavily towards the river Trueba, which swept with a bound round the rear—the men endeavoring to escape, some by the fords, some by the town, some by the hills on the right; but the weather was bad, the road steep, the overthrow fatal. Those whom the sword missed, went to their own provinces, carrying dismay into the remotest parts of Gallicia, Leon, Castile, and the Asturias. Blake himself reached Reynosa on the 12th, and then rallied about seven thousand fugitives, without artillery, without arms, without spirit, and without hope.

It has been said that, Spartan-like, Romana's soldiers died to a man in their ranks; yet, in 1812, Captain Hill, of the royal navy, being at Cronstadt to receive Spaniards taken by the Russians during Napoleon's retreat, found that the greater portion were men who had escaped with Romana from the Danish Isles in 1808. Captives at Espinosa, they had served Napoleon for four years, passed the ordeal of the Moscow retreat, and were still above four thousand strong!

A line of retreat by Aguilar del Campo, where his artillery remained, was still open to Blake, who thought to remain at Reynosa, to restore order, and then retire through Leon upon Sir David Baird's division, the head of which was now near Astorga. But his total ignorance of the French operations and strength again misled him; he looked only to the side of Espinosa, and already Soult's cavalry was upon his line of retreat, and the Duke of Dantzic was hastening by the valley of Villarcayo towards Reynosa.* Upon the 13th, he was attacked by Soult's advanced guard, and being now utterly confounded, he fled with four or five thousand men through the valley of Cabuerniga, and took refuge at Arnedo, in the heart of the Asturian mountains, where the Marquis of Romana joined him, and assumed the command of all that remained of this unfortunate army.

Blake being thus disposed of, Marshal Lefebre, after a halt of a few days to refresh his troops, took the road of Carrion and Valladolid, while Soult concentrated the 2d corps at Reynosa, and seized

* S. Journal of Operations, MS.

Santander, where he captured a quantity of English stores. This done, the Duke of Dalmatia spread his columns over the whole of the Montaña, pursuing, attacking, and dispersing every body of Spaniards which yet held together, and filling all places with alarm. Everything military belonging to the patriots was thus driven over the snowy barrier of the Asturian hills; and Soult, having left a detachment at San Vincente de Barqueira, scoured the banks of the Deba, took the town of Potes, and overrun Leon with his cavalry as far as Sahagun and Saldana. Meanwhile the Duke of Belluno, quitting Espinosa, joined the Emperor, whose head-quarters were fixed at Burgos, after the defeat of Belvedere.*

These battles of Espinosa and Gamonal, and the subsequent operations of Marshal Soult, laid the north of Spain prostrate, secured the whole coast from St. Sebastian to the frontier of the Asturias, and by a judicious arrangement of small garrisons and movable columns, the provinces of Guipuscoa, Navarre, Biscay, and the Baston de Laredo, were fettered. Thus the communication of the army with France could no longer be endangered by insurrection in the rear; the wide and fertile plains of Old Castile and Leon were thrown open to the French, and forbidden to the separated divisions of the British army. These great advantages, the result of Napoleon's admirable combinations, the fruits of ten days of active exertion, obtained so easily, and yet so decisive of the fate of the campaign, prove the weakness of the system upon which the Spanish and British governments were at this time acting—if that can be called a system where no one general knew what another had done, was doing, or intended to do.

But Burgos, instead of Vittoria, was now become the pivot of operations; and the right of the army being secured, the Emperor prepared to change his front, and bear down against the armies of Castaños and Palafox, with a similar impetuosity. It was however first necessary to ascertain the exact situation of the British force. Napoleon believed that it was concentrated at Valladolid, and he detached three divisions of cavalry and twenty-four pieces of artillery, by Lerma and Palencia, with orders to cross the Duero, to turn the flank of the English, threaten their communications with Portugal, and thus force them to retire. It was, however, soon discovered that the heads of their columns had not penetrated beyond Salamanca and Astorga, and that many days must elapse before they could be concentrated and in a condition to act offensively. Certain of this fact, the Emperor let loose his three divisions of cavalry, and eight thousand horsemen, sweeping over the plains, vexed all Leon and Castile; the Captain General Pigna-

* S. Journal of Operations, MS.

telli shamefully fled, and the authorities everywhere shrunk from the tempest. The people displayed no enthusiasm, and, disconcerted by the rapid movements of the French, spread a thousand confused and contradictory reports, while the incursions of the cavalry extended to the neighborhood of Astorga, to Benevente, Zamora, Toro, Tordesilla, and even to the vicinity of Salamanca. Such was the fear or the apathy of the inhabitants, that thirty dragoons were sufficient to raise contributions at the gates of the largest towns;* and after the overthrow of Espinosa was known, ten troopers could safely traverse the country in any direction.

The front of the French army being now changed, the second corps, hitherto the leading column of attack, became a corps of observation, covering the right flank and protecting the important point of Burgos, where large magazines were establishing, and upon which the reinforcements continually arriving from France were directed. Of the other corps, the first, the guards, and a part of the reserve were at Burgos; Ney, with the sixth, was at Aranda de Duero. This officer's march from Ebro had been made to intercept the Estremadurans on the side of Madrid; and although their sudden destruction at Gamonal rendered this unnecessary, Ney was equally well placed to cut Castaños off from the capital. Meanwhile, as Lagrange had occupied Logroño, and Moncey was with three divisions of infantry and one of cavalry at Lodosa, the Spanish army of the centre was turned, menaced, and excised from Madrid, before Castaños was even aware that the campaign had commenced.

In passing the mountains near Tolosa, Lasnes, Duke of Montebello, fell from his horse, and was left at Vittoria, and his hurts were dangerous; a rapid and interesting cure was however effected by wrapping him in the skin of a sheep newly slain,† and the Emperor then directed him to assume the command of Lagrange's division and Colbert's light cavalry, to unite them with the third corps at Lodosa, and to fall upon Castaños in front. At the same time he ordered Ney to ascend the course of the Duero with the light cavalry and two divisions of the sixth corps, to connect his left with the right of Lasnes, and to gain Agreda by the road of Osma and Soria, from whence he could intercept the retreat of Castaños, and place himself on the rear of the Spanish army. To support this operation, the first corps, and Latour Maubourg's division of heavy cavalry being drawn from the reserve, proceeded by Lerma and Aranda, and from thence slowly followed the direction of Ney's march. The Emperor, with the guards, and the

* Sir John Moore's Papers, MS.
† Baron Larrey's Surgical Campaigns.

remainder of the reserve, continued at Burgos, where the citadel was repaired and armed, magazines formed, and arrangements made to render it the great dépôt of the army; and all the reinforcements coming from France were directed upon this town, and proclamations were issued, assuring the country people of protection, if they would be tranquil and remain in their houses.

Ten days had now elapsed since Napoleon, breaking forth from Vittoria, had deluged the country with his troops, and each day was marked by some advantage gained over the Spaniards, but these misfortunes were still unknown at Tudela and disregarded at the capital. The remnants of Belvedere's army had rallied in the pass of the Somosierra, and on the side of Segovia;* the troops belonging to the army of the centre, which had been detained in Madrid, were forwarded to the former place, those left behind from Cuesta's levies were ordered to the latter. General St. Juan, an officer of reputation, took the command at the Somosierra,† General Heredia repaired to Segovia, an intermediate camp of detachments was formed at Sepulveda, and the men thus collected were, by the Junta, magnified into a great army sufficient to protect Madrid. That the left wing of the French army was still unbroken upon the Ebro, the Central Junta attributed, not to the enemy's strength, but to the dilatory proceedings of Castaños;‡ wherefore, depriving him of the command, they gave it to Romana, precisely at the moment when it was impossible for the latter General to reach the army he was to lead; but the Junta wanted a battle, and uncorrected by Blake's destruction, doubted not of victory.

The proceedings at Tudela also continued to be worthy of the time, for the madness of the generals and the folly of the deputy had increased rather than abated. The freaks of Francisco Palafox, and their ridiculous termination on the 12th of November, I have already related, and a few days sufficed to give birth to new plans equally absurd, but more dangerous, as the crisis approached nearer. This time Castaños took the lead. He knew upon the 10th that the Estremaduran army was at Burgos, and that the French were marching on that town; from that moment, despairing of the junction of the British army, and likewise of his own first and third divisions which had been left in Madrid, he sent orders to Belvedere to unite himself with Blake.§ His letters never reached that officer, who was defeated before they were written, and Castaños, feeling that he himself was in a dangerous position,

* Mr. Stuart. Lord W. Bentinck, MSS.
† Ibid.
‡ Ibid.
§ Castaños' Vindication.

and that some decided measure was required, conceived so extra-ordinary a plan, that it would be difficult to credit it upon any au-thority but his own. He proposed to carry the army of the centre, reduced in numbers and ill-disciplined as it was, by the Concha de Haro and Soria, towards Burgos, to fall upon the Emperor's rear-guard, and, as a preliminary step, he determined to beat the army in his front;* but Palafox had also a plan for attacking Moncey on the side of Sanguessa, and the first measure necessay was to com-bine these double operations. It was agreed therefore that Capa-rosa should be garrisoned by four thousand infantry, that the bridge head at that place should be fortified, and that O'Neil should be reinforced at Sanguessa by detachments from the centre until his troops amounted to nineteen thousand infantry and twelve hundred cavalry;† he was then to break down the bridge, place guards at all the passages on the Aragon, come down to Caparosa, cross the river, and threaten Peraltes and Olite on the 17th; but on the 18th, he was to turn suddenly to the left, and get in rear of Lodosa, while La Peña and Coupigny, marching from Centruenigo, should attack Moncey in front.

This great movement was openly talked of at the head-quarters of the Spanish generals for several days before its execution;‡ and these extraordinary commanders, who were ignorant of Blake's disasters, announced their intention of afterwards marching towards Vittoria to lighten the pressure on that officer if he should be in difficulty; or if, as his despatches of the 5th had assured them, he was successful, to join in a general pursuit. Castaños, however, concealed his real project, which was to move by the Concha de Haro towards Burgos.

It was found impossible to procure a sufficient number of boats to lay a bridge over the Ebro at Alfaro, thus the reinforcements intended for O'Neil were forced to make a circuit by Tudela, and lost three or four days;§ however, on the 14th O'Neil arrived at Caparosa, after breaking the bridge of Sanguessa, and on the 15th the reinforcements joined him. The 17th, the day appointed for the execution of the plan, Castaños received notice of his own dis-missal from the command, yet he persevered in his project. La Peña and Coupigny were put in motion to pass the bridges of Logroño and Lodosa, and the fords between them, but General O'Neil, instead of executing his part, first refused to stir without an order from Joseph Palafox, who was at Zaragoza, and then chang-

* Castaños' Vindication,
† Colonel Graham's Correspondence, MSS.
‡ Ibid.
§ Ibid.

ing his ground, complained that he was without bread.*   Castaños besought him to move upon the 18th, urging the necessity of the measure, and the danger of delay; but the deputy, Palafox, who had hitherto approved of the project, suddenly quitted the head-quarters, and went to Caparosa, from whence, in concert with O'Neil, he wrote to demand a further reinforcement from the centre, of six thousand infantry and some more cavalry, without which they affirmed that it would be dangerous to pass the Aragon river. Castaños preserved his temper, invited the deputy to return to the right bank of the Ebro, and opposed the demand for more troops on the ground of the delay it would cause; but now the Captain-General Palafox, agreeing with neither side, proposed a new plan, and it is difficult to say how long these strange disputes would have continued, if an umpire had not interposed, whose award was too strongly enforced to be disregarded.

Castaños was with the divisions of Coupigny and La Peña at Calahorra on the 19th, when he received information that a French corps was advancing upon Logroño;† it was Lasnes, with La-grange's and Colbert's troops, yet the Spaniard concluded it to be Ney, for he was ignorant of the changes which had taken place since the 8th of the month. It was likewise reported that Moncey, whose force he estimated at twelve thousand, when it really was above twenty thousand, had concentrated at Lodosa, and, at the same time, the Bishop of Osma announced that twelve thousand men, under Dessolles, were marching from the side of Aranda de Duero. On the 21st, the intelligence that Dessolles had passed Almazan, and that Moncey was in motion, was confirmed.‡ Castaños then, relinquishing his offensive projects, prepared to retire, and it was full time; for Marshal Ney, who left Aranda on the 19th, had passed Almazan on the 20th, dispersed several small bands of insurgents, and entered Soria on the 21st, so that when Castaños determined to fall back on the 21st, his flank was already turned, and his retreat upon Madrid in the enemy's power. The Spanish artillery was at Centruenigo, and a large detachment was with O'Neil at Caparosa; but during the night of the 21st and 22d Castaños retired to the heights which extend from Tudela by Cascante, Novellas, Taranzona, and Monteguda.§

On the morning of the 22d Lasnes was seen marching upon Calahorra; at this moment the only supply of money which the Central Junta had transmitted for his army arrived at Tudela, and,

* Castanos' Vindication.
† Ibid.
‡ Castanos's account of the Battle of Tudela.
§ Ibid.

to complete the picture of distracted councils, O'Neil refused to fall back upon Caparosa without the order of Palafox. Fortunately the latter arrived at the moment in Tudela, and a conference taking place between him and Castaños the same day, they agreed that the Aragonese army should cross the Ebro, and occupy the heights over Tudela, while the rest of the troops should stretch away in line as far as Taranzona; nevertheless, in defiance of all orders, entreaties, or reasoning, the obstinate O'Neil remained in an olive-wood on the right bank of the river during the night of the 22d, leaving the key of the position open to the enemy.

A council of war was held, the discussion was turbulent, and the opinions discordant. Palafox insisted on the defence of Aragon, as the principal or rather the only object to be attended to;* and he wished the whole army to pass to the left bank of the Ebro, and confine its operations to the protection of Zaragoza on that side,— a proposal which alone was sufficient to demonstrate his total incapacity for military affairs. Castaños reasoned justly against this absurdity, but the important moments passed in useless disputation, and the generals came to no concluion. Meanwhile Marshal Lasnes, bringing with him Maurice Mathieu's division of the sixth corps, which had just arrived from France, concentrated above thirty thousand infantry, four or five thousand cavalry, and sixty pieces of artillery, and marching by Alfaro, appeared, at eight o'clock in the morning of the 23d, in front of the Spanish outposts, close to Tudela, just at the moment when the Aragonese were passing the bridge and ascending their position.

BATTLE OF TUDELA.

From forty to fifty guns were distributed along the front of the Spanish army, which, numbering about forty-five thousand fighting men, was extended on a range of easy hills from Tudela to Taranzona, a distance of more than ten miles. Two divisions of the army of the centre connected the Aragonese with the fourth division, which occupied Cascante, three divisions were in Taranzona, and there were no intermediate posts between these scattered bodies. The weakness attendant on such an arrangement being visible to the enemy at the first glance, Lasnes hastened to make his dispositions, and at nine o'clock General Morlot with one division attacked the heights above the town. Maurice Mathieu, supported by the cavalry of Lefebre Desnouettes, assailed the centre, and General Lagrange advanced against Cascante. The Aragonese resisted Morlot with vigor, and even pressed him in the plain at the foot of

* Ibid, and his Vindication.
† Mr. Stuart's Letters, MS. Lord W. Bentinck's ditto.

the hills, but Maurice Mathieu having gained possession of an olive-wood, and a small ridge which was connected with the centre of the Spanish position, after some sharp fighting pierced the line, and then Lefebre, breaking through the opening with his cavalry, wheeled up to the left, and threw the right wing into hopeless confusion. The defeated soldiers fled towards the bridge of Tudela, pursued by the victorious horsemen. In the mean time La Peña, descending from Cascante with the fourth division, drove in Lagrange's advanced guard of cavalry, yet he was soon encountered at a charging pace by the infantry, was beaten and fell back to Taranzona, where three divisions had remained during the whole of the action, which, strictly speaking, was confined to the heights above Tudela. Palafox was not in the battle, and O'Neil, with the right wing and the centre, fled to Zaragoza with such speed, that some of the fugitives are said to have arrived there the same evening.

When La Peña was driven back upon Taranzona, the left wing had commenced an orderly retreat towards Borja, when some cavalry, detached by Ney from the side of Soria, coming in sight, caused great confusion; a magazine blew up, in the midst of the disorder cries of treason were heard, the columns dissolved in a few moments, and the road to Borja was covered with a disorganized multitude. This ended the celebrated battle of Tudela, in which forty thousand men were beaten and dispersed by an effort that, being in itself neither very vigorous nor well sustained, was nevertheless sufficient to demonstrate the incapacity of Spanish generals, and the want of steadiness in Spanish soldiers.

Several thousand prisoners, thirty pieces of artillery, and all the ammunition and baggage, fell into the hands of the French, who rated the killed and wounded very high. The total loss may be estimated at eight or nine thousand men.* Fifteen thousand escaped to Zaragoza; a detachment of two thousand, under the Conde de Cartoajal and General Lilli, left in the mountains of Nalda, were cut off by the result of the action, and two divisions, whose numbers were increased by fugitives from the others, were rallied at Calatayud on the 25th, but they were half starved and mutinous. At Calatayud, Castaños received two despatches from the Central Junta, virtually restoring him to the command, for the first empowered him to unite the Aragonese army with his own, and the second desired him to co-operate with St. Juan in the Somosierra to protect the capital.† The battle of Tudela disposed of the first despatch; the seconnd induced Castaños to march by Siguenza upon Madrid.

* Eleventh Bullettin. Victoires et Conquêtes.
† Castanos' Account of the Battle of Tudela, and Vindication.

In the mean time, Napoleon, recalling the greatest part of his cavalry from the open country of Castile, and having left seven or eight thousand men in Burgos, had fixed his head-quarters at Aranda de Duero on the 23d; but from the difficulty of transmitting despatches through a country in a state of insurrection, intelligence of the victory at Tudela only reached him on the 26th, and he was exceedingly discontented that Castaños should have escaped the hands of Ney.* That Marshal had been instructed to reach Soria by the 21st, to remain there until Lasnas should be in front of the Spaniards, and then to pass by Agreda, and intercept the retreat of the latter; and on the evening of the 21st, General Jomini and Colonel D'Esmenard, staff-officers of the sixth corps, arrived with an escort of eighty cavalry at Soria. This town is situated upon a rocky height, with a suburb below, and the Conde de Cartoajal, who was retiring from the mountains of Nalda, happening to be in the upper part, the magistrates endeavored to entrap the French officers. For this purpose, they were met at dusk by the municipality, and invited to enter the town with great appearance of cordiality; but their suspicions were excited, the plan failed, Cartoajal marched during the night, and the next day the sixth corps occupied the place.

General Jomini, whose profound knowledge of the theory of war enabled him to judge accurately of the events that were likely to occur, urged Ney to continue his march upon Calatayud, without any rest; the Marshal, however, either offended with the heat of Jomini's manner, or from some other cause, resolved to follow the letter of his instructions, and remained at Soria the 23d and 24th, merely sending out some light cavalry on the side of Medina Celi and Agreda. On the 25th he marched to the latter town, and the 26th crossed the field of battle, passing through Cascante; the 27th, he arrived, with one division, at Mallan, a town between Tudela and Zaragoza, his advanced guard being at Arlazon on the Xalon.* To the erroneous direction and dilatory nature of these movements, Castaños owed the safety of the troops, which were re-assembled at Calatayud.

Ney must have been acquainted with the result of the battle on the 25th, and it is remarkable that he should have continued on the road towards Agreda, when a single march by Medina Celi would have brought him upon the line of retreat from Calatayud to Siguenza. By some writers these errors have been attributed to Ney's jealousy of Marshal Lasnes; by others it has been asserted that the plunder of Soria detained him. The falsehood of the

* S. Journal of Operations, MS. Eleventh Bulletin.
† S. Journal of Operations, MS.

latter charge is, however, evident from the fact, that with the exception of a requisition for some shoes and great-coats, no contribution was exacted from Soria, and no pillage took place at all; and with respect to the former accusation, a better explanation may be found in the peculiar disposition of this extraordinary man, who was notoriously indolent, and unlearned in the abstract science of war. It was necessary for him to see, in order to act, and his character seemed to be asleep until some imminent danger aroused all the marvellous energy and fortitude with which nature had endowed him.

The success at Tudela fell short of what Napoleon had a right to expect from his previous dispositions, yet it sufficed to break the Spanish strength on that side, and to lay open Aragon, Navarre, and New Castile, as the northern part of Spain had before been opened by the victory of Espinosa. From the frontiers of France to those of Portugal, from the sea-coast to the Tagus, the country was now overwhelmed; Madrid, Zaragoza, and the British army, indeed, lifted their heads a little way above the rising waters, but the eye looked in vain for an efficient barrier against the flood, which still poured on with unabated fury. And as the divided, weak state of the English troops led the Emperor to conclude that Sir John Moore would instantly retire into Portugal, he ordered Lasnes to pursue Palafox—to seize the important position of Monte Torrero—to summon Zaragoza, and to offer a complete amnesty to all persons in the town, without reservation, thus bearing testimony to the gallantry of the first defence. His own attention was fixed on Madrid. That capital was the rallying point of all the broken Spanish, and of all his own pursuing divisions, and it was the centre of all interests; a commanding height from whence a beneficial stream of political benefits might descend to allay, or a driving storm of war pour down to extinguish the fire of insurrection.*

* S. Journal of Operations, MS.

CHAPTER II.

Napoleon marches against the capital ; forces the pass of the Somosierra—St.
Juan murdered by his men—Tumults in Madrid—French army arrives there ;
the Retiro stormed—Town capitulates—Remains of Castaños' army driven
across the Tagus ; retire to Cuença—Napoleon explains his policy to the nobles,
clergy, and tribunals of Madrid—His vast plans, enormous force—Defenceless
state of Spain.

THE French patrols sent towards the Somosierra ascertained,
on the 21st, that above six thousand men were intrenching themselves in the gorge of the mountains ; that a small camp at Sepulveda blocked the roads leading upon Segovia ; and that General
Heredia was preparing to secure the passes of the Guadarama.
Napoleon having, however, resolved to force the Somosierra, and
reach the capital before Castaños could arrive there, ordered Ney
to pursue the army of the centre without intermission, and directed
the fourth corps to continue its march from Carrion by Palencia,
Valladolid, Olmedo, and Segovia.   The movement of this corps is
worthy of the attention of military men.   We shall find it confus-
ing the spies and the country people—overawing the flat country
of Leon and Castile—protecting the right flank of the army—
menacing Gallicia and Salamanca—keeping the heads of Moore's
and Baird's columns from advancing, and rendering it dangerous
for them to attempt a junction—threatening the line of Hope's
march from the Tagus to the Guadarama—dispersing Heredia's
corps, and finally turning the pass of Somosierra, without ever ceasing to belong to the concentric movement of the great army upon
Madrid.

But the time lost in transmitting intelligence of the victory at
Tudela was productive of serious consequences.*   The officer
despatched with these fresh instructions, found Ney and Moncey
(Lasnes was sick at Tudela) each advanced two days' march in
the wrong direction.   The first, as we have seen, was at Mallen,
preparing to attack Zaragoza ; the second was at Almunio, near
Calatayud, pursuing Castaños.   They were consequently obliged
to countermarch, and during the time thus lost, the people of Zaragoza, recovering from the consternation into which they were at first
thrown by the appearance of the flying troops, made arrangements
for a vigorous defence.   Castaños also escaped to Siguenza, without any further loss than what was inflicted in a slight action at
Burvieca, where General Maurice Mathieu's division came up with
his rear-guard.

* S. Journal of Operations, MS.

The Emperor quitted Aranda on the 28th with the guards, the first corps, and the reserve, and marched towards Somosierra. Head-quarters were at Boucequillas on the 29th, and a detachment being sent to attack the camp at Sepulveda, was beaten, with a loss of fifty or sixty men; yet the Spaniards, struck with a panic after the action, quitted their post, which was very strong, and fled in disorder towards Segovia.   The 30th, the French advanced guard reached the foot of the Somosierra, where General St. Juan, whose force now amounted to ten or twelve thousand men, was judiciously posted.   Sixteen pieces of artillery, planted in the neck of the pass, swept the road along the whole ascent, which was exceedingly steep and favorable for the defence; the infantry, advantageously placed on the right and left, were in lines, one above another, and some intrenchments, made in the more open parts, strengthened the whole position.

PASSAGE OF THE SOMOSIERRA.

At daybreak, three French battalions attacked St. Juan's right, three more assailed his left, and as many marched along the causeway in the centre, supported by six guns.   The French wings, spreading over the mountain side, commenced a warm skirmishing fire, which was as warmly returned, while the frowning battery at the top of the causeway was held in readiness to crush the central column, when it should come within range.   At that moment Napoleon rode into the mouth of the pass, and attentively examined the scene before him; the infantry were making no progress, and a thick fog mixed with smoke hung upon the ascent; suddenly, as if by inspiration, he ordered the Polish cavalry of his guard to charge up the causeway, and seize the Spanish battery.   In an instant the foremost ranks of the first squadron were levelled with the earth by the fire of the great battery, and the remainder were thrown into confusion, but General Krazinski as suddenly rallied them, and covered by the smoke and the morning vapor led them sword in hand up to the mountain.   As these gallant horsemen passed, the Spanish infantry on each side fired and fled towards the summit of the causeway, and when the Poles, cutting down the gunners, took the battery, the whole army was in flight, abandoning arms, ammunition and baggage.

This surprising exploit, in the glory it conferred upon one party, and the disgrace it heaped upon the other, can hardly be paralleled in the annals of war.   It is indeed almost incredible, even to those who are acquainted with Spanish armies, that a position, in itself nearly impregnable, and defended by twelve thousand men, should, without any panic, but merely from a deliberate sense of danger, be abandoned, at the wild charge of a few squadrons, which two companies of good infantry would have effectually stopped: yet some of the Spanish regiments so shamefully beaten here, had been victorious at Baylen a few months before, and General St. Juan's dispositions at Somosierra were far better than Reding's at the former battle! The charge itself, viewed as a simple military operation, was extravagantly rash; but taken as the result of Napoleon's sagacious estimate of the real value of Spanish troops, and his promptitude in seizing the advantage offered by the smoke and fog that clung to the side of the mountain, it was a most felicitous example of intuitive genius. The routed troops were pursued towards Buitrago by the French cavalry. St. Juan himself broke through the French on the side of Sepulveda, and gained the camp of Heredia at Segovia; but the cavalry of the fourth corps approached, and the two Generals crossing the Guadarama, united some of the fugitives from Somosierra on the Madrid side of the mountains, and were about to enter that capital, when the appearance of a French patrol terrified the vile cowards that followed them; the multitude once more fled to Talavera de la Reyna, and there consummated their intolerable villany by murdering their unfortunate General, and fixing his mangled body to a tree, after which, dispersing, they carried dishonor and fear into their respective provinces.*

The Somosierra being forced, the imperial army came down from the mountains; the sixth corps hastened on from the side of Alcala and Guadalaxara; the Central Junta fled from Aranjuez, and the remnant of the forces under Castaños, being intercepted on the side of Madrid, and pressed by Ney in the rear, turned towards the Tagus. The Junta, flying with indecent haste, spread a thousand false reports, and with more than ordinary pertinacity, endeavored to deceive the people and the English General; a task in which they were strongly aided by the weak credulity of Mr. Frere, the British plenipotentiary, who accompanied them in their flight toward Badajos; Mr. Stuart, however, being endowed with greater discretion and firmness, remained at Madrid until the enemy had actually commenced the investment of that town.

Castaños, after the combat of Burvieca, had continued his retreat unmolested by Ney, who never recovered the time lost by the false movement upon Mallen; but although the Spaniards escaped the sword, their numbers daily diminished, their sufferings increased, and their insubordination kept pace with their privations. At Alcazar del Rey, Castaños resigned the command to General La Peña, and proceeded to Truxillo himself, with an escort of thirty

* Colonel Graham's Correspondence.

infantry and fifteen dragoons, a number scarcely sufficient to protect his life from the ferocity of the peasants, who were stirred up
and prepared, by the falsehoods of the Central Junta, and the villany of the deserters, to murder him.* Meanwhile Madrid was in a
state of anarchy seldom equalled. A local and military junta were
formed to conduct the defence, the inhabitants took arms, a multitude of peasants from the neighborhood entered the place, and the
regular forces, commanded by the Marquis of Castellar, amounted
to six thousand men, with a train of sixteen guns; the pavement
was taken up, the streets were barricadoed, the houses were pierced,
and the Retiro, a weak irregular work, which commanded the city,
was occupied in strength. Don Thomas Morla and the Prince of
Castelfranco were the chief men in authority; the people demanded
ammunition, and when they received it, discovered, or said, that it
was mixed with sand, and as some person accused the Marquis of
Perales, a respectable old general, of the deed, a mob rushed to
his house, murdered him, and dragged his body about the streets;
many others of inferior note also fell victims to this fury, for no
man was safe, none dared assume authority to control, none dared
give honest advice; the houses were thrown open, the bells of the
convents and churches rung incessantly, and a band of ferocious
armed men traversed the streets in all the madness of popular
insurrection. Eight days had now elapsed since the first preparations for defence were made, and each day the public effervescence
had increased, the dominion of the mob had become more decisive,
their violence more uncontrollable; the hubbub was extreme, when,
on the morning of the 2d of December, three heavy divisions of
French cavalry suddenly appeared on the high ground to the north-
west, and like a dark cloud overhung the troubled city.

At twelve o'clock the Emperor arrived, and the Duke of Istria,
by his command, summoned the town, but the officer employed was
upon the point of being massacred by the irregulars, when the
Spanish soldiers, ashamed of such conduct, rescued him. This determination to resist was, however, nothwithstanding the fierceness
displayed at the gates, very unpalatable to many of the household-
ers, numbers of whom escaped from different quarters;† deserters
also came over to the French, and Napoleon, while waiting for his
infantry, examined all the weak points of the city.

Madrid was for many reasons incapable of defence. There were
no bulwarks; the houses, although strong and well built, were not,
like many Spanish towns, fire proof; there were no outworks, and
the heights on which the French cavalry were posted, the palace,

* Castaños' Vindication.
† Fourteenth Bulletin.

and the Retiro, completely commanded the city; the perfectly open country around would have enabled the French cavalry to discover and cut off all convoys, and no precaution had been taken to provide subsistence for the hundred and fifty thousand people contained within the circuit of the place. The desire of the Central Junta, that this metropolis should risk the horrors of a storm, was therefore equally silly and barbarous; their own criminal apathy had deprived Madrid of the power of procrastinating its defence until relieved from without, and there was no sort of analogy between the situation of Zaragoza and this capital. Napoleon knew it well; he was not a man to plunge headlong into the streets of a great city, among an armed and excited people; he knew that address in negotiation, a little patience, and a judicious employment of artillery, would soon reduce the most outrageous to submission, and he had no wish to destroy the capital of his brother's kingdom.

In the evening the infantry and artillery arrived, and were posted at the most favorable points. The night was clear and bright, and in the French camp all was silent and watchful, but a tumultuous noise was heard from every quarter of the city, as if some mighty beast was struggling and howling in the toils.* At midnight a second summons was sent through the medium of a prisoner, and the Captain-General Castellar attempted to gain time by an equivocal reply; but the French light troops stormed the nearest houses, and one battery of thirty guns opened against the Retiro, while another threw shells from the opposite quarter, to distract the attention of the inhabitants. This building, situated on a rising ground, was connected with another range of buildings erected on the same side of the Prado, which is a public walk nearly encircling the town, and into which some of the principal streets opened, upon the above-mentioned range. In the morning a practicable breach was made in the Retiro wall, and the difference between military courage and ferocity became apparent; for Villatte's division, breaking in, easily routed the garrison, and, pursuing its success, seized all the public buildings connected with it, and then crossing the Prado, gained the barriers erected at the entrance of the streets, and took possession of the immense palace of the Duke of Medina Celi, which was in itself the key to the city on that side.

Such a vigorous commencement created great terror; the town was summoned for the third time, and in the afternoon, Morla and another officer came out to demand a suspension of arms, necessary, they said, to persuade the people to surrender. The Emperor addressed Morla in terms of great severity, reproaching him for

* Fourteenth Bulletin.

his scandalous conduct towards Dupont's army. "Injustice and bad faith," he exclaimed, "always recoil upon those who are guilty of either." A saying well applied to that Spaniard, and Napoleon himself confirmed its philosophic truth in after times. "The Spanish ulcer destroyed me!" was an expression of deep anguish which escaped from him in his own hour of misfortune.

Morla returned to the town, his story was soon told: before six o'clock the next morning Madrid must surrender or perish! Dissensions arose. The violent excitement of the populace was considerably abated, but the armed peasantry from the country and the poorest inhabitants still demanded to be led against the enemy, and a constant fire was kept up from the houses in the neighborhood of the Prado, by which the French General Maison was wounded, and General Bruyères killed. Nevertheless the disposition to fight became each moment weaker, and finally Morla and Castelfranco prepared a capitulation; the Captain-General Castellar, however, refused to sign it, and as the town was only invested on one side, he effected his escape with the regular troops during the night, carrying with him sixteen guns. The people then sunk into a quiescent state, and at eight o'clock in the morning of the 4th, Madrid surrendered.

That Morla was a traitor there is no doubt, and his personal cowardice was excessive; but Castelfranco appears to have been rather weak and ignorant than treacherous, and certainly the surrender of Madrid was no proof of his guilt; that event was inevitable. The boasting uproar of the multitude, when they are permitted to domineer for a few days, is not enthusiasm; the retreat of Castellar with the troops of the line during the progress of the negotiation was the wisest course to pursue, and proves that he acquiesced in the propriety of surrendering. That the people neither could nor would defend the city is quite evident; for it is incredible that Morla and Castelfranco should have been able to carry through a capitulation in so short a period, if the generals, the regular troops, the armed peasantry, and the inhabitants, had been all, or even a part of them, determined to resist.

Napoleon, cautious of giving offence to a population so lately and so violently excited, carefully provided against any sudden reaction, and preserved the strictest discipline; a soldier of the imperial guard was shot in one of the squares for having a plundered watch in his possession; the infantry were placed in barracks and convents, the cavalry were kept ready to scour the streets on the first alarm, and the Spaniards were all disarmed. The Emperor then fixed his own quarters at Chamartin, a country house four miles from Madrid, and in a few days everything presented the most tranquil appearance, the shops were opened, the public amusements recommenced, and the theatres were frequented. The inhabitants of capital cities are easily moved, and easily calmed; self-interest and sensual indulgence unfit them for noble and sustained efforts ; they can be violent, ferocious, cruel, but are seldom constant and firm.

During the operations against Madrid, La Peña, after escaping from the sixth corps, arrived at Guadalaxara with about five thousand men ; on the 2d, the Dukes of Infantado and Albuquerque leaving the capital, joined him ; and, on the 4th, Venegas came up with two thousand men. While these generals were hesitating what course to pursue, Napoleon, apprised of their vicinity, directed Bessières with sixteen squadrons upon Guadalaxara, supporting him by Ruffin's division of the first corps ; at the approach of this cavalry, the main body retired through the hills by Sanctorcaz towards Aranjuez, and the artillery crossed the Tagus at Sacedon ; Ruffin's division immediately changed its direction, and cut the Spaniards off from La Mancha by the line of Ocaña. Meanwhile a mutiny among the Spanish troops forced La Peña to resign, and the Duke of Infantado was chosen in his place. The Tagus was then crossed at several points, and after some slight actions with the advanced cavalry of the French, this miserable body of men finally saved themselves at Cuença, where many deserters and fugitives, and the brigades of Cartoajal and Lilli, which had escaped the different French columns, also arrived, and the Duke proceeded to organize another army.

On the French side, the fourth corps reached Segovia, passed the Guadarama, dispersed some armed peasants assembled at the Escurial, and then marched toward Almaraz, to attack General Galluzzo, who, having assembled five or six thousand men to defend the left bank of the Tagus, had, with the usual skill of a Spanish general, occupied a line of forty miles.* The first French corps entered La Mancha at the same time, and Toledo immediately shut its gates; but, although the Junta of that town publicly proclaimed their resolution to bury themselves under the ruins of the city, at the approach of a French division, they betrayed a most contemptible cowardice. Thus, six weeks had sufficed to dissipate the Spanish armies; the glittering bubble was bursted, and a terrible reality remained. From St. Sebastian to the Asturias, from the Asturias to Talavera de la Reyna, from Talavera to the gates of the noble city of Zaragoza, all was submission, and beyond that boundary, all was apathy or dread. Ten thousand French soldiers

* Sir John Moore's Papers.

could safely, as regarded the Spaniards, have marched from one extremity of the Peninsula to the other.

After the fall of Madrid, King Joseph remained at Burgos, issuing proclamations, and carrying on a sort of underplot, through the medium of his native ministers; the views of the latter naturally turned towards the Spanish interests as distinct from the French, and a source of infinite mischief to Joseph's cause was thus opened, for that monarch, anxious to please and conciliate his subjects, ceased to be a Frenchman without becoming a Spaniard. At this time, however, Napoleon assumed and exercised all the rights of conquest, and it is evident, from the tenor of his speeches, proclamations, and decrees, that some ulterior project, in which the King's personal interests were not concerned, was contemplated by him. It appeared as if he wished the nation, in imitation of the old King, to offer the crown to himself a second time, that he might obtain a plausible excuse for adopting a new line of policy by which to attract the people, or at least to soften their pride, which was now the main obstacle to his success.

An assemblage of the nobles, the clergy, the corporations, and the tribunals of Madrid, waited upon him at Chamartin, and presented an address, in which they expressed their desire to have Joseph among them again.* The Emperor's reply was an exposition of the principles upon which Spain was to be governed, and offers a fine field for reflection upon the violence of those passions which induce men to resist positive good, and eagerly seek for danger, misery, and death, rather than resign their prejudices.

"I accept," said he, "the sentiments of the town of Madrid. I regret the misfortunes that have befallen it, and I hold it as a particular good fortune that I am enabled, under the circumstances of the moment, to spare that city, and to save it from yet greater misfortunes.

"I have hastened to take measures fit to tranquillize all classes of citizens, knowing well that to all people, and to all men, uncertainty is intolerable.

"I have preserved the religious orders, but I have restrained the number of monks; no sane person can doubt that they are too numerous. Those who are truly called to this vocation by the grace of God will remain in their convents; those who have lightly or from worldly motives adopted it, will have their existence secured among the secular ecclesiastics, from the surplus of the convents.

"I have provided for the wants of the most interesting and useful of the clergy, the parish priests.

"I have abolished that tribunal against which Europe and the

* Moniteur.

age alike exclaimed. Priests ought to guide consciences, but they should not exercise any exterior or corporal jurisdiction over men.

"I have taken the satisfaction which was due to myself and to my nation, and the part of vengeance is completed. Ten of the principal criminals bend their heads before me; but for all others there is absolute and entire pardon.

"I have suppressed the rights usurped by the nobles during civil wars, when the kings have been too often obliged to abandon their own rights to purchase tranquillity and the repose of their people.

"I have suppressed the feudal rights, and every person can now establish inns, mills, ovens, weirs, and fisheries, and give free play to their industry; only observing the laws and customs of the place. The self-love, the riches, and the prosperity of a small number of men, was more hurtful to your agriculture than the heats of the dog-days.

"As there is but one God, there should be in one state but one justice; wherefore, all the particular jurisdictions having been usurped, and being contrary to the national rights, I have destroyed them. I have also made known to all persons that which each can have to fear, and that which they may hope for.

"The English armies I will drive from the Peninsula. Zaragoza, Valencia, Seville, shall be reduced either by persuasion or by force of arms.

"There is no obstacle capable of retarding for any length of time the execution of my will. But that which is above my power, is to constitute the Spaniards a nation, under the orders of the King, if they continue to be imbued with the principles of division, and of hatred towards France, such as the English partisans and the enemies of the continent have instilled into them. I cannot establish a nation, a King, and Spanish independence, if that King is not sure of the affection and fidelity of his subjects.

"The Bourbons can never again reign in Europe. The divisions in the royal family were concerted by the English; it was not either King Charles or his favorite, but the Duke of Infantado, the instrument of England, that was upon the point of overturning the throne. The papers recently found in his house prove this; it was the preponderance of England that they wished to establish in Spain. Insensate project! which would have produced a land war without end, and caused torrents of blood to be shed.

"No power influenced by England can exist upon the continent; if any desire it, their desire is folly, and sooner or later will ruin them. I shall be obliged to govern Spain, and it will be easy for me to do it by establishing a viceroy in each province. However, I will not refuse to concede my rights of conquest to the King, and to establish him in Madrid, when the thirty thousand citizens assemble in the churches, and on the holy sacrament take an oath, not with the mouth alone, but with the heart, and without any jesuitical restriction, ' to be true to the King, to love and support him.' Let the priests from the pulpit and in the confessional, the tradesmen in their correspondence and their discourses, inculcate these sentiments in the people; then I will relinquish my rights of conquest, then I will place the King upon the throne, and I will take a pleasure in showing myself the faithful friend of the Spaniards.

"The present generation may differ in opinions; too many passions have been excited; but your descendants will bless me as the regenerator of the nation; they will mark my sojourn among you as memorable days, and from those days they will date the prosperity of Spain. These are my sentiments; go consult your fellow citizens, choose your part, but do it frankly, and exhibit only true colors."

The ten criminals were the Dukes of Infantado, of Hijar, Medina Celi, and Ossuna; Marquis Santa Cruz; Counts Fernan, Miñez, and Altamira; Prince of Castello Franco, Pedro Cevallos, and the Bisop of Santander, who were proscribed, body and goods, as traitors to France and Spain.

Napoleon now made dispositions indicating a vast plan of operations. It would appear that he intended to invade Gallicia, Andalusia, and Valencia, by his lieutenants, and to carry his arms to Lisbon in person. Upon the 20th December the sixth corps, the guards, and the reserve, were assembled under his own immediate control. The first corps was stationed at Toledo, and the light cavalry attached to it scoured the roads leading to Andalusia, up to the foot of the Sierra Morena. The fourth corps was at Talavera, on the march towards the frontier of Portugal. The second corps was on the Carrion river, preparing to advance against Gallicia. The eighth corps was broken up: the divisions composing it were ordered to join the second, and Junot, who commanded it, repaired to the third corps, to supply the place of Marshal Moncey, who was called to Madrid for a particular service,—doubtless an expedition against Valencia. The fifth corps, which had arrived at Vittoria, was directed to reinforce the third, then employed against Zaragoza. The seventh was always in Catalonia.

Vast as this plan of campaign appears, it was not beyond the Emperor's means; for, without taking into consideration his own genius, activity, and vigor, there were on his muster rolls above three hundred and thirty thousand men, and above sixty thousand horses. Two hundred pieces of field artillery followed the corps to battle, and as many more remained in reserve. Of this monstrous army, two hundred and fifty-five thousand men and fifty thousand horses were actually under arms, with their different regiments, while thirty-two thousand were detached or in garrisons, preserving tranquillity in the rear and guarding the communications of the active force. The remainder were in hospital, and so slight had been the resistance of the Spanish armies, that only nineteen hundred prisoners were to be deducted from this multitude. Of the whole host, two hundred and thirteen thousand were native Frenchmen; the residue were Poles, Germans, and Italians; thirty-five thousand men and five thousand horses were available for fresh enterprise, without taking a single man from the service of the lines of communication. What was there to oppose this fearful array? What consistency or vigor in the councils? What numbers? What discipline and spirit in the armies of Spain? What enthusiasm among the people? What was the disposition, the means, what the activity of the allies of that country? The answers to these questions demonstrate that the fate of the Peninsula hung at this moment upon a thread, and that the deliverance of that country was due to other causes than the courage, the patriotism, or the constancy of the Spaniards.

First, with regard to their armies. The Duke of Infantado resided with, rather than commanded, a few thousand wretched fugitives at Cuença, destitute, mutinous, and cowed in spirit. At Valencia there was no army; for that which belonged to the province was shut up in Zaragoza, and dissensions had arisen between Palafox and the local Junta in consequence.* In the passes of the Sierra Morena were five thousand raw levies, hastily made by the Junta of Seville, after the defeat of St. Juan. Galluzzo, who had undertaken to defend the Tagus with six thousand timid and ill-armed soldiers, was at this time in flight, having been suddenly attacked and defeated at Almarez, by a detachment of the fourth corps. Romana was near Leon, at the head of eighteen or twenty thousand runaways, collected by him after the dispersion at Reynosa;† but of this number only five thousand were armed, and none were subordinate, or capable of being disciplined; for, when checked for misconduct, the Marquis complained that they deserted. In Gallicia there was no army, and in the Asturias the local government were so corrupt, so faithless, and so oppressive, that the spirit of the people was crushed and patriotism reduced to a name.

The members of the Central Junta had at first thought of going to Badajos, but, being terrified, fled to Seville, and their inactivity

* Infantado's Letters. Narrative of Moore's Campaign. Stuart's and Frere's Letters.
† Sir John Moore's Papers.

was more conspicuous in this season of adversity than before, contrasting strangely with the pompous and inflated language of their public papers : all their promises were fallacious, their incapacity glaring, their exertions ridiculous, abortive, and the Junta of Seville, still actuated by their own ambitious views, had now openly reassumed all their former authority. In short, the strength and spirit of Spain were broken; the enthusiasm was null, except in a few places ; and the Emperor was, with respect to the Spaniards, perfectly master of operations. He was in the centre of the country ; he held the capital, the fortresses, the command of the great lines of communication between the provinces; and on the wide military horizon no cloud intercepted his view, save the heroic city of Zaragoza on the one side, and a feeble British army on the other. Sooner or later, he observed, and with truth, that the former must fall, as it was an affair of artillery calculation. The latter he naturally supposed to be in full retreat for Portugal ; but as the fourth corps was nearer to Lisbon than the British General, a hurried retreat alone could bring the latter in time to that capital, and consequently no preparations for defence could be made sufficient to arrest the sixty thousand Frenchmen which the Emperor could carry there at the same moment. The subjugation of Spain appeared inevitable, when the genius and vigor of Sir J. Moore frustrated Napoleon's plans at the very moment of execution. The Austrian war breaking out at the instant, drew the master-spirit from the scene of contention, and England then put forth her vast resources, which being fortunately wielded by a general equal to the task of delivering the Peninsula, it was delivered. But through what changes of fortune, by what unexpected helps, by what unlooked-for and extraordinary events, under what difficulties, by whose perseverance, and in despite of whose errors, let posterity judge ; for in that judgment only will impartiality and justice be found.

CHAPTER III.

Sir John Moore arrives at Salamanca; hears of the battle of Espinosa—His dangerous position; discovers the real state of affairs; contemplates a hardy enterprise; hears of the defeat at Tudela; resolves to retreat; waits for General Hope's division—Danger of that General; his able conduct—Central Junta fly to Badajos—Mr. Frere, incapable of judging rightly, opposes the retreat; his weakness and levity; insults the General; sends Colonel Charmilly to Salamanca—Manly conduct of Sir John Moore; his able and bold plan of operations.

OPERATIONS OF THE BRITISH ARMY.

WHILE at Madrid, Napoleon heard that Sir John Moore, having relinquished his communication with Lisbon, was menacing the French line of operations on the side of Burgos. This intelligence obliged him to suspend all his designs against the south of Spain and Portugal, and to fix his whole attention upon that General's movements. The reasons which induced Moore to divide his army, and to send General Hope with one column by the Tagus, while the other marched under his own personal command, by Almeida and Ciudad Rodrigo, have been already related; as likewise the arrangements which brought Sir David Baird to Coruña, without having permission to land his troops, and without money to equip them, when they were suffered to disembark.

The 8th of November, Sir John Moore was at Almeida, on the frontier of Portugal; his artillery was at Truxillo, in Spanish Estremadura, and Sir David Baird's division was at Coruña. General Blake, pursued by fifty thousand enemies, was that day flying from Nava to Espinosa; Castaños and Palafox were quarrelling at Tudela. The Conde de Belvedere was at Burgos with thirteen thousand bad troops, and Napoleon was at Vittoria with one hundred and seventy thousand good troops.

At this time the letters of Lord William Bentinck and Colonel Graham, exposing all the imprudence of the Spanish generals, were received, and disquieted the English General. He already foresaw that his junction with the other divisions of his army might be impeded by the result of an action, which the Spaniards appeared to be courting, contrary to all sound policy; but as no misfortune had yet befallen them, he continued his march, hoping " that all the bad which might happen, would not happen."

The 11th he crossed the frontier of Spain, and marched to Ciudad Rodrigo; on that day Blake was completely discomfited at Espinosa, and the Estremaduran army, beaten the day before at Gamonal, was utterly ruined and dispersed.

The 13th, the head of the British columns entered Salamanca, at the moment when Blake's fugitive force was finally disorganized at Reynosa, leaving the first, second, and fourth French corps, amounting to near seventy thousand men, free to act against any quarter.

Sir John Moore participated at first in the universal belief that the nation was enthusiastic, and fixed in a determination to dispute every step with the invaders; and after he had detected the exaggerations of the military agents, and perceived the want of capacity in the Spanish generals and rulers, he still trusted that the spirit of the people would compensate for their deficiency of skill. What then was his surprise to find, that the defeat of the Conde de Belvedere, an event which laid Castile open to the incursions of the enemy, which uncovered the march of the British, and compromised their safety, had created no sensation among the people; that the authorities had spread no alarm, taken no precautions, delivered out no arms, although many thousands were stored in the principal towns, and neither encouraged the inhabitants by proclamations, nor enrolled any of them for defence! He himself was not informed of this important occurrence until a week after it happened, and then only through a single official channel.

Valladolid, where the enemy's cavalry were, was but three marches from Salamanca, and as not more than four thousand of Moore's infantry had come up to the latter town, it was evident that if the French advanced in force, the British must fall back towards Ciudad Rodrigo. Nevertheless the General, assembling the local authorities, explained the nature of his position, endeavored to excite their ardor, and, notwithstanding the apathetic state of the public mind, resolved not to retire unless forced back by superior numbers; he even hastened the arrival of his rear divisions, but sent orders to both Hope and Baird to concentrate their troops and be prepared for a retreat. His exhortations produced no effect upon the Junta or the people; the former were stupefied and timid, the latter, although declaring their hatred of the invaders, would not stir in defence; the first feeling of indignation against the French was exhausted, and there was nothing to supply its place; the fugitives from the armies passed daily without shame, and unreproached by their countrymen. In this state the English General remained until the 18th; his army was closing up, and the French cavalry withdrew from Valladolid to Palencia, when the news of Blake's defeat reached Salamanca, not by rumor, or by any direct communication from the Montaña Santander, but through Mr. Stuart, eight days subsequent to the date of the action; the Central Junta did not even inform the minister plenipotentiary until thirty hours after having received official intelligence of it themselves.*

Want of transport and supplies had obliged the British to march in small and successive divisions; it was, therefore, the 23d of November before the centre, consisting of twelve thousand infantry, and a battery of six guns, was concentrated at Salamanca. On that day, Castaños and Palafox being defeated at Tudela, and their armies scattered without a chance of rallying again in the field, the third and sixth French corps became disposable. The Emperor also, victorious on both flanks, and with a fresh base of operations fixed at Burgos, was then free to move, with the guards and the reserve, either against Madrid or in the direction of Salamanca; detachments of his army were already in possession of Valladolid, the very town which, a few days before, the Spanish government had indicated for the base of Sir John Moore's operations, and the formation of his magazines.† The 26th, the head of Sir David Baird's column was in Astorga, but the rear extended beyond Lugo, while the head of Hope's division was at the Escurial, and the rear at Talavera. But the second French corps was on the Deba, threatening Leon and the Asturias; the cavalry covered the plains; the fourth corps was descending by Carrion and Valladolid, to seize the pass of the Guadarama; the Emperor himself was preparing to force the Somosierra.

From this summary of contemporary events, it is evident that, notwithstanding Sir John Moore had organized, equipped, and supplied his army, and marched four hundred miles, all in the space of six weeks, he was too late in the field; the campaign was decided against the Spaniards before the British had, strictly speaking, entered Spain as an army. And it is certain that if, instead of being at Salamanca, Escurial, and Astorga, on the 23d, the troops had been united at Burgos on the 8th, such was the weakness of the Spanish forces, the strength of the enemy, and such the skill with which Napoleon directed his movements, that a difficult and precarious retreat was the utmost favor that could be expected from fortune by the English.

Sir John Moore's situation on his arrival at Salamanca, gave rise to serious reflections. He had been sent forward without a plan of operations, or any data upon which to found one; his instructions merely directed him to open communication with the Spanish authorities, for the purpose of "framing the plan of campaign." But General Castaños, with whom he was desired to correspond, was superseded immediately afterwards, and the Marquis of Ro-

* Mr. Frere's Letter to the Junta.
† Sir John Moore's Papers.

mana, his successor, was engaged in rallying the remains of Blake's force in the Asturias, at a distance of two hundred miles from the only army with which any plan of co-operation could be formed, and of whose proceedings he also was ignorant. No channel of intelligence had been pointed out to Moore, and, as yet a stranger in the country, and without money, he could not establish any certain one for himself. It was the will of the people of England, and the orders of the government, that he should push forward to the assistance of the Spaniards, and he had done so, without magazines, and without money to form them; trusting to the official assurance of the minister, that above a hundred thousand Spanish soldiers covered his march, that the people were enthusiastic and prepared for any exertion to secure their own deliverance, but he found them supine and unprepared; the French cavalry, in parties as weak as twelve men, traversed the country, and raised contributions, without difficulty or opposition. This was the state of Castile, and the letters of Mr. Stuart and Lord William Bentinck amply exposed the incapacity, selfishness, and apathy of the supreme government at Aranjuez. The correspondence of Colonel Graham painted in the strongest colors the confusion of affairs on the Ebro, the jealousy, the discord of the generals, the worse than childish folly of the deputy Palafox and his creatures. Sir David Baird's experience proved, that in Gallicia the people were inert as in Castile and Leon, and the authorities more absurd and more interested. General Hope expressed a like opinion as to the ineptitude of the Central Junta; and even the military agents, hitherto so sanguine, had lowered their tone of exultation in a remarkable manner.

Napoleon's enormous force was unknown to Sir John Moore, but he knew that it could not be less than eighty thousand fighting men, and that thirty thousand more were momentarily expected, and might have arrived; he knew that Blake and the Conde de Belvedere were totally defeated, and that Castaños must inevitably be so if he hesitated to retreat. The only conclusion to be drawn from these facts was, that the Spaniards were unable, or unwilling, to resist the enemy, and that the British would have to support the contest alone, unless they could form a junction with Castaños, before the latter was entirely discomfited and destroyed; but there was no time for such an operation, and the first object was, to unite the parcelled divisions of the English army.

From Astorga to Salamanca was five marches; from Salamanca to the Escurial was six marches; but it would have required five days to close up the rear upon Salamanca, six days to enable Hope to concentrate at the Escurial, and sixteen to enable Baird to assemble at Astorga. Hence twenty days were required for the

English army to unite and act in a body; and to have advanced in their divided state, would have been equally contrary to military principle and to common sense. A retreat, although it was prescribed by the rules of scientific war, and in unison with the instructions of the government, which forbade the General to commit his troops in any serious affair before the whole were united, would have been, while the Spanish army of the centre still held the field, ungenerous: the idea was repugnant to the bold and daring spirit of Moore. Rather than resort to such a remedy for the false position his government had placed him in, he contemplated a hardy and dangerous enterprise, such as none but great minds are capable of. He proposed, if he could draw the extended wings of his army together in good time, to abandon all communication with Portugal, and throwing himself into the heart of Spain, to rally Castaños' army, if it yet existed, upon his own, to defend the southern provinces, and trust to the effect which such an appeal to the patriotism and courage of the Spaniards would produce.

But Moore also considered that the question was not purely military; the Spanish cause was not one which could be decided by the marches of a few auxiliary troops; its fate rested on the vigor of the rulers, the concert of the generals, the unity of the exertions, and the fixed resolution of the people to suffer all privations, and die rather than submit; to him it appeared doubtful that such a spirit, or the means of creating it, existed, and more doubtful that there was capacity in the government to excite or to direct it when aroused; no men of talent had yet appeared, and good-will was in itself nothing if improperly treated. Wherefore, he turned to the English plenipotentiary, who had just superseded Mr. Stuart near the Central Junta; for he had been directed by the ministers to communicate with him upon all important points,—to receive with deference his opinion and advice; and the present was an occasion to which those instructions were peculiarly applicable. Mr. Frere had come fresh from the English government; he was acquainted with its views; he was in the most suitable position to ascertain what degree of elasticity the Spanish cause really possessed, and the decision of the question belonged as much to him as to the General, because it involved the whole policy of the English Cabinet with respect to Spain; it was likewise the more proper to consult him because, as a simple operation of war, the proposed movement was rash. All the military, and many political reasons, called for a retreat upon Portugal, which would take the army back upon its own resources, insure its concentration, increase its strength, protect British interests, and leave it free either to return to Spain, if a favorable opportunity should occur, or to pass by sea to Andalusia, and commence the campaign in the south.

Such were the reflections that induced Sir John Moore to solicit Mr. Frere's opinion upon the general policy of the proposed operation. But in so doing he never had the least intention of consulting him upon the mode of executing the military part, of which he conceived himself to be the best judge; and while awaiting the reply, he directed Sir David Baird, if the enemy showed no disposition to molest him, to push the troops on to Salamanca as fast as they should arrive at Astorga. Sir David was proceeding to do so, when Blake advised him that a considerable French force was collecting at Rio Seco and Ampudia, with a view of interrupting the march; this arrested his movement; he was even preparing to fall back, when he was stopped by Moore, whose information led him to believe that Blake's report was false. Valuable time was thus lost, but it was the march of the fourth corps, then traversing the line from Carrion to the Guadarama, that gave rise to this contradictory intelligence, for the many various changes in the French positions, and the continual circulation of their light cavalry through the plains, bewildered the spies and the peasants. The force of the enemy on different points also confused the higher agents, who, believing the greatest amount of the invading army to be from a hundred to a hundred and twenty thousand men, could never reconcile the reports with this standard, and therefore concluded that Napoleon exaggerated his real numbers to create terror.

Moore had written to Mr. Frere on the 27th of November, Baird was to march by Benevente on the 1st, and Hope by Tordesillas, the troops at Salamanca by Zamora and Toro; and all the arrangements for the execution of the project were completed when, in the night of the 28th, a despatch from Mr. Stuart made known the disaster at Tudela. This again changed the aspect of affairs; the question proposed to Mr. Frere was no longer doubtful. The projected movement had been founded upon *the chance of rallying the Spanish armies behind the Tagus*, a hazardous and daring experiment when first conceived, but now that Castaños had no longer an army—now that the strength of Spain was utterly broken—to have persisted in it would have been insanity; the French could be over the Tagus before the British, and there were no Spanish armies to rally. The defeat at Tudela took place the 23d of November; Baird's brigades could not be united at Astorga before the 4th of December, and to concentrate the whole of the army at Salamanca required a flank march of several days over an open plain; an operation not to be thought of, within a few marches of a skilful enemy, who possessed such an overwhelming force of artillery and cavalry.

As long as Castaños and Palafox kept the field, there was reason to believe that the French stationed at Burgos would not make any serious attempt on the side of Astorga, but that check being now removed, an unmilitary flank march would naturally draw their attention, and bring them down upon the parcelled divisions of the English troops. The object of succoring the Spaniards called for great, but not for useless sacrifices. The English General was prepared to confront any danger and to execute any enterprise which held out a chance of utility, but he also remembered that the best blood of England was committed to his charge; that not an English army, but the very heart, the pith of the military power of his country was in his keeping; it was intrusted to his prudence, and his patriotism spurned the idea of seeking personal renown by betraying that sacred trust. The political reasons in favor of marching towards Madrid scarcely balanced the military objections before the battle of Tudela; and after that event, the latter requiring double force, left no room for hesitation in the mind of any man capable of reasoning at all, and Sir John Moore resolved to fall back into Portugal.

He ordered Sir David Baird to regain Coruña or Vigo, and to carry his troops by sea to Lisbon; yet wishing, if possible, to unite with Hope before the retrograde movement commenced, he directed Baird to show a bold front for a few days in order to attract the enemy's attention. The negligence, the false intelligence, the frauds, the opposition approaching to hostility, experienced by Sir David Beard during his march from Coruña, had so reduced that General's hopes, that he prepared for this retreat without reluctance; he was in direct communication with Romana, but the intercourse between them had rather confirmed than weakened the impression on Baird's mind, that it was impossible to depend upon the promises, the information, or the judgment of any Spanish general. In the mean time, Napoleon forced the Somosierra, and summoned Madrid; the Supreme Junta fled towards Badajos; St. Juan was murdered at Talavera, the remnant of Castaños' army was driven towards the Tagus; the fourth corps approached Segovia, and Sir John Hope's situation became very critical.

His column, consisting of three thousand infantry, nine hundred cavalry, the artillery, and the great parc of ammunition, had been obliged, from the want of money and supplies, to move in six divisions, each being a day's march behind the other.* At Almaraz he endeavored to discover a way across the mountains to

* Sir John Moore's Papers. Hope's Letters.

Ciudad Rodrigo, and a road did exist, but the peasants and mule-teers declared it to be impracticable for carriages, and consequently unfit for the convoy; the truth of their assertions was much doubted, but Sir John was daily losing horses from the glanders, and with a number but just sufficient to drag his guns and convoy along a good road, he feared to explore a difficult passage over the sierras.

When his leading division had reached Talavera, Don Thomas Morla, then Secretary of War, anxious to have the troops more minutely divided, proposed that the regiments should march through Madrid in ten divisions on as many successive days, the first to reach the capital on the 22d of November, which would exactly have brought the convoy into the jaws of the French army.*   Hope immediately repaired in person to Madrid, held a conference with Morla, and quickly satisfied himself that every-thing was in confusion, and that the Spanish government had nei-ther arranged a general plan, nor was capable of conducting one. Convinced of this unfortunate truth, he paid no attention to Mor-la's proposition, but carried his troops at once by the road of Naval Carnero to the Escurial, where he halted to close up the rear, and to obtain bullocks to assist in dragging the parc over the Guada-rama.   The 28th, he crossed the mountain, and entered the open flat country; the 28th and 29th the infantry and guns were at Villa Castin and St. Antonia, the parc was at Espinar, and the cavalry advanced on the road to Arevalo.   General Heredia was then at Segovia, but the Duke of Dantzic was at Valladolid and Placentia, and his patrols were heard of at Coca, only a few miles from Arevalo, and in the course of the day a despatch from Mr. Stuart announced the catastrophe at Tudela, and the dispersion of the camp at Sepulveda; at the same time the outposts of cavalry in the front reported that four hundred French horse were at Ol-medo, only twelve miles from Arevalo, and that four thousand others were in the neighborhood; the scouts at St. Garcia, on the right, also tracked the French again at Anaya, near Segovia.

Hope's situation was now truly embarrassing.   If he fell back to the Guadarama, the army at Salamanca would be without am-munition or artillery.†   If he advanced, it must be by a flank move-ment of three days, with a heavy convoy, over a flat country, and within a few hours' march of a very superior cavalry.   If he de-layed where he was, even for a few hours, the French on the side of Segovia might get between him and the pass of Guadarama, and then, attacked in front, flank, and rear, he would be reduced to

* Lord W. Bentinck's Letters.
† Gen. Hope's Reports, MS.

the shameful necessity of abandoning his convoy and guns to save his men in the mountains of Avila. A man of less intrepidity and calmness would have been ruined. Hope, as enterprising as he was prudent, without any hesitation ordered the cavalry to throw out parties cautiously towards the French, and maintain a confident front if the latter approached; then moving the infantry and guns from Villacastin, and the convoy from Espinosa by cross roads to Avila, he continued his march day and night until they reached Peneranda. Meanwhile the cavalry to cover this movement closed gradually to the left, and finally occupied Fontiveros on the 2d of December. The infantry and the draught animals were greatly fatigued; but the danger was not over; the patrols reported that the enemy, to the number of ten thousand infantry, two thousand cavalry, and forty guns, were still in Olmedo; this was the eternal fourth corps, which, thus traversing the country, continually crossed the heads of the English columns, and seemed to multiply the forces of the French at all points. Hope immediately drew his infantry and cavalry up in position, and obliged the artillery and the convoy to proceed without rest to Alba de Tormes, where a detachment from Salamanca met them, and covered their march to that town. This vigorous and skilful march was thus concluded, for the division remaining at Peneranda collected its stragglers, and pushed outposts to Medina del Campo, Madrigal, and Torecilla, while the fourth corps unwittingly pursued its march to the Guadarama.

Sir John Moore's resolution to retreat upon Portugal created a great sensation at Madrid and at Aranjuez. The Junta feared, and with reason, that such a palpable proof of the state to which their negligence and incapacity had reduced the country, would endanger their authority and perhaps their lives;* and although they were on the point of flying to Badajos themselves, they were anxious that others should rush headlong into danger. Morla, and those who, like him, were prepared to abandon the cause of their country, felt mortified at losing an opportunity of commemorating their defection by a single act of perfidy; and the English plenipotentiary was surprised and indignant that a general of experience and reputation should think for himself, and decide upon a military operation without a reference to his opinion.

Mr. Frere, although a person of some scholastic attainments, was very ill qualified for the duties of his situation, which at this moment required temper, sagacity, and judgment. Greatly overrating his own talents for public affairs, he had come out to Spain impressed with false notions of what was passing in that

* Mr. Stuart's Correspondence.

country, and tenaciously clinging to the pictures of his imagination, resented the intrusion of reason, and petulantly spurned at
facts. The defeat of the Conde de Belvedere at Gamonal, a
defeat that broke the centre of the Spanish line, uncovered the
flank and rear of Castaños' army, opened a way to Madrid, and
rendered the concentration of the British divisions unsafe, if not
impossible, he curiously called the "unlucky affair of the 10th at
Burgos." After the battle of Tudela he estimated the whole
French army on the side of Burgos and Valladolid at eleven
thousand men, when they were above one hundred thousand; and
yet, with information so absurdly defective, he was prompt to interfere with, and eager to control the military combinations of the
General, which were founded upon the true and acknowledged
principles of the art of war.*

Moore, while anxiously watching the dangerous progress of Sir
John Hope, was suddenly assailed by the representations and remonstrances of all these offended, mortified, and disappointed persons; and as the question of retiring was, by the defeat of Tudela,
rendered so purely military, and the necessity of it so palpable, the
General, although anticipating some expressions of discontent from
the Spanish government, was totally unprepared for the torrent of
puerile impertinences with which he was overwhelmed.

Morla, a subtle man, endeavored first to deceive Mr. Stuart, by
treating the defeat of Castaños lightly, and stating officially that he
had saved the greatest part of his army at Siguenza, and was on
the march to join St. Juan at the Somosierra;† to this he added,
that there were only small bodies of French cavalry in the flat
country of Castile and Leon, and no force on that side capable of
preventing the junction of Sir John Moore's army. This was on
the evening of the 30th, but the Emperor had forced the pass of
the Somosierra on that morning, and the Duke of Dantzic was at
Valladolid. The same day Mr. Frere, writing from Aranjuez in
answer to the General's formal communication, and before he was
acquainted with his intention to fall back, deprecated a retreat upon
Portugal, and asserted that the enthusiasm of the Spanish was
unbounded, except in Castile and Leon, where, he admitted, they
were more passive than they should be.‡ He even stated that
twenty thousand men were actually assembled in the vicinity of
the capital, and that Castaños was falling back upon them; that
reinforcements were arriving daily from the southern provinces, and
that the addition of the British army would form a force greatly

---

* Narrative of Moore's Campaign.
† Moore's Papers. Mr. Stuart's Correspondence.
‡ Moore's Papers. Frere's Correspondence.

superior to any the French could bring against that quarter, in sufficient time. It was certain, he said, that the latter were very
weak, and would be afraid to advance, while the whole country,
from the Pyrenees to the capital, was in arms upon their left flank.
Rumors also were rife that the conscription had been resisted, and
this was the more probable, because every great effort made by
France was accompanied by weakness and internal disturbance,
and a pastoral letter of the Bishop of Carcassonne seemed to imply
that it was so at that time. "Good policy, therefore, required, that
the French should be attacked before their reinforcements joined
them, as any success obtained at that moment would render a conscription for a third attempt infinitely difficult, if not impracticable;
but if, on the other hand," said this inconsiderate person, "the
French are allowed, with their present forces, to retain their present advantages, and to wait the completion of their conscription,
they would pour into Spain with a number of troops which would
give them immediate possession of the capital and the central provinces." Two days after the date of this letter, the Emperor was
actually at the capital; and Mr. Frere, notwithstanding the superior
Spanish force which his imagination had conjured up, was with
the Junta, flying in all haste from those very central provinces,
France remaining, meanwhile, strong, and free from internal dissension.

This rambling epistle was not despatched when the General's
intention to fall back upon Portugal was made known to Mr. Frere,
but he thought it so admirably calculated to prevent a retreat, that
he forwarded it, accompanied by a short explanatory note, which
was offensive in style, and indicative of a petulant disposition. At
the same time, Augustin Bueno and Ventura Escalente, two generals deputed by the Junta to remonstrate against Sir John Moore's
intended retreat, arrived at head-quarters, and they justified the
choice of their employers, being in folly and presumptuous ignorance
the very types of the government they represented. Asserting that
St. Juan, with twenty thousand men under his command, had so
fortified the pass of the Somosierra, that it could not be forced by
any number of enemies, and that reinforcements were daily joining
him, they were proceeding to create immense Spanish armies, when
the General stopped their garrulity by introducing Colonel Graham, who had been a witness of the dispersion of Castaños' army,
and had just left the unfortunate St. Juan at Talavera, surrounded
by the villanous runagates, who murdered him the next day.* It
may be easily supposed that such representations, and from such
men, could have no weight with the commander of an army; in

* Moore's Papers.

fact, the necessity of retreating was rendered more imperious by these glaring proofs that the Junta and the English plenipotentiary were totally ignorant of what was passing around them.

But Napoleon was now in full career; he had raised a hurricane of war, and, directing his fury as he pleased, his adversaries were obliged to conform their movements to his, and as the circumstances varied from hour to hour, the determination of one moment was rendered useless in the next. The appearance of the French cavalry in the plains of Madrid had sent the Junta and Mr. Frere headlong towards Badajos, yet the people of Madrid, as we have seen, shut their gates, and displayed the outward signs of a resolution to imitate Zaragoza; the neighboring peasants flocked in to aid the citizens, and a military Junta, composed of the Duke of Infantado, the Prince of Castel Franco, the Marquis of Castellar, and Don Thomas Morla, was appointed to manage the defence. Morla, being resolved to make a final effort to involve the British army in the destruction of his own country, easily persuaded the Duke of Infantado to quit Madrid on a mission to the army of the centre; and thus the traitor was left sole master of the town, because the Duke and himself only had any influence with that armed mob which had murdered the Marquis de Perales, and filled the city with tumult.

When the French Emperor summoned the Junta to surrender, Morla, in concert with the Prince of Castel Franco, addressed a paper to Sir John Moore, in which it was stated that "twenty-five thousand men under Castaños, and ten thousand from the Somosierra, were marching in all haste to the capital, where forty thousand others were in arms. Nevertheless, apprehending an increase of force on the enemy's side, the Junta hoped the English army would either march to the assistance of Madrid, or take a direction to fall upon the rear of the French; and not doubting that the English General had already formed a junction with Blake's army," which they well knew had been dispersed, "they hoped he would be quick in his operations." This paper was sent by a government messenger to Salamanca, but ere he could reach that place, Morla, who had commenced negotiations before the despatch was written, capitulated, and Napoleon was in Madrid. This communication alone would not have been sufficient to arrest Moore's retrograde movement, for he was become too well acquainted with what facility Spanish armies were created on paper, to rely on any statement of their numbers; but Mr. Stuart also expressed a belief that Madrid would make a vigorous resistance, and the tide of false information having set in with a strong current, every moment brought fresh assurances that a great spirit had arisen.

On the day that Morla's communication arrived, there also appeared at head-quarters one Charmilly, a French adventurer. This man, who has been since denounced in the British Parliament as an organizer of assassination in St. Domingo, and a fraudulent bankrupt in London, came as the confidential agent of Mr. Frere. He had been in Madrid during the night of the first, and left it immediately after having held a conference with Morla, the next morning. Taking the road to Talavera, he met with the plenipotentiary, to whom he spoke with such enthusiasm of the spirit and preparations of the inhabitants in the capital, that Mr. Frere, readily confiding in him, and imparting his own views, not only intrusted him, a stranger, with letters to the British General, but charged him with a mission to obstruct the retreat into Portugal. Thus instructed, Charmilly hastened to Salamanca, and presented Mr. Frere's first missive, in which that gentleman, after alluding to former representations, and to the information of which Colonel Charmilly was the bearer, viz., the enthusiasm in the capital, made a formal remonstrance, to the effect that propriety and policy demanded an immediate advance of the British to support this generous effort. Charmilly also demanded a personal interview, which was granted; yet Moore, having some suspicion of the man, whom he had seen before, listened to his tale of the enthusiasm and vigorous character displayed at Madrid, with an appearance of coldness that baffled the penetration of the adventurer, who retired under the impression that a retreat was certain.

But for many years so much ridicule had been attached to the name of an English expedition, that weak-headed men claimed a sort of prescriptive right to censure, without regard to subordination, the conduct of their general. It had been so in Egypt, where a cabal was formed to deprive Lord Hutchinson of the command; it had been so at Buenos Ayres, at Ferrol, and in Portugal; it was so at this time in Sir John Moore's army; and it will be found, in the course of this work, that the superlative talents, vigor, and success of the Duke of Wellington, could not, even at a late period of the war, secure him from such vexatious folly. The three generals who commanded the separate divisions of the army, and who were in consequence acquainted with all the circumstances of the moment, were perfectly agreed as to the propriety of a retreat; but in other quarters indecent murmurs were so prevalent among officers of rank as to call for rebuke; and Charmilly, ignorant of the decided character of the general-in-chief, concluding that this temper was favorable to the object of his mission, presented a second letter, which Mr. Frere had charged him to deliver, should the first fail of effect. The purport of it was to desire that if Sir John Moore still persisted in his intention of retreating, *"the bearer might be previously examined before a council of war;"* in other words, that Mr. Frere, convinced of Sir John Moore's incapacity and want of zeal, was determined to control his proceedings even by force. And this to a British general, of long experience and confirmed reputation, and by the hands of a foreign adventurer!!! The indignation of a high spirit at such a foolish, wanton insult, may be easily imagined. He ordered Charmilly to quit the cantonments of the British army instantly. His anger, however, soon subsided. Quarrels, among the servants of the public, could only prove detrimental to his country, and he put his personal feelings on one side. The information brought by Charmilly, separated from the indecorum of his mission, was in itself important; it confirmed the essential fact, that Madrid was actually resisting, and that the spirit and energy of the country was awaking.

Hitherto his own observation had led Sir John Moore to doubt if the people took sufficient interest in the cause to make any effectual effort; all around himself was apathetic and incapable; his correspondents, with the exception of Mr. Frere, nay, even the intercepted letters of French officers, had agreed in describing the general feeling of the country as subsiding into indifference, and, to use his own words, *" Spain was without armies, generals, or a government."* But now the fire essential to the salvation of the nation seemed to be kindling, and Moore, feeling conscious of ability to lead a British army, hailed the appearance of an enthusiasm which promised success to a just cause, and a brilliant career of glory to himself. That the metropolis should thus abide the fury of the conqueror was indeed surprising; it was a great event and full of promise, and the situation of the army was likewise improved. General Hope's junction was accomplished; and as the attention of the French was turned towards Madrid, there was no reason to doubt that Baird's junction could likewise be effected. On the other hand, there was no certainty that the capital would remain firm when danger pressed, none that it would be able to resist, none that the example would spread; yet without it did so nothing was gained, because it was only by a union of heart and hand throughout the whole country, that the great power of the French could be successfully resisted.

In a matter so balanced, Moore, as might be expected from an enterprising general, adopted the boldest and most generous side. He ordered Baird, who, after destroying some stores, had fallen back to Villa Franca, to concentrate his troops at Astorga, and he himself prepared for an advance; but as he remained without any further information of the fate of Madrid, he sent Colonel Graham to obtain intelligence of what was passing, and to carry his answer to Morla. This resolution being taken, he wrote to Mr. Frere, calmly explaining the reasons for his past conduct, and those which actuated him in forming a fresh plan of operation. " I wish anxiously," said this noble-minded man in conclusion, "I wish axiously, as the King's minister, to continue upon the most confidential footing with you, and I hope, as we have but one interest, the public welfare, though we occasionally see it in different aspects, that this will not disturb the harmony which should subsist between us. Fully impressed as I am with these sentiments, I shall abstain from any remarks upon the two letters from you, delivered to me last night and this morning by Colonel Charmilly, or on the message which accompanied them. I certainly at first did feel and expressed much indignation at a person like him being made the channel of a communication of that sort from you to me. These feelings are at an end, and I dare say they never will be created towards you again."

The plan of operations now occupied his mind. The Somosierra and the Guadarama were both in possession of the enemy, wherefore no direct movement could be made towards Madrid; and as the rear of Baird's troops was still several marches behind Astorga, a general movement on the side of the capital could not commence before the 12th of the month. Zaragoza, the General knew, was determined to stand a second siege, and he had the guarantee of the first that it would be an obstinate stand; he had received from the Junta of Toledo a formal assurance of their resolution to bury themselves under the ruins of the town sooner than submit; and he was informed from several quarters that the southern provinces were forwarding crowds of fresh levies. Romana at this time also was in correspondence with him, and, with the usual exaggeration of a Spaniard, declared his ability to aid him with an army of twenty thousand men. Upon these data Sir John Moore formed a plan, bearing the stamp of genuine talent and enterprise, whether it be examined as a political or military measure.

He supposed the French Emperor to be more anxious to strike a heavy blow against the English, and to shut them out of Spain, than to overrun any particular province, or get possession of any town in the Peninsula. He resolved, therefore, to throw himself upon the communications of the French army, hoping, if fortune was favorable, to inflict a severe loss upon the troops which guarded them, before aid could arrive. If Napoleon, suspending his operations against the south, should detach them largely, Madrid would thereby be succored; if he did not detach largely, the British could hold their ground. Moore knew well that a great com-

mander would in such a case be more likely to unite his whole
army, and fall upon the troops which thus ventured to place themselves on his line of operations; but, to relieve the Spaniards at a
critical moment, and to give time for the southern provinces to organize their defence and to recover courage, he was willing thus to
draw the whole of the enemy upon himself. He felt that, in doing
so, he compromised the safety of his own army, that he must glide
along the edge of a precipice, that he must cross a gulf on a rotten
plank; but he also knew the martial qualities of his soldiers, he had
confidence in his own genius, and the occasion being worthy of a
great deed, he dared essay it even against Napoleon.

Colonel Graham returned on the 9th, bringing the first intimation
of the capitulation of the capital. He had been able to proceed no
farther than Talavera, where he encountered two members of the
Supreme Junta. By them he was told that the French, being
from twenty to thirty thousand strong, possessed the Retiro; that
the people retained their arms, and that La Peña, with thirty
thousand men of the army of the centre, was at Guadalaxara; that
fourteen thousand of St. Juan's and Heredia's forces were assembled
at Almarez; and that Romana, with whom they anxiously desired
the English should unite, had likewise an army of thirty thousand
fighting men: finally, they assured Colonel Graham that the most
energetic measures were in activity wherever the enemy's presence
did not control the patriots.

Mortifying as it was to find that Madrid, after so much boasting,
should have held out but one day, the event itself did not destroy
the ground of Moore's resolution to advance. Undoubtedly it was
so much lost; it diminished the hope of arousing the nation, and it
increased the danger of the British army, by letting loose a greater
number of the enemy's troops; but as a diversion for the south it
might still succeed, and as long as there was any hope, the resolution of the English General was fixed, to prove that he would not
abandon the cause, even when the Spaniards were abandoning it
themselves.

CHAPTER IV.

British army advances towards Burgos—French outposts surprised at Rueda—
Letter from Berthier to Soult intercepted—Direction of the march changed—
Mr. Stuart and a member of the Junta arrive at head-quarters—Arrogant and
insulting letter of Mr. Frere—Noble answer of Sir John Moore—British army
united at Mayorga; their force and composition—Inconsistent conduct of Ro-
mana; his character—Soult's position and forces; concentrates his army at
Carrion—Combat of cavalry at Sahagun—The British army retires to Benevente
—The Emperor moves from Madrid, passes the Guadarama, arrives at Tordesillas, expects to interrupt the British line of retreat, fails—Bridge of Castro
Gonzalo destroyed—Combat of cavalry at Benevente—General Lefebre taken
—Soult forces the bridge of Mansilla; takes Leon—The Emperor unites his
army at Astorga; hears of the Austrian war; orders Marshal Soult to pursue
the English army, and returns to France.

THE forward movement of the British army commenced on the
11th of December. Moore's first intention was to march with his
own and Hope's division to Valladolid, with a view to cover the
advance of his stores and to protect the junction of Sir David
Baird's troops, the rear of which was still behind Astorga; nevertheless preparations for a retreat upon Portugal were continued,
and Sir David was ordered to form magazines at Benevente,
Astorga, Villa Franca, and Lugo, by which arrangement two lines of
operation were secured, and a greater freedom of action obtained.

The 13th head-quarters were at Alaejos; two brigades and Lord
Paget's cavalry at Toro; General Hope at Torrecilla; General
Charles Stewart's horsemen at Rueda, having the night before surprised there fifty infantry and thirty dragoons, who declared that in
the French army it was believed that the English were retreating
to Portugal.

At Alaejos an intercepted despatch of the Prince of Neufchâtel
was brought to head-quarters, and the contents were important
enough to change the direction of the march. It was addressed to
the Duke of Dalmatia, and described Madrid as perfectly tranquil,
the shops open, and the public amusements going forward as in a
time of profound peace. The fourth corps of the army was said
to be at Talavera, on its way towards Badajos, and this movement,
it was observed, would force the English to retire to Portugal, if,
contrary to the Emperor's belief, they had not already done so.
The fifth corps was on the march to Zaragoza, and the eighth to
Burgos. Soult was therefore directed to drive the Spaniards into
Gallicia, to occupy Leon, Benevente, and Zamora, and to keep the
flat country in subjection; for which purpose his two divisions of
infantry, and the cavalry brigades of Franceschi and Debelle, were
considered sufficient.

It is remarkable that the first correct information of the capitulation of Madrid should have been thus acquired from the enemy, ten days after the event had taken place; nor is it less curious, that while Mr. Frere's letters were filled with vivid descriptions of Spanish enthusiasm, Napoleon should have been so convinced of their passiveness, as to send this important despatch by an officer, who rode post, without an escort, and in safety, until his abusive language to the post-master at Valdestillos created a tumult, in which he lost his life. Captain Waters, an English officer sent to obtain intelligence, happening to arrive in that place, heard of the murder, and immediately purchased the despatch for twenty dollars; and the accidental information thus obtained was the more valuable, as neither money nor patriotism had hitherto induced the Spaniards to bring any intelligence of the enemy's situation, and each step the army had made was in the dark. It was now however certain that Burgos was or would be strongly protected, and that Baird's line of march was unsafe if Soult, following these instructions, advanced. On the other hand, as the French appeared to be ignorant of the British movements, there was some chance of surprising and beating the second corps before Napoleon could come to its succor. Hope, therefore, was ordered to pass the Duero at Tordesillas, and direct his march upon Villepando; head-quarters were removed to Toro; and Valderas was given as the point of junction to Baird's division, the head of which was now at Benevente.

The 16th Mr. Stuart arrived at Toro, accompanied by Don F. X. Caro, a member of the Spanish government, who brought two letters, the one from the Junta, the other from Mr. Frere.* That from the Junta complained, that when Romana proposed to unite fourteen thousand picked men to the British army, with a view to make a forward movement, his offer had been disregarded, and a retreat determined upon, in despite of his earnest remonstrances; this retreat they declared to be uncalled for, and highly impolitic, "as the enemy was never so near his ruin as in that moment." If the Spanish and British armies should unite, they said, it would give "liberty to the Peninsula," that "Romana, with his fourteen thousand select men," was still ready to join Sir John Moore, and that "thirty thousand fresh levies would, in a month, be added to the ranks of the allied force."

This tissue of falsehoods—for Romana had approved of the intention to retreat, and never had above six thousand men armed—was addressed to Mr. Frere, and by him transmitted to the General, together with one from himself, which, in allusion to the retreat

* Sir John Moore's Papers, MS.

upon Portugal, contained the following extraordinary passages :* " I mean the immense responsibility with which you charge your-self by adopting, upon a supposed military necessity, a measure which must be followed by immediate if not final ruin to our ally, and by indelible disgrace to the country with whose resources you are intrusted." " I am unwilling to enlarge upon a subject in which my feelings must be stifled, or expressed at the risk of offence, which, with such an interest at stake, I should feel unwilling to ex-cite ; but this much I must say, that if the British army had been sent abroad for the express purpose of doing the utmost possible mischief to the Spanish cause, with the single exception of not firing a shot against their troops, they would, according to the measures now announced as about to be pursued, have completely fulfilled their purpose."

These letters were dated at Truxillo ; for the Junta, not think-ing themselves safe at Badajos, had proceeded so far on their way to Seville, and on that side the French had continued to advance, the remnants of the Spanish armies to fly, and everything bore the most gloomy appearance. Mr. Frere knew this. In a subsequent letter he acknowledged that the enthusiasm was extinguished, and a general panic commencing at the moment when he was penning these offensive passages. He was utterly ignorant of the numbers, the situation, and the resources of the enemy ; but he formed hypotheses, and upon the strength of them insulted Sir John Moore, and endangered the interests of his country. In this manner the British General, while struggling with unavoidable difficulties, had his mind harassed by a repetition of remonstrances and represent-ations, in which common sense, truth, and decency were alike dis-regarded ; but he did not fail to show how little personal feelings weighed with him in opposition to the public welfare. He had reason to suppose Mr. Frere had received his letter relative to Charmilly's mission, yet, as it was not acknowledged, he took ad-vantage of the omission, and, with singular propriety and dignity, thus noticed the plenipotentiary's second insulting communication : " With respect to your letter delivered to me at Toro by Mr. Stuart, I shall not remark upon it. It is in the style of the two which were brought to me by Colonel Charmilly, and consequently was answered by my letter of the 6th, of which I send you a duplicate ; that subject is, I hope, at rest !"

At Toro Sir John Moore ascertained that Romana, although aware of the advance of the British, and engaged to support them, was retiring into Gallicia. Nominally commander-in-chief of the Spanish armies, he was at the head of a few thousand miserable

* Sir John Moore's Papers, MS.

soldiers ; for the Spaniards, with great ingenuity, contrived to have no general when they had an army, and no army when they had a general.* After the dispersion of Blake's people at Reynosa, Romana rallied about five thousand men at Renedo, in the valley of Cabernuigo, and endeavored to make a stand on the borders of the Asturias ; but without any success, for the vile conduct of the Asturian Junta, joined to the terror created by the French victories, had completely subdued the spirit of the peasantry, and ruined the resources of that province. Romana complained that, when checked for misconduct, his soldiers quitted their standards : indeed, that any should have been found to join their colors is to be admired ; for, among the sores of Spain, there was none more cankered, more disgusting, than the venality, the injustice, the profligate corruption of the Asturian authorities. Without a blush, they openly divided the English subsidies, and defrauded not only the soldiers of their pay and equipments, but the miserable peasants of their hire, doubling the wretchedness of poverty, and deriding the misery they occasioned by pompous declarations of their own virtue.

From the Asturias Romana had led the remnants of Blake's force to Leon, about the period of Moore's arrival at Salamanca. Like others, he had been deceived as to the real state of the country, and at this time repented that he had returned to Spain. He was a person of talent, quickness, and information, but disqualified by nature for military command ; a lively principle of error pervaded all his notions of war, and no man ever bore the title of general who was less capable of commanding an army. Neither was he exempt from the prevailing weakness of his countrymen. At this moment, when he had not strength to stand upright, his letters were teeming with gigantic offensive projects ; and although he had before approved of the intention to retreat, he was now as ready to urge a forward movement, promising to co-operate with twenty thousand soldiers, when he could scarcely muster a third of that number, and those only half armed, and scarcely capable of distinguishing their own standards : and, at the very time he made the promise, he was retiring into Gallicia—not meaning to deceive, for he was as ready to advance as to retreat ; but this species of boasting is inherent in his nation. It has been asserted that Caro offered the chief command of the Spanish armies to Sir John Moore, and that the latter refused it. This is not true. Caro had no power to do so, and there were no armies to command ; but that gentleman, in his interview, either was or affected to be satisfied of the sound-

* Ibid. Colonel Syme's Correspondence. General Leith.

ness of the English General's views, and ashamed of the folly of
the Junta.

The 18th, head-quarters were at Castro Nuevo, from which place
Moore wrote to Romana, informing him of his intention to fall upon
Soult. He desired his co-operation, and requested that the Marquis would, according to his own plan given to the British minister
in London, reserve the Asturias for his own line of communication,
and leave Gallicia to the British. The latter were now in full
march. Baird was at Benevente, Hope at Villepando, and the
cavalry scouring the country on the side of Valladolid, had several
successful skirmishes and took a number of prisoners. The French
could be no longer ignorant of the movement, and the English General brought forward his columns rapidly. On the 20th the whole
of the forces were united, the cavalry at Melgar Abaxo, the infantry
at Mayorga, and as much concentrated as the necessity of obtaining
cover in a country devoid of fuel and deep with snow would permit. The weather was exceedingly severe and the marches long;
but a more robust set of men never took the field. Their discipline
was admirable, and there were very few stragglers; the experience
of one or two campaigns alone was wanting to make a perfect
army. The number was however small; nominally it was nearly
thirty-five thousand, but four regiments were still in Portugal, and
three more were left by Sir David Baird at Lugo and Astorga;
one thousand six hundred and eighty-seven men were detached,
and four thousand and five were in hospital. Hence the actual
number present under arms on the 19th of December was only
nineteen thousand and fifty-three infantry, two thousand two hundred and seventy-eight cavalry, and one thousand three hundred
and fifty-eight gunners—forming a total of twenty-three thousand
five hundred and eighty-three men, with sixty pieces of artillery.
They were organized in three divisions—a reserve, two light brigades of infantry, and one division of cavalry; four batteries were
attached to the infantry, two to the cavalry, and one was kept in
reserve. Meanwhile Romana, who had been able to bring forward
very few men, promised to march in two columns by Almanzer and
Guarda, and sent some information of the enemy's position. But
Sir John Moore depended little upon his intelligence, when he found
him, even so late as the 19th of December, upon the faith of information from the Junta, representing Madrid as still holding out; and,
when the advanced posts were already engaged at Sahagun, proposing an interview at Benevente to arrange the plan of operations.

On the French side, Soult was concentrating his force on the
Carrion. After his rapid and brilliant success at the opening of the

campaign, his corps was ordered to remain on the defensive, until the movements against Tudela and Madrid were completed, and the despatches directing him to recommence his offensive operations, were, as we have seen, intercepted on the 12th; but on the 16th, he became acquainted with the advance of the English army.* At that period, General Bonnet's division occupied Barquera de San Vincente and Potes, on the Deba, watching some thousand Asturians whom Ballasteros had collected near Llanes; Merle's and Mermet's divisions were on the Carrion, Franceschi's dragoons at Valladolid, Debelle's at Sahagun. The whole formed a total of sixteen or seventeen thousand infantry, and twelve hundred cavalry, present under arms, of which only eleven thousand infantry and twelve hundred cavalry could, without uncovering the important post of Santander, be opposed to the advance of the British.† Soult, alarmed at this disparity of force, required General Mathieu Dumas, commandant at Burgos, to direct all the divisions and detachments passing through that town, whatever might be their original destination, upon the Carrion, and this decisive conduct was approved by the Emperor.‡

On the 21st, Bonnet's division was still on the Deba, but Mermet's was in the town of Carrion, Merle's at Saldaña; Franceschi's cavalry had retired from Valladolid to Riberos de la Cuesca, Debelle's continued at Sahagun, and thirteen hundred dragoons, under General Lorge, arrived at Palencia from Burgos. Meantime, the fifteenth and tenth British hussars, having quitted Melgar Abaxo during the night, came close to Sahagun before daylight on the 21st. The tenth marched straight to the town, while the fifteenth turned it by the right, and endeavored to cut off the enemy; a patrol gave the alarm, and when four hundred of the fifteenth had reached the rear of the village, they were opposed by a line of six hundred French dragoons. The tenth were not in sight, but Lord Paget, after a few moments, charged with the fifteenth, broke the enemy's line, and pursued them for some distance. Some twenty killed, two lieutenant-colonels, and eleven other officers, with a hundred and fifty-four men prisoners, were the result of this affair, which lasted about twenty minutes. Debelle then retired to Santerbas; the English infantry occupied Sahagun, and head-quarters were established there. During these events Romana remained at Mancilla, and it was evident that no assistance could be expected from him. The truth was, that, ashamed of exposing the weakness and misery of his troops, he kept away, for, after all his

* S. Journal of Operations, MS.
† Ibid.
‡ Ibid.

promises, he could not produce six thousand fighting men. His letters however were, as usual, extremely encouraging. *The French force in Spain was exceedingly weak, Palafox had not been defeated at Tudela; Soult, including Bonnet's division, had scarcely nine thousand men of all arms; it was an object to surround and destroy him before he could be succored;*—and other follies of this nature.

The English troops having now outmarched their supplies, halted the 22d and 23d, and Soult, whose intention was to act on the defensive, hastened the march of the reinforcements from the side of Burgos; yet being fearful for his communication with Placentia, he abandoned Saldaña on the 23d, and concentrated his infantry at Carrion.* Debelle's cavalry again advanced to Villatilla and Villa-cuenda, Franceschi remained at Riberos, the dragoons of General Lorge occupied Paredes, and General Dumas pushed on the divisions of the eighth corps, of which Laborde's was already arrived at Palencia; Loison's and Heudelet's followed at the distance of two days' march, but they were weak. Sir John Moore's plan was to move during the night of the 23d, so as to arrive at Carrion by daylight on the 24th, to force the bridge, and afterwards, ascending the river, to fall upon the main body of the enemy, which, his information led him to believe, was still at Saldaña. This attack was, however, but a secondary object; his attention was constantly directed towards Madrid. To beat the troops in his front would be a victory of little value beyond the honor, because the third and fourth corps were so near; the pith of the operation was to tempt the Emperor from Madrid, and his march from that capital was to be the signal for a retreat, which sooner or later was inevitable.

To draw Napoleon from the south was Moore's design, and it behoves the man to be alert who interposes between the lion and his prey. On the 23d, Romana first gave notice that the French were in motion from the side of Madrid; and in the night of the 23d, when the troops were actually in march towards Carrion, this intelligence was confirmed by the General's own spies,—all their reports agreed that the whole French army was in movement to crush the English: the fourth corps had been halted at Talavera, the fifth at Vittoria, the eighth was closing up to reinforce the second, and the Emperor in person was marching towards the Guadarama. The principal objects of Sir John Moore's advance were thus attained; the siege of Zaragoza was delayed, the southern provinces were allowed to breathe, and it only remained for him to prove, by a timely retreat, that this offensive operation, although hazardous, was not the result of improvident rashness,

* S. Journal of Operations, MS.

nor weakness of mind, but the hardy enterprise of a great commander acting under peculiar circumstances. As a military measure, his judgment condemned it; as a political one, he thought it
of doubtful advantage, because Spain was really passive; but he
had desired to give the Spaniards an opportunity of making one
more struggle for independence. That was done. If they could
not, or would not profit of the occasion, if their hearts were faint
or their hands feeble, the shame and the loss were their own; the
British General had done enough—enough for honor, enough for
utility, more than enough for prudence; the madness of the times
required it. His army was already on the verge of destruction, the
enemy's force was hourly increasing in his front, the first symptoms of a retreat would bring it headlong on, and in the mean time
the Emperor threatened the line of communication with Gallicia,
and by the rapidity of his march left no time for consideration.

After the first burst, by which he swept the northern provinces,
and planted his standards on the banks of the Tagus, that monarch
had put all the resources of his subtle genius into activity, endeavoring to soften the public mind, and by engrafting benefits on the
terror his victories had created, to gain over the people; but, at
the same time, he was gathering in his extended wings, and preparing for a new flight, which would have carried him over the
southern kingdoms of the Peninsula, and given him the rocks of
Lisbon as a resting place for his eagles. Madrid was tranquil,
and Toledo, notwithstanding her heroic promises, had never shut
her gates; one division of the first corps occupied that town, another was in Ocaña, and the light cavalry scoured the whole of La
Mancha, even to the borders of Andalusia; the fourth corps, and
Milhaud's and Lasalle's horsemen, were at Talavera, preparing to
march to Badajos, and sixty thousand men, with one hundred and
fifty guns and fifteen days' provisions in carts, were reviewed at
the gates of Madrid upon the 19th; three days afterwards they
were in full march to intercept the line of Sir John Moore's retreat.

Napoleon was informed of that General's advance on the 21st,
and in an instant the Spaniards, their juntas, and their armies, were
dismissed fom his thoughts; his corps were arrested in their different movements, ten thousand men were left to control the capital,
and on the evening of the 22d fifty thousand men were at the foot
of the Guadarama. A deep snow choked the passes of the Sierra,
and, after twelve hours of ineffectual toil, the advanced guards were
still on the wrong side. The general commanding reported that
the road was impracticable; but Napoleon, dismounting, placed
himself at the head of the column, and, amidst storms of hail and
drifting snow, led his soldiers over the mountain.• Many men and

animals died during the passage, which lasted two days; but the Emperor, personally urging on the troops with unceasing vehemence, reached Villacastin, fifty miles from Madrid, on the 24th, and the 26th he was at Tordesillas with the guards and the divisions of Lapisse and Dessolles; the dragoons of La Houssaye entered Valladolid on the same day, and Marshal Ney, with the sixth corps, was at Rio Seco.

From Tordesillas Napoleon, communicating with Soult, informed him of these movements, concluding his despatch thus: " *Our cavalry scouts are already at Benevente. If the English pass to-day in their position, they are lost; if, on the contrary, they attack you with all their force, retire one day's march; the farther they proceed, the better for us. If they retreat, pursue them closely.*"* Then, full of hope, he hastened himself to Valderas, but had the mortification to learn that, notwithstanding his rapid march, having scarcely rested night or day, he was twelve hours too late. The British were across the Esla! In fact Soult was in full pursuit when this letter was written; for Sir John Moore, well aware of his own situation, had given orders to retreat the moment the intelligence of Napoleon's march from Madrid reached him, and the heavy baggage was immediately moved to the rear, while the reserve, the light brigades, and the cavalry, remained at Sahagun—the latter pushing patrols up to the enemy's lines, and skirmishing to hide the retrograde march.

The 24th, General Hope, with two divisions, had gone back by the road of Mayorga, Baird, with another, by that of Valencia de San Juan, where there was a ferry-boat to cross the Esla river. The Marquis of Romana undertook to guard the bridge of Mansilla. The enemy's dragoons, under Lorge, arrived the same day at Frechilla, and the division of Laborde entered Paredes. The 25th the General-in-chief, with the reserve and light brigades, followed the route of Hope's column to Valderas, and the 26th, Baird passed the Esla at Valencia, and took post on the other side, but with some difficulty, for the boat was small, the fords deep, and the river rising. The troops, under the commander-in-chief, approached the bridge of Castro Gonzalo early in the morning of the 26th, but the stores were a long time passing, a dense fog intercepted the view, and so nicely timed was the march, that the scouts of the imperial horsemen were already infesting the flank of the column, and even carried off some of the baggage.

As the left bank of the river commanded the bridge, General Robert Crawfurd remained with a brigade of infantry and two guns to protect the passage; for the cavalry was still in the rear, watch-

* S. Journal of Operations, MS.

ing Soult, who, aware of the retreat, was pressing forward in pursuit. Meanwhile Lord Paget, after passing Mayorga, was intercepted by a strong body of horse, which belonged to Ney's corps, and was embattled on a swelling ground close to the road. Though the soil was deep and soaked with snow and rain, two squadrons of the tenth, riding stiffly up, gained the summit, and notwithstanding the enemy's advantage of numbers and position, killed twenty men and captured one hundred. This was a bold and hardy action; but the English cavalry had been engaged more or less for twelve successive days, with such fortune and bravery that above five hundred prisoners had already fallen into their hands; and their leaders being excellent, their confidence was unbounded.

From Mayorga Lord Paget proceeded to Benevente; but the Duke of Dalmatia, with great judgment, now pushed for Astorga by the road of Mancilla, whereupon Romana, leaving three thousand men and two guns to defend the bridge at the latter place, fell back to Leon.* Thus, by a critical march, Moore recovered his communications with Gallicia, and had so far baffled the Emperor; but his position was by no means safe, or even tenable.

The town of Benevente, a rich open place, remarkable for a small, but curious Moorish castle, containing a fine collection of ancient armor, is situated in a plain that, extending from the Gallician mountains to the neighborhood of Burgos, appears to be boundless. The river Esla wound through it, about four miles in front of Benevente, and the bridge of Castro Gonzalo was the key to the town; but the right bank of the Esla was completely commanded from the further side, and there were many fords. Eighteen miles higher up, at Valencia de San Juan, a shorter road from Mayorga to Astorga crossed the river by the ferry-boat; and at Mancilla, the passage being only defended by Spaniards, was in a manner open to Soult, for Romana had not destroyed the arches of the bridge. Beyond Mancilla, under the hills skirting this great plain, stood the town of Leon, which was inclosed with walls, and capable of resisting a sudden assault.

Moore, aware of his incapacity, resolved to remain no longer than was necessary to clear out his magazines at Benevente, and to cover the march of his stores. But the road to Astorga by Leon was much shorter than that through Benevente; and as Romana was inclined to retreat to Gallicia, Sir John requested that he would maintain himself at Leon as long as he could, and repeated his desire to have that province left open for the English army. Romana, who assented to both these requests, had a great rabble with him; and as Leon was a walled place, and a number of citizens

* S. Journal of Operations, MS.

and volunteers were willing and even eager to fight, the town might have made resistance.   Moore hoped that it would do so, and gave orders to break down the bridge at Castro Gonzalo in his own front, the moment the stragglers and baggage should have passed; but at this time the bad example of murmuring given by men of high rank had descended lower, many regimental officers neglected their duty, and what with the dislike to a retreat, the severity of the weather, and the inexperience of the army, the previous fine discipline of the troops was broken down.   Such disgraceful excesses had been committed at Valderas, that the General issued severe orders, justly reproaching the soldiers for their evil deeds, and appealing to the honor of the army to amend them.

On the night of the 26th, the light cavalry of the imperial guard, riding close up to the bridge of Castro Gonzalo, captured some women and baggage, and endeavored to surprise the post, which gave rise to a remarkable display of courage and discipline.   John Walton and Richard Jackson, private soldiers of the forty-third, being posted beyond the bridge, were directed, on the approach of an enemy, the one to stand firm, the other to fire and run back to the brow of the hill, to give notice whether there were many or few.   Jackson fired, but was overtaken, and received twelve or fourteen sabre cuts in an instant; nevertheless he came staggering on, and gave the signal, while Walton, with equal resolution, stood his ground and wounded several of the assailants, who then retired, leaving him unhurt; but his cap, knapsack, belts, and musket, were cut in above twenty places, and his bayonet was bent double and notched like a saw.   The 27th, the cavalry and the stragglers being all over the river, General Crawfurd commenced the destruction of the bridge amidst torrents of rain and snow; and while half the troops worked, the other half kept the enemy at bay from the heights on the left bank, for the cavalry scouts of the imperial guard were spread over the plain.

At ten o'clock at night a large party of French, following some wagons, again endeavored to pass the piquets and gallop down to the bridge; that failing, a few dismounted, and extending to the right and left, commenced a skirmishing fire, while others remained ready to charge, if the position of the troops, which they expected to ascertain by this scheme, should offer an opportunity.   The event did not answer their expectations, and this anxiety to interrupt the work induced General Crawfurd to destroy two arches of the bridge, and to blow up the connecting buttress; yet the masonry was so solid and difficult to pierce, that it was not until twelve o'clock in the night of the 28th that all the preparations were completed. The troops then descended the heights on the left bank, and passing with the greatest silence, by single files, over planks laid across the broken arches, gained the other side without loss; an instance of singular good fortune, for the night was dark and tempestuous, the river, rising rapidly with a roaring noise, was threatening to burst over the planks, and the enemy was close at hand. To have resisted an attack in such an awkward situation would have been impossible, but happily the retreat of the troops was undiscovered, and the mine was sprung with good effect.

Crawfurd marched to Benevente, where the cavalry and the reserve still remained. Here several thousand infantry slept in the upper part of an immense convent built round a square, and a frightful catastrophe was impending; for the lower galleries were so thickly stowed with the horses of the cavalry, that it was scarcely possible to pass them; there was but one entrance, and two officers of the forty-third, returning from the bridge, on entering the convent, perceived that a large window-shutter was on fire, that in a few moments the straw under the horses would ignite, and six thousand men and animals must inevitably perish in the flames. One of these officers, Captain Lloyd, a man of great strength, activity, and of a presence of mind which never failed, made a sign of silence to his companion, and then springing on to the nearest horse, ran along the backs of the others, until he reached the blazing shutter, which he tore off its hinges and cast out of the window, and then awakening a few men, cleared the passage without any alarm, which in such a case would have been as destructive as the fire.

Two days' rest had been gained at Benevente, but as very little could be done to remove the stores, the greatest part were destroyed. The army was and had been from the first without sufficient means of transport, the General had no money to procure it, and the ill-will of the Spaniards and the shuffling conduct of the Juntas added infinitely to their difficulties. But time pressed. Hope and Fraser marched by La Baneza, and reached Astorga the 29th, where Baird joined them from Valencia de San Juan; on the same day the reserve and Crawfurd's brigade quitted Benevente. The cavalry remained in the town, leaving parties to watch the fords of the Esla. In this state of affairs General Lefebre Desnouettes, seeing only a few cavalry posts on the great plain, rather hastily concluded that there was nothing to support them, and crossing the river at daybreak, by a ford a little way above the bridge, with six hundred horsemen of the imperial guard, advanced into the plain. The piquets under Major Loftus Otway retired fighting, and being joined by a part of the third German hussars, even charged the leading French squadrons with some effect.

General C. Stewart then took the command, and the ground was obstinately disputed, but the enemy advanced. At this moment the plain was covered with stragglers, baggage-mules, and followers of the army, the town was filled with tumult, the distant piquets and videttes were seen galloping in from the right and left, the French were pressing forward boldly, and every appearance indicated that the enemy's whole army was coming up and passing the river.

Lord Paget ordered the tenth hussars to mount and form under the cover of some houses at the edge of the town, for he desired to draw the enemy, whose real situation he had detected at once, well into the plain before he attacked; in half an hour, everything was ready, and he gave the signal. Then the tenth hussars galloped forward, the piquets that were already engaged closed together, and the whole charged. The scene changed instantly; the enemy were seen flying at full speed towards the river, the British following close at their heels, until the French squadrons, without breaking their ranks, plunged into the stream, and gained the opposite heights, where, like experienced soldiers, they wheeled instantly, and seemed inclined to come forward a second time; but a battery of two guns opened upon them, and after a few rounds they retired. During the pursuit in the plain, an officer was observed separating himself from the main body, and making towards another part of the river; being followed, and refusing to stop, he was wounded and brought in a prisoner. It was General Lefebre Desnouettes.

Although the imperial guards were outnumbered in the end, they were very superior at the commencement of this action, which was stiffly fought on both sides, for the British lost fifty men, and the French left fifty-five killed and wounded on the field, besides the General and other officers; according to Baron Larrey, seventy of those who recrossed the river were also wounded, making a total loss of above two hundred excellent soldiers.* Lord Paget maintained his posts on the Esla, under an occasional cannonade, until the evening, and then withdrew to La Baneza; and while these things were passing, Napoleon arrived at Valderas, Ney at Villaton, and Lapisse at Toro. The French troops were worn down with fatigue, yet the Emperor still urged them on. The Duke of Dalmatia, he said, would intercept the English at Astorga, and their labors would be finally rewarded. Nevertheless, the destruction of the bridge of Castro Gonzalo was so well accomplished, that twenty-four hours were required to repair it, the fords were now impassable, and it was the 30th before Bessières could cross the Esla; but on that day he passed through Benevente with nine thousand

* Larrey's Surgical Campaign.

cavalry, and bent his course towards La Baneza;* the same day Franceschi carried the bridge of Mansilla de las Mulas by a single charge of his light horsemen, and captured the artillery and one half of the Spanish division left to protect it. Romana immediately abandoned Leon and many stores, and the 31st the Duke of Dalmatia entered that town without firing a shot, while the Duke of Istria, with his cavalry, took possession of La Baneza; the advanced posts were then pushed forward to the Puente d'Orvigo on one side, and the Puente de Valembre on the other.† The rear of the English army was still in Astorga, the head-quarters having arrived there only the day before.

In the preceding month large stores had been gradually brought up to this town by Sir David Baird, and as there were no means of transport to remove them, orders were given, after supplying the immediate wants of the army, to destroy them; but Romana, who would neither defend Leon nor Mansilla, had, contrary to his promises, pre-occupied Astorga with his fugitive army, and when the English divisions marched in, such a tumult and confusion arose, that no orders could be executed with regularity, no distribution made, nor the destruction of the stores be effected. The disorder thus unexpectedly produced was very detrimental to the discipline of the troops, which the unwearied efforts of the General had partly restored; the resources which he had depended on for the support of his soldiers became mischievous, and contributed to disorganize instead of nourishing them. And he had the further vexation to hear Romana, the principal cause of this misfortune, proposing, with troops unable to resist a thousand light infantry, to recommence offensive operations on a plan, in comparison with which the visions of Don Quixote were wisdom.

On the 31st, the flank brigades separated from the army at Bonillas, and bent their course by cross-roads towards Orense and Vigo, being detached to lessen the pressure on the commissariat, and to cover the flanks of the army; Fraser's and Hope's divisions entered Villa Franca, and Baird's division was at Bembibre; the reserve, with the head-quarters, halted at Cambarros, a village six miles from Astorga, until the cavalry fell back in the night to the same place, and then the reserve marched to Bembibre. The Marquis of Romana, after doing so much mischief by crossing the line of march, left his infantry to wander as they pleased, and retired with his cavalry and some guns to the valley of the Minho, and the rest of his artillery mixed with the British army, but most of it was captured before reaching Lugo.

* Bulletin.
† S. Journal of Operations, MS.

Upon the 1st of January the Emperor took possession of Astorga, where seventy thousand French infantry, ten thousand cavalry, and two hundred pieces of artillery, after many days of incessant marching, were now united. The congregation of this mighty force, while it evinced the power and energy of the French monarch, attested also the genius of the English General, who, with a handful of men, had found the means to arrest the course of the conqueror, and to draw him, with the flower of his army, to this remote and unimportant part of the Peninsula, at the moment when Portugal, and the fairest provinces of Spain, were prostrate beneath the strength of his hand. That Spain, being in her extremity, Sir John Moore succored her, and in the hour of weakness intercepted the blow which was descending to crush her, no man of candor and honesty can deny. For what troops, what preparations, what courage, what capacity was there in the south to have resisted, even for an instant, the progress of a man who, in ten days, and in the depth of winter, crossing the snowy ridge of the Carpentinos, had traversed two hundred miles of hostile country, and transported fifty thousand men from Madrid to Astorga, in a shorter time than a Spanish courier would have taken to travel the same distance?

This stupendous march was rendered fruitless by the quickness of his adversary; but Napoleon, though he had failed to destroy the English army, resolved, nevertheless, to cast it forth of the Peninsula, and being himself recalled to France by tidings that the Austrian storm was ready to burst, had fixed upon the Duke of Dalmatia to continue the pursuit. For this purpose three divisions of cavalry and three of infantry were added to his former command; but of these last, the two commanded by Generals Loison and Heudelet were several marches in the rear, and General Bonnet's remained always in the Montaña de Santander. Hence the whole number bearing arms which the Duke led immediately to the pursuit, was about twenty-five thousand men, of which four thousand two hundred were cavalry, composing the divisions of Lorges, La Houssaye, and Franceschi.* Fifty-four guns were with the columns, Loison's and Heudelet's divisions followed by forced marches, and Soult was supported by Ney with the sixth corps, wanting its third division, but mustering above sixteen thousand men under arms, the flower of the French army, together with thirty-seven pieces of artillery. Thus, including Laborde, Heudelet, and Loison's division, nearly sixty thousand men and ninety-one guns were put on the track of the English army. Meanwhile the Emperor returned to Valladolid, where he received the addresses of the notables and deputies from Madrid and other great towns,

* S. Journal of Operations, MS.

and strove, by promises and other means, to win the good opinion
of the public. Appointing Joseph to be his lieutenant-general, he
allotted separate provinces for each "corps d'armée," and directing
the imperial guard to return to France, after three days' delay he
departed himself with scarcely an escort, but with an astonishing
speed that frustrated the designs which the Spaniards had, as some
say, formed against his person.

CHAPTER V.

Sir John Moore retreats towards Vigo ; is closely pursued—Miserable scene at
Bembibre—Excesses at Villa Franca—Combat at Calcabellos—Death of Gen-
eral Colbert—March to Nogales—Line of retreat changed from Vigo to Coruña
—Skilful passage of the bridge of Constantino ; skirmish there—The army
halts at Lugo—Sir John Moore offers battle ; it is not accepted ; he makes a
forced march to Betenzos ; loses many stragglers ; rallies the army ; reaches
Coruña—The army takes a position—Two large stores of powder exploded—
Fleet arrives in the harbor ; army commences embarking—Battle of Coruña—
Death of Sir John Moore—His character.

THE Duke of Dalmatia, a general who, if the Emperor be
excepted, was no wise inferior to any of his nation, commenced his
pursuit of the English army with a vigor that marked his eager
desire to finish the campaign in a manner suitable to the brilliant
opening at Gamonal. The main body of his troops followed the
route of Foncevadon and Ponteferrada ; a second column took the
road of Cambarros and Bembibre ; Franceschi entered the valley of
Syl, and moving up that river, turned the position of Villa Franca
del Bierzo.[*]

Thus Sir John Moore, after having twice baffled the Emperor's
combinations, was still pressed in his retreat with a fury that seemed
to increase every moment. The separation of his light brigades, a
measure which he reluctantly adopted by the advice of his quartermaster-general, had weakened the army by three thousand men,
yet he still possessed nineteen thousand of all arms, good soldiers
to fight, and strong to march, although shaken in discipline by the
disorders at Valderas and Astorga ; for the General's exertions to
restore order and regularity were by many officers slightly seconded,
and by some with scandalous levity disregarded. There was no
choice but to retreat. The astonishing rapidity with which the
Emperor had brought up his overbearing numbers, and thrust the
English army into Gallicia, had rendered the natural strength of

* S. Journal of Operations, MS.

that country unavailing; the resources were few, even for an army in winter quarters, and for a campaign in that season, there were none at all. All the draught cattle that could be procured would scarcely have supplied the means to transport ammunition for two battles, whereas the French, sweeping the rich plains of Castile with their powerful cavalry, might have formed magazines at Astorga and Leon, and from thence have been supplied in abundance, while the English were starving.

Before he advanced from Salamanca, Moore, foreseeing that his movement must sooner or later end in a retreat, had sent officers to examine the roads of Gallicia and the harbors which offered the greatest advantages for embarkation; by the reports of those officers, which arrived from day to day, and by the state of the magazines which he had directed to be formed, his measures were constantly regulated.* The magazines of Astorga, Benevente, and Labaneza, were, by untoward circumstances, and the deficiency of transport, rendered, as we have seen, of no avail beyond the momentary supply they afforded, and part of their contents falling into the enemy's hands, gave him some cause of triumph; but those at Villa Franca and Lugo contained about fourteen days' consumption, and there were other small magazines formed on the line of Orense and Vigo.

More than this could not have been accomplished. It was now only the fifteenth day since Sir John Moore had left Salamanca, and already the torrent of war, diverted from the south, was foaming among the rocks of Gallicia. Nineteen thousand British troops, posted in strong ground, might have offered battle to very superior numbers, but where was the use of merely fighting an enemy who had three hundred thousand men in Spain? Nothing could be gained by such a display of courage, and the English General, by a quick retreat, might reach his ships unmolested, embark, and carrying his army from the narrow corner in which it was cooped to the southern provinces, establish there a good base of operations, and renew the war under favorable circumstances. It was by this combination of a fleet and army that the greatest assistance could be given to Spain, and the strength of England become most formidable. A few days' sailing would carry the troops to Cadiz, but six weeks' constant marching would not bring the French army from Gallicia to that neighborhood. The northern provinces were broken, subdued in spirit, and possessed few resources; the southern provinces had scarcely seen an enemy, were rich and fertile, and there also was the seat of government. Sir John Moore, reasoning thus, resolved to fall down to the coast and embark, with as little

* Sir John Moore's Papers, MS.

loss or delay as might be; but Vigo, Coruña, and Ferrol were the principal harbors, and their relative advantages could not be determined except by the reports of the engineers, none of which, so rapidly had the crisis of affairs come on, were yet received; and as those reports could only be obtained from day to day, the line of retreat became of necessity subject to daily change.

When the Duke of Dalmatia took the command of the pursuing army, Hope's and Fraser's divisions were, as I have said, at Villa Franca, Baird's at Bembibre, the reserve and cavalry at Cambarros, six miles from Astorga. Behind Cambarros, the mountains of Gallicia rose abruptly, but there was no position, because, after the first rise at the village of Rodrigatos, the ground continually descended to Calcabellos, a small town, only four miles from Villa Franca, and the old road of Foncevadon and Ponteferrada, which turned the whole line, was choked with the advancing columns of the enemy.* The reserve and the cavalry therefore marched during the night to Bembibre, and on their arrival Baird's division proceeded to Calcabellos; but in the immense wine vaults of Bembibre many hundred of his men remained behind inebriated, the followers of the army crowded the houses, and a number of Romana's disbanded men were mixed with this heterogeneous mass of marauders, drunkards, muleteers, women, and children; the weather was dreadful, and, notwithstanding the utmost exertions of the General-in-chief, when the reserve marched the next morning, the number of those unfortunate wretches was not diminished. Leaving a small guard to protect them, Sir John Moore proceeded to Calcabellos, yet scarcely had the reserve marched out of the village, when some French cavalry appeared, and in a moment the road was filled with the miserable stragglers, who came crowding after the troops, some with shrieks of distress and wild gestures, others with brutal exclamations, while many, overcome with fear, threw away their arms, while those who preserved them were too stupidly intoxicated to fire, and kept reeling to and fro, alike insensible to their danger and to their disgrace. The enemy's horsemen, perceiving this, bore at a gallop through the disorderly mob, cutting to the right and left as they passed, and riding so close to the columns, that the infantry were forced to halt in order to check their audacity.

At Calcabellos the reserve took up a position. Baird then marched to Herrerias, and the General-in-chief went on to Villa Franca. But in that town great excesses had been committed by the preceding divisions; the magazines were plundered, the bakers driven away from the ovens, the wine stores forced, and the com-

* See Colonel Carmichael Smith's report.

missaries prevented from making the regular distributions; the doors of the houses were broken, and the scandalous insubordination of the soldiers proved that a discreditable relaxation of discipline on the part of the officers had taken place. Moore arrested this disorder, and caused one man taken in the act of plundering a magazine to be hanged in the market-place; then issuing severe orders to prevent a recurrence of such inexcusable conduct, he returned to Calcabellos, which the enemy were now approaching.

The Guia, a small, but at this season of the year a deep stream, ran through that town, and was crossed by a stone bridge. On the Villa Franca side a lofty ridge, rough with vineyards and stone walls, was occupied by two thousand five hundred infantry, with a battery of six guns; four hundred riflemen, and about the same number of cavalry, were posted on a hill two miles beyond the river, to watch the two roads of Bembibre and Foncevadon. In this situation, on the 3d of January, a little after noon, the French General Colbert approached with six or eight squadrons, but observing the ground behind Calcabellos so strongly occupied, demanded reinforcements. Soult, believing that the English did not mean to make a stand, replied by ordering Colbert to charge without delay, and the latter, stung by the message, obeyed with precipitate fury. From one of those errors so frequent in war, the British cavalry, thinking a greater force was riding against them, retired at speed to Calcabellos, and the riflemen, who, following their orders, had withdrawn when the French first came in sight, were just passing the bridge, when a crowd of staff-officers, the cavalry, and the enemy, came in upon them in one mass; in the confusion thirty or forty men were taken, and Colbert, then crossing the river, charged on the spur up the road. The remainder of the riflemen had however thrown themselves into the vineyards, and when the enemy approached within a few yards, opened such a deadly fire, that the greatest number of the French horsemen were killed on the spot, and among the rest Colbert himself; his fine martial figure, his voice, his gestures, and, above all, his great valor, had excited the admiration of the British, and a general feeling of sorrow was predominant when the gallant soldier fell. Some French voltigeurs now crossed the river, and a few of the 52d regiment descended from the upper part of the ridge to the assistance of the riflemen, when a sharp skirmish commenced, in which two or three hundred men of both sides were killed or wounded. Towards evening, Merle's division of infantry appeared on the hills in front of the town, and made a demonstration of crossing opposite to the left of the English position, but the battery of the latter checked this movement, and night coming on the combat ceased.

As the road from Villa Franca to Lugo led through a rugged country, the cavalry were now sent on to the latter town at once, and during the night the French patrols breaking in upon the rifle piquets, wounded some men, but were beaten back without being able to discover that the English troops had abandoned the position. This however was the case, and the reserve reached Herrerias, a distance of eighteen miles, on the morning of the 4th, Baird's division being then at Nogales, Hope's and Fraser's near Lugo.

At Herrerias, the English General, who constantly directed the movements of the rear-guard himself, received the first reports of the engineers relative to the harbors. It appeared that Vigo, besides its greater distance, offered no position to cover the embarkation, but Coruña and Betanzos did. The march to Vigo was of necessity abandoned, the ships were directed round to Coruña, and Moore, who now deeply regretted the separation of his light brigades, sent forward instructions for the leading division to halt at Lugo, where he designed to rally the army, and give battle if the enemy would accept it. These important orders were carried to Sir David Baird by one of the aides-de-camp of the commander-in-chief, but Sir David forwarded them by a private dragoon, who got drunk and lost the despatch. This blamable irregularity was ruinous to General Fraser's troops; in lieu of resting two days at Lugo, that General, unwitting of the order, pursued his toilsome journey towards St. Jago de Compostella, and then returning without food or rest, lost more than four hundred stragglers.

On the 5th, the reserve having, by a forced march of thirty-six miles, gained twelve hours' start of the enemy, reached Nogales, at which place they met a large convoy of English clothing, shoes and ammunition, intended for Romana's army, yet moving towards the enemy—a circumstance characteristic of the Spanish mode of conducting public affairs. There was a bridge at Nogales which the engineers failed to destroy, but this was a matter of little consequence; the river was fordable above and below, and the General was unwilling, unless for some palpable advantage, which seldom presented itself, to injure the communications of a country that he was unable to serve: moreover, the bridges were commonly very solidly constructed, and the arches having little span, could be rendered passable again in a shorter time than they could be destroyed. At this period of the retreat also the road was covered with baggage, sick men, women, and plunderers, all of whom would have been thus sacrificed; for the peasantry, although armed, did not molest the enemy, but fearing both sides alike, carried their effects into the mountains: even there the villanous marauders followed them, and in some cases were by the Spaniards killed—a just punishment for quitting their colors. Under the most favorable circumstances, the tail of a retreating force exhibits terrible scenes of distress, and on the road near Nogales the followers of the army were dying fast from cold and hunger. The soldiers, barefooted, harassed, and weakened by their excesses at Bembibre and Villa Franca, were dropping to the rear by hundreds, while broken carts, dead animals, and the piteous appearance of women and children, struggling or falling exhausted in the snow, completed a picture of war, which, like Janus, has a double face.

Franceschi, who, after turning Villa Franca, had scoured the valley of the Syl and captured many Spanish prisoners and baggage, now regained the line of march at Becerea, and towards evening the French army, recovering their lost ground, passed Nogales, galling the rear-guard with a continual skirmish; and here it was that dollars to the amount of twenty-five thousand pounds were abandoned.* This small sum was kept near head-quarters to answer sudden emergencies, and the bullocks that drew it being tired, the General, who could not save the money without risking an ill-timed action, had it rolled down the side of the mountain, whence part of it was gathered by the enemy, part by the Gallician peasants. The returns laid before Parliament in 1809 made the sum £60,000, and the whole loss during the campaign nearly £77,000, but it is easier to make an entry of one sum for a treasury return, than to state the details accurately; the money-agents were, like the military agents, acting independently, and all losses went down under the head of abandoned treasure. Officers actually present agree, that the only treasure *abandoned* by the army was that at Nogales, and that the sum was £25,000. When it was ordered to be rolled over the brink of the hill, two guns and a battalion of infantry were engaged with the enemy to protect it, and some person in whose charge the treasure was, exclaiming, "It is *money!*" the General replied, "So are shot and shells." Accidents will happen in wars. An officer of the guards had charge of the cars that drew this treasure, and in passing a village, another officer, observing that the bullocks were exhausted, took the pains to point out where fresh and strong animals were to be found; but the escorting officer, either ignorant of, or indifferent to his duty, took no notice of this recommendation, and continued his march with the exhausted cattle.

Towards evening the reserve approached Constantino; the French were close upon the rear, and a hill within pistol-shot of

* S. Journal of Operations, MS.

the bridge offered them such an advantage, that there was little hope to effect the passage without great loss. Moore, however, posted the riflemen and the artillery on the hill, so as to mask the hasty passage of the reserve, and the enemy, ignorant of the vicinity of a river, were cautious, until they saw the guns go off at a trot, and the riflemen follow at full speed; then they pursued briskly, but when they reached the bridge the British were over, and a good line of battle was formed on the other side. A fight commenced, and the assailants were continually reinforced as their columns of march arrived; yet General Paget maintained the post with two regiments until nightfall, and then retired to Lugo, in front of which the whole army was now assembled.

A few of the French cavalry showed themselves on the 6th, but the infantry did not appear, and the 7th Sir John Moore, in a general order, gave a severe but just rebuke to the officers and soldiers for their previous want of discipline, at the same time announcing his intention to offer battle. It has been well said, that a British army may be gleaned in a retreat, but cannot be reaped; whatever may be their misery, the soldiers will always be found clean at review, ready at a fight; and scarcely was this order issued, when the line of battle, so attenuated before, was filled with vigorous men, full of confidence and valor. Fifteen hundred had fallen in action or dropped to the rear, but as three fresh battalions, left by Sir David Baird when he first advanced from Astorga, had rejoined the army between Villa Franca and Lugo, nineteen thousand combatants were still under arms.

The right of the English position was in comparatively flat ground, and partially protected by a bend of the Minho. The centre was amongst vineyards, with low stone walls. The left, which was somewhat withdrawn, rested on the mountains, being supported and covered by the cavalry. It was the intention of the General to engage deeply with his right and centre, before he closed with his left wing, in which he had posted the flower of his troops, thinking thus to bring on a decisive battle, and trusting to the valor of the men to handle the enemy in such sort as that he should be glad to let the army continue its retreat unmolested. Other hope, to re-embark the troops without loss, there was none, save by stratagem. Soult, an experienced general, commanding soldiers habituated to war, might be tempted, but could never be forced, to engage in a decisive battle among those rugged mountains, where whole days would pass in skirmishing, without any progress being made towards crippling an adversary.

It was mid-day before the French Marshal arrived in person at the head of ten or twelve thousand men, and the remainder of his power followed in some disarray, for the marches had not been so easy but that many even of the oldest soldiers had dropped behind. As the columns came up, they formed in order of battle along a strong mountainous ridge fronting the English, and as the latter were not distinctly seen, from the inequalities of the ground, Soult doubted if they were all before him; wherefore taking four guns, and some squadrons commanded by Colonel Lallemande, he advanced towards the centre, and opened a fire, which was immediately silenced by a reply from fifteen pieces. The Marshal, being then satisfied that something more than a rear-guard was in his front, retired. About an hour after he made a feint on the right, and at the same time sent a column of infantry and five guns against the left. On that side the three regiments which had lately joined were drawn up, and the French, pushing the outposts hard, were gaining the advantage, when Moore arrived, rallied the light troops, and with a vigorous charge breaking the adverse column, treated it very roughly in the pursuit. The estimated loss of the French was between three and four hundred men.

As it was now evident that the British meant to give battle, the Duke of Dalmatia hastened the march of Laborde's division, which was still in the rear, and requested Marshal Ney, who was then at Villa Franca, to detach a division of the sixth corps by the Val des Orres to Orense; Ney, however, merely sent some troops into the valley of the Syl, and pushed his advance posts in front as far as Nogales, Poyo, and Dancos.* At daybreak on the 8th the two armies were still embattled. On the French side seventeen thousand infantry, four thousand cavalry, and fifty pieces of artillery were in line, but Soult deferred the attack until the 9th.† On the English part, sixteen thousand infantry, eighteen hundred cavalry, and forty pieces of artillery impatiently awaited the assault, and blamed their adversary for delaying a contest which they ardently desired; yet the darkness fell without a shot having been fired, and with it fell the English General's hope to engage the enemy on equal terms. What was to be done? assail the French position? remain another day in expectation of a battle? or, in secresy, gain a march, and get on board without being molested, or at least obtain time to establish the army in a good situation to cover the embarkation? The first operation was warranted neither by present nor by future advantages, for how could an inferior army expect to cripple a superior one, posted, as the French were, on a strong mountain, with an overbearing cavalry to protect their infantry, should the latter be beaten; and when twenty thousand fresh troops were at the distance

* S. Journal of Operations, MS.
† Ibid.

of two short marches in the rear? The British army was not provided to fight above one battle; there were no draught cattle, no means of transporting reserve ammunition, no magazines, no hospitals, no second line, no provisions; a defeat would have been ruin, a victory useless. A battle is always a serious affair, but two battles, under such circumstances, though both should be victories, would have been destruction. But why fight at all, after the army had been rallied, and the disasters of the march from Astorga had been remedied? What if, beating first Soult and then Ney, the British had arrived once more above Astorga, with perhaps ten thousand infantry, and half as many hundred cavalry? From the mountains of Gallicia their General might have cast his eyes as far as the Sierra Morena, without being cheered by the sight of a single Spanish army; none existed to aid him, none to whom he might give aid. Even Mr. Frere acknowledged that at this period six thousand ill-armed men collected at Despeñas Peros, formed the only barrier between the French and Seville, and Sir John Moore was sent out, not to waste English blood in fruitless battles, but to assist the universal Spanish nation!

The second proposition was decided by the state of the magazines; there was not bread for another day's consumption remaining in the stores at Lugo. It was true that the army was in heart for fighting, but distressed by fatigue and bad weather, and each moment of delay increased privations that would soon have rendered it inefficient for a campaign in the south, the only point where its services could now be effectual.* For two whole days Moore had offered battle; this was sufficient to rally the troops, to restore order, and to preserve the reputation of the army. Lugo was strong ground in itself, but it did not cover Coruña, the road leading from Orense to St. Jago de Compostella turned it; the French ought to have been on that line, and there was no reason to suppose that they were not; Soult, as we have seen, pressed Ney to follow it. It was then impossible to remain at Lugo, and useless if it had been possible. The General adopted the third plan, and prepared to decamp in the night; he ordered the fires to be kept bright, and exhorted the troops to make a great exertion, which he trusted would be the last required of them.

The country immediately in the rear of the position was intersected by stone walls and a number of intricate lanes; precautions were taken to mark the right tracks, by placing bundles of straw at certain distances, and officers were appointed to guide the columns. At ten o'clock the regiments silently quitted their ground and retired in excellent order; but a moody fortune pursued Sir John

* Sir John Moore's Papers.

Moore throughout this campaign, baffling his prudence, and thwarting his views, as if resolved to prove the unyielding firmness of his mind. A terrible storm of wind and rain, mixed with sleet, commenced as the army broke up from the position, the marks were destroyed, and the guides lost the true direction; only one of the divisions gained the main road, the other two were bewildered, and when daylight broke, the rear column was still near to Lugo. The fatigue, the depression of mind occasioned by this misfortune, and the want of shoes, broke the order of the march, and the stragglers were becoming numerous, when, unfortunately, Baird, who was with the leading division, thinking to relieve the men during a halt which took place in the night, desired them to take refuge from the weather in some houses a little way off the road. Complete disorganization followed this imprudent act; from that moment it became impossible to make the soldiers keep their ranks; plunder succeeded, the example was infectious, and what with real suffering, and evil propensity encouraged by this error of inexperience, the main body of the army, which had bivouacked for six hours in the rain, arrived at Betanzos on the evening of the 9th, in a state very discreditable to its discipline.

The commander-in-chief, with the reserve and the cavalry, as usual, covered the march, and in the course of it he ordered several bridges to be destroyed, but the engineers failed of success in every attempt.* Fortunately, the enemy did not come up with the rear before the evening, and then only with the cavalry, otherwise many prisoners must have fallen into their hands; for the number of stragglers uncovered by the passage of the reserve was so numerous, that when pressed, they united, under Sergeant Newman, of the 43d regiment, and repulsed the French cavalry themselves: a signal proof that the disorder was occasioned as much by insubordination in the regiments as by the fatigue of the march. The reserve, commanded by General Edward Paget, an officer distinguished during the retreat by his firmness, ability, and ardent zeal, remained in position during the night a few miles from Betanzos; the rest of the army was quartered in that town, and as the enemy could not gather in strength on the 10th, the commander-in-chief halted that day, and the cavalry passed from the rear-guard to the head of the column. The 11th, the French interrupted those employed to destroy the bridge of Betanzos, but from some mismanagement, although the twenty-eighth regiment repulsed the first skirmishers, the bridge, constructed of wood, was only partially destroyed. In the mean time Sir John Moore assembled the army in one solid mass. The loss of men in the march from Lugo to Betanzos had been greater

* Mr. James Moore's Narrative.

than that in all the former part of the retreat, added to all the waste of the movement in advance and the loss sustained in the different actions; nevertheless, fourteen or fifteen thousand infantry were still in column, and by an orderly march to Coruña under the personal direction of the commander-in-chief, demonstrated that inattention and the want of experience in the officers was the true cause of those disorders, which had afflicted the army far more than the sword of the enemy or the rigor of the elements.

As the troops approached Coruña, the General's looks were directed towards the harbor, but an open expanse of water painfully convinced him, that to fortune at least he was no way beholden; contrary winds still detained the fleet at Vigo, and the last consuming exertion made by the army was rendered fruitless! The men were put into quarters, and their leader awaited the progress of events.

The bridge of El Burgo was destroyed, and also that of Cambria, situated a few miles up the Mero river; but the engineer employed at the latter, mortified at the former failures, was so anxious to perform his duty in an effectual manner, that he remained too near the mine, and was killed by the explosion. Meanwhile three divisions occupied the town and suburbs of Coruña, and the reserve was posted between the village of El Burgo and the road of St. Jago de Compostella. For twelve days these hardy soldiers had covered the retreat, during which time they had traversed eighty miles of road in two marches, passed several nights under arms in the snow of the mountains, were seven times engaged with the enemy, and now assembled at the outposts, having fewer men missing from the ranks, including those who had fallen in battle, than any other division in the army: an admirable instance of the value of good discipline, and a manifest proof of the malignant injustice with which Sir John Moore has been accused of precipitating his retreat beyond the measure of human strength.

The town of Coruña, although sufficiently strong to oblige an enemy to break ground before it, was weakly fortified, and to the southward commanded by some heights close to the walls. Sir John Moore therefore caused the land front to be strengthened, and occupied the citadel, but disarmed the sea face of the works; and the inhabitants cheerfully and honorably joined in the labor, although they were fully aware that the English intended to embark, and that they would incur the enemy's anger by taking a part in the military operations. Such flashes of light from the dark cloud which at this moment covered Spain may startle the reader, and make him doubt if the Spaniards could have been so insufficient to their own defence as they have been represented in the

course of this history. I answer, that the facts were as I have told
them, and that it was such paradoxical indications of character that
deceived the world at the time, and induced men to believe that
that reckless, daring defiance of the power of France so loudly
proclaimed by the patriots would be strenuously supported. Of
proverbially vivid imagination and quick resentments, the Spaniards
feel and act individually rather than nationally, and during this
war, that which appeared constancy of purpose was but a repetition of momentary fury ; a succession of electric sparks, generated
by constant collision with the French army, and daily becoming
fainter as custom reconciled them to those injuries and insults
which are commonly the attendants of war.

Procrastination and improvidence are the besetting sins of the
nation. At this moment large magazines of arms and ammunition,
which had been sent in the early part of the preceding year from
England, were still in Coruña unappropriated and unregarded by
a nation infested with three hundred thousand enemies, and having
a hundred thousand soldiers unclothed and without weapons. Three
miles from the town they had piled four thousand barrels of powder
in a magazine built upon a hill, and a smaller quantity, collected
in another storehouse, was at some distance from the first. To
prevent them from falling a prey to the enemy, Moore caused both
to be exploded on the 13th, and the inferior one blew up with a
terrible noise, which shook the houses in the town ; but when the
train reached the great store, there ensued a crash like the bursting
forth of a volcano ; the earth trembled for miles, the rocks were
torn from their bases, and the agitated waters rolled the vessels as
in a storm ; a vast column of smoke and dust, shooting out fiery
sparks from its sides, arose perpendicularly and slowly to a great
height, and then a shower of stones, and fragments of all kinds,
bursting out of it with a roaring sound, killed many persons who
remained too near the spot. Stillness, slightly interrupted by the
lashing of the waves on the shore, succeeded, and the business of
war went on. The next measure was a painful one ; for the ground
in front of Coruña is impracticable for cavalry, and as the horses
were generally foundered, and it was impossible to embark them
all in the face of an enemy, a great number were reluctantly ordered
to be shot ; these poor animals, already worn down and feet broken,
would otherwise have been distributed among the French cavalry,
or used as draft cattle, until death relieved them from procrastinated
sufferings.

But the French were now collecting in force on the Mero, and
it became necessary to choose a position of battle. A chain of
rocky elevations, commencing on the sea-coast north-west of the

Sketch of the
BATTLE OF CORUÑA
16th January 1809

English
French

Burgo

Gl Laborde

Gl Merle

Gl Mermet

Palavia
Abaxo

Great French
Battery

Carlos

Elvina

Laborde's
dragoons

Gl Hope's divn

Baird's
divn

Lorge's
dragoons

Bat. of the
reserve

Franceschi's
Lt Cavalry

French Battery
firing on the Shipping

Airis

Mechristophers

St Lucia

Road to St Jago

S Diego Pt

Gl Frazer's divn

HARBOR

MESCADERIA

CORUÑA

ORSON
BAY

Scale
¼   ½   ¾   1 Mile
2   6   8   Furlongs

place, and ending on the Mero just behind the village of El Burgo, offered an advantageous line of defence, covered by a branch of the Mero, which, washing a part of the base, would have obliged the enemy to advance by the road of Compostella. This ridge was however too extensive for the English army, and if not wholly occupied, the French might have turned it by the right, and moved along a succession of eminences to the very gates of Coruña. There was no alternative, but to take possession of an inferior range, inclosed as it were within the other, and completely commanded by it within cannon-shot; here, therefore, the army was posted. Meanwhile the French army had been so exhausted with continual toil, that it was not completely assembled on the Mero before the 12th. On that day the infantry took post opposite El Burgo, the cavalry of La Houssaye lined the river as far as the ocean, and Franceschi, crossing at the bridge of Celas, seven miles higher up the river, intercepted some stores arriving from St. Jago, and made a few prisoners. The 14th, the bridges at El Burgo being rendered practicable for artillery, two divisions of infantry, and one of cavalry, passed the river, and to cover this march some guns opened on the English posts, but were soon silenced by a superior fire. In the evening the transports from Vigo hove in sight, and soon after entered the harbor of Coruña, and the dismounted cavalry, the sick, all the best horses, and fifty-two pieces of artillery, were embarked during the night, eight British and four Spanish guns only being retained on shore ready for action.

On the 15th, Laborde's division arrived. The French then occupied the great ridge inclosing the British position, placed their right on the intersection of the roads leading from St. Jago and Betanzos, and their left upon a rocky eminence which overlooked both lines;* after this they extended their cavalry, supported by some troops on their own left, and a slight skirmish took place in the valley below. The English piquets opposite the right of the French also got engaged, and were so galled by the fire of two guns, that Colonel M'Kenzie, of the fifth regiment, pushed out with some companies to seize the battery; a line of infantry, hitherto concealed by some stone walls, immediately arose, and poured in such a fire of musketry, that the Colonel was killed, and his men force back with loss.

In the course of the night, Soult with great difficulty established a battery of eleven heavy guns on the rocks which closed the left of his line of battle, and then formed his order of battle.† Laborde's division was posted on the right, having one half on the high ground,

* Noble's Expedition de Gallice.
† Ibid.

and the other half on the descent towards the river. Merle's division was in the centre. Mermet's division formed the left. The position was covered in front of the right by the villages of Pala-via Abaxo and Portosa, and in front of the centre by a wood. The left was secured by the rugged heights where the great battery was established, which was about twelve hundred yards from the right of the British line, and midway the little village of Elvina was held by the piquets of the fiftieth British regiment.* The late arrival of the transports, the increasing force of the enemy, and the disadvantageous nature of the ground had greatly augmented the difficulty and danger of the embarkation, and several general officers now proposed to the commander-in-chief, that he should negotiate for leave to retire to his ships upon terms. There was little chance of such a proposal being agreed to by the enemy, and there was no reason to try. The army had suffered, but not from defeat; its situation was dangerous, but far from desperate; wherefore the General would not consent to remove the stamp of energy and prudence, which marked his retreat, by a negotiation that would have given an appearance of timidity and indecision to his previous operations, as opposite to their real character as light is to darkness; his high spirit and clear judgment revolted at the idea, and he rejected the degrading advice without hesitation.

All the encumbrances of the army were shipped in the night of the 15th and morning of the 16th, and everything was prepared to withdraw the fighting men as soon as the darkness would permit them to move without being perceived; and the precautions taken would, without doubt, have insured the success of this difficult operation, but a more glorious event was destined to give a melancholy but graceful termination to the campaign. About two o'clock in the afternoon a general movement along the French line gave notice of an approaching battle, and the British infantry, fourteen thousand five hundred strong, immediately occupied the inferior range of hills already spoken of. The right was formed by Baird's division, and, from the oblique direction of the ridge, approached the enemy, while the centre and left were of necessity withheld in such a manner that the French battery on the rocks raked the whole of the line.† General Hope's division, crossing the main road, prolonged Baird's line to the left, and occupied strong ground abutting on the muddy bank of the Mero. A brigade of Baird's division remained in column behind the right wing, and in like manner a brigade of Hope's division was behind the left wing, while Paget's reserve, posted at Airis, a small village in rear of

* Sir John Moore's Letter to Lord Castlereagh.
† Vide Plan of the Battle.

the centre, looked down the valley which separated Baird's right from the hills occupied by Franceschi's cavalry; a battalion detached from the reserve kept these horsemen in check, and was itself connected with the main body by a chain of skirmishers extended across the valley. Fraser's division held the heights immediately before the gates of Coruña, watching the coast road, but it was also ready to succor any point.

These dispositions were dictated by the nature of the ground, which was very favorable to the enemy; for Franceschi's cavalry reached nearly to the village of San Cristoval, a mile beyond Baird's right, and hence Sir John Moore was forced to weaken his front and keep Fraser's division in reserve until Soult's attack should be completely unfolded. There was, however, one advantage on the British side: many thousand new English muskets, found in the Spanish stores, were given to the troops in lieu of their rusty, battered arms, and as their ammunition was also fresh, their fire was far better sustained than that of the enemy.

BATTLE OF CORUNA.

When Laborde's division arrived, the French force was not less than twenty thousand men, and the Duke of Dalmatia made no idle evolutions of display, for distributing his lighter guns along the front of his position, he opened a fire from the heavy battery on his left, and instantly descended the mountain with three columns, covered by clouds of skirmishers. The British piquets were driven back in disorder, and the village of Elvina was carried by the first French column, which then, dividing, attempted to turn Baird's right by the valley, and to break his front at the same time. The second column made against the English centre, and the third attacked Hope's left at the village of Palavia Abaxo. The weight of Soult's guns overmatched the English six-pounders, and the shot swept the position to the centre; but Sir John Moore, observing that, according to his expectations, the enemy did not show any body of infantry beyond that which moving up the valley outflanked Baird's right, ordered General Paget to carry the whole of the reserve to where the detached regiment was posted, and, as he had before arranged with him, to turn the left of the French attack and menace the great battery. Meanwhile, he directed Fraser to support Paget, and then throwing back the fourth regiment, which formed the right of Baird's division, he opened a heavy fire upon the flank of the troops penetrating up the valley, while the fiftieth and forty-second regiments met those breaking through Elvina. The ground about that village being intersected by stone walls and hollow roads, a severe scrambling fight ensued, the French were forced back with great loss, and the fiftieth regiment, entering the village with them, after a second struggle drove them beyond it. Seeing this, the General ordered up a battalion of the guards to fill the void in the line made by the advance of those regiments, whereupon the forty-second, with the exception of its grenadiers, mistaking his intention, retired, and at that moment the enemy, being reinforced, renewed the fight beyond the village; the officer commanding the fiftieth* was wounded and taken prisoner, and Elvina then became the scene of a second struggle, which being observed by the commander-in-chief, he addressed a few animating words to the forty-second, and caused it to return to the attack. During this time Paget, with the reserve, had descended into the valley, and the line of the skirmishers being thus supported, vigorously checked the advance of the enemy's troops in that quarter, while the fourth regiment galled their flank; at the same time the centre and left of the army also became engaged, Sir David Baird was severely wounded, and a furious action ensued along the line, in the valley, and on the hills.

Sir John Moore, while earnestly watching the result of the fight about the village of Elvina, was struck on the left breast by a cannon shot; the shock threw him from his horse with violence, but he rose again in a sitting posture, his countenance unchanged, and his steadfast eye still fixed upon the regiments engaged in his front, no sigh betraying a sensation of pain. In a few moments, when

---

* The author's eldest brother; he was said to be slain. When the French renewed the attack on Elvina, he was somewhat in advance of that village, and alone, for the troops were scattered by the nature of the ground. Being hurt in the leg, he endeavored to retire, but was overtaken, and thrown to the ground with five wounds; a French drummer rescued him, and when a soldier with whom he had been struggling made a second attempt to kill him, the drummer once more interfered. The morning after the battle Marshal Soult sent his own surgeon to Major Napier, and, with a kindness and consideration very uncommon, wrote to Napoleon, desiring that his prisoner might not be sent to France, which, from the system of refusing exchanges, would have ruined his professional prospects; the drummer also received the cross of the Legion of Honor. When the second corps quitted Coruña, Marshal Soult recommended his prisoner to the attention of Marshal Ney, and the latter treated him rather with the kindness of a friend than the civility of an enemy; he lodged him with the French Consul, supplied him with money, gave him a general invitation to his house, and not only refrained from sending him to France, but when by a flag of truce he knew that Major Napier's mother was mourning for him as dead, he permitted him, and with him the few soldiers taken in the action, to go at once to England, merely exacting a promise that none should serve until exchanged. I would not have touched at all upon these private adventures, were it not that gratitude demands a public acknowledgment of such generosity, and that demand is rendered more imperative by the after misfortunes of Marshal Ney. That brave and noble-minded man's fate is but too well known! He who had fought five hundred battles for France, not one against her, was shot as a traitor! Could the bitterest enemy of the Bourbons have more strongly marked the difference between their interests and those of the nation?

he was satisfied that the troops were gaining ground, his countenance brightened, and he suffered himself to be taken to the rear. Then was seen the dreadful nature of his hurt. The shoulder was shattered to pieces, the arm was hanging by a piece of skin, the ribs over the heart were broken and bared of flesh, and the muscles of the breast torn into long strips, which were interlaced by their recoil from the dragging of the shot. As the soldiers placed him in a blanket his sword got entangled, and the hilt entered the wound; Captain Hardinge, a staff officer, who was near, attempted to take it off, but the dying man stopped him, saying, "*It is as well as it is. I had rather it should go out of the field with me;*" and in that manner, so becoming to a soldier, Moore was borne from the fight.*

Meanwhile the army was rapidly gaining ground. The reserve, overthrowing everything in the valley, obliged La Houssaye's dragoons, who had dismounted, to retire, turned the enemy on that side, and even approached the eminence upon which the great battery was posted; on the left, Colonel Nicholls, at the head of some companies of the fourteenth, carried Palavia Abaxo, which General Foy defended but feebly; in the centre, the obstinate dispute for Elvina had terminated in favor of the British, and when the night set in, their line was considerably advanced beyond the original position of the morning, while the French were falling back in confusion. If at this time General Fraser's division had been brought into action along with the reserve, the enemy could hardly have escaped a signal overthrow; for the little ammunition Soult had been able to bring up was nearly exhausted, the river Mero, with a full tide, was behind him, and the difficult communication by the bridge of El Burgo was alone open for a retreat. On the other hand, to continue the action in the dark was to tempt fortune; the French were still the most numerous, and their ground was strong; moreover the disorder they were in offered such a favorable opportunity to get on board the ships, that Sir John Hope, upon whom the command of the army had devolved, satisfied with having repulsed the attack, judged it more prudent to pursue the original plan of embarking during the night. This operation was effected without delay, the arrangements being so complete that neither confusion nor difficulty occurred. The piquets, kindling a number of fires, covered the retreat of the columns, and being themselves withdrawn at daybreak, were embarked, under the protection of General Hill's brigade, which was posted near the ramparts of the town.

* Mr. James Moore's Narrative. Hardinge's Letter.

When the morning dawned, the French, observing that the British had abandoned their position, pushed forward some battalions to the heights of St. Lucie, and about midday succeeded in establishing a battery, which playing upon the shipping in the harbor caused a great deal of disorder among the transports ; several masters cut their cables, and four vessels went ashore, but the troops being immediately removed by the men-of-war's boats, the stranded vessels were burnt, and the whole fleet at last got out of harbor. General Hill's brigade then embarked from the citadel, while General Beresford, with a rear-guard, kept possession of that work until the 18th, when the wounded being all put on board, his troops likewise embarked ; the inhabitants faithfully maintained the town against the French, and the fleet sailed for England. The loss of the British was never officially published, but was estimated at eight hundred, and that of the French at three thousand. The latter is undoubtedly an exaggeration, yet it must have been very great, for the arms of the English were all new, the ammunition fresh, and whether from the peculiar construction of our muskets, the physical strength and coolness of the men, or from all combined, it is certain that the fire of an English line is the most destructive known. The nature of the ground also prevented any movement of artillery on either side, and the French columns in their attack were exposed to grape, which they could not return because of the distance of their batteries.

Thus ended the retreat to Coruña; a transaction which, up to this day, has called forth as much of falsehood and malignity as servile and interested writers could offer to the unprincipled leaders of a base faction, but which posterity will regard as a genuine example of ability and patriotism. From the spot where he fell, the General who had conducted it was carried to the town by a party of soldiers ; his blood flowed fast, and the torture of his wound was great, yet such was the unshaken firmness of his mind, that those about him, judging from the resolution of his countenance that his hurt was not mortal, expressed a hope of his recovery ; hearing this, he looked steadfastly at the injury for a moment, and then said, "*No, I feel that to be impossible.*"* Several times he caused his attendants to stop and turn him round, that he might behold the field of battle ; and when the firing indicated the advance of the British, he discovered his satisfaction, and permitted the bearers to proceed. Being brought to his lodgings, the surgeons examined his wound, but there was no hope, the pain increased, and he spoke with great difficulty. At intervals he asked if the French were beaten, and addressing his old friend, Colonel Anderson, he said,

* Captain Hardinge's Letter.

" *You know that I always wished to die this way.*"* Again he asked if the enemy were defeated, and being told they were, observed, " *It is a great satisfaction to me, to know we have beaten the French.*" His countenance continued firm and his thoughts clear ; once only, when he spoke of his mother, he became agitated ; but he often inquired after the safety of his friends, and the officers of his staff, and he did not even in this moment forget to recommend those whose merit had given them claims to promotion. His strength failed fast, and life was just extinct, when with an unsubdued spirit, as if anticipating the baseness of his posthumous calumniators, he exclaimed, "*I hope the people of England will be satisfied! I hope my country will do me justice!*" In a few minutes afterwards he died, and his corpse, wrapped in a military cloak, was interred by the officers of his staff in the citadel of Coruña, the guns of the enemy paid his funeral honors, and Soult, with a noble feeling of respect for his valor, raised a monument to his memory.

Thus ended the career of Sir John Moore, a man whose uncommon capacity was sustained by the purest virtue, and governed by a disinterested patriotism more in keeping with the primitive than the luxurious age of a great nation. His tall graceful person, his dark searching eyes, strongly defined forehead, and singularly expressive mouth, indicated a noble disposition and a refined understanding, while the lofty sentiments of honor habitual to his mind, being adorned by a subtle playful wit, gave him, in conversation, an ascendency that he always preserved by the decisive vigor of his actions. He maintained the right with a vehemence bordering on fierceness, and every important transaction in which he was engaged increased his reputation for talent, and confirmed his character as a stern enemy to vice, a steadfast friend to merit, a just and faithful servant of his country. The honest loved him, the dishonest feared him ; for while he lived he did not shun, but scorned and spurned the base, and with characteristic propriety, they spurned at him when he was dead.

A soldier from his earliest youth, Moore thirsted for the honors of his profession, and feeling that he was worthy to lead a British army, hailed the fortune that placed him at the head of the troops destined for Spain. As the stream of time passed, the inspiring hopes of triumph disappeared, but the austerer glory of suffering remained, and with a firm heart he accepted that gift of a severe fate. Confiding in the strength of his genius, he disregarded the clamors of presumptuous ignorance, and opposing sound military views to the foolish project so insolently thrust upon him by the

* Mr. James Moore's Narrative.

ambassador, he conducted his long and arduous retreat with sagacity, intelligence, and fortitude; no insult disturbed, no falsehood
deceived him, no remonstrance shook his determination; fortune
frowned without subduing his constancy; death struck, but the
spirit of the man remained unbroken when his shattered body
scarcely afforded it a habitation. Having done all that was just
towards others, he remembered what was due to himself; neither
the shock of the mortal blow, nor the lingering hours of acute pain
which preceded his dissolution, could quell the pride of his gallant
heart, or lower the dignified feeling with which, conscious of merit,
he at the last moment asserted his right to the gratitude of the
country he had served so truly.

If glory be a distinction, for such a man death is not a leveller

CHAPTER VI.

OBSERVATIONS—GENERAL VIEW OF THE CAMPAIGN.

Observations—The conduct of Napoleon and that of the English Cabinet compared—The Emperor's military dispositions examined—Propriety of Sir John
Moore's operations discussed—Diagram, exposing the relative positions of the
Spanish, French, and English armies—Propriety of Sir John Moore's retreat
discussed; and the question, whether he should have fallen back on Portugal
or Gallicia, investigated—Sir John Moore's judgment defended; his conduct
calumniated by interested men for party purposes; eulogized by Marshal Soult,
by Napoleon, by the Duke of Wellington.

Mr. Canning, in an official communication to the Spanish deputies in London, observed, that "the conduct of the campaign in
Portugal was unsatisfactory, and inadequate to the brilliant successes with which it opened." In the relation of that campaign, it
has been shown how little the activity and foresight of the Cabinet
contributed to those successes, and the following short analysis will
prove that, with respect to the campaign in Spain also, the proceedings of the ministers were marked alike by tardiness and incapacity.

Joseph abandoned Madrid the 3d of August, and on the 11th of
the same month, the French troops from the most distant parts of
Europe were in motion to remedy the disasters in the Peninsula.

The 1st of September a double conscription, furnishing one hundred and sixty thousand men, was called out to replace the troops
withdrawn from Poland and Germany.

The 4th of September the Emperor announced to the Senate,
that "he was resolved to push the affairs of the Peninsula with the

greatest activity, and to destroy the armies which the English had disembarked in that country."

The 11th, the advanced guard of the army coming from Germany reached Paris, and was there publicly harangued by the Emperor.

The 8th of November that monarch broke into Spain at the head of three hundred thousand men, and the 5th of December, not a vestige of the Spanish armies remaining, he took possession of Madrid.

Now the Asturian deputies arrived in London the 6th of June, and yet on the 20th of August—the battle of Vimiero being then unfought, and, consequently, the fate of the campaign in Portugal uncertain—the English minister invited Sir Hew Dalrymple to discuss three plans of operations in Spain, each founded upon data utterly false, and all objectionable in detail. He also desired that Sir Arthur Wellesley should go to the Asturias to ascertain what facilities that country offered for the disembarkation of an English army; and the whole number of troops disposable for the campaign, exclusive of those already in Portugal, he stated to be twenty thousand, of which one half was in England and the other in Sicily. He acknowledged that no information yet received had enabled the Cabinet to decide as to the application of the forces at home, or the ulterior use to be made of those in Portugal, yet, with singular rashness, the whole of the southern provinces, containing the richest cities, finest harbors, and most numerous armies, were discarded from consideration; and Sir Hew Dalrymple, who was well acquainted with that part of Spain, and in close and friendly correspondence with the chiefs, was directed to confine his attention to the northern provinces, of which he knew nothing.

The reduction of Junot's army in Portugal, and the discomfiture of Joseph on the Ebro, were regarded as certain events, and the observations of the minister were principally directed, not to the best mode of attack, but to the choice of a line of march that would insure the utter destruction or captivity of the whole French army; nay, elated with extravagant hopes, and strangely despising Napoleon's power, he instructed Lord William Bentinck to urge the Central Junta to an invasion of France, as soon as the army on the Ebro should be annihilated. Thus it appears that the English ministers were either profoundly ignorant of the real state of affairs, or that, with a force scattered in England, Portugal, and Sicily, and not exceeding forty-five thousand men, they expected in one campaign, first to subdue twenty-six thousand French under Junot, then to destroy eighty thousand under Joseph, and turning the tide of war, to invade France.

The battle of Vimiero took place, and Sir Arthur Wellesley naturally declined a mission more suitable to a staff captain than a victorious commander; but before Sir Hew's answer, exposing the false calculations of the minister's plans, could be received in England, a despatch, dated the 2d of September, announced the resolution of the government to employ an army in the northern provinces of Spain, and directed twenty thousand men to be held in readiness to unite with other forces to be sent from England. Nevertheless, this project also was so immature, that no intimation was given how the junction was to be effected, whether by sea or land; nor had the minister even ascertained that the Spaniards would permit English troops to enter Spain at all. Three weeks later, Lord William Bentinck, writing from Madrid, says, "I had an interview with Florida Blanca; he expressed his surprise that there should be a doubt of the Spaniards wishing for the assistance of the English army." Such also was the confusion at home, that Lord Castlereagh repeatedly expressed his fears lest the embarkation of Junot's troops should have absorbed all the means of transport in the Tagus, when a simple reference to the transport office in London would have satisfied him that, although the English army should also be embarked, there would still remain a surplus of twelve thousand tons.

When the popular cry rose against the convention of Cintra, the generals-in-chief were recalled in succession, as rapidly as they had been appointed; the despatches addressed to one generally fell into the hands of his successor; but the plans of the ministers becoming at last mature, on the 6th of October Sir John Moore was finally appointed to lead the forces into Spain. At this period the head of the grand French army was already in the passes of the Pyrenees, the hostile troops on the Ebro coming to blows, the Spaniards weak and divided, and the English forty marches from the scene of action: yet, said the minister to Sir John Moore, "there will be full time to concert your plan of operations with the Spanish generals before the equipment of your army can be completed." Was this the way to oppose Napoleon? Could such proceedings lead to aught but disaster? It has been said that Sir Hew Dalrymple's negligence was the cause of this delay—that he should have had the troops in readiness. But that general could not prudently incur the expense of equipping, for a march, an army that was likely to be embarked; he could not, in short, divine the plans of the ministers before they were formed, and it is evident that the error attaches entirely to the government.

The incapacity of the Spanish generals has been already sufficiently exposed by occasional observations in the narrative; their faults, glaring and fatal, call for no further remark ; but the exact combinations, the energy and rapidity of the French Emperor, merit the most careful examination. His operations were not— as they have been generally considered—a pompous display of power, to create an appearance of conquest that was unreal; not a mere violent irruption with a multitude of men, but a series of skilful and scientific movements, worthy of so great a general and politician. It is true that his force was immense, and that the Spaniards were but contemptible soldiers, yet he never neglected the lessons of experience, nor deviated from the strictest rules of art. With astonishing activity, and, when we consider the state of his political relations on the continent, we may add, with astonishing boldness, he first collected ample means to attain his object, then, deceiving his enemies with regard to his numbers, position, and intentions, and choosing his time with admirable judgment, he broke through the weak part of their line and seized Burgos, a central point, which enabled him to envelop and destroy the left wing of the Spaniards before their right could hear of his attack, the latter being itself turned by the same movement, and exposed to a like fate. This position also enabled him to menace the capital, to keep the English army in check, and to cover the formation of those magazines and stores which were necessary to render Burgos the base and pivot of further operations.

Napoleon's forces were numerous enough to have attacked Castaños and Palafox, while Blake was being pursued by the first and fourth corps ; but trusting nothing to chance, he waited for twelve days, until the position of the English army was ascertained, the strength of the northern provinces quite broken, and a secure place of arms established. Then leaving the second corps to cover his communication, and sending the fourth corps into the flat country, to coast, as it were, the heads of the English columns, and to turn the passes of the Carpentino mountains, he caused the Spanish right wing to be destroyed, and himself approached the capital at a moment when not a vestige of a national army was left—when he had good reason to think that the English were in full retreat—when the whole of his own corps were close at hand—and consequently when the greatest moral effect could be produced, and the greatest physical power concentrated at the same time to take advantage of it. Napoleon's dispositions were indeed surprisingly skilful; for, although Marshal Lefebre's precipitation at Zornoza, by prolonging Blake's agony, lost six days of promise, it is certain that even reverses in battle could neither have checked the Emperor nor helped the Spaniards.

If Soult had been beaten at Gamonal, Napoleon was close at

hand to support the second corps, and the sixth corps would have fallen upon the flank and rear of the Spaniards.

If the first corps had been defeated at Espinosa, the second and fourth corps and the Emperor's troops would have taken Blake in flank and rear.

If Lasnes had been defeated at Tudela, he could have fallen back on Pampeluna. The fifth and eighth corps were marching to support him, and the sixth corps would have taken the Spaniards in flank.

If the Emperor had been repulsed at the Somosierra, the sixth corps would have turned that position by Guadalaxara, and the fourth corps by Guadarama.

If Sir John Moore had retreated on Portugal, the fourth corps was nearer to Lisbon than he was ; and if he had overthrown Soult, the fifth and eighth corps were ready to sustain that Marshal, while Napoleon, with fifty thousand men, as we have seen, was prepared to cut the British line of retreat into Gallicia. In short, no possible event could have divided the Emperor's forces ; and he constantly preserved a central position, which enabled him to unite his masses in sufficient time to repair any momentary disaster. By a judicious mixture of force and policy also, he obliged Madrid to surrender in two days, and thus prevented the enthusiasm which would doubtless have arisen if the capital had been defended for any time, and the heart-burnings if it had been stormed. The second sweep that he was preparing to make when Sir John Moore's march called off his attention from the south, would undoubtedly have put him in possession of the remaining great cities of the Peninsula. Then the civil benefits promised in his decrees and speeches would have produced their full effect, and the result may be judged of by the fact that, in 1811 and '12, Aragon, Valencia, and Andalusia were, under the able administration of Marshals Soult and Suchet, as submissive as any department of France. Both generals raised Spanish battalions, and employed them not only to preserve the public peace, but to chase and put down the guerillas of the neighboring provinces.

Sir John Moore's talents saved the Peninsula at this crisis ; and here only a military error of Napoleon's may be detected. Forgetting his own maxim that war is not a conjectural art, he took for granted that the English army was falling back to Portugal, and without ascertaining that it was so, acted upon the supposition. This apparent negligence, so unlike his usual circumspection, leads to the notion that through Morla he might have become acquainted with the peculiar opinions and rash temper of Mr. Frere, and trusted that the treacherous arts of the Spaniard, in conjunction with the presumptuous disposition of the plenipotentiary, would so mislead the English General as to induce him to carry his army to Madrid, and thus deliver it up entire and bound. It was an error; but Napoleon could be deceived or negligent only for a moment. With what vigor he recovered himself, and hastened to remedy his error! How instantaneously he relinquished his intentions against the south, turned his face away from the glittering prize, and bent his whole force against the only man among his adversaries that had discovered talent and decision! Let those who have seen the preparations necessary to enable a small army to act, even on a preconceived plan, say what uncontrollable energy that man possessed, who, suddenly interrupted in such great designs, could, in the course of a few hours, put fifty thousand men in movement on a totally new line of operations, and in the midst of winter execute a march of two hundred miles, with a rapidity hardly to be equalled under the most favorable circumstances.

The indefatigable activity of the Duke of Dalmatia greatly contributed to the success of the whole campaign; and it is a remarkable circumstance, that Soult and Napoleon, advancing from different bases, should have so combined their movements, that, after marching, the one above a hundred, and the other above two hundred miles, through a hostile country, they effected their junction at a given point, and at a given hour, without failure: nor is it less remarkable, that such a decided and well-conducted operation should have been baffled by a general at the head of an inexperienced army.

When Sylla, after all his victories, styled himself a happy, rather than a great general, he discovered his profound knowledge of the military art. Experience had taught him that the speed of one legion, the inactivity of another, the obstinacy, the ignorance, or the treachery of a subordinate officer, was sufficient to mar the best concerted plan—nay, that the intervention of a shower of rain, an unexpected ditch, or any apparently trivial accident, might determine the fate of a whole army. It taught him that the vicissitudes of war are so many, that disappointment will attend the wisest combinations; that a ruinous defeat, the work of chance, often closes the career of the boldest and most sagacious of generals, and that to judge of a commander's conduct by the event alone, is equally unjust and unphilosophical, a refuge for vanity and ignorance.

These reflections seem to be peculiarly applicable to Sir John Moore's campaign, which has by sundry writers been so unfairly discussed. Many of the subsequent disasters of the French can now be distinctly traced to the operations of the British army. It can be demonstrated that the reputation of that excellent man was basely

15*

sacrificed at the period of his death, and that the virulent censures passed upon his conduct have been as inconsiderate as they were unmerited and cruel. The nature of the commands held by Sir John Moore in the years 1807–8–9 forced him into a series of embarrassments, from which few men could have extricated themselves. After refusing the charge of the absurd expedition to Egypt in 1806, which ended, as he judged it must do, unfavorably, he succeeded to the command of the troops in Sicily, a situation which immediately involved him in unpleasant discussions with the Queen of Naples and the British envoy; discussions to which the subsequent well-known enmity of the Cabinet of that day may be traced. By his frank conduct, clear judgment, and firm spirit, he soon obtained an influence over the wretched court of Palermo, that promised the happiest results; the Queen's repugnance to a reform was overcome, the ministers were awed, and the miserable intrigues of the day abated; the Sicilian army was reorganized, and a good military system was commenced under the advice of the British general.

This promising state of affairs lasted but a short time; the Russian fleet put into the Tagus, the French threatened Portugal, and Sicily was no longer considered! Sir John Moore was ordered to quit that island, and to assemble a large force at Gibraltar for a special service; but the troops to be gathered were dispersed in the Mediterranean from Egypt to the Straits, and their junction could not be effected at all, unless the English ambassador at Constantinople should succeed in bringing a negotiation, then pending between the Turks and Russia, to a happy issue.* Now this special service in question had two objects: 1, to aid Sir Sidney Smith in carrying off the royal family of Portugal to the Brazils; 2, to take possession of Madeira; yet neither was made known to the General before his arrival at Gibraltar, which was not until after Junot had taken possession of Lisbon. Sir John Moore then, following his instructions, proceeded home, and thus our interests in Sicily were again abandoned to the vices and intrigues of the court of Palermo. On the passage he crossed General Spencer going with a force against Ceuta, and soon after he had reached England he was despatched to Sweden, without any specific object, and with such vague instructions, that an immediate collision with the unfortunate Gustavus was the consequence.

Having with much dexterity and judgment withdrawn himself and his army from the capricious violence of that monarch, Sir John was superseded and sent to Portugal, with the third rank in an army which at that time no man had such good claims to command as himself; the mode of doing this was also offensive, and it was

* Sir John Moore's Journal, MS.

evident that the ministers desired to drive him into private life.
Their efforts were, however, powerless against his pure and elevated
patriotism. In a personal conference with Lord Castlereagh, he
expressed his indignation at the insults offered to him, and then
repaired to his station at Portsmouth, where an official letter followed him, the purport being, that his remonstrance being disre-
spectful, it would be referred to the King for reprehension, and that
measures would be taken to remove him from what appeared to be
a disagreeable situation: in other words, that his resignation was
demanded. Without a moment's hesitation he replied to this menace, in a letter which breathed the very spirit of manly dignity and
patriotism. "I am," he wrote, "this moment honored with your
Lordship's letter (by messenger) of yesterday's date. As I have
already had the honor to express my sentiments to your Lordship
fully at my last interview, it is, I think, unnecessary to trouble you
with a repetition of them now. I am about to proceed on the service on which I have been ordered, and it shall be my endeavor to
acquit myself with the same zeal by which I have ever been actuated when employed in the service of my country. The communication which it has been thought proper to make to his Majesty
cannot fail to give me pleasure; I have the most perfect reliance
on his Majesty's justice, and shall never feel greater security than
when my conduct, my character, and my honor are under his Majesty's protection." He heard no more on that subject.

The good fortune of England was never more conspicuous than
at this period, when her armies and fleets were thus bandied about,
and a blind chance governed the councils at home. For first a force
collected from all parts of the Mediterranean was transported to
the Baltic at a time when an expedition composed of troops, which
had but a short time before come back from the Baltic, was sailing from England to the Mediterranean. An army intended to
conquer South America was happily assembled in Ireland at the
moment when an unexpected event called for their services in Portugal. A division destined to attack the Spaniards at Ceuta, arrived at Gibraltar at the instant when the insurrection of Andalusia
fortunately prevented them from making an attempt that would
have materially aided Napoleon's schemes against the Peninsula.
Again, three days after Sir John Moore had withdrawn his army
from Sweden, orders arrived to employ it in carrying off the Spanish troops under Romana—an operation for which it was not
required, and which would have retarded, if not entirely frustrated,
the campaign in Portugal; but the ministers were resolved at any
cost to prevent Moore from commanding the army destined for
Portugal. Nor was it the least part of England's fortune that in

such long-continued voyages in bad seasons, no disaster befell the huge fleets thus employed in bearing her strength from one extremity of Europe to the other.

After the convention of Cintra, Moore was again placed at the head of an army, an appointment unexpected by him, for the frank and bold manner in which he expressed himself to the ministers left him little to hope; but the personal good-will of the King, and his own towering reputation, crushed all opposition. Thus, in a few months after he had quitted Sweden, Moore, with an army not exceeding twenty-four thousand men, was in the heart of Spain, opposed to Napoleon, who, having passed the Pyrenees at the head of three hundred and thirty thousand men, could readily bring two hundred thousand to bear on the British; a vast disproportion of numbers, and a sufficient answer to all the idle censures passed upon the retreat to Coruña.

The most plausible grounds of accusation against Sir John Moore's conduct, rest on three alleged errors :—

1st. That he divided his forces.

2dly. That he advanced against Soult.

3dly. That he made a precipitate and unnecessary retreat.

When a general, aware of the strength of his adversary, and of the resources to be placed at his own disposal, arranges a plan of campaign, he may be strictly judged by the rules of art; but if, as in the case of Sir John Moore, he is suddenly appointed to conduct important operations without a plan being arranged, or the means given to arrange one, then it is evident that his capacity or incapacity must be judged of by the energy he displays, the comprehensive view he takes of affairs, and the rapidity with which he accommodates his measures to events, that the original vice of his appointment will not permit him to control. Sir Walter Scott, in his Life of Napoleon, with that intrepidity of error which marks the work, has asserted, "that Moore sent ten thousand men, under Sir D. Baird, by sea, to Coruña." That "the general science of war, upon the most extended scale, seems to have been so little understood or practised by the English generals at this time, that instead of the country being carefully reconnoitred by officers of skill, the march of the army was arranged by such hasty and inaccurate information as could be collected from the peasants;" and that "by these reports Sir John Moore was induced to divide his army."

The second of these assertions is devoid of reason, and both are contrary to fact. Sir David Baird was never at Lisbon, but was sent with his troops by the ministers direct from England to Coruña. The "general science of war upon the most extended scale," is an inflated and unmeaning expression; the most contracted operation requires that good information should be obtained; and as to the fact, Sir John Moore employed his own staff officers to examine the roads, sought information equally from noble and peasant, and, like all great commanders, regulated his proceedings by the general result of his inquiries.

The first dividing of the army was, therefore, the act of the ministers, who sent Baird to Coruña; the after separation of the artillery was Sir John Moore's, the reasons for which have been already stated; but it is worth while to examine what the effect of that measure was, and what it might have been. And here it may be observed, that, although a brigade of light six-pounders did accompany the troops to Almeida, the road, in a military sense, was *not practicable*, for the guns were in some places let down the rocks by ropes, and in others carried over the difficult places! a practicable affair with one brigade, but how could the great train of guns and ammunition-wagons that accompanied Sir John Hope, have passed such places without a loss of time that would have proved more injurious to the operations than the separation of the artillery? The advance of the army was guided by three contingent cases, any one of which arising would have immediately influenced the operations: 1. Blake on the left, or Castaños and Palafox upon the right, might have beaten the French, and advanced to the Pyrenees. 2. They might have maintained their position on the Ebro. 3. The arrival of reinforcements from France might have forced the Spaniards to fall back upon the upper Duero, on one side, and to the mountains of Guadalaxara on the other. In the first case, there was no risk of marching by divisions towards Burgos, which was the point of concentration given by the British and Spanish ministers. In the second case, the army could safely unite at Valladolid. In the third case, if the division of Sir David Baird had reached Toro early in November,—and this it was reasonable to expect, because that General arrived at Coruña the 13th of October,—the retrograde movement of the Spanish armies would probably have drawn the English to the Guadarama, as a safe and central point between the retiring Spanish wings.

Now the artillery, marching from the Alemtejo by the roads of Talavera and Naval Carnero to Burgos, would pass over one hundred and two Spanish leagues; to Aranda de Duero, eighty-nine leagues; to Valladolid, ninety-two leagues; while the columns that marched by Almeida and Salamanca would pass over one hundred and sixteen leagues to Burgos, and ninety-eight to Valladolid. Wherefore, supposing the Spaniards successful, or even holding their own, the separation of the artillery was an advantage, and if the

Spaniards were driven back, their natural line of retreat would have brought them towards Madrid, Blake by Aranda to the Somosierra, and Castaños and Palafox by Siguenza and Tarancon, to cover the capital, and to maintain an interior communication between the Somosierra and the Henares river. The British artillery would then have halted at Espinar, after a march of only eighty leagues, and Baird and Moore's corps, uniting at Salamanca early in November, might, by a flank march to Arevalo, have insured the concentration of the whole army.

Thus, in the three anticipated cases, the separation of the artillery was prudent, and promised to be advantageous. There was, indeed, a fourth case, that which really happened. All the Spanish armies were dispersed in an instant! utterly effaced! But Sir John Moore could not have divined such a catastrophe, while his ears were ringing with the universal clamor about the numbers and enthusiasm of the patriots; and if he had foreseen even a part of such disasters, he would never have advanced from Portugal. With the plans of the Spanish government he was unacquainted, but he was officially informed that above one hundred and forty thousand Spanish soldiers were between him and a feeble dispirited enemy; and as the intercepted letter from the Governor of Bayonne stated that the reinforcements would only arrive between the 18th of October and the 18th of November, it was reasonable to suppose the French would not commence offensive operations before the latter period, and that ample time would be afforded to concentrate the English troops under the protection of the Spanish armies.

If Sir John Moore could have suspected the delusion under which the British government acted; if he could have divined the incredible folly of the Central Junta and the Spanish generals, or the inaccuracy of the military agents; if he could have supposed that the Spanish armies were weak in numbers, weaker in spirit, and destitute of food and clothing, or that, while the Spanish authorities were pressing him to advance, they would wantonly detain Sir David Baird's troops seventeen days on board the transports; if he could have imagined all this, undoubtedly his arrangements ought and would have been different, his army would have been kept together, and the road to Salamanca through Coria, however difficult, would have been preferred to a divided march.

Now the dangerous and absurd position of the Spanish armies, and the remote situation of the British troops in October, may be explained by the annexed diagram. Lisbon being taken as a centre, and the distance A between Lisbon and Coruña being the radius, let a circle passing through Madrid be described, and let

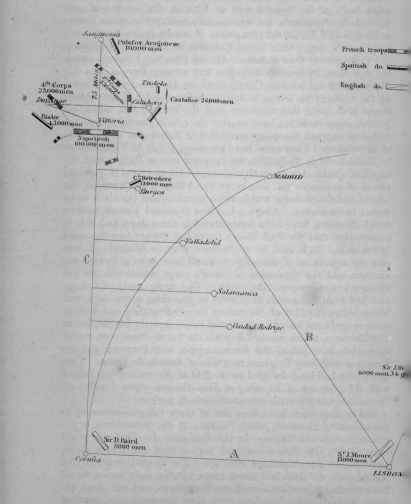

Sangnessa

Palafox. Aragonese
16000 men

4ᵗʰ Corps
25,000 men

3ʳᵈ
25,000 men

Tudela

75 Miles

Dan Argo

Calahora

Castaños 26000 men

Blake
45.000 men

Vittoria

Napoleon
100.000 men

MADRID

Cᵗ Belvedere
13000 men

Burgos

Valladolid

C

Salamanca

Ciudad Rodrigo

B

Sir J.H
4000 men 34 g

Sir D. Baird
8000 men

Coruña

A

Sᵗ J. Moore
15000 men

LISBON

French troops

Spanish do.

English do.

the tangential line c be drawn perpendicular to the radius A, meeting the secant B at Sanguessa.   Then it will be seen that as the extreme right of the Spaniards was posted at Sanguessa, and Castaños at Calahorra, while Blake was near Durango, and the main body of the French was at Vittoria, the latter not only divided the Spaniards, but was actually twenty-five miles nearer to Burgos and Valladolid (the points of concentration for Moore's and Baird's corps) than either Castaños or Blake; and seventy-five miles nearer than Palafox. On the 10th, the Emperor struck the first blow, by beating Belvedere and seizing Burgos; but Sir David Baird did not quit Coruña until the 12th, and did not bring up the whole of his troops to Astorga before the 4th of December; hence it is clear, that whatever road the artillery had taken, the British army could not have averted the ruin of the Spaniards.

Let us suppose the troops assembled at Salamanca on the 13th of November. They must have advanced either to Valladolid or to Madrid. If to Valladolid, the Emperor was at Burgos with the imperial guards, ten or twelve thousand cavalry, and a hundred pieces of artillery; the first corps was within a day's march, the second and fourth corps within three marches, and the sixth corps within two marches. Above a hundred thousand French soldiers could, therefore, have been concentrated in three days, and it is to be observed that Sir John Moore never had twenty-five thousand in the field. It is said, he might have gone to Madrid; in that case the separation of the artillery would have been a decided advantage, and the separation of Baird's corps, which was not the General's arrangement, the error. The army could not have marched from Salamanca to Madrid in less than seven days, and hence before the 21st of November, twenty-four thousand British soldiers could not have been collected in the capital; but the fourth French corps, which reached Segovia the 1st of December, would meanwhile have cut off the communication with Portugal, and the Emperor with forty thousand men was at Aranda de Duero. Castaños, who had been defeated on the 23d of November, was indeed with the remnant of an army at Guadalaxara about the 1st of December, but the sixth corps was close in pursuit.

Moore must then have done one of three things—advanced to the succor of Castaños, joined St. Juan at the Somosierra, or retreated across the Tagus. In the first case, the Emperor would have forced the Somosierra, and uniting with the fourth corps, have placed sixty thousand men upon the English rear; in the second case, the sixth and fourth corps, turning both flanks, would have effected a junction behind the Somosierra, and cut them off from Madrid, while Napoleon, with forty thousand men, assailed them in front. To retreat over the Tagus was to adopt the southern provinces for a new base of operations, and might have been useful if the Spaniards would have rallied round him with enthusiasm and courage; but would they have done so when the Emperor was advancing with his enormous force? After-experience proves that they would not. The Duke of Dalmatia, in 1810, with an army very inferior to that under Napoleon, reached the gates of Cadiz without a serious blow being struck to oppose him, and at this time the people of the south were reckless of the opportunity procured for them by Sir John Moore's march on Sahagun.

It has, however, been said, that twenty-four thousand British troops, acting vigorously, could have checked the Emperor, and raised the courage of the Spaniards. To such an observation I will oppose a fact. In 1815, Napoleon crossed the Sambre with one hundred and fifteen thousand men, and the two hundred and ten thousand regular troops in his front, among which were more than thirty thousand English, could with difficulty stop his progress after four days' fighting, in three of which he was successful. If Sir John Moore, at a subsequent period, was willing to risk the danger of a movement on the capital, it was because he was misinformed of the French strength, and the Spaniards were represented to be numerous and confident; he was also unacquainted with the defeat at Tudela. His object was, by assisting Castaños, to arouse the spirit of the patriots, and nothing more strongly evinces his hardihood and prompt judgment; for, in his letter to Mr. Frere, he distinctly stated the danger to be incurred, and carefully separating the military from the political reasons, only proposed to venture the army, if the envoy was satisfied that the Spanish government and people would answer to such an appeal, and that the British Cabinet would be willing to incur the risk for such an object. If he did not follow up his own proposal, it was because he had discovered that the army of Castaños was, not simply defeated, but destroyed; because the Somosierra had been forced by a charge of cavalry; and because the passes of the Guadarama, on his line of march to Madrid, were seized by the enemy before his own army could be concentrated.

Why then did he not retreat into Portugal? Because, Napoleon having directed his forces against the capital, the British army was unable to concentrate; because Madrid had shut her gates; because Mr. Frere and the Spanish authorities endeavored to deceive him by false information; because the solemn declaration of the Junta of Toledo, that they would bury themselves under the ruins of that town rather than surrender, joined to the fact that Zaragoza was fighting heroically, seemed to guarantee the constancy and vigor of that patriotic spirit which was apparently once more excited; because the question was again become political, and it was necessary to satisfy the English people, that nothing was left undone to aid a cause which they had so much at heart; because the peculiar position of the French army at the moment, afforded the means of creating a powerful diversion in favor of the southern provinces. These are the unanswerable reasons for the advance towards Sahagun. In the details of execution, that movement may be liable to some trifling objections; perhaps it would have been better to have carried the army on the 21st at once to Carrion and neglected Sahagun and Saldanha; but in its strategic and political character, it was well conceived and well timed, hardy and successful.

The irritating interference that Sir John Moore was called upon to repel, and the treachery and the folly, equal in its effects to treachery, that he was obliged to guard against, have been sufficiently dwelt upon already; yet before discussing the retreat from Astorga, it may be of some military interest to show that the line of Portugal, although the natural one for the British army to retire upon, was not at this period necessarily either safe or useful, and that greater evils than those incurred by a retreat through Gallicia would probably have attended a retrograde march upon Lisbon.

The rugged frontier of Portugal, lying between the Duero and the Tagus, is vulnerable in many points to an invading army of superior force. It may be penetrated between the Duero and Pinhel, and between Pinhel and Guarda, by roads leading into the valleys of the Zezere and the Mondego; between the Sierra de Estrella and the Sierra de Gata, by the road from Alfayates to Sabugal and Panamacor, or that by Guarda and Coria. Again, it may be pierced between the Sierra de Gata and the Tagus by Idanha Velha, Castello Branco, and Sobreira Formosa; and from the Tagus to the Guadiana, a distance of about twenty leagues, the Alemtejo presents an open country without any strong fortress, save La Lippe, which may be disregarded and passed without danger. Now Sir John Moore commenced his forward movement from Salamanca on the 12th of December, and at that period the fourth corps, being at Talavera de la Reyna, was much nearer to Lisbon than the British army was, and the Emperor was preparing to march on that capital with the sixth corps, the guards, and the reserve. He could, as the Duke of Berwick did, penetrate by both sides of the Tagus; and what was to prevent him from reaching Lisbon before the British force, if the latter had retreated from Salamanca? He marched on a shorter line and a better road, and he could supply his troops by requisitions, a system that, however fatal it may be in the end, is always advantageous at first; but Moore must, from a scanty military chest, have purchased his supplies from a suspicious peasantry, rendered more distrustful by the retreat.

It is true that in Lisbon, Sir John Cradock commanded six thousand infantry and two hundred and fifty-eight cavalry; but the Portuguese provisional government, who had only organized a few ill-composed battalions, were so inactive, that it was not until the 11th of December that a proclamation, calling on the people to arm, was issued. In the arsenal there were scarcely muskets and equipments for eight thousand men, and the new levies were only required to assemble when the country should be actually invaded. Sir Robert Wilson, having with great activity organized about two thousand of the Lusitanian legion, had marched in the middle of December from Oporto, and this was all that could be opposed to an army more numerous, and more favorably situated for invasion, and incomparably better commanded than that with which Massena invaded the country in 1810. Thus it may be affirmed, that if a retreat upon Lisbon was advisable before Napoleon took Madrid, it was not a safe operation after that event, and it is clear that Sir John Moore neither lightly nor injudiciously adopted the line of Gallicia.

The arguments of those who deny the necessity of falling back, even behind the Esla, are scarcely worth notice; a simple reference to the numbers under the Emperor, and the direction of his march, is sufficient to expose their futility; but the necessity of the continued and, as it has been unjustly called, the precipitate retreat to Coruña, may not be quite so obvious. The advance to Sahagun was intended to create a diversion, and give the Spaniards an opportunity of making head in the south; it succeeded in drawing away the enemy, yet the Spaniards did not make any head, the Central Junta displayed no energy or wisdom; a few slight demonstrations by the Marquis of Palacios, on the side of the Sierra Morena, and by the Duke of Infantado on the side of Cuença, scarcely disturbed the first corps which remained in La Mancha; ten thousand men were sufficient to maintain Madrid in perfect tranquillity, and a part of the fourth corps even marched from Talavera by Placentia on Salamanca. By the letters of Mr. Stuart, and the reports of his own spies, the English General was informed of all these disheartening circumstances, yet the intelligence arrived slowly and at intervals, and he, hoping that the Spaniards would finally make an effort, announced his intention to hold the Gallicias; Mr. Stuart's correspondence at last deprived him of that hope, and the presence of the Emperor, the great amount of his force, and the vehemence with which he pressed forward, confirmed the unhappy truth that nothing could be expected from the south.

Sir John Moore could not with twenty-three thousand men maintain himself against the whole French army, and until he reached Astorga his flanks were always exposed; from thence he retreated in comparative security, but the natural strength of the country between that town and Coruña misled persons of shallow judgment, who have since inconsiderately advanced many vague accusations, such as that passes where a hundred men could stop an amy were lightly abandoned; that the retreat was a flight, and the General's judgment clouded by the danger of his situation. There might be some foundation for such observations if military commanders were like prize-fighters, bound to strike always at the front; but as long as armies are dependent for their subsistence and ammunition upon lines of communication, the safety of their flanks and rear must be considered as of consequence. Moore was perfectly aware that he could fight any number of men in some of the mountainous positions on the road to Coruña; yet unless he could make a permanent defence, such battles would have been worse than useless, and a permanent defence was impossible, inasmuch as there were none but temporary magazines nearer than Coruña, and there were neither carriages of transport, nor money to procure them; moreover a severe winter had just set in, the people were disinclined to aid the troops, and as the province was poor, few resources could be drawn from the vicinity. Neither was there a single position that could be maintained for more than a few days against a superior force.

That of Rodrigatos could be turned by the old road leading to Villa Franca, Villa Franca itself by the valley of the Syl, and from thence the whole line to Coruña might be turned by the road of Orense, which also led directly to Vigo; and until he reached Nogales, Moore's intention was to retire to Vigo. The French could have marched through the richest part of Gallicia to St. Jago and Coruña on the left, or from the Asturias, by the way of Mondonedo, on the right; and if it be asked, why they did not do so? the answer is prompt: the Emperor having quitted the army, the jealousies and misunderstandings usual between generals of equal rank impeded the operations. A coolness subsisted between Marshal Ney and the Duke of Dalmatia, and without entering into the grounds of their difference, it is plain that, in a military point of view, the judgment of the latter was the soundest. The former committed a great error by remaining at Villa Franca instead of pushing his corps, or a part of it, as recommended by Soult, along the valley of Orense to St. Jago de Compostella; the British army would have been lost if the sixth corps had reached Coruña before it; and what would have been the chances in the battle if three additional French divisions had been engaged? Granting, therefore, that the troops could have been nourished during the winter, Villa Franca, Nogales, Constantino and Lugo were not permanently defensible by any army whose base of operations was at Coruña. Hence it was that Sir John Moore resolved to regain his ships with the view to renew the war in the south, and Hannibal himself could have done no more.

Nor was the mode of executing the retreat at all unbecoming the character of an able officer. Lord Bacon observes that " honorable retreats are no ways inferior to brave charges, as having less of fortune, more of discipline, and as much of valor." That is an honorable retreat in which the retiring general loses no trophies in flight sustains every charge without being broken, and finally, after a severe action, re-embarks his army in the face of a superior enemy, without being seriously molested. It would be honorable to effect this before a foe only formidable from numbers, but it is infinitely more creditable, when the commander, while struggling with bad weather and worse fortune, has to oppose veterans with inexperienced troops, and to contend against an antagonist of eminent ability, who scarcely suffers a single advantage to escape him during this long and vigorous pursuit. All this Sir John Moore did, and finished his work by a death as firm and glorious as any that antiquity can boast of.

Put to Lord Bacon's test, in what shall the retreat to Coruña be found deficient? Something in discipline perhaps, but that fault does not attach to the general. Those commanders who have been celebrated for making fine retreats were in most instances well acquainted with their armies; and Hannibal, speaking of the elder Scipio, derided him, although a brave and skilful man, for that, being unknown to his own soldiers, he should presume to oppose himself to a general who could call to each man under his command by name; thus inculcating, that unless troops be trained in the peculiar method of a commander, the latter can scarcely achieve anything great. Now Moore had a young army suddenly placed under his guidance, and it was scarcely united, when the superior numbers of the enemy forced it to a retrograde movement under very harassing circumstances; he had not time, therefore, to establish a system of discipline, and it is in the leading events, not the minor details, that the just criterion of his merits is to be sought for.

Was the retreat uncalled for? Was it unnecessarily precipitate? Was any opportunity of crippling the enemy lost? Was any weakness to be discovered in the personal character of the General? These are the questions that sensible men will ask. The first has been already examined; the second is a matter of simple calcula-

tion. The rear-guard quitted Astorga on the 1st of January; on
the 3d it repulsed the enemy in a sharp skirmish at Calcabellos;
the 6th it rejoined the main body at Lugo, having three times
checked the pursuers during the march; it was unbroken, had lost
no gun, suffered no misfortune. The whole army offered battle at
Lugo for two successive days, and it was not accepted, and the
retreat recommencing, the troops reached Betanzos on the morning
of the 10th, and Coruña on the 11th; thus in eleven days, three
of which were days of rest, a small army passed over a hundred
and fifty miles of good road. Now Napoleon, with fifty thousand
men, left Madrid on the 22d of December, and the 28th he was at
Villepando, having performed a march, on bad roads, of a hundred
and sixty-four miles in seven days. The retreat to Coruña was
consequently not precipitate, unless it can be shown that it was
unnecessary to retreat at all beyond Villa Franca; neither can it
be asserted, that any opportunity of crippling the enemy was lost.
To fight a battle was the game of the French Marshal, and if any
censure will apply to his able campaign, it is that he delayed to
attack at Lugo; victorious or beaten, it would have increased the
embarrassments of his adversary, who must have continued his
retreat encumbered with the wounded, or the latter must have been
abandoned without succor in the midst of winter.

At Coruña the absence of the fleet necessarily brought on a
battle. That it was honorable to the British troops is clear from
the fact that they embarked without loss after the action. That it
was absolutely necessary to embark notwithstanding the success, is
a certain proof how little advantage could have been derived from
any battle fought farther inland, and of Sir John Moore's prudence
in declining an action the moment he had rallied his army at Lugo and
restored that discipline which the previous movements had shaken.
But, notwithstanding the clamor with which this campaign has
been assailed, as if no army had ever yet suffered such misfortunes, it is certain that the nominal loss was small—the real loss
smaller—and that it sinks into nothing when compared with the
advantages gained. An army which, after marching in advance or
retreat above five hundred miles before an enemy of immensely
superior force, has only lost, including those killed in battle, four
thousand men, or a sixth part of its numbers, cannot be said to
have suffered severely; nor would the loss have been so great but
for the intervention of the accidental occurrences mentioned in the
narrative. Night marches are seldom happy; that from Lugo to
Betanzos cost the army in stragglers more than double the number
of men lost in all the preceding operations; nevertheless, the
reserve in that, as in all the other movements, suffered little, and

it is a fact, that the light brigades detached by the Vigo road, which were not pursued, made no forced marches, slept under cover, and were well supplied, left, in proportion to their strength, as many men behind as any other part of the army; thus proof upon proof accumulates that inexperience was the primary and principal cause of the disorders which attended the retreat. Those disorders were sufficiently great, but many circumstances contributed to produce an appearance of suffering and disorganization which was not real.

Sir John Moore's intention was to have proceeded to Vigo, in order to restore order before he sailed for England, instead of which the fleet steered home directly from Coruña, and a terrible storm scattered it; many ships were wrecked; and the remainder, driving up the channel, were glad to put into any port. The soldiers, thus thrown on shore, were spread from the Land's End to Dover. Their haggard appearance, ragged clothing, and dirty accutrements, things common enough in war, struck a people only used to the daintiness of parade with surprise; the usual exaggerations of men just escaped from perils and distresses were increased by the uncertainty in which all were as to the fate of their comrades; a deadly fever, the result of anxiety, and of the sudden change from fatigue to the confinement of a ship, filled the hospitals at every port with officers and soldiers, and thus the miserable state of Sir John Moore's army became the topic of every letter, and the theme for every country newspaper along the coast. The nation, at that time unused to great operations, forgot that war is not a harmless game, and judging of the loss positively, instead of comparatively, was thus disposed to believe the calumnies of interested men, who were eager to cast a shade over one of the brightest characters that ever adorned the country. Those calumnies triumphed for a moment, but Moore's last appeal to his country for justice will be successful; posterity, revering and cherishing his name, will visit such of his odious calumniators as are not too contemptible to be remembered, with a just and severe retribution; for thus it is that time freshens the beauty of virtue and withers the efforts of baseness. And if authority be sought for in a case where reason speaks so plainly, future historians will not fail to remark, that the man whose talents exacted the praises of Soult, of Wellington, and of Napoleon, could be no ordinary soldier.

"Sir John Moore," says the first, "took every advantage that the country afforded to oppose an active and vigorous resistance, and he finished by dying in a combat that must do credit to his memory."

Napoleon more than once affirmed, that if he committed a few trifling errors, they were to be attributed to his peculiar situation, for that his talents and firmness alone had saved the English army from destruction.*

"In Sir John Moore's campaign," said the Duke of Wellington, "I can see but one error : when he advanced to Sahagun, he should have considered it as a movement of retreat, and sent officers to the rear to mark and prepare the halting places for every brigade. But this opinion I have formed after long experience of war, and especially of the peculiarities of a Spanish war, which must have been seen to be understood : finally, it is an opinion formed after the event."

* Vivian's Conversations at Elba.   Voice from St Helena.

BOOK V.

CHAPTER I.

Slight effect produced in England by the result of the campaign—Debates in Parliament—Treaty with Spain—Napoleon receives addresses at Valladolid—Joseph enters Madrid—Appointed the Emperor's lieutenant—Distribution of the French army—The Duke of Dantzic forces the bridge of Almaraz—Toledo entered by the first corps—Infantado and Palacios ordered to advance upon Madrid—Cuesta appointed to the command of Galluzzo's troops—Florida Blanca dies at Seville—Succeeded in the presidency by the Marquis of Astorga—Money arrives at Cadiz from Mexico—Bad conduct of the Central Junta—State of the Spanish army—Constancy of the soldiers—Infantado moves on Tarancon—His advanced guard defeated there—French retire towards Toledo—Disputes in the Spanish army—Battle of Ucles—Retreat of Infantado—Cartoajal supersedes him, and advances to Ciudad Real—Cuesta takes post on the Tagus, and breaks down the bridge of Almaraz.

THE effect produced in England, by the unfortunate issue of Sir John Moore's campaign, was not in proportion with the importance of the subject. The people, trained to party politics and possessed of no real power to rebuke the folly of the Cabinet, regarded both disasters and triumphs with factious rather than with national feelings, and it was alike easy to draw their attention from affairs of weight or to fix it on matters of little moment. Thus, the Duke of York's conduct being at this time made the object of parliamentary inquiry, to drag his private frailties before the world was thought essential to the welfare of the nation, while the incapacity which had caused England and Spain to mourn in tears of blood, was left unprobed. An insular people, who are by their situation protected from the worst evils of war, may suffer themselves to be thus deluded; but if an unfortunate campaign were to bring a devastating enemy into the heart of the country, the honor of a general and the military policy of the Cabinet would no longer be considered as mere subjects for a vile sophist's talents in misrepresentation.

It is true that the misfortunes of the campaign were by many orators, in both houses of Parliament, treated with great warmth, but the discussions were chiefly remarkable as examples of astute eloquence without any knowledge of facts. The opposition speakers, eager to criminate the government, exaggerated the disasters of the retreat, and comprehending neither the motives nor the movements of Sir John Moore, urged several untenable charges against the ministers, who, disunited by personal feelings, did not all adopt the same grounds of defence. Thus, Lord Castlereagh and Lord Liverpool, passing over those errors of the Cabinet which left the General only a choice of difficulties at his outset, asserted, and truly, that the advantages derived from the advance to Sahagun more than compensated the loss in the subsequent retreat; and both those statesmen paid an honorable tribute to the merits of the commander; but Mr. Canning, unscrupulously resolute to defend Mr. Frere, assented to all the erroneous statements of the opposition, and then with malignant dexterity endeavored to convert them into charges against the fallen general. Sir John Moore was, he said, wholly answerable for the campaign. Whether glorious or distressing, whether to be admired or deplored, it was his own; he had kept the government quite ignorant of his proceedings! Being closely pressed on this point by Mr. C. Hutchinson and Mr. Whitbread, Mr. Canning deliberately repeated the assertion; yet, not long afterwards, Sir John Moore's letters to the ministers, written almost daily, and furnishing exact and copious information of all that was passing in the Peninsula, were laid before the house!

While the dearest interests of the nation were thus treated in Parliament, the ardor of the English people was somewhat abated; yet the Spanish cause, so rightful in itself, was still popular, and a treaty was concluded with the Supreme Junta, by which the contracting powers bound themselves to make common cause against France, and to agree to no peace except by common consent. But the ministers, although professing unbounded confidence in the result of the struggle, already looked upon the Peninsula as a secondary object; for the warlike preparations of Austria, and the reputation of the Archduke Charles, whose talents were foolishly said to exceed Napoleon's, had awakened the dormant spirit of coalitions; and it was more agreeable to the aristocatic feeling of the English Cabinet, that the French should be defeated by a monarch in Germany than by a plebeian insurrection in Spain. The obscure intrigues of the Princess of Tour and Taxis, and the secret societies on the Continent emanating as they did from patrician sources, excited the sympathy of the ministers, engaged their attention, and nourished those distempered feelings which made them see only weakness and disaffection in France, when throughout that mighty empire few desired and none dared to oppose the Emperor's wishes; when even secret discontent was confined to some royalist chiefs and splenetic republicans, whose influence was never felt until after Napoleon had suffered the direst reverses.

Unable to conceive the extent of that monarch's views, or to measure the grandeur of his genius, the ministers attributed the results of his profound calculations to a blind chance, his victories to treason, to corruption, to anything but that admirable skill with which he wielded the most powerful military force that ever obeyed the orders of a single chief. Thus self-deluded, and mis-judging the difficulties to be encountered, they adopted every idle project, and squandered their resources without any great or decided effort. While negotiating with the Spanish Junta for the occupa-tion of Cadiz, they were planning an expedition against Italy, and while loudly asserting their resolution to defend Portugal, reserved their principal force for a secret blow in Holland; their prepara-tions being however marked by a pomp and publicity totally unsuited to war. With what a mortal calamity that pageant closed, shall be noticed hereafter; at present it is fitting to trace the operations in Spain, which were coincident with the retreat of Sir John Moore.

It has already been stated that when Madrid surrendered, Napo-leon refused to permit Joseph to return there unless the public bodies and the heads of families would unite to demand his resto-ration, and swear, without any mental reservation, to be true to him.* Registers had consequently been opened in the different quarters of the city, and twenty-eight thousand six hundred heads of families inscribed their names, and voluntarily swore in presence of the host, that they were sincere in their desire to receive Joseph.† After this, deputations from all the councils, from the junta of com-merce and money, the hall of the Alcaldes, and from the corporation, waited on the Emperor at Valladolid, and being there joined by the municipality of that town, and by deputies from Astorga, Leon, and other places, presented the oath, and prayed that Joseph might be king. Napoleon, thus entreated, consented that his brother should reassume his kingly functions.

It would be idle to argue from this apparently voluntary submis-sion to the French Emperor, that a change favorable to the usur-pation had been produced in the feelings of the Spanish people; but it is evident that Napoleon's victories and policy had been so far effectual, that in the capital, and many other great towns, the multitude as well as the notables were, either from fear or convic-tion, submissive to his will; and it is but reasonable to suppose, that if his conquests had not been interrupted by extraneous cir-cumstances, this example would have been generally followed, in preference to the more glorious, but ineffectual, resistance made by the inhabitants of those cities, whose fortitude and whose calami-

* Nellerto.
† Azanza and O'Farril.

ties have forced from mankind a sorrowful admiration. The cause of Spain at this moment was in truth lost, if any cause, depending upon war, which is but a succession of violent changes, can be called so ; for the armies were dispersed, the government bewildered, the people dismayed, the cry of resistance hushed, and the stern voice of Napoleon, answered by the tread of three hundred thousand French veterans, was heard throughout the land. But the hostility of Austria arrested the conqueror's career, and the Spanish energy revived at the abrupt cessation of his terrific warfare.

Joseph, escorted by his French guards, in number between five and six thousand, entered Madrid the 23d of January. He was, however, a king without revenues, and he would have been without even the semblance of authority, if he had not been likewise nominated the Emperor's lieutenant in Spain, by virtue of which title he was empowered to move the French army at his will. This power was one extremely unacceptable to the marshals, and he would have found it difficult to enforce it, even though he had restrained the exercise to the limits prescribed by his brother ; but disdaining to separate the general from the monarch, he conveyed his orders to the French army through his Spanish ministers, and the army in its turn disdained and resisted the assumed authority of men, who, despised for their want of military knowledge, were also suspected as favoring interests essentially differing from those of the troops.*

The iron grasp that had compressed the pride and the ambitious jealousy of the marshals being thus relaxed, the passions which had ruined the patriots began to work among their enemies, producing indeed less fatal effects, because their scope was more circumscribed, but sufficiently pernicious to stop the course of conquest. The French army, no longer a compact body, terrible alike from its massive strength and its flexible activity, became a collection of independent bands, each formidable in itself, but, from the disunion of the generals, slow to combine for any great object ; and plainly discovering, by irregularities and insubordination, that they knew when a warrior and when a voluptuous monarch was at their head. These evils were however only felt at a later period, and the distribution of the troops, when Napoleon quitted Valladolid, still bore the impress of his genius.

The first corps was quartered in La Mancha.

The second corps was destined to invade Portugal.

The third and fifth corps carried on the siege of Zaragoza.

The fourth corps remained in the valley of the Tagus.

* King's Correspondence captured at Vittoria, MSS.

The sixth corps, wanting its third division, was appointed to hold Gallicia.

The seventh corps continued always in Catalonia.

The imperial guards, directed on Vittoria, contributed to the security of the great communication with France until Zaragoza should fall, and were yet ready to march when wanted for the Austrian war.

General Dessolles, with the third division of the sixth corps, returned to Madrid. General Bonnet, with the fifth division of the second corps, remained in the Montaña Santander.

General Lapisse, with the second division of the first corps, was sent to Salamanca, where he was joined by Maupetit's brigade of cavalry, which had crossed the Sierra de Bejar.

The reserve of heavy cavalry, being broken up, was distributed by divisions, in the following order :—

Latour Maubourg's joined the first corps. Lorge's and La Houssaye's were attached to the second corps. Lassalle's was sent to the fourth corps. The sixth corps was reinforced with two brigades. Milhaud's division remained at Madrid, and Kellermann's guarded the lines of communication between Tudela, Burgos, and Palencia.

Thus, Madrid being still the centre of operations, the French were so distributed, that by a concentric movement on that capital, they could crush every insurrection within the circle of their positions ; and the great masses, being kept upon the principal roads diverging from Madrid to the extremities of the Peninsula, intercepted all communication between the provinces ; while the second corps, thrust out, as it were, beyond the circumference, and destined, as the fourth corps had been, to sweep round from point to point, was sure of finding a supporting army, and a good line of retreat, at every great route leading from Madrid to the yet unsubdued provinces of the Peninsula. The communication with France was, at the same time, secured by the fortresses of Burgos, Pampeluna, and St. Sebastian, and by the divisions posted at Santander, Burgos, Bilbao, and Vittoria ; it was also supported by a reserve at Bayonne.

The northern provinces were parcelled out into military governments, the chiefs of which corresponded with each other, and by the means of movable columns, repressed every petty insurrection. The third and fifth corps, having their base at Pampeluna, and their line of operations directed against Zaragoza, served as an additional covering force to the communication with France, and were themselves exposed to no flank attacks, except from the side of Cuença, where the Duke of Infantado commanded; but that general was himself watched by the first corps.

All the lines of correspondence, not only from France but between the different corps, were maintained by fortified posts, having greater or lesser garrisons, according to their importance. Between Bayonne and Burgos there were eleven military stations. Between Burgos and Madrid, by the road of Aranda and Somosierra, there were eight; and eleven others protected the more circuitous route to the capital, by Valladolid, Segovia, and the Guadarama.* Between Valladolid and Zaragoza, the line was secured by fifteen intermediate points. The communication between Valladolid and Santander contained eight posts; and nine others connected the former town with Villa Franca del Bierzo, by the route of Benevente and Astorga; finally, two were established between Benevente and Leon.

At this period, the force of the army, exclusive of Joseph's French guards, was three hundred and twenty-four thousand four hundred and eleven men, about thirty-nine thousand being cavalry.

Fifty-eight thousand men were in hospital.

The dépôts, governments, garrisons, posts of correspondence, prisoners, and "*battalions of march*," composed of stragglers, absorbed about twenty-five thousand men.

The remainder were under arms, with their regiments, and consequently more than two hundred and forty thousand men were in the field; while the great line of communication with France (the military reader will do well to mark this, the key-stone of Napoleon's system) was protected by above fifty thousand men, whose positions were strengthened by three fortresses and sixty-four posts of correspondence, each more or less fortified.

Having thus shown the military state of the French, I shall now proceed with the narrative of their operations, following, as heretofore, a local rather than a chronological arrangement of events.

OPERATIONS IN ESTREMADURA AND LA MANCHA.

The defeat of Galluzzo has been incidentally touched upon before. The Duke of Dantzic, having observed that the Spanish general pretended with six thousand raw levies to defend a river line of forty miles, made a feint of crossing the Tagus at Arzobispo, and then suddenly descending to Almaraz, forced a passage over that bridge on the 24th of December, killing and wounding many Spaniards and capturing four guns; and so complete was the dispersion, that for a long time after, not a man was to be found in

* Muster-rolls of the French army, MSS.

arms throughout Estremadura. The French cavalry followed the fugitives, but intelligence of Sir John Moore's advance to Sahagun being received, the pursuit ceased at Merida, and the fourth corps, which had left eight hundred men in garrison at Segovia, then occupied Talavera and Placentia; the Duke of Dantzic was recalled to France, and Sebastiani succeeded to his command. At this period also, the first corps (of which Lapisse's division only had followed the Emperor to Astorga) entered Toledo without opposition, and the French outposts were pushed towards Cuença, and towards the Sierra Morena.

Meanwhile, the Central Junta, changing its first design, retired to Seville instead of Badajos, and being continually urged, both by Mr. Stuart and Mr. Frere, to make some effort to lighten the pressure on the English army, ordered Palafox and the Duke of Infantado to advance; the one from Zaragoza towards Tudela, the other from Cuença towards Madrid. The Marquis of Palacios, who had been removed from Catalonia, and was now at the head of five or six thousand levies in the Sierra Morena, was also directed to advance into La Mancha; and Galluzzo, deprived of his command, was constituted a prisoner, along with Cuesta, Castaños, and a number of other culpable or unfortunate officers, who, vainly demanding a judgment on their cases, were dragged from place to place by the government.

Cuesta was, however, so popular in Estremadura, that the Central Junta, although fearing and detesting him, were forced to place him at the head of Galluzzo's fugitives, part of whom had, when the pursuit ceased, rallied behind the Guadiana, and were now, with the aid of fresh levies, again taking the form, rather than the consistence of an army. This appointment was an act of deplorable incapacity; the moral effect was to degrade the government by exposing its fears and weakness, and, in a military view, it was destructive, because Cuesta was physically and mentally incapable of command. Obstinate, jealous, and stricken in years, he was heedless of time, circumstances, dispositions or fitness; to punish with a barbarous severity, and to rush headlong into battle, constituted, in his mind, all the functions of a general.

The President, Florida Blanca, eighty-one years of age, died at Seville, and the Marquis of Astorga succeeded him, but the character of the Junta was in no manner affected by the change. Some fleeting indications of vigor had been produced by the imminence of the danger during the flight from Aranjuez, but a large remittance of silver from South America having arrived at Cadiz, the attention of the members was absorbed by this object, and the public weal was blotted from their remembrance; even Mr. Frere, ashamed of their conduct, appeared to acquiesce in the justness of Sir John Moore's estimate of the value of Spanish co-operation.

The number of men to be enrolled for the defence of the country had been early fixed at five hundred thousand, but scarcely one third had joined their colors; nevertheless, considerable bodies were assembling at different points, because the people, especially those of the southern provinces, although dismayed, were obedient, and the local authorities, at a distance from the actual scene of war, rigorously enforcing the law of enrolment, sent the recruits to the armies; hoping thereby either to stave the war off from their own districts, or to have the excuse of being without fighting men, to plead for quiet submission. The fugitive troops also readily collected again at any given point, partly from patriotism, partly because the French were in possession of their native provinces, partly that they attributed their defeats to the treachery of their generals, and partly that, being deceived by the gross falsehoods and boasting of the government, they, with ready vanity, imagined that the enemy had invariably suffered enormous losses. In fine, for the reasons mentioned in the commencement of this history, men were to be had in abundance, but, beyond assembling them and appointing some incapable person to command, nothing was done for defence. The officers, who were not deceived, had no confidence either in their own troops or in the government, nor were they themselves confided in or respected by their men : the latter, starved, misused, ill-handled, possessed neither the compact strength of discipline nor the daring of enthusiasm. Under such a system, the peasantry could not be rendered energetic soldiers, nor were they active supporters of the cause; but with a wonderful constancy they endured for it fatigue, sickness, nakedness and famine, displaying in all their actions, and in all their sentiments, a distinct and powerful national character. This constancy, although rendered nugatory by the vices and follies of the juntas and leading men, hallowed the people's efforts, and the flagitious violence of the invasion almost justified their ferocity.

Palacios, on the receipt of the orders above mentioned, advanced with five thousand men to Vilharta, in La Mancha; and the Duke of Infantado, anticipating the instructions of the Junta, was already in motion from Cuença, his army, reinforced by the divisions of Cartoajal and Lilli, and by fresh levies, being about twenty thousand men, of which two thousand were cavalry. To check the incursions of the French horsemen, he had, a few days after the departure of Napoleon from Madrid, detached General Senra and General Venegas, with eight thousand infantry and all the horse, to scour the country around Tarancon and Aranjuez; and the former entered Horcajada, while the latter endeavored to cut off a French detachment, but was himself surprised and beaten by a very inferior force. Marshal Victor, nevertheless, withdrew his advanced posts, and, concentrating Ruffin's and Villatte's divisions of infantry and Latour Maubourg's cavalry at Villa de Alorna, in the vicinity of Toledo, left Venegas in possession of Tarancon. But, among the Spanish generals, mutual recriminations succeeded their failure. The Duke of Infantado possessed neither authority nor talents to repress their disputes, and in this untoward state of affairs, receiving the orders of the Junta, he projected a movement on Toledo, intending to seize that place and Aranjuez, break down the bridges, and maintain the line of the Tagus.

The 10th he quitted Cuença with ten thousand men, intending to join Venegas, who, with the rest of the army, was at Tarancon.

The 13th, he met a crowd of fugitives near Carascosa, and heard, with equal surprise and consternation, that the division under Venegas was beaten, and the pursuers close at hand.

ROUT OF UCLES.

It appeared that Victor, ignorant of the exact situation and intention of the Spanish generals, and yet uneasy at their movements, had marched from Toledo to Ocaña the 10th, and that Venegas then abandoned Tarancon and took post at Ucles. The French again advanced on the 12th in two columns, of which one, composed of Ruffin's division and a brigade of cavalry, lost its way, and arrived at Alcazar; the other, led by Victor in person, arrived in front of the Spanish position at Ucles early in the morning of the 13th. This meeting was unexpected by either party, but the French attacked without hesitation, and the Spaniards, making towards Alcazar, were cut off by Ruffin, and totally discomfited. Several thousand were taken, others fled across the fields, and one body, preserving some order, marched towards Ocaña, where, meeting the French parc, it received a heavy discharge of grape, and dispersed. Of the whole force, only one small detachment, under General Giron, forced a passage by the road of Carascosa, and so reached the Duke of Infantado, who immediately retreated safely to Cuença, as the French cavalry was too much fatigued to pursue him briskly.

From Cuença he sent his guns towards Valencia by the road of Tortola, but marched his infantry and cavalry by Chinchilla to Tobarra on the frontiers of Murcia, and then to Santa Cruz de Mudela, a town situated near the entrance to the defiles of the Sierra Morena. This place he reached in the beginning of February, having made a painful and circuitous retreat of more than two hundred miles, in a bad season; his artillery had been captured at Tortola, and his force was reduced by desertion and straggling to a handful of discontented officers and a few thousand men, worn out with fatigue and misery. Meanwhile, Victor, after scouring a part of the province of Cuença and disposing of his prisoners, made a sudden march upon Vilharta, intending to surprise Palacios, but that officer, aware of Infantado's retreat, had already effected a junction with the latter at Santa Cruz de Mudela; wherefore the French Marshal relinquished the atttempt, and re-occupied his former position at Toledo.

The captives taken at Ucles were marched to Madrid; those who were weak and unable to walk, being, says Mr. Rocca, shot by order of Victor, because the Spaniards had hanged some French prisoners.* If so, it was a barbarous and a shameful retaliation, unworthy of a soldier; for what justice or propriety is shown in revenging the death of one innocent person by the murder of another?

After the French had thus withdrawn, Infantado and Palacios proceeded to re-organize their forces, under the name of the Carolina Army, and when the levies in Granada and other parts came up, the Duke of Albuquerque, at the head of the cavalry, endeavored to surprise a French regiment of dragoons at Mora, but the latter rallied quickly, fought stoutly, and effected a retreat with scarcely any loss. Albuquerque then retired to Consuegra, where he was attacked the next day by superior numbers, and got off with difficulty. The Duke of Infantado was now displaced by the Junta, and General Urbina, Conde de Cartoajal, the new commander, having restored some discipline, advanced to Ciudad Real, and took post on the left bank of the upper Guadina. From thence he opened a communication with Cuesta, whose army had been increased to sixteen thousand men, of which three thousand were cavalry; for the Spaniards suffered more in flight than in action, and the horsemen, escaping with little damage, were more easily rallied, and in greater relative numbers than the infantry. With these forces, Cuesta had advanced to the Tagus, when Moore's march upon Sahagun had drawn the fourth corps across that river; the latter, however, by fortifying an old tower, still held the bridge of Arzobisbo. Cuesta extended his line from the mountains in front of that place, to the Puerto de Mirabete, and broke down the bridge of Almaraz, a magnificent structure, the centre arch of which was above one hundred and fifty feet high.

In these positions both sides remained tranquil in La Mancha and in Estremadura, and so ended the Spanish exertions to lighten

* Rocca's Memoirs.

the pressure upon the British army. Two French divisions of infantry, and as many brigades of cavalry, had more than sufficed to baffle them; and thus the imminent danger of the southern provinces, when Sir John Moore's vigorous operations drew the Emperor to the north, may be justly estimated.

CHAPTER II.

Operations in Aragon—Confusion in Zaragoza—The third and fifth corps invest that city—Fortification described—Monte Torrero taken—Attack on the suburb repulsed—Mortier takes post at Calatayud—The convent of San Joseph taken—The bridge-head carried—Huerba passed—Device of the Spanish leaders to encourage the besieged—Marquis of Lazan takes post on the Sierra de Alcubierre—Lasnes arrives in the French camp—Recalls Mortier—Lazan defeated—Gallant exploit of Mariano Galindo—The walls of the town taken by assault—General Lacoste and Colonel San Genis slain.

CONTINUATION OF THE OPERATIONS IN ARAGON.

FROM the field of battle at Tudela, all the fugitives from O'Neil's, and a great part of those from Castaños' army, fled to Zaragoza, and with such speed as to bring the first news of their own disaster. With the troops, also, came an immense number of carriages, and the military chests, for the roads were wide and excellent, and the pursuit was slack. The citizens and the neighboring peasantry were astounded at this quick and unexpected calamity. They had, with a natural credulity, relied on the boasting promises of their chiefs, and being necessarily ignorant of the true state of affairs, never doubted that their vengeance would be sated by a speedy and complete destruction of the French. When their hopes were thus suddenly blasted, when they beheld troops from whom they expected nothing but victory, come pouring into the town with all the tumult of panic; when the peasants of all the villages through which the fugitives passed, came rushing into the city along with the scared multitude of flying soldiers and camp followers, every heart was filled with consternation, and the date of Zaragoza's glory would have ended with the first siege, if the success at Tudela had been followed up by the French with that celerity and vigor which the occasion required.

Napoleon, foreseeing that this moment of confusion and terror would arrive, had, with his usual prudence, provided the means, and given directions for such an instantaneous and powerful attack as would inevitably have overthrown the bulwark of the eastern provinces: but the sickness of Marshal Lasnes, the difficulty of communication, the consequent false movements of Moncey and Ney—in fine, the intervention of fortune, omnipotent as she is in war, baffled the Emperor's long-sighted calculations. The leaders had time to restore order amongst the multitude, to provide stores, to complete the defensive works, and, by a ferocious exercise of power, to insure implicit obedience: the danger of resisting the enemy appeared light, when a suspicious word or gesture was instantly punished by death.

The third corps having missed the favorable moment for a sudden assault, and being reduced by sickness, by losses in battle, and by detachments, to seventeen thousand four hundred men, including the engineers and artillery,* was too weak to invest the city in form, and therefore remained in observation on the Xalon river, while a battering train of sixty guns, with well-furnished parcs, which had been by Napoleon's orders previously collected in Pampeluna, was carried to Tudela and embarked upon the canal leading to Zaragoza. Marshal Mortier, with the fifth corps, was directed to assist in the siege, and he was in march to join Moncey, when his progress also was arrested by Sir John Moore's advance towards Burgos; but the scope of that General's operation being determined by Napoleon's counter movement, Mortier resumed his march to reinforce Moncey, and, on the 20th of December, 1808, their united corps, forming an army of thirty-five thousand men of all arms, advanced against Zaragoza. At this time, however, confidence had been restored in the town, and all the preparations necessary for a vigorous defence were completed.†

The nature of the plain in which Zaragoza is situated, the course of the rivers, the peculiar construction of the houses, and the multitude of convents have been already described, but the difficulties to be encountered by the French troops were no longer the same as in the first siege. At that time little assistance had been derived from science; now, instructed by experience, and inspired as it were by the greatness of their resolution, neither the rules of art nor the resources of genius were neglected by the defenders.

Zaragoza offered four irregular fronts. The first, reckoning from the right of the town, extended from the Ebro to a convent of barefooted Carmelites, and was about three hundred yards wide.

The second, twelve hundred yards in extent, reached from the Carmelites to a bridge over the Huerba.

The third, likewise of twelve hundred yards, stretched from this bridge to an oil manufactory built beyond the walls.

---

* Muster-roll of the French army, MS.
† Cavallero. Doyle's Correspondence, MS.

The fourth, being on an opening of four hundred yards, reached from the oil manufactory to the Ebro.

The first front, fortified by an ancient wall and flanked by the guns on the Carmelite, was strengthened by new batteries and ramparts, and by the Castle of Aljaferia, commonly called the Castle of the Inquisition, which, standing a little in advance, was a square fort, having a bastion and tower at each corner, and a good stone ditch, and it was connected with the body of the place by certain walls loop-holed for musketry.*

The second front was defended by a double wall, the exterior one of recent erection, faced with sun-dried bricks, and covered by a ditch, with perpendicular sides, fifteen feet deep and twenty feet wide. The flanks of this front were formed from the convent of the Carmelites, by a large circular battery standing in the centre of the line, by a fortified convent of the Capuchins, called the Trinity, and by some earthen works protecting the head of the bridge over the Huerba.

The third front was covered by the river Huerba, the deep bed of which was close to the foot of the ramparts. Behind this stream a double intrenchment was carried from the bridge head to a large projecting convent of Santa Engracia, a distance of two hundred yards. Santa Engracia itself was very strongly fortified and armed, and from thence to the oil manufactory the line of defence was prolonged by an ancient Moorish wall, on which several terraced batteries were raised, to sweep all the space between the rampart and the Huerba. These batteries, and the guns in the convent of Santa Engracia, likewise overlooked some works raised to protect a second bridge that crossed the river about cannot-shot below the first.

Upon the right bank of the Huerba, and a little below the second bridge, stood the convent of San Joseph, the walls of which had been strengthened and protected by a deep ditch with a covered way and palisade. It was well placed, as an advanced work, to impede the enemy's approach, and to facilitate sallies on the right bank of the river, and it was open in the rear, to the fire from the works at the second bridge, both being overlooked by the terraced batteries, and by the guns of Santa Engracia.

The fourth front was protected by the Huerba, by the continuation of the old city wall, by new batteries and intrenchments, and by several armed convents and large houses.

Beyond the walls, the Monte Torrero, which commanded all the plain of Zaragoza, was crowned by a large ill-constructed fort, raised at the distance of eighteen hundred yards from the convent of San Joseph. This work was covered by the royal canal, the

* Rogniat's Siege of Zaragoza.   Cavallero's Siege of Zaragoza.

sluices of which were defended by some field-works open to the fire of the fort itself.

On the left bank of the Ebro, the suburb, built in a low marshy plain, was protected by a chain of redoubts and fortified houses, and some gun-boats, manned by seamen from the naval arsenal of Carthagena, completed the circuit of defence. The artillery of the place was, however, of too small a calibre.* There were only sixty guns carrying more than twelve-pound balls, and there were but eight large mortars. There was, however, no want of small arms, and Colonel Doyle had furnished many English muskets.

These were the regular external defences of Zaragoza, most of which were constructed at the time, according to the skill and means of the engineers ; but the experience of the former siege had taught the people not to trust to the ordinary resources of art, and, with equal genius and resolution, they had prepared an internal system of defence infinitely more efficacious.

It has already been observed that the houses of Zaragoza were fire-proof, and generally of only two stories ; that in all the quarters of the city, the massive convents and churches rose like castles above the low buildings, and that the greater streets, running into the broad-way called the Cosso, divided the town into a variety of districts, unequal in size, but each containing one or more large structures. Now, the citizens, sacrificing all personal convenience, and resigning all idea of private property, gave up their goods, their bodies, and their houses to the war, and being promiscuously mingled with the peasantry and the regular soldiers, the whole formed one mighty garrison, well suited to the vast fortress into which Zaragoza was transformed : for the doors and windows of the houses were built up, their fronts loop-holed, internal communications broken through the party walls, the streets trenched and crossed by earthen ramparts mounted with cannon, and every strong building turned into a separate fortification. There was no weak point, because there could be none in a town which was all fortress, and where the space covered by the city was the measurement for the thickness of the ramparts.

Nor in this emergency were the leaders unmindful of moral force. The people were cheered by a constant reference to the former successful resistance ; their confidence was raised by the contemplation of the vast works that had been executed, and it was recalled to their recollection that the wet, usual at that season of the year, would spread disease among the enemy's ranks, impairing, if not entirely frustrating, his efforts. Neither was the aid of superstition neglected ; processions imposed upon the sight, false

* Cavallero.

miracles bewildered the imagination, and terrible denunciations of the divine wrath shook the minds of men whose former habits and present situation rendered them peculiarly susceptible of such impressions. Finally, the leaders were themselves so prompt and terrible in their punishments, that the greatest cowards were likely to show the boldest bearing in their wish to escape suspicion.

To avoid the danger of any great explosion, the powder was made as occasion required, which was the more easily effected, because Zaragoza contained a royal dépôt and refinery for salt-petre, and there were powder-mills in the neighborhood which furnished workmen familiar with the process. The houses and trees beyond the walls were all demolished and cut down, and the materials carried into the town. The public magazines contained six months' provisions, the convents were well stocked, the inhabitants had laid up their own stores for several months, and General Doyle sent a convoy into the town from the side of Catalonia; and there was abundance of money, because, in addition to the resources of the town, the military chest of Castaños' army, which had been filled only the night before the battle of Tudela, was, in the flight, carried to Zaragoza.[*] Some companies of women were enrolled to attend the hospitals and to carry provisions and ammunition to the combatants; they were commanded by the Countess of Burita, a lady of an heroic disposition, who is said to have displayed the greatest intelligence and the noblest character during both sieges.

There were thirteen engineer officers, eight hundred sappers and miners, composed of excavators formerly employed on the canal, and from fifteen hundred to two thousand cannoneers.[†] The regular troops that fled from Tudela, being joined by two small divisions which retreated, at the same time, from Sanguessa and Caparosa, formed a garrison of thirty thousand men, and, with the inhabitants and peasantry, presented a mass of fifty thousand combatants, who, with passions excited almost to phrensy, awaited an assault amidst those mighty intrenchments, where each man's home was a fortress and his family a garrison. To besiege, with only thirty-five thousand men, a city so prepared, was truly a gigantic undertaking!

SECOND SIEGE OF ZARAGOZA.

The 20th of December, the two Marshals, Moncey and Mortier, having established their hospitals and magazines at Alagon on the Xalon, advanced in three columns against Zaragoza.[‡]

[*] Doyle's Correspondence, MS.
[†] Cavallero, Siege of Zaragoza.
[‡] Rogniat.

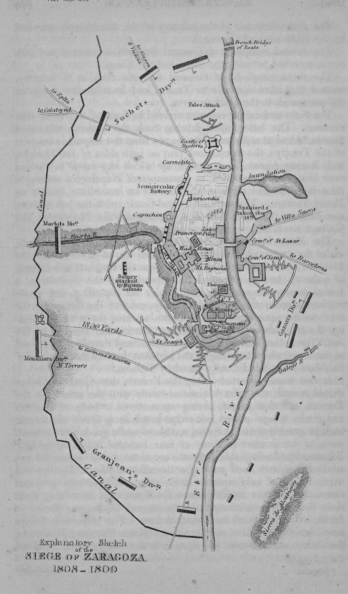

French Bridge of Boats

to Alagon & Tudela

to Epila

to Calatayud

Suchets Div.n

False Attack

Castle of Alaferia

Carmelite

Canal

Semicircular Battery

Misericordia

Capuchin

Cosso

Inundation

Spaniards taken the 18.th

to Villa Nueva

Marlots Div.n

Huerba R.

Francisco Pino

Mad House

Mines

St. Engracia

Conv.t of St Lazar

Conv.t of Jesus

to Barcelona

Battery attacked by Marimon Gallindo

University

St. Monica

St. Augustin

Gazans Div.n

1800 Yards

Meaumiers Div.n

M. Terrero

St. Joseph

to Carinena & Bourtas

Galego R.

Sierra de Alcabicro

Granjean's Div.n

Canal

Ebro River

Explanatory Sketch
of the
SIEGE OF ZARAGOZA
1808 – 1809

The first, composed of the infantry of the third corps, marched by the right bank of the canal.

The second, composed of General Suchet's division of the fifth corps, marched between the canal and the Ebro.

The third, composed of General Gazan's division of infantry, crossed the Ebro opposite to Tauste, and from thence made an oblique march to the Gallego river.

The right and centre columns arrived in front of the town that evening. The latter, after driving back the Spanish advanced guards, halted at a distance of a league from the Capuchin convent of the Trinity; the former took post on both sides of the Huerba, and, having seized the aqueduct by which the canal is carried over that river, proceeded, in pursuance of Napoleon's orders, to raise batteries and make dispositions for an immediate assault on Monte Torrero. Meanwhile General Gazan, with the left column, marching by Cartejon and Zuera, reached Villa Nueva, on the Gallego river, without encountering an enemy.

The Monte Torrero was defended by five thousand Spaniards, under the command of General St. Marc; but at daybreak on the 21st, the French opened their fire against the fort, and one column of infantry having attracted the attention of the Spaniards, a second, unseen, crossed the canal under the aqueduct, and penetrating between the fort and the city, entered the former by the rear; at the same time a third column stormed the works protecting the great sluices. These sudden attacks, and the loss of the fort,* threw the Spaniards into confusion, and they hastily retired to the town, which so enraged the blebeian leaders that the life of St. Marc was with difficulty saved by Palafox.

It had been concerted among the French that General Gazan should assault the suburb, simultaneously with the attack on the Torrero, and that officer, having encountered a body of Spanish and Swiss troops placed somewhat in advance, drove the former back so quickly that the Swiss, unable to make good their retreat, were, to the number of three or four hundred, killed or taken.† But notwithstanding this fortunate commencement, Gazan did not attack the suburb itself until after the affair at Monte Torrero was over, and then only upon a single point, without any previous examination of the works; hence the Spaniards, recovering from their first alarm, reinforced this point, and Gazan was forced to desist, with the loss of four hundred men. This important failure more than balanced the success against Monte Torrero; it restored the shaken confidence of the Spaniards at a most critical moment,

* Cavallero.
† Rogniat.

and checking in the French, at the outset, that impetuous spirit, that impulse of victory which great generals so carefully watch and improve, threw them back upon the tedious and chilling process of the engineer.

The 24th of December the investment of Zaragoza was completed on both sides of the Ebro. Gazan occupied the bridge over the Gallego with his left, and covered his front from sorties by inundations and cuts, that the low marshy plain where he was posted enabled him to make without difficulty.

General Suchet occupied the space between the upper Ebro and the Huerba.

Morlot's division of the 3d corps encamped in the broken hollow that formed the bed of that stream.

Meunier's division crowned the Monte Torrero, and General Grandjean, continuing the circuit to the lower Ebro, communicated with Gazan's post on the other side. Several Spanish detachments that had been sent out to forage were thus cut off, and could never re-enter the town, and a bridge of boats constructed on the upper Ebro completed the circle of investments, insuring a free intercourse between the different quarters of the army.

General Lacoste, an engineer of reputation and aid-de-camp to the Emperor, directed the siege. His plan was, that one false and two real attacks should be conducted by regular approaches on the right bank of the Ebro; and he still hoped to take the suburb by a sudden assault. The trenches were opened the night of the 29th; the 30th the place was summoned, and the terms dictated by Napoleon when he was at Aranda de Duero being offered, the example of Madrid was cited to induce a surrender. Palafox replied, that if Madrid had surrendered, Madrid had been sold: Zaragoza would neither be sold nor surrender! On the receipt of this haughty answer the attacks were commenced, the right being directed against the convent of San Joseph, the centre against the upper bridge over the Huerba, the left, which was the false one, against the castle of Aljaferia.

The 31st Palafox made sorties against all the three attacks. From the right and centre he was beaten back with loss, and he was likewise repulsed on the left at the trenches; but some of his cavalry, gliding between the French parallel and the Ebro, surprised and cut down a post of infantry, stationed behind some ditches that intersected the low ground on the bank of that river. This trifling success exalted the enthusiasm of the besieged, and Palafox gratified his personal vanity by boasting proclamations, some of which bore the marks of genius, but the greater part were ridiculous.

The 1st of January the second parallels of the true attacks were commenced, and the next day Palafox caused the attention of the besiegers to be occupied on the right bank of the Ebro by slight skirmishes, while he made a serious attack from the side of the suburb on Gazan's lines of contravallation. This sally was repulsed with loss, but, on the right bank, the Spaniards obtained some success.

Marshal Moncey being called to Madrid, Junot now assumed the command of the third corps, and, about the same time, Marshal Mortier was directed to take post at Calatayud, with Suchet's division, for the purpose of securing the communication with Madrid. The gap in the circle of investment left by this draft of eight thousand men, being but scantily stopped by extending Morlot's division, a line of contravallation was constructed at that part to supply the place of numbers. Meanwhile the besieged, hoping and expecting each day that the usual falls of rain would render the besiegers' situation intolerable, continued their fire briskly, and worked counter approaches to the right of the French attacks; but the season was unusually dry, and a thick fog rising each morning covered the besiegers' advances and protected their workmen, both from the fire and from the sorties of the Spaniards.

The 10th of January, thirty-two pieces of French artillery battered in breach both the convent of San Joseph and the head of the second bridge on the Huerba, and the town also was bombarded. San Joseph was so much injured by this fire that the Spaniards, resolving to evacuate it, withdrew their guns; nevertheless, two hundred of their men, making a vigorous sally at midnight, pushed close up to the French batteries, but being taken in flank with a discharge of grape, retired, with loss of half their number.

The 11th, the besiegers' batteries having continued to play on San Joseph, the breach became practicable, and, at four o'clock in the evening, some companies of infantry with two field-pieces attacked by the right, while a column was kept in readiness to assail the front, when this attack should have shaken the defence, and two other companies of chosen men were directed to search for an entrance by the rear, between the fort and the river.

The defences of the convent were now reduced to a ditch eighteen feet deep, and a covered way, which, falling back on both flanks to the Huerba, extended along the bank for some distance, and was occupied by a considerable number of men; but when some French guns raked it from the right, the Spaniards, crossing the bed of the river in confusion, took refuge in the town, and at that moment the front of the convent was assaulted. The depth of the ditch and the Spanish fire checked the assailants a moment, yet the chosen companies, passing round the works, found a small bridge, crossed it, and entered by the rear, and the next instant the front was stormed, and the defenders were all killed or taken.

The French, who had suffered but little in this assault, immediately lodged themselves in the convent, raised a rampart along the edge of the Huerba, and commenced batteries against the body of the place and against the works at the head of the upper bridge, from whence, as well as from the town, they were incommoded by the fire that played into the convent.

The 15th, the bridge-head in front of Santa Engracia was carried with the loss of only three men; the Spaniards cut the bridge itself, and sprung a mine under the works, but the explosion occasioned no mischief, and the third parallels being soon completed, the trenches of the two attacks were united, and the defences of the besieged were confined to the town itself; they could no longer make sallies on the right bank of the Huerba, without overcoming the greatest difficulties. The passage of the Huerba was then effected by the French, and breaching and counter-batteries, mounting fifty pieces of artillery, were constructed against the body of the place, and as the fire also reached the bridge over the Ebro, the communication between the suburb and the town was interrupted.

Unshaken by this aspect of affairs, the Spanish leaders, with great readiness of mind, immediately forged intelligence of the defeat of the Emperor, and, with the sound of music, and amidst the shouts of the populace, proclaimed the names of the marshals who had been killed; asserting, also, that Palafox's brother, the Marquis of Lazan, was already wasting France. This intelligence, extravagant as it was, met with implicit credence; for such was the disposition of the Spaniards throughout this war, that the imaginations of the chiefs were taxed to produce absurdities proportionable to the credulity of their followers; hence the boasting of the leaders and the confidence of the besieged augmented as the danger increased, and their anticipations of victory seemed realized when the night-fires of a succoring force were discerned, blazing on the hills behind Gazan's troops.

The difficulties of the French were indeed fast increasing; for while inclosing Zaragoza, they were themselves encircled by insurrections, and their supplies so straitened that famine was felt in their camp. Disputes among the generals also diminished the vigor of the operations, and the bonds of discipline being relaxed, the military ardor of the troops naturally became depressed. The soldiers reasoned openly upon the chances of success, which in times of danger is only one degree removed from mutiny.

The nature of the country about Zaragoza was exceedingly favorable to the Spaniards. The town, although situated in a plain, is surrounded at some miles' distance by high mountains, and to the south, the fortresses of Mequinenza and Lerida afforded a double base of operations for any forces that might come from Catalonia and Valencia. The besiegers drew their supplies from Pampeluna, and their line of operation, running through Alagon, Tudela, and Caparosa, was harassed by the insurgents, who were in considerable numbers, on the side of Epila and in the Sierra de Muela, threatening Alagon; while others, descending from the mountains of Soria, menaced the important point of Tudela. The Marquis of Lazan also, anxious to assist his brother, had drafted five thousand men from the Catalonian army, and taking post in the Sierra de Liciñena, or Alcubierre, on the left of the Ebro, drew together all the armed peasantry of the valleys as high as Sanguessa. Extending his line from Villa Franca on the Ebro to Zuera on the Gallego, he hemmed in the division of Gazan, and sent detachments as far as Caparosa, to harass the French convoys coming from Pampeluna.

To maintain their communications and to procure provisions, the besiegers had placed between two and three thousand men in Tudela, Caparosa, and Tafalla, and some hundreds in Alagon and at Montalbarra. Between the latter town and the investing army, six hundred and fifty cavalry were stationed; a like number were posted at Santa Fé to watch the openings of the Sierra de Muela; finally, sixteen hundred cavalry and twelve hundred infantry, under the command of General Wathier, were pushed towards the south as far as Fuentes. Wathier, falling suddenly upon an assemblage of four or five thousand insurgents at Belchite, dispersed them, and then taking the town of Alcanitz, established himself there, in observation, for the rest of the siege. Lazan, however, still maintained himself in the Alcubierre.

In this state of affairs Marshal Lannes, having recovered from his long sickness, arrived before Zaragoza, and took the supreme command of both corps on the 22d of January. The influence of his firm and vigorous character was immediately perceptible. Recalling Suchet's division from Calatayud, where it had been lingering without necessity, he sent it across the Ebro, ordered Mortier to attack Lazan, and at the same time directed a smaller detachment against the insurgents in Zuera;* meanwhile, repressing all disputes, he restored discipline in the army, and pressed the siege with infinite resolution.

The detachment sent to Zuera defeated the insurgents, and took

* Rogniat.

possession of that place and of the bridge over the Gallego. Mortier encountered the Spanish advanced guard at Perdeguera, and pushed it back to Nuestra Señora de Vagallar, where the main body, several thousand strong, was posted, and where, after a short fight, he defeated it, took four guns, and then spreading his troops in a half circle, extending from Huesca to Pina on the Ebro, awed the country between those places and Zaragoza, and checked further insurrection.

Before Lannes arrived, the besieged had been much galled by a mortar battery, situated behind the second parallel of the centre attack, and one Mariano Galindo undertook, with eighty volunteers, to silence it. He surprised the guard of the trenches, and entered the battery, but the French reserve arrived in his front, the guard of the trenches rallied, and, thus surrounded, Galindo, fighting bravely, was wounded and taken, and his comrades perished, with as much glory as simple soldiers can attain to. After this, the armed vessels in the river attempted to flank the batteries raised against the Aljaferia, but the French guns obliged them to retire, and the besiegers' works being carried over the Huerba, in the nights between the 21st and 26th of January, the third parallels of the true attack were completed. The oil manufactory, and other advantageous posts on the left bank of that river, were then incorporated with the lines of approach, and the second parallel of the false attack was commenced at one hundred and fifty yards from the Aljaferia. These advantages were, however, not obtained without pain; for the Spaniards frequently sallied, spiked two guns, and burnt a post on the right of the besiegers' line.

The French fire now broke the walls rapidly; two practicable breaches were opened in front of the San Joseph, a third was commenced in the San Augustin, facing the oil manufactory, a broad way was made into the Santa Engracia, and at twelve o'clock on the 29th of January, four chosen columns, rushing forth from the trenches, burst upon the ruined walls of Zaragoza.

On the right, the assailants twice stormed an isolated stone house that defended the breach of San Augustin, and twice they were driven back with loss.

In the centre, regardless of two small mines that exploded at the foot of the walls, they carried the breach fronting the oil manufactory, and then endeavored to break into the town; but the Spaniards retrenched within the place opened such a fire of grape and musketry, that the French were finally content to establish themselves on the summit of the breach, and to connect their lodgment with the trenches by new works.

The third column was more successful; the breach was carried, and the neighboring houses also, as far as the first large cross street; beyond that the French could not penetrate, but they were enabled to establish themselves within the walls of the town, and immediately brought forward their trenches, so as to comprehend the lodgment within their works.

The fourth column, composed of the Polish soldiers of the Vistula, vigorously stormed the Santa Engracia and the convent adjoining it; and then, unchecked by the fire from the houses, and undaunted by the explosion of six small mines planted on their path, swept the ramparts to the left, as far as the first bridge on the Huerba. The guards of the trenches, excited by this success, now rushed forward tumultuously, mounted the walls, bayoneted the artillery men at the guns in the Capuchin, and then continuing their career, endeavored, some to reach the semicircular battery and the Misericordia, others to break into the city.

This wild assault was soon checked, by grape from two guns planted behind a traverse on the ramparts, and by a murderous fire from the houses, and as the ranks of the assailants were thinned, their ardor sunk, while the courage of their adversaries increased. The French were driven back upon the Capuchins, and the Spaniards were already breaking into that convent in pursuit, when two battalions, detached by General Morlot from the trenches of the false attack, arrived, and secured possession of that point, which was moreover untenable by the Spaniards, inasmuch as the guns of the convent of Santa Engracia saw it in reverse. The French lost, on this day, more than six hundred men, but Lacoste immediately abandoned the false attack against the castle, fortified the Capuchin convent and a house situated at an angle of the wall abutting upon the bridge over the Huerba, and then joining them by works to his trenches, the ramparts of the town became the front line of the besiegers.

The walls of Zaragoza thus went to the ground, but Zaragoza herself remained erect, and as the broken girdle fell from the heroic city, the besiegers started at the view of her naked strength. The regular defences had, indeed, crumbled before the skill of the assailants, but the popular resistance was immediately called, with all its terrors, into action! and, as if Fortune had resolved to mark the exact moment when the ordinary calculations of science should cease, the chief engineers on both sides were simultaneously slain. The French General, Lacoste, a young man, intrepid, skilful, and endowed with genius, perished like a brave soldier. The Spanish Colonel, San Genis, died, not only with the honor of a soldier, but the glory of a patriot. Falling in the noblest cause, his blood stained the ramparts which he had himself raised for the protection of his native place.

CHAPTER III.

System of terror—The convent of St. Monica taken—Spaniards attempt to retake it, but fail—St. Augustin taken—French change their mode of attack—Spaniards change their mode of defence—Terrible nature of the contest—Convent of Jesus taken on the side of the suburb—Attack of the suburb repulsed—Convent of Francisco taken—Mine exploded under the university fails, and the besieged are repulsed—The Cosso passed—Fresh mines worked under the university, and in six other places—French soldiers dispirited—Lannes encourages them—The houses leading down to the quay carried by storm—An enormous mine under the university being sprung, that building is carried by assault—The suburb is taken—Baron Versage killed, and two thousand Spaniards surrender—Successful attack on the right bank of the Ebro—Palafox demands terms, which are refused—Fire resumed—Miserable condition of the city—Terrible pestilence, and horrible sufferings of the besieged—Zaragoza surrenders—Observations.

THE war being now in the streets of Zaragoza, the sound of the alarm-bell was heard in every quarter; the people crowded into the houses nearest to the lodgments of the enemy, additional barricades were constructed across the principal thoroughfares, mines were prepared in the more open spaces, and the internal communications from house to house were multiplied, until they formed a vast labyrinth, the intricate windings of which were only to be traced by the weapons and the dead bodies of the defenders. The Junta, become more powerful from the cessation of regular warfare, urged the defence with redoubled energy, yet increased the horrors of the siege by a ferocity pushed to the verge of phrensy; every person who excited the suspicions of these furious men, or of those immediately about them, was instantly put to death. Amidst the noble bulwarks of war, a horrid array of gibbets was seen, on which crowds of wretches were each night suspended, because their courage sunk under accumulating dangers, or that some doubtful expression, some gesture of distress, had been misconstrued by their barbarous chiefs.*

From the height of the walls which he had conquered, Lannes contemplated this terrific scene, and judging that men so passionate and so prepared could not be prudently encountered in open battle, he resolved to proceed by the slow, certain process of the mattock

* Cavallero.

and the mine;* this also was in unison with the Emperor's instructions, and hence until the 2d of February, the efforts of the French were only directed to the enlargement of their lodgments on the ramparts. This they effected with severe fighting and by means of explosions, working through the nearest houses, and sustaining many counter-assaults, of which the most noted and furious was made by a friar on the Capuchins' convent.

It has been already observed, that the large streets divided the town into certain small districts, or islands of houses. To gain possession of these, it was necessary not only to mine but to fight for each house; and to cross the great intersecting streets it was indispensable to construct traverses above, or to work by underground galleries; a battery raked each street, and each house was defended by a garrison that, generally speaking, had only the option of repelling the enemy in front or dying on the gibbet erected behind. As long as the convents and churches remained in possession of the Spaniards, the progress of the French among the islands of small houses was of little advantage to them; the strong garrisons in the greater buildings enabled the defenders, not only to make continual and successful sallies, but to countermine their enemies, whose superior skill in that kind of warfare was often frustrated by the numbers and persevering energy of the besieged.

To overcome these obstacles, the batteries opposite the fourth front had breached the convents of Augustin and Santa Monica, and the latter had been taken the 31st of January; for while the attack was hot, a part of the wall in another direction was blown in by a petard, and the besiegers pouring through took the main breach in rear, cleared the convent and several houses behind it. Nevertheless the Spaniards opened a gallery from the Augustins and worked a mine that night under Santa Monica, but the French discovered it and stifled the miners. The next day, the breach in the Augustin becoming practicable, the attention of the defenders was drawn to it, while the French springing a mine, which they had carried under the wall, from the side of Santa Monica, entered by the opening, and the Spaniards, thus again unexpectedly taken in the rear, were easily driven out. Rallying a few hours after, they vainly attempted to retake the structure, and the besiegers then broke into the neighboring houses, and at one push reached the point where the Quemada-street joined the Cosso; but the Spaniards renewed the combat with such a fury, that the French were beaten out of the houses again, and lost more than two hundred men.

On the side of Santa Engracia a contest still more severe took

* Rogniat.

place; the houses in the vicinity were blown up, yet the Spaniards fought so obstinately for the ruins, that the Polish troops were scarcely able to make good their lodgment—although two successive and powerful explosions had, with the buildings, destroyed a number of the defenders.

The experience of these attacks induced a change in the mode of fighting on both sides. Hitherto the play of the French mines had reduced the houses to ruins, leaving the soldiers exposed to the fire from the next Spanish posts; the engineers, therefore, diminished the quantity of powder, that the interior only might fall and the outward walls stand, and this method was found successful. Whereupon the Spaniards, with ready ingenuity, saturated the timbers of the houses with rosin and pitch, and setting fire to those which could no longer be maintained, interposed a burning barrier, which often delayed the assailants for two days, and always prevented them from pushing their successes during the confusion that necessarily followed the bursting of the mines. The fighting was, however, incessant; a constant bombardment, the explosion of mines, the crash of falling buildings, clamorous shouts, and the continued echo of musketry deafened the ear, while volumes of smoke and dust clouding the atmosphere, lowered continually over the heads of the combatants, as hour by hour the French, with a terrible perseverance, pushed forward their approaches to the heart of the miserable but glorious city.

Their efforts were chiefly directed from two points, namely, Santa Engracia, which may be denominated the left attack, and Saint Augustin, which constituted the right attack. At Santa Engracia they labored on a line perpendicular to the Cosso, from which they were only separated by the large convent of the Daughters of Jerusalem, and by the hospital for madmen, which was intrenched, although in ruins since the first siege; the line of this attack was protected on the left by the convent of the Capuchins, which Lacoste had fortified to repel the counter-assaults of the Spaniards. The attack from the Augustin was more diffused, because the localities presented less prominent features to determine the direction of the approaches. But the French, having mounted a number of light six-inch mortars, on peculiar carriages, drew them from street to street, and house to house, as occasion offered; on the other hand the Spaniards continually plied their enemies with hand grenades, which seem to have produced a surprising effect. In this manner the never-ceasing combat was prolonged until the 7th of February, when the besiegers, by dint of alternate mines and assaults, had worked their perilous way at either attack to the

Cosso, yet not without several changes of fortune and considerable loss; and they were not able to obtain a footing on that public walk, for the Spaniards still disputed every house with undiminished resolution. Meanwhile, Lannes, having caused trenches to be opened on the left bank of the Ebro, played twenty guns against an isolated structure called the Convent of Jesus, which covered the right of the suburb line; on the 7th of February this convent was carried by storm, with so little difficulty that the French, supposing the Spaniards to be panic-stricken, entered the suburb itself, but were quickly driven back; they, however, made good their lodgment in the convent.

On the town side the 8th, 9th, and 10th were wasted by the besiegers in vain attempts to pass the Cosso. They then extended their flanks; to the right with a view to reach the quay, and so connect this attack with that against the suburb; to the left to obtain possession of the large and strongly built convent of St. Francisco, in which, after exploding an immense mine and making two assaults, they finally established themselves.

The 11th and 12th, mines, in the line of the right attack, were exploded under the university, a large building on the Spanish side of the Cosso, yet their play was insufficient to open the walls, and the storming party was beaten, with the loss of fifty men. Nevertheless, the besiegers continuing their labors during the 13th, 14th, 15th, 16th, and 17th, passed the Cosso by means of traverses, and prepared fresh mines under the university, yet deferred their explosion until a simultaneous effort could be combined on the side of the suburb. At the left attack also, a number of houses, bordering on the Cosso, being gained, a battery was established that raked that great thoroughfare above ground, while under it six galleries were carried, and six mines loaded to explode at the same moment.

But the spirit of the French army was now exhausted. They had labored and fought without intermission for fifty days; they had crumbled the walls with their bullets, burst the convents with their mines, and carried the breaches with their bayonets; fighting above and beneath the surface of the earth, they had spared neither fire nor sword; their bravest men were falling in the obscurity of a subterranean warfare, famine pinched them, and Zaragoza was still unconquered!

"Before this siege," they exclaimed, "was it ever known that twenty thousand men should besiege fifty thousand? Scarcely a fourth of the town is won, and we are already exhausted. We must wait for reinforcements, or we shall all perish among these cursed

ruins, which will become our own tombs, before we can force the
last of these fanatics from the last of their dens."*

Marshal Lannes, unshaken by these murmurs, and obstinate to
conquer, endeavored to raise the soldiers' hopes. He told them
that the losses of the besieged so far exceeded their own, that the
Spaniards' strength would soon be exhausted and their courage
sink, that the fierceness of their defence was already abating; and
that if, contrary to expectation, they should renew the example of
Numantia, their utter destruction must quickly be effected, by the
united evils of battle, pestilence, and misery. His exhortations
were successful, and on the 18th of February, all combinations
being completed, a general assault took place.

The French at the right attack opened a party-wall by the explosion of a petard, made a sudden rush through some burning
ruins, and then carried, without a check, the whole island of houses
leading down to the quay, with the exception of two buildings;
the Spaniards were thus forced to abandon all the external fortifications between St. Augustin and the Ebro, which they had preserved until that day. During this assault the mines under the
university containing three thousand pounds of powder were
sprung, and the walls tumbling with a terrific crash, a column
of the besiegers entered the place, and after one repulse secured a
lodgment. Meanwhile fifty pieces of artillery thundered upon the
suburb, ploughed up the bridge over the Ebro, and by midday
opened a practicable breach in the great convent of Saint Lazar,
which was the principal defence on that side. Lannes, observing
that the Spaniards seemed to be shaken by this overwhelming fire,
ordered an assault there also, and Saint Lazar being carried forthwith, the retreat to the bridge was thus intercepted, and the besieged falling into confusion, and their commander, Baron Versage,
being killed, were all destroyed or taken, with the exception of
three hundred men, who, braving the terrible fire to which they
were exposed, got back into the town. General Gazan immediately occupied the abandoned works, and having thus cut off
more than two thousand men that were stationed on the Ebro,
above the suburb, forced them also to surrender.

This important success being followed, on the 19th, by another
fortunate attack on the right bank of the Ebro, and by the devastating explosion of sixteen hundred pounds of powder, the constancy of the besieged was at last shaken. An aide-de-camp of
Palafox came forth to demand certain terms, before offered by the
Marshal, adding thereto, that the garrison should be allowed to
join the Spanish armies, and that a certain number of covered

* Rogniat.

carriages should follow them. Lannes rejected these proposals, and the fire continued, but the hour of surrender was come! Fifty pieces of artillery on the left bank of the Ebro laid the houses on the quay in ruins. The church of Our Lady of the Pillar, under whose especial protection the city was supposed to exist, was nearly effaced by the bombardment, and six mines under the Cosso, loaded with many thousand pounds of powder, were ready for a simultaneous explosion, which would have laid a quarter of the remaining houses in dust. In fine, war had done its work, and the misery of Zaragoza could no longer be endured.

The bombardment, which had never ceased since the 10th of January, had forced the women and children to take refuge in the vaults, with which the city abounded; there the constant combustion of oil, the closeness of the atmosphere, unusual diet, and fear and restlessness of mind, had combined to produce a pestilence which soon spread to the garrison. The strong and the weak, the daring soldier and the shrinking child, fell before it alike; and such was the state of the atmosphere and the predisposition to disease, that the slightest wound gangrened and became incurable. In the beginning of February the daily deaths were from four to five hundred; the living were unable to bury the dead; and thousands of carcasses, scattered about the streets and court-yards, or piled in heaps at the doors of the churches, were left to dissolve in their own corruption, or to be licked up by the flames of the burning houses as the defence became contracted. The suburb, the greatest part of the walls, and one fourth of the houses were in the hands of the French; sixteen thousand shells, thrown during the bombardment, and the explosion of forty-five thousand pounds of powder in the mines, had shaken the city to its foundations, and the bones of more than forty thousand persons of every age and sex, bore dreadful testimony to the constancy of the besieged.*

Palafox was sick, and of the plebeian chiefs, the curate of St. Gil, the lemonade seller of the Cosso, and the Tios, Jorge and Marin, having been slain in battle, or swept away by the pestilence, the obdurate violence of the remaining leaders was so abated, that a fresh junta was formed, and after a stormy consultation, the majority being for a surrender, a deputation waited upon Marshal Lannes on the 20th of February, to negotiate a capitulation. They proposed that the garrison should march out with the honors of war; that the peasantry should not be considered as prisoners; and at the particular request of the clergy, they also demanded that the latter should have their full revenues guaranteed to them, and punctually paid. This article was rejected with indignation, and,

* Cavallero. Rogniat. Suchet.

according to the French writers, the place surrendered at discretion; but the Spanish writers assert, that Lannes granted certain terms, drawn up by the deputation at the moment, the name of Ferdinand the 7th being purposely omitted in the instrument, which in substance ran thus:—

The garrison to march out with the honors of war; to be constituted prisoners, and marched to France; the officers to retain their swords, baggage, and horses; the men their knapsacks; persons of either class, wishing to serve Joseph, to be immediately enrolled in his ranks; the peasants to be sent to their homes; property and religion to be guaranteed.

With this understanding the deputies returned to the city, where fresh commotions had arisen during their absence. The party for protracting the defence, although the least numerous, were the most energetic; they had before seized all the boats on the Ebro, fearing that Palafox and others, of whom they entertained suspicions, would endeavor to quit the town; and they were still so menacing and so powerful, that the deputies, not daring to pass through the streets, retired outside the walls to the castle of Aljaferia, and from thence sent notice to the junta of their proceedings. The dissentient party would, however, have fallen upon the others the next day, if the junta had not taken prompt measures to enforce the surrender; the officer in command of the walls near the castle, by their orders, gave up his post to the French during the night, and on the 21st of February, from twelve to fifteen thousand sickly beings laid down those arms which they were scarcely able to handle, and this cruel and memorable siege was finished.

OBSERVATIONS.—1. When the other events of the Spanish war shall be lost in the obscurity of time, or only traced by disconnected fragments, the story of Zaragoza, like some ancient triumphal pillar standing amidst ruins, will tell a tale of past glory, and already men point to the heroic city, and call her Spain, as if her spirit were common to the whole nation; yet it was not so, nor was the defence of Zaragoza itself the effect of unalloyed virtue. It was not patriotism, nor was it courage, nor skill, nor fortitude, nor a system of terror, but all these combined under peculiar circumstances, that upheld the defence; and this combination, and how it was brought about, should be well considered; for it is not so much by catching at the leading resemblances, as by studying the differences of great affairs, that the exploits of one age can be made to serve as models for another.

2. The defence of Zaragoza may be examined under two points of view—as an isolated event, and as a transaction bearing on the general struggle in the Peninsula. With respect to the

latter, it was a manifest proof, that neither the Spanish people nor the government partook of the Zaragozan energy. It would be absurd to suppose that, in the midst of eleven millions of people animated by an ardent enthusiasm, fifty thousand armed men could for two months be besieged, shut in, destroyed, they and their works, houses and bodies mingled in one terrible ruin, by less than thirty-five thousand adversaries, without one effort being made to save them! Deprive the transaction of its dazzling colors, and the outline comes to this: Thirty-five thousand French, in the midst of insurrections, did, in despite of a combination of circumstances peculiarly favorable to the defence, reduce fifty thousand of the bravest and most energetic men in Spain. It is true, the latter suffered nobly; but was their example imitated? Gerona, indeed, although less celebrated, rivalled, and perhaps more than rivalled, the glory of Zaragoza; elsewhere her fate spoke, not trumpet-tongued to arouse, but with a wailing voice, that carried dismay to the heart of the nation.

3. As an isolated transaction, the siege of Zaragoza is very remarkable, yet it would be a great error to suppose that any town, the inhabitants of which were equally resolute, might be as well defended. Fortune and bravery will do much, but the combinations of science are not to be defied with impunity. There are no miracles in war! If the houses of Zaragoza had not been nearly incombustible, the bombardment alone would have caused the besieged to surrender, or to perish with their flaming city.

4. That the advantages offered by the peculiar structure of the houses, and the number of convents and churches, were ably seized by the Spaniards, is beyond doubt. General Rogniat, Lacoste's successor, treats his opponents' skill in fortification with contempt; but Colonel San Genis' talents are not to be judged of by the faulty construction of a few out-works, at a time when he was under the control of a disorderly and ferocious mob; he knew how to adapt his system of defence to the circumstances of the moment, and no stronger proof of real genius can be given. "Do not consult me about a capitulation," was his common expression. "*I shall never be of opinion that Zaragaza can make no further defence.*" Yet neither the talents of San Genis nor the construction of the houses would have availed, if the people within had not been of a temper adequate to the occasion; and to trace the passions by which they were animated to their true causes is a proper subject for historical and military research. That they did not possess any superior courage is evident from the facts: the besieged, although twice the number of the besiegers, never made any serious impression by their sallies, and they were unable to

defend the breaches. In large masses, the standard of courage which is established by discipline, may be often inferior to that produced by fanaticism or any other peculiar excitement; but the latter never lasts long, neither is it equitable, because men are of different susceptibility, following their physical and mental conformation; hence a system of terror has always been the resource of those leaders who, being engaged in great undertakings, were unable to recur to discipline. Enthusiasm stalked in front of their bands, but punishment brought up the rear, and Zaragoza was no exception to this practice.

5. It may be said that, the majority of the besieged not being animated by any peculiar fury, a system of terror could not be carried to any great length; a close examination explains this seeming mystery. The defenders were composed of three distinct parties,—the regular troops, the peasantry from the country, and the citizens; the citizens, who had most to lose, were naturally the fiercest, and, accordingly, amongst them the system of terror was generated. The peasantry followed the example, as all ignorant men, under no regular control, will do. The soldiers meddled but little in the interior arrangements, and the division of the town into islands of posts rendered it perfectly feasible for violent persons, already possessed of authority, to follow the bent of their inclinations: there was no want of men, and the garrisons of each island found it their own interest to keep those in front of them to their posts, that the danger might be the longer staved off from themselves.

6. Palafox was only the nominal chief of Zaragoza; the laurels gathered in both sieges should adorn plebeian brows, but those laurels dripped with kindred as well as foreign blood. The energy of the real chiefs, and the cause in which that energy was exerted, may be admired; the acts perpetrated were, in themselves, atrocious, and Palafox, although unable to arrest their savage proceedings, can claim but little credit for his own conduct. For more than a month preceding the surrender, he never came forth of a vaulted building, which was impervious to shells, and in which there is too much reason to believe that he and others, of both sexes, lived in a state of sensuality, forming a disgusting contrast to the wretchedness that surrounded them.

OBSERVATIONS ON THE FRENCH OPERATIONS.

1. Before the arrival of Marshal Lannes, these operations were conducted with little vigor. The want of unity, as to time, in the double attack of the Monte Torrero and the suburb, was a flagrant

error, which was not redeemed by any subsequent activity.   After the arrival of that Marshal, the siege was pursued with singular intrepidity and firmness; and although General Rogniat appears to disapprove of Suchet's division having been sent to Calatayud, it seems to have been a judicious measure, inasmuch as it was necessary,—1. To protect the line of correspondence with Madrid. 2. To have a corps at hand, lest the Duke of Infantado should quit Cuença, and throw himself into the Guadalaxara district, a movement that would have been extremely embarrassing to the King. Suchet's division, while at Calatayud, fulfilled these objects, without losing the power of succoring Tudela, or of intercepting the Duke of Infantado if he attempted to raise the siege of Zaragoza; but, when the Spanish army at Cuença was directed to Ucles, and that the Marquis of Lazan was gathering strength on the left bank of the Ebro, it was undoubtedly proper to recall Suchet.

2. It may not be misplaced here to point out the errors of Infantado's operations.   If, instead of bringing on a battle with the first corps, he had marched to the Ebro, established his dépôts, and placed arms at Mequinenza and Lerida, opened a communication with Murcia, Valencia, and Catalonia, and joined the Marquis of Lazan's troops to his own; he might have formed an intrenched camp in the Sierra de Alcubierre, and from thence have carried on a methodical war with, at least, twenty-five thousand regular troops. The insurrections on the French flanks and line of communication with Pampeluna would then have become formidable, and, in this situation, having the fortresses of Catalonia behind him, with activity and prudence he might have raised the siege.

3. From a review of all the circumstances attending the siege of Zaragoza, we may conclude that fortune was extremely favorable to the French.   They were brave, persevering, and skilful, and they did not lose above four thousand men; but their success, partly resulting from the errors of their opponents, was principally due to the destruction caused by the pestilence within the town; for, of all that multitude said to have fallen, six thousand Spaniards only were slain in battle; and although thirteen convents and churches had been taken, yet, when the town surrendered, forty remained to be forced!*

Such were the principal circumstances of this memorable siege. I shall now relate the contemporary operations in Catalonia.

* Rogniat.

CHAPTER IV.

Operations in Catalonia—St Cyr commands the seventh corps—Passes the frontier—State of Catalonia—Palacios fixes his head-quarters at Villa Franca—Duhesme forces the line of the Llobregat—Returns to Barcelona—English army from Sicily designed to act in Catalonia—Prevented by Murat—Duhesme forages El Vallés—Action of San Culgat—General Vives supersedes Palacios—Spanish army augments—Blockade of Barcelona—Siege of Rosas—Folly and negligence of the Junta—Intrenchments in the town carried by the besiegers—Marquis of Lazan, with six thousand men, reaches Gerona—Lord Cochrane enters the Trinity—Repulses several assaults—Citadel surrenders 5th December—St. Cyr marches on Barcelona—Crosses the Ter—Deceives Lazan—Turns Hostalrich—Defeats Milans at San Celoni—Battle of Cardadeu—Caldagnes retires behind the Llobregat—Negligence of Duhesme—Battle of Molino del Rey.

OPERATIONS IN CATALONIA.

It will be remembered, that when the second siege of Gerona was raised, in August, 1808, General Duhesme returned to Barcelona, and General Reille to Figueras, after which the state of affairs obliged those generals to remain on the defensive. Napoleon's measures to aid them were as prompt as the occasion required; for while the siege of Gerona was yet in progress, he had directed troops to assemble at Perpignan in such numbers as to form, with those already in Catalonia, an army of more than forty thousand men, to be called the "*7th corps,*" and to be commanded by General Gouvion St. Cyr, to whom he gave this short but emphatic order: "*Preserve Barcelona for me. If that place be lost, I cannot retake it with* 80,000 *men.*"*

The troops assembled at Perpignan were, the greatest part, raw levies—Neapolitans, Etruscans, Romans, and Swiss, mixed, however, with some old regiments; but as the preparations for the grand army under the Emperor absorbed the principal attention of the administration in France, General St. Cyr was straitened in the means necessary to take the field, and his undisciplined troops, suffering severe privations, were depressed in spirit, and inclined to desert. On the 1st of November, Napoleon, who was at Bayonne, sent orders to the "*7th corps*" to commence operations; St. Cyr, therefore, put his division in motion on the 3d, and crossing the frontier, established his head-quarters at Figueras on the 5th.

Meanwhile in Catalonia, as in other parts of Spain, lethargic vanity, and abuses of the most fatal kind, had succeeded the first enthusiasm and withered the energy of the people. The local Junta had, indeed, issued abundance of decrees, and despatched agents to the Supreme Junta, and to the English commanders in the

* St. Cyr's Journal of Operations.

Mediterranean and Portugal, all charged with the same instructions, namely, to demand arms, ammunition, and money; and although the Central Junta treated their demands with contempt, the English authorities answered them generously and freely. Lord Collingwood lent the assistance of his fleet; from Malta and Sicily arms were obtained, and Sir Hew Dalrymple, having completely equipped the Spanish regiments released by the convention of Cintra, despatched them to Catalonia in British transports. Yet it may be doubted if the conduct of the Central Junta were not the wisest; for the local government established at Tarragona had already become so negligent, or so corrupt, that the arms thus supplied were, instead of being used in defence of the country, sold to foreign merchants!* Such being the political state of Catalonia, it naturally followed that the military affairs should be ill-conducted.

The Count of Caldagues, after having relieved Gerona, returned by Hostalrich, and resumed the line of the Llobregat; fifteen hundred men, drawn from the garrison of Carthagena, reached Tarragona, and the Marquis of Palacios, accompanied by the Junta, quitted the latter town, and fixed his quarters at Villa Franca, within twenty miles of Caldagues, and the latter then disposed his troops, five thousand in number, on different points between Martorel and San Boy, covering a line of eighteen miles, along the left bank of the river.†

Meanwhile Duhesme, who had rested but a few days, marched in the night from Barcelona with six thousand men, and having arrived the 2d of September at day-break on the Llobregat, attacked Caldagues' line on several points, but principally at San Boy and Molino del Rey. The former post was carried, and the Spaniards were pursued to Vegas, a distance of seven or eight miles, but at Molino del Rey the French were repulsed, and Duhesme then returned to Barcelona.

It was the intention of the British ministers, that an auxiliary force should have sailed from Sicily about this period, to aid the Catalans, and doubtless it would have been a wise and timely effort, but Napoleon's foresight prevented the execution. He directed Murat to menace Sicily, and that prince, feigning to collect forces on the coast of Calabria, spread many reports of armaments being in preparation, while, as a preliminary measure, General Lamarque carried the island of Capræ; here, Sir Hudson Lowe first became known to history by losing, in a few days, a post that, without any pretensions to celebrity, might have been defended for as many years. Murat's demonstrations sufficed to impose upon Sir John

* Lord Collingwood's Correspondence.
† Cabanes.

17*

Stuart, and from ten to twelve thousand British troops were thus paralyzed at a most critical period; and such will always be the result of a policy which has no fixed, definite object in view. When statesmen cannot see their own way clearly, the executive officers will seldom act with vigor.

During September the Spanish army daily increased, the tercios of Migueletes were augmented, and a regiment of hussars that had been most absurdly kept in Majorca ever since the beginning of the insurrection, arrived at Tarragona. Palacios, however, remained at Villa Franca; Caldagues continued to guard the Llobregat, and Mariano Alvarez commanded the advanced guard, composed of the garrisons of Gerona and Rosas, the corps of Juan Claros, and other partisan chiefs. Francisco Milans and Milans de Bosch, with six thousand Migueletes, kept the mountains northward and eastward of Barcelona; the latter hemming in the French right, the former covering the district of El Vallés, and watching, like a bird of prey, the enemy's foragers in the plain of Barcelona. The little port of Filieu de Quixols, near Palamos Bay, was filled with privateers, and the English frigates off the coast, besides aiding the Spanish enterprises, carried on a littoral warfare in the gulf of Lyons with great spirit and success. Many petty skirmishes happened between the Migueletes and the French; but on the 10th of October, Duhesme attacked Milans de Bosch at St. Gerony beyond the Besos, and completely dispersed his corps, and the 11th, sent Colonel Devaux, with two thousand men, against Granollers, which the Spaniards deserted, although it was their chief dépôt. Devaux, having captured and destroyed a considerable quantity of stores, returned the 12th to Mollet, where a column of equal strength was stationed in support, and then occupied the pass of Moncada, while General Millossewitz proceeded with the second column to forage El Vallés. Meanwhile Caldagues, drawing together three thousand infantry, two squadrons of cavalry, and six guns, marched by the back of the hills towards Moncada, hoping to intercept the French on their return to Barcelona; thus Millossewitz and he met unexpectedly at San Culgat.* In the confused action which ensued, the French were beaten, and retreated across the mountains to Barcelona, while Caldagues, justly proud of his soldier-like movement, returned to his camp on the Llobregat.†

The 28th of October, Palacios was ordered to take the command of the levies then collecting in the Sierra Morena, and General Vives succeeded him in Catalonia. The army was now reinforced with more infantry from Majorca; the Spanish troops, released by

* Lafaille, Campagne de Catalonia.
† Vacani.

the convention of Cintra, arrived at Villa Franca; seven or eight thousand Granadian levies were brought up to Tarragona by General Reding, and at the same time six thousand men, drafted from the army of Aragon, reached Lerida, under the command of the Marquis of Lazan. The whole were organized in six divisions; the troops in the Ampurdan forming one, and including the garrisons of Hostalrich, Gerona, and Rosas, this *army of the right*, as it was called, amounted to thirty-six thousand men, of which twenty-two thousand foot and twelve hundred horse were near Barcelona, or in march for it.

Vives, seeing himself at the head of such a power, and in possession of all the hills and rivers surrounding Barcelona, resolved to storm that city, and all things seemed to favor the attempt. The inhabitants were ready to rise; a battalion of the Walloon guards, who had been suffered to remain in the city in a species of neutrality, plotted to seize one of the gates, and the French were so uneasy that Duhesme actually resolved to abandon the town and confine his defence to the citadel and Montjouik; a resolution from which he was only diverted by the remonstrances of the chief engineer Lafaille. In this state of affairs, Vives, transferring his quarters to Martorel, directed a general attack on the French outposts, but he was repulsed at every point, and returned to the mountains; the Walloon guards were then disarmed, the inhabitants awed, and the defences of the town increased. From that period to the raising of the blockade, the warfare of the Spanish General was contemptible, although disputes among his adversaries had arisen to such a height that Duhesme was advised to send Lecchi a prisoner to France.

Catalonia was now a prey to innumerable disorders. Vives, a weak, indolent man, had been the friend of Godoy, and was not popular. He had, when commanding in the islands, retained the troops in them with such tenacity as to create doubts of his attachment to the cause; yet the Supreme Junta, while privately expressing their suspicions, and requesting Lord Collingwood to force him to an avowal of his true sentiments, wrote publicly to Vives in the most flattering terms, and finally appointed him Captain-General of Catalonia.* By the people, however, he and others were vehemently suspected, and, as the mob governed throughout Spain, the authorities, civil and military, were more careful to avoid giving offence to the multitude than anxious to molest the enemy; and hence, although Catalonia was full of strong places, they were neither armed nor provisioned, for all persons were confident that the French only thought of retreating.

* Lord Collingwood's Correspondence.

Such was the state of the province and of the armies, when Napoleon, being ready to break into the northern parts of Spain, ordered St. Cyr to commence operations.   His force (including a German division of six thousand men, not yet arrived at Perpignan) amounted to more than thirty thousand men; ill-composed, however, and badly provided, and St. Cyr himself was extremely discontented with his situation.*   The Emperor had given him discretionary powers to act as he judged fitting, only bearing in mind the importance of relieving Barcelona; but Marshal Berthier neglected the equipment of the troops, and Duhesme declared that his magazines would not hold out longer than December.   To march directly to Barcelona was neither an easy nor an advantageous movement.   That city could only be provisioned from France, and, until the road was cleared by the taking of Gerona and Hostalrich, no convoys could pass except by sea.   To attack those places with prudence, it was essential to get possession of Rosas; not only to secure an intermediate port for French vessels passing with supplies to Barcelona, but to deprive the English of a secure harbor, and the Spaniards of a point from whence they could, in concert with their allies, intercept the communications of the French army, and even blockade Figueras, which, from the want of transport, could not be provisioned at this period.   These considerations having determined St. Cyr to commence by the siege of Rosas, he repaired to Figueras in person, the 6th of November, and on the 7th, General Reille, being charged to conduct the operation, after a sharp action, drove in the Spaniards before that place, and completed the investment.

SIEGE OF ROSAS.

This town was but a narrow slip of houses built along the water's edge, at the head of the gulf of the same name.   The citadel, a large irregular pentagon, stood on one side, and, on the other, the mountains that skirt the flat and swampy plain of the Ampurdan, rose, bluff and rocky, at the distance of half a mile.   An old redoubt was built at the foot of the hills, and, from thence to the citadel, an intrenchment had been drawn to cover the houses; hence Rosas, looking towards the land, had the citadel on the left hand, the mountains on the right, and the front covered by this intrenchment.   The roadstead permitted ships of the line to anchor within cannon-shot of the place, and on the right hand, coming up the gulf, a star fort, called the Trinity, crowned a rugged hill about a mile and a quarter distant from the citadel; the communication between it and the

* Muster rolls of the French army, MSS. St. Cyr.

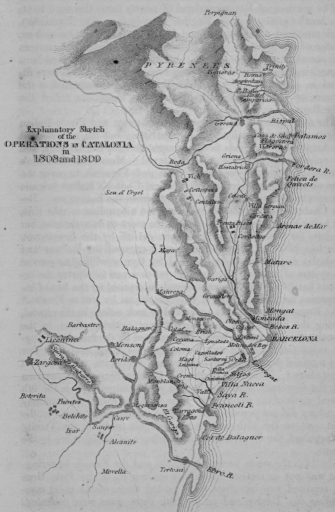

Perpignan

PYRENEES

Figueras
Rosas
Ampurdam
R.Fluvia
Castel
Fongueras

Trinity

Bispal

Gerona

Casa de Selva
Palamos
Flagestera
Vidreras

Explanatory Sketch
of the
OPERATIONS in CATALONIA
in
1808 and 1809

Roda

Orions

Hostalrich

St.Felieu de
Quixols

Ter dera R.

Seu d'Urgel

Vich
Collespina
Centellas

Colони

Villa Gorman
Cordera

Arenas de Mar

Venta Pisca

Cordedме

Maya

Mongat
Monbada
Besos R.

Manresa

Gariga

Granulers

Oleston
Calsat
Ledrori

BARCELONA

Barbastro
Balagner

Vala

Monbsanor

Cervera
Agnatada

Molins de Rey

Licenina

Monson

Coloma
Capellades

Lerida

Maqt
Lusuma

Sardarni
Ordel

Villa
Franca
Christina

Llobregat

Sitjes

Monblando
Pla

Villa Nueva

Zarjesa Medhena

Valls

Saya R.

Fuentes

Botorita

Maquinghsa

Francoli R.

Belchite

Casye

Zarragona
Reus

Ixar
Sanper

El Garin

Alcanits

Col de Balagner

Morella

Tortosa

Ebro R.

town being by a narrow road carried between the foot of the mountain and the water's edge.

The garrison of Rosas consisted of nearly three thousand men; two bomb-vessels, and an English seventy-four (the Excellent), were anchored off the town, and Captain West, the Commodore, reinforced the garrisons of the Trinity and the citadel with marines and seamen from these vessels; but the damages sustained in a former siege had been only partially repaired; both places were ill-found in guns and stores, and the Trinity was commanded at the distance of pistol-shot from a point of the mountains called the Puig Rom.

The force under Reille, consisting of his own and Pino's Italian division, skirmished daily with the garrison; but the rain flooded the Ampurdan, the roads became impassable for the artillery, and the opening of the trenches was delayed. Meanwhile Souham's division took post between the Fluvia and Figueras, to cover the siege on the side of Gerona, and General Chabot's Italian brigade was sent to Rabos and Espollas, to keep down the Somatenes. Before Chabot's arrival, Reille had detached a battalion to that side, and being uneasy for its safety sent three more to its assistance, but too late, for two companies had been cut off by the Somatenes. This loss, however, proved beneficial, it enraged the Italians and checked a disposition to desert; and St. Cyr, unwilling to pursue the system of burning villages and yet desirous to repress the insidious hostility of the peasants, seized, in reprisal for the loss of his companies, an equal number of villagers, whom he sent to France.*

At Rosas the inhabitants embarked or took refuge in the citadel, leaving the houses, and the intrenchment covering them, to the French; the latter were however prevented by the fire of the English ships from making any permanent lodgment, and in a few days a mixed detachment of soldiers and townsmen re-established a post there.† This done, on the 8th Captain West, in conjunction with the Governor, made a sally, but was repulsed, and on the 9th several yards of the citadel's ramparts crumbled away. Fortunately the enemy did not perceive the accident, which was repaired in the night, and on the 15th an obstinate assault made on the Trinity was repulsed, the English seamen bearing a principal share in the success.

The 16th the roads became passable, and the French battering-train was put in motion. The way leading up to the Puig Rom was repaired, two battalions were posted there, on the point commanding the Trinity, and on the 19th three guns were mounted.

* St. Cyr.
† Captain West's despatch.

The trenches were then opened at the distance of four hundred yards from the citadel, and the 20th the fire of the French mortars obliged the vessels of war to anchor beyond the range of the shells.

During this time Souham was harassed by the Migueletes from the side of Gerona, and the French cavalry, unable to find forage, were sent back to France. Napoleon, meanwhile, rendered uneasy by the reports of General Duhesme, directed the seventh corps to advance to Barcelona, so as to arrive there by the 26th of November, yet St. Cyr refused to abandon the siege of Rosas without a more positive order.* On the other side, the assistance afforded to the besieged by Captain West was represented to the Catalonian government as an attempt to possess himself of the place, and the Junta, readily believing the tale, entered into an angry correspondence with Don Pedro O'Daly, the Governor, relative to the supposed treachery, yet took no measures to raise the siege. Pending the correspondence, however, the Excellent sailed from Rosas, and was succeeded by the Fame, Capain Bennet, who immediately landed some men under the Trinity, and endeavored, but ineffectually, to take the battery opposed to that fort.

The 27th the besiegers assaulted the Spaniards, who had intrenched themselves in the deserted houses of the town; a hundred and sixty were taken, fifty escaped into the citadel, and the rest were slain. Breaching batteries were then commenced among the ruins of the houses, and the communication with the shipping rendered so unsafe, that Lazan, who had come from Lerida to Gerona with six thousand men, and had collected provisions and stores at the mouth of the Fluvia, with the intention of supplying Rosas by sea, abandoned his design.†

Reille, observing the dilapidated state of the citadel, now sent another summons; but the governor was firm, and meanwhile, as the engineers reported the breach in the Trinity to be practicable, an assault there was ordered for the 30th of November. An Italian officer, who had formerly served in the fort, being appointed to lead the storming party, asserted that the breach was a false one; his remonstrance was unheeded, and indeed the Spanish commandant thought the post so untenable, that two days before, the marines of the Fame had been withdrawn by Captain Bennet. But at this moment Lord Cochrane, a man of infinite talent in his profession, and of surpassing courage and enterprise, threw himself with eighty seamen into the fort. He found the breach really practicable, yet broken into an old gallery, which he immediately filled with earth and hammocks, and so cut off the opening; hence

* St Cyr.
† Doyle's Correspondence, MS.

the unfortunate Italian could do nothing, and fell with all his followers, except two who escaped to their own side, and two who, being spared by the seamen, were drawn up with ropes. A second assault, made a few days after, was likewise repulsed.

While this passed at the Trinity, the breaching batteries opened against the citadel, and a false attack was commenced on the opposite side; the next night the garrison made a sally with some success, but the walls were completely broken by the French fire, and the 5th of December, O'Daly, hopeless of relief, surrendered with two thousand four hundred men. Lord Cochrane then abandoned the Trinity, first blowing up the magazine.

St. Cyr observes that the garrison of Rosas might have been easily carried off, at night, by the British shipping. To embark two thousand five hundred men, in the boats of two ships, and under a heavy fire, whether by night or day, is not an easy operation, yet the censure seems well founded, because sufficient preparation might have been previously made. Nor can the defence of the place (with the exception of Lord Cochrane's exploit) be deemed brilliant, whether with relation to the importance of the place, the assistance that might have been rendered from the sea, or the number of the garrison compared with that of the besiegers. It held out, however, thirty days, and, if that time had been well employed by the Spaniards outside, the loss of the garrison would have been amply repaid; but Vives, wholly occupied with Barcelona, was indifferent to the fate of Rosas; a fruitless attack on Souham's posts, by Mariano Alvarez, was the only effort made to interrupt the siege, or to impede the farther progress of the enemy. Lazan, although at the head of six or seven thousand men, could not rely upon more than three thousand, and his applications to Vives for a reinforcement were unheeded.*

The fall of Rosas enabled St. Cyr to march to the relief of Barcelona, and he resolved to do so, although the project, at first sight, appeared rather insane than hardy; for the roads, by which Gerona and Hostalrich were to be turned, being mere paths impervious to carriages, no artillery, and little ammunition, could be carried, and the country was full of strong positions. The Germans had not yet arrived at Perpignan; it was indispensable to leave Reille in the Ampurdan, to protect Rosas and Figueras; and these deductions being made, less than eighteen thousand men, including the cavalry, which had been recalled from France, remained disposable for the operation: but, on the Spanish side, Reding having come up, there were twenty-five thousand men in the camp before Barcelona, and ten thousand others, under Lazan

* Doyle's Correspondence, MS.

and Alvarez, were at Gerona. The Spanish troops were, however, exceedingly ill organized. Two-thirds of the Migueletes carried pikes, and many were without any arms at all; there was no sound military system; the Spanish generals were ignorant of the French movements and strength, and their own indolence and want of vigilance drew upon them the contempt and suspicion of the people.*

The 8th of December St. Cyr united his army on the left bank of the Fluvia. The 9th he passed that river, and driving the Spaniards over the Ter, established his head-quarters at Mediñya, ten miles from Gerona. He wished, before pursuing his own march, to defeat Lazan, lest the latter should harass the rear of the army; but, finding that the Marquis would not engage in a serious affair, he made a show of sitting down before Gerona on the 10th, hoping thereby to mislead Vives, and render him slow to break up the blockade of Barcelona:† this succeeded, the Spaniard remained in his camp, irresolute and helpless, while his enemy was rapidly passing the defiles and rivers between Gerona and the Besos.

The nature of the country between Figueras and Barcelona has been described in a former place, and referring to that description, the reader will find that the only carriage routes by which St. Cyr could march were, one by the sea-coast, and one leading through Gerona and Hostalrich. The first, exposed to the fire of the English vessels, had been broken up by Lord Cochrane, in August; and to use the second, it was necessary, either to take the fortresses, or to turn them by marching for three days through the mountains. St. Cyr adopted the last plan, trusting that rapidity and superior knowledge of war would enable him to separate Lazan and Alvarez from Vives, and so defeat them all in succession.

The 11th of December he crossed the Ter and reached La Bisbal; here he left the last of his carriages, delivered out four days' biscuit and fifty rounds of ammunition to the soldiers, and with this provision, a drove of cattle, and a reserve of only ten rounds of ammunition for each man, he commenced his hardy march, making for Palamos. On the route he encountered and beat some Migueletes that Juan Claros had brought to oppose him, and, when near Palamos, he suffered a little from the fire of the English ships; but he had gained the first step, and his hopes were high.

The 13th, he turned his back upon the coast, and, by a forced march, reached Vidreras and Llagostera, thus placing himself between Vives and Lazan, for the latter had not yet passed the heights of Casa de Selva.

* Cabanes.
† St. Cyr.

The 14th, marching by Mazanet de Selva and Martorel, he reached the heights above Hostalrich, and encamped at Grions and Masanas. During this day's journey, his rear was slightly harassed by Lazan and Claros, but he was well content to find the strong banks of the Tordera undefended by Vives. His situation was, however, extremely critical. Lazan and Claros had, the one on the 11th, the other on the 12th, informed Vives of the movement; hence the bulk of the Spanish force before Barcelona might be expected, at any moment, in some of the strong positions in which the country abounded; the troops from Gerona were, as we have seen, in the rear, the Somatenes were gathering thickly on the flanks, Hostalrich was in front, and the French soldiers had only sixteen rounds of ammunition.

St. Cyr's design was to turn Hostalrich, and get into the main road again behind that fortress. The smugglers of Perpignan had affirmed that there was no pathway, but a shepherd assured him that there was a track by which it could be effected; and, when the efforts of the staff officers to trace it failed, St. Cyr himself discovered it, but nearly fell into the hands of the Somatenes during the search.

The 15th, at daybreak, the troops being put in motion, turned the fortress and gained the main road, and the garrison of the place, endeavoring to harass their rear, was repulsed; yet the Somatenes on the flanks, emboldened because the French, to save ammunition, did not return their fire, became exceedingly troublesome, and near San Celoni the head of the column encountered some battalions of Migueletes, which Francisco Milans had brought up from Arenas de Mar, by the pass of Villa Gorguin.

Milans, not being aware of St. Cyr's approach, was soon beaten, and his men fell back, part to Villa Gorguin, part to the heights of Nuestra Señora de Cordera: the French thus gained the defile of Treintapasos, but they were now so fatigued that all desired to halt, save the General, who insisted upon the troops clearing that defile, and reaching a plain on the other side, which was not effected before ten o'clock. Lazan's troops did not appear during the day, but Vives' army was in front, and its fires were seen on the hills between Cardadeu and Llinas.

Information of St. Cyr's march, as I have already observed, had been transmitted to Vives on the 11th, and there was time for him to have carried the bulk of his forces to the Tordera, before the French could pass that river; but intelligence of the battle of Tudela, and of the appearance of the French near Zaragoza, arrived at the same moment, and the Spanish General betrayed the greatest weakness and indecision; at one moment resolving to continue before Barcelona, at another designing to march against St. Cyr.* He had, on the 9th, sent Reding, with six guns, six hundred cavalry, and one thousand infantry, to take the command in the Ampurdan; and the 12th, after receiving Lazan's report, he reinforced Reding, who was still at Granollers, and directed him upon Cardadeu. The 14th, he ordered Francisco Milans to march by Mattaro and Arenas de Mar, to examine the coast road, and, if the enemy was not in that line, to repair also to Cardadeu. The 15th, Milans, as we have seen, was beaten at St. Celoni, but, in the night, he rallied his whole division on the heights of Cordera, thus flanking the left of the French forces at Llinas.

A Spanish council of war had been held on the 13th. Caldagues advised that four thousaud Migueletes should be left to observe Duhesme, and that the rest of the army should march at once to fight St. Cyr: good and soldier-like counsel; but Vives was loth to abandon the siege of Barcelona, and adopting half measures, left Caldagues, with the right wing of the army, to watch Duhesme, and carried the centre and the left, by the route of Granollers, to the heights between Cardadeu and Llinas, where, exclusive of Milans' division, he united, in the night of the 15th, about eight thousand regulars, besides several thousand Somatenes. Duhesme immediately occupied the posts abandoned by Vives, and thus separated him from Caldagues; yet St. Cyr's position, on the morning of the 16th, would have been very dangerous, if he had been opposed by any but Spanish generals and Spanish troops.

Vives and those about him, irresolute and weak as they were in action, were not deficient in boasting words; they called the French army, in derision, "*the succor;*" and, in allusion to the battle of Baylen, announced that a second "*bull-fight,*" in which Reding was again the "*matador,*" would be exhibited.† Dupont and St. Cyr were, however, men of a different temper: the latter, knowing that the Spaniards were not troops to stand the shock of a good column, united his army in one solid mass at daybreak on the 16th, and without hesitation marched against the centre of the enemy, ordering the head of the column to go headlong on, without either firing or forming line.

BATTLE OF CARDADEU.

The hills occupied by the Spanish army were high and wooded. Vives, in person, commanded on the left; the other wing was under Reding, and the Somatenes clustered upon a lofty ridge which was separated from the right of the position by the little river Mo-

---

* Cabanes. Doyle's Correspondence, MS.
† St. Cyr.

gent. The main road from Llinas led through the centre of the line, and a second road branching off from the first, and running between the Mogent and Reding's ground, went to Mattaro.

The flank of the French attacking column was galled by the Somatenes, and halted. General Pino, who led it, instead of falling on briskly, sent for fresh instructions, and meanwhile extended his first brigade in a line to his left. St. Cyr reiterated the order to fight in column ; but he was sorely troubled at Pino's error, for Reding, advancing against the front and flank of the extended brigade, obliged it to commence a fire, which it could not nourish from the want of ammunition.

In this difficulty the French General acted with great ability and vigor. Pino's second brigade was directed to do that which the first should have done ; two companies were sent to menace the left of the Spaniards, and St. Cyr himself rapidly carried Souham's division, by the Mattaro road, against Reding's extreme right. The effect was instantaneous and complete ; the Spaniards, overthrown on their centre and right, and charged by the cavalry, were beaten, and dispersed in every direction, leaving their artillery, ammunition, and two thousand prisoners behind.

Vives escaped on foot across the mountain to Mattaro, where he was taken on board an English vessel ; but Reding fled on horseback by the main road, and the next day, having rallied some of the fugitives at Monmalo, retreated by the route of San Culgat to Molino del Rey. The loss of the French was only six hundred men, and the battle, which lasted one hour, was so decisive, that St. Cyr resolved to push on to Barcelona immediately, without seeking to defeat Milans or Lazan, whom he judged too timid to venture an action : moreover, he hoped that Duhesme, who had been informed on the 7th of the intended march, and who could hear the sound of the artillery, would intercept and turn back the flying troops.

The French had scarcely quitted the field of battle when Milans arrived, and, finding how matters stood, retired to Arenas de Mar, giving notice to Lazan, who retreated to Gerona ; St. Cyr's rear was thus cleared. Meanwhile Duhesme, heedless of what was passing at Cardadeu, instead of intercepting the beaten army, sent Lecchi to attack Caldagues, who, having concentrated his division on the evening of the 16th, repulsed Lecchi, and then retired behind the Llobregat, leaving behind some artillery and the large magazines which Vives had collected for the siege. Thus St. Cyr reached Barcelona without encountering any of Duhesme's troops, and, in his Memoirs of this campaign, he represents that General as astonishingly negligent ; seeking neither to molest the enemy nor

to meet the French army; treating everything belonging to the
service with indifference; making false returns, and conniving at
gross malversation in his generals. Duhesme, however, has not
wanted defenders.

St. Cyr, now reflecting upon the facility with which his opponents could be defeated, and the difficulty of pursuing them,
resolved to rest a few days at Barcelona, in hopes that the
Spaniards, if unmolested, would re-assemble in numbers behind the
Llobregat, and enable him to strike an effectual blow, for his design
was to disperse their forces so that they should be unable to interrupt the sieges which he meditated; nor was he deceived in his
calculations. Reding joined Caldagues, rallied from twelve to
fifteen thousand men behind the Llobregat, and Vives, who had
relanded at Sitjes, sent orders to Lazan and Milans to join him
there by the way of Vallés; the arrival of the latter was, however,
so uncertain that the French General, who knew of these orders,
judging it better to attack Reding at once, united Chabran's
division to his own, and on the 20th advanced to St. Felieu de
Llobregat.

The Spaniards were drawn up on the heights behind the village
of San Vincente, and their position, lofty and rugged, commanded
a free view of the approaches from Barcelona; the Llobregat
covered the front, and the left was secured from attack, except at
the bridge of Molino del Rey, which was intrenched, guarded by a
strong detachment, and protected by heavy guns. Reding's cavalry
amounted to one thousand, and he had fifty pieces of artillery, the
greatest part of which were in battery at the bridge of Molino del
Rey; his right was, however, accessible, because the river was
fordable in several places. The main road to Villa Franca led
through this position, and, at the distance of ten or twelve miles in
the rear, the pass of Ordal offered another post of great strength.

Vives was at San Vincente on the 19th, but returned to Villa
Franca the same day; hence, when the French appeared on the
20th, the camp was thrown into confusion, and a council of war
being held, one party was for fighting, another for retreating to
Ordal;* finally an officer was sent to Vives for orders, and he
returned with a message, that Reding might retreat if he could not
defend his post; but the latter fearing that he should be accused,
and perhaps sacrificed for returning without reason, resolved to
fight, although he anticipated nothing but disaster. The season
was extremely severe, snow was falling, and both armies suffered
from cold and wet; but the Spanish soldiers were dispirited by past
defeats, and the despondency and irresolution of their generals

* Cabanes.

could not escape observation, while the French and Italian troops were confident in their commander, and flushed with success. In these dispositions the two armies passed the night.

BATTLE OF MOLINO DEL REY.

St. Cyr, observing that Reding's attention was principally directed to the bridge of Molino, ordered Chabran's division to that side, with instructions to create a diversion by opening a fire from some artillery, and then retiring as if his guns could not resist the weight of the Spanish metal; in short, to persuade the enemy that a powerful effort would be made there; but when the centre and right of the Spaniards should be attacked, Chabran was to force the passage of the bridge, and assail the heights beyond it. The stratagem succeeded; Reding accumulated troops on his left, and neglected his right, which was the real point of attack.

The 21st, Pino's division crossing the Llobregat at daylight, by a ford in front of St. Felieu, marched against the right of the Spanish position; Chabot's division followed; Souham's, which had passed at a ford lower down, and then ascended by the right bank, covered Pino's passage; the light cavalry were held in reserve behind Chabot's division, and a regiment of cuirassiers was sent to support Chabran at Molino del Rey.

The Spanish position consisted of two mountain heads, separated by a narrow ravine and a torrent, and as the troops of the right wing were exceedingly weakened, they were immediately chased off their headland by the leading brigade of Pino's division. Reding then, seeing his error, changed his front, drawing up on the other mountain, on a new line, nearly perpendicular to the Llobregat, but he still kept a strong detachment at the bridge of Molino, which was thus in rear of his left. The French divisions formed rapidly for a fresh effort, Souham was on the right, Pino in the centre, and Chabot on the left; and the latter gained ground in the direction of Villa Franca, endeavoring to turn the Spaniards' right, and cut off their retreat, while the light cavalry, making way between the mountain and the river, sought to connect themselves with Chabran at Molino. The other two columns, having crossed the ravine that separated them from the Spaniards, ascended the opposite mountain. The Catalans, forming quickly, opposed their enemies with an orderly but ill-directed fire, and their front line advancing, offered to charge with an appearance of great intrepidity; but their courage sinking, they turned as the hostile masses approached, and the reserve immediately opened a confused volley upon both parties. In this disorder, the road to Villa Franca being intercepted by Chabot, the right was forced upon the centre, the

centre upon the left, and the whole pushed back in confusion upon
Molino del Rey. Meantime a detachment from Chabran's division,
passing the Llobregat above Molino, blocked the road to Martorel,
and in this miserable situation, the Spaniards being charged by the
light cavalry, scarcely a man would have escaped if Chabran had
obeyed his orders, by pushing across the bridge of Molino upon
their rear. But that General, at all times feeble in execution,
remained a tranquil spectator of the action, until the right of Souham's division reached the bridge; thus the routed troops escaped
by dispersion, throwing away everything that could impede their
flight across the mountains. Vives reached the field of battle
just as the rout was complete, and was forced to fly with the rest.
The victorious army pursued in three columns; Chabran's in the
direction of Igualada; Chabot's by the road of San Sadurni,
which turned the pass of Ordal; Souham's by the royal route of
Villa Franca, at which place the head-quarters were established
on the 22d. The posts of Villa Nueva and Sitjes were immediately occupied by Pino, while Souham pushed the fugitives to the
gates of Tarragona.

The loss of the Spaniards, owing to their swiftness, was less than
might have been expected; not more than twelve hundred fell into
the hands of the French, but many superior officers were killed or
wounded, and, on the 22d, the Count de Caldagues was taken, a
man apparently pedantic in military affairs, and wanting in
modesty, but evidently possessed of both courage and talent. The
whole of the artillery, vast quantities of powder, and a magazine
of English muskets quite new, were captured, yet many of the
Migueletes were unarmed, and the Junta were unceasing in their
demands for succors of this nature! but the history of any one
province was the history of all Spain.

CHAPTER V.

BARCELONA was now completely relieved, and the captured
magazines supplied it for several months; there was no longer a
Spanish army in the field, and in Tarragona, where some eight or
nine thousand of the Spanish fugitives from this and the former
battle had taken refuge, there was terrible disorder. The people
rose tumultuously, broke open the public stores, and laying hands
on all the weapons they could find, rushed from place to place, as
if searching for something to vent their fury upon; they called
aloud for the head of Vives, and to save his life he was cast into
prison by Reding, who was proclaimed General-in-chief.* The
regular officers were insulted by the populace, and there was as
usual a general cry to defend the city, mixed with furious menaces
against traitors; but there were neither guns, nor ammunition, nor
provisions, and during the first moment of anarchy, St. Cyr might
certainly have rendered himself master of Tarragona, by a vigorous effort.† The opportunity soon passed away; the French
General, seeking only to procure subsistence, occupied himself in
forming a train of field artillery, while Reding, who had been
almost without hope, proceeded to rally the army, and place the
town in a state o defence.

The 1st of January eleven thousand infantry and eight hundred
cavalry re-assembled at Tarragona and Reus; a Swiss regiment
from Majorca, and two Spanish regiments from Granada, increased

* Cabanes.
† St. Cyr.

this force, and the 5th three thousand four hundred men arrived from Valencia, from whence also five thousand muskets, ammunition in proportion, and ten thousand pikes fresh from England, were forwarded to Tarragona, and a supply of money, obtained from the British agents at Seville, completed the list of fortuitous events following the disaster of Molino del Rey.* These fortunate circumstances, and the inactivity of St. Cyr, who seemed paralyzed, restored the confidence of the Catalans, yet their system remained unchanged, for in Spain confidence often led to insubordination, but never to victory.

A part of the fugitives from Molino had taken refuge at Bruch, where, being joined by the Somatenes, they chose Major Green, an English military agent, for their general, thinking to hold that post, which was considered impregnable ever since the defeats of Chabran and Swartz. St. Cyr, glad of this opportunity to retrieve the honor of the French arms, detached Chabran himself the 11th January to take his own revenge; but as that General was still depressed by the recollection of his former defeat, to encourage him, Chabot was directed from San Sadurni upon Igualada, by which the defile of Bruch was turned, and a permanent defence rendered impossible.† Green made little or no resistance; eight guns were taken, a considerable number of men were killed, the French pursued to Igualada, and a detachment, without orders, even assailed and took Montserrat itself, and rejoined the main body without loss. Chabot was then recalled to San Sadurni, and Chabran was quartered at Martorel.

While these events were passing beyond the Llobregat, the Marquis of Lazan advanced, with seven or eight thousand men, towards Castellon de Ampurias. The 1st of January he drove back a battalion of infantry upon Rosas with considerable loss, but the next day General Reille, having assembled about three thousand men, intercepted his communications, and attacked him in his position behind the Muga; the victory seems to have been undecided, and in the night Lazan, regaining his communications, returned to Gerona.

The battle of Molino del Rey having abated, for a time, the ardor of the Catalans, Reding was enabled to avoid serious actions, while the Somatenes harassed the enemy; and this plan, being followed during the months of January and February, was exceedingly troublesome to St. Cyr, because he was obliged to send small parties continually to seek for provision, which the country people hid with great care, striving hard to protect their scanty

* Doyle's Correspondence, MS.
† St. Cyr.

stores. In the beginning of February the country between the Llobregat and Tarragona was almost exhausted of food; the English ships continued to vex the coast-line, and the French, besides deserters, lost many men, killed and wounded, in the innumerable petty skirmishes sustained by the marauding parties. Still St. Cyr maintained his positions, until the country people, tired of a warfare in which they were the chief sufferers, clamored against Reding, that he, with a large regular force, should look calmly on, until the last morsel of food was discovered, and torn from their starving families; the townspeople, also feeling the burden of supporting the troops, impatiently urged the General to fight, nor was this insubordination confined to the rude multitude. Lazan, although at the head of nine thousand men, remained perfectly inactive after the skirmish at Castellon de Ampurias; but when Reding required him to leave a suitable garrison in Gerona, and bring the rest of his troops to Igualada, he would not obey, and their dispute was only terminated by Lazan's marching, with five thousand men, to the assistance of Zaragoza. His operations there have been related in the narrative of that siege.

The army immediately under Reding was very considerable, the Swiss battalions were numerous and good, and some of the most experienced of the Spanish regiments were in Catalonia; every fifth man of the robust population had been called out after the defeat of Molino del Rey, and, although the people, averse to serve as regular soldiers, did not readily answer the call, the force under Reding was, in the beginning of February, not less than twenty-eight thousand men. The urban guards were also put in activity, and above fifteen thousand Somatenes assisted the regular troops; but there was more show than real power, for Reding was incapable of wielding the regular troops skilfully, and the Migueletes, being ill armed, without clothing and insubordinate, devastated the country equally with the enemy. The Somatenes, who only took arms for local interests, would not fight, except at the times, in the manner, and in the place that suited themselves; they neglected the advice of the regular officers, reviled all who would not adopt their own views, and caused many to be removed from their commands. The Spanish generals never obtained from them good information of the enemy's movements; yet their own plans were always made known to the French, for at Reding's head-quarters, as at those of Castaños before the battle of Tudela, every project was openly and ostentatiously discussed. Reding himself was a man of no military talent, his activity was of body, not of mind; but he was brave and honorable; and popular, because, being without system, arrangement, or deep design, and easy in his nature, he thwarted no man's humors, and thus floated in the troubled waters until their sudden reflux left him on the rocks.

The Catalonian army was now divided into four distinct corps.

Alvarez, with four thousand men, held Gerona and the Ampurdan.

Lazan, with five thousand, was near Zaragoza.

Don Juan Castro, an officer accused by the Spaniards of treachery, and who afterwards did attach himself to Joseph's party, occupied, with sixteen thousand men, a line extending from Olessa, on the upper Llobregat, to the pass of San Cristina, near Tarragona; this line, running through Bruch, Igualada, and Llacuna, was above sixty miles long.

The remainder of the army, amounting to ten or twelve thousand men under Reding himself, was quartered at Tarragona, Reus, and the vicinity of those places.

The troops were fed from Valencia and Aragon, the convoys from the former being conveyed in vessels along the coast; but the magazines being accumulated on one or two points of the line, and chosen without judgment, fettered Reding's movements and regulated those of the French, whose only difficulty, in fact, was to procure food.

Early in February, St. Cyr, having exhausted the country about him, and finding his communications much vexed by the Somatenes, and by descents from the English ships, concentrated his divisions in masses at Vendril, Villa Franca, San Sadurni, and Martorel. The seventh corps, having been reinforced by the German division, and by some conscripts, amounted at this period to forty-eight thousand men, of which forty-one thousand were under arms, but the force immediately with St. Cyr did not exceed twenty-three thousand combatants. The relative position of the two armies was, however, entirely in favor of the French General; his line, extending from Vendril, by Villa Franca, to Martorel, was not more than thirty miles, and he had a royal road by which to retreat on Barcelona; whereas the Spanish posts, covering an extent of above sixty miles, formed a half-circle round the French line, and their communications were more rugged than those of St. Cyr. Nevertheless, it is not to be doubted that, by avoiding any serious action, the Catalans might have obliged the French to abandon the country between the Llobregat and Tarragona; famine, and the continued drain of men in a mountain warfare, would have forced the latter away, nor could they have struck any formidable blow to relieve themselves, seeing that all the important places were fortified towns requiring a regular siege. The never-failing arrogance of the Spanish character, and the unstable judgment of Reding, induced him to forego these advantages. The closing of the French posts, and some success in a few petty skirmishes, were magnified, the last into victories, and the first into a design on the part of the enemy to fly; and an intercourse opened with some of the inhabitants of Barcelona, gave hopes of regaining that city by means of a conspiracy within the walls. The Catalans had before made proposals to General Lecchi to deliver up the citadel of that place; nor is there anything that more strongly marks the absurd self-sufficiency of the Spaniards during this war, than the repeated attempts they made to corrupt the French commanders. As late as the year 1810, Martin Carrera, being at the head of about two thousand ragged peasants, half-armed, and only existing under the protection of the English outposts, offered to Marshal Ney, then investing Ciudad Rodrigo, rank and honors in the Spanish army if he would desert!

Reding, swayed by the popular clamor which this state of affairs produced, resolved to attack; and in this view directed Castro to collect his sixteen thousand men, to fall upon the right flank and rear of St. Cyr, by the routes of Llacuna and Igualada, and to send a detachment to seize the pass of Ordal, to cut off the French line of retreat to Barcelona; meanwhile, advancing with eight thousand by the road of Vendril and St. Cristina, he himself was to attack the enemy in front. All the Migueletes and Somatenes between Gerona and the Besos were to aid in these operations, the object being to surround the French, a favorite project with the Spaniards at all times; and as they publicly announced this intention, the joy was universal the destruction of the hostile army being as usual anticipated with the utmost confidence.

The Catalans were in motion on the 14th of February, but St. Cyr had kept his army well in hand, and seeing the Spaniards were ready to break in upon him, resolved to strike first. Wherefore, leaving Souham's division at Vendril, to hold Reding in check, on the 16th St. Cyr marched from Villa Franca, with Pino's division, and overthrew Castro's advanced posts which were at Lacuña and Saint Quinti. The Spanish centre was thus pierced, their wings completely separated, and Castro's right was thrown back upon Capellades.

The 17th, the French General, continuing his movement with Pino's division, reached Capellades, where he expected to unite with Chabot and Chabran, who had orders to concentrate there,— the one from San Sadurni, the other from Martorel. By this skilful movement he avoided the pass of Bruch, and concentrated three divisions on the extreme right of Castro's left wing and close to his magazines, which were at Igualada.

Chabot arrived the first, and being for a little time unsupported, was attacked and driven back with loss; but when the other divisions came up, the action was restored and the Spaniards put to flight. They rallied again at Pobla de Claramunt, between Capellades and Igualada, a circumstance agreeable to St. Cyr, because he had sent Mazzuchelli's brigade from Llacuna direct upon Igualada, and if Chabot had not been so hard pressed, the action of Capellades was to have been delayed until Mazzuchelli had got into the rear; scarcely, however, was the head of that General's column descried, when Castro, who was at Igualada with his reserves, recalled the troops from Pobla de Claramunt.* The French were close at their heels, and the whole passed through Igualada, fighting and in disorder; after which, losing all courage, the Spaniards threw away their arms, and fled by the three routes of Cervera, Calaf, and Manresa. They were pursued all the 17th, yet the French returned the next day with few prisoners, because, says St. Cyr, *the Catalans are endowed by nature with strong knees.*

Having thus broken through the centre of the Spanish line, defeated a part of the left wing and taken the magazines, St. Cyr posted Chabot and Chabran at Igualada, to keep the beaten troops in check, while himself, with Pino's division, marched on the 18th to fight Reding, whose extreme left was now at St. Magi. Souham also had been instructed, when by preconcerted signals he should know that the attack at Igualada had succeeded, to force the pass of Cristina, and push forward to Villa Radoña, upon which town St. Cyr was now marching.

The position of St. Magi, being attacked at four o'clock in the evening of the 18th, was carried without difficulty, but it was impossible to find a single peasant to guide the troops on the next day's march to the abbey of Santa Creus. In this perplexity, a wounded Spanish captain, who was prisoner, having demanded to be allowed to go to Tarragona, St. Cyr assented, offering to carry him to the Creus, and thus the prisoner unconsciously acted as a guide to his enemies.* The march was long and difficult, and it was late ere they reached the abbey, which was a strong point, occupied in force by the troops that had been beaten in San Magi the evening before, wherefore the French, after a fruitless demonstration of assaulting it, took a position for the night. Meanwhile Reding, hearing of Castro's defeat, made a draft of men and guns from the right wing, and was marching by Pla and the pass of Cabra, intending to rally his left; his road ran just behind St. Creus, and he was passing at the moment when the French appeared

* St. Cyr.
† Ibid.

before that place; but as neither general was aware of the other's presence, each continued his particular movement.

The 20th St. Cyr, crossing the Gaya river under a fire from the abbey, continued his rapid march upon Villa Radoña, near which place he dispersed a small corps; but finding that Souham was not come up, he sent an officer, escorted by a battalion, to hasten that General, whose non-arrival gave reason to believe that the staff officers and spies, sent with the previous instructions, had all been intercepted. This caused the delay of a day and a half, which would otherwise have sufficed to crush Reding's right wing, surprised as it would have been, without a chief, in the plain of Tarragona.

While the French rested at Villa Radoña, Reding pursued his march to St. Coloma de Querault, where he rallied many of Castro's fugitives, and thus the aspect of affairs was totally changed; for Souham, after forcing the pass of San Cristina, reached Villa Radoña the 21st, and, at the same time, the weakly men, who had been left at Villa Franca, also arrived; hence more than two-thirds of the whole French army were concentrated at Villa Radoña at the moment when the Spanish commander, being joined by the detachment beaten from San Cristina and by the troops from the abbey of Creus, had also rallied the greatest part of his forces at St. Coloma de Querault. Each general could now, by a rapid march, overwhelm his adversary's right wing; but the troops left by Reding, in the plain of Tarragona, could retire upon that fortress, while those left by St. Cyr at Igualada were without support. When, therefore, the French General, who, continuing his movement on Tarragona, had reached Valls the 22d, heard of Reding's march, he immediately returned with Pino's division to Pla, resolved, if the Spanish General should advance towards Igualada, to follow him with a sharp spur.

The 23d the French halted; Souham at Valls to watch the Spanish troops in the plain of Tarragona; Pino's division at Pla, but sending detachments to the abbey of Creus and towards Santa Coloma to feel for Reding. In the evening these detachments returned with some prisoners; the one reported that the abbey was abandoned; the other that the Spanish General was making his way back to Tarragona, by the route of Sarreal and Momblanch. St. Cyr, therefore, retaining Pino's division at Pla, pushed his advanced posts on the right to the abbey, and in front to the defile of Cabra, designing to encounter the Spaniards, if they returned by either of these roads; and he ordered Souham to take post in front of Valls, with his left on the Francoli river, his right towards Pla, and his advanced guard at Pixa Moxons, to watch for Reding by the road of Momblanch.

The 24th the Spanish General, being in St. Coloma, called a council of war, at which Colonel Doyle, the British military agent, assisted. One party was for fighting St. Cyr, another for retreating to Lerida, a third for attacking Chabran at Igualada, a fourth for regaining the plain of Tarragona. There were many opinions, but neither wisdom nor resolution, and finally Reding, leaving General Wimpfen, with four thousand men, at Santa Coloma, decided to regain Tarragona, and took the route of Momblanch with ten thousand of his best troops, following the Spanish accounts, but St. Cyr says with fifteen thousand. The Captain-General knew that Valls was occupied, and his line of march intercepted; but he imagined the French to be only five or six thousand, for the exact situation and strength of an enemy were particulars that seldom troubled Spanish commanders.

BATTLE OF VALLS.

While in full march without any scouts, at daybreak on the 25th of February, the head of Reding's column was suddenly fired upon at Pixa Moxons by Souham's detachment, which was immediately driven in upon the main body; and this attack being vigorously followed, the whole of that General's division gave way. Under cover of this fight the Spanish baggage and artillery passed the Francoli river, and the road to Tarragona being thus opened, Reding might have effected his retreat without difficulty; but he continued to press Souham until St. Cyr, who had early intelligence of what was passing, came down from Pla upon the left flank of the Spanish army. When the French dragoons, which preceded their infantry, appeared in Souham's line, Reding re-crossed the Francoli and took a position behind that river, intending to retreat from thence in the evening, but his able opponent obliged him again to fight.

At three o'clock the action recommenced. The banks of the Francoli were steep and rugged, and the positions beyond strong and difficult of access, yet the French General wishing, as he himself states, to increase the moral ascendency of his soldiers, forbade the artillery, although well placed for execution, to play on Reding's battalions, lest they should fly before the infantry could reach them! Under this curious arrangement the action was begun by the light troops.

The French, or rather Italian infantry, were superior in number to the Spaniards, and the columns, covered by the skirmishers, passed the river with great alacrity, and ascended the heights under an exceedingly regular fire, which was continued until the attacking troops had nearly reached the summit of the position; then both Swiss and Catalans wavered, and breaking ere the infantry could close with them, were instantly charged by the French cavalry. Reding, after receiving several sabre wounds, saved himself at Tarragona, where the greatest number of the vanquished also took refuge, while the remainder fled in the greatest disorder by the routes of Tortosa and Lerida; the Count of Castel d'Orius and many other superior officers, the artillery and baggage were taken, and four thousand men were killed or wounded. During all these movements and actions, Reding received no assistance from the Somatenes; nor is this surprising, for it may be received as an axiom in war, that armed peasants are only formidable to stragglers and small detachments: when the regular forces engage, the poor countryman, sensible of his own weakness, wisely quits the field.

St. Cyr lost only a thousand men, and on the 26th Souham entered the rich town of Reus, where, contrary to the general custom, the inhabitants remained. Pino then occupied Pla, Alcover and Valls; detachments were sent to Salou and Villa Seca, on the sea-coast west of Tarragona, and Chabot, recalled from Igualada, was posted at Santa Cruz, to watch Wimpfen, who still remained at Santa Coloma de Querault.

The battle of Valls finished the regular warfare in Catalonia. Those detachments, which by the previous movements had been cut off from the main body of the army, joined the Somatenes, and as partisan corps, troubled the communications of the French; but St. Cyr had no longer a regular army to deal with in the field, and Tortosa, which was in a miserably defenceless condition, without provisions, must have fallen, if after the battle any attempt had been made against it. Lazan, indeed, after his defeat near Zaragoza, carried a few men to Tortosa, where he declared himself independent of Reding's command; but this battle and the fall of Zaragoza had stricken terror far and wide; the neighboring provinces, fearing and acting each for its own safety, had no regard to any general plan, and the confusion was universal.

Meanwhile, the fugitives from Valls, joined to the troops already in Tarragona, crowded the latter place, and an infectious disorder breaking out, a great mortality ensued; wherefore St. Cyr, satisfied that sickness should do the work of the sword, begirt the city with a resolution to hold his positions while food could be procured. In this policy he remained steadfast until the middle of March, although Wimpfen attacked and drove Chabran in succession from Igualada, Llacuna, and St. Quinti, to Villa Franca; and although the two Milans and Claros, acting between the Besos and the Llobregat, had cut his communication with Barcelona, and in conjunction with the English squadron, renewed the blockade of that city. This plan appears injudicious; the sickness in Tarragona did not cause it to surrender, and the subjugation of Catalonia was certainly retarded by the cessation of offensive operations. The object of the French General should have been to seize some strong places, such as Tortosa, Tarragona, Gerona, or Lerida, while the terror of defeat was fresh; his inactivity after the battle of Molino del Rey and at this period, enabled the Catalonians to recover confidence, and to put those towns in a state of defence; thus he gained nothing but the barren glory of victory.

Towards the middle of March, the resources of the country being all exhausted, he at last determined to abandon the plains of Tarragona, and take some position where he could feed his troops, cover the projected siege of Gerona, and yet be at hand to relieve Barcelona. The valleys about Vich alone offered all these advantages, but as Claros and the Milans were in force at Molino del Rey, he ordered Chabran to drive them from that point, that the sick and wounded men might be first transferred from Valls to Barcelona.

The 10th of March, Chabran sent a battalion with one piece of artillery on that service, and the Migueletes, thinking it was the advanced guard of a greater force, abandoned the post, but being undeceived, returned, beat the battalion, and took the gun. The 12th, Chabran received orders to march with his whole division, consisting of eight battalions and three squadrons, and he reached the bridge, yet he returned without daring to attack. St. Cyr repeated his orders, and on the 14th the troops, apparently ashamed of their General's irresolution, fell on vigorously, carried the bridge and established themselves on the heights at both sides of the river.*

The communication thus opened, it was found that Duhesme, pressed by the Migueletes without, was also extremely fearful of conspiracies within the walls; his fears, and the villainous conduct of his police, had at last excited the inhabitants to attempt that which their enemies seemed so much to dread.† In March, an insurrection was planned in concert with the Migueletes and the English squadron, and the latter coming close in cannonaded the town on the 10th, expecting that Wimpfen, the Milans, and Claros would have assaulted the gates, which was to have been the signal for the insurrection within. The inhabitants were sanguine of success, because there were above two thousand Spanish pris-

* St. Cyr.
† Ibid.

oners in the city, and outside the walls there were two tercios secretly recruited and maintained by the citizens ; and these men, being without uniforms, constantly passed in and out of the town, yet Duhesme was never able to discover or to prevent them. This curious circumstance is illustrative of the peculiar genius of the Spaniards, which in all matters of surprise and stratagem is unrivalled. The project against the city was, however, baffled by Chabran's actions at Molino del Rey, which occupied the partisan corps outside the walls, and the British squadron, exposed to a heavy gale, and disappointed in the co-operation from the land side, sailed away the 11th.

St. Cyr intended to commence his retrograde movement the 18th, but the 17th a cannonade was heard on the side of Momblanch, which was ascertained to proceed from a detachment of six hundred men, with two guns, under the command of Colonel Briche. This officer, being sent by Mortier to open the communication after the fall of Zaragoza, had forced his way through the Spanish partisan corps, and to favor his return the army halted two days ; but the enterprise, after a trial, appeared so dangerous, that he relinquished it, and attached himself to the seventh corps.

Meanwhile the inactivity that succeeded the battle of Valls, and the timidity displayed by Chabran in the subsequent skirmishes, had depressed the spirits of the troops ; they contemplated the approaching retreat with great uneasiness, and many officers infected with fear advised the General to hide his movements from the enemy ; but he, anxious to restore their confidence, took the part of giving the Spaniards a formal notice of his intentions, desiring Reding to send proper officers to take over the hospitals which had been fitted up at Valls, as well as some French, wounded, that could not be moved. This done, the army commenced its retreat, reached Villa Franca the 21st of March, and the 22d passed the Llobregat, followed, but not molested, by some feeble Spanish detachments. The 23d, Wimpfen, who had rallied the Migueletes of Claros and the Milans, at Tarrasa after the affair of the 24th, was beaten by General Pino, who pursued him to near Manresa, and then foraging the country, returned with provisions sufficient to feed the army without drawing on the magazines of Barcelona.

During these proceedings, Reding died in Tarragona of his wounds. He had been received there with such dissatisfaction after the battle of Valls, that the interference of the British consul was necessary to save him from the first fury of the populace, who were always ready to attribute a defeat to the treachery of the General. His military conduct was, by his own officers, generally and justly condemned, and his skill in war was slight, but his courage and honesty were unquestionable, and he was of distinguisded humanity; at this unhappy period, when the French prisoners in every part of Spain were tortured with the most savage cruelty, and when to refrain from such deeds was to incur suspicion, Reding had the manliness, not only to repress all barbarities within the range of his command, but even to conclude a convention with St. Cyr, under which the wounded men on both sides were to receive decent treatment, and to be exchanged as soon as their hurts were cured.* In his last moments he complained that he had been ill-served as a general; that the Somatenes had not supported him; that his orders were neglected, his plans disclosed to the enemy, and that he could never get true intelligence; complaints which the experience of Moore, Baird, Cradock, and, above all, of Wellington, proved to be applicable to every part of Spain, at every period of the war. Coupigny succeeded Reding, but was soon superseded by Blake, who was appointed Captain-General of the Coronilla, or little crown, a title given to the union of Valencia, Aragon, and Catalonia. The warfare in Aragon being thus ultimately connected with that in Catalonia, a short account of what was passing in the former province will be useful.

When Zaragoza fell, Lannes returned to France, and Mortier, who succeeded him, sent detachments against Monzon, Jaca, Mequinenza, and Lerida. The fort of Monzon, commanding a passage over the Cinca river, was abandoned by the Spaniards, and Jaca surrendered, by which a new and important line of communication was opened with France; but the demonstration against Mequinenza failed, and the summons to Lerida was fruitless. Mortier then quartered his troops on both sides of the Ebro, from Barbastro to Alcañitz, and sent Colonel Briche, as we have seen, to open a communication with the seventh corps. This was in March, and in April Mortier moved with the fifth corps to Castile, leaving Junot with the third corps to hold Aragon; but that officer being sick, soon returned to France, and was replaced by General Suchet. The third corps was now very much reduced; one brigade was employed to protect the communication with Navarre, another was escorting the prisoners from Zaragoza to Bayonne, and many artillery-men and non-commissioned officers had been withdrawn to serve in Germany: thus the number of disposable troops in Aragon did not exceed twelve thousand men under arms.

The weakness of the army gave the new General great uneasiness, which was not allayed when he found that men and officers were discontented and dispirited. Suchet was, however, no ordinary man; with equal vigor and prudence he commenced a system

* St. Cyr.

of discipline in his corps, and of order in his government, that afterwards carried him, with scarcely a check, from one success to another, until he obtained for himself the rank of Marshal, and for his troops the honor of belonging to the only French army in Spain that never suffered any signal reverse. He at first hoped that the battle of Valls, and other defeats sustained by the Spaniards at this period, would give him time to re-organize his corps in tranquillity; but this hope soon vanished. The peasantry, observing the weakness of the third corps, only waited for a favorable opportunity to rise, and the Migueletes and Somatenes of the mountains about Lerida and Mequinenza were, under the command of Pereña and Baget, already in activity.

While Junot still held the command, Blake, drawing troops from Valencia and Tarragona, had joined Lazan, and fixed his quarters at Morella, on the frontier of Aragon. Designing to operate in that province rather than in Catalonia, he endeavored to re-kindle the fire of insurrection; nor was fortune adverse to him, for a part of the garrison of Monzon having made an unsuccessful marauding excursion beyond the Cinca, the citizens fell upon those who remained, and obliged them to abandon that post, which was immediately occupied by Pereña. The Duke of Abrantes then sent eight companies of infantry and thirty cuirassiers to retake the place, but Baget reinforced Pereña, the French were repulsed, and the Cinca suddenly overflowing behind them cut off their retreat; the cavalry, plunging with their horses into the river, escaped by swimming; the infantry, finding the lower passages guarded by the garrison of Lerida, and the upper cut off by the partisan corps, after three days' marching and skirmishing, surrendered. The prisoners were carried to Tarragona, and soon afterwards exchanged, in pursuance of a convention made by Reding and St. Cyr.

This slight success excited the most extravagant hopes, and the garrison of Mequinenza having contrived to burn the bridge of boats which the French had thrown over the Ebro at Caspe, Blake drove the French from Beceyta and Val de Ajorfa, and entered Alcañitz. The beaten troops retired with loss to Samper and Ixar; and it was at this moment, when the quarters on both sides of the Ebro were harassed, and the wings of the third corps separated by the destruction of the bridge at Caspe, that Suchet arrived to take the command of the third corps. Finding his troops spread over a great tract of country, and in danger of being beaten in detail, he immediately ordered General Habert to abandon the left bank of the Ebro, cross that river at Fuentes, and follow in reserve upon Ixar, where Suchet himself rallied all the rest of the troops, with the exception of a small garrison left in Zaragoza.

BATTLE OF ALCANITZ.

The French battalions were fearful and disorderly; but the General, anxious to raise their spirits, marched towards Blake on the 23d of May.* The latter was in position in front of Alcañitz; a bridge over the Guadalupe was immediately behind his centre, which was covered by a hill, and his left was well posted near some pools of water, but his right was rather exposed. The French had about eight thousand infantry and seven hundred cavalry in the field, and the Spaniards about twelve thousand of all arms.

Suchet, observing Blake's dispositions, judged that, if he could carry the hill in the centre and so separate the Spanish wings, the latter would be cut off from the bridge of Alcañitz, and obliged to surrender. In this design he directed a column against each wing to draw Blake's attention to his flanks, and when the skirmishers were well engaged, three thousand men, pushing rapidly along the main road, attacked the hillock; but a brisk fire of musketry and artillery checked their progress, the Spaniards stood firm, and the French, after a feeble effort to ascend the hill, began to waver, and finally fled outright. Suchet, who was himself slightly wounded, rallied them in the plain, and remained there for the rest of the day, but without daring to renew the action. In the night he retreated, but, although not pursued, his troops were seized with panic, and, at daylight, came pouring into Samper with all the tumult and disorder of a rout. Blake's inactivity enabled the French General to restore order, and he caused the man who first commenced the alarm to be shot; then encouraging the troops, that they might not seem to fly, he rested in position two whole days, after which he retreated to Zaragoza.

This action at Alcañitz was a subject of triumph and rejoicing all over Spain; the Supreme Junta conferred an estate upon Blake; the kingdom of Murcia was added to his command, his army rapidly augmented, and he, greatly elated and confirmed in a design he had formed to retake Zaragoza, turned his whole attention to Aragon, and totally neglected Catalonia. To the affairs of that province it is now time to return.

St. Cyr remained in Barcelona for a considerable period, during which he endeavored to remedy the evils of Duhesme's government, and to make himself acquainted with the political disposition of the inhabitants. He also filled the magazines with three months' provisions, and, as the prisoners within the walls were an encumbrance on account of their subsistence, and a source of uneasiness from their numbers, he resolved to send them to France. The 15th of

* Suchet's Memoirs,

April, having transferred his sick and weakly men to the charge of Duhesme, and exchanged Chabran's for Lecchi's division, he marched to Granollers, giving out that he was returning to the frontier of France, lest the Catalans should remove their provisions from Vich, and thus frustrate his principal object.

The Migueletes, under Milans and Claros, had taken post on each side of the long and narrow defile of Garriga, in the valley of the Congosto, which they barricadoed with trees and pieces of rock, and mined in several places; Wimpfen with his corps was also at a little distance, ready to join them at the first alarm. Hence, when on the 16th Lecchi's division, escorting two thousand prisoners, appeared at the head of the defile, an action commenced, but in an hour the Migueletes fled on all sides; for St. Cyr, fully aware of the strength of the position, had secretly detached Pino to attack Wimpfen, and, while Lecchi was engaged at the entrance, Souham and Chabot, traversing the mountains, arrived, the one upon the flank, the other at the further end of this formidable pass.

The 18th, the French were established at Vich; the inhabitants had fled to the hills with their effects, but left their provisions behind. Chabot's and Pino's division were immediately posted at Centellas, San Martin, Tona, and Col de Sespino, to guard the entrances into the valley, but Souham's division remained near the town, his right being at Roda and Manlieu on the Ter, and his advanced posts at Gurp, St. Sebastian, and St. Eularia. General Lecchi then marched with the prisoners by Filieu de Pallerols to Besalu, and although he was attacked several times on the march, delivered his charge to General Reille, and returned without loss, bringing news of Napoleon's arrival in Paris, and of the approaching war with Austria. On the other side, a movable column sent to Barcelona brought back the pleasing intelligence that Admiral Cosmao's squadron, baffling the extreme vigilance of Lord Collingwood, had reached that city with ample supplies. Thus, in May, what may be called the irregular movements in Catalonia terminated, and the more methodical warfare of sieges commenced; but this part was committed to other hands; General Verdier had succeeded Reille in the Ampurdan, and Marshal Augereau was on the road to supersede St. Cyr.

OBSERVATIONS.—1. Although his marches were hardy, his battles vigorous, and delivered in right time and place, St. Cyr's campaign may be characterized as one of great efforts without corresponding advantages. He himself attributes this to the condition of the seventh corps, destitute and neglected, because *the Emperor disliked and wished to ruin its chief;* a strange accusation, and unsustained by reason or facts. What! Napoleon wilfully

destroy his own armies! sacrifice forty thousand men, to disgrace
a general whom he was not obliged to employ at all! St. Cyr
acknowledges that when he received his instructions from the Emperor, he observed the affliction of the latter at the recent loss of
Dupont's force, yet he would have it believed, that, in the midst
of this regret, that monarch, with a singular malice, was preparing
greater disasters for himself, merely to disgrace the commander he
was talking to; and why? because the latter had formerly served
with the army of the Rhine! Yet St. Cyr met with no reverses in
Catalonia, and was afterwards made a Marshal by this implacable
enemy.

2. That the seventh corps was not well supplied, and its commander thereby placed in a difficult situation, is not to be disputed
in the face of the facts stated by St. Cyr; but if war were a state
of ease and smoothness, the fame which attends successful generals
would be unmerited. Napoleon selected St. Cyr because he
thought him a capable commander; in feeble hands, he knew the
seventh corps would be weak, but, with St Cyr at its head, he
judged it sufficient to overcome the Catalonians, nor was he much
mistaken. Barcelona, the great object of solicitude, was saved;
Rosas was taken; and if Tarragona and Tortosa did not also
fall, the one after the battle of Molino del Rey, the other after that
of Valls, it was because the French General did not choose to attack
them. Those towns were without the slightest preparation for
defence, moral or physical, and must have surrendered; nor can
the unexpected and stubborn resistance of Gerona, Zaragoza, and
Valencia be cited against this opinion; these cities were previously
prepared and expectant of a siege, yet, in two instances, there was
a moment of dismay and confusion, not fatal, only because the besieging generals wanted that ready vigor which is the characteristic of great captains.

3. St. Cyr, aware that a mere calculation of numbers and equipment is but a poor measure of the strength of armies, exalts the
enthusiasm and the courage of the Catalans, and seems to tremble
at the danger which, owing to Napoleon's suicidal jealousy, menaced, at that period, not only the seventh corps but even the south
of France. In answer to this, it may be observed that M. de St.
Cyr did not hesitate, with eighteen thousand men, having no artillery and carrying only sixty rounds of musket-ammunition, to
plunge into the midst of those terrible armies; to march through
the mountains for whole weeks; to attack the strongest positions
with the bayonet alone, nay, even to dispense with the use of his
artillery, when he did bring it into action, lest his men should not
have a sufficient contempt for their enemies. And who were these

undaunted soldiers, so high in courage, so confident, so regardless of the great weapon of modern warfare? Not the select of the imperial guards, the conquerors in a hundred battles, but raw levies; the dregs and scrapings of Italy, the refuse of Naples and of Rome; states which to name as military was to ridicule. With such soldiers, the battles of Cardadeu, Molino, Igualada, and Valls were gained; yet St. Cyr does not hesitate to call the Migueletes, who were beaten at those places, the best light troops in the world. The best *light troops* are neither more nor less than the best troops in the world; but if, instead of fifteen thousand Migueletes, the four thousand men composing Wellington's light division had been on the heights of Cardadeu, St. Cyr's sixty rounds of ammunition would scarcely have carried him to Barcelona. The injurious force with which personal feelings act upon the judgment are well known, or it might excite wonder that so good a writer and so able a soldier should advance such fallacies.

4. St. Cyr's work, admirable in many respects, bears, nevertheless, the stamp of carelessness. Thus, he affirms that Dupont's march to Andalusia encouraged the tumults of Aranjuez, yet the tumults of Aranjuez happened in the month of March, nearly three months previous to Dupont's movement, which took place in May and June. Again, he says that Napoleon, to make a solid conquest in the Peninsula, should have commenced with Catalonia, instead of overrunning Spain by the northern line of operations; an opinion quite unsustainable. The progress of the seventh corps was impeded by the want of provisions, not by the enemy's force; twenty thousand men could beat the Spaniards in the field, but they could not subsist. To have increased the number would only have increased the difficulty. Would it have given a just idea of Napoleon's power, to employ the strength of his empire against the fortified towns in Catalonia? In what would the greater solidity of this plan have consisted? While the French were thus engaged, the patriots would have been organizing their armies; England would have had time to bring all her troops into line, and two hundred thousand men placed between Zaragoza and Tortosa, or breaking into France by the western Pyrenees, while the Austrians were advancing to the Rhine, would have sorely shaken the solidity of General St. Cyr's plan.

5. The French Emperor better understood what he was about. He saw a nation intrinsically powerful and vehemently excited, yet ignorant of war and wanting the aid which England was eager to give. All the elements of power existed in the Peninsula, and they were fast approximating to a centre, when Napoleon burst upon that country, and as the gathering of a water-spout is said to

be sometimes prevented by the explosion of a gun, so the rising strength of Spain was dissipated by his sudden and dreadful assault; if the war was not then finished, it was because his lieutenants were tardy and jealous of each other. St. Cyr also appears to have fallen into an error, common enough in all times, and one very prevalent among the French generals in Spain. He considered his task as a whole in itself, instead of a constituent part of a greater system. He judged very well what was wanting for the seventh corps, to subjugate Catalonia in a solid manner, but he did not discern that it was fitting that the seventh corps should forget Catalonia, to aid the general plan against the Peninsula. Rosas surrendered at the very moment when Napoleon, after the victories of Baylen, Espinosa, Tudela, and the Somosierra, was entering Madrid as a conqueror; the battles of Cardadeu and Molino del Rey may, therefore, be said to have completely prostrated Spain, because the English army was isolated, the Spanish armies destroyed, and Zaragoza invested. Was that a time to calculate the weight of powder and the number of pick-axes required for a formal siege of Tarragona? The whole Peninsula was shaken to the centre, the proud hearts of the Spaniards sunk with terror, and in that great consternation, to be daring was, on the part of the French generals, to be prudent. St. Cyr was not in a condition to besiege Tarragona formally, but he might have assaulted it with less danger than he incurred by his march to Barcelona. The battle of Valls was another epoch of the same kind; the English army had re-embarked, and the rout of Ucles had taken place; Portugal was invaded and Zaragoza had just fallen. That was a time to render victory fruitful, yet no attempt was made against Tortosa.

6. St. Cyr, who justly blames Palacios and Vives for remaining before Barcelona instead of carrying their army to the Ter and the Fluvia, seems inclined to applaud Reding for conduct equally at variance with the true principles of war. It was his own inactivity after the battle of Molino that produced the army of Reding, and the impatient folly of that army, and of the people, produced the plan which led to the rout of Igualada and the battle of Valls. Instead of disseminating thirty thousand men in a line of sixty miles, from Tarragona to the upper Llobregat, Reding should have put Tarragona and Tortosa into a state of defence, and leaving a small corps of observation near the former, have made Lerida the base of his operations. In that position, keeping the bulk of his force in one mass, he might have acted on St. Cyr's flanks and rear effectually, by the lines of Cervera and Momblanch—and without

danger to himself; nor could the French General have attempted aught against Tarragona.

But it is not with reference to the seventh corps alone that Lerida was the proper base of the Spanish army. Let us suppose that the Supreme Junta had acted for a moment upon a rational system; that the Valencian troops, instead of remaining at Morella, had been directed on Lerida, and that the Duke of Infantado's force had been carried from Cuença to the same place instead of being routed at Ucles. Thus, in the beginning of February, more than fifty thousand regular troops would have been assembled at Lerida, encircled by the fortresses of Monzon, Belaguer, Mequinenza, Tarragona, and Tortosa. Its lines of operations would have been as numerous as the roads. The Seu d'Urgel, called the granary of Catalonia, would have supplied corn, and the communication with Valencia would have been direct and open. From this central and menacing position, such a force might have held the seventh corps in check, and even raised the siege of Zaragoza; nor could the first corps have followed Infantado's movements without uncovering Madrid and abandoning the system of the Emperor's operations against Portugal and Andalusia.

7. The French General praises Reding's project for surrounding the French, and very gravely observes that the *only method* of defeating it was by taking the offensive himself. Nothing can be juster; but he should have added that it was a *certain method;* and, until we find a great commander acting upon Reding's principles, this praise can only be taken as an expression of civility towards a brave adversary. His own movements were very different; he disliked Napoleon personally, but he did not dislike his manner of making war. Bonaparte's campaign in the Alps against Beaulieu was not unheeded by his lieutenant. For one proceeding of St. Cyr's, however, there is no precedent, nor is it likely that it will ever be imitated. He stopped the fire of his artillery, when it was doing infinite execution, the better to establish the moral ascendency of his troops. What a sarcasm on the courage of his enemies! What a complete answer to his own complaints that Napoleon had maliciously given him a hopeless task! But, he says, his adversaries were numerous and fought bravely! Surely he could not have commanded so long without knowing *that there is in all battles a decisive moment, when every weapon, every man, every combination of force that can be brought to bear, is necessary to gain the victory.* Wilfully to neglect the means of reducing the enemy's strength, previous to that critical period of an action, is a gross folly.

8. If General St. Cyr's own marches and battles did not sufficiently expose the fallacy of his opinions relative to the vigor of
the Catalans, Lord Collingwood's correspondence would supply
the deficiency. That able and sagacious man, writing at this
period, says:

"In Catalonia, everything seems to have gone wrong since the
fall of Rosas. The Spaniards are in considerable force, yet are
dispersed and panic-struck whenever the enemy appears."—"The
applications for supplies are unlimited; they want money, arms,
and ammunition, of which no use appears to be made when they
get them."—"In the English papers, I see accounts of successes,
and convoys cut off, and wagons destroyed, which are not true.
What has been done in that way has been by the boats of our
frigates, which have, in two or three instances, landed men and
attacked the enemy with great gallantry. The Somatenes range the
hills in a disorderly way, and fire at a distance, but retire on being
approached."—"The multitudes of men do not make a force."

Add to this the Spanish historian Cabanes' statements that the
Migueletes were always insubordinate, detested the service of the
line, and were many of them armed only with staves, and we have
the full measure of the Catalans' resistance.

It was not the vigor of the Catalans, but of the English, that in
this province, as in every part of the Peninsula, retarded the progress of the French. Would St. Cyr have wasted a month before
Rosas; would he have been hampered in his movements by his
fears for the safety of Barcelona; would he have failed to besiege
and take Tarragona and Tortosa, if a French fleet had attended
his progress by the coast, or if it could even have made two runs
in safety? To Lord Collingwood, who, like the Roman Bibulus,
perished of sickness on his decks rather than relax in his watching,—to his keen judgment, his unceasing vigilance, the resistance
made by the Catalans was due. His fleet it was that interdicted
the coast line to the French, protected the transport of the Spanish
supplies from Valencia, assisted in the defence of the towns, aided
the retreat of the beaten armies; in short, did that which the
Spanish fleets in Cadiz and Carthagena should have done. But
the Supreme Junta, equally disregarding the remonstrances of
Lord Collingwood, the good of their own country, and the treaty
with England, by which they were bound to prevent their ships
from falling into the hands of the enemy, left their fleets to rot in
harbor, although money was advanced, and the assistance of the
British seamen offered to fit them out for sea.

Having now related the principal operations that took place in the eastern and central provinces of Spain, which were so suddenly overrun by the French Emperor; having shown that, however restless the Spaniards were under the yoke imposed upon them, they were unable to throw it off; I shall turn to Portugal, where the tide of invasion, still flowing onward, although with diminished volume, was first stayed, and finally forced back, by a counter flood of mightier strength.

BOOK VI.

CHAPTER I.

TRANSACTIONS IN PORTUGAL.

When Sir John Moore marched from Portugal, the Regency, established by Sir Hew Dalrymple, nominally governed that country; but the weak character of the members, the listless habits engendered by the ancient system of misrule, the intrigues of the Oporto faction, and the general turbulence of the people, soon produced an alarming state of anarchy. Private persons usurped the functions of government, justice was disregarded, insubordination and murder were hailed as indications of patriotism, and war was the universal cry; yet military preparations were wholly neglected, for the nation, in its foolish pride, believed that the French had neither strength nor spirit for a second invasion.

In Lisbon there was a French faction; the merchants were apprehensive, the Regency unpopular, and the public mind unsettled; in Oporto, the violence of both people and soldiers was such that Sir Harry Burrard sent two British regiments there by sea, to preserve tranquillity; in fine, the seeds of disorder were widely cast and sprouting vigorously before the English Cabinet thought fit to accredit a responsible diplomatist near the government, or to place a permanent chief at the head of the forces left by Sir John Moore. The convention of Cintra was known in England in September; the Regency was established and the frontier fortresses occupied by British troops in the same month; yet it was not until the middle of December that Mr. Villiers and Sir John Cradock, charged with the conduct of the political and military proceedings in Portugal, reached Lisbon; thus the important interval between the departure of Junot and their arrival was totally neglected by the English Cabinet.

Sir Hew Dalrymple, who had nominated the Regency; Sir Arthur Wellesley, who to local knowledge and powerful talents added the influence of a victorious commander, Burrard, Spencer, were all removed from Portugal at the very moment when the presence of persons acquainted with the real state of affairs was essential to the well-being of the British interests in that country. And this error was the offspring of passion and incapacity; for, if the convention of Cintra had been rightly understood, the ministers, appreciating the advantages of that treaty, would have resisted the clamor of the moment, and the generals would not have been withdrawn from the public service abroad, to meet unjust and groundless charges at home.

It may be disputed whether Portugal was the fittest theatre for the first operations of a British army; but, when that country was actually freed from the presence of an enemy; when the capital and the frontier fortresses were occupied by English troops; when Sir John Moore, leaving his hospitals, baggage, and magazines there, as in a place of arms, had marched to Spain, the question was no longer doubtful. The ancient relations between England and Portugal, the greatness of the port of Lisbon, the warlike disposition of the Portuguese; above all, the singularly happy circumstance, that there was neither court nor monarch to balance the English influence, and that even the nomination of the Regency was the work of an English General, offered such great and obvious advantages as could nowhere else be obtained. It was a miserable policy that, neglecting such an occasion, retained Sir Arthur Wellesley in England, while Portugal, like a drunken man, at once weak and turbulent, was reeling on the edge of a precipice.

The 5th of December, 1808, Sir John Cradock, being on his voyage to Lisbon, touched at Coruña. Fifteen hundred thousand dollars had just arrived there in the Lavinia frigate, but Sir John Moore's intention to retreat upon Portugal being known, Cradock divided this sum, and carried away eight hundred thousand dollars; proposing to leave a portion at Oporto, and to take the remainder to Lisbon, that Moore might find, on whatever line he retreated, a supply of money.

From Coruña he proceeded to Oporto, where he found that Sir Robert Wilson had succeeded in organizing, under the title of the Lusitanian Legion, about thirteen hundred men, and that others were on their way to reinforce him; but this excepted, nothing civil or military bespoke either arrangement or common sense. The Bishop, still intent upon acquiring supreme rule, was deeply engaged with secret intrigues, and under him, a number of factious and designing persons instigated the populace to violent actions with a view to profit from their excesses.

The formation of this Lusitanian Legion was originally a project of the Chevalier da Souza, Portuguese Minister in London ; he was one of the Bishop's faction, and this force was raised not so much to repel the enemy, as to support that party against the government. The men were promised higher pay than any other Portuguese soldiers, to the great discontent of the latter ; and they were clad in uniforms differing in color from the national troops. The Regency, who dreaded the machinations of the turbulent priest, entertained the utmost jealousy of this legion, which, in truth, was a most anomalous force, and, as might be expected from its peculiar constitution, was productive of much embarrassment.

Sir John Cradock left three hundred thousand dollars at Oporto, and directed the two British battalions which were in that neighborhood to march to Almeida ; then taking on board a small detachment of German troops, he set sail for Lisbon. Before his departure, he strongly advised Sir Robert Wilson to move such of his legionaries as were sufficiently organized to Villa Real, in Tras os Montes, a place appointed by the Regency for the assembly of the forces in the north ; Sir Robert, tired of the folly and disgusted with the insolence and excesses of the ruling mob, readily adopted this advice, so far as to quit Oporto, but having views of his own, went to Almeida instead of Villa Real.

The state of the capital was little better than that of Oporto. There was arrangement neither for present nor for future defence, and the populace, albeit less openly encouraged to commit excesses, were quite uncontrolled by the government. The Regency had a keener dread of domestic insurrection than of the return of the French, whose operations they regarded with even less anxiety than the Bishop did, as being further removed than he was from the immediate theatre of war. Their want of system and vigilance was evinced by the following fact. Sattaro and another person, having contracted for the supply of the British troops, demanded, in the name of the English General, all the provisions in the public stores of Portugal, and then sold them to the English commissaries for his own profit.

Sir John Cradock's instructions directed him to reinforce Moore's army, and not to interfere with that General's command if the course of events brought him back to Portugal. In fact, his operations were limited to the holding of Elvas, Almeida, and the capital; for, although he was directed to encourage the formation of a native army upon a good and regular system, and even to act in concert with it on the frontier, he was debarred from political interference; even his relative situation as to rank was left unsettled until the arrival of Mr. Villiers, to whose direction all political and many military arrangements were intrusted.

It is evident that the influence of a general thus fettered, and commanding only a small scattered force, must be feeble and insufficient to produce any real amelioration in the military situation of the country; yet the English ministers, attentive only to the false information obtained from interested agents, still imagined that not only the Spanish, but the Portuguese armies were numerous, and to be relied upon; and they confidently expected that the latter would be able to take an active part in the Spanish campaign. Cradock, feeling the danger of this illusion, made it his first object to transmit home exact information of the real strength and efficiency of the native regular troops. They were nominally twenty thousand; but Miguel Pereira Forjas, military secretary to the Regency, and the ablest public man Portugal possessed, acknowledged that this force was a nullity, and that there were not more than ten thousand stand of serviceable arms in the kingdom, the greatest part of which were English.* The troops themselves were undisciplined and unruly; the militia and the "ordenanza," or armed peasantry, animated by the spirit of outrage rather than of enthusiasm, evinced no disposition to submit to regulation; neither was there any branch of administration free from the grossest disorder.

The Spanish dollar had a general acceptance in Portugal. The Regency, under the pretence that a debased foreign coin would drive the Portuguese coin out of circulation, deprived the dollar of its current value. This regulation, true in principle, and applicable, as far as the Portuguese gold coin (which is of peculiar fineness) was concerned, had, however, a most injurious effect. The Spanish dollar was in reality finer than the Portuguese silver cruzado-nova, and would finally have maintained its value, notwithstanding this decree, if the slur thus thrown upon it by the government had not enabled the money changers to run its value down for the moment; a matter of infinite importance, for the English soldiers and sailors being all paid in these dollars, at four shillings and sixpence, which was the true value, were thus suddenly mulcted fourpence in each, by the artificial depreciation of the moment. The men attributed this to fraud in the shop-keepers, the retail trade of Lisbon was interrupted, and quarrels between the tradesmen and the soldiers

* Cradock's Correspondence, MS.

took place hourly. To calm this effervescence, a second decree was promulgated, directing that the dollar should be received at the mint and in the public offices at its real value; it then appeared that the government could profit by coining the dollar of four shillings and sixpence into cruzado-novas, a circumstance which gave the whole affair the appearance of an unworthy trick to recruit the treasury. This happened in October, and as the financial affairs were ill-managed, and the Regency destitute of vigor or capacity, the taxes were unpaid, the hard cash exhausted, and the treasury paper at a heavy discount when Cradock arrived.

Upon the scroll thus unfolded he could only read confusion, danger and misfortune; such being the fruits of victory, what could be expected from disaster! And at this period (the middle of December) Sir John Moore was supposed to be in full retreat upon Portugal, followed by the Emperor with one French army, while another threatened Lisbon by the line of the Tagus. The English troops in the kingdom did not amount to ten thousand men, including the sick, and they were ill-equipped and scattered; moreover, the capital was crowded with women and children, with baggage and non-combatants, belonging as well to the army in Spain as to that in Portugal. There were in the river three Portuguese ships of the line, two frigates, and eight other smaller vessels of war; but none were in a state for sea, and the whole likely to fall into the hands of the enemy, for in the midst of this confusion Sir Charles Cotton was recalled, without a successor being appointed. The zeal and talents of Captain Halket, the senior officer on the station, amply compensated for the departure of the Admiral, as far as professional duties were concerned; but he could not aid the General, nor deal with the Regency, as vigorously as an officer of higher rank, and formally accredited, could have done.

Sir John Cradock, although fully sensible of his own difficulties, with a very disinterested zeal, resolved to make the reinforcing of Sir John Moore's army his first care, but his force at this time was, as I have already said, less than ten thousand men of all arms. It consisted of eight British and four German battalions of infantry, four troops of dragoons, and thirty pieces of artillery, of which, however, only six were horsed so as to take the field. There was, also, a battalion of the 60th regiment, composed principally of Frenchmen recruited from the prison ships, but it had been sent back from Spain, as the soldiers could not be trusted near their countrymen.* Of these thirteen battalions two were in Abrantes, one in Elvas, three at Lamego on the Duero, one in Almeida, and the remaining six at Lisbon. Three of the four battalions in

* Sir J. Cradock's Papers, MS.

the north were immediately directed to join Sir John Moore by the route of Salamanca, and of those in the south, two, accompanied by a demi-brigade of artillery, were sent to him from Abrantes, by the road of Castello Branco and Ciudad Rodrigo.

Meanwhile Mr. Villiers arrived, and Sir John Cradock forwarded to the Regency a strong representation of the dangerous state of Portugal. He observed that there was neither activity in the government nor enthusiasm among the people; that the army, deficient in numbers, and still more in discipline, was scattered and neglected, and, notwithstanding that the aspect of affairs was so threatening, the Regency were apparently without any system, or fixed principle of action. He proposed, therefore, that a general enrolment of all the people should take place, and from the British stores he offered a supply of a thousand muskets and ten thousand pikes.* This giving of pikes to the people, which appears to have been in compliance with Mr. Villiers' wishes, betrayed more zeal than prudence; a general levy, and arming with pikes of the turbulent populace of a capital city, at such a conjuncture, was more likely to lead to confusion and mischief than to any effectual defence. The main objects pressing upon the General's attention were however sufficiently numerous and contradictory, to render it difficult for him to avoid errors.

It was a part of his instructions, and of manifest importance, to send reinforcements to Sir John Moore; yet it was equally necessary to keep a force towards the frontier on the line of the Tagus, seeing that the fourth French corps had just passed that river at Almaraz, had defeated Galluzzo's army and menaced Badajos, which was without arms, ammunition, or provisions; moreover, the populace there were in commotion and slaying the chief persons. Now, Sir John Cradock's instructions directed him to keep his troops in a position that would enable him to abandon Portugal, if a very superior force should press him; but as, in such a case, he was to carry off the British army and the Portuguese navy and stores, destroying what he could not remove, and to receive on board his vessels all the natives who might be desirous of escaping, it was of pressing necessity to ship the women, children, baggage, and other encumbrances belonging to Moore's army, immediately, that his own rear might be clear for a sudden embarkation. In short, he was to send his troops to Spain, and yet defend Portugal; to excite confidence in the Portuguese, and yet openly to carry on the preparations for abandoning that country.

The populace of Lisbon were, however, already uneasy at the rumors of an embarkation, and it was doubtful if they would per-

* Sir J. Cradock's Correspondence, MS.

mit even the British non-combatants to get on board quietly, much less suffer the forts to be dismantled, and the ships of war to be carried off, without a tumult, which, at such a conjuncture, would have been fatal to all parties. Hence it was imperative to maintain a strong garrison in Lisbon and in the forts commanding the mouth of the river, and this draft, together with the troops absorbed by the fortresses of Almeida and Elvas, reduced the fighting men in the field to insignificance.

The Regency, knowing the temper of the people, and fearing to arm them, were not very eager to enforce the levy; anxious, however, to hide their weakness, they promised, at the urgent solicitations of the English General, to send six thousand troops to Alcantara, on the Spanish frontier, with a view to observe the march of the fourth corps, a promise which they never intended, and indeed were unable to perform. Forjas, who was supposed to be very inimical to the British influence, frankly declared that they neither could nor would move without an advance of money, and Sir John Cradock, although he recommended that this aid should be given, had no power to grant it himself.

Letters from Sir John Moore, dated at Salamanca, now reached Lisbon; they increased the anxiety to reinforce the army in Spain, but, as they clearly showed that reverses were to be expected, Cradock, although resolved to maintain himself in Portugal as long as it was possible to do so without a breach of his instructions, felt more strongly that timely preparation for an embarkation should be made; especially as the rainy season, in which the south-west winds prevail, had set in, and rendered the departure of vessels from the Tagus very uncertain.* Meanwhile the internal state of Portugal was in no wise amended, or likely to amend.

The government had, indeed, issued a decree, on the 23d of December, for organizing the population of Lisbon in sixteen legions, but only one battalion of each was to parade at the same moment for exercise, and those only on Sundays, nor were the legions, at any time, to assemble without the order of the general commanding the province; this regulation, which rendered the whole measure absurd, was dictated by the fears of the Regency. A proposal to prepare the Portuguese vessels for sea was acceded to, without any apparent dissatisfaction, but the government, secretly jealous of their allies, fomented or encouraged discontent and suspicion among the people. No efforts were made to improve the regular force, none to forward the march of troops to Alcantara, and so inactive or so callous were the Regency to the rights of humanity, that a number of French prisoners, captured at various

* Sir J. Cradock's Correspondence, MS.

periods by the Portuguese, and accumulated at Lisbon, were denied subsistence; Sir John Cradock, after many fruitless representations, was forced to charge himself with their supply, to avert the horror of seeing them starved to death. The provisions necessary for Fort La Lippe were also withheld, and General Leite, acting upon the authority of the Regency, strenuously urged that the British troops should evacuate that fortress.

The march of the reinforcements for Sir John Moore left only three hundred dragoons and seven battalions available for the defence of Portugal, of which four were necessarily in garrison, and the remainder were unable to take the field in default of mules, of which animal the country seemed bereft; yet, at this moment, as if in derision, Mr. Frere, the Central Junta, the Junta of Badajos, and the Regency of Portugal, were, with common and characteristic foolishness, pressing Sir John Cradock to march into the south of Spain, although there was scarcely a Spanish soldier there in arms to assist him; and such a movement, if it had been either prudent or practicable, was directly against his instructions.*

Towards the end of December, the communication with Sir John Moore was suddenly interrupted, and the line of the Tagus acquired great importance. The troops going from Elvas to the army in Spain were therefore directed to halt at Castello Branco, and General Richard Stewart, who commanded them, being reinforced with two hundred cavalry, was ordered, for the moment, to watch the roads by Salvatierra and the two Idanhas, and to protect the flying bridges at Abrantes and Vilha Velha from the enemy's incursions. At the same time, a promise was obtained from the Regency that all the Portuguese troops in the Alemtejo should be collected at Campo Mayor and Portalegre.

Sir John Cradock fixed upon Sacavem as the position in which his main body should be concentrated, intending to defend that point as long as he could with so few troops; and as he knew that Almeida, although full of British stores, and important in every way, was, with respect to its own defence, utterly neglected by the Regency, who regarded with jealousy even the presence of a British force there, he sent Brigadier-General A. Cameron, with instructions collect the convalescents of Moore's army, to unite them with the two battalions still at Almeida, and then to make his way to the army in Spain; but if that should be judged too dangerous, he was to return to Lisbon.† In either case, the stores and the sick men lying at Almeida were to be directed upon Oporto.

The paucity of cavalry was severely felt on the frontier; it pre-

* Sir J. Cradock's Correspondence, MS.
† Ibid.

vented the General from ascertaining the real strength and objects of the enemy's parties, and the Portuguese reports were notoriously contradictory and false. The 14th dragoons, seven hundred strong, commanded by Major-General Cotton, had been disembarked since the 22d of December, and were destined for the army in Spain. But the commissary doubted if he could forward that small body even by detachments, such was the penury of the country, or rather the difficulty of drawing forth its resources; many debts of Sir John Moore's army were also still unpaid, and a want of confidence prevented the country people from bringing in supplies upon credit.

In the midst of these difficulties rumors of reverses in Spain became rife, and acquired importance, when it became known that four thousand infantry and two thousand cavalry, the advanced guard of thirty thousand French troops, were actually at Merida, on the road to Badajos; the latter town being, not only in a state of anarchy, but destitute of provisions, arms, and ammunition. Had the Portuguese force been assembled at Alcantara, Sir John Cradock would have supported it with the Britsh brigades from Abrantes and Castello Branco, but not a man had been put in motion, and he, feeling no confidence either in the troops or promises of the Regency, resolved to concentrate his own army near Lisbon. General Stewart was, therefore, directed to destroy the bridges of Vilha Velha and Abrantes, and fall back to Sacavem. Meanwhile, the Lisbon populace, supposing that the English General designed to abandon them without necessity, were violently excited. The Regency, either from fear or folly, made no effort to preserve tranquillity, and the people proceeded from one excess to another, until it became evident that, in a forced embarkation, the British would have to fight their allies as well as their enemies. At this gloomy period, when ten marches would have brought the French to Lisbon, when a stamp of Napoleon's foot would have extinguished that spark of war which afterwards blazed over the Peninsula, Sir John Moore made his daring movement upon Sahagun, and Portugal, gasping as in a mortal agony, was instantly relieved.

CHAPTER II.

It was the advanced guard of the fourth corps that had approached Merida with the intention of proceeding to Badajos, and
the Emperor was, as we have seen, preparing to follow; but, in the
night of the 26th of December, an officer carrying the intelligence
of Moore's movement reached Merida, and, next morning, the
French marching hastily to the Tagus, crossed it, and rejoined their
main body, from which another powerful detachment was immediately directed upon Placentia. This retrograde movement obviated
the immediate danger, and Sir John Cradock endeavored to pacify
the people of Lisbon. Ordering Stewart's brigade, which had been
strengthened by two German battalions, to halt at Santarem, he explained his own motives to the Portuguse, and urged the Regency
to a more frank and vigorous system than they had hitherto fol-
followed; for, like the Spanish juntas, they promised everything,
and performed nothing; neither would they, although consenting
verbally to all the measures proposed, ever commit themselves by
writing, having the despicable intention of afterwards disclaiming
that which might prove disagreeable to the populace, or even to the
French. Sir John Cradock, however, had no power beyond his
own personal influence to enforce attention to his wishes; no successor to Sir Charles Cotton had yet arrived, and Mr. Villiers seems
to have wanted the decision and judgment required to meet such a
momentous crisis.

In the north, General Cameron, having sent the sick men and
part of the stores from Almeida towards Oporto, gave up that fortress to Sir Robert Wilson, and on the 5th of January marched,
with two British battalions and a detachment of convalescents, by
the Tras os Montes, to join the army in Spain. On the 9th, hearing of Sir John Moore's retreat to Coruña, he would have returned
to Almeida, but Lapisse, who had taken Zamora, threatened to in-

tercept his line of march, whereupon he made for Lamego, and advised Sir R. Wilson to retire to the same place. Colonel Blunt, with seven companies, escorting a convoy for Moore's army, was likewise forced to take the road to Oporto, and on that city all the British stores and detachments were now directed.

Notwithstanding the general dismay, Sir R. Wilson, who had been reinforced by some Spanish troops, Portuguese volunteers, and straggling convalescents of the British army, rejected Cameron's advice, and proceeded to practise all the arts of an able partisan—that is to say, enticing the French to desert, spreading false reports of his own numbers, and, by petty enterprises and great activity, arousing a spirit of resistance throughout the Ciudad Rodrigo country.

The continued influx of sick men and stores at Oporto, together with the prospect of General Cameron's arrival there, became a source of uneasiness to Sir John Cradock. Oporto, with a shifting bar and shoal water, is the worst possible harbor for vessels to clear out, and one of the most dangerous for vessels to lie off, at that season of the year; hence, if the enemy advanced in force, a great loss, both of men and stores, was to be anticipated. The departure of Sir Charles Cotton had diminished the naval means, and, for seventeen successive days, such was the state of the wind that no vessel could leave the Tagus; Captain Halket, however, contrived at last to send to Oporto tonnage for two thousand persons, and undertook to keep a sloop of war off that place.* Sir Samuel Hood also dispatched some vessels from Vigo, but the weather continued for a long time so unfavorable that these transports could not enter the harbor, and the encumbrances hourly increasing, at last produced the most serious embarrassments.

Sir John Moore having now relinquished his communications with Portugal, Sir John Cradock had to consider how, relying on his own resources, he could best fulfil his instructions and maintain his hold of that country, without risking the utter destruction of the troops intrusted to his care. For an inferior army Portugal has no defencible frontier. The rivers generally running east and west, are fordable in most places, subject to sudden rises and falls, offering but weak lines of resistance, and, with the exception of the Zezere, presenting no obstacles to the advance of an enemy penetrating by the eastern frontier. The mountains, indeed, afford many fine and some impregnable positions, but such is the length of the frontier line and the difficulty of lateral communications, that a general who should attempt to defend it against superior forces would risk to be cut off from the capital if he concentrated

* Sir J. Cradock's Correspondence, MS.

his troops; and if he extended them his line would be immediately broken. The possession of Lisbon constitutes, in fact, the possession of Portugal, south of the Duero, and an inferior army can only protect Lisbon by keeping close to the capital.

Sensible of this truth, Sir John Cradock adopted the French Colonel Vincente's views for the defence of Lisbon, and proceeded, on the 4th of January, with seventeen hundred men, to occupy the heights behind the creek of Sacavem, leaving, however, three thousand men in the forts and batteries of Lisbon. At the earnest request of the Regency, who in return promised to assemble the native troops at Thomar, Abrantes, and Vilha Velha, he ordered General Stewart's brigade, two thousand seven hundred strong, to halt at Santarem; but the men had been marching for a month under incessant rain, their clothes were worn out, their equipments ruined, and, in common with the rest of the army, they wanted shoes.*

Cameron being now on the Douro, Kemmis, with the 40th regiment at Elvas, and the main body under Cradock between Santarem and Lisbon, this army not exceeding ten thousand men, but with the encumbrances of an army of forty thousand, was placed on the three points of a triangle, the shortest side of which was above a hundred and fifty miles. The general commanding could not bring into the field above five thousand men, nor could that number be assembled in a condition for service at any one point of the frontier, under three weeks or a month; moreover, the uncertainty of remaining in the country at all, rendered it difficult to feed the troops, for the commissioners, being unable to make large contracts for a fixed time, were forced to carry on, as it were, a retail system of supply.

At this moment of extreme weakness, Mr. Frere, with indefatigable folly, was urging Sir John Cradock to make a diversion in Spain, by the line of the Tagus, and Mr. Villiers was as earnest that he should send a force by sea to Vigo. His own instructions prescribed the preservation of Lisbon, Elvas, and Almeida, the assembling, in concert with the native government, of an Anglo-Portuguese army on the frontier, and the sending of succors to Sir John Moore. Cradock's means were so scanty that the attainment of any one of those objects was scarcely possible, yet Mr. Canning, writing officially to Mr. Villiers, at this epoch, as if a mighty and well furnished army was in Portugal, enforced the "*necessity of continuing to maintain possession of Portugal as long as could be done with the force intrusted to Sir John Cradock's command, remembering always that not the defence of Portugal alone, but the employment of the enemy's military force, and the diver-*

* Sir John Cradock's Correspondence, MS.

sion which would be thus created in favor of the south of Spain, were objects not to be abandoned, except in case of the most extreme necessity." The enemy's military force! It was three hundred thousand men, and this despatch was a pompous absurdity. The ministers and their agents, eternally haunted by the phantoms of Spanish and Portuguese armies, were incapable of perceiving the palpable bulk and substance of the French hosts; the whole system of the Cabinet was one of shifts and expedients; every week produced a fresh project, and minister and agent alike followed his own views, without reference to any fixed principle; the generals were the only persons not empowered to arrange military operations.

The number of officers employed to discover the French movements enabled Cradock, although his direct communications were interrupted, to obtain intelligence of Moore's advance toward Sahagun; wherefore, he again endeavored to send a reinforcement into Spain by the way of Almeida. The difficulty of getting supplies, however, finally induced him to accede to Mr. Villiers' wishes, and on the 12th of January he shipped six hundred cavalry and thirteen hundred infantry, meaning to send them to Vigo; but while they were still in the Tagus, intelligence of the retreat upon Coruña was received, and the troops were disembarked.[*]

The 14th of January the Conqueror line-of-battle-ship, having Admiral Berkeley on board, reached Lisbon; and for the first time since Sir John Cradock took the command of the troops in Portugal, he received a communication from the ministers in England.[†] It now appeared that their thoughts were less intently fixed upon the defence of Portugal than upon getting possession of Cadiz. Their anxiety upon this subject had somewhat subsided after the battle of Vimiero, but it revived with greater vigor when Sir John Moore, contemplating a movement in the south, suggested the propriety of securing Cadiz as a place of arms; and in January an expedition was prepared to sail for that town, with the design of establishing a new base of operations for the English army. This project failed, but the following particulars of the transaction afford ample proof of the perplexed, unstable nature of the minister's policy.

NEGOTIATION FOR THE OCCUPATION OF CADIZ.

While it was still unknown in England that the Supreme Junta had fled from Aranjuez, Sir George Smith, who had conducted Spencer's negotiation in 1808, was again sent to Cadiz to prepare

* Sir John Cradock's Correspondence, MS.
† Cradock's Papers, MS.

the way for the reception of an English garrison.* Four thousand men destined for this service were then embarked at Portsmouth. General Sherbrooke, who commanded them, was first directed to touch at Lisbon on his way to Cadiz; he was afterwards desired to make for Coruña to be at the order of Sir John Moore; yet finally, his force being increased to five thousand men, he sailed on the 14th of January for Cadiz, under his first instructions. Mr. Frere was then directed to negotiate for the admission of these troops into Cadiz, as the only condition upon which a British army could be employed to aid the Spanish cause in that part of the Peninsula.

As the reverses in the north of Spain became known, the importance of Cadiz increased, and the importance of Portugal decreased, in the eyes of the English ministers. Sir John Cradock was made acquainted with Sherbrooke's destination, and was himself commanded to obey any requisition for troops that might be made by the Spanish Junta; and so independent of the real state of affairs were the ministerial arrangements, that Cradock, whose despatches had been one continued complaint of his inability to procure horses for his own artillery, was directed to furnish them for Sherbrooke's.

Sir George Smith, a man somewhat hasty, but of remarkable zeal and acuteness, left England about the middle of December; and on his arrival at Cadiz, at once discovered that there, as in every other part of the Peninsula, all persons being engaged in theories or intrigues, nothing useful for defence was executed. The ramparts of the city were in tolerable condition, but scarcely any guns were mounted, while, two miles in front of the town, an outwork had been commenced upon such a scale that it could not possibly be finished under four months, and, after the slow mode of Spanish proceedings, would have taken as many years to complete.

For a solid defence of all the fortifications, Sir George Smith judged that twenty thousand good troops would be requisite, but that ten thousand would suffice for the city; there were, however, only five thousand militia and volunteers in the place, and not a regular soldier under arms, neither any within reach. The number of guns mounted and to be mounted exceeded four hundred; to serve them, two hundred and fifty peasants and volunteers were enrolled, and, being clothed in uniforms, were called artillerymen.

Knowing nothing of Sir John Moore's march to Sahagun, Sir George Smith naturally calculated upon the immediate approach of the French; wherefore, seeing the helpless state of Cadiz, and

* Papers laid before Parliament, 1810.

being assured that the people would willingly admit an English garrison, he wrote to Sir John Cradock for troops. The latter, little thinking that, at such a conjuncture, the Supreme Junta would be more jealous of their allies than fearful of their enemies—judging also from the tenor of his latest instructions, that obedience to this requisition would be consonant to the minister's wishes—immediately ordered Colonel Kemmis to proceed from Elvas with the fortieth regiment, by the route of Seville, and at the same time, embarking three thousand of the best troops at Lisbon, sent them to Cadiz.* This force, commanded by Major-General Mackenzie, sailed the 2d February, and reached their destination the 5th of the same month.

Meanwhile, Mr. Frere, although acquainted with the sailing of Mackenzie's armament, was ignorant that Sir George Smith had applied to the governor of Cadiz for permission to take military possession of that town;† for Smith had no instructions to correspond with Mr. Frere, and the latter had opened a separate negotiation with the Central Junta at Seville, in which he endeavored to pave the way for the occupation by proposing to have the troops admitted as guests; and he sent Mr. Stuart to arrange this with the local authorities. Mr. Frere had, however, meddled much with the personal intrigues of the day; he was, moreover, of too slender a capacity to uphold the dignity and just influence of a great power on such an occasion, and the flimsy thread of his negotiation snapped under the hasty touch of Sir George Smith. The Supreme Junta, averse to everything that threatened to interrupt their course of sluggish indolence, had sent the Marquis de Villel, a member of their own body, to Cadiz, avowedly to prepare the way for the admission of the troops, but, in reality, to thwart that measure; hence the circumstance of Mackenzie's arrival, with an object different from that announced by Mr. Frere, was instantly taken advantage of to charge England with treachery. The Junta, knowing Mr. Frere to be their own dupe, believed, or affected to believe, that he was also the dupe of the English minister, and that the whole transaction was an artifice, on the part of the latter, to get possession of the city with a felonious intent.‡ The admission of the British troops was nevertheless earnestly desired by the inhabitants of Cadiz, and of the neighboring towns; and this feeling was so well understood by Mr. Stuart and Sir George Smith, that they would, notwithstanding the reluctance of the Supreme Junta, have brought the affair to a good conclusion; but, at the most critical

---

* Sir J. Cradock's Correspondence, MS.
† Parl. Papers, 1810.
‡ Ibid.

period of the negotiation, the former was sent on a secret mission to Vienna, by the way of Trieste, and the latter, who was in bad health, died about the same period. Thus the negotiation failed for want of a head to conduct it.

General Mackenzie, like Sir George Smith, thought that the object might be attained. He observed, indeed, that the people, far from suspecting any danger, were ignorant or incredulous of the reverses in the north, that nothing had been done towards equipping the fleet for sea, and that, notwithstanding the earnest remonstrances of Admiral Purvis and Mr. Stuart, the Spaniards would neither work themselves nor permit the English sailors to work for them; but he also saw that the public feeling was favorable to the British troops, and the good will of the people openly expressed. The affair was, however, now in the hands of Mr. Frere.

In the course of the negotiations carried on by that minister, the Supreme Junta had proposed—

1. That the troops should land at Port St. Mary's, to be quartered there and in the neighboring towns. 2. That they should join Cuesta's army. 3. That they should go to Catalonia. 4. That they should be parcelled out in small divisions, to be attached to the different Spanish armies. Nay, untaught by their repeated disasters, and pretending to hold the English soldiery cheap, those self-sufficient men proposed that the British should garrison the minor fortresses on the coast, in order to release an equal number of Spaniards for the field.

Mr. Frere wished to accept the first of these proposals, but General Mackenzie, Sir George Smith, and Mr. Stuart agreed that it would be injurious for many reasons; not the least urgent of which was that, as the troops could not have been embarked again without some national dishonor, they must have marched towards Cuesta, and thus have been involved in the campaign without obtaining that which was their sole object—*the possession of Cadiz as a place of arms.*

Mr. Frere then suggested a modification of the second proposal, namely, to leave a small garrison in Cadiz, and to join Cuesta with the remainder of the troops. At this time Sir G. Smith was dead, Mr. Stuart had embarked for Trieste, and General Mackenzie, reluctant to oppose Mr. Frere's wishes, consented to march, if the necessary equipments for his force could be procured; but he observed, that the plan was contrary to his instructions, and to the known wishes of the English government, and liable, in part, to the same objections as the first proposition. This was on the 18th of February; on the 22d, a popular tumult commenced in Cadiz.

The Supreme Junta, desirous to show that the city did not require an English garrison for its protection, had sent there two regiments, composed of Poles, Germans, and Swiss, deserters or prisoners. The people, aware that the Junta disliked and intended to disarm the volunteers of Cadiz, were justly offended that deserters should be trusted in preference to themselves; they stopped the courier, opened the despatches from Seville, and imprisoned the Marquis of Villel, who was obnoxious, because, while mild to persons suspected of favoring the French, he had harshly or rather brutally punished some ladies of rank. Proceeding from one violence to another, the populace endeavored to kill the state prisoner, and being prevented in that, committed other excesses, and murdered Don Joseph Heredia, the collector of public rents. During the tumult, which lasted two days, the disembarkation of the English troops was repeatedly called for by the mob; and two British officers being sent on shore as mediators, were received with enthusiasm, and obeyed with respect—a manifest proof of the correct view taken by Sir George Smith.

The 24th, tranquillity was restored; the 25th, General Mackenzie, not having received from Mr. Frere an answer to his letter of the 18th, suggested that of the three English battalions then in the harbor, two should be placed in Cadiz, and that the third, proceeding to Seville, should there unite with the 40th regiment, and both together march to join Cuesta. Mr. Frere, however, instead of addressing the Junta with an authority and dignity becoming the representative of a great nation, on whose support the independence of the whole Peninsula rested, had been endeavoring to gain his end by subtlety. The object was one that England had a right to seek, the Spanish rulers no right to refuse; for the people wished to further it, and the threat of an appeal to them would soon have silenced the feeble negative of such a despicable and suspected government. Mr. Frere, incapable of taking a single and enlarged view, pressed a variety of trifling points, and discussed them with the secretary of the Junta, with more regard to epistolary dexterity than to useful diplomacy; and when his opponent conceded the great point of admitting troops at all, broke off the negotiation, upon the question; whether the number to be admitted should be one or two thousand men; as if the way to drive a wedge was with the broad end foremost.

Self-baffled in that quarter, the British plenipotentiary, turning towards Cuesta, the avowed enemy of the Junta, and one much feared by them, sought to secure his assistance by holding out the lure of having a British force added to his command; but the sarcastic old General derided the diplomatist. "Although I do not," said he, "discover any great difficulty in the actual state of

things, which should prevent his British Majesty's troops from
garrisoning Cadiz under such terms, and for the purpose which
your excellency proposes, I am far from supposing that the Supreme
Junta, which is fully persuaded of the importance of our union
with England, is not grounded in its objections; and your excellency
knows that it is sufficient that they should have them, to prevent
my giving any opinion on so important a measure, *unless they should
consult me.** With regard to the 4,300 men, which your excellency
is pleased to mention, there is no doubt that I stand in need of
them; but I flatter myself, England, sensible of the importance of
Estremadura, will even lend me much greater assistance, particularly if, from any change of circumstances, the Supreme Junta
should no longer manifest the repugnance we speak of."

This answer having frustrated the projected intrigue, Mr. Frere,
conscious perhaps of diplomatic incapacity, returned with renewed
ardor to the task of directing the military affairs, in every part of
the Peninsula. He had seen an intercepted letter of Soult's
addressed to the King, in which the project of penetrating into
Portugal was mentioned; and immediately concluding that General
Mackenzie's troops would be wanted for the defence of that kingdom, counselled him to abandon Cadiz and return to Lisbon; but
the General, who knew that, even should he return, a successful
defence of Portugal with so few troops would be impossible, and
that every precaution was already taken for an embarkation in the
last extremity, observed, that "the danger of Lisbon rendered the
occupation of Cadiz more important."

General Mackenzie's reply was written the 26th of February.
On the 3d of March he received another despatch from Mr. Frere.
Cadiz, and the danger of Portugal, seemed to have passed from
the writer's mind, and were unnoticed; entering into a minutely
inaccurate statement of the situation of the French and Spanish
armies, he observed, that Soult having failed in an attempt to
penetrate Portugal by the Minho, *it was impossible from the position of the Spanish forces, assisted as they were by the Portuguese,
that he could persevere in his plan.* Wherefore, he proposed that
the British force then in the harbor of Cadiz should proceed immediately to Tarragona, to aid Reding; and this wild scheme was
only frustrated by an unexpected despatch from Sir John Cradock,
recalling the troops to Lisbon. They arrived there on the 12th of
March; and thus ended a transaction clearly indicating an unsettled
policy, shallow combinations, and a bad choice of agents on the
part of the English Cabinet, and a most unwise and unworthy disposition in the Supreme Junta.

* Parl. Papers, 1810.

General Mackenzie attributed the jealousy of the latter to French influence; Mr. Frere to the abrupt proceedings of Sir George Smith, and to fear, lest the Junta of Seville, who were continually on the watch to recover their ancient power, should represent the admission of the British troops as a treasonable proceeding on the part of the supreme government. It is, however, evident that the true cause was the false position in which the English ministers had originally placed themselves by inundating Spain with arms and money, without at the same time asserting a just influence, and making their assistance the price of good order and useful exertion.

CHAPTER III.

Weakness of the British army in Portugal—General Cameron marches to Lisbon —Sir R. Wilson remains near Ciudad Rodrigo—Sir J. Cradock prepares to take a defensive position at Passa d'Arcos—Double dealing of the Regency—The populace murder foreigners, and insult the British troops—Anarchy in Oporto —British government ready to abandon Portugal—Change their intention— Military system of Portugal—The Regency demand an English general—Beresford is sent to them—Sherbrooke's and Mackenzie's troops arrive at Lisbon— Beresford arrives there, and takes the command of the native force—Change in the aspect of affairs—Sir J. Cradock encamps at Lumiar—Relative positions of the allied and French armies—Marshal Beresford desires Sir J. Cradock to march against Soult—Cradock refuses—Various unwise projects broached by different persons.

THE effort made to secure Cadiz was an act of disinterested zeal on the part of Sir John Cradock. The absence of his best troops exposed him to the most galling peevishness from the Regency, and to the grossest insults from the populace; with his reduced force, he could not expect to hold even a contracted position at the extremity of the rock of Lisbon against the weakest army likely to invade Portugal; and as there was neither a native force nor a government to be depended upon, there remained for him only the prospect of a forced and, consequently, disgraceful embarkation, and the undeserved obloquy that never fails to follow disaster.

In this disagreeable situation, as Elvas and Almeida no longer contained British troops, his attention was necessarily fixed upon Lisbon and upon Oporto, which the violence of the gales had rendered a sealed port; meanwhile, the hospitals and magazines of Almeida, and even those of Salamanca, being sent to Lamego, had crowded that place with fifteen hundred sick men, besides escorts and hourly accumulating stores. The Douro had overflowed, the craft could not ply, one large boat attempting to descend was overset, and eighty persons, soldiers and others, had perished. General Cameron also, hearing of this confusion, relinquished the idea of embarking at Oporto, and, recrossing the Douro, made for Lisbon, where he arrived the beginning of February, with two thousand men, who were worn with fatigue, having marched eight hundred miles under continued rains. Sir Robert Wilson had sent his guns to Abrantes, by the road of Idanha Nova; but partly from a spirit of adventure, partly from an erroneous idea that Sir John Cradock wished him to defend the frontier, he remained with his infantry in the neighborhood of Ciudad Rodrigo. His force had been increased by a Spanish detachment under Don Carlos d'España, and by some volunteers, but it was still weak, and his operations were necessarily confined to a few trifling skirmishes: yet, like many others, his imagination so far outstripped his judgment, that, when he had only felt the advanced post of a single division, he expressed his conviction that the French were going to abandon Spain altogether.

Sir John Cradock entertained no such false expectations. He was informed of the battle of Coruña and the death of Moore, and he knew too well the vigor and talent of that General to doubt that he had been oppressed by an overwhelming force; he knew also that Zaragoza had fallen, and that twenty-five thousand French troops were thus free to act in other quarters; he knew that Soult, with at least twenty thousand men, was on the Minho; that Romana was incapable of making any head; that Portugal was one wide scene of helpless confusion, and that a French army was again in the neighborhood of Merida, threatening Lisbon by the line of the Tagus; in fine, that his own embarrassments were hourly increasing, and that the moment was arrived when the safety of his troops was the chief consideration. The tenor of the few despatches he had received from England led him to suppose that the ministers designed to abandon Portugal; but, as their intentions on that head were never clearly explained, he resolved to abide by the literal interpretation of his first instructions, and to keep his hold of the country as long as it was possible to do so without risking the utter destruction of his army. To avoid that danger, he put every encumbrance at Lisbon on board the transports in the Tagus; proceeded to dismantle the batteries at the mouth of the river, and in concert with the Admiral, made preparations for carrying away or destroying the military and naval stores in the arsenal. At the same time, he renewed his efforts to embark the sick men and stores at Oporto; but the weather continued so unfavorable, that he was finally obliged to remove the invalids and stores by land, yet he could not procure carriages for the whole.

After the arrival of Cameron's detachment, the effective British force under arms, including convalescents and fifteen hundred stragglers from Sir John Moore's army, was about eight thousand men; yet when the security of the forts and magazines and the tranquillity of Lisbon were provided for, only five thousand men, and those not in the best order, could be brought into the field. As this force was infinitely too weak to cover such a town as Lisbon, the General judged that it would be unwise to take up a position in advance, whence he should be obliged to retreat through the midst of a turbulent and excited population, which had already given too many indications of ill-temper to leave any doubt of its hostility under such circumstances. He, therefore, came to the resolution of withdrawing from Saccavem and Lisbon, to concentrate his whole force on a position at Passa d'Arcos, near the mouth of the river, where he could embark with least danger, and where he had the best chance of defending himself, if necessary, against superior numbers.

This reasoning was sound, and Cradock's intention was, undoubtedly, not to quit Portugal, unless driven from it by force, or in pursuance of orders from England; his arrangements, however, seem to have carried more the appearance of alarm than was either politic or necessary; the position of Passa d'Arcos might have been prepared, and the means necessary for an embarkation secured, and yet the bulk of the troops kept in advance until the last moment. To display a bold and confident front in war is, of all things, the most essential, as well to impose upon friends as upon enemies; Sir John Cradock did not fail to experience the truth of this maxim. The population of Lisbon, alarmed by the reverses in Spain, yet, like all the people in the Peninsula, confident in their own prowess and resolution until the very moment of attack, became extremly exasperated; the Regency, partly from their natural folly and insincerity, but more from the dread of the lower orders, countenanced, if they did not instigate, the latter to commit excesses, and to interrupt the proceedings of the British naval and military authorities. The measures of precaution relative to the forts had originated with the Regency, yet they now formally protested against them, and, with a view to hamper the General, encouraged their subalterns to make many false and even ridiculous charges against the British executive officers; and it would appear that the remonstrances of the Admiral and Generals were but imperfectly supported by Mr. Villiers.

In this manner the people's violence was nourished until the city was filled with tumult; mobs, armed with English pikes and muskets, collected night and day in the streets and on the high-roads, and under the pretext of seeking for and killing Frenchmen, attacked indiscriminately all foreigners, even those in the British service wearing the British uniform. The guards, who endeavored to protect the victims of this ferocity, were insulted; couriers, passing with despatches, were intercepted and deprived of their papers; English officers were outraged in the streets, and such was the audacity of the people that the artillery was placed in the squares, in expectation of an affray. The state of Lisbon was similar to what it had been at the period of Junot's convention, and if the British had abandoned the country at this time, they would have been assailed with as much obloquy by the Portuguese; for such has been, and will be, the fate of all unsuccessful auxiliaries,—a reflection that should render historians cautions of adopting accusations upon the authority of native writers on the like occasions.

This spirit was not confined to Lisbon. In Oporto the disposition to insult the British was more openly encouraged than in the capital; the government of the multitude was more decidedly pronounced. From the cities it spread to the villages. The people of the Alemtejo frontier were, indeed, remarkably apathetic; but, from the Minho to the Tagus, the country was in horrible confusion; the soldiers were scattered, without regard to military system, and, being unpaid, lived at free quarters; the peasantry of the country assembling in bands, and the populace of the towns in mobs, intercepted the communications, appointed or displaced the generals at their pleasure, and massacred all persons of whom they were suspicious; the ammunition which had been supplied from England was wasted by constant firing in token of insubordination, and, as if the very genius of confusion was abroad, some of the British troops, principally *malingerers*,* of Sir John Moore's army, added their quota of misconduct, to increase the general distress.

The leading instigator of the excesses at Oporto was one Raymundo, a coadjutor and creature of the Bishop's, a turbulent and cruel fellow, who, by taking a share in the first insurrection against the French, obtained a momentary influence, and has since been elevated, by a very credulous writer, into a patriotic hero. He was, however, a worthless coward, fitted for secret villany, and incapable of a noble action.

This state of affairs, productive of so much misery and danger, continuing without intermission, caused many of the upper classes to despair of their country's safety by war, and increased the number of those who, wishing to attach themselves to the fortune of France, were ready to accept of a foreign prince for their sovereign,

---

* An appellation given among soldiers to men who, under pretence of sickness, shrink from the performance of their duties in the field.

if with him they could obtain tranquillity and an ameliorated constitution ; and when, soon afterwards, the edge of the enemy's sword,
falling upon the senseless multitude, filled the streets of Oporto
with blood, there was a powerful French party in Portugal. The
bulk of the people were, however, stanch in their country's cause ;
they were furious and disorderly, but imbued with hatred of the
French, ready at the call of honor, and susceptible of discipline,
without any loss of energy.

The turbulence of the citizens, the remonstrances of the Regency,
and the representations of Mr. Villiers, who was in doubt for the
personal safety of the British subjects residing in Lisbon, convinced
Sir John Cradock that political circumspection and adroitness were
as important as military arrangements to prevent a catastrophe at
this critical period ; hence, as, contrary to what might have been
expected, the enemy had not yet made any actual movement across
the frontier, he suspended his design of falling back to Passa d'Arcos.

In this unsettled state affairs remained until March, when intelligence arrived that the French fleet was at sea, whereupon two of
the line-of-battle ships in the Tagus were despatched to reinforce
Sir Thomas Duckworth's squadron, and the batteries at the mouth
of the river were again armed. Meanwhile, Soult was making
progress in the north, the anarchy at Oporto was continually increasing, and the English government had certainly come to the
resolution of abandoning Portugal if the enemy advanced ; for,
although Sir John Cradock was not informed of their views, an
officer in England, well acquainted with Portuguese customs, actually received orders, and was embarking, to aid the execution of this
measure, when suddenly the policy of the Cabinet once more
changed, and it was resolved to reinforce the army. This resolution, which may be attributed partly to the Austrian war, partly
to the failure at Cadiz, partly to the necessity of satisfying public
opinion in England, was accompanied by a measure which laid the
first solid basis on which to build a reasonable hope of success.

The Portuguese government, either spontaneously, or brought
thereto by previous negotiation, had offered the command of their
troops, with the title of Marshal, to an English general, and the
British ministers accepted this offer, promised supplies of arms,
ammunition, clothing, and a subsidy for the payment of a certain
number of regular soldiers ; thus obtaining a firm hold of the military resources of Portugal, and gaining for the first time a position
in the Peninsula suitable to the dignity of England and the contest in which she was engaged. The Portuguese desired to have Sir
Arthur Wellesley, but he refused the offer, and it is said that Sir John
Murray, (he who afterwards failed at Tarragona,) Sir John Doyle,

and even the Marquis of Hastings, a man undoubtedly well qualified, sought for the office, but that powerful parliamentary interest
prevailing, Major-General Beresford was finally chosen, and at the
same time received the local rank of Lieutenant-General; to the
great discontent of several officers of superior rank, who were displeased that a man without any visible claim to superiority should
be placed over their heads.

Information of this change was immediately sent to Sir John
Cradock, and General Sherbrooke was ordered to repair to Lisbon.
The latter was close to Cadiz harbor when the orders overtook
him, and his and Mackenzie's divisions arrived together in the Tagus on the 12th of March; thus the fate of Portugal was again fixed
by England. But if Mr. Frere's plan had been followed—if Mackenzie had proceeded to Tarragona, and nothing but foul weather
prevented him—if Sherbrooke's voyage had not been delayed by
storms, and that sailing about from port to port, he had, as is most
probable, been engaged in some other enterprise—if Victor, obeying his orders, had marched to Abrantes—if any of these events
had happened, Sir John Cradock must have abandoned Portugal,
and then how infinitely absurd the proceedings of the English ministers would have appeared, and how justly their puerile combinations would have excited the scorn of Europe!

Marshal Beresford reached Lisbon early in March, and after
some negotiation, received from the Regency power to appoint
British officers to the command of regiments, and to act without
control in any manner he should judge fitting to ameliorate the
condition and discipline of the Portuguese forces; and this was
the more important, as the military polity of Portugal, although
fallen into disuse, was severe, precise, and admirably calculated to
draw forth the whole strength of the nation. The army could be
completed by coercion; the militia were bound to assemble by
regiments, and liable to any service within the frontiers; and the
whole of the remaining male population could be enrolled under
the name of *ordenancas*, numbered by battalions in their different
districts, and obliged under very severe penalties to assemble, at
the orders of the local magistrates, either to work, to fight, to escort
convoys, or in any manner to aid the operations of the army.

This affair arranged, Beresford fixed his quarters at Thomar,
collected the Portuguese troops in masses, and proceeded to recast
their system on the model of the British army; commencing, with
stern but wholesome rigor, a reform that, in process of time, raised
out of chaos an obedient, well disciplined, and gallant force, worthy
of a high place among the best in Europe; for the Portuguese
people, though easily misled and excited to wrath, are of a docile

orderly disposition, and very sensible of just and honorable conduct in their officers. This reform was, however, not effected at
once, nor without many crosses and difficulties being raised by the
higher orders and by the government—difficulties that General
Beresford could never have overcome, if he had not been directed,
sustained, and shielded by the master spirit under whom he was
destined to work. The plan of giving to English officers the command of the Portuguese troops was at first proceeded on with
caution; but after a time, the ground being supposed safe, it was
gradually enlarged, until almost all the military situations of importance were held by Englishmen, which, combined with other causes,
gave rise to numerous intrigues, not confined to the natives, and, as
we shall find, in after times, seriously threatening the power of the
Marshal, the existence of the British influence, and the success of
the war.

Sir John Cradock's situation was now materially alleviated. The
certainty of the Austrian war produced a marked change in the
disposition of the Regency; the arrival of Sherbrooke's and Mackenzie's divisions increased the British force to fourteen thousand
men, and the populace became more cautious of offering insults.
About the middle of March, two thousand men being left to maintain tranquillity in Lisbon, the remainder of the army was encamped at Lumiar and Saccavem, and while these things were
passing at Lisbon, the aspect of affairs changed also in other parts
of the kingdom.

The bulk of the Portuguese regular troops, amounting to ten or
twelve thousand men, was collected by Marshal Beresford between
the Tagus and the Mondego. Beyond the valley of the Mondego,
Colonel Trant had assembled a small corps of volunteers, students
from the university, and General Vittoria was at the head of two
regular battalions in Upper Beira. The Bishop of Oporto was
preparing to defend that town, with a mixed, but ferocious and insubordinate multitude. General Silveira, with four or five thousand men, had taken post in the Tras os Montes, and Romana, who
had collected seven or eight thousand at Monterey, was in communication with him. Sir Robert Wilson, who was at the head of
about three thousand men, had withdrawn the legion from Almeida,
and sent a detachment to Bejar, but remained himself on the
Agueda, watching the advanced posts of Lapisse. A few Portuguese regiments were extended from Salvatierra and Idanha to
Alcantara. A permanent bridge of boats was laid over the Tagus
at Abrantes, and there were small garrisons in that town and at
Elvas.

All these forces united would not, however, with the exception of the British, have been capable of sustaining the shock of ten thousand French soldiers for half an hour, and the whole mass of the latter, then hanging on the frontier of Portugal, was above fifty thousand; gathering like clouds on the horizon, they threatened many points, but gave no certain indication of where the storm would break. Soult, indeed, with about twenty thousand men, was endeavoring to pass the Minho; but Lapisse, although constantly menacing Ciudad Rodrigo, kept his principal masses at Salamanca and Ledesma, and Victor had concentrated his between the Alberche and the Tietar. Hence Lapisse might join either Soult or Victor, and the latter could march by Placentia against Ciudad Rodrigo, while Soult attacked Oporto; or he might draw Lapisse to him, and penetrate Portugal by Alcantara; he might pass the Tagus, attack Cuesta, and pursue him to Seville; or, after defeating him, he might turn short to the right, and enter the Alemtejo.

In this uncertainty, Sir John Cradock, keeping the British concentrated at Lumiar and Saccavem, waited for the enemy to develop his plans, and, in the mean time, endeavored to procure the necessary equipments for an active campaign. He directed magazines to be formed at Coimbra and Abrantes; urged the Regency to exertion, took measures to raise money, and despatched officers to Barbary to procure mules. But while thus engaged, intelligence arrived that Victor, having suddenly forced the passage of the Tagus at Almaraz, was in pursuit of Cuesta on the road to Merida; that Soult, having crossed the Minho, and defeated Romana and Silveira, was within a few leagues of Oporto, and that Lapisse had made a demonstration of assaulting Ciudad Rodrigo. The Junta of Oporto now vehemently demanded aid from the Regency, and the latter, although not much inclined to the Bishop's party, proposed that Sir John Cradock, uniting a part of the British forces to the Portuguese troops under Marshal Beresford, should march to the succor of Oporto.[*] Beresford was averse to trust the Portuguese under his immediate command among the disorderly multitude of that city, but he thought the whole of the British army should move in a body to Leiria, and from thence either push on to Oporto, or return, according to the events that might occur in the latter town, and he endeavored to persuade Cradock to follow this plan.

It was doubtful, he said, if Victor and Soult intended to co-operate in a single plan, but, on the supposition that it was so, he considered it essential to drive back or to overcome one before the other could come to his assistance. Victor was then in pursuit of Cuesta; if he continued that pursuit, it must be to enter Seville, or to cripple

* Sir J. Cradock's Correspondence, MS.

his opponent previous to the invasion of Portugal; in either case he would be in the Sierra Morena before he could hear of the march from Leiria, and, as Cradock had daily intelligence of his movements, there would be full time to relieve Oporto, and return again to the defence of Lisbon. If, however, Soult depended on the co-operation of Victor, he would probably remain on the right of the Duero until the other was on the Tagus, and Lapisse also would be contented for the present with capturing Ciudad Rodrigo and Almeida.

This unsound reasoning did not weigh with Sir John Cradock, who resolved to preserve his central position, covering the capital at such a distance as to preclude the danger of being cut off from it by one army while he was engaged with another. Portugal, he observed, was in a state of anarchy equally incompatible with firm resistance and rapid movements; the peasantry were tumultuous and formidable to everybody but the enemy; Beresford himself acknowledged that the regular forces were mutinous, disregarding their officers, choosing when and where to rest, when to fight, when to remain in quarters, and altogether unfit to be trusted within the circle of the Oporto mischief. The British troops, therefore, were the only solid resource; but they were too few to divide, and must act in a body, or not at all. Lisbon and Oporto were the enemy's objects; which was it most desirable to protect?—the former was of incomparably greater importance than the latter; the first was near, the second two hundred miles off; and, although the utmost exertions had been made, the army was not yet equipped for an active campaign. The troops were ill-clothed, and wanted shoes; the artillery was unhorsed; the commissariat possessed only a fourth part of the transport necessary for the conveyance of provisions and ammunition, and no activity could immediately supply these deficiencies, inasmuch as some of the articles required were not to be had in the country; to obtain others, the interference of the Regency was necessary, but hitherto all application to that quarter had been without any effect. Was it wise then to commence offensive operations in the north? The troops of Soult and Lapisse united were estimated at thirty thousand men, of which above five thousand were cavalry; the British could only bring fifteen guns and twelve thousand men, of all arms, into the field; yet, if they marched with the avowed intention of relieving Oporto, they must accomplish it, or be dishonored!

Was it consistent with reason to march two hundred miles in search of a combat, which the very state of Oporto would render it almost impossible to gain, and for an object perhaps already lost? Suspicion was alive everywhere; if Oporto was already taken, the army must come back; that would be the signal for fresh tumults, for renewed cries that the country was to be abandoned; Lisbon would instantly be in a state of insurrection, and would be even more formidable to the British than the enemy. Besides, it was impossible to reckon upon Cuesta's aid in keeping Victor employed. He was personally inimical to the English, and his principal object was to gain time for the increase and discipline of his own force. Victor was apparently pursuing Cuesta, but his parties had already appeared in the neighborhood of Badajos, and there was nothing but a weak Portuguese garrison in Elvas to impede his march through the Alemtejo. To cover Lisbon and the Tagus was the wisest plan; fixed in some favorable position, at a prudent distance from that capital, he could wait for the reinforcements he expected from England. He invited the Portuguese troops to unite with him; a short time would suffice to establish subordination; and then the certainty that the capital could not be approached, except in the face of a really formidable army, would not only keep the enemy in check, but, by obliging him to collect in greater numbers for the attempt, would operate as a diversion in favor of Spain.

The general soundness of this reasoning is apparent, and it must not be objected to Sir John Cradock that he disregarded the value of a central position, which might enable him to forestall the enemy: if the latter should march on his flank against Lisbon, the difficulty of obtaining true intelligence from the natives and his own want of cavalry, rendered it utterly unsafe for him to divide his army, or to trust it any distance from the capital. Marshal Beresford's plan, founded on the supposition that Cradock could engage Soult at Oporto, and yet quit him and return at his pleasure to Lisbon, if Victor advanced, was certainly fallacious; the advantages rested on conjectural, the disadvantages on positive data; it was conjectural that they could relieve Oporto, it was positive that they would endanger Lisbon. The proposition was, however, not made upon partial views; but at this period other men, less qualified to advise, pestered Sir John Cradock with projects of a different stamp, yet deserving of notice, as showing that the mania for grand operations, which I have before marked as the malady of the times, was still raging.

To make a suitable use of the British army was the object of all these projectors, but there was a marvellous variety in their plans. The Regency desired that the Portuguese and British troops should co-operate for the relief of Oporto, and yet protect Lisbon, objects which were incompatible. Beresford advised that the whole English army should march. The Bishop was importunate to have some British soldiers placed under his command, and he recalled Sir Robert Wilson to the defence of Oporto. It appeared reasonable that the legion should defend the city in which it was raised, but Mr. Frere wrote from Seville, that Sir Robert would do better to remain; he therefore accepted Spanish rank, and refusing obedience to the prelate's orders, retained his troops. The Regency, glad of the opportunity, approved of this proceeding, and adopted the legion as a national corps. Meanwhile, Romana was earnest with Cradock for money, and wanted to have a thousand British soldiers sent to aid the insurrection at Vigo; but at the same time, Mr. Frere, and Colonel D'Urban, a corresponding officer placed by Cradock at Cuesta's head-quarters, proposed other plans of higher pretensions.*

Zaragoza, said the latter, has fallen, and ten thousand French troops being thus released, are marching towards Toledo; this is the moment to give a fatal blow to Marshal Victor! It is one of those critical occasions that seldom recur in war! In a day or two Sir Robert Wilson will be on the Tietar with two thousand five hundred men;† augment his force with a like number of Portuguese, who may be drawn from Sobreira, Idanha, and Salvatierra; he shall thus turn the right and rear of Victor's army, and his movement cannot be interrupted by the French force now at Salamanca and Alva, because the communication from thence to the Tagus by the passes of Banos and Tornevecas is sealed up. While Sir Robert Wilson thus gets in the rear of Victor with five thousand men, Cuesta, with twelve thousand infantry and two thousand cavalry, shall attack the latter in front; a matter of easy execution, because Cuesta can throw a pontoon bridge over the Tagus, near Almaraz, in an hour and a half, and the Conde de Cartoajal, who is at Manzanares in La Mancha, with ten thousand infantry and two thousand horse, will keep Sebastiani in check. The hope is great, the danger small, and if a few British troops can be added to the force on the Tietar, the success will be infallible.

There were, however, some grave objections to this infallible plan. General Cuesta was near Almaraz, Sir John Cradock was at Lisbon, and Sir Robert Wilson was at Ciudad Rodrigo. Their circuitous line of correspondence was thus above four hundred miles long, and it is not very clear how the combination was to be effected with that rapidity which was said to be essential to the success; neither is it very evident, that operations to be combined at such a distance, and executed by soldiers of different nations, would have been successful at all. On the one side, twenty thousand raw Portuguese and Spanish levies were to act on double ex-

* Sir J. Cradock's Correspondence, MS.
† Ibid.

ternal lines of operation; on the other, twenty-five thousand French veterans waited in a central position, with their front and flanks covered by the Tagus and the Tietar. In such a contest it is possible to conceive a different result from that anticipated by Colonel d'Urban.

Mr. Frere's plans were not less extensive, or less sanguine. When his project for assisting Catalonia had been frustrated, by the recall of General Mackenzie from Cadiz, he turned his attention to the north. Soult, he wrote to Sir John Cradock, tired of the resistance he has met with, will probably desist from his *"unaccountable project of entering Portugal, and occupying Gallicia at the same time."* Let the British army, therefore, make a push to drive the enemy out of Salamanca, and the neighboring towns, while the Asturians, on their side, shall take possession of Leon and Astorga, and thus open the communication between the northern and southern provinces. Fearing, however, that if this proposal should not be adopted, the English General might be at a loss for some enterprise, Mr. Frere also recommended that the British army should march to Alcantara, and that the fortieth regiment, which hitherto he had retained at Seville, contrary to Sir John Cradock's wishes, should join it at that place ; and then, said he, the whole operating by the northern bank of the Tagus, may, in concert with Cuesta, *"beat the French out of Toledo, and consequently out of Madrid."*

Now, with respect to the first of these plans, Soult never had the intention of holding Gallicia, which was Marshal Ney's province ; but he did propose to penetrate into Portugal, and he was not likely to abandon his purpose, because the only army capable of opposing him was quitting that kingdom, and making a *"push"* of four hundred miles to drive Lapisse out of Salamanca ; moreover, the Asturians were watched by General Bonnet's division on one side, and by Kellermann on the other, and the fifth corps, not ten but fifteen thousand strong, having quitted Zaragoza, were at this time in the Valladolid country, close to Leon and Astorga.*

With respect to the operations by the line of the Tagus, which were to drive Joseph out of Madrid, and consequently to attract the attention of all the French corps, it is to be observed, that Sir John Cradock could command about twelve thousand men, Cuesta sixteen thousand, Cartoajal twelve thousand, making a total of forty thousand.   But Soult had twenty-three thousand, Lapisse nine thousand, Victor was at the head of twenty-five thousand, Sebastiani could dispose of fifteen thousand, Mortier of a like number, the King's guards and the garrison of Madrid were twelve thou-

* Muster rolls of the French army, MS.

sand; making a total of nearly a hundred thousand men.   Hence, while Mr. Frere and Colonel D'Urban, confiding in Soult's inactivity, were thus plotting the destruction of Victor and Sebastiani, the first Marshal stormed Oporto; the second, unconscious of his danger, crossed the Tagus, and defeated Cuesta's army at Medellin, and at the same moment Sebastiani routed Cartoajal's at Ciudad Real.

JUSTIFICATORY PIECES.

No. 1.

To the Editor of the "Times."

Sir,—M. Thiers, in his 9th volume of the "Consulate and Empire," claims for himself the secret of the Peninsular war, having found it in certain papers to which he only has had access. That may be; but I ask if he is incapable of drawing false conclusions from secret materials to support perverse assertions? To answer with good warrant, let us examine how he deals with authentic documents, not confined to his secret repertory.

Thiers.—"3,000 brisk resolute Frenchmen" opposed 15,000 English at Roriça.

Reply.—The Duke of Wellington judged the French to be 6,000. Laborde, their commander, denied he had 6,000, thus tacitly admitting he had 5,000 or more.

Thiers.—The English had 400 cavalry.

Reply.—The English Adjutant-General's return gives 250.

Thiers.—Laborde wounded or killed 1,200 or 1,500 English at Roriça.

Reply.—The Adjutant-General's return gives 479 killed, wounded, and missing.

Thiers.—"Junot collected 9,000 some hundred men to fight at Vimiero."

Reply.—The French order of battle found on the field gave 14,000.

Thiers.—22,000 French embarked under the convention.

Reply.—The official French embarkation return gives nearly 26,000 men and officers.

Thiers.—"Only 26,000 men followed Junot into Portugal."

Reply.—The Imperial muster-rolls give 29,584 effective in Portugal, 23d of May, 1808.

Thiers.—The French army of Spain under Napoleon was 250,000 strong, of which 200,000 only were assembled there the end of October, 1808.

Reply.—The Imperial muster-rolls show, on the 25th of October, more than 319,000 effective; on the 15th of November, more than 335,000 effective.

Thiers.—Sir John Moore's troops arrived at Salamanca, exhausted by their long march, and by privations.

Reply.—Moore's despatches say his troops were in better case than when they started from Lisbon; they suffered no privations, and their excellent condition up to Sahagun was notorious.

Thiers.—"Moore advanced to Sahagun with 29,000 English troops, and about 10,000 Spaniards."

Reply.—The Adjutant-General's return of the 19th of December gives

23,583 of all arms: Moore had no Spaniards, and Romana, who did not act in concert, had only 6,000.

M. Thiers cannot deny the authenticity of my numbers, seeing they were taken from the original Imperial muster-rolls in the French War-office; not the yellow, but the green rolls; the officers of that office will appreciate the distinction of colors.

M. Thiers cannot plead ignorance. All the documents are printed in my history, and he had access to the French originals.

So much for quantities. Let us examine him as to qualities.

Thiers.—Wellington has a "contracted intellect;" Sir John Moore was "irresolute in council;" the English soldier is "beaten almost to death for the least fault;" "he is little practised to march;" "is inanimate, feeble, when forced to move to attack;" "he has no vivacity, no audacity, no enthusiasm, no hardihood, no enterprise;" "to beat him he must be forced to take the initiative in attack," &c.

Reply.—Wellington's intellect, measured by M. Thiers' imagination, must appear very contracted. Yet it is strange that with a few troops having no enterprise, no hardihood, and fearing to be beaten to death for trifling offences, he should have maintained the war for five years successfully in Spain, against enormous numbers of soldiers and officers the best and most skilful in the world, according to M. Thiers, and, finally, should carry that war into France! Strange that troops unable to march should have moved, in face of an enemy, from Lisbon to the Agueda, from the Agueda to Madrid, from the Douro to the Adour, from the Adour to the Upper Garonne. Stranger still, if to beat those troops it was only necessary to make them attack, that they should have attacked successfully at Roriça, where the French hill was five times more steep, rugged, and difficult than the English hill at Vimiero, which the French unsuccessfully attacked; that they forced the passage of the Douro and drove Soult out of Portugal; that they attacked Massena at Redinha, at Casal Nova, at Fonte d'Aronce, at Sabugal, and drove him also out of Portugal; that they attacked and retook the key of the position at Albuera, which the Spaniards had lost; that they attacked and defeated Marmont at Salamanca—the King at Vittoria, driving him out of Spain; that in the second fight, near Pampeluna, they attacked Soult's mountain position, and drove him out of Spain; that they forced the intrenched mountain position at Vera, and his fortified mountain lines on the Nivelle, covering Bayonne; that they passed the Gave de Pau in face of the French army, and defeated that army at Orthes —that they passed the Garonne and forced the intrenched camp at Toulouse, thus terminating the war! M. Thiers is not happy in his military reveries. Brilliant phrases condemnatory of revolutions which he could neither arrest nor guide are more consonant to his genius.

Thiers.—Sir John Moore was "irresolute in council"—"he yielded to the imperious admonitions of Mr. Frere"—"papers published by his family prove this."

Reply.—The papers published by Moore's family prove that he repelled Mr. Frere's arrogance with calm dignity, did not follow his plans, and changed his own because fresh events called for change. His irresolution in council exists in M. Thiers' imagination,—nowhere else. Those who knew Sir John Moore will laugh at such a silly assertion. M. Thiers has not been so remarkable for political resolution himself as to give him a right to censure others. In what council known to him did Sir John Moore display irresolution? Those who have read that General's journals know of several held with Mr. Pitt, Lord Melville, and others, wherein his ability, unhesitating vigor, and readiness to undertake what he advised, the sure sign of resolution, were signally manifested. But M. Thiers speaks afterwards of his "prudent firmness." Prudent firmness combined with irresolution! Indomitable resolution, both in council and in the field, was Moore's characteristic. Napoleon himself was not more decided.

One more example of unfounded censure.

"Sir John Moore said his advance served the Spanish cause by drawing Napoleon to the north, and giving the south time to rally." This M. Thiers calls a "presumptuous manner of presenting the affair to cover a disastrous campaign."

The best reply to that presumptuous remark is M. Thiers' history, wherein he distinctly shows that Napoleon did turn all his forces from the south to the north in consequence of Moore's advance to Sahagun—an advance which that General had previously declared he would make to produce such a result.

Verily, M. Thiers must amend his manner of treating known accessible facts, if he would have his authority accepted for the unknown and inaccessible. WILLIAM NAPIER, Major-General.

No. 2.

Paris, le 26 Fevrier, 1850.

MONSIEUR,—Je vous remercie de la communication que vous avez bien voulu me faire. Il est impossible d'écrire l'histoire sans rencontrer des critiques, mais l'opinion que tous les hommes bien informés au sujet de la guerre de la Peninsule ont depuis longtemps conçue de l'ouvrage du major-général Napier me permet de ne pas m'arrêter aux attaques qu'il dirige contre mon livre dans le *Times* du 11 de ce mois. Partout où j'ai eu à indiquer un nombre de troupes, j'ai toujours consulté avant de me prononcer la correspondance des gouvernements et celle des généraux placés à la tête de ces troupes ; c'est à l'aide de ces documents contradictoires que j'ai établi les nombres que j'ai donnés. M. Napier n'a eu pour écrire son histoire aucun document Français officiel, et ce n'est qu'à des officers du maréchale Soult qu'il a dû peut-être quelques communications sans caractère authentique.

Quant aux jugements que j'ai émis sur le duc de Wellington et sur l'armée Anglaise, ils sont exprimés dans des termes qui marquent toute mon estime et pour les troupes Anglaises et pour le grand homme de guerre qui les a commandés dans la Peninsule. Je me suis prescrit la loi d'être toujours impartial et juste ; aussi de tous les écrivains de l'Europe je crois être celui qui a parlé des armées étrangères et de leurs capitaines avec la plus grande impartialité, et qui leur a rendu le plus largement justice. Je n'ai donc rien à retirer ni des chiffres qui se trouvent dans le neuvième volume de mon "Histoire du Consulat et de l'Empire," ni des appréciations aux quelles je me suis livré à l'égard des généraux et de leurs troupes ; je tiendrais en conscience mon temps pour mal employé si je consacrais une partie á refuter les assertions de certains critiques ignorants ou interessés.

Agréez, Monsieur, l'assurance de ma considération très distinguée,

A. THIERS.

A Monsieur W. Jeffs, à Londres.

No. 3.

To the Editor of the " Times."

Sir,—Previous to noticing M. Thiers' observations which Mr. Jeffs (his bookseller) has published in your journal of this day, I offer the following consolation to the last-named gentleman :—A person wishing to purchase M. Thiers' ninth volume was told that my criticism in *The Times* had caused every copy to be sold off; there was not one remaining ! I heartily wish it had done as much for my own work. My conscience not being burdened, therefore, with sin or sorrow on account of Mr. Jeffs, I can with greater ease of mind meet M. Thiers, whose work, sparkling with paste brilliants, wants that real jewel—truth. My present reply need not, however, be long or labored. M. Thiers has himself confirmed my judgment of his infidelity to facts, and his unsound peremptory assertions.

What does the analysis of his letter to Mr. Jeffs present in answer to the long list of errors I charged him with ?

1. That he has always consulted for his numbers the government correspondence and that of the generals commanding the armies.

2. That I had no official French document to guide me, but had *perhaps* some communications non-authentic from some of Marshal Soult's officers.

3. That his judgments on the Duke of Wellington and the British troops were expressed in terms marking his esteem for both.

It is, then, a mark of esteem for a general and his troops to deny to the first an enlarged capacity, and to the last nearly all the essential qualities of soldiers ! Perhaps it is a proof also of his esteem for French generals and soldiers to tell them by implication, as M. Thiers has certainly done, that they were overcome not once and accidentally, but during a series of years, by a military chief of a contracted mind, and an army incapable of doing anything better than standing still to be shot ; for to that conclusion M. Thiers' history inevitably leads.

But I, an English historian, having seen what French generals and soldiers can do in the field, tell M. Thiers, the French historian, who has not, I believe, ever served, that his country's generals and soldiers are most formidable men to deal with in the field ; and that the general and soldiers who face them must be fitted to encounter all that genius and the sternest hardihood can effect in war.

M. Thiers speaks of French government's and French generals' correspondence, as conclusive in support of his statement of numbers. They could not be conclusive as to the English numbers, which he has misrepresented as much as he has the French numbers. The question is, however, not what M. Thiers consulted, but what he has published. And there I am forced again to say that he must amend his treatment of known accessible facts, if he would have his authority accepted for the unknown and inaccessible.

He says I had no official documents, meaning of course the correspondence he has consulted, to guide me—nay, that I had only some unauthentic communications from some of Marshal Soult's officers. But if I show him that I also have seen most of his government's and generals' correspondence, and that my communications were with Marshal Soult direct—not with his officers—he will perhaps allow some weight to my authority. Any person looking at my history will find all my obligations to French generals and officers acknowledged. But my business here is to show how

M. Thiers, while thinking to dispose of me as lightly as he does of facts, entirely confirms my judgment of his reckless dogmatism, when he says I had no authentic official French documents.

1. I had direct communications from Marshal Soult, who, when Minister of War, sent me, through General Pelet, with whom I also had personal communication, an immense mass of official correspondence upon most of the great operations in the Peninsula.

2. I had the correspondence of King Joseph with the French marshals and generals, and with the Emperor, during the greatest part of the war. This correspondence, ciphered and deciphered, was captured at Vittoria, and was lent to me by the Duke of Wellington.

3. I had a direct correspondence with Marshal Jourdan.

4. I had personal acquaintance with, and received information from officers high on the staff of Marshal Ney and Marshal Massena; and I had copies of the official journals of military operations kept by the chief of Marshal Victor's staff, and General Dupont's staff, and several others, as may be seen in my history.

From all these authentic documents I also was enabled to establish the numbers I have given. I was also enabled to compare them with the information obtained in the field by the Duke of Wellington. But I did not rely, as M. Thiers seems to have done, upon an estimate obtained from a comparison of *contradictory documents*—" documens contradictoires "—these are his words. I went directly to the fountain-head ; I got admission to the French " *bureau de la guerre.*" I worked there for many weeks with General Pelet, who was then engaged in seeking authority for his really sound and truly excellent history of the Emperor's German campaign of 1809—a work I recommend to M. Thiers as having no false brilliants, but yet of inestimable worth. Well, then, from the Emperor Napoleon's muster-rolls, made every fifteen days by Marshal Berthier—not those bound in yellow, as I have before said, but those bound in green for his peculiar information—I extracted most carefully the numbers of the French armies throughout the war, and I have published them in my history.

Comparing them with the Duke of Wellington's field estimates, and with statements of the generals commanding corps found in Joseph's portfolios, with the official journals of operations, and with the Emperor's plans of operations transmitted to the King, in which he details the numbers even to a squad of a few men—for I found a correction even of such a small matter in his own hand-writing on one of these memoirs ;—comparing, I say, all documents together, I found the accuracy of the muster-rolls confirmed, as indeed they were sure to be, for what general dared to make a false return of numbers to the Emperor?

If, then, the correspondence of Napoleon, of Wellington, of Soult, Jourdan, and King Joseph, be official authentic French documents, I was in as good a position as M. Thiers to arrive at accuracy; and I repeat my censures upon his inaccuracy, leaving the world to judge.

M. Thiers says his time would be ill employed if he devoted a part of it to refute the assertions of ignorant or interested critics. I entirely agree with him ; it would be much better to employ it in writing his own history in a manner to avoid the just censures of honest and well-informed critics.

W. NAPIER, Major-General.

March 27th, 1850.

OBSERVATIONS ON SOME PASSAGES IN CHAPTERS II. AND IV.

WITH respect to the tumult of the 2d of May, 1808, I drew my information from officers, some French, some Italian, who were present. On the veracity of my informants I had the firmest reliance, their accounts agreed well, and the principal facts were confirmed by the result of my personal inquiries at Madrid in the year 1812. But since the first edition of this work the following notes from General Harispe have been sent to me, and I insert them in justice to the colonel of the Imperial Guard. At the same time I have to remark that my statement in respect to the latter was made upon the authority of an officer of Murat's staff.

Bayonne, May 22, 1831.

Au Colonel (Anglais) George Napier.

" MONSIEUR,—J'ai lu avec un véritable intérêt les passages de l'ouvrage de monsieur votre frère, que vous m'aviez prié d'examiner. Je vous remercie de cette communication. J'ai porté en marge les rectifications nécessaires pour rétablir la vérité.—Recevez, monsieur, &c., &c.

" Le Lieut.-Général, Comte HARISPE."

Marginal Notes by General Harispe.

Chap. II., page 15.   Aucun des quartiers de troupes Françaises à Madrid ne fut attaqué, mais 350 à 400 hommes environ, qui se trouvaient isolés ou occupés à des distributions de pain, furent assassinés.

Page 15.   Le colonel de la Garde Impériale ne fit mettre à mort personne.

Chap. VI., page 58.   Le bataillon Suisse ne fût pas pris au pont de Pajaso, mais bien le lendemain de l'attaque de los Cabrillas.*

Page 59.   L'attaque de la ville (Valencia) se termina à la nuit, sans que les Espagnols eussent fait aucune sortie.

* This error has been corrected.

APPENDIX.

[The following five Notes, dictated by the Emperor Napoleon, and signed by General Bertrand, were found in King Joseph's portfolio, at the battle of Vittoria.]

No. I.

OBSERVATIONS ADDRESSEES AU GENERAL SAVARY SUR LES AFFAIRES D'ESPAGNE.

Le 13 *Juillet,* 1808.

1ere *Observation.*—LES affaires des Français en Espagne seroient dans une excellente position si la division Gobert avait marché sur Valladolid, et si la division Frère eut occupé San Clemente, ayant une colonne mobile à trois ou quatre journées sur la route du général Dupont.

Le g^{al} Gobert ayant été dirigé sur le général Dupont, le g^{al} Frère étant avec le maréchal Moncey, harassé et affaibli par des marches et des contremarches, la position de l'armée Française est devenue moins belle.

2e *Observation.*—Le maréchal Bessières est aujourd'hui à Medina del Rio Secco avec 15 mille hommes, infanterie, cavalerie, artillerie. Le 15 ou le 16, il attaquera Bénavente, se mettra en communication avec le Portugal, jettera les rebelles en Galice, et s'emparera de Léon. Si toutes les opérations réussissent ainsi, et d'une manière brillante, la position de l'armée Française redeviendra ce qu'elle était.

Si le général Cuesta se retire de Bénavente sans combattre, il se retirait sur Zamora, Salamanque, pour venir gagner Avila et Segovia, certain qu'alors le maréchal Bessiéres ne pourrait point le poursuivre, puisque, dans cette supposition, il serait menacé par l'armée de Galice, dont l'avant garde est réunie à Léon.

Alors il faut que le général qui commande à Madrid puisse promptement réunir 6 à 7000 hommes pour marcher sur le général Cuesta. Il faut que la citadelle de Ségovie soit occupée par quelques pièces de canon, trois à 400 convalescens avec six semaines de biscuit.

C'est une grande faute de n'avoir pas occupé cette citadelle quand le major-général l'a mandé. De toutes les positions possibles, Ségovie est la plus dangereuse pour l'armée : capitale d'une province, assise entre les deux routes, elle ôterait à l'armée toutes ses communications, et l'ennemi une fois posté dans cette citadelle, l'armée Française ne pourrait plus l'en déloger. Trois ou 400 convalescens et un bon chef de bataillon, une escouade d'artillerie, rendront le château de Ségovie imprenable pendant bien de temps, et assureront à l'armée l'importante position de Ségovie.

Si le général Cuesta se jette en Galice, sans combattre, sans éprouver de défaite, la position de l'armée devient toujours meilleure ; à plus forte raison, s'il est jetté en Galice après avoir éprouvé une forte défaite.

20*

3e *Observation.*—Si le maréchal Bessières, arrivé devant Bénavente, reste en présence sans attaquer le g^{al} Cuesta, ou s'il est repoussé, son but sera toujours de couvrir Burgos, en tenant le plus possible l'ennemi en échec ; il peut être renforcé de 3000 hommes de troupes de ligne, qui accompagnent le roi, mais alors il n'y a point à hésiter. Si le maréchal Bessières a fait une marche rétrograde sans bataille, il faut sur le champ lui envoyer 6000 hommes de renforts. S'il a fait son mouvement après une bataille, où il ait éprouvé de grandes pertes, il faudra faire de grandes dispositions : rappeller à marches forcées sur Madrid le g^{al} Frère, le g^{al} Caulaincourt, le g^{al} Gobert, le g^{al} Vedel, et laisser le g^{al} Dupont sur les montagnes de la Sierra Morena, ou le rapprocher même de Madrid, en le tenant toujours, cependant, à sept ou huit marches, afin de pouvoir écraser le g^{al} Cuesta et toute l'armée de Galice pendant que le g^{al} Dupont servira d'avant-garde pour tenir l'armée d'Andalousie en échec.

4e *Observation.*—Si le général Dupont éprouvait un échec, cela serait de peu de conséquence. Il n'aurait d'autre résultat que de lui faire repasser les montagnes ; mais le coup qui serait porté au maréchal Bessières serait un coup porté au cœur de l'armée, qui donnerait le *tetanos*, et qui se ferait sentir à touts les points extrêmes de l'armée. Voilà pourquoi il est très malheureux que toutes les dispositions ordonnées n'aient pas été suivies. L'armée du maréchal Bessières devrait se trouver avoir au moins huit mille hommes de plus, afin qu'il n'y eut aucune espèce de chance contre l'armée du maréchal Bessières.

La vraie manière de renforcer le général Dupont, ce n'est pas de lui envoyer des troupes, mais c'est d'envoyer des troupes au maréchal Bessières. Le général Dupont et le général Vedel sont suffisans pour se maintenir dans les positions qu'ils ont retranchées ; et si le maréchal Bessières avait été renforcé, et l'armée de Galice écrasée, le général Dupont immédiatement après se trouverait dans la meilleure position, non seulement par des forces qu'on pourrait alors lui envoyer, mais encore par la situation morale des affaires. Il n'y a pas un habitant de Madrid, pas un paysan des vallées qui ne sente que toutes les affaires d'Espagne aujourd'hui sont dans l'affaire du maréchal Bessières. Combien n'est-il pas malheureux que dans cette grande affaire on se soit donné volontairement 20 chances contre soi.

5e *Observation.*—L'affaire de Valence n'a jamais été d'aucune considération. Le maréchal Moncey seul était suffisant. C'était une folie que de songer à le secourir. Si le m^{al} Moncey ne pouvait pas prendre Valence, 20 mille hommes de plus ne le lui auraient pas fait prendre, parcequ'alors c'était une affaire d'artillerie, et non une affaire d'hommes : car on ne prend pas d'un coup de collier une ville de 80 ou 100 mille âmes, qui a barricadé ses rues, mis de l'artillerie à toutes les portes et dans toutes les maisons. Or, dans cette hypothèse, le m^{al} Moncey était suffisant pour former une colonne mobile, faire face à l'armée de Valence, et faire sentir dans toute leur force les horreurs de la guerre.

Le g^{al} Frère ne pouvait donc rien pour faire prendre Valence, et le g^{al} Frère pouvait beaucoup posté à San Clemente, soit qu'il dût revenir à Madrid, soit qu'il dût prendre une position intermédiaire pour secourir le g^{al} Dupont.

C'était une autre erreur que de songer à faire aller le m^{al} Moncey à Valence pour ensuite le faire marcher en Murcie et sur Grenade. C'était vouloir fondre ce corps d'armée en détail et sans fruit. Comme le dit fort bien le général Dupont, il valait mieux lui envoyer directement un régiment que de lui envoyer trois dans cette direction là.

Dans les guerres civiles ce sont les points importans qu'il faut garder : il ne faut pas aller partout. Si cependant on a dirigé le m^{al} Moncey sur Valence, c'était à une époque où la situation des affaires n'était pas la même ; c'était lorsque l'armée de Valence pouvait envoyer en Catalogne ou à Saragosse comme elle en menaçait.

6e *Observation.*—Le but de tous les efforts de l'armée doit être de conserver Madrid. C'est là qu'est tout. Madrid ne peut être menacé que par l'armée de Galice. Elle peut l'être aussi par l'armée de l'Andalousie, mais d'une manière beaucoup moins dangereuse, parcequ'elle est simple et directe, et que par toutes les marches que fait le g^{al} Dupont sur ses derrières, il se renforce. Les généraux Dupont et Vedel étaient suffisans, ayant plus de 20,000 hommes : le m^{al} Bessières ne l'est pas proportionellement, vû que sa position est plus dangereuse. Un échec que recevrait le g^{al} Dupont serait peu de chose ; un échec que recevrait le m^{al} Bessières serait plus considérable et se ferait sentir à l'extremité de la ligne.

Résumé.—Faire reposer et rapprocher de Madrid le g^{al} Frère, le g^{al} Caulaincourt, le g^{al} Gobert, afin qu'ils puissent arriver à Madrid avant le g^{al} Cuesta, si celui-ci battait le m^{al} Bessières. Immédiatement après l'événement qui aura lieu de 15 ou le 16, prendre une part selon les événemens qui auront eu lieu, et dans le but d'écraser l'armée ennemie en Galice. Si le maréchal Bessières a eu grand succès, sans éprouver de grandes pertes, tout sera bien dans la direction actuelle. S'il a un succès après avoir éprouvé beaucoup de pertes, il faut se mettre en mesure de la renforcer. S'il se tient en observation sans attaquer, il faut le renforcer. S'il a été défait et bien battu, il faut se concentrer et rassembler toutes ses troupes dans le cercle le sept ou huit journées de Madrid, et étudier les dispositions dans les différentes directions pour savoir où placer les avant-gardes, afin de profiter de l'avantage qu'on a d'être au milieu, pour écraser successivement avec toutes ses forces les divers corps de l'ennemi. Si on n'ordonne pas sur le champ au g^{al} Dupont de repasser les montagnes, c'est qu'on espère que malgré la faute faite, le m^{al} Bessières a la confiance (qu'on partage) qu'à la rigueur il est suffisant pour écraser l'ennemi. Le m^{al} Bessières a eu le bon esprit de tellement réunir toutes ses forces, qu'il n'a pas même laissé un seul homme à St. Ander. Quelqu'avantage qu'il y eût à laisser là un millier d'hommes, il a senti qu'un millier d'hommes pouvait décider sa victoire.

Quant à la division du g^{al} Verdier devant Saragosse, elle a rempli aux trois quarts son but. Elle a désorganisé tous les Arragoniens, a porté le découragement parmi eux, les a réduits à défendre les maisons de leur capitale, a soumis tous les environs, a bloqué la ville, et réuni tous les moyens pour s'en emparer sans que cela devienne trop couteux.

Voilà l'esprit de la guerre d'Espagne.

[Dictated by the Emperor Napoleon.]

No. II.

NOTE POUR LE ROI D'ESPAGNE.

Bayonne, Juillet, 1808.

L'armée d'Espagne a son quartier-général à Madrid; voici sa composition actuelle:

1°. *Corps des Pyrénées Occidentales.*

Le maréchal Bessières commande le corps des Pyrénées Occidentales, qui est fort de 23 mille hommes, infanterie, cavalerie, artillerie, occupe la place de St. Sébastien, les troys Biscayes, les montagnes de St. Ander, la place de Burgos, et est chargée de combattre l'armée ennemie des Asturies et de Galice.

Toutes les troupes sont en mouvement pour composer l'armée de la manière suivante:

Division du g^{al} Mouton	1ere *brigade,* le g^{al} Reynaud. { le 4 reg^t d'infanterie légère / 15e d'infanterie de ligne / 1er bat^{on} de Paris en marche total 3000 hom. présens sous les armes, et 6 pièces de canon, ci .... 3000 h^{es} (*Cette brigade marche sur Bénévente.*) 2e *brigade,* le g^{al} Rey. { 2e reg^t d'infanterie légère / 12e idem total 2100 hommes et 6 pièces de canon, ci 2100 (*Cette brigade est à Burgos avec le roi, et doit joindre sa division.*)		5100 h^{es}
Division du g^{al} Merle.	Brigade d'Armagnac . . . . 1800 Brigade Gaulois . . . . 1800 Brigade Sabathier . . . . 2800 Brigade Ducos . . . . 2000 _____ Total . . . 8400 et 16 pièces de canon.		8400 h^{es}
Garde.	{ Infanterie . . . . et 6 pièces de canon		1900 h^{es}

(*Toutes ces troupes marchent sur Bénévente.*)

Cavalerie.	10e de chasseurs . . . . 450 22e id. . . . . 450 Garde . . . . 300 (*Ces troupes marchent sur Bénévente.*) Escadrons de dragons . . . . . 200 (*Ces escadrons sont en marche et ont dépassé la frontière.*) 26e de chasseurs . . . . 450 (*Arrivant à Bayonne sous peu de jours.*) —— Total de la cavalerie . . . . 1950 h^{es}	1950 h^{es}

A reporter   17,350 h^{es}

De l'autre part . . . . 17,350 h^{es}

Les forces actives du maréchal Bessières sont donc de 17,000 h^{es}. Il n'en a guères que 15,000 pour l'affaire de Bénévente.

S'il obtenait à Bénévente et à Léon un grand succès contre l'armée de Galice, peut-être serait-il convenable pour profiter de la victoire et de la terreur des premiers momens de se jetter dans la Galice. Toutefois, il devrait d'abord prendre position à Léon, en s'emparant de la plaine, jettant l'ennemi dans les montagnes, et interceptant au moins à Astorga la communication de la grande route.

Garnison de Burgos.—Il y a dans le château de Burgos une garnison *de dépôt** . . . . 600 h^{es}

Colonne du général Bonnet.—Il y a encore à Burgos le g^{al} de division Bonnet, faisant partie du corps du m^{al} Bessières: ce g^{al} va avoir sous ses ordres une colonne mobile de 1200 hommes, pour maintenir la tranquillité dans la ville et ses environs. Cette colonne est composée comme il suit:

4e bataillon du 118e formant	450 h^{es}	
(*Actuellement existant à Burgos.*)		
3e bataillon du dépôt g^{al} actuellement à Vitoria . .	450	1500 h^{es}
2 comp^{ies} du 4e infanterie légère, formant un petit bataillon	400	
(*En marche, ayant passé la frontière.*)	———	
	1300 h^{es}	
Escadron de dragons (en marche)	200	
2 pièces de canon en marche	———	
	1500 h^{es}	

Colonne d'Aranda.—Cette colonne, formée du 1er bataillon de marche, fort de 1000 h^{es} et de 4 pièces de canon, peut se réunir au besoin avec la colonne du g^{al} Bonnet: elles doivent assurer la communication jusqu'aux montagnes en avant d'Aranda, ci 1000 h^{es}

Colonne de Vitoria.—Le général de brigade Monthion, et le colonel Barerre, occupent Vitoria avec une colonne composée comme il suit:

2 compagnies du 15e de ligne, formant un petit bataillon de	300 h^{es}	
Le 2e bat^{on} du 12e d'infanterie légère.	600	
Le 2e bat^{on} du 2e id.	600	
	———	
(Ce qui fait en infanterie)	1500 h^{es}	
1 escadron de dragons (en marche)	200	
2 pièces de canon.	———	
(Tous ces corps sont en marche)	1700 ci	1700 h^{es}

Garnison de St. Sébastien.—Le général Thouvenot commande à St. Sébastien avec mille hommes de garnison, ci . . . . . 1000 h^{es}

Récapitulation.—Le corps du m^{al} Bessières est de . . . . . 23,150 h^{es}
et 36 pièces de canon.

Les détachemens et troisièmes bataillons des corps qui sont aux divisions actives du m^{al} Bessières pourront sous 15 jours le rejoindre, vû qu'ils seront remplacés à Vitoria et à Burgos par d'autres corps.

* Note.—These two words are added in Napoleon's own handwriting.

2°. *Arragon.*

Jusqu'à cette heure les troupes qui sont en Arragon faisaient partie du corps des Pyrénées Occidentales. Mais le corps des Pyrénées Occidentales se portant sur la Galice, il devient indispensable d'en faire une division à part.

Aujourd'hui, ce commandement comprend Pampelune, la Navarre, et les troupes qui forment le siège de Saragosse, sous les ordres du général Verdier.

Ces troupes sont divisées en quatre brigades, et sont composées ainsi qu'il suit :

3 régiments d'infanterie de ligne de la Vistule, ayant sous les

armes	3600 h⁻ˢ
Les 4ᵉ, 6ᵉ et 7ᵉ bataillons de marche	1500
Le 3ᵉ bataillon du 14ᵉ provisoire	1300
Le 1ᵉʳ regiment supplémentaire	900
Les 47ᵉ, 15ᵉ et 70ᵉ	1600
Un bataillon des gardes nationales d'élite	600

Total . . . . . 9500 hˢ

La cavalerie consiste dans un régiment de lanciers Polonais . . . . 700 }
Plus un escadron de marche . . . . 400 } 1100

A Pampelune le gᵃˡ Dagout commande. Indépendamment d'un dépôt de 800 hommes, formant la garnison de la citadelle, il a (ci 800 une colonne mobile composée du 1ᵉʳ bataillon de marche du Portugal, du troisième bataillon du 118ᵉ, fort de 650 hommes, et d'un escadron de dragons, ce qui forme un total de 1400 hommes disponibles pour se porter sur tous les points de la Navarre, et sur les communications de Saragosse, pour y mettre l'ordre : ci 1400

Artillerie 200

Il y a donc encernement en Arragon et en Navarre . . . . . 13,000 hˢ

Aussitôt que Saragosse sera pris, et que le corps de l'Arragon sera constitué, il sera nécessaire de faire entrer au corps du marˡ Bessières le bataillon du 47ᵉ, celui du 15ᵉ, et les trois bataillons du 14ᵉ provisoire ; ce qui augmentera le mᵃˡ Bessières de deux mille hommes, afin de tenir les corps réunis. Il est possible qu'on fasse partir de Bayonne les 19,300 hommes de bonnes troupes de ligne, pour se diriger sur Saragosse et enlever la prise de cette place, si toutefois elle n'est pas encore prise.

Si Saragosse était pris, le corps du mᵃˡ Bessières pourrait être renforcé de ces trois mille hommes d'élite et de 2000 hommes du corps de Saragosse, ce qui lui ferait un corps nombreux pour la campagne de Galice.

Indépendamment de Saragosse, les rebelles occupent la ville de Jaca et plusieurs ponts dans les vallées. A tous les débouchés des vallées en France il y a un général de brigade avec une colonne mobile. On attendra la prise de Saragosse pour entrer dans ces vallées et y marcher dans les deux sens. En général l'esprit des vallées est bon ; mais des troupes de contrebandiers que les chefs des rebelles ont enregimentés les vexent.

3°. *Catalogne.*

Le général Duhesme occupe Barcelone, qui est une place qui a deux très belles forteresses, qui la dominent. C'est la plus grande ville de la monarchie.

Le général Duhesme a deux divisions, la division Chabran et la division Lechi, formant 11,000 h^es d'infanterie, 1600 h^es de cavalerie et 18 pièces de canon.

Le général Duhesme a eu plusieurs événemens ; il a brûlé un grand nombre de villages, et maintenu en respect le pays à 15 lieues à la ronde.

La ville de Géronne, n'ayant pas été occupée, les insurgés de la Catalogne ont établis là leur Junte, d'où ils donnent le mouvement au reste de la province. 2000 insurgés assiégeaient le fort de Figuéras. On y avait heureusement laissé 300 Français : ils ont été obligés de tirer beaucoup de coups de canon et de brûler le village.

Le g^al de division Reille, avec deux bataillons Toscans, a marché sur Figuéras, l'a débloqué, le 6 du mois, et y a fait entrer une grande quantité de vivres, dont on manquait. Le 10, il réunissait sa division, qui arrivait de divers points de la France ; il avait déjà 6000 hommes, et il doit avoir aujourd'hui 9000 h^es ; il doit s'assurer de Rosas et marcher sur Géronne, établir ses communications avec le général Duhesme et ersemble pacifier la Catalogne.

Les forces réunies des généraux Duhesme et Reille s'élèvent
donc à 22,000 h^es.

Ainsi le corps des Pyrénées Occidentales est fort de 23,000
Celui d'Arragon, de 13,000
Celui de Catalogne, de 22,000

Total . . 58,000 h^es

Nous venons de faire connaître la situation de l'armée dans les provinces de la Biscaye, de St. Ander, de la Castille, de la Navarre, de l'Arragon, et de la Catalogne ; c'est à dire, sur toute la frontière de France.

Voici actuellement la situation dans les autres points :

Les deux corps qui se sont rendus à Madrid sous les ordres du général Dupont et du m^al Moncey portaient, et portent encore : le premier, le nom de corps d'observation de la Gironde commandé par le g^al Dupont ; le second, le nom de corps d'observation des Côtés de l'Océan, commandé par le m^al Moncey.

Le corps d'observation de la Gironde est composé de trois divisions : deux sont en Andalousie avec le général Dupont ; la 3eme, celle du général Frère, doit être à présent à San Clemente.

Le corps d'observation des Côtés de l'Océan est composé également de trois divisions. La première est avec le maréchal Moncey, sous Valence : les deux autres sont à Madrid, et disséminés en différentes colonnes, pour maintenir la communication avec le général Dupont. Les états de situation vous feront connaître la force de ces divisions : mais on peut en général les considérer les unes dans les autres comme fortes de 6000 hommes présens sous les armes.

Il y a *à Madrid* deux bataillons de la garde, formant 1000 hommes, et à-peu-près 900 hommes de cavalerie de la garde.

Ainsi il y a *à Madrid*, et du côté *de Valence et de l'Andalousie*, le valeur de 40,000 hommes d'infanterie, huit mille hommes de cavalerie et 80 pièces de canon attelées.

Le général Junot a en Portugal trois divisions, formant présens sous les armes, compris son artillerie, sa cavalerie, 23 mille hommes.*

Telle est la situation de l'armée en Espagne et en Portugal.

1ere *Observation.*—Les événemens qui se passent aujourd'hui et demain amélioreront beaucoup la situation de toutes les affaires, en jettant dans la Galice le général Cuesta, en lui ôtant ses communications avec l'Estremadure, Madrid et l'Andalousie, en assurant notre communication avec le Portugal, et en assurant la soumission des provinces de Salamanque, Zamora, Toro, &ª.

La manière dont ces événemens auront lieu décideront à entrer sur le champ en Galice, à soumettre les Asturies, ou à différer encore quelques jours.

2e *Observation.*—La Navarre et la Biscaye se sont maintenues tranquilles.

En Arragon le plat pays a été soumis, les rebelles ont été battus plusieurs fois ; avec deux seuls bataillons, 8 à 10 mille insurgés ont été détruits ou dispersés; le découragement est au dernier point parmi eux. Ils se sont défendus dans leurs maisons à Saragosse ; on les a bombardé ; on leur a fait beaucoup de mal; on a achevé aujourd'hui de bloquer la ville en jettant un pont sur l'Ebre. Une fois cette ville soumise, il n'y a pas de doute que toute l'Arragon ne devienne tranquille. Une partie des troupes sera cependant nécessaire pour maintenir la province ; une petite partie pourra aider à la soumission de la Catalogne. La partie qui est nécessaire pour le bien du service du maréchal Bessières ira le rejoindre. Ainsi cet événement équivaudra à un secours considérable.

3eme *Observation.*—La première opération du général Reille a débloqué Figuéras: il soumet à present tous les environs. Il ne tardera pas sans doute à s'emparer de Géronne et à établir sa communication par terre avec le général Duhesme. La réduction de Géronne entamera probablement celle de Lerida; on pourra avoir alors une colonne de deux ou trois mille hommes, qu'on dirigera par Tortose sur Valence.

4eme *Observation.*—On n'a point de nouvelles de l'expédition de Valence, et le maréchal Moncey a huit mille hommes. Avec ces forces il n'a rien à craindre. Il ne peut pas prendre la ville, qui est très grande, si les paysans s'y sont renfermés et ne craignent point de la ruiner: mais le maˡ Moncey se maintiendra dans le plat pays, occupera les révoltés, qu'il empêchera de se porter ailleurs, et fera porter au pays tout le poids de la guerre.

5e *Observation.*—On compte que le général Dupont a aujourd'hui prés de 20,000 hommes. Si les opérations du maréchal Bessiéres réussissent bien, il n'y aura pas d'inconvénient à appuyer encore le général Dupont et à lui permettre de reprendre l'offensive. Ainsi les deux points importans, et où on fera une véritable guerre réglée, sont la Galice et l'Andalousie, parceque les troupes du camp de St. Roche, de Cadiz, des Algarves, sont prés de 25 mille hommes, qu'elles ont pris parti pour la sédition de Seville en Andalousie, et que tout ce qui était à Porto a pris parti pour les rebelles de Galice.

Le point le plus important de tous est celui du maˡ Bessiéres, comme on l'a déjà vu dans la note qu'on a envoyé. On doit tout faire pour que ce corps n'éprouve aucun mouvement rétrograde, aucun échec; celui du général Dupont vient après.

Les affaires de Saragosse sont au 3e ordre; celles de Valence ne sont qu'au 4me.

Voilà le véritable situation des affaires militaires du royaume.

* *Note by the Author.*—This calculation was made under the supposition that General Avrel had joined Dupont.

Il parait convenable de former dans l'Arragon une division de 10 à 12 mille hommes que pourra commander le g^{al} Verdier. Il devra correspondre directement avec l'état major du roi, avec le m^{al} Bessiéres (pour s'entendre), avec le g^{al} Duhesme pour se concerter, et avec le général de la 11e division militaire, qui se tiendra à Bayonne, afin de connaître toujours la situation de cette frontiére. Son commandement doit embrasser la Navarre et tout l'Arragon.

Alors l'armée sera composée du corps des Pyrénées Occidentales, de la division de l'Arragon (il est inutile d'en faire un corps), du corps de la Catalogne composé de trois divisions, y compris celle du général Reille, et des six divisions que forment les corps d'observation de la Gironde et des Côtés de l'Océan.

Cela fera à-peu-près 12 divisions réunies, et en outre un certain nombre de petites colonnes mobiles et de garnisons.

[Dictated by the Emperor Napoleon.]

No. III.

NOTE SUR LA POSITION ACTUELLE DE L'ARMEE EN ESPAGNE.

Bayonne, ce 21 Juillet, 1808.

1ere *Observation.*—La bataille de Medina del Rio Seco a mis les affaires de l'armée dans la meilleure situation. Le maréchal Bessiéres ne donne plus aucune inquiétude, et toutes les sollicitudes doivent se tourner du côté du général Dupont.

2e *Observation.*—Dans la position actuelle des affaires, l'armée Française occupe le centre; l'ennemi, un grand nombre de points de la circonférence.

3me *Observation.*—Dans une guerre de cette nature, il faut du sang froid, de la patience, et du calcul, et il ne faut pas épuiser les troupes en fausses marches et contremarches; il ne faut pas croire, quand on a fait une fausse marche de trois à quatre jours, qu'on l'ait réparée par une contremarche: c'est ordinairement deux fautes au lieu d'une.

4me *Observation.*—Toutes les opérations de l'armée ont réussies jusqu'à cette heure, autant qu'elles devaient réussir. Le général Dupont s'est maintenu au-delà des montagnes, et dans le bassin de l'Andalousie; trois fois il a défait les insurgés. Le maréchal Moncey a défait les insurgés à Valence; il n'a pas pu prendre la ville, ce qui est une chose qui n'est pas extraordinaire. Peut-être eût-on pu désirer qu'il eût pu se camper à une journée de la ville, comme a fait le général Dupont; mais, enfin, qu'il soit à une journée ou à cinq, comme à Saint Clémente, la différence n'est pas trés grande. En Arragon, on a battu sur tous les points, et dans toutes les circonstances, l'ennemi, et porté le découragement partout. Saragosse n'a pas été pris; il est aujourd'hui cerné; et une ville de 40 à 50 mille âmes, défendue par un mouvement populaire, ne se prend qu'avec du temps et de la patience. Les histoires des guerres sont pleines des catastrophes les plus considérables pour avoir brusqué et s'être enfourré dans les rues étroites des villes. L'example de Buenos Ayres, et des 12 milles Anglais d'élite qui y ont péri, en est une preuve.

5me *Observation.*—Ainsi la position de l'armée est bonne, le maréchal Moncey étant à Saint Clémente, ou environ, et les généraux Gobert et Vedel réunis au général Dupont en Andalousie; ce serait une faute, à moins d'incidens et d'un emploi immédiat à donner à ces troupes dans un autre point, que de concentrer toutes les troupes trop près de Madrid. L'incertitude des événemens du maréchal Bessières, et les 25 chances qu'il avoit contre lui sur cent, pouvaient déterminer à faire arrêter la marche de toutes les troupes qui s'éloignaient de la capitale, afin que les colonnes pussent être rappellées à Madrid si le maréchal Bessières était battu, et pussent arriver dans cette ville avant l'ennemi; mais ce serait une faute si on eût fait rétrograder ces colonnes, et si on eût agi comme si le maréchal Bessières avait été battu, lorsque quelques jours avant on agissait comme si l'armée de Galice n'existait pas. 500 chevaux et 1800 hommes d'infanterie dirigés sur Valladolid étaient tous ce qu'il fallait. Si cette colonne était partie trois jours plutôt, elle y serait arrivé le 15. Le maréchal Bessières a été vainqueur, et avait pour être vainqueur 75 chances contre 25; mais la fatigue qu'on a donné à l'armée, et les mouvemens rétrogrades qu'on a ordonné inutilement, puisque même le maréchal Bessières battu, on avait 8 à 10 jours pour réunir l'armée, ont fait un mal moral et physique. Il faut espérer que la nouvelle de la victoire arrivée à temps aura mis l'état major à même d'arrêter tout mouvement sur Madrid, et que chaque colonne se trouvere plus près du point où elle doit se trouver.

6me *Observation.*—Dans la situation actuelle des affaires, le plus important de tous est le général Dupont. On doit lui envoyer le reste de la division Gobert, et employer d'autres troupes pour maintenir la communication; il faut tenir la tête de la division du maréchal Moncey sur Saint Clémente, et menacer toujours la province de Valence. Si le maréchal Bessières a battu sans effort et avec peu de perte l'armée de Galice, et a eu moins de huit milles hommes engagés, il n'y a pas de doute qu'avec 20 milles la général Dupont ne culbute tout ce qu'il a devant lui.

7me *Observation.*—La brigade du général Rey rend à l'armée plus qu'elle n'a perdu par le détachement qui a été fait sur Valladolid. Toutes les probabilités humaines sont que le maréchal Bessières n'a plus besoin d'aucun renfort, du moins pour être maître de toute la Castille et du royaume de Léon. Ce n'est que lorsqu'on aura reçu la nouvelle de ce qu'il aura fait à Bénévente et à Léon qu'on pourra décider s'il doit attaquer la Galice.

8me *Observation.*—Le général Verdier, en Arragon, a cerné Saragosse: le 14eme et le 44eme de ligne partent demain pour s'y rendre. Les partis Français vont jusqu'à moitié chemin de Lerida, de Barbastro, et de Jaca. Dans dix jours toute l'artillerie sera arrivée. Cette belle et bonne brigade de troupes de ligne porte à près des quinze mille hommes l'armée du général Verdier. Il est probable que Saragosse tombera bientôt, et que les deux tiers de ces 15 mille hommes deviendront disponibles.

9me *Observation.*—Ainsi le corps du maréchal Bessières a pris l'offensive, il est dépuis sa victoire renforcé de la brigade Lefebre et de la brigade Gaulois; il est donc dans le cas de conserver l'offensive. Le corps du général Verdier en Arragon a battu partout les insurgés, a cerné la ville avec des forces beaucoup moindres; il vient d'être considérablement renforcé; ainsi il peut donner une nouvelle activité aux opérations du siège, et conserver son activité offensive sur les deux rives de l'Ebre. La corps de Catalogne a joliment agi, ayant pour point d'appui Barcelonne, la jonction sera faite aujourd'hui ou demain devant Géronne, avec le gén[1] Reille.

10eme *Observation.*—Voilà pour les trois corps d'armée situés du côté de la France. La communication de Madrid avec la France est importante sous tous les points de vue. Il faut donc que les colonnes qui viennent d'être organisées à Burgos, et à Vitoria et qui seront journellement renforcées et augmentées, soient laissées dans ces stations.

Ci-joint la note de la formation de ces colonnes. Elles sont presque toutes composées de 3eme bataillons et de conscrits, mais avec de bons cadres; 15 à 20 jours de stations à Burgos et à Vitoria les mettront à-peu-près à l'école de battaillon. Ce serait une très grande faute que de rappeler trop tôt ces troupes pour en renforcer les cadres principaux; il faut attendre jusqu'à ce qu'on ait pu les remplacer à Vitoria et à Burgos par de nouvelles troupes.

11eme *Observation.*—Il n'y a donc rien à craindre du côté du maréchal Bessières, ni dans le nord de la Castille, ni dans le royaume de Léon.

Il n'y a rien à craindre en Arragon; Saragosse tombera un jour plus tôt ou un jour plus tard.

Il n'y a rien à craindre en Catalogne.

Il n'y a rien à craindre pour les communications de Burgos à Bayonne, moyennant les deux colonnes organisées dans ces deux villes, et qui seront renforcées. S'il y avait des événemens en Biscaye, la force qui se réunit à Bayonne, formant une réserve, seroit suffisante pour mettre tout en ordre.

S'il arrive à Burgos quelque événement trop considérable pour que la colonne mobile qui est à Burgos puisse y mettre ordre, le maréchal Bessières ne sera pas assez loin pour n'y pouvoir faire un détachement.

Le général Monthion a la surveillance de toutes les Biscayes. Le général Bonnet à Burgos est chargé de maintenir la communication de Vitoria avec le maréchal Bessières et avec Madrid. Il est nécessaire que ces deux généraux correspondent tous les jours entr'eux et avec le général Drouet, qui est laissé en réserve à Bayonne, de même que le génl Verdier de Saragosse et le génl Dagoult de Pampelune doivent correspondre tous les jours avec le général Drouet à Bayonne, et avec Madrid, par le canal de Bayonne et de Vitoria; jusqu'à ce que les communications directes soient rétablies, un courrier partant de Madrid peut se rendre par Vitoria, Tolosa, Pampelune, devant Saragosse. Le seul point important donc aujourd'hui est le général Dupont. Si l'ennemi parvenait jamais à s'emparer des défilés de la Sierra Morena, il serait difficile de l'en chasser; il faut donc renforcer le génl Dupont, de manière qu'il ait 25 mille hommes, compris ce qu'il faudra pour garder les passages des montagnes, et une partie du chemin de La Manche. Il pourra disposer les troupes de manière que le jour où il voudra attaquer, la brigade de deux à trois mille hommes, destinée à garder les montagnes, arrive au camp du génl Dupont à marches forcées, et soit successivement remplacée par les colonnes qui seraient en arrière, de sorte que le génl Dupont ait pour le jour de la bataille plus de 23 mille hommes à mettre en ligne.

Une fois qu'on aura bien battu l'ennemi, une partie des troupes se dissipera, et selon que la victoire sera plus ou moins décidée, on pourra faire continuer le mouvement à d'autres troupes sur le général Dupont.

12eme *Observation.*—Saragosse pris, on aura des troupes disponible, soit pour renforcer l'armée de Catalogne, soit pour marcher sur Valence de concert avec le maréchal Moncey, soit pour renforcer le maréchal Bessières et marcher en Galice, si après la victoire qu'il a déjà remporté, et celle qu'il remportera à Léon, il ne croit pas assez fort pour s'y porter d'abord.

13eme *Observation.*—Il serait important de choisir deux points intermédiaires entre Andujar et Madrid, pour pouvoir y laisser garnison permanente, un commandant, un dépôt de cartouches, munitions, canons, magasins de biscuit, des fours, du farine, et un hôpital, de sorte que de 3 à 400 hommes défendent le magasin et l'hôpital contre tout une insurrection. Il est difficile de croire qu'il n'y ait point quelque château ou donjon, pouvant être retranché promptement et propre à cela. C'est par ce seul moyen qu'on peut raccourcir la ligne d'opération, et être sûr d'avoir toutes les trois ou quatre grandes marches, une manutention et un point de repos.

14eme *Observation.*—En résumé, le partage de l'armée paraît devoir être celui-ci:

Corps de Catalogne, tel qu'il existe à-peu-près . . .		20,000 h^{es}
Corps d'Arragon, tel qu'il existe à-peu-près, 15 mille hommes, jusqu'à ce que Saragosse soit prit		15,000
Corps du maréchal Bessières, ce qu'il a à-peu-près .	17,000	
Colonne de Burgos	2,000	
Colonne de Vitoria	2,000	
Garnison de St. Sébastien	1,500	
Corps d'Aranda	1,000	
Total du corps du mar^d Bessières		24,000 h^{es}

Après la prise de Saragosse, lorsque les affaires de Catalogne seront un peu appaisées, on pourra, selon les circonstances, ou renforcer le maréchal Bessières, ou renforcer le général Dupont, ou entreprendre l'opération de Valence.

Aujourd'hui, le seul point qui menace, où il faut promptement avoir un succés, c'est du côté du général Dupont, avec 25 mille hommes, infanterie, cavalerie, et artillerie comprise : il a beaucoup plus qu'il ne faut pour avoir de grands résultats ; à la rigueur, avec 21 mille hommes présens sur le champ de battaille, il peut hardiment prendre l'offensive, il ne sera pas battu, et il aura pour lui plus de 80 chances.

[Dictated by Napoleon.]

No. IV.

NOTE SUR LES AFFAIRES D'ESPAGNE.

St. Cloud, ce 30 *Août,* 1808.

1ere *Observation.*—Dans la position de l'armée d'Espagne on a à craindre d'être attaqué sur la droite par l'armée de Galice, sur le centre par l'armée venant de Madrid, sur la gauche par l'armée venant de Saragosse et de Valence. Ce serait une grande faute que de laisser l'armée de Saragosse et de Valence prendre position à Tudela.

Tudela doit être occupé, parceque c'est une position honorable, et Milagro une position obscure.

Tudela est sur les communications de Pampelune, a un beau pont en pierre, et est l'aboutissant d'un canal sur Saragosse. C'est une position offensive sur Saragosse telle que l'ennemi ne peut pas la négliger ; cette position seule couvre la Navarre. En gardant Tudela, on garde une grande quantité de bateaux, qui nous seront bientôt nécessaires pour le siège de Saragosse.

Si l'ennemi était maître de Tudela, toute la Navarre s'insurgerait, l'ennemi pourrait arriver à Estella, en négligeant la position de Milagro et en coupant la communication avec Pampelune.

D'Estella il serait sur Tolosa ; il y serait sans donner le temps de faire les dispositions convenables ; il n'est pas à craindre, au contraire, que l'ennemi fasse aucune opération sur Pampelune ; tant que nous aurons Tudela, il serait lui-même coupé sur Saragosse.

Le général qui commande à Tudela peut couvrir les hauteurs de redoutes ; si c'est une armée d'insurgés, s'en approcher et la battre, la tenir constamment sur la défensive par les reconnoissances et ses mouvemens sur Saragosse.

Et si, au lieu de cela, une partie de l'armée de ligne Espagnole marchait sur Tudela, le général Français repassera l'Ebre s'il y est forcé, disputera la terrein sur Pampelune, et donnera le temps au général en chef de l'armée Française de prendre ses mesures. Ce corps d'observation remplira alors son but, et aucune opération prompte sur Tolosa ni Estella n'est à craindre.

Au lieu qu'en occupant la position de Milagro, l'ennemi sera à Estella, le même jour qu'on l'apprendra au quartier-général. Si on occupe Tudela, il faut s'y aider de redoutes, et s'y établir, n'y conserver aucune espèce d'embarras, et les tenir tous dans Pampelune. Si l'ennemi l'occupe, il faut l'en chasser, et s'y établir ; car dans l'ordre défensif, ce serait une grande faute, qui entraînerait de fâcheuses conséquences.

2e *Observation.*—La position de Burgos était également importante à tenir, comme ville de haute réputation, comme centre de communication et de rapports.

De là des partis non seulement de cavalerie, mais encore de deux ou de trois mille hommes d'infanterie, et même quatre ou cinq mille hommes en échelons, peuvent poster les premières patrouilles d'hussards dans toutes les directions jusqu'à deux marches, et parfaitement informés de tout ce qui se fait, en instruire le quartier-général, de manière que si l'ennemi se présente en force sur Burgos, les différentes divisions puissent à temps s'y porter pour le soutenir et livrer la bataille, ou si cela n'est pas jugé convenable, éclairer les mouvemens d'ennemi, lui laisser croire qu'on veut se porter sur Burgos, et pouvoir ensuite faire sa retraite pour se porter ailleurs.

Un corps de 12 à 15 mille hommes ne prend-il pas 20 positions dans la journée au seul commandement d'un adjutant major ? et nos troupes seraient-elles devenues des levées en masse, qu'il faudroit placer 15 jours d'avance dans les positions où on voudroit qu'elles se battent ?

Si cela eût été jugé ainsi, le corps du maréchal Bessières eût pris la position de Miranda ou de Briviesca ; mais lorsque l'ennemi est encore à Madrid, lorsqu'on ignore où est l'armée de Galice, et qu'on a le soupçon que les rebelles pourront employer une partie de leurs efforts contre le Portugal, prendre, au lieu d'une position menaçante, offensive, honorable, comme Burgos, une position honteuse, borgne comme Trevino, c'est dire à l'ennemi, " Vous n'avez rien à craindre ; portez vous ailleurs ; nous avons fait nos dispositions pour aller plus loin, ou bien nous avons choisi un champ de bataille pour nous battre ; venez ici, vous ne craignez pas d'être inquiétés." Mais que fera le général Français, si l'on marche demain sur Burgos ? laissera-t-il prendre par 6000 insurgés la citadelle de cette ville, ou si les Français ont laissés garnison dans le château (car on ignore la position et la situation de l'armée), comment une garnison de 4, 6, ou 800 hommes se retira-t-elle dans une si vaste plaine ? Et dès lors c'est comme s'il n'y avoit rien : l'ennemi maître de cette citadelle, on ne la reprendra plus.

Si, au contraire, on veut garder la citadelle, on veut donc livrer bataille à l'ennemi ; car cette citadelle ne peut pas tenir plus de trois jours ; et si on veut livrer bataille à l'ennemi, pourquoi le maréchal[1] Bessières abandonne-t-il le terrein où on veut livrer bataille ?

Ces dispositions paraissent mal raisonnées, et quand l'ennemi marchera on fera essuyer à l'armée un affront qui démoralisera les troupes, n'y eût-il que des corps légers un des insurgés qui marchassent.

En résumé, la position de Burgos devait être gardée ; tous les jours à trois heures du matin on devait être sous les armes, et à une heure du matin il devait partir des reconnaissances dans toutes les directions. On devait ainsi recueillir des nouvelles à huit ou dix lieues à la ronde, pour qu'on peût prendre ensuite le parti que les circonstances indiqueraient.

C'est la première fois qu'il arrive à une armée de quitter toutes les positions offensives, pour se mettre dans de mauvaises positions défensives, d'avoir l'air de choisir des champs de bataille, lorsque l'éloignement de l'ennemi, les mille et une combinaisons différentes qui peuvent avoir lieu, ne laissent point la probabilité de prévoir si la bataille aura lieu à Tudela, entre Tudela et Pampelune, entre Soria et l'Ebre, ou entre Burgos et Miranda.

La position de Burgos, tenue en force et d'une manière offensive, menace Palencia, Valladolid, Aranda, Madrid même. Il faut avoir longtemps fait la guerre pour la concevoir ; il faut avoir entrepris un grand nombre d'opérations offensives pour savoir comme le moindre événement ou indice encourage ou décourage, décide une opération ou une autre.

En deux mots, si 15 mille insurgés entrent dans Burgos, se retranchent dans la ville, et occupent le château, il faut calculer une marche de plusieurs jours pour pouvoir s'y poster et reprendre la ville ; ce qui ne sera pas sans quelque inconvénient ; si pendant ce temps-là la véritable attaque est sur Logroño ou Pampelune, on aura fait des contremarches inutiles, qui auront fatigué l'armée : et enfin, si l'ennemi occupe Logroño, Tudela, et Burgos, l'armée Française serait dans une triste et mauvaise position.

Quand on tient à Burgos de la cavalerie sans infanterie, n'est-ce pas dire à l'ennemi qu'on ne veut pas y tenir ; n'est-ce pas l'engager à y venir ? Burgos a une grande influence dans le monde par son nom, dans la Castille parceque c'en est la capitale, dans les opérations parcequ'elle donne une communication directe avec St. Ander. Il n'est pas permis à 300 lieues, et n'ayant pas même un état de situation de l'armée, de prescrire ce qu'on doit faire ; mais on doit dire que si aucune force majeure ne l'empêche, il faut occuper Burgos et Tudela.

Le corps détaché de Tudela a son mouvement assuré sur Pampelune, a le rôle de garder la Navarre, a ses ennemis à tenir en échec, Saragosse et tous les insurgés. Il était plus que suffisant pour surveiller Tudela, l'Ebre, et Pampelune, pour dissiper les rassemblemens s'il n'y avait que des insurgés, contenir l'ennemi, donner des renseignemens, et retarder la marche sur Pampelune. Si, au lieu des insurgés, c'est l'armée ennemie qui marche de ce côté, il suffit encore pour donner le temps à l'armée de Burgos, à celle de Miranda, de marcher réunie avec 36 mille hommes, soit pour prendre l'offensive, soit pour prendre en flanc l'ennemi qui marche sur Pampelune, soit pour se replier et rentrer dans la Navarre, si toute l'armée ennemie avait pris cette direction.

Si ces observations paraissent bonnes et qu'on les adopte, que l'ennemi n'ait encore montré aucun plan, il faut que le général qui commande le corps de Saragosse fasse construire quelques redoutes autour de Tudela, pour favoriser ses champs de bataille, réunisse des vivres de tous les côtés, et soit là dans une position offensive sur Saragosse en maintenant sa communication avec Logroño par sa droite, mais au moins par la rive gauche de l'Ebre. Il faut que le maréchal Bessières, avec tout son corps, renforcé de la cavalerie légère, soit campé dans le bois près Burgos, la citadelle bien occupée ; que tous les hôpitaux, les dépôts, les embarras soient au delà de l'Ebre ; qu'il soit là en position de manœuvre, tous les jours, à trois heures du matin, sous les armes, jusqu'au retour de toutes les reconnaissances, et éclairant le pays dans la plus grande étendue ; que le corps du ma¹ Moncey soit à Miranda et à Briviesca, tous ses embarras et hôpitaux derrière Vitoria, toujours en bataille avant le jour, et envoyant des reconnaissances sur Soria et les autres directions de l'ennemi.

Il ne faut pas perdre de vue que les corps des maréchaux Bessières et Moncey devant être réunis, il faut se lier le moins possible avec Logroño, et cependant considérer le corps du général Lefebre comme un corps détaché, que a une ligne d'opération particulière sur Pampelune et un rôle séparé ; vouloir conserver Tudela comme une partie contigue de la ligne, c'est se disséminer beaucoup. Enfin, faire la guerre, c'est à dire, avoir des nouvelles par les curés, les alcaldes, les chefs de couvent, les principaux propriétaires, les postes : on sera alors parfaitement informé.

Les reconnaissances qui tous les jours se dirigeront du côté de Soria, de Burgos, sur Palencia, et du côté d'Aranda, peuvent former tous les jours trois postes d'interception, trois rapports d'hommes arrêtés, qu'on traitera bien, et qu'on relachera quand ils auront donné les renseignemens qu'on désire. On verra alors venir l'ennemi, on pourra réunir toutes ses forces, lui dérober des marches, et tomber sur ses flancs au moment où il méditera un projet offensif.

3ᵐᵉ *Observation.*—L'armée Espagnole d'Andalousie était peu nombreuse. Toutes les Gazettes Anglaises, et les rapports de l'officier Anglais qui était au camp, nous le prouvent. L'inconcevable ineptie du général Dupont, sa profonde ignorance des calculs d'un général en chef, son tâtonnement, l'ont perdu : 18 mille hommes ont posé les armes, six mille seulement se sont battus, et encore ces 6000 hommes que le gén¹ Dupont a fait battre à la pointe du jour, après les avoir fait marcher toute la nuit, étaient un contre trois. Malgré tout cela, l'ennemi s'est si mal battu, qu'il n'a pas fait un prisonnier, pris une pièce de canon, gagné un pouce de terrein, et l'armée de Dupont est restée intacte dans sa position : ce qui sans doute a été une malheur ; car il eût mieux valu que cette division eût été mise en déroute, éparpillée, et détruite, puisque les divisions Vedel et Dufour, au lieu de se rendre par la capitulation, auraient fait leur retraite. Comment ces deux divisions ont-elles été comprises dans la capitulation ? c'est par la lâcheté insultante et l'imbécilité des hommes qui ont négocié, et qui porteront sur l'échaffaud la peine de ce grand crime national.

Ce que l'on vient de dire prouve que les Espagnoles ne sont pas à craindre ; toutes les forces Espagnoles ne sont pas capables de culbuter 25 mille Français, dans une position raisonnable.

Depuis le 12 jusqu'au 19, le général Dupont n'a fait que des bêtises, et malgré tout cela, s'il n'avait pas fait la faute de se séparer de Vedel, et qu'il eût marché avec lui, les Espagnols auraient été battus et culbutés. À la guerre les hommes ne sont rien, c'est un homme qui est tout. Jusqu'à cett heure nous n'avons trouvé ces exemples que dans l'histoire de nos ennemis aujourd'hui, il est fâcheux que nous puissions les trouver dans la notre.

Une rivière, fût-elle aussi large que la Vistule, aussi rapide que le Danub à son embouchure, n'est rien si on n'a des débouchés sur l'autre rive, et un téte prompte à reprendre l'offensive. Quant à l'Ebre, c'est moins que rien on ne la regarde que comme une trace.

Dans toutes ces observations, on a parlé dans la position où se trouvai l'armée du 20 au 26, lorsqu'elle n'avait nulle part nouvelle de l'ennemi.

Si on continue à ne prendre aucune mesure pour avoir des nouvelles, o: n'apprendra que l'armée de ligne Espagnole est arrivée sur Tudela et Pampe

lune, qu'elle est sur les communications, sur Tolosa, que lorsqu'elle y sera déjà
rendue.   On a fait connaître dans la note précédente comment on faisait à
la guerre pour avoir des nouvelles.   Si la position de Tudela est occupée
par l'ennemi, on ne voit pas que l'Ebre soit tenable.   Comment a-t-on évacué
Tudela, lorsqu'on avait mandé dans des notes précédentes qu'il fallait garder
ce point, et que l'opinion même des généraux qui venaient de Saragosse
était d'occuper cette importante position ?

[Dictated by Napoleon.]

No. V.

NOTE SUR LES AFFAIRES D'ESPAGNE.

St. Cloud, Août, 1808.

1ere *Observation.*—Tudela est important sous plusieurs points de vue : il a
un pont sur l'Ebre, et protège parfaitement la Navarre ; c'est le point d'intersection du canal qui va à Saragosse.

Les convois d'artillerie et de vivres mettent pour se rendre de Pampelune
à Tudela trois jours, de Tudela à Saragosse trois jours.   Mais en se servant
du canal, on va de Tudela à Saragosse en 14 heures.   Lorsque donc les vivres,
les hôpitaux, sont à Tudela, c'est comme s'ils étaient à Saragosse.

La première opération que doit faire l'armée lorsqu'elle reprendra son système d'offensif, et qu'elle sera forte de tous ses moyens, ce doit être d'investir
et de prendre Saragosse ; et si cette ville résiste comme elle l'a fait la pre-
miére fois, en donner un exemple qui retentisse dans toute l'Espagne.

Une vingtaine de pièces de 12 de campagne, une vingtaine d'obusiers de six
pièces de campagne, une douzaine de mortiers, et une douzaine de pièces de
16 et de 24, parfaitement approvisionées, seront nécessaires, ainsi que des
mineurs pour remplir ce but.

Il n'est aucun de ces bouches à feu qui doive consommer son approvisionnement de campagne.

Un approvisionnement extraordinaire de 80 mille coups de canon, bombes
ou obus, parait nécessaire pour prendre cette ville.

Il faudrait donc, pour ne pas retarder la marche de la grande armée, 15
jours avant qu'elle ne puisse arriver, commencer le transport de Pampelune
à Tudela, et que dans les 48 heures après l'investissement de Saragosse,
l'artillerie y arrivât sur des bâteaux, de manière que quatre jours après on
pût commencer trois attaques à la fois, et avoir cette ville en peu de jours,
ce qui serait une partie des succès, en y employant 25 à 30 mille hommes,
ou plus s'il était nécessaire.

On suppose que, si l'ennemi a pris position entre Madrid et Burgos, il aura
été battu.

Il faut donc occuper Tudela.   Ce point est tellement important qu'il serait
à désirer qu'on pût employer un mois à le fortifier et à s'y retrancher, de
manière qu'un millier d'hommes avec 8 à 10 pièces de canon s'y trouvassent
en sûreté et à l'abri de toutes les insurrections possibles.   Il ne faut pas surtout souffrir que les révoltés s'y retranchassent ; ce serait deux sièges au
lieu d'un ; et il serait impossible de prendre Saragosse avant d'avoir Tudela,
à cause du canal.

On trouvera ci-joint des observations du colonel Lacoste sur Tudela ;

puisque les localités empêchent de penser à le fortifier, il eût été utile de l'occuper au lieu de Milagro, qui n'aboutit à rien.

2e. Soria n'est je crois qu'à deux petites marches des positions actuelles de l'armée. Cette ville s'est constamment mal comportée. Une expédition qui se porterait sur Soria, la désarmerait, en prendrait une trentaine d'hommes des plus considérables, qu'on enverrait en France pour ôtages, et qui enfin lui ferait fournir des vivres pour l'armée, serait d'un bon effet.

3me. Une troisième opération qui serait utile serait l'occupation de St. Ander. Il serait bien avantageux qu'elle pût se faire par la route directe de Bilbao à St. Ander.

4me. Il faut s'occuper de désarmer la Biscaye et la Navarre ; c'est un point important ; tout Espagnol pris les armes à la main doit être fusillé.

Il faut veiller sur la fabrique d'armes de Placencia, ne point laisser travailler les ouvriers pour les rebelles.

Le fort de Pancorvo doit être armé et fortifié avec la plus grande activité. Il doit y avoir dans ce fort des fours, des magasins de bouches et de guerre. Situé presqu'à mi-chemin de Bayonne à Madrid, c'est un poste intermédiaire pour l'armée, et un point d'appui pour les opérations de la Galice.

Il y a dans l'armée plus de généraux qu'il n'en faut : deux seraient nécessaires au corps qui était sous Saragosse. Les généraux de division La Grange, Belliard, et Grandjean sont sans emploi, et tous trois bons généraux.

Il faut renvoyer le plus promptement possible, le régiment et le général Portugais pour joindre leurs corps à Grenoble, où il doit se former.

5me. On ne discutera pas ici si la ligne de l'Ebre est bonne, si elle a la configuration requise pour être défendue avec avantage.

On discutera encore moins si on eût pu ne pas évacuer Madrid, conserver la ligne du Duero, ou prendre une position qui eût couvert le siège de Saragosse et eût permis d'attendre que cette ville fût prise ; toutes ces questions sont oiseuses.

Nous nous contenterons de dire, puisqu'on a pris la ligne de l'Ebre, que les troupes s'y dissous et s'y reposent, qu'elle a au moins l'avantage que le pays est plus sain, étant plus élevé, et qu'on peut y attendre que les chaleurs soient passées.

Il faut surtout ne point quitter cette ligne sans avoir un projet déterminé, qui ne laisse aucune incertitude dans les opérations à suivre. Ce serait un grand malheur de quitter cette ligne pour être ensuite obligé de la reprendre.

A la guerre les trois quarts sont des affaires morales ; la balance des forces réelles n'est que pour un autre quart.

6me. En gardant la ligne de l'Ebre il faut que le général ait bien prévu toute ce que l'ennemi peut faire dans tous les hypothèses.

L'ennemi peut se présenter devant Burgos, partir de Soria, et marcher sur Logroño, ou, en partant de Saragosse, se porter sur Estella, et menacer ainsi Tolosa. Il faut, dans toutes ces hypothèses, qu'il n'y ait point un long-temps perdu en délibérations, qu'on puisse se ployer de sa droite à sa gauche, et de sa gauche à sa droite, sans faire aucun sacrifice : car dans les manœuvres combinées, les tâtonnemens, l'irrésolution qui naissent des nouvelles contradictoires qui se succèdent rapidement, conduisent à des malheurs.

Cette diversion de Saragosse sur Tolosa est une des raisons qui a long-temps fait penser que la position de Tudela devait être gardée, soit sur la rive droite, soit avec la faculté de repasser sur la rive gauche. Elle est offensive sur Saragosse, elle previent à temps de tous les mouvemens qui pourraient se faire de ce côté.

7me. Une observation qu'il n'est pas hors de propos de faire ici c'est, que l'ennemi, qui a intérêt de masquer ses forces, en cachant le véritable point

21

de son attaque, opère de manière que le coup qu'il veut porter n'est jamais indiqué d'une manière positive, et le général ne peut deviner que par la connaissance bien approfondie de sa position, et la manière dont il fait entrer son système offensif, pour protéger et garantir son système défensif.

8me. On n'a point de renseignemens sur ce que fait l'ennemi. On dit toujours qu'on ne peut pas avoir des nouvelles, comme si cette position était extraordinaire dans une armée, comme si on trouvait ordinairement des espions. Il faut en Espagne, comme partout ailleurs, envoyer des parties qui enlèvent tantôt le curé ou l'alcalde, tantôt un chef de couvent ou le maître de poste, et surtout toutes les lettres ; quelquefois le maître de la poste, aux douanes, ou celui qui en fait les fonctions ; on les met aux arrêts jusqu'à ce qu'ils parlent, en les faisant interroger deux fois par jour, on les garde en tage, et on les charge d'envoyer des piétons, et de donner des nouvelles. Quand on saura prendre des mesures de force et de vigueur, on aura des nouvelles.

Il faut intercepter toutes les postes, toutes les lettres. Le seul motif d'avoir des nouvelles peut déterminer à faire un gros détachement de quatre à cinq mille hommes, qui se portent dans une grande ville, prennent les lettres à la poste, se saisissent des citoyens les plus aisés, de leurs lettres, papiers, gazettes, etc. Il est hors de doute que même dans la ligne des Français les habitans sont tous informés de ce qui se passe : à plus forte raison hors de la ligne. Qui empêche donc, qu'on prenne les hommes marquans, et qu'on les renvoye ensuite sans les maltraiter ?

Il est donc de fait, lorsqu'on n'est point dans un désert, et qu'on est dans un pays peuplé, que si le général n'est pas instruit, c'est qu'il n'a pas su prendre les mesures convenables pour l'être.

Les services que les habitans rendent à un général ennemi, ils ne le font jamais par affection, ni même pour avoir de l'argent ; les plus réels qu'on obtient c'est pour avoir des sauve-gardes, et des protections ; c'est pour conserver ses biens, ses jours, sa ville, son monastère.

[The original of the following memoir is a rough draft, written by King Joseph. It has many erasures and interlineations, and was evidently composed to excuse his retreat from Madrid. The number of the French troops was undoubtedly greater than is here set down, unless the infantry alone be meant.]

No. VI.

Lorsqu'on a quitté Madrid à la nouvelle de *la défection* d'un corps de vingt-deux mille hommes, il y avoit dans Madrid dix sept mille hommes, au corps du maréchal Bessières quinze mille cinq cent, au corps de Saragosse onze mille sept cent : l'armée se composait donc de quarante-cinq mille hommes ; mais ces trois corps étaint distans entre eux de près de cent lieues. La première idée fut de réunir le corps de Madrid à celui de Léon, à Burgos, et par suite d'entrer en communication avec celui de Saragosse, avec lequel l'état major de Madrid n'avait jamais eu aucune relation directe, et dont il ignorait absolument la situation et la composition.

Vingt jours après sa sortie de Madrid le roi s'est trouvé à la tête d'une armée de cinquante mille hommes. Le feu de la sédition n'a pas pu se communiquer sur les points parcourus par les trois corps d'armée alors réunis ; les communications avec la France ont été gardées ; l'insurrection de Bilbao a été éteinte dans le sang de 1200 insurgés. Peu de jours après, 20,000 d'entre

l'ennemi, et d'attendre dans une noble attitude le mouvement général qui sera imprimé par votre majesté lors de l'arrivée de toutes les troupes dans ce pays.

De tous les projets le dernier parait préférable; il est plus noble et aussi sûr que le 5ème.

Ces deux projets sont seuls absolument offensifs ou absolument défensifs. On peut les regarder, l'un et l'autre, comme propres à assurer la conservation de l'armée jusqu'à l'arrivée des renforts. Le dernier a sur l'autre l'avantage d'arrêter le progrès de l'ordre nouveau qui s'établit en Espagne; il est plus digne des troupes Françaises, et du frère de votre majesté. Il est aussi sûr que celui de la sévère et honteuse défensive proposée par l'article cinq. Je l'ai communiqué au mar^{al} Jourdan et au mar^{al} Ney, qui l'un et l'autre sont de cet avis. Je ne doute point que les autres maréchaux ne partagent leur opinion.

Au premier Octobre je puis avoir la réponse de V. M., et même avant, puisque je lui ai manifesté cette opinion par ma lettre du 14 Septembre.

Si V. M. approuve ce plan, il sera possible qu'elle n'ait pas de mes nouvelles jusqu'a l'arrivée des troupes; mais je suis convaincu qu'elle trouvera les affaires dans une bien meilleure situation qu'en suivant aucun des autres cinq projets.

Miranda, le 16 *Sept.* 1808.

No. VII.

S.

EXTRAITS DES LETTRES DU MAJOR GENERAL AU GENERAL SAVARY, A MADRID.

Bayonne, 12 *Juillet,* 1808.

Section 1.—J'ai rendu compte à l'empereur, général, de votre lettre du 8. S. M. trouve que vous vous êtes dégarni, de trop de monde à Madrid, que vous avez fait marcher trop de troupes au secours du g^{al} Dupont, qu'on ne doit pas agir offensivement jusqu'à ce que les affaires de la Galice soient éclairées. De tous les points de l'armée, général, le plus important est la Galice, parceque c'est la seule province qui ait réellement conclu un traité avec l'Angleterre. La division de ligne des troupes Espagnoles qui était à Oporto s'est joint à celle qui était en Galice, et enfin par la position de cette province extrêmement près de l'Angleterre. Indépendamment de ces considérations, la position la rend encore plus intéressante; car les communications de l'armée se trouveraient compromises si le maréchal Bessiéres n'avait pas un entier succès, et il faudrait bien alors reployer toutes vos troupes, et marcher isolément au secours du maréchal Bessières. Encore une fois, général, vous vous êtes trop dégarni de Madrid, et si un bon régiment de cuirassiers, quelques pièces d'artillerie et 1000 à 1200 hommes d'infanterie avaient pu arriver à l'appui du maréchal Bessières, le 14, cela lui aurait été d'un éminent secours. *Qu'importe que Valence soit soumis? Qu'importe que Saragosse soit soumis?* Mais, général, le moindre succès de l'ennemi du côté de la Galice aurait des inconvéniens immenses. Instruit comme vous l'étiez des forces du général Cuesta, de la désertion des troupes d'Oporto, &^a. . . . .

S.M. trouve que pour bien manœuvrer il aurait fallu vous arranger de manière à avoir du 12ᵉ au 15ᵉ 8000 hommes pour renforcer le maréchal Bessières. Une fois nos derrières débarassées, et cette armée de Galice détruite, tout le reste tombe et se soumet de soi-même, &c., &c.

S.

EXTRAIT DE LA LETTRE, &c.

Bayonne, 13 *Juillet,* 1808.

Section 2.—Nous recevons vos lettres de 9 et du 10, général. L'empereur me charge de vous faire connaître que si le général Gobert était à Valladolid, le général Frère à San Clémente, ayant une colonne dans la Manche ; si 300 à 400 convalescens, un bon commandant, 4 pièces de canon, une escouade d'artillerie, et vingt mille rations de biscuit étaient dans le château de Ségovie, la position de l'armée serait superbe et à l'abri de toute sollicitude. La conduite du général Frère ne paraît pas claire. Les nouvelles qu'il a eues du maréchal Moncey paraissent apocryphes. Il est possible que ses 8000 hommes et son artillerie n'aient pas été suffisans pour enlever la ville de Valence. Cela étant, le maréchal Moncey ne l'enleverait pas d'avantage avec 20,000 hommes, parcequ'alors c'est une affaire de canons et de mortiers, &ª. &ª. . . . *Valence est comme la Catalogne et l'Arragon ; ces trois points sont secondaires.* Les deux vrais points importans sont le général Dupont et particulièrement le maréchal Bessières, parceque le premier a devant lui le corps du camp de St. Roche et le corps de Cadiz, et le maréchal Bessières parcequ'il a devant lui les troupes de la Galice et celles qui étaient à Oporto. Le général Dupont a près de 20,000 hommes ; il ne peut pas avoir contre lui un pareil nombre de troupes ; il a déjà obtenu des succès très marquans, et au pis aller il ne peut être contraint qu'a repasser les montagnes, ce qui n'est qu'un événement de guerre. Le maréchal Bessières est beaucoup moins fort que le général Dupont, et les troupes Espagnoles d'Oporto et de la Galice sont plus nombreuses que celles de l'Andalousie, et les troupes de la Galice n'ont pas encore été entamées. Enfin le moindre insuccès du maréchal Bessières intercepte toutes les communications de l'armée et compromettrait même sa sûreté. Le général Dupont se bat pour Andujar, et le maréchal Bessières se bat pour les communications de l'armée et pour les opèrations le plus importantes aux affaires d'Espagne, &c. &c.

S.

EXTRAIT DE LA LETTRE, &c. &c.

Bayonne, 18 *Juillet,* 1808, *à dix heures du soir.*

Section 3.—Je reçois, général, vos lettres du 14. L'aide-de-camp du maréchal Moncey a donné à sa majesté tous les détails sur ce qui s'est passé. La conduite du maréchal a été belle. Il a bien battu les rebelles en campagne. Il est tout simple qu'il n'ait pu entrer à Valence ; c'était une affaire de mortiers et de pièces de siège. Sa position à San Clémente est bonne, de là il est à même de remarcher sur Valence. Du reste, général, *l'affaire de Valence est une affaire du second ordre, même celle de Saragosse,* qui cependant est plus importante. L'affaire du maréchal Bessières était d'un intérêt majeur pour les affaires d'Espagne, et la première après cette affaire c'est celle du général Dupont, et c'est le moment de laisser le général Gobert suivre la

route. Le maréchal Moncey se repose ; le général Reille marche sur Géronne : ainsi trois colonnes pourront marcher ensemble sur Valence ; le corps
du général Reille, celui de Saragosse, et celui du maréchal Moncey, ce qui
formera les 20,000 hommes que ce maréchal croit nécessaires. Mais l'empereur, général, trouve que vous avez tort de dire qu'il n'y a rien été fait
depuis six semaines. On a battu les rassemblemens de la Galice, de St.
Ander, ceux d'Arragon et de Catalogne, qui dans leur aveuglement croyaient
qu'ils n'avaient qu'à marcher pour détruire les Français : le maréchal Moncey, les généraux Duhesme, Dupont, Verdier, ont fait de bonne besogne, et
tous les hommes sensés en Espagne ont changé dans le fonds de leur opinion,
et voient avec la plus grande peine l'insurrection. Au reste, général, les affaires d'Espagne sont dans la situation la plus prospère depuis la bataille de
Medina del Rio Seco, &c. &c. Le 14ᵉ et le 44ᵉ arrivent demain ; après demain ils partent pour le camp de Saragosse ; *non pas que ses troupes puissent
avancer la reddition, qui est une affaire de canon*, mais elles serviraient contre
les insurgés de Valence, s'ils voulaient renforcer ceux de Saragosse. Enfin,
si le général Gobert et les détachements qui sont à moitié chemin pour rejoindre le général Dupont font juger à ce général qu'il a des forces suffisantes
pour battre le général Castaños, il faut qu'elles continuent leur direction, et
qu'il attaque l'ennemi, s'il croit devoir le faire, &ᵃ. &ᵃ.

(Cette lettre a été écrite le jour de la bataille de Baylen.)

Extrait de la Lettre, &c.

Bordeaux, 3 Août, 1808.

Section 4.—Les événemens du général Dupont sont une chose sans exemple, et la rédaction de sa capitulation est de niveau avec la conduite tenue
jusqu'à cette catastrophe. L'empereur pense qu'on n'a pas tenu compte du
vague de la rédaction de l'acte, en permettant que les corps en échellons sur
la communication entre vous et le général Dupont aient marché pour se
rendre aux Anglais : car on ne doit pas présumer qu'ils aient la loyauté de
laisser passer les troupes qui s'embarquent. Comme vous ne parlez pas de
cela, on pense que vous avez retiré ces échellons sur Madrid. Après avoir lu
attentivement la relation du général Dupont, on voit qu'il n'a capitulé que
le lendemain de la bataille, et que les corps des généraux Vedel et Dufour,
qui se trouvent compris pour quelque chose dans la capitulation (on ne sait
pourquoi), ne se sont pas battus. Par la relation même du général Dupont,
tout laisse penser que l'armée du général Castaños n'était pas à beaucoup
près aussi forte qu'on le dit, et qu'il avait réuni à Baylen tout ce qu'il avait
de forces. S. M. ne lui calcule pas plus de 25,000 hommes de troupes de
ligne et plus de 15,000 paysans. Par la lettre du général Belliard *il paraît
que l'ordre est donné de lever le siège de Saragosse*, ce qui serait prématuré ;
car vous comprendrez qu'il n'est pas possible qu'on ne laisse un corps d'armée,
qui couvre Pampelune, et contienne la Navarre, sans quoi l'ennemi peut cer-
ner Pampelune, insurger la Navarre, et alors la communication de France
par Tolosa serait coupée, et l'ennemi sur les derrières de l'armée. Suppposant
l'ennemi réuni à Pampelune, la ville bloquée, il peut se trouver en cinq à six
marches sur les derrières de Burgos. L'armée qui assiège Saragosse est
donc à peu près nécessaire pour contenir la Navarre, les insurgés de l'Arragon et de Valence, et pour empêcher de percer sur notre flanc gauche ; car
si, comme le dit le général Belliard, le général Verdier se porte avec ses
troupes à Logroño, en jettant 2000 hommes dans Pampelune, la communication de Bayonne, qu'eut sur le champ interceptée le général Verdier, serait

mieux à Tudela qu'à Logroño. Si le général Castaños s'avance, et que vous puissiez lui livrer la bataille, on ne peut en prévoir que les plus heureux résultats : mais de la manière dont il a marché vis-à-vis du général Dupont, tout donne à croire qu'il mettra la plus grande circonspection dans ses mouvemens. Si par le canal des parlementaires l'on peut établir une suspension d'armes sans que le roi y soit pour rien en apparence, cette espèce d'armistice pourrait se rompre en se prévenant de part et d'autre huit jours d'avance, donnant aux Français la ligne du Duero passant par Almazan pour joindre l'Ebre. Cette suspension d'armes, que les insurgés pourraient regarder comme avantageuse, afin de s'organiser à Madrid, ne nous serait pas défavorable, parcequ'on verrait pendant ce temps l'organisation que prendraient les parties insurgés de l'Espagne, et ce que veut la nation, &c. &c.

LE MAJOR GENERAL AU ROI D'ESPAGNE.

Nantes, 11 Août, 1808.

Section 5.—Sire, le général Savary ni vos ministres Azanza et Urquijo ne sont arrivés : il paraît qu'il y a des rassemblemens à Bilbao d'après les nouvelles que nous recevons. S. M. pense qu'il est important d'y faire marcher le plutôt possible une colonne pour y rétablir l'ordre. *V. M. sait que la moitié de Saragosse était en notre pouvoir, et que sous peu on espérait avoir le reste de la ville. Lorsque le général Belliard a donné l'ordre de lever le siège, il eût été à désirer que cet ordre fût conditionnel, comme cela paraissait être l'intention de V. M., ainsi qu'on le voit dans sa correspondance ; c'est à dire, que le siège ne fût levé que dans le cas où l'on n'aurait pas cru être maitre de la ville avant cinq ou six jours.* Cela aurait présenté des circonstances meilleures ; car si le général Verdier évacue en entier la Navarre et l'Arragon, il est à craindre que la Navarre ne s'insurge, et Pampelune ne tarderait pas à être cernée. J'ai mandé à V. M. que déjà des corps entiers de la grande armée sont en mouvement pour se rendre en poste en Espagne. Les dispositions les plus vigoureuses sont prises de tous côtés, et *dans six semaines ou deux mois l'Espagne sera soumise.* L'empereur, qui continue à jouir d'une bonne santé, quoiqu'il soit très occupé, part dans une heure pour continuer sa route sur Angers, Tours, et Paris. V. M. doit être persuadée que toutes nos pensées sont sur elle et sur l'armée qu'elle commande.

No. VIII.

LETTER FROM MR. DRUMMOND TO SIR ALEXANDER BALL.

Palermo, July 4th, 1808.

MY DEAR SIR,—His Highness the Duke of Orleans has applied to me to write to you on a subject about which he appears to be extremely interested. I take it for granted that you are acquainted with all the events which have lately happened in Spain. The Duke thinks that the appearance of a member of the house of Bourbon, in that country, might be acceptable to the Spaniards, and of great service to the common cause. In this I perfectly concur with his Highness, and if you shall be of the same opinion you will probably have no objection to send a ship here to carry his Highness to Gibraltar. He himself is exceedingly sanguine. We have letters from London down to the 5th of June. Portugal has followed the example of Spain, and Lisbon is probably now in other hands. An invitation has been sent to Sir Charles Cotton. (Signed) WILLIAM DRUMMOND.

P. S. Weigh well what is said here, written at the side of the person.

MR. DRUMMOND TO SIR HEW DALRYMPLE.

Palermo, July 24th, 1808.

DEAR SIR,—This letter will be delivered to you by his Royal Highness Prince Leopold, second son of the King of the Two Sicilies. This Prince goes immediately to Gibraltar to communicate immediately with the loyal Spaniards, and to notify to them that his father will accept the regency, if they desire it, until his nephew Ferdinand the Seventh be delivered from captivity. Don Leopold and his cousin the Duke of Orleans will offer themselves as soldiers to the Spaniards, and will accept such situations as may be given to them suitable to their illustrious rank. If their visit should not be acceptable to the Spaniards, Don Leopold will return to Sicily, and his Serene Highness the Duke of Orleans will proceed to England. Being of opinion that the appearance of an Infant of Spain may be of the greatest utility at the present crisis, and in all events can hardly be productive of harm, I have urged his Sicilian Majesty to determine upon this measure, which I conceive to be required at his hands, in consequence of the manifesto of Palafox, which you have probably seen. At the distance of 1000 miles, however, we cannot be supposed to be accurately informed here of many circumstances with which you probably may be intimately acquainted; Prince Leopold therefore will be directed to consult with you, and to follow your advice, which I have no doubt you will readily and cheerfully give him. I take the liberty at the same time of recommending him to your care and protection. (Signed) WM. DRUMMOND.

EXTRACT OF A LETTER FROM SIR HEW DALRYMPLE TO LORD CASTLEREAGH.

Gibraltar, August 10th, 1808.

MY LORD,—Last night the Thunderer arrived here, having on board the Duke of Orleans, the second Prince of the Two Sicilies, and a considerable number of noblemen and others, the suite of the latter. As the ship came to anchor at a late hour, I had not the honor of seeing the Duke of Orleans until near ten at night, when he came accompanied by Captain Talbot. The Duke first put into my hands a letter from Mr. Drummond, as the Captain did a despatch from Sir Alexander Ball, copies of which I have the honor to inclose. As the latter seemed bulky, I did not immediately open it, and therefore did not immediately remark that Sir Alexander Ball *did not seem aware* that the Prince of the Two Sicilies was coming down, much less that he meditated establishing his residence at Gibraltar for the avowed purpose of negotiating for the regency of Spain. Of this object the Duke of Orleans made no mystery, and proceeded to arrange the time and manner of the Prince's reception in the morning, and the accommodation that should be prepared for him, suited to his rank, and capable of containing his attendants. I took early occasion first to remark the ill effect this measure might produce in Spain at the moment when the establishment of a central government had become obviously necessary, and would naturally lead to much intrigue and disunion, until the sentiments of the people and the armies (which would naturally assemble for the purpose of expelling the enemy from their territory) should be pronounced. . . . .

EXTRACT OF A LETTER FROM LORD CASTLEREAGH TO SIR HEW DALRYMPLE.

Downing Street, Nov. 4th, 1808.

"I have great pleasure, however, in assuring you that the measures pursued by you on that delicate and important subject" (the unexpected arrival of Prince Leopold and the Duke of Orleans at Gibraltar) "received his Majesty's entire approbation."

(Signed)

CASTLEREAGH.

No. IX.

SIR ARTHUR WELLESLEY TO SIR HARRY BURRARD.

Head-quarters, at Laos, August 8th, 1808.

SIR,—Having received instructions from the Secretary of State that you were likely to arrive on the coast of Portugal with a corps of 10,000 men, lately employed in the north of Europe under the orders of Sir John Moore, I now submit to you such information as I have received regarding the general state of the war in Portugal and Spain, and the plan of operations which I am about to carry into execution.

The enemy's force at present in Portugal consists, as far as I am able to form an opinion, of from 16,000 to 18,000 men, of which number there are about 500 in the fort of Almeida, about the same number in Elvas, about 6 or 800 in Peniché, and 16 or 1800 in the province of Alemtejo, at Setuval, &c. ; and the remainder are disposable for the defence of Lisbon, and are in the forts of St. Julian and Cascaes, in the batteries along the coast as far as the rock of Lisbon, and the old citadel at Lisbon, to which the enemy have lately added some works.

Of the force disposable for the defence of Lisbon, the enemy have lately detached a corps of about 2000, under General Thomières, principally I believe to watch my movements, which corps is now at Alcobaça ; and another corps of 4000 men, under General Loison, was sent across the Tagus into Alemtejo on the 26th of last month, the object of which detachment was to disperse the Portuguese insurgents in that quarter, to force the Spanish corps, consisting of about 2000 men, which had advanced into Portugal as far as Evora from Estremadura, to retire, and then to be enabled to add to the force destined for the defence of Lisbon the corps of French troops which had been stationed at Setuval and in the province of Alemtejo ; at all events Loison's corps will return to Lisbon, and the French corps disposable for the defence of that place will probably be about 14,000 men, of which at least 3000 must be left in the garrisons and forts on the coast and in the river.

The French army under Dupont, in Andalusia, surrendered on the 20th of last month to the Spanish army under Castaños ; so that there are now no French troops in the south of Spain. The Spanish army of Gallicia and Castile, to the northward, received a check at Rio Seco, in the province of Valladolid, on the 14th of July, from a French corps supposed to be under the command of General Bessières, which had advanced from Burgos.

The Spanish troops retired on the 15th to Benevente, and I understand there has since been an affair between the advanced posts in that neighborhood, but I am not certain of it; nor am I acquainted with the position of the Spanish army, or of that of the French, since the 14th July. When you will have been a short time in this country, and will have observed the degree to which the deficiency of real information is supplied by the circulation of unfounded reports, you will not be surprised at my want of accurate knowledge on these subjects.

It is, however, certain that nothing of importance has occurred in that quarter since the 14th of July; and from this circumstance I conclude that the corps called Bessières' attacked the Spanish army at Rio Seco solely with a view to cover the march of King Joseph Bonaparte to Madrid, where he arrived on the 21st July. Besides their defeat at Andalusia, the enemy, as you may probably have heard, have been beat off in an attack upon Zaragoza, in Aragon, in another upon the city of Valencia; (in both of which it is said that they have lost many men;) and it is reported that, in Catalonia, two of their detachments have been cut off, and that they have lost the fort of Figueras in the Pyrenees, and that Barcelona is blockaded. Of these last mentioned actions and operations I have seen no official accounts, but the report of them is generally circulated and believed; and at all events, whether these reports are founded or otherwise, it is obvious that the insurrection against the French is general throughout Spain; that large parties of Spaniards are in arms; amongst others, in particular, an army of 20,000 men, including 4000 cavalry, at Almaraz on the Tagus, in Estremadura, and that the French cannot carry on their operations by means of small corps, I should imagine, from their inactivity, and from the misfortunes they have suffered, that they have not the means of collecting a force sufficiently large to oppose the progress of the insurrection and the efforts of the insurgents, and to afford supplies to their different detached corps, or that they find that they cannot carry on their operations with armies so numerous as they must find it necessary to employ without magazines.

In respect to Portugal, the whole kingdom, with the exception of the neighborhood of Lisbon, is in a state of insurrection against the French; their means of resistance are, however, less powerful than those of the Spaniards, their troops have been completely dispersed, their officers had gone off to the Brazils, and their arsenals pillaged, or in the power of the enemy, and their revolt under the circumstances in which it had taken place is still more extraordinary than that of the Spanish naiton.

The Portuguese may have in the northern part of the kingdom about 10,000 men in arms, of which number 5000 are to march with me towards Lisbon. The remainder, with a Spanish detachment of about 1500 men which came from Gallicia, are employed in a distant blockade of Almeida, and in the protection of Oporto, which is now the seat of government.

The insurrection is general throughout Alemtejo and Algarve to the southward, and Entre Minho e Duero and Tras os Montes and Beira to the northward; but for want of arms the people can do nothing against the enemy.

Having consulted Sir C. Cotton, it appeared to him and to me that the attack proposed upon Cascaes-bay was impracticable, because the bay is well defended by the fort of Cascaes and the other works constructed for its defence, and the ships of war could not approach sufficiently near to silence them. The landing in the Passa d'Arcos in the Tagus could not be effected without silencing fort St. Julian, which appeared to be impracticable to those who were to carry that operation into execution.

There are small bays within, which might admit of landing troops, and others to the northward of the rock of Lisbon, but they are all defended by works which must have been silenced; they are of small extent, and but few men could have landed at the same time. There is always a surf on them which affects the facility of landing at different times so materially, as to render it very doubtful whether the troops first landed could be supported in sufficient time by others, and whether the horses for the artillery and cavalry, and the necessary stores and provisions could be landed at all. These inconveniences attending a landing in any of the bays near the rock of Lisbon would have been aggravated by the neighborhood of the enemy to the landing-place, and by the exhausted state of the country in which the troops would have been landed. It was obviously the best plan, therefore, to land in the northern parts of Portugal, and I fixed upon Mondego bay as the nearest place which afforded any facility for landing, excepting Peniché, the landing-place of which peninsula is defended by a fort occupied by the enemy, which it would be necessary to attack regularly, in order to place the ships in safety.

A landing to the northward was further recommended, as it would insure the co-operation of the Portuguese troops in the expedition to Lisbon. The whole of the corps placed under my command, including those under the command of General Spencer, having landed, I propose to march on Wednesday, and I shall take the road by Alcobaça and Obidos, with a view to keep up my communication by the sea-coast, and to examine the situation of Peniché, and I shall proceed towards Lisbon by the route of Mafra, and by the hills to the northward of that city.

As I understand from the Secretary of State that a body of troops under the command of Brigadier-General Ackland may be expected on the coast of Portugal before you arrive, I have written to desire he will proceed from hence along the coast of Portugal to the southward; and I propose to communicate with him by the means of Captain Bligh of the Alfred, who will attend the movements of the army with a few transports, having on board provisions and military stores. I intend to order Brigadier-General Ackland to attack Peniché, if I should find it necessary to obtain possession of that place, and if not, I propose to order him to join the fleet stationed off the Tagus, with a view to disembark in one of the bays near the rock of Lisbon, as soon as I shall approach sufficiently near to enable him to perform that operation. If I imagined that General Ackland's corps was equipped in such a manner as to be enabled to move from the coast, I should have directed him to land at Mondego, and to march upon Santarem, from which station he would have been at hand either to assist my operations, or to cut off the retreat of the enemy, if he should endeavor to make it either by the north of the Tagus and Almeida, or by the south of the Tagus and Elvas; but as I am convinced that General Ackland's corps is intended to form a part of some other corps which is provided with a commissariat, that he will have none with him, and consequently that his corps must depend upon the country, and as no reliance can be placed upon the resources of this country, I have considered it best to direct the General's attention to the sea-coast; if, however, the command of the army remained in my hands, I should certainly land the corps which has lately been under the command of Sir John Moore at Mondego, and should move it upon Santarem. I have the honor to inclose a return of the troops, &c. &c.

(Signed)   ARTHUR WELLESLEY.

SIR ARTHUR WELLESLEY TO SIR HARRY BURRARD.

Camp at Lugar, 8 miles north of Lerya, August 10, 1808.

SIR,—Since I wrote to you on the 8th inst., I have received letters from Mr. Stuart and Colonel Doyle at Coruña, of which I inclose copies. From them you will learn the state of the war in that part of Spain, and you will observe that Mr. Stuart and Colonel Doyle are of opinion that Marshal Bessières will take advantage of the inefficiency of the Gallician army under General Blake to detach a corps to Portugal to the assistance of General Junot; we have not heard yet of that detachment, and I am convinced it will not be made till King Joseph Bonaparte will either be reinforced to such a degree as to be in safety in Madrid, or till he shall have effected his retreat into France, with which view it is reported that he left Madrid on the 29th of last month.

I conceive, therefore, that I have time for the operations which I propose to carry on before a reinforcement can arrive from Leon, even supposing that no obstacles would be opposed to its march in Spain or Portugal; but it is not probable that it can arrive before the different reinforcements will arrive from England; and as Marshal Bessières had not more than 20,000 men in the action at Rio Seco on the 14th July, I conceive that the British troops, which will be in Portugal, will be equal to contend with any part of that corps which he may detach.

The possibility that, in the present state of affairs, the French corps at present in Portugal may be reinforced, affords an additional reason for taking the position at Santarem, which I apprised you, in my letter of the 8th, I should occupy, if the command of the army remained in my hands after the reinforcements should arrive. If you should occupy it, you will not only be in the best situation to support my operations, and to cut off the retreat of the enemy, but if any reinforcements of the French troops should enter Portugal, you will be in the best situation to collect your whole force to oppose him, &c. &c.   (Signed)   ARTHUR WELLESLEY.

No. X.

ARTICLES OF THE DEFINITIVE CONVENTION FOR THE EVACUATION OF PORTUGAL BY THE FRENCH ARMY.

The generals commanding in chief, &c., &c., being determined to negotiate, &c., &c.

Article 1. All the places and forts in the kingdom of Portugal occupied by the French troops shall be given up to the British army in the state in which they are at the period of the signature of the present convention.

Art. 2. The French troops shall evacuate Portugal with their arms and baggage, they shall not be considered as prisoners of war, and on their arrival in France they shall be at liberty to serve.

Art. 3. The English government shall furnish the means of conveyance for the French army, which shall be disembarked in any of the ports of France between Rochefort and L'Orient inclusively.

Art. 4. The French army shall carry with it all its artillery of French calibre, with the horses belonging thereunto, and the tumbrils supplied with sixty rounds per gun: all other artillery arms, and ammunition, as also the military and naval arsenals, shall be given up to the British army and navy, in the state in which they may be at the period of the ratification of the convention.

Art. 5. The French army shall carry with it all its equipments, and all that is comprehended under the name of property of the army; that is to say, its military chest, and carriages attached to the field commissariat and field hospital; or shall be allowed to dispose of such part of the same on its accounts, as the commander-in-chief may judge it unnecessary to embark. In like manner, all individuals of the army shall be at liberty to dispose of their private property of every description, with full security hereafter for the purchasers.

Art. 6. The cavalry are to embark their horses, as also the generals and other officers of all ranks. It is, however, fully understood that the means of conveyance for horses, at the disposal of the British commanders, are very limited; some additional conveyance may be procured in the port of Lisbon. The number of horses to be embarked by the troops shall not exceed 600, and the number embarked by the staff shall not exceed 200. At all events, every facility will be given to the French army to dispose of the horses belonging to it which cannot be embarked.

Art. 7. In order to facilitate the embarkation, it shall take place in three divisions, the last of which will be principally composed of the garrisons of the place, of the cavalry, the artillery, the sick, and the equipments of the army. The first division shall embark within seven days of the date of the ratification, or sooner if possible.

Art. 8. The garrison of Elvas and its forts, and of Peniché and Palmela, will be embarked at Lisbon. That of Almeida at Oporto, or the nearest harbor. They will be accompanied on their march by British commissaries, charged with providing for their subsistence and accommodation.

Art. 9. All the sick and wounded who cannot be embarked with the troops are intrusted to the British army. They are to be taken care of whilst they remain in this country at the expense of the British government, under the condition of the same being reimbursed by France when the final evacuation is effected. The English government will provide for their return to France, which will take place by detachments of about one hundred and fifty or two hundred men at a time. A sufficient number of French medical officers shall be left behind to attend them.

Art. 10. As soon as the vessels employed to carry the army to France shall have disembarked in the harbors specified, or in any other of the ports of France to which the stress of weather may force them, every facility shall be given to them to return to England without delay, and security against capture until their arrival in a friendly port.

Art. 11. The French army shall be concentrated in Lisbon, and within a distance of about two leagues from it. The English army will approach within three leagues of the capital, and will be so placed as to leave about one league between the two armies.

Art. 12. The forts of St. Julian, the Bugio, and Cascaes, shall be occupied by the British troops on the ratification of the convention. Lisbon and its citadel, together with the forts and batteries as far as the lazaretta or Trafaria on one side, and Fort St. Joseph on the other, inclusively, shall be given up on the embarkation of the 2d division; as shall also the harbor and all armed vessels in it of every description, with their rigging, sails, stores, and ammunition. The fortresses of Elvas, Almeida, Peniché, and

Palmela, shall be given up as soon as the British troops can arrive to occupy them. In the mean time, the general-in-chief of the British army will give notice of the present convention to the garrisons of those places, as also to the troops before them, in order to put a stop to all further hostilities.

Art. 13. Commissioners shall be named on both sides to regulate and accelerate the execution of the arrangements agreed upon.

Art. 14. Should there arise doubts as to the meaning of any article, it will be explained favorably to the French army.

Art. 15. From the date of the ratification of the present convention, all arrears of contributions, requisitions, or claims whatever, of the French government against subjects of Portugal, or any other individuals residing in this country, founded on the occupation of Portugal by the French troops, in the month of December, 1807, which may not have been paid up, are cancelled; and all sequestrations laid upon their property, movable or immovable, are removed, and the free disposal of the same is restored to the proper owners.

Art. 16. All subjects of France, or of powers in friendship or alliance, domiciliated in Portugal, or accidentally in this country, shall be protected; their property of every kind, movable and immovable, shall be respected; and they shall be at liberty either to accompany the French army or to remain in Portugal. In either case their property is guarantied to them, with the liberty of retaining or of disposing of it, and passing the produce of the sale thereof into France, or any other country where they may fix their residence, the space of one year being allowed them for that purpose. It is fully understood that shipping is excepted from this arrangement, only however in as far as regards leaving the port, and that none of the stipulations above mentioned can be made the pretext of any commercial speculations.

Art. 17. No native of Portugal shall be rendered accountable for his political conduct during the period of the occupation of this country by the French army; and all those who have continued in the exercise of their employments, or who have accepted situations under the French government, are placed under the protection of the British commanders; they shall sustain no injury in their persons or property: it not having been at their option to be obedient or not to the French government, they are also at liberty to avail themselves of the stipulations of the 16th article.

Art. 18. The Spanish troops detained on board ship, in the port of Lisbon, shall be given up to the commander-in-chief of the British army, who engages to obtain of the Spaniards to restore such French subjects, either military or civil, as may have been detained in Spain without having been taken in battle, or in consequence of military operations, but on occasion of the occurrences of the 29th of last May, and the days immediately following.

Art. 19. There shall be an immediate exchange established for all ranks of prisoners made in Portugal since the commencement of the present hostilities.

Art. 20. Hostages of the rank of field officers shall be mutually furnished, on the part of the British army and navy, and on that of the French army, for the reciprocal guarantee of the present convention. The officer of the British army shall be restored on the completion of the articles which concern the army; and the officer of the navy on the disembarkation of the French troops in their own country. The like is to take place on the part of the French army.

Art. 21. It shall be allowed to the general-in-chief of the French army to send an officer to France with intelligence of the present convention. A vessel will be furnished by the British Admiral to convey him to Bordeaux or Rochefort.

Art. 22. The British Admiral will be invited to accommodate his excellency the commander-in-chief and the other principal officers of the French army on board ships of war.

Done and concluded at Lisbon this 30th day of August, 1808.

(Signed)   GEORGE MURRAY, Quartermaster-General.
KELLERMANN, le Général de Division.

ADDITIONAL ARTICLES.

Art. 1. The individuals in the civil employment of the army made prisoners either by the British troops or by the Portuguese, in any part of Portugal, will be restored as is customary, without exchange.

Art. 2. The French army shall be subsisted from its own magazines up to the day of embarkation. The garrisons up to the day of the evacuation of the fortresses. The remainder of the magazines shall be delivered over in the usual forms to the British government, which charges itself with the subsistence of the men and horses of the army from the above-mentioned periods till their arrival in France, under the condition of being reimbursed by the French government for the excess of the expense beyond the estimation to be made by both parties, of the value of the magazines delivered up to the British army. The provisions on board the ships of war in the possession of the French army will be taken on account by the British government, in like manner with the magazines of the fortresses.

Art. 3. The general commanding the British troops will take the necessary measures for re-establishing the free circulation of the means of subsistence between the country and the capital.

Done and concluded at Lisbon this 30th day of August, 1808.

(Signed)   GEORGE MURRAY, Quartermaster-General.
KELLEMANN, le Général de Division.

Ratified, &c. &c.

No. XI.

1st. LETTER FROM BARON VON DECKEN TO THE GENERAL COMMANDING THE ARMY IN PORTUGAL.

Oporto, August 18, 1808.

SIR,—The Bishop of Oporto having expressed to me his wish to see me in private, in order to make me an important communication, which he desired to be kept secret, I went to his palace last night at a late hour. The Bishop told me that he had taken the government of Portugal in his hands to satisfy the wish of the people, but with the intention to re-establish the government of his lawful sovereign; and he hoped that his Majesty the King of Great Britain had no other point in view in sending troops to this country. After having given him all possible assurance on that head, the Bishop continued that as the Prince Regent, in leaving Portugal, had established a regency for the government of this country during his absence, he considered it his duty to resign the government into the hands of that regency as soon as possible. My answer was, that I had no instruction from my government on that head, but that I begged him to consider whether the cause of his sovereign would not be hurt in resigning the government into the hands of a Regency which, from its having acted under the influence of the French, had lost the confidence of the nation, and whether it would not be more advisable for him to keep the government until the pleasure of the Prince Regent was known. The Bishop allowed that the Regency appointed by the Prince Regent did not possess the confidence of the people, that several members of it had acted in such a manner as to show themselves as friends and partisans of the French, and that, at all events, all the members of the late Regency could not be re-established in their former power; but he was afraid that the provinces of Estremadura, Alemtejo, and Algarvé would not acknowledge his authority if the British government did not interfere. After a very long conversation, it was agreed that I should inform our ministers with what the Bishop had communicated to me, and in order to lose no time in waiting for an answer, the Bishop desired me to communicate the same to you, expressing a wish that you would be pleased to write to him an official letter, in order to express your desire that he might continue the government until the pleasure of his sovereign was known, for the sake of the operations of the British and Portuguese troops under your command.

The secretary of the Bishop, who acted as interpreter, told me afterwards in private, that the utmost confusion would arise from the Bishop resigning the government at this moment, or associating with people who were neither liked nor esteemed by the nation.

I beg leave to add, that although the Bishop expressed the contrary, yet it appeared to me that he was not averse to his keeping the government in his hands, if it could be done by the interference of our government. I have the honor to be, &c. &c.

  (Signed)   FREDERICK VON DECKEN, Brig-Gen.

2nd. DITTO TO DITTO.

Oporto, August 22, 1808.

SIR,—Your Excellency will have received the secret letter which I had the honor to send you by Brigadier-General Stuart, on the 18th, respecting the communication of his Excellency the Bishop of Oporto relative to his resignation of the government into the hands of the Regency established by the Prince Regent. In addition to what I have had the honor to state upon that subject, I beg leave to add, that his Excellency the Bishop has this day desired me to make your Excellency aware, in case it might be wished that he should keep the government in his hands until the pleasure of the Prince Regent may be known, that he could not leave Oporto; and the seat of government must in that case necessarily remain in this town. His Excellency the Bishop thinks it his duty to inform you of this circumstance as soon as possible, as he foresees that the city of Lisbon will be preferred for the seat of government, as soon as the British army have got possession of it. If the seat of the temporary government should remain at Oporto, the best method to adopt with respect to the other provinces of Portugal appears to be, to cause them to send deputies to that place for the purpose of transacting business relative to their own provinces; in the same manner as the provinces of Entre Douro y Minho and Tras os Montes now send their representatives. One of the principal reasons why his Excellency the Bishop can only accede to continue at the head of the government under the condition of remaining at Oporto is, because he is persuaded that the inhabitants of this town will not permit him to leave it, unless by order of the Prince Regent. It might also be advisable to keep the seat of government at Oporto, as it may be supposed that Lisbon will be in a state of great confusion for the first two months after the French have left it. I have the honor to be, sir, &c. &c.

(Signed)   FREDERICK VON DECKEN, Brig.-Gen.

3rd.

Oporto, August 28.

SIR,—Your Excellency will have received my secret letters of the 18th and 22d instant relative to the temporary government of this kingdom. His Excellency the Bishop of Oporto has received lately deputies from the province of Alemtejo and the kingdom of Algarve. Part of Estremadura, viz., the town of Leiria, has also submitted to his authority; and it may be therefore said that the whole kingdom of Portugal has acknowledged the authority of the temporary government, of which the Bishop of Oporto is at the head, with the exception of Lisbon and the town of Setubal, (St. Ubes.) Although the reasons why these towns have not yet acknowledged the authority of the temporary government may be explained by their being in possession of the French; yet the Bishop is convinced that the inhabitants of Lisbon will refuse to submit to the temporary government of Oporto, in which they will be strongly supported by the members of the former Regency established by the Prince Regent, who of course will be very anxious to resume their former power. The Bishop in assuming the temporary government complied only with the wishes of the people: he was sure that it was the only means of saving the country; but having had no interest of his own in view, he is willing to resign the authority, which he has accepted with reluctance, as soon as he is convinced that it can be done without hurting the cause of his sovereign, and throwing the country into confusion. There is every reason to apprehend that the inhabitants of the three northern provinces of Portugal will never permit the Bishop to resign the government, and submit to the former Regency. They feel extremely proud of having first taken to arms, and consider themselves as the deliverers and saviors of their country; and as the inhabitants of Lisbon will be as much disinclined to submit to the temporary government of Oporto, a division of the provinces, which will excite internal commotion, will naturally follow, if not supported by your Excellency. It has appeared to me that the best way to reconcile these opposite parties would be in endeavoring to unite the present government at Oporto with such of the members of the former Regency who have not forfeited by their conduct the confidence of the people; and having opened my idea to the Bishop, his answer was, that he would not object to it if proposed by you. I therefore take the liberty of suggesting, that the difficulty above mentioned would be in a great measure removed if your Excellency would be pleased to make it known after Lisbon has surrendered, that until the pleasure of the Prince Regent was known, you would consider the temporary government established at Oporto as the lawful government, with the addition of the four members of the late Regency, who have been pointed out to me by the Bishop as such who have behaved faithfully to their sovereign and country —viz., *Don Francisco Noronha, Francisco da Cunha, the Monteiro Mor, and the Principal Castro.* These members to be placed at the head of the different departments, and to consider the Bishop as the President, whose directions they are to follow—a plan which will meet with the less difficulty, as the President of the former Regency, named by the Prince Regent, has quitted Portugal, and is now in France. The circumstance that Lisbon is now in a state of the greatest confusion will furnish a fair pretext for fixing the seat of the temporary government in the first instance at Oporto, to which place the gentlemen above-named would be ordered to repair without loss of time, and to report themselves to the Bishop. Independent of the reasons which I had the honor of stating to your Excellency in my letter of the 22d instant, why it is impossible for the Bishop to leave Oporto, I must beg leave to add, that, from what I understand, the greater part of the inhabitants of Lisbon are in the French interest, and that it will require a garrison of British troops to keep that city in order. The Bishop of Oporto, although convinced of the necessity of considering Lisbon at present as a military station, and of placing a British commandant and a British garrison there, yet from a desire that the feelings of the inhabitants might be wounded as little as possible, wishes that you would be pleased to put also some Portuguese troops in garrison at Lisbon, together with a Portuguese commandant, who, though entirely under the orders of the British governor, might direct the police in that town, or at least be charged with putting into execution such orders as he may receive from the British governor under that head. If your Excellency should be pleased to approve of this proposal, the Bishop thinks Brigadier Antonio Pinto Bacelar to be the properest officer of those who are now with the Portuguese army to be stationed at Lisbon, and who might also be directed to organize the military force of the province of Estremadura. The Bishop is fully convinced that the temporary government of the country cannot exist without the support of British troops: he hopes that our government will leave a corps of 6000 men in Portugal after the French have been subdued, until the Portuguese troops may be sufficiently organized and disciplined to be able to protect their own government. I have the honor to be, sir, your most obedient and humble servant,

FREDERICK VON DECKEN, Brig.-Gen.

No. XII.

[Translation.]

LETTER FROM GENERAL LEITE TO SIR HEW DALRYMPLE.

MOST ILLUSTRIOUS AND MOST EXCELLENT SIR,—Strength is the result of union, and those who have reason to be grateful should be most urgent in their endeavors to promote it. I therefore feel it to be my duty to have recourse to your Excellency to know how I should act without disturbing the union so advantageous to my country. The Supreme Junta of the Portuguese government established at Oporto, which I have hitherto obeyed as the representatives of my sovereign, have sent me orders by an officer, dated the 1st instant, to take possession of the fortress of Elvas, as soon as it shall be evacuated. After having seen those same Spaniards who got possession of our strong places as friends, take so much upon themselves as even to prevent the march of the garrison which I had ordered to replace the losses sustained in the battle of Evora, which deprived me of the little obedience that was shown by the city of Beja, always favored by the Spanish authorities; after having seen the Portuguese artillery, which was saved after the said battle, taken possession of by those same Spaniards, who had lost their own, without being willing even to lend me two three-pounders to enable me to join his Excellency the Monteiro Mor; after having seen the arms which were saved from the destructive grasp of the common enemy made use of by those same Spaniards *who promised much and did nothing ;* after having seen a Spanish brigadier dispute my authority at Campo Mayor, where I was President of the Junta, and from whence his predecessor had taken away 60,000 crowns without rendering any account; in a word, after having seen the march of these Spaniards marked by the devastation of our fields, and the country deserted to avoid the plunder of their light troops, I cannot for a moment mistake the cause of the orders given by the Supreme Junta of Oporto. A corps of English troops having yesterday passed Estrémos, on their road to Elvas, knowing that in a combined army no officer should undertake any operation which may be intended for others, thereby counteracting each other, I consulted Lieutenant-General Hierre (Hope), who has referred me to your Excellency, to whom in consequence I send Lieutenant-Colonel the Marquis of Terney, my quartermaster-general, that he may deliver you this letter, and explain verbally everything you may wish to know which relates to my sovereign and the good of my country, already so much indebted to the English nation.

God preserve your Excellency many years.

(Signed)   FRANCISCO DE PAULO LEITE, Lieutenant-General.

(Dated) *Estrémos,* 16th *September,* 1808.

To the most illustrious and most excellent
    Sir Hew Dalrymple.

EXTRACT OF A LETTER FROM SIR HEW DALRYMPLE TO LIEUTENANT-GENERAL SIR JOHN HOPE.

Head-quarters, Benefico, 25th *Sept.,* 1808.

SIR,—Impediments having arisen to the fulfilment of that article of the convention which relates to the cession of Elvas by the French to the British army, in consequence of the unexpected and unaccountable conduct of the commander-in-chief of the army of Estremadura, in bombarding that place and endeavoring to impose upon the French garrison terms of capitulation different from those which were agreed upon by the British and French generals in chief; and as the British corps sent to take possession of the above fortress, and to hold it in the name of the Prince Regent until reinforced by a body of Portuguese troops, is not of sufficient strength to preclude the possibility of insult, should the General above mentioned persevere in the contemptuous and hostile disposition he has hitherto shown; I have therefore thought it advisable to order the remainder of your division, and General Paget's advanced guard, to cross the Tagus, and to occupy cantonments as near as possible to the place above-mentioned. In the mean time Colonel Graham is gone to Badajos to expostulate with General Galluzzo on the singular and very inexplicable line of conduct he has seen cause to adopt. . .

No. XIII.

JUSTIFICATORY EXTRACTS FROM THE CORRESPONDENCE OF SIR JOHN MOORE AND OTHER PERSONS.

SECTION I.—RELATING TO WANT OF MONEY.

Sir John Moore to Lord William Bentinck, October 22, 1808.

"Sir David Baird has unfortunately been sent out without money. He has applied to me, and I have none to give him." . . . "I undertake my march in the hope that some will arrive; if it does not, it will add to the number of a great many distresses."

Sir John Moore to General Hope, October 22, 1808.

"Baird has sent his aide-de-camp Gordon to me: he is without money, and his troops only paid to September. He can get none at Coruña."

Sir John Moore to Sir David Baird, October 22, 1808.

"We are in such want of money at this place, that it is with difficulty I have been able to spare 8000*l.*, which went to you in the Champion this day."

Sir John Moore to Lord Castlereagh, October 27.

"It is upon the general assurance of the Spanish government that I am leading the army into Spain without any established magazines. In this situation nothing is more essentially requisite than money, and unfortunately we have been able to procure very little here."

Sir John Moore to Mr. Frere, November 10, 1808.

"I understand from Sir David Baird that you were kind enough to lend him 40,000*l.* from the money you brought with you from England. We are in the greatest distress for money. I doubt if there is wherewithal after the 24th of this month to pay the troops their subsistence."

Sir John Moore to Lord Castlereagh, November 24, 1808.

"I am without a shilling of money to pay, and I am in daily apprehension that from the want of it our supplies will be stopped. It is impossible to describe the embarrassments we are thrown into from the want of that essential article."

Admiral de Courcy to Mr. Stuart, Coruña, October 21, 1808.

"Mr. Frere will have told you that the Semiramis has brought a million of dollars, in order to be at his disposal, besides 50,000*l.* in dollars, which are to be presented to the Marquis of Romana's army. In the mean time, the British troops remain in their transports at Coruña, uncertain whether they shall be invited to the war, and *without a shilling to pay their expenses.*"

SECTION II.—RELATING TO ROADS.

Sir John Moore to General Anstruther, at Almeida, dated Lisbon, October 12, 1808.

"A division under Beresford is marching upon Coimbra, and a part of it will proceed on to Oporto or not, as information is received from you that the road from thence to Almeida is or is not practicable. Some officers of the Spanish engineers, employed in the quartermaster-general's department, with commissaries, are sent from Madrid to obtain information on the subjects you will want with respect to roads, subsistence, &c. &c., from Almeida to Burgos."

Sir John Moore to Lord William Bentinck, October 22, 1808.

"Colonel Lopez has no personal knowledge of this part of Spain; but what he has told me accords with other information I had before received, that the great Madrid road was the only one by which artillery could travel; the French brought theirs from Ciudad Rodrigo to Alcantara, but by this *it was destroyed.*" . . . . "The difficulty of obtaining correct information of roads, and the difficulties attending the subsistence of troops through Portugal, are greater than you can believe."

Sir John Hope to Sir John Moore, Madrid, November 20.

"I sent Wills of the engineers by Placentia to Salamanca, and before this time I suppose he may have made his report to you of the roads from the Tagus at Almarez and Puente de Cardinal to Salamanaca." . . . . . . "Delancy is upon this road, and I have directed him to communicate with you at Salamanca, as soon as possible."

Sir John Moore to Lord Castlereagh, October 27, 1808.

"I am under the necessity of sending Lieutenant-General Hope, with the artillery, &c., by the great road leading from Badajos to Madrid, as *every information* agreed that no other was fit for the artillery."

Substance of a report from Captain Carmichael Smyth, of the Engineers, 26th December, 1808.

"The country round about Astorga is perfectly open, and affords no advantage whatsoever to a small corps to enable it to oppose a large force with any prospect of success. In retreating, however, towards Villa Franca, at the distance of about two leagues from Astorga, the hills approaching each other form some strong ground; and the high ground in particular in the rear of the village of Rodrigatos appears at first sight to offer a most advantageous position. One very serious objection presents itself nevertheless to our making a stand near Rodrigatos, or indeed at any position before we come to the village of Las Torres (about one league from Bembibre), as the talus or slope of the ground, from Manzanel (close to Rodrigatos) until Las Torres, would be in favor of an enemy, should we be forced at Rodrigatos, and we should be consequently obliged to retreat down hill for nearly two leagues, the enemy having every advantage that such a circumstance would naturally give them.

"From Las Torres to Bembibre the ground becomes more open, but with the disadvantage, however, of the slope being still against us. From Bembibre to Villa Franca there is great variety of ground, but no position that cannot easily be turned, excepting the ground in the rear of Calcavellos, and about one league in front of Villa Franca. This is by far the strongest position between Astorga and Villa Franca. It is also necessary to add, that the position at Rodrigatos can easily be turned by the Foncevadon road (which, before the establishment of the Camina Real, was the high road towards Coruña). This is not the case with the position in front of Villa Franca, as the Foncevadon road joins the Camina Real to Calcavellos in front of the proposed position."

Major Fletcher, Royal Engineers, to Sir John Moore, Betanzos, Jan. 5, 1809.

"I have the honor to report to your Excellency that, in obedience to your orders, I have examined the neck of land between the harbor of Ferrol and the bridge of Puente de Humo. This ground does not appear to possess any position that has not several defects." . . "I did not find any ground so decidedly advantageous and containing a small space, as to render it tenable for the vanguard of an army to cover the embarkation of the main body." . . "I should have sent this report much sooner, but found it impossible to procure post-horses until my arrival at Lugo, and since that time I have had very bad ones."

Ditto to Ditto, Coruña, Jan. 6, 1809.

"I am therefore led to suggest, that as Coruña is fortified, riveted, and tolerably flanked (though the ground about it is certainly not favorable), as it could not be carried by a coup-de-main if properly defended, as it contains a great quantity of cover for men, and as, even against artillery, it might make resistance of some days, it may be worth consideration whether, under present circumstances, it may not be desirable to occupy it in preference to the peninsula of Betanzos, should the army not turn off for Vigo."

SECTION III.—RELATING TO EQUIPMENT AND SUPPLIES.

Sir John Moore to Lord Castlereagh, Oct. 9, 1808.

"At this instant the army is without equipment of any kind, either for the carriage of the light baggage of regiments, artillery stores, commissariat stores, or other appendages of an army, and not a magazine is formed on any of the routes by which we are to march."

Sir John Moore to Lord Castlereagh, Oct. 18, 1808.

"In none of the departments is there any want of zeal, but in some important ones there is much want of experience." . . "I have no hope of getting forward at present with more than the light baggage of the troops, the ammunition immediately necessary for the service of the artillery, and a very scanty supply of medicines."

Sir John Moore's Journal.

"My anxiety is to get out of the ragged roads of Portugal before the rains."

Sir John Moore to Lord Wm. Bentinck, Oct. 22, 1808.

"The season of the year admitting of no delay, there was a necessity for beginning the march, and trusting for information and supplies as we got on ; unfortunately, our commissariat is inexperienced, and a scoundrel of a contractor, Mr. Sattaro, has deceived us."

Sir David Baird to Sir John Moore, Oct. 29, 1808.

"The want of provisions for the men and forage for the horses has been one of the most serious obstacles we have had to contend with. Nor do I at present feel at all easy upon that subject." . . "The horses are suffering very severely, both for want of proper accommodations and food." . . "From Lord Castlereagh's letter, I was led to expect that every preparation for our equipment had been made previous to our leaving England ; I need hardly say how different the case was, and how much I have been disappointed."

"The continued slowness of the Junta is the only explanation I can offer for the want of proper arrangements on the routes for the reception of the English troops."

Section IV.—Relating to the Want of Information.

Sir John Moore's Journal, November 28, 1808.

"I am not in communication with any of the (Spanish) generals, and neither know their plans nor those of the government. No channel of information has been opened to me, and I have no knowledge of the force or situation of the enemy, but what, as a stranger, I pick up."

Ditto, Salamanca.

"It is singular that the French have penetrated so far (Valladolid), and yet no sensation has been made upon the people. They seem to remain quiet, and the information was not known through any other channel but that of a letter from the Captain-General of the province to me."

Sir David Baird to Sir John Moore, Astorga, Nov. 19, 1808.

"The local authorities have not only failed in affording us the least benefit in that respect (supplies), but have neglected to give us any kind of information as to the proceedings of the armies or the motions of the enemy."

Ditto, Astorga, 23d November.

"It is clearly apparent how very much exaggerated the accounts generally circulated of the strength of the Spanish armies have been." . . "It is very remarkable that I have not procured the least intelligence, or received any sort of communication from any of the official authorities at Madrid, or either of the Spanish generals."

Sir David Baird to Sir John Moore, Villafranca, Dec. 12, 1808.

"I also inclose a letter from the Marquis of Romana; you will be fully able to appreciate the degree of reliance that may be placed on the *verbal* communication made to him by the extraordinary courier from Madrid. It was from the same kind of authority that he derived the information he conveyed to me of a *supposed* brilliant affair at Somosierra, which turned out to be an inconsiderable skirmish altogether undeserving of notice."

Colonel Graham to Sir John Moore, Madrid, Oct. 4, 1808.

"The deputies sent over knew nothing but just concerning their own provinces, and *pour se faire valoir*, they exaggerated everything; for example, those of the Asturias talked louder than anybody, and Asturias as yet has never produced a man to the army; thus government, with all their wish to get information (which cannot be doubted), fail in the proper means."

Lord Wm. Bentinck to Sir John Moore, Madrid, Nov. 20, 1808.

"I must at the same time take the liberty of stating my belief, that reliance cannot be placed upon the correctness of information, even if such

,information should not be kept back, which does not come through the channel of a British officer. It is the choice of officers rather than the system, that seems to have failed."

Mr. Stuart to Sir John Moore, Madrid, Nov. 19, 1808.

"In your direct communications with Spanish generals, you must, however, be contented with their version of the state of affairs, which I do not think can always be relied on, because they only put matters in the view in which they wish you to see them."

Ditto, Nov. 29.

"The calculation of force which the Junta hope may be united in the army under your command will be as follows, if no impediment prevents the different corps reaching the points selected for their junction."

		Remarks by Colonel Napier.
British	35,000	They were only 23,500.
La Romana.	20,000	. . only 5000 armed.
San Juan	15,000	Totally dispersed.
Levies from the south, say	10,000	None ever arrived.
	80,000	Real total, 28,500.

Lieut. Boothby, Royal Engineers, to Sir John Moore, La Puebla, Jan. 1, 1809.

"I shall consider of any means that may more completely insure the earliest information of the enemy's movements towards this quarter; but the Spaniards are the most difficult people in the world to employ in this way, they are so slow, so talkative, and so credulous."

Section V.—Relating to the Conduct of the Local Juntas.

Sir David Baird to Sir John Moore, Coruña, Oct. 24, 1808.

"The answer of the supreme government to our application, as read by Mr. Frere last night in the presence of the Junta of this province, is certainly very different from what I expected. Instead of expressing an anxiety to promote our views, and dissatisfaction at the impediments thrown in the way of our measures by the Gallician government, it merely permits us to land here in the event of its being found impracticable to send us by sea to St. Andero, and directs that, if our disembarkation takes place, it should be made in detachments of 2000 or 3000 men each! to be successively pushed on into Castile, without waiting for the necessary equipment of mules and horses."

Sir David Baird to Sir John Moore, Coruña, Nov. 7.

"We have received no sort of assistance from the government."

Sir David Baird to Sir John Moore, Astorga, Nov. 19.

"Had the Spanish government afforded us any active assistance, the state of our equipments would have been much more advanced."

Colonel Graham to Sir John Moore, Madrid, Oct. 4, 1808.

"All this, instead of at once appointing the fittest men in the country to be ministers, looks much like private interest and patronage being the objects more than the public good."

22

Ditto, Tudela, Nov. 9, 1808.

"*It is hoped* that the Aragonese army will come over to fill it " (the line) " up, but being an independent command, no order has yet been sent. An express went after Palafox, who will return here this morning, and *then it is hoped* that he will send an order to General O'Neil at Sanguessa to march instantly ; and *further it is hoped* that General O'Neil will obey this order without waiting for one from his immediate chief, Palafox, the Captain-General of Aragon, who is at Zaragoza ; at all events, there is a loss of above twenty-four hours by the happy system of independent commands, which may make the difference of our having 18,000 men more or less in the battle that may be fought whenever the French are ready." . . " Making me compliments of there being no secrets with their allies, they " (the members of the council of war) " obliged me to sit down, which I did for a quarter of an hour, enough to be quite satisfied of the miserable system established by this Junta." . . " In short, I pitied poor Castaños and poor Spain, and came away disgusted to the greatest degree."

Colonel Graham to Lord W. Bentinck, Centruenigo, Nov. 13, 1808.

" If anything can make the Junta sensible of the absurdity of their conduct, this will. It would indeed have been more felt if a great part of the division had been lost, as might well have happened. But the difficulty of passing so many men with artillery, and in small boats, and the time that would have been required so great, that I can hardly persuade myself these people can be so foolish as ever seriously to have entertained the idea. But with whatever intentions, whether merely as a pretence for assuming the command for the purpose of irritating Castaños ; whether from the silly vanity of exercising power, and doing something which, if by great good luck it had succeeded, might have proved what might be done with a more active commander ; or whether from a real conviction of the excellence of the scheme,—it must be equally evident to every military man, indeed to every man of common sense, that it is impossible things can succeed in this way ; and then the Junta itself interferes, and to worse purpose."

Castaños' Vindication.

" The nation is deceived in a thousand ways ; as an example, it is believed that our armies were greatly superior to those of the enemy, reckoning 80,000 men that of the centre, when your excellencies " (the Junta) " knew that it only amounted to 26,000 men." . . " Madrid possessed money and riches ; the noble and loyal inhabitants of that capital wished to give both the one and the other ; but whilst the armies were suffering the horrors of famine, naked, and miserable, the possessions and jewels of the good Spaniards remained quiet in Madrid, and they might be soon seized by the tyrant, as they were in the end."

Stuart's Despatch, August 7, 1808.

" No province shares the succors granted by Great Britain, although they may not be actually useful to themselves. No gun-boats have been sent from Ferrol to protect Santander or the coast of Biscay ; and the Asturians have in vain asked for artillery from the dépôts of Gallicia. The stores landed at Gihon, and not used by the Asturians, have remained in that port and in Oviedo, although they would have afforded a seasonable relief to the army of General Blake. The money brought by the Pluto for Leon, which has not raised a man, remains in the port where it was landed."

Major Cox to Sir Hew Dalrymple, Seville, August 3, 1808.

"I freely confess that I cannot help feeling some degree of apprehension that this great and glorious cause may be ruined by the baneful effects of jealousy and division."

Ditto, August 27.

"The fact is, their" (the Junta of Seville) "attention has been for some time past so much occupied by vain and frivolous disputes, and by views of private interest and advantage, and they seem to have neglected entirely every concern of real importance, and almost to have lost sight of the general interests of the country." . . . "A million of dollars have, I understand, been sent out." . . . "It certainly would not be prudent to intrust so large a sum to the management of the temporary government of a particular province, without having a sufficient security for its proper application. My own opinion is, that the less money which is given to them the better, until the general government is formed. This Junta has shown too evident signs of a wish to aggrandize themselves, and a disinclination to afford those aids to other provinces, which they had it in their power to grant, not to afford just grounds of suspicion, that their boasted loyalty and patriotism have at times been mixed with unworthy considerations of self-interest and personal advantage."

Ditto, Sept. 5.

"By Mr. Duff's present instructions, he would have had no option" (distributing the money), "even though the *iniquitous project of partition*, which your Excellency knows was once contemplated, were still in existence."

Major Cox to Sir Hew Dalrymple, Sept. 7.

"A dispute between the two Juntas" (Seville and Granada), "which had nearly been productive of the most serious consequences, and would probably have ended in open hostility, had it not been prevented by the moderate, but decided, conduct of General Castaños."

Ditto, Seville, Sept. 10.

"The Supreme Junta of Seville have latterly manifested very different views, and, I am sorry to say, they seem almost to have lost sight of the common cause, and to be wholly addicted to their particular interest. Instead of directing their efforts to the restoration of their legitimate sovereign and the established form of a national government, they are seeking the means of fixing the permanency of their own, and endeavoring to separate its interests from those of the other parts of Spain. To what other purposes can be attributed the order given to General Castaños, not to march on any account beyond Madrid? To what the instructions given to their deputy, Don Andrea Miniano, to uphold the authority and preserve the integrity of the Junta of Seville; to distinguish the army to which he is attached by the name of the army of Andalusia; to preserve constantly the appellation, and not to receive any orders but what came directly from this government? And above all, what other motive could induce the strong and decided measure of enforcing obedience to those orders, by withholding from General Castaños the means of maintaining his troops, in case of his refusing to comply with them?" . . . "What has been the late occupation of the Junta of Seville? Setting aside the plans which were formed for augmenting the Spanish army in those provinces, and neglecting the consideration of those which have been proposed in their stead, their attention has been taken up in the appointment of secretaries to the different departments, in disposing of places of emolument, in making promotions in the army, appointing canons in the church, and instituting orders of knighthood. Such steps as these make their designs too evident."

Captain Carrol to Sir David Baird, Llanes, Dec. 17, 1808.

"This province" (Asturias), "the first to declare war with France, has during seven months taken no steps that I can discover to make arrangements against the event of the enemy's entering the province." . . . . "What has been done with the vast sums of money that came from England? you will naturally ask. Plundered and misapplied: every person who had or has anything to do with money concerns endeavoring to keep in hand all he can, and be ready, let affairs turn out as they may, to help himself."

General Broderick to Mr. Stuart, Reynosa, 11th Sept., 1808.

"The fact is, the Junta of Gallicia thinks that this army having marched to the assistance and protection of these countries, the latter ought to pay the expense, and therefore refuse the supplies, which Blake is unwilling to press."

Lord William Bentinck to Sir Hew Dalrymple, Seville, Sept. 19, 1808.

"Notwithstanding the professions of the Junta, their conduct has evidently fallen short of them, and I think it would be very desirable that more money should not fall into their hands."

Major Coxe to Sir Hew Dalrymple, Seville, 10th and 27th July.

"The proclamation of Florida Blanca was received here some time ago, but was carefully suppressed by the government."
"Other publications, containing maxims similar to those inculcated by the proclamation of Florida Blanca, have appeared, but are suppressed here with equal care."

SECTION VI.—CENTRAL JUNTA.

Mr. Stuart to Mr. Canning, Sept. 26, 1808.

"I have heard of several circumstances since my arrival at Aranjuez, which throw a light upon the conduct of General Cuesta, and, if well founded, go far to prove the existence of projects incompatible with the formation of any regular government in the country. I cannot say they are openly avowed by either party, although the measures of precaution, which the leading members of the Junta have deemed expedient, go far to prove that the whispers which circulate are not altogether without foundation. It is said that the difficulty of forming a Central Junta induced Cuesta to propose to Castaños the establishment of a military power, alleging that, in the present situation of the corps under his command, he would take on himself to prevent the union of the Central Junta, and that his influence with the officers in other parts of Spain would enable him to crush all opposition, by the instant disorganization of the provisional government in the provinces of the kingdom. And I know, indeed, that the movement of Cuesta from Arevola to Segovia gave so much alarm at Madrid, and so fully convinced the public that he was going to carry this design into execution, that Castaños was formally requested to give orders for the approach of a division to Madrid, to be ready to oppose any act of violence calculated to bias the determination of the persons about to form the government."

Mr. Stuart to Mr. Canning, Oct. 9, 1808.

" I have received the paper (of which I inclose a copy) from the Supreme Junta. Although somewhat startled at the exorbitancy of the demand, I was no less so at the language in which the demand is conveyed, and the conversation I have subsequently had upon the subject. However willing I am to make every possible allowance for the embarrassments of this rising government, and the inexperience or intemperance of many among its members, I cannot but feel that the generosity of Great Brittain not only called for some acknowledgment of what has been already done in favor of Spain, but that it likewise might have deserved a petition couched in terms less resembling a military requisition. When it was observed to Mr. de Villar (the author of the note) that the demand for specie much exceeded the means of any country in the world, he said, credit or specie was indifferent, provided they could obtain a part of what was requisite for present services. Mr. de Jovellanos was not so moderate, and *literally* proposed that I should draw bills at once on the treasury for the whole, or at least engage the faith of his Majesty's government by such a promise as should enable them to raise money by anticipation, upon my signature, until the arrival of a British subsidy." . . . . " It was seriously demanded also, that the English government should seize the sums which the Prince of Peace and other friends of the French interest *are supposed* to have in the English funds; nor could my explanation, citing several well-known instances to prove the impossibility of such a measure, and the determination to keep inviolable whatever was deposited under the guardianship of the public faith, prevent Mr. de Jovellanos and others from testifying some ill-humor and incredulity at my answer."

Lord William Bentinck to Sir John Moore, Madrid, Oct. 4, 1808.

" I am sorry to say that the new government do not seem to proceed with the despatch and energy which the critical situation of the country demands."

Ditto to Sir H. Burrard, Madrid, Oct. 8.

" In my last letter I adverted to the inactivity and apparent supineness which prevailed in the Central Council in regard to the military, as well as to the other business of the other government."

Ditto to Sir John Moore, Nov. 8.

" But it is upon the spot where the exact state of the armies, and the extraordinary inefficiency of the government, whose past conduct promises so little for the future, are known, that the danger must be more justly appreciated." . . . " The most simple order, however urgent the case, cannot be obtained from the government without a difficulty, solicitation, and delay that is quite incredible."

Sir John Hope to Sir John Moore, Madrid, Nov. 20, 1808.

" It is perfectly evident that they " (the Junta) " are altogether without a plan as to their future military operations, either in the case of success or misfortune. Every branch is affected by the disjointed and inefficient construction of their government."

Mr. Stuart to Sir John Moore, Madrid, Oct. 18, 1808.

" Lord William Bentinck, as well as myself, have made repeated representations, and I have given in paper after paper to obtain something like promptitude and vigor; but though loaded with fair promises in the commencement, we scarcely quit the members of the Junta before their attention is absorbed in petty pursuits, and the wrangling which impedes even the simplest arrangements necessary for the interior government of a country." . . . " In short, we are doing what we can, not what we wish; and I assure you we have infamous tools to work with."

Ditto, Seville, Jan. 2, 1809.

" Morla's treason is abused, but passed over; and the arrival of money from Mexico, which is really the arrival of spoil for the French, seems to have extinguished every sentiment the bad views and the desperate state of things ought to have created."

Ditto, Jan. 10, 1809.

" Castaños, Heredia, Castelar, and Galluzzo are all here. These unfortunate officers are either prisoners or culprits, waiting the decision of government on their conduct in the late transactions. If the state of affairs should allow the government to continue in existence, they will probably wait many months, for no determination is to be expected from people who have in no one instance punished guilt or rewarded merit since they ruled the country. The Junta indeed, to say the truth, is at present absolutely null, and although they represent the sovereign authority, I have never witnessed the exercise of their power for the public good."

Mr. Frere to Sir John Moore, Las Santos, Dec. 16, 1808.

" The subject of the ships in Cadiz had not escaped me, but I thought it so *very dangerous* to suggest to the Junta any idea except that of living and dying on Spanish ground, that I avoided the mention of any subject that could seem to imply that I entertained any other prospects."

Section VII.—Relating to the Passive State of the People.

Sir John Moore's Journal, Dec. 9, 1808.

" In this part the people are passive. We find the greatest difficulty to get people to bring in information."

Sir John Moore to Mr. Frere, Sahagun, Dec. 23, 1808.

" If the Spaniards are enthusiastic, or much interested in this cause, their conduct is the most extraordinary that was ever exhibited."

Sir John Moore to Lord Castlereagh, Astorga, Dec. 31, 1808.

" I arrived here yesterday, where, contrary to his promise, and to my expectation, I found the Marquis la Romana, with a great part of his troops. Nobody can describe his troops to be worse than he does, and he complains as much as we do of the indifference of the inhabitants, his disappointment at their want of enthusaism; and said to me in direct terms, that had he known how things were, he would neither have accepted the command, nor have returned to Spain. With all this, however, he talks of attacks and movements which are quite absurd, and then returns to the helpless state of his army and of the country."

Mr. Stuart to Sir John Moore, Nov. 17, 1808.

"The tranquillity of Madrid is truly wonderful."

Sir David Baird to Sir John Moore, Dec. 6.

"Destitute as we are of magazines, and without receiving even a show of assistance, either from the government or inhabitants of the country, who, on the contrary, in many instances, even thwarted our plans and measures, we could not have advanced without exposing ourselves to almost certain destruction."

Sir David Baird to Lord Castlereagh, Astorga, Nov. 22, 1808.

"Major Stuart, of the 95th regiment, who was despatched in front of this place to obtain information, reports that the inhabitants appear perfectly depressed by their losses, and seem to abandon all hope of making a successful resistance."

Captain Carrol to Sir John Moore, Dec. 17, 1808.

"On my arrival at Oviedo all was confusion and dismay; the confidence between the people, the army, and the Junta destroyed." . . "Is it to be expected that the peasantry can be as hearty in the cause of patriotism as if they were treated with justice?"

Lieut. Boothby to Sir John Moore, La Puebla, Jan. 1, 1809.

"The Spanish soldiers now here (about 700) are merely on their way to the Marquis de la Romana; and as to any neighboring passes, there are no people whom I can call upon to occupy them, or should expect to defend them, however naturally strong they may be, for I see no people who are thinking of the enemy's advance with any sentiments beyond passive dislike, and hopes of protection from God and the English army."

Extract from General Fane's Journal, 1808–9.

"Five hundred and twenty-nine miles of our marches have been in Spain, and notwithstanding all we have read about Spanish patriotism, we have never been joined by *one man*, nor have we seen *one corps in arms*. The people have offered us *no* assistance; while not even a cart or a guide have been to be procured but by *force*, and by that measure we have generally been obliged to obtain our quarters. How our ministers could have been so deceived as to the state of the country is inconceivable."

The Prince of Neufchatel to the Duke of Dalmatia, Dec. 10, 1808.

"The city of Madrid is quite tranquil, the shops are all open, the public amusements are resumed."

General Thouvenot to the Prince of Neufchatel, St. Sebastian, 29th Nov., 1808.

"The successes obtained by the armies of the Emperor, and those which are also foreseen, begin to make a sensible impression upon the authorities of the country, who become from day to day more affable towards the French, and more disposed to consider the King as their legitimate sovereign."

The Commandant Meslin to the Prince of Neufchatel, Vittoria, 29th Nov., 1808.

" The public feeling is still bad, still incredulous of our successes." . . . " As to the tranquillity of the country, it appears certain."

Mr. Frere to Sir John Moore, Merida, Dec. 14, 1808.

" A thousand barriers would be interposed against that deluge of panic which sometimes overwhelms a whole nation, and of which at one time I was afraid I saw the beginning in this country." . . *"The extinction of the popular enthusiasm in this country,* and the means which exist for reviving it, would lead to a very long discussion."

SECTION VIII.—MISCELLANEOUS.

Lord Collingwood to Sir H. Dalrymple, Ocean, Cadiz, June 23, 1808.

" At Minorca and Majorca they describe themselves to be strong, and having nothing to apprehend. However, they made the proposal for entering into a convention with us for their defence, and in the course of it demanded money, arms, and the protection of the fleet. When, in return for them, it was required that their fleet should be given up to us, to be held for their King Ferdinand, or that a part of them should join our squadron against the enemy, they rejected all those proposals: so that whatever we did for them was to be solely for the honor of having their friendship."

Captain Whittingham to Sir Hew Dalrymple, June 12, 1808.

" 12th June. I returned to Xeres at 3 o'clock, A. M. The General sent for me, and requested I would go without delay to Gibraltar, and inform Lieut.-General Sir Hew Dalrymple that he at present occupied Carmona with three thousand men (regulars), having his head-quarters at Utrera, where his regular force would amount to twelve thousand men; that it was not his intention to attempt to defend Seville; that the heavy train of artillery, consisting of eighty pieces, was already embarked for Cadiz, under the pretext that they were wanting for the defence of its works; and that everything was prepared for burning the harness, timbers, &c., &c., of the field-pieces; that he intended to fall gradually back upon Cadiz, if forced to retreat; and that he did not at present desire that any English troops should be landed till their numbers should amount to eight or ten thousand men, lest the ardor of the people should oblige him to commence an offensive system of warfare before the concentration of a considerable Spanish and English force should afford reasonable hopes of success."

Captain Whittingham to Sir Hew Dalrymple, Utrera, June 29, 1808.

" The President approved of the idea, condemned the policy which had led Spain to attempt to establish manufactures by force, and showed clearly that the result had been the loss of a considerable branch of the revenue, the increase of smuggling, and consequently an enormous expense, in the payment of nearly *one hundred thousand* custom or rather excise officers, distri buted about the country, and the ruin of numberless families seduced by the prospect of immediate profit to engage in illicit traffic."

Lord William Bentinck to Sir Hew Dalrymple, Madrid, Oct. 2, 1808.

"A passage of Lord Castlereagh's letter, of which I received from you a copy, instructed you, if possible, to ascertain the intentions of the Spanish government after the expulsion of the French. Though not positively directed by you to ask this information, yet the occasion appeared to make the question so natural, and seemingly of course, and even necessary, that I availed myself of it, and gave to General Castaños, to be laid before Count Florida Blanca, a memorandum of which I inclose a copy, marked A."

Extract from the copy marked A.

"It seems probable, in such case, that no diversion could be more effectual or more formidable to Bonaparte than the march of a large combined British and Spanish army over the Pyrenees, into that part of France where there are no fortified places to resist their passage into the very heart of the country, and into that part where great disaffection is still believed to exist."

No. XIV.

JUSTIFICATORY EXTRACTS FROM SIR JOHN MOORE'S CORRESPONDENCE.

Sir John Moore to Mr. Frere, Salamanca, Nov. 27, 1808.

"The movements of the French give us little time for discussion. As soon as the British army has formed a junction, I must, upon the supposition that Castaños is either beaten or retreated, march upon Madrid, and throw myself into the heart of Spain, and thus run all risks and share the fortunes of the Spanish nation, or I must fall back upon Portugal." . . . "The movement into Spain is one of greater hazard, as my retreat to Cadiz or Gibraltar must be very uncertain. I shall be entirely in the power of the Spaniards; but perhaps this is worthy of risk, if the government and people of Spain are thought to have still sufficient energy, and the means to recover from their defeats; and by collecting in the south be able, with the aid of the British army, to resist, and finally repel, the formidable attack which is prepared against them."

Sir John Moore's Journal, Salamanca, Nov. 30, 1808.

"In the night of the 28th I received an express from Mr. Stuart, at Madrid, containing a letter from Lieutenant-Colonel Doyle, announcing the defeat of Castaños' army near Tudela. They seem to have made but little resistance, and are, like Blake's, flying; this renders my junction with Baird so extremely hazardous that I dare not attempt it; but even were it made, what chance has this army, now that all those of Spain are beaten, to stand against the force which must be brought against it? The French have eighty thousand in Spain, and thirty thousand were to arrive in twenty days from the 15th of this month. As long as Castaños' army remained there was a hope, but I now see none. I am therefore determined to withdraw the army."

Ditto, Dec. 9.

" After Castaños' defeat, the French marched from Madrid, the inhabitants flew to arms, barricadoed their streets, and swore to die rather than submit. This has arrested the progress of the French, and Madrid still holds out: this is the first instance of enthusiasm shown ; there is a chance that the example may be followed, and the people be roused ; in which case there is still a chance that this country may be saved.   Upon this chance I have stopped Baird's retreat, and am taking measures to form our junction whilst the French are wholly occupied with Madrid.   We are bound not to abandon the cause as long as there is hope ; but the courage of the populace of Madrid may fail, or at any rate they may not be able to resist : in short, in a moment things may be as bad as ever, unless the whole country is animated and flock to the aid of the capital, and in this part the people are passive."

Sir John Moore to Lord Castlereagh, Salamanca, Dec. 10, 1808.

"I certainly think the cause desperate, because I see no determined spirit anywhere, unless it be at Zaragoza.   There is, however, a chance, and whilst there is that I think myself bound to run all risks to support it.   I am now differently situated from what I was when Castaños was defeated : I have been joined by General Hope, the artillery, and all the cavalry (Lord Paget, with three regiments, is at Toro) ; and my junction with Sir David Baird is secure, though I have not heard from him since I ordered him to return to Astorga."

Sir John Moore to Lord Castlereagh, Sahagun, Dec. 12.

" I shall threaten the French communications and create a diversion, if the Spaniards can avail themselves of it ; but the French have in the north of Spain from eighty to ninety thousand men, and more are expected.   Your lordship may, therefore, judge what will be our situation if the Spaniards do not display a determination very different to any they have shown hitherto."

Sir John Moore's Journal.   Sahagun, Dec. 24, 1808.

" I gave up the march on Carrion, which had never been undertaken but with a view of attracting the enemy's attention from the armies assembling in the south, and in the hope of being able to strike a blow at a weak corps, whilst it was still thought the British army was retreating into Portugal ; for this I was aware I risked infinitely too much, but something, I thought, was to be risked for the honor of the service, and to make it apparent that we stuck to the Spaniards long after they themselves had given up their cause as lost."

Sir John Moore to Lord Castlereagh, Coruña, Jan. 13, 1809.

" Your lordship knows that had I followed my own opinion as a military man, I should have retired with the army from Salamanca.   The Spanish armies were then beaten ; there was no Spanish force to which we could unite ; and from the character of the government, and the disposition of the inhabitants, I was satisfied that no efforts would be made to aid us, or favor the cause in which they were engaged.   I was sensible, however, that the apathy and indifference of the Spaniards would never have been believed ; that had the British been withdrawn, the loss of the cause would have been imputed to their retreat ; and it was necessary to risk this army to convince the people of England, as well as the rest of Europe, that the

Spaniards had neither the power nor the inclination to make any efforts for themselves. It was for this reason that I marched to Sahagun. As a diversion it has succeeded. I brought the whole disposable force of the French against this army, and it has been allowed to follow it, without a single movement being made by any of what the Spaniards call armies to favor its retreat."

No. XV.

This despatch from the Count of Belvedere to the Count of Florida Blanca, relative to the battle of Gamonal, is an example of the habitual exaggerations of the Spanish generals:

[Translation.]

Since my arrival at Burgos I have been attacked by the enemy; in two affairs I repulsed him; but to-day, after having sustained his fire for thirteen hours, he charged me with double my force, besides cavalry, as I believe he had three thousand of the latter, and six thousand infantry at least, and I have suffered so much that I have retired on Lerma, and mean to assemble my army at Aranda de Duero. I have sustained a great loss in men, equipage, and artillery; some guns have been saved, but very few. Don Juan Henestrosa, who commanded in the action, distinguished himself, and made a most glorious retreat; but as soon as the cavalry attacked, all was confusion and disorder. I shall send your Excellency the particulars by an officer when they can be procured. The volunteers of Zafra, of Sezena, of Valencia, and the first battalion of infantry of Truxillo, and the provincials of Badajos, had not arrived at Burgos, and consequently I shall be able to sustain myself at Aranda, but they are without cartridges and ammunition. I lament that the ammunition at Burgos could not be brought off. The enemy followed me in small numbers: I am now retiring (10 p. m.), fearing they may follow me in the morning. I yesterday heard from General Blake, that he feared the enemy would attack him to-day, but his dispositions frustrated the enemy's designs, beginning the action at eleven at night.

(Signed)   Conde de Belvedere.

No. XVI.

EXTRACT FROM A LETTER FROM THE DUKE OF DALMATIA TO THE AUTHOR.

" Dans la même lettre que vous m'avez fait l'honneur de m'écrire, vous me priez aussi, Monsieur, de vous donner quelques lumières sur la poursuite de Mr. le général Sir John Moore, quand il fit sa retraite sur la Corogne en 1809. Je ne pense pas que vous desiriez des détails sur cette opération, car ils doivent vous être parfaitement connus, mais je saisirai avec empressement l'occasion que vous me procurez pour rendre à la mémoire de Sir John Moore le témoignage que ses dispositions furent toujours les plus convenables aux circonstances, et qu'en profittant habillement des avantages que les localités pouvaient lui offrir pour seconder sa valeur, il m'opposa partout la resistance la plus énergique et la mieux calculée; c'est ainsi qu'il trouva une mort glorieuse devant la Corogne au milieu d'un combat qui doit honorer son souvenir.

"*Paris, ce 15 Novembre*, 1824."

No. XVII.

LETTER FROM MR. CANNING TO MR. FRERE.

London, Dec. 10, 1808.

SIR,—The messenger, Mills, arrived here yesterday with your despatches, No. 19 to 26 inclusive; and at the same time advices were received from Lieutenant-General Sir David Baird, dated on the 29th ultimo, at Astorga, which state that General to have received intelligence from Sir John Moore of the complete defeat of General Castaños' army, and of the determination taken by Sir John Moore, in consequence, to fall back upon Portugal, while Sir David Baird is directed by Sir John Moore to re-embark his troops, and to proceed to the Tagus. Thus, at the same moment at which I receive from you the caution entertained in your No. 20, that a retreat into Portugal would be considered by the Central Junta as indicating an intention to abandon the cause of Spain, his Majesty's government receive the information that this measure has actually been adopted, but under circumstances which, it is to be supposed, could not have been in the contemplation of the Central Junta. To obviate, however, the possibility of such an impression as you apprehend being produced upon the Spanish government by the retreat of the British armies, I lose no time in conveying to you his Majesty's commands, that you should forthwith give the most positive assurance, that the object of this retreat is no other than that of effecting in Portugal the junction which the events of the war have unfortunately rendered impracticable in Spain, with the purpose of preparing the whole army to move forward again into Spain, whenever and in whatever direction their services may be best employed in support of the common cause. In proof of this intention, you will inform the Spanish government, that an additional reinforcement of cavalry is at this moment sailing for Lisbon, and that the British army in Portugal will be still further augmented, if necessary, so as to make up a substantive and effective force, adequate to any operation for which an opportunity may be offered in the centre or south of Spain, according to the course which the war may take. But while you make this communication to the Spanish government, it is extremely necessary that you should accompany it with a distinct and pressing demand for the communication to you and to the British General of whatever be the plan of operations of the Spanish armies. Sir John Moore complains that he had not received the slightest intimation of any such plan at the date of his last despatch of the 20th ultimo; and I am afraid the appointment which you mention in your No. 20, of General Morla, to discuss with the British commanders the mode of co-operation between the British and Spanish armies, will not have taken place till after the defeat of the Spanish armies will have entirely disposed of that question for the present. The language of Sir David Baird, with respect to defect of information, is precisely the same as that of Sir John Moore. Sir David Baird has indeed had the advantage of some intercourse with the Marquis de la Romana; but the Marquis de la Romana himself does not appear to have been in possession of any part of views of his government, nor to have received any distinct account of the numbers, state, or destination even, of either of the armies which he was himself appointed to command. The British government has most cautiously and scrupulously abstained from interfering in any of the councils of the Junta, or presuming to suggest to them by what plan they should defend their country. But when the question is as to the co-operation of a British force, they have a right and it is their duty to require that some plan should have been formed, and being formed, should be communicated to the British commander, in order that he may judge of, and (if he shall approve) may be prepared to execute the share intended to be assigned to him. You will recollect, that the army which has been appropriated by his Majesty to the defence of Spain and Portugal is not merely a considerable part of the disposable force of this country; it is, in fact, the British army. The country has no other force disposable. It may, by a great effort, reinforce the army for an adequate purpose; but another army it has not to send. The proposals, therefore, which are made, somewhat too lightly, for appending parts of this force, sometimes to one of the Spanish armies, sometimes to another, and the facility with which its services are called for, wherever the exigency of the moment happens to press, are by no means suited to the nature of the force itself, or consonant to the views with which his Majesty has consented to employ it in Spain. You are already apprised by my former despatch (inclosing a copy of General Moore's instructions), that the British army must be kept together under its own commander, must act as one body for some distinct object, and on some settled plan.

It will decline no difficulty, it will shrink from no danger, when, through that difficulty and danger, the commander is enabled to see his way to some definite purpose. But, in order to this, it will be necessary that such purpose should have been previously arranged, and that the British army should not again be left, as that of Sir John Moore and Sir David Baird have recently been, in the heart of Spain, without one word of information, except such as they could pick up from common rumor, of the events passing around them. Previously, therefore, to General Sir John Moore's again entering Spain, it will be expected that some clear exposition should be made to him of the system upon which the Spaniards intend to conduct the war; the points which they mean to contest with the advancing enemy, and those which, if pressed, by a series of reverse, they ultimately propose to defend.

The part assigned to the British army in the combined operation must be settled with Sir John Moore, and he will be found not unambitious of that in which he may be opposed most directly to the enemy. The courage and constancy displayed by the Junta, under the first reverses, are in the highest degree worthy of admiration.* And if they shall persevere in the same spirit, and can rouse the country to adequate exertions, there is no reason to despair of the ultimate safety of Spain. But it is most earnestly to be hoped that the same confidence which they appear to have placed in the ability of their armies, under Blake and Castaños, to resist the attacks of the enemy, will not be again adopted as their guide, again to deceive them in the ulterior operations of the war. It is to be hoped that they will weigh well their really existing means of defence against the means of attack on the part of the enemy, and that if they find them unequal to maintain a line of defence as extended as they have hitherto attempted to main-

* The extract which follows this letter furnishes a curious comment on this passage.

tain, they will at once fall back to that point, wherever it may be, at which they can be sure that their stand will be permanent and their resistance effectual. It is obvious, that unless they can resist effectually in the passes of the Guadarama, or in the Sierra Morena, the ultimate point of retreat, after a series of defeats more or less numerous and exhausting, according as they shall the sooner or the later make up their minds to retreat, is Cadiz. Supported by Cadiz on one side, and by the fortress of Gibraltar on the other, the remaining armies of Spain might unquestionably make such a stand, as no force waich France could bring against them could overpower; and the assistance of the British army would be in this situation incalculably augmented by the communication with Gibraltar and the sea. I am aware of the jealousy with which the mention of a British force of any sort, coupled with the name of Cadiz, will be received. But the time seems to be arrived at which we must communicate with each other (the Spanish government and England) without jealousy or reserve. His Majesty has abjured, in the face of the world, any motive of interested policy,—you are authorized to repeat in the most solemn manner, if necessary, that abjuration. But if, in the midst of such sacrifices and such exertions as Great Britain is making for Spain—if, after having foregone all objects of partial benefit, many of which the state of Spain (if we had been so ungenerous as to take that advantage of it) would have brought within our reach, the fair opinion of the British government cannot be received without suspicion; there is little hope of real cordiality continuing to subsist under reverses and misfortunes, such as Spain must but too surely expect, and such as are at all times the tests of sincerity and confidence. It is the opinion of the British government, that the last stand (if all else fail) must be made at Cadiz. It is the opinion of the British government, that this stand will be made in vain *only* if the necessity of resorting to it is too late acknowledged, and the means of making it effectually not providently prepared. It is the opinion of the British government, that on no account should the naval means of Spain be suffered to fall into the hands of France, or those of France to be recovered by her. It is their opinion that this may be prevented; but to prevent it, the object must be fairly looked at beforehand; and it is hoped that a spirit of distrust unworthy both of those who entertain it, and of those with respect to whom it is entertained, will not be suffered to interfere between an object of so great importance and the means of insuring its accomplishment. It is absolutely necessary to lose no time in bringing this subject fairly before the Spanish government; and if, in doing so, you should see either in M. Cevallos, or in Count Florida Blanca, marks of that distrust and suspicion which must fatally affect any measure of co-operation between the British and Spanish forces, it will be right that you should at once anticipate the subject, and you are at liberty to communicate this despatch *in extenso*, as the surest mode of proving the openness with which the British government is desirous of acting, and the disdain which it would feel of any imputation upon its disinterestedness and sincerity. But while this object is thus to be stated to the Central Government, it is not to this object alone that the services of the British army are to be appropriated. The Commander-in-Chief will have both the authority and the inclination to listen to any proposal for any other practical undertaking. And it is only in the event of no such object or undertaking being presented to him in Spain, that he is directed to confine himself to the defence of Portugal.   I am, &c. &c. &c.,

                    (Signed)   GEORGE CANNING.

EXTRACTS FROM A LETTER FROM MR. CANNING TO MR. FRERE OF THE SAME DATE AS THE ABOVE.

December 10, 1808.

"The timely preparation of the fleets of France and Spain, now in the harbor of Cadiz, is also a point to be pressed by you with earnestness, but, at the same time, with all the delicacy which belongs to it. In the event of *an emigration to America*, it is obvious that this preparation should be made beforehand. And in the case of this project not being adopted, and of a resolution being taken to defend Cadiz to the utmost, it would still be desirable that the fleets should be prepared for removal to Minorca, in order to be out of the reach of any use which the disaffected in Cadiz (of whom General Morla is represented to have expressed considerable apprehension) might be disposed to make of them for compromise with the enemy."

EXTRACT FROM A LETTER FROM MR. CANNING TO MR. FRERE.

December 11, 1808.

"SIR,—Complaints have been justly made of the manner in which the British troops, particularly those under Sir David Baird, have been received in Spain.

"The long detention of Sir David Baird's corps on board the transports at Coruña may but too probably have contributed to render the difficulties of a junction between the two parts of the British army insurmountable, by giving the enemy time to advance between them. In addition to this, it is slated, that there was a total want of preparation for supply of any sort, and the unwillingness with which those supplies appeared to have been administered, have undoubtedly occasioned as much disappointment as inconvenience to the British commanders. Unless some change is effected in these particulars when the army again moves into Spain, the advance of the British troops through that country will be attended with more difficulty than a march through a hostile country."

No. XVIII.

ABSTRACT OF THE MILITARY FORCE OF GREAT BRITAIN IN 1808.

Extracted from the Adjutant-General's returns.

Cavalry	30,000
Foot guards	6,000
Infantry of the line	170,000
Artillery	14,000
Total	220,000

Of these, between 50 and 60,000 were employed in the Colonies in India, the remainder were disposable, because from 80 to 100,000 militia, differing from the regular troops in nothing but the name, were sufficient for the home duties. If to this force we add 30,000 marines, the military power of England must be considered prodigious.

RETURN OF BRITISH TROOPS EMBARKED FOR PORTUGAL AND SPAIN IN 1808.

Artillery.	Cavalry.	Infantry.	Total.	
357	349	8688	9394	Commanded by Sir A. Wellesley; embarked at Cork the 15th, 16th, and 17th June, 1808; sailed 12th of July; landed at Mondego, August 1st.
379	...	4323	4702	Commanded by Generals Acland and Anstruther; embarked at Harwich, July 18th and 19th; landed at Maceira, Aug. 20th, 1808.
66	...	4647	4713	Commanded by Gen. Spencer; embarked at Cadiz; landed at Mondego, Aug. 3d.
712	563	10,049	11,324	Commanded first by Sir John Moore; secondly by Sir Harry Burrard; embarked at Portsmouth, April, 1808; sailed to the Baltic; returned, and sailed to Portugal, July 31st; landed at Maceira, August 29th.
...	672	...	672	Landed at Lisbon, Dec. 31st, 1808.
186	...	943	1129	Embarked at Gibraltar; sailed Aug. 14; landed at the Tagus in September.
94	...	929	1023	Commanded by General Beresford; embarked at Madeira, sailed Aug. 17th; landed at the Tagus in September.
...	672	...	672	Commanded by General C. Stewart; embarked at Gravesend; landed at Lisbon, September 1st.
798	...	10,271	11,069	Commanded by Sir D. Baird; embarked at Falmouth, sailed Oct. 9; arrived at Coruña 19th Oct.; landed 29th do.
...	...	1622	1622	Two regiments sent round to Lisbon from Sir D. Baird's force.
...	2021	...	2021	Commanded by Lord Paget; embarked at Portsmouth; landed at Coruña, Oct. 30th.
2592	4277	41,472	46,719	
			1,622	Add two regiments sent to Lisbon from Coruña.
			48,341	Grand total, of which 800 were artificers, wagon train, and commissariat.

No. XIX.

RETURNS OF KILLED, WOUNDED, AND MISSING, OF THE ARMY
UNDER THE COMMAND OF SIR A. WELLESLEY.

1808. August.	OFFICERS.			MEN.			Total.
	Killed.	Wounded.	Missing.	Killed.	Wounded.	Missing.	
15th—Brillos	1	1	0	1	5	21	29
17th—Roriça	4	19	4	66	316	70	479
21st —Vimiero	4	35	2	131	499	49	720
Grand total for the campaign	9	55	6	198	820	140	1228

No. XX.

BRITISH ORDER OF BATTLE. RORICA, 17th AUGUST, 1808.

Extracted from the Adjutant-General's states.

		Regiments.			
Right Wing.	1st brigade, Major-General Hill....	5th / 9th / 38th	2780		
	3d ditto, Major-General Nightingale.	29th / 82d	1722	7246	
	5th ditto, C. Crawfurd...........	45th / 50th / 91st	2744		
Left Wing.	4th brigade, Brigadier-Gen. Bowes..	6th / 32d	1829		
	2d ditto, Major-General Ferguson...	36th / 40th / 71st	2681	5846	
	6th ditto (light), Brigadier-General Fane.....................	95th, 2d bn. / 60th, 5th bn.	1336		

Artillery, 18 guns, 6 and 9 lbs............................. 660   660
Cavalry... 240   240

Total British................ 13,992

Portuguese, Colonel Trant... { Infantry of the line...... 1000 / Light troops........... 400 / Cavalry............... 250 } ... 1,650

Grand total, British and Portuguese, including sick men, &c. &c... 15,642

No. XXI.

BRITISH ORDER OF BATTLE. VIMIERO, 21st AUGUST, 1808.

Extracted from the Adjutant-General's states.

		Regiments.		
Right wing.	1st brigade, General Hill..........	5th 9th 38th	2780	2780
Centre.	6th ditto, Brigadier-General Fane...	50th 60th 95th, 2d bn.	2293	4953
	7th ditto, Brigadier-General Anstruther	9th 43d, 2d bn. 52d, 2d bn. 97th	2660	
Left wing.	2d brigade, Major-General Ferguson..	36th 40th 71st	2681	7612
	3d ditto, Major-General Nightingale..	29th 82d	1722	
	4th ditto, Brigadier-General Bowes...	6th 32d	1829	
	8th ditto, Major-General Acland	2d 20th	1380	
Reserve 5th brigade Brig.-Gen. C. Crawfurd..		45th 50th 91st	2744	2744

Artillery, 18 guns, 6 and 9 lbs................................ 660   660
Cavalry, 20th light dragoons............................. 240   240

Total British.............. 18,989

Portuguese, Colonel Trant........ { Infantry, 1,400 } 1,650
                                 { Cavalry,   250 }

Grand total, including sick, wounded, and missing............ 20,639

No. XXII.

RETURN OF SIR HEW DALRYMPLE'S ARMY, OCT. 1, 1808.

Head-quarters, Bemfica.

	Fit for duty.	Hospital.	Detached.	Total.
Cavalry........................	1,402	128	28	1,558
Artillery.......................	2,091	146	6	2,243
Infantry.......................	25,678	3196	454	29,328
Total.....................	29,171	3470	488	

Grand total, including artificers, wagon train, &c., &c........ 33,129

No. XXIII.

EMBARKATION RETURN OF THE FRENCH ARMY UNDER GENERAL JUNOT.

| | PRESENT UNDER ARMS. | | | DETACHED. | | | ABSENT WITHOUT PAY. | | | | | TOTAL. | | CRIMINALS. |
| | | | | | | | Hospital | | Prisons. | | | | | |
	Officers.	Men.	Horses.	Officers.	Men.	Horses.	Officers.	Men.	Officers.	Men.	Officers.	Men.	Horses.	Men.
Infantry......	273	15,860	....	52	2078	0	46	3281	17	895	..	22,635	..	13
Cavalry.....	48	1,722	1176	..	1	1	..	195	1	....	..	1,974	..	..
Artillery.....	21	1,015	472	..	6	..	..	....	3	....	..	1,121	..	..
Engineers....	14	.....	.....	..	..	..	..	....	..	....	..	17	..	..

```
Guns..............................10    8 lbs.  ⎫
Ditto.............................16    4 lbs.  ⎬ 30
Howitzers ........................ 4    6 inch. ⎭
```

Grand total, 25,747 men, 1655 horses, and 30 pieces of artillery.

NOTE.—On the staff of each division there are—

1 General of division.	1 Inspector of reviews.
2 Generals of brigade.	1 Commissary of engineers.
7 Aides-de-camp.	2 Officers of engineers.

Artillery................... { 1 General. / 4 Colonels. / 2 Chefs-de-bataillon.

Engineers.................. { 1 Colonel. / 2 Captains. } The remainder in the divisions.

No. XXIV.

THE FOLLOWING EXTRACT FROM A MINUTE MADE BY HIS ROYAL HIGHNESS THE DUKE OF YORK IN 1808

Proves that sixty thousand men could have been provided for the campaign of 1808–9 in *Spain*, without detriment to other services :

"There are at present in Portugal { Cavalry.............. 1,640 / Infantry, 34 battalions . 29,806 } 31,446

"Under orders to embark........ { Cavalry.............. 3,410 / Infantry.............11,419 } 14,829

Total.................... 46,275

"Of this force the 20th dragoons and eight battalions should remain in Portugal. The disposable force would then be—

	Cavalry.	Infantry.
From Portugal	1,313	23,575
Under orders	3,200	11,419
Force to be drawn from Sicily		8,000
Total	4,513	42,994
"To this may be added, four regiments of cavalry and the two brigades of guards	2,560	2,434
Grand total	7,073	45,428

"When to this you add four battalions of infantry, which may be spared, and the artillery, it will form a corps of about sixty thousand rank and file."

Note.—The details of names and strength of the regiments are omitted to save space.

No. XXV.

SIR JOHN MOORE'S ORDER OF BATTLE.

Third division.	*Second division.*	*First division.*
Lt.-Gen. M'Kenzie Fraser.	Lieut.-Gen. Sir John Hope.	Lieut.-Gen. Sir David Baird.
79th, 38th, 3d, 43d, 23d, 9th, 6th. Wilmot's brig. of artillery, 6 pieces.	76th, 59th, 51st, 92d, 71st, 36th, 32d, 14th, 5th, 2d. Drummond's brigade of art., 6 pieces.	81st, 26th, 1st, 50th, 42d, 4th, 1st, & 3d battalion guards, Bean's brigade of artillery, 6 pieces.
Second Flank Brigade.	*Reserve.*	*First Flank Brigade.*
Brigadier-General C. Alten.	Major-General E. Paget.	Colonel R. Crawfurd.
1st battalion 2d battalion K.G.L. K.G.L.	21st, 28th, 1st battal'n 95th, 52d, 20th. Carthew's brigade of artillery, 6 pieces.	2d bat. 95th, 2d bat. 52d, 1st battalion 43d.

Cavalry.

Lieutenant-General Lord Paget.

3d light dragoons K.G.L., 15th light dragoons, 10th, 18th, 7th hussars. Dowman's and Evelin's troops of horse artillery, 12 pieces.

Artillery Parc and Reserve.

Colonel Harding.

---

5 brigades	30 pieces
6 ditto, attached to the divisions	36 "

RETURN OF SIR JOHN MOORE'S ARMY, DECEMBER 19, 1808.

Extracted from the Adjutant-General's morning state of that day.

	Fit for Duty.	Hospital.	Detached.	Total.	
Cavalry.	2,278	182	794	3,254	
Artillery.	1,358	97	...	1,455	
Infantry.	22,222	3,756	893	26,871	
	25,858	4,035	1,687	31,580	
Deduct..	2,275	{ Men composing four battalions, viz:		{ 3d regt. left in Portugal. 76th } Between Villa 51st } Franca and Lugo. 59th }	
	23,583	Total number under arms.			

Note.—Of 66 guns, 42 were attached to the divisions, the remainder in reserve, with the exception of one brigade of 3 lbs.

No. XXVI.

The following General Return, extracted from especial regimental reports, received at the Horse Guards, contains the whole number of non-commissioned officers and men, cavalry and infantry, lost during Sir John Moore's campaign :—

Total.

Lost at or previous to the arrival of the } Cavalry...... 95 } 1397
army at the position of Lugo....... { Infantry...... 1302 }

Of this number 200 were left in the wine-vaults of Bembibre, and nearly 500 were stragglers from the troops that marched to Vigo.

Lost between the departure of the army } Cavalry...... 9 } 2636
from Lugo and the embarkation at { Infantry...... 2627 }
Coruña ....

Grand total.......................... 4033

Of the whole number, above 800 contrived to escape to Portugal, and being united with the sick left by the regiments in that country, they formed a corps of 1876 men, which being re-embodied under the name of the battalions of detachments, did good service at Oporto and Talavera.

The pieces of artillery abandoned during the retreat were six 3-pounders.

These guns were landed at Coruña without the General's knowledge : they never went beyond Villa Franca, and not being horsed, they were thrown down the rocks when the troops quitted that town.

The guns used in the battle of Coruña were spiked and thrown into the sea.

N. B. Some trifling errors may possibly have crept into the regimental states in consequence of the difficulty of ascertaining exactly where each man was lost, but the inaccuracies could not affect the total amount above fifty men more or less.

No. XXVII.

The following states of the Spanish armies are not strictly accurate, because the original reports from whence they have been drawn were generally very loose, often inconsistent, and sometimes contradictory: nevertheless, it is believed that the approximation is sufficiently close for any useful purpose.

State I.

Army of Andalusia.

	Armed Peasantry.	Regulars.
1808.		
19th July, Baylen.....................	Unknown	29,000
1st Sept. { Madrid / La Mancha / Sierra Morena }.............	——	30,600

State II.

Numbers of the Spanish armies in October, 1809, according to the reports transmitted to Sir John Moore by the military agents.

	Regulars.	Armed peasantry incorporated with the regular troops.	
Troops upon the Ebro, and in Biscay....	75,300	70,000	145,000
In Catalonia.........................	20,000	....	20,000
In march from Aragon to Catalonia.....	10,000	....	10,000
Ditto new levies from Granada.........	....	10,000	10,000
In the Asturias.......................	18,000	....	18,000
Total.................123,000	80,000	——
Grand total....................................203,000

State III.

Real numbers of the Spanish armies in line of battle, in the months of October, November, and December, 1808.

1st Line.

	Cavalry.	Infantry.	Guns.	
Army of Palafox................	550	17,500	20	} Defeated and dispersed at Tudela.
Army of Castaños.............	2200	24,500	48	
Army of Blake.................	100	30,000	26	} Ditto at the battles of Zornosa and Espinosa.
Army of Romana...............	1404	8,000	25	
Asturians......................	....	8,000	..	
Army of Count Belvedere.......	1150	11,150	30	Ditto at Gamonal.
Total........................	5404	99,150	149	
Deduct Romana's cavalry and guns, which never came into the line of battle................	1404	....	25	
Total brought into first line of battle......................	4000	99,150	124	103,150

2d Line.

	Infantry.	Cavalry.	
General St. Juan's division.....	12,000	..	Were beaten at the Somosierra, 30th November; murdered their General at Talavera, December 7th, and dispersed.
Fugitives from Gamonal, commanded by General Heredia.	4000	..	Fled from Segovia and Sepulveda, Dec. 2d, and dispersed at Talvera,7th.
Fugitives from Blake's army re-organized by Romana...	6000	1400	Beaten at Mancilla, 20th Dec.; retired into Gallicia. Infantry dispersed there.
Asturian levies under Ballesteros.....................	5000	..	Were not engaged.
Fugitives assembled by Galluzzo behind the Tagus.....	6000	..	Defeated and dispersed, 24th Dec., by the 4th corps, at Almaraz.

Total, brought into 2d line...	33,000	1400

To cover Moore's advance there were on the Ebro, in Biscay, and in the Asturias, according to the Spanish and the military agents' reports...	173,000
The real number brought into the field was...................	103,150

Exaggeration.....................	69,850

Note.—The real amount includes the sick in the field hospitals.

No. XXVIII.

SECTION I.—STATE OF THE FRENCH ARMY, CALLED "THE FIRST PART OF THE ARMY OF SPAIN," OCT. 1, 1808.

Head-quarters, Vittoria. King Joseph, Commander-in-Chief. General Jourdan, Major-General. General Belliard, Chief of the Staff. Recapitulation, extracted from the Imperial states, signed by the Prince of Neufchatel.

Officers included, present under arms.

	Men.	Horses.
Division imperial guard, commanded by General Dorsenne.	2,423	786
Do. reserve cavalry, imperial gendarmes, and other troops....... } General Saligny......	5,417	944
Corps of Marshal Bessières.............................	15,595	2,923
Corps of Marshal Ney..................................	13,756	2,417
Corps of Marshal Moncey.. 16,636 } Garrison of Pampeluna.... 6,004 }	22,640	3,132
Garrisons of Vittoria, Bilbao, St. Sebastian, Tolosa, Montdragon, Salinas, Bergara, Villa Real, Yrun, and other places of less note .... } General Lagrange....	8,479	1,458
To carry over......	68,310	11,660

	Men.	Horses.
Brought over........................	68,310	11,660
Troops disposable at Bayonne and vicinity or in march upon that place........................ (General Drouet, commanding 11th military division......)	20,005	5,196
Troops employed as movable columns in the defence of the frontier from Bayonne to Belgarde..	6,042	261
In Catalonia, General Duhesme....................	10,142	1,638
Fort of Fernando, Figueras, General Reille...........	4,027	557
Division of General Chabot......................	1,434	....
Total..............................	109,960	19,312

Note.—At this period the Spaniards and the military agents always asserted that the French had only from 35 to 45,000 men of all weapons.

STATE OF THE FRENCH ARMY CALLED THE "SECOND PART OF THE ARMY OF SPAIN," OCTOBER 1, 1808.

THIS army, composed of the troops coming from the grand army and from Italy, was by an imperial decree, dated 7th September, divided into six corps and a reserve.

Present under arms.

	Men.	Horses.
1st corps, Marshal Victor, Duke of Belluno	29,547	5,552
5th do. " Mortier, Duke of Treviso	24,405	3,495
6th do., destined for Ney, Duke of Elchingen . . .	22,694	3,945
Infantry of the Viceroy of Spain's guards	1,213	....
Cavalry ditto	456	551
1st division of dragoons	3,695	3,994
2d ditto	2,940	3,069
3d ditto	2,020	2,238
4th ditto	3,101	3,316
5th ditto	2,903	3,068
Division of General Sebastiani	5,808	185
5th regiment of dragoons	556	531
German division	6,067	381
Polish ditto	6,818	...
Dutch brigade	2,280	751
Westphalian light horse	522	559
General Souham's division	7,259	...
General Pino's ditto	6,803	...
24th regiment of dragoons	664	731
Regiment of royal Italian chasseurs	560	512
Regiment of Napoleon's dragoons	500	474
Artillery and engineers in march for Perpignan . .	1,706	1,430
Total of second part	132,517	34,782
Total of first part	109,960	19,312
Grand total	242,477	54,094

SECTION II.—GENERAL STATE OF THE FRENCH ARMY, OCTOBER 10th, 1808.

	PRESENT UNDER ARMS.		DETACHED.		HOSPITAL.	PRISONERS.	EFFECTIVE.		
	Men.	Horses.	Men.	Horses	Men.	Men.	Men.	Cav. Hor.	Art. Hor.
1st corps, Duke of Belluno	28,797	5,615	2,201	219	2,939	...	33,937	3,329	2,501
2d ditto, — Istria	20,093	3,219	7,394	1,199	5,536	30	33,054	3,616	802
3d ditto, — Conegliano	18,867	3,186	11,082	2,472	7,522	219	37,690	4,537	821
4th ditto, — Dantzic	22,859	2,410	955	40	2,170	...	25,984	1,791	659
5th ditto, — Treviso	24,552	3,833	188	6	1,971	2	26,713	1,805	2,034
6th ditto, — Elchingen	29,568	4,304	3,381	257	5,051	33	38,033	2,465	2,096
7th ditto, General St Cyr	35,657	5,254	1,302	198	4,948	200	42,107	4,045	1,404
8th ditto, Duke of Abrantes	19,059	2,247	2,137	1	3,528	1,006	25,730	1,776	472
Reserve	34,924	23,604	3,533	733	3,553	392	42,382	21,225	3,112
1st hussars and 27th chasseurs	1,424	1,463	256	208	74	...	1,754	1,675	...
Artillery and engineers in march, coming from Germany	3,446	958	107	...	...	...	3,446	...	958
Movable columns for defence of the frontiers of France	8,588	477	107	...	146	19	8,860	268	209
Total	247,834	56,670	32,643	5,333	37,488	1,901	319,690	46,822	15,068

	UNDER ARMS.						DETACHED.		HOSPITAL.	PRISONERS.	EFFECTIVE.		
	Artillery.		Cavalry.		Infantry.		Men.	Horses	Men.	Men.	Men.	Cav. Hor.	Art. Hor.
	Men.	Horses.	Men.	Horses.	Men.	Men.							
Of this number { French	17,868	15,107	34,172	35,761	152,770		29,647	5,052	31,401	1,771	267,629	41,565	14,253
Auxiliaries	1,503	968	4,782	4,831	36,739		2,889	277	6,018	130	52,061	5,263	815
Total	19,371	16,075	38,954	40,592	189,509		32,536	5,329	37,419	1,901	319,690	46,828	15,068

Grand total............319,690 men and 61,896 horses.

SECTION III.—STATE OF THE FRENCH ARMY OF SPAIN, THE
EMPEROR NAPOLEON COMMANDING IN PERSON,
25th OCTOBER, 1808.

1148 Officers of the Staff.   298 Battalions.   184 Squadrons.

Present under arms.		Detached.		Hospital.	Prisoners.	Total.		
Men.	Horses.	Men.	Horses.	Men.	Men.	Men.	Cav. H.	Art. H.
249,046	55,759	33,438	4,943	34,558	1,892	318,934	45,242	15,498

Grand total.....318,934 men and 60,740 horses.

STATE OF THE FRENCH ARMY IN SPAIN, THE EMPEROR
NAPOLEON COMMANDING, 15th NOVEMBER, 1808.

Officers of the Staff, 1064.   Battalions, 290.   Squadrons, 181.

Present under arms.		Detached.		Hospital.	Prisoners.	Total.		
Men.	Horses.	Men.	Horses.	Men.	Men.	Men.	Cav. H.	Art. H.
255,876	52,430	32,245	8,295	45,107	1,995	335,223	43,920	16,808

Grand total.....335,223 men and 60,728 horses.

SECTION IV.—STATE OF THE FRENCH ARMY IN PORTUGAL,
1st JANUARY, 1808.

[Extracted from the Imperial returns.]

General Junot, Commander-in-Chief.   General Thiebault, Chief of the Staff.

1st division, General De Laborde ⎫
2d   "   "   Loison   ⎬ 26 battalions, 7 squadrons.
3d   "   "   Travot   ⎪
Cavalry   "   Kellermann ⎭

10 guns of 8 lbs. ⎫
22 guns of 4 lbs. ⎬ 36 pieces.
4 6-inch howitzers ⎭

	Under arms.		Effective.	
	Men.	Horses.	Men.	Horses.
	16,190	1,114	27,735	1,377
At Salamanca, or in march to join the army in Portugal...............	4,795	1,296	4,795	1,296
Total.............	20,985	2,310	29,530	2,673

STATE OF THE FRENCH ARMY IN PORTUGAL,
23d MAY, 1808.

	Under arms.		Detached.		Hospital.		Effective.		
	Men.	Horses.	Men.	Horses.	Men.	Men.	Horses.	Art.	
French..........	24,446	2,789	...	...	2,449	29,684	3,586	629	
Spanish division of Gen. Quesnel...	9,281	101	1,087	...	651	11,019	...	...	
Do. Gen. Caraffa...	6,399	844	174	13	141	6,624	13	...	
Portuguese troops..	4,621	483	570	234	116	5,307	234	...	
Total......	44,657	4,217	1,831	247	3,357	52,634	3,833	629	

Grand total.....52,634 men, 4454 horses, and 36 guns.

SECTION V.—STATE OF "THE SECOND ARMY OF OBSERVATION OF THE GIRONDE," 1st FEB., 1808, SPAIN.

General Dupont commanding.

20 battalions and 1 division of cavalry.

Headquarters, Valladolid.

Present under arms.		Detached.		Hospital.	Effective.	
Men.	Horses.	Men.	Horses.	Men.	Men.	Horses.
20,729	2,884	1,303	334	2,277	24,309	3,218

Total....24,309 men and 3,218 horses.

SECTION VI.—STATE OF "THE ARMY OF OBSERVATION DE COTE D'OCEAN," 1st FEB., 1808, SPAIN.

Marshal Moncey, commanding.

Head-quarters, Vittoria.

Present under arms.		Detached.		Hospital.	Effective.	
Men.	Horses.	Men.	Horses.	Men.	Men.	Horses.
21,878	2,547	2,144	...	4,464	28,486	2,547
Train of the guard.....................					225	509

Grand total....28,711 men and 3,391 horses.

No. XXIX.

THE following letters from Lord Collingwood did not come into my possession before the first edition of the present volume was in the press. It will be seen that they corroborate many of the opinions and some of the facts that I have stated, and they will doubtless be read with the attention due to the observations of such an honorable and able man.

To SIR HEW DALRYMPLE.

Ocean, Gibraltar, 30th August, 1808.

MY DEAR SIR,—I have been in great expectation of hearing of your progress with the army, and hope the first account will be of your success whenever you move. I have heard nothing lately of Junot at Cadiz; but there have been accounts, not very well authenticated, that Joseph Bonaparte, in his retiring to France, was stopped by the mass rising in Biscay, to the amount of fourteen thousand well-armed men, which obliged him to return to Burgos, where the body of the French army was stationed.

At Zaragoza, the French, in making their fourteenth attack upon the town, were defeated, repulsed with great loss, and had retired from it. There is a deputy here from that city with a commission from the Marquis de Palafox to request supplies. The first aid upon their list is for ten or fifteen thousand troops. The deputy states they have few regulars in the province, and the war has hitherto been carried on by all being armed. In this gentleman's conversation I observe, what I had before remarked in others, that he had no view of Spain beyond the kingdom of Aragon; and in reply to the observations I made on the necessity of a central government, he had little to say, as if that had not yet been a subject of much consideration. I have great hope that General Castaños, Cuesta, and those captains-general who will now meet at Madrid, will do something effectual in simplifying the government. In a conversation I had with Morla on the necessity of this, he seemed to think the Juntas would make many difficulties, and retain their present power as long as they could.

I hope, my dear sir, you will give some directions about this puzzling island (*Perexil*), which it appears to me will not be of any future use; but the people who are on it will suffer much in the winter, without habitations, except tents; I conceive the purpose for which it was occupied is past, and will probably never return; whenever they quit it, they should bring the stores away as quietly as possible; for, if I am not mistaken, the Emperor has an intention to keep them, and will remonstrate against their going. I hope you have received good accounts from Lady Dalrymple, &c.

* * * * * * *

I am to sail to-day for Toulon, where everything indicates an intention in the French to sail. Mr. Duff brought a million of dollars to Seville, and has instructions to communicate with the Junta; but he appears to me to be too old to do it as Major Cox has done; he is still there, and I conclude will wait for your instructions. Mr. Markland would accept with great thankfulness the proposal you made to him to go to Valencia.

I beg my kind regards, &c.

COLLINGWOOD.

P.S. Prince Leopold is still here, and I understand intends to stay until he hears from England. I have given passports for Dupont and a number of French officers to go to France on parole, ninety-three in number. General Morla was impatient to get them out of the country. The Spaniards were much irritated against them; they were not safe from their revenge, except in St. Sebastian's castle.

To SIR HEW DALRYMPLE.

Ocean, off Toulon, October 18, 1808.

MY DEAR SIR,—I have received the favor of your letters of the 27th August and 5th September, and beg to offer you my sincere congratulations on the success of the British army in Portugal, which I hope will have satisfied the French that they are not those invincible creatures which Bonaparte had endeavored to persuade them they were.

It is a happy event to have rescued Portugal from the government of France; and their carrying off a little plunder is a matter of very secondary consideration; perhaps it may have the good effect of keeping up the animosity of the Portuguese who suffer, and incite them to more resistance in future.

The great business now is to endeavor to establish that sort of government, and organize that sort of military force, which may give security to the country; and the great difficulty in Portugal will be to find men who are of ability, to place at the head of the several departments, who have patriotism to devote themselves to its service, and vigor to maintain its independence. In a country exhausted like Portugal, it will require much ingenious expedient to supply the want of wealth and of everything military. If it is not found in the breasts of those to whom the people look up, Portugal will remain in a hapless and uncertain state still.

I have not heard from Sir Charles Cotton how he settled his terms with the Russian Admiral; but as he has got possession of the ships to be sent to England, they cannot but be good. The hoisting of the English flag on the fort which surrendered to our troops, I conclude, would be explained to the Portuguese as not to be understood as taking possession by England for other purpose than to be restored to its Prince, as was done at Madeira; but in this instance it ought to have been thought necessary to deprive Siniavin of the argument he would have used of the neutrality of the Portuguese flag, with whom his nation was not at *war*.

I left Cadiz the moment everything in that quarter was pacific; and Mr. Duff arrived there with a million of dollars for their use; this money was sent to the Junta of Seville, where I am afraid there are many members unworthy of the trust.

I have only heard once from Cox since I left that quarter. After getting the money, Father Gil seemed to have dropped his communications with Major C., and their discussions were not of a nature to excite much public interest; they consisted more in private bickerings than of grave consult for the public weal. Tilly seems to have been entirely disappointed in his project, both in respect to the annexation of Southern Portugal to Andalusia, and the pension of 12,000 dollars for his service in the Supreme Council; of those you will be informed by Major Cox. I am afraid I related the proceedings to his Majesty's ministers of events which were passing almost under my eye, and gave my opinion on them with too great freedom; I mean with a freedom that is not usual; but they were facts of which, without being possessed, his Majesty's ministers could not have a knowledge of the real state of affairs in Spain; and the sentiments those facts inspired were necessary to explain my motives, and the rule of conduct which I pursued. And still I consider the great and only danger to which Spain is now exposed, is the supposition that the whole nation is possessed of the same patriotism which, in Andalusia, Aragon, and Valencia, led to such glorious results. It is far otherwise. There are not many Castañoses, nor Cuestas, nor Palafoxes; and take from Spain the influence of the clergy, and its best source of power would be lost; wherever this influence is least, the war is languid.

I wrote to you, some time since, to represent the state of Catalonia. Nothing can be more indifferent to the cause than they appear to be; yet the common peasantry have not less spirit nor less desire to repel their enemy. They have no leaders. Palacios, the Captain-General, stays at Villa Franca, west of Barcelona, talking of what he intends to do; and the people speak of him as either wanting zeal in their cause or ability to direct them; while the French from Barcelona and Figueras do just what they please. When the French attacked Gerona, he did nothing to succor it. The greatest discomfiture they suffered was from Lord Cochrane, who, while they were employed at the siege, blew up the road, making deep trenches in a part where the fire of his ships could be brought upon; and when they came there he drove them from their guns, killed many, and took some cannon.

The French fleet is here quite ready for sea, and I am doing all that is in my power to meet them when they do come out. It is an arduous service; the last ten days we have had gales of wind incessantly; the difficulty of keeping a sufficient squadron is very great. I think the storms from those Alpine mountains are harder than in England, and of more duration.

I beg my best regards to Captain Dalrymple, and my sincerest wishes for every success to attend you.

I am, my dear Sir Hew,

Your obedient and most humble servant,

COLLINGWOOD.

P.S. In the letter which I wrote to you on the state of Catalonia I represented the necessity of sending a body of British troops to Catalonia. There is no other prospect of the French being kept in any bounds. The avenues to France are as open now as at any time they have been. I have kept a ship always as Rosas Bay; her marines have garrisoned the castle, and her company assisted in repairing the works. The French appear to have designs on that place. The presence of the English alone prevents them. If 18,000 men were here of our army, I think they would make Mr. Palacio come forward, and put the whole country into activity, which till then I don't think they ever will be.   COLLINGWOOD.

They want an English resident at Gerona, that they may have somebody to apply to for succor . . .

[The rest torn off in the original.]

To SIR HEW DALRYMPLE.

Ocean, off Minorca, April 8, 1809.

MY DEAR SIR,—I received the favor of your letter a few days ago, which gave me great pleasure, after all the trouble and vexations you have had, to hear you were all well.

I was exceedingly sorry when I saw the angry mood in which the convention in Portugal was taken up, even before the circumstances which led to it were at all known. Before our army landed in Portugal, the French force was reported to be very small. I remember its being said that a body of 5000 troops was all that was necessary to dispossess Junot. I conclude the same sort of report went to England; and this, with the victory that was obtained, led people to expect the extermination of the few French which were supposed to be there; and when once the idea is entertained, people shut their eyes to difficulties.

I remember what you told me the last time I saw you off Cadiz, of the communication which might be made to you by an officer who possessed the entire confidence of ministers. I thought then, that whatever ministers had to communicate to a commander-in-chief, could not be done better than by themselves; for intermediate communications are always in danger of being misunderstood, and never fail to cause doubts and disturb the judgment. I hope now it is all over, and your uneasiness on that subject at an end.

My labors I think will never cease. I am worn down by fatigue of my mind, with anxiety and sorrow; my health is very much impaired; and while our affairs require an increased energy, I find myself less able to conduct them from natural causes. I give all my thoughts and time, but have interruptions, from my weak state of body, which the service will scarcely admit of. I never felt the severity of winter more than this last. They were not gales of wind, but hurricanes; and the consequence is, that the fleet has suffered very much, and many of the ships very infirm. I would not have kept the sea so long, because I know the system of blockading must be ruinous to our fleet at last, and in no instance that I can recollect has prevented the enemy from sailing. In the spring we are found all rags, while they, nursed through the tempest, are all trim. I would not have done it; but what would have become of me if, in my preserving the ships, the French had sailed, and effected anything in any quarter! The clamor would have been loud, and they would have sought only for the cause in my treachery or folly, for none can understand that there is any bad weather in the Mediterranean. The system of blockade is ruinous; but it has continued so long, and so much to the advantage of the mercantile part of the nation, that I fear no minister will be found bold enough to discontinue it. We undertake nothing against the enemy, but seem to think it enough to prevent him taking our brigs; his fleet is growing to a monstrous force, while ours every day gives more proof of its increasing decrepitude.

Of the Spaniards I would not say much; I was never sanguine in the prospect of success, and have no reason to change my opinion; the lower class of people, those who are under the influence of priests, would do anything were they under proper direction; but directors are difficult to be found. There is a canker in the state; none of the superior orders are serious in their resistance to the French, and have only taken a part against them thus far from the apprehension of the resentment of the people. I believe the Junta is not free from the taint of the infection, or would they have continued Don Miguel Vives in high and important command after such evident proofs as he gave of want of loyalty? I do not know what is thought of Infantado in England; but in my mind, the man, the Duke (for his rank has a great deal to do with it), who would seat himself in Bonaparte's council at Bayonne, sign his decrees, which were distributed in Spain, and then say he was forced to do it, is not the man who will do much in maintaining the glory or the independence of any country; no such man should be trusted now. The French troops are mostly withdrawn from Spain, except such as are necessary to hold certain strong posts, and enable them to return without impediment. Figueras, Barcelona, and Rosas, are held here in Catalonia, and of course the country quite open to them. Will the Spaniards dispossess them? The Junta does not seem to know anything of the provinces at a distance from them. At Tarragona the troops are ill-clothed, and without pay; on one occasion they could not march against the enemy, having no shoes, and yet at Cadiz they have fifty-one millions of dollars. Cadiz seems to be a general dépôt of everything they can get from England. If they are not active the next two months, Spain is lost.

I hope Lady Dalrymple, &c., &c.

I ever am, my dear sir,

Your very faithful and obedient servant,

COLLINGWOOD.

No. XXX.

SECTION I.—GENERAL STATE OF THE FRENCH ARMY IN SPAIN,

EXTRACTED FROM THE IMPERIAL MUSTER-ROLLS, SIGNED BY THE PRINCE OF NEUFCHATEL.

Commanded by the Emperor Napoleon, in person, 15th Jan., 1809.

Present under arms.		Detached.		Hospital.	Prisoners.	Total.	
Men.	Horses.	Men.	Horses.	Men.	Men.	Men.	Horses.
241,010	48,821	24,549	3,521	58,026	826	324,411	52,342

King Joseph commanding—15th Feb., 1809.

Present under arms.		Detached.		Hospital.	Prisoners.	Total effective.	
Men.	Horses.	Men.	Horses.	Men.	Men.	Men.	Horses.
193,446	33,203	36,326	9,523	56,404	1,843	288,019	42,726

Note.—The imperial guards, the reserve of infantry, and several thousand non-commissioned officers and old soldiers, wanted for the war in Austria, in all about 40,000 men, were struck off the rolls since the last returns.

1st July, 1809.

Pesent under arms.		Detached.		Hospital.	Prisoners and Stragglers.	Total effectiv.	
Men.	Horses.	Men.	Horses.	Men.	Men.	Men.	Horses.
201,082	31,537	19,596	4,513	60,785	7,301	288,766	36,050
		Deduct detached men comprised in governments				19,596	4,513
		Real total............				269,170	31,537

15th July, 1809.

196,144	31,131	19,122	4,608	58,230	8,089	281,585	35,739
		Deduct detached in governments..				19,122	4,608
		Real total............				262,463	31,131

15th August, 1809.

187,560	30,319	12,697	3,930	58,588	7,403	266,248	34,880
		Deduct for governments.........				12,697	3,930
		Real total............				253,551	30,950

SECTION II.—RETURN OF THE FRENCH ARMY BY CORPS.

Troops immediately under the King—1st June, 1809.
The King's guards, about 5000 men, of all arms, are never borne on the rolls.
First corps, Marshal Victor commanding.
Head-quarters, Torremocha.

		Present under arms. Men.	Total. Men.
4 divisions of infantry	41 battalions	21,268	32,819
2 do cavalry	27 squadrons	5,232	7,344
Artillery and equipage	40 companies	2,984	3,610
Number of guns, 48			
	Total present under arms.....	29,484	Grand total 43,773

First corps—21st June, 1809.

Head-quarters, Almaraz.

3 divisions of infantry	33 battalions	18,367	25,633
2 do. cavalry	20 squadrons	4,259	5,762
Artillery and equipage	"	2,535	2,860
	Total present under arms.....	25,161	Grand total 34,255

First corps—15th July, 1809.

Head-quarters, Cazalegas.

3 divisions of infantry	33 battalions	18,890	26,373
2 do cavalry	18 squadrons	3,781	5,080
Artillery and equipage	"	2,586	3,005
	Total present under arms.....	25,257	Grand total 34,458

First corps—1st August, 1809.
Head-quarters, Maqueda.

		Present under arms. Men.	Total. Men.
3 divisions of infantry	33 battalions	15,066	25,068
2 do. cavalry	18 squadrons	4,987	4,983
Artillery and equipage	"	2,362	2,873

Total present under arms..... 22,415 Grand total 32,924

Fourth corps, General Sebastiani—10th July, 1809.
Head-quarters, Alcala.

3 divisions of infantry	27 battalions	17,100	25,960
2 do. cavalry	25 squadrons	3,670	5,859
Number of artillerymen omitted in the returns 30 guns.		"	"

Total present under arms..... 20,770 Grand total 31,819

15th August, 1809.

3 divisions of infantry	27 battalions	14,259	25,801
2 do. cavalry	25 squadrons	3,420	5,801

Total present under arms..... 17,679 Grand total 31,602

Division of Reserve, General Dessolles—15th July, 1809.
Head-quarters, Madrid.

		Present under arms. Men.	Total. Men
1 division of infantry	10 battalions	7,681	10,254
Number of guns unknown.			

Kellermann's division—21st April, 1809.
Head-quarters, Astorga.

	Men.	Horses.	Guns.
Total, composed of detachments	8,753	805	8

10th June, 1809.
Head-quarters, Oviedo.

	Under arms. Men.	Horses.	Total. Men.	Horses.
Total, composed of detachments	7,423	2,549	7,681	2,690

15th July, 1809.
Head-quarters, Valladolid.

8 squadrons 6 guns	2,291	2,360	2,469	2,393

SECTION III.

1st February, 1809.

			Under arms—Men.
Division Lapisse	infantry	12 battalions	7,692
Brigade Maupetit	cavalry	6 squadrons	910

Total under General Lapisse at Salamanca 8,602 sabres and bayonets.
Number of guns and artillerymen unknown.

SECTION IV.—RETURN OF TROOPS UNDER THE IMMEDIATE COMMAND OF
MARSHAL SOULT.

Second corps, Soult—15th July, 1809.

Head-quarters, Toro.

		Present under arms. Men.	Total. Men.
4 divisions of infantry	47 battalions	16,626	35,188
3 do. cavalry	19 squadrons	2,883	4,540
Artillery 40 guns	"	1,081	1,620
	Total present under arms.....	20,590	Grand total 41,348

Fifth corps, Mortier.

Head-quarters, Valladolid.

2 divisions of infantry	24 battalions	15,036	19,541
1 brigade of cavalry	6 squadrons	896	1,491
Artillery 30 guns	"	648	803
	Total present under arms.....	16,580	Grand total 21,835

Sixth corps, Ney.

Head-quarters, Benevente.

2 divisions of infantry	24 battalions	13,700	17,587
1 do. cavalry	10 squadrons	1,446	2,092
Artillery 37 guns	"	1,113	1,293
	Total present under arms.....	16,259	Grand total 20,972

General total under Soult, 15th July, 1809.

95 battalions—35 squadrons 107 guns		53,529	84,155

SECTION V.—TROOPS EMPLOYED IN THE SIEGE OF ZARAGOZA, UNDER MARSHAL
LASNES.

15th January, 1809.

	Present under arms. Men.	Detached. Men.	Hospital. Men.	Total effective. Men.
Third corps	17,406	5,789	13,668	36,863
Fifth corps	18,284	"	4,189	22,473
Total......	35,690	5,789	17,857	59,336

15th February, 1809.

Third corps	16,035	5,891	13,259	35,269
Fifth corps	17,933	1,735	3,859	23,626
Total......	33,968	7,626	17,118	58,895

15th January, 1809.

Present under arms. Men.	Detached. Men.	Hospital. Men.	Prisoners. Men.	Total. Men.	Horses.
41,386	"	6,589	543	48,518	5,403

15th May, 1809.

42,246	2,341	10,243	435	55,265	5,537

15th June, 1809.

42,146	1,699	10,222	406	54,473	5,365

No. XXXI.

SECTION I.—STATE OF SPAIN.

Colonel Kemmis to Sir J. Cradock, December 17, 1808.

" In consequence of the unfavorable news from Spain, yesterday, the populace in Badajos murdered a Spanish colonel, and one or two more of note."

Lieutenant Ellis (an officer employed to gain intelligence) to Colonel Kemmis, Loboa, December 27.

" The French entered Truxillo yesterday, at eleven o'clock ; and from the circumstance of their having reconnoitred the intermediate villages, might be expected to arrive at Merida in two hours after we left it."

Colonel Kemmis to Sir John Cradock, Elvas, December 28.

" Badajos cannot make resistance in any degree, either to check or to stop the progress of the enemy. From the statement made to me last night by the governor, they want *arms, ammunition,* and *provisions.*"—" The enemy marched into Truxillo on the 26th, at half-past twelve o'clock in the day ; but at two on the following morning, a French officer arrived there, and they fell back four leagues."

Lieutenant Ellis to Colonel Kemmis, December 28.

" I proceeded cautiously to Truxillo. The main body of the enemy, six thousand in number, had retired across the bridge of Almaraz, and had not taken the road to Madrid, but had proceeded to Placentia, leaving behind more than half the requisition for money which had been imposed on the town of Truxillo."

Mr. Stuart to Sir John Moore, Seville, January 2, 1809.

" The corps of four thousand infantry and two thousand cavalry, which had marched from Talavera, and had actually passed the bridge of Almaraz, has fallen back, and is already near Placentia, on its way nothward."—"The extreme attention of Bonaparte being at this moment directed to the English army, everything which can be collected is opposed to you alone."

Section II.

Mr. Stuart to Sir J. Moore, December 27, 1808.

" You will receive together with this, several letters from Doyle, which describe events in Catalonia *no way differing from what we have witnessed in other parts of Spain !*"—" The Junta have established themselves here, and whatever may have been the expectation which their alarm on the road may have induced Mr. Frere to form of their future proceedings, *a culpable relapse into their former apathy* seems susceptible of no other remedies but such as will be much stronger than any Spaniard is likely to adopt."—"Although Caro promised to write every particular of his conversation with you to the Junta, I have hitherto been unable to see his letter. I therefore thought it expedient to put the whole to writing, and, *at the same time, to express my conviction both of the justice and propriety of your whole conduct during the late events, when it was impossible, under any circumstances, to have adopted other determination consistently with the safety of the army committed to your charge.* Though I doubt if this will stop the clamor which has been raised on the subject; and though events have probably since taken place, which may materially change the state of affairs, it may be satisfactory to tell you that Mr. Frere *appears* to enter into the reasons alleged by you, and to feel, in their full force, the motives which induced you to act so cautiously, and to ground no operation on the hope of any effectual support from the Spaniards."

Ditto, Seville, January 2.

" The President, Florida Blanca, died two days since, and I was in hopes that the Junta would have availed themselves of this event to make some change in their government. I see, however, little but good disposition, and *am still to look for that* energy in rewarding service and punishing treachery which can alone mend matters."

Ditto, Seville, January 10.

" Reding is at *Tarragona*, expecting to be attacked, and possessing a force composed chiefly of peasantry, but of which he certainly cannot command above ten thousand men in a situation to face his opponents at any given point."—" Whittingham arrived here yesterday, last from the Duke of Infantado's headquarters. He assures me the Duke had already twenty thousand men when he *left Cuenca.*"—" *On the side of Estremadura,* matters are not going on well : Galluzo, who allowed the enemy to pass the bridges, is here prisoner, and his corps is placed under the command of Cuesta. I cannot say, however, that I see much activity since the change ; parties of the enemy cover the country between Madrid and Almaraz, while the corps of six thousand men, which had been pushed forward from Madrid, have, I understand, already passed Placentia, and probably are on the other side of the Puerto, for the purpose of falling on the Salamanca country, and if possible cutting off your communication with Ciudad Rodrigo."

Section III.

Mr. Frere to Mr. Canning, Seville, May 8.

" Besides the advantages which may be looked for from placing so extensive a command under a person of such tried abilities as General Blake, it is to be hoped that it will put an end to the distractions arising from the contracted views of those who directed the provincial Juntas, particularly that of Valencia, which have been so embarrassing to his predecessors."

Ditto, Seville, July 10, 1809.

" As the devastations which have been committed have, in many instances, deprived the peasants of the means of paying what is due to the proprietors and to the church, a general spirit of resistance to all claims of this kind has begun to show itself."

Sir John Cradock to Lord Castlereagh, December 24, 1808.

" I much fear that alarm and despondency have gained ground about Badajos and that part of Spain, and that there is so little co-operation in the acts of their several juntas, and such a want of subordination and common consent among the armed bodies to which the defence of the country is intrusted, against such an united force as that of the French, that extreme confusion prevails every where."

Colonel Kemmis to Sir John Cradock, Elvas, December 30.

" He (Lieutenant Ellis) has been living with General Cuesta for the last two days,"—" who has assured him that the Spanish troops in Madrid forced their way through the French army; and he expressed great sorrow in adding that, though a Spanish force is often collected, the smallest check disperses them; that in few instances dépôts were provided, and those ill supplied," &c.—" that, such was the dispersion and flight of the Spanish armies, between Badajos and Madrid, there did not remain a single man."

Colonel Kemmis to Lieut.-Colonel Reynel, Military Secretary to Sir John Cradock, Seville, February 7, 1809.

" In passing through the Sierra Morena mountains, where nature has done much for the defence of this province, it was painful to observe the pitiful works they were about to throw up. In this whole direction there is but one body that has anything like the appearance of a soldier, viz., dismounted cavalry."

General Mackenzie to Sir John Cradock, Cadiz, February 9, 1809.

" The Spaniards here seemed lulled in the most fatal security. They are ignorant of the events in the North of Spain, or will not give credit when they do hear them. Vague reports of the Emperor of Austria's having declared war, and Bonaparte's return to France, gain unlimited credit." . .
" The equipment of the fleet goes on very slowly, though there is no want of exertion now on the part of Admiral Purvis or Mr. Stuart; offers of every assistance are daily made, but they will neither work themselves, nor permit our people to work for them. The preparations of the ships for carrying off the French prisoners go on equally ill."

Duc de Albuquerque to Mr. Frere, Talavera, July 31, 1809.

" During our marches we stop to repose, like flocks of sheep, without taking up any position, so that, if the enemy knew the condition we were in, they would defeat us wherever they attacked us. If, in the evening of the 26th, I had not gone out directly with my division, and succeeded in checking the enemy, the whole army would have dispersed, and all the artillery and baggage which were in the streets of St. Ollalla would have been lost;

and as a proof of what would have happened, had not the enemy, who was within musket-shot, been checked, for many had already thrown away their arms, &c., the commissaries, abandoning more than fifteen hundred rations of bread, the carts occupying and blocking up the streets of the town; and to this, I repeat, we are daily exposed, as we march as if it were on a pilgrimage, without any regard to distance, order, or method, and with the whole parc of artillery, which ought always to remain at the distance of two, three, or more leagues."

Sir Arthur Wellesley to Lord Wellesley, Merida, September 1, 1809.

"I am much afraid, from what I have seen of the proceedings of the Central Junta, that, in the distribution of their forces, they do not consider military defence and military operations so much as they do political intrigue and the attainment of trifling political objects."

Lord Wellesley to Mr. Canning, Seville, September 2, 1809.

"While the intelligence received from Sir Arthur Wellesley, to the date of the 24th instant, continued to furnish irresistible proofs of the failure of every promise or effort made by this government for the immediate relief of our troops, no satisfaction was afforded to me respecting any permanent plan for their future supply."—"The troops of Portugal, which entered Spain, under General Beresford, suffered similar distress, and experienced similar ill-treatment; although the efforts of Portugal, in the cause of Spain, have been as gratuitous as those of Great Britain; and although Spain possesses no claim, of any description, to the aid of a Portuguese army."—"In this calamity, the people of Spain cannot fail to acknowledge the natural consequences of their own weakness, nor to discover the urgent necessity of enforcing a more steady, pure, and vigorous system, both of counsel and action. A relaxed state of domestic government, and an indolent reliance on the activity of foreign assistance, have endangered all the high and virtuous objects for which Spain has armed and bled. It must now be evident that no alliance can protect her from the inevitable results of internal disorder and national infirmity. She must amend and strengthen her government; she must improve the administration of her resources, and the structure and discipline of her armies, before she can become capable of deriving benefit from foreign aid. Spain has proved untrue to our alliance, because she is not true to herself."—"Until some great change shall be effected in the conduct of the military resources of Spain, and in the state of her armies, no British army can safely attempt to co-operate with the Spanish troops in the territory of Spain."

No. XXXII.

JUSTIFICATORY EXTRACTS FROM SIR J. CRADOCK'S CORRESPONDENCE, MSS.

Section I.—State of Portugal.

Sir J. Cradock to Sir R. Wilson, Oporto, December 8, 1808.

"I press this measure" (to move the legion from Oporto to Villa Real) "upon your adoption, for many reasons, &c., &c.; but the more especially that it will give an impulse to military preparation in general, and tend to eradicate *the notion that, since the evacuation of Portugal by the French, the prospect of a future war is at an end."*

Sir J. Cradock to Sir John Moore, December 9, 1808.

"I have pressed the adoption of such measures as appeared most likely *to revive some notion of danger,* and the necessity of activity and energy."

Sir J. Cradock to Lord Castlereagh, December 14, 1808, Lisbon.

"The inaction of the Regency was apparent at Oporto to a lamentable degree; and, though I saw General Bernadim Freire, I could not gain from him any information as to the state or numbers of the Portuguese troops, where they were stationed, or who commanded them. I apprehend, from his conversation, that the general officers are all of equal authority; and that even seniority had not its usual effect. He concluded his observations to me with the strong expression, '*That, from the evacuation of Portugal by the French, the nation had thought all war at an end.'* "

Sir J. Cradock to Sir John Moore, December 28, 1808.

"Mr. Villiers and myself have both concurred upon the *absolute necessity to arouse and animate the Portuguese to some sense of their situation.*"

Colonel Kemmis to Sir J. Cradock, Elvas, December 30, 1808.

"*The apathy of the Portuguese is not to be expressed.* Their General, Leite, is a most excellent character; a theorist, and, like his countrymen, *supine.*"

Extract from the Report of Lieutenant Brotherton, (an officer employed to obtain intelligence in the north of Portugal,) February 11, 1809. Head-quarters of Romana's army.

"From the totally defenceless state in which the two northern provinces are left, it will require at least eight days (I speak from authority) to prepare anything like adequate means of defence."

Section II.—Lusitanian Legion.

Lord Castlereagh to Sir J. Cradock, November 27, 1808.

"Its formation was proposed by the Chevalier de Souza.—The pay, allowances, and clothing, were settled by the Chevalier de Souza. The former regulated, as I understood, upon the scale *of increased pay, which the provisional government of Oporto had adopted for all the troops they were in progress of levying.*"

Sir J. Cradock to Lord Castlereagh, December 24, 1808.

"I have considerable doubt if ever they " (the legion) " can be incorporated, with effect and conciliation, with the body of the Portuguese army." "They are viewed with *extreme jealousy by the Regency ; and the commanding officers of the Portuguese battalion resisted, universally, the allowing of volunteers from their regiments to enter into the legion.*"

Sir J. Cradock to Lord Castlereagh, January 19, 1809.

" The Lusitanian legion continues to give considerable uneasiness, from its peculiar state, under present circumstances."

Captain Morgan (Lusitanian legion) to Sir J. Cradock, January 19, 1809.

" Should a retreat be adopted, Sir Robert would not retire to Oporto. *It is the government of a mob, of which he has had too much experience.*"

SECTION III.—PORTUGUESE ARMY.

Sir J. Cradock to Sir J. Moore, December 9, 1808.

" I am sorry to state that I find, as far as my limited observation reaches, the Portuguese army, and every other military concern, *in the worst possible state.*"

Sir J. Cradock to Mr. Villiers, December 18, 1809.

" I am sure that the state of the Portuguese army is quite misunderstood in England ; *and that a reliance is placed upon it for the defence of the country that is entirely without foundation.* Their " (Portuguese) " ministers will avow this to you after ten minutes' conversation."—" Even of the reduced numbers of their men enrolled, (not amounting to twenty thousand, at the very highest computation,) to make anything out of them, it is necessary to recur to first principles, and give them *officers, arms, clothing, accoutrements, horses,* &c. ; and I need not say that money is wanting to effect this ; and the ministers positively declare that they have none ; and that no collection of their forces can take place, much less a movement to the frontier, without a supply."—" M. Forjas, secretary to the government, in answer to a strong question from me, stated that *their army have not in their possession ten thousand firelocks fit for use.*"

Sir J. Cradock to Lord Castlereagh, December 24, 1808.

" I am exerting myself to bring to account ' the *supposed* Portuguese army.' "—" Your lordship will perceive that *I talk of the regulars as if it were a regular force ;* but I should be guilty of a deceit, that might lead to bad consequences, if I did not fairly state that *I conceive them to be of no moment at this time.*"

Sir J. Cradock to Mr. Villiers, January 8, 1809.

" I am ready to go to the utmost verge of prudence ; but *Mr. Frere, when he talks of Portuguese troops and arrangements, really* (as I believe you will allow) *fait bâtir les châteaux.*"

Major-General Cotton to Sir J. Cradock, April 7, 1809.

" I yesterday inspected the Portuguese cavalry."—" This cavalry is unformed, and totally unfit for any sort of service."

Sir J. Cradock to Lord Castlereagh, February 12.

" It appears that a report has reached your lordship that a conscription for horses in this country had been attended with great effect, and that above three thousand had been collected. It is, indeed, a matter of serious concern that such *serious misrepresentations* should be transmitted ; for it is a well-known fact that many of the Portuguese regiments of cavalry are *without horses;* and if I am to pursue the subject, their *battalions of infantry are one-half without arms or clothing!* But the total want of all means of regulations for subsistence forms so deplorable a view, in the event of co-operation, that the result, in my opinion, cannot be attended with success. *It is, however, but justice to say, that the disposition of the Portuguese seems well-inclined and faithful to the common cause; and that a very efficient soldiery may be formed under more favorable circumstances.*"

Sir J. Cradock to Mr. Frere, February 27, 1809.

" I fear that your Excellency is led to entertain a more favorable notion of the efficacy of the Portuguese army than, in any shape, it is entitled to. In short, my opinion is that they want everything that constitutes a respectable force, except about ten thousand English arms. I believe they have no others. Many of their *cavalry regiments are without horses, without swords, pistols, &c. Their battalions are not clothed; and, as to subsistence, they live at free quarters upon the villages where they are stationed.* To take the field with effect, or an assurance of food, seems to me out of the question. Since the first moment of my arrival, I wished to procure the advance of a small Portuguese force to Alcantara; but it has been impossible. It is a matter of serious lamentation that such misrepresentations of the Portuguese force should go home, or reach your Excellency."

Sir J. Cradock to Lord Castlereagh, April 3.

" No reliance whatever can be placed upon the Portuguese troops in their present state. *If I said that the whole were ready to mutiny or revolt, I believe I speak General Beresford's sentiments. They will not be commanded by their own officers, and they do just as they please.*"

Section IV.—Conduct of the Regency—Treatment of French Prisoners.

Sir J. Cradock to Mr. Villiers, January 26, 1809.

" I have hitherto directed that these prisoners should be subsisted at our charge, but I have no authority in this measure; they are *in a most deplorable state,* and really are a *disgrace to all concerned.*"

Sir J. Cradock to Mr. Villiers, February 5, 1809.

" It is absolutely necessary that the Regency should give in an answer about the French prisoners. The whole is an unauthorized heavy charge, for which I give my warrant; and I see no end to the case; and, added to this, *their situation is a reflection upon humanity.*"

Section V.—Neglect, Duplicity, and Timidity.

Colonel Kemmis to Sir J. Cradock, Elvas, December 17.

" Lalyppe, on which the very existence of Elvas depends, has not been supplied with provisions as I have been taught to expect."

Colonel Kemmis to Sir J. Cradock, Elvas, December 25.

" The great importance of this fort" (Lalyppe) " is well known to the Portuguese; and, therefore, they are jealous, notwithstanding the miserable condition of their troops, and total incapacity to defend the fort, if attacked."

Sir J. Cradock to Mr. Villiers, December 26, 1808.

"*The promises and apparently satisfactory language of the Portuguese government* are, in my opinion, by no means sufficient to meet the case. *I want to see* some steps actually taken before my mind is decided that the nation will defend itself."—"Indeed, I am told, on good authority, that *the government are afraid to allow the people to arm.*"—"The moment I see any materials to work upon, it will be my most anxious duty to give every effect, &c."—"But, under the present *inactivity and indifference,* it is, &c."

Reports of Colonel Donkin (Quartermaster-General) to Sir John Cradock, March 21.

"I cannot, however, order officers of my department to check this irregularity" (forcing quarters) "*when it originates solely in the neglect of the Portuguese civil magistrates;* for troops will not obey orders, which expose them wantonly to great privations."

Sir J. Cradock to Mr. Villiers, March 25.

"I have repeatedly urged this subject" (quarters of troops) "to the Regency, in the strongest manner, but, as you perceive, without effect."

Sir J. Cradock to Lord Castlereagh, March 17.

"Whatever suits the momentary purpose, upon the most superficial view, seems to be the guide in the Portuguese counsels. Ultimate objects, which, in the course of things, must arrive, are never brought into the calculation."

Cradock to Berkeley, January 17.

"The Regency seems to decline giving any specific directions relative to the guns in fort St. Julian and the river batteries, and, *above all, not to write anything;* but they are very willing to acquiesce in anything we shall do, only anxious that, on a future day, it *shall appear to be our act, not theirs.*"

Admiral Berkeley to Sir J. Cradock, February 19, 1809.

"I imagine Mr. Villiers has transmitted a copy of the extraordinary note sent him by the Regency, in which they complain of the conduct of the artillery officer who dismantled the Bugio fort, and intimate their intention of sending for all the guns and powder from fort St. Julian; and add many particulars, as novel as they are suspicious."—"Whether the language of this note arises from duplicity, or any other cause, it is equally to be resisted; and, therefore, I have stated some facts which may be retorted upon them, and which will not place their conduct in the *most favorable point of view towards either their own sovereign or Great Britain.*"

Extract from an official note, drawn up by Sir John Cradock, Lisbon, February 20, 1809.

"It was told me two or three times, by Mr. Villiers, that M. Forjas, or some other member of the Regency, had expressed extreme solicitude about the forts on the Tagus, &c."—"I always urged Mr. Villiers to get from M. Forjas, or any other member, a declaration of what they wished, that we might exactly conform to it; for they seemed to be anxious to go beyond what we should venture to propose. Mr. Villiers, after some time, told me that the Portuguese government were *unwilling to put down anything upon paper,* or give any specific instruction; but they would willingly leave all the arrangement to us."—"After the above statement, which I declare, upon my honor, to be the accurate description of what has passed, I must express my surprise, and even indignation, at the protest now made by the Regency: and when it is considered that the Bugio fort is often inaccessible for a week together, this part of their complaint is shameful to the highest degree. *Their general object is, however, to be distinguished.*"

Section VI.—Anarchy in Portugal.

Sir J. Cradock to Lord Castlereagh, February 20, 1809.

"*Northern parts.*—It may be difficult to manage any money-transactions in Oporto, for the populace in that town have been suffered to become the masters; and it was only by an exchange of public and private property that the commissariat money has been lately secured."

Sir J. Cradock to Mr. Villiers, February, 1809.

"To gratify a mob, the other day, at Oporto, a guard of the sixtieth regiment was given up, and disarmed by Baron Eben."

Captain Brotherton to Sir J. Cradock, March 17, 1809, Lamego.

"Considering the tumults, and the state of effervescence of the public mind, and the blind fury of the populace—it will neither be so useful nor safe to remain amongst them."

Sir J. Cradock to Lord Castlereagh, March 26, 1809.

"The disposition is good, but the proceedings are those of an ungovernable mob, *exposed to the evil effects of designing persons.*"—"I confine myself to the north of Portugal and Oporto, for the same excesses have not taken place at this side the Douro; but the principles of insubordination, I should fear, would prevail."—"If the confusion and anarchy that prevail at Oporto will permit a defence, some exertion may be expected."—"Ammunition has been abundantly supplied, *but no quantity would meet the consumption expended in the manner it has been in the Tras os Montes;* an attempt to save which was, I believe, the occasion of Bernadim Freire's death."

Sir J. Cradock to Lord Castlereagh, March 30, 1809.

"The anarchy that prevails at Oporto must, I fear, render every exertion unavailable for defence; and such is the ungovernable spirit of the populace, *that it is very difficult to say what part they might take if the proceedings of the British did not suit their views.*"

Sir J. Cradock to Mr. Frere, March 29.

"Oporto and all its concerns, with the Bishop, nominally, at its head, is in the hands of a wild ungovernable populace, *that has already committed the most cruel excesses.* I fear the same spirit exists in what is called the Portuguese army."

Sir J. Cradock to Mr. Frere, January 29, Lisbon.

"Without a British force in Lisbon, the authority of the Regency would pass away, and the scenes of Oporto would take place here."

Report of Captain Lawson, January 30, Lisbon.

"Last night, my servant returning from the post-office was attacked by a party of Portuguese pikemen, headed by one of their own officers, who severely wounded the horse in two places, and slightly in several places, and obliged him, the servant, to put himself under the protection of the guard at the town-major's office, to save his own life; the outrage was committed without the slightest provocation."

General Langworth to Sir J. Cradock, February 1, *Lisbon.*

" The orderly with the general orders, on his way to St. Julian's, was stopped by a Portuguese serjeant and twenty men with pikes; the serjeant forced the orderly to deliver the letter containing the orders, broke it open, read the contents, and returned the inclosed receipt; the same guard stopped Captain Clives, Royal Grenadiers, and Lieutenants Beurman and Liners; these officers were in full uniform."

General Sontag's Official Report, January 3.

" Mr. Usher, deputy-purveyor, and Mr. M'Carty, interpreter, both British subjects, arrived this day from Oporto, went to Moore's hotel, where they were arrested and brought to the Minister of Police. Mr. Usher was in his British uniform."

Sir J. Cradock to Lord Castlereagh, January 30.

" Some unpleasant incidents have lately occurred on the part of the Portuguese armed inhabitants of Lisbon towards British individuals, but I cannot persuade myself that they have proceeded from any fixed evil disposition."—" The British army has not, in any instance, departed from the most regular discipline, and continues to manifest the greatest temper and moderation."—" The excesses on the part of the Portuguese commence by an *uncontrolled pursuit, without any authority from the police, after all persons whom they please to call Frenchmen*, and, in their indiscriminate career, they *often attack every foreigner, and will not even abstain from* those in our service. Those *persons seek refuge in our guard-room*, and though the guards and patrols have positive orders not to interfere under any pretext with the police, yet it is very difficult to smother the feelings of humanity when the wretched persons are flying from a furious and unauthorized rabble. *Mr. Villiers has exerted himself much with the Regency to check this disorder, and prevent the assembly of armed persons in the streets at night, who beat drums and discharge their pieces at all hours; but as yet his remonstrances have not had the desired effect.*"

Mr. Villiers to Sir J. Cradock, January 30.

" Finding the people beat to arms, and paraded about the streets after dark, *on the very evening after the Regency had settled that these irregularities should be restrained*, I addressed the ministers of the home department upon the subject; and as other excesses came to my knowledge, I followed up my complaint."

Sir J. Cradock to Mr. Villiers, January 30.

" I have, this morning, been taking such steps as appear necessary to secure our general situation from insult; and, at the same time, if practicable, not to manifest a distrust in the Portuguese nation, which, if sanctioned from head-quarters, would destroy any reason for our being here. I can assure you, every officer and soldier has received impressions that it is most difficult to act against, but I am determined to persevere in keeping the army from aggression to the last moment."

Sir J. Cradock to Mr. Villiers, February.

" When I reflect upon the frequent declarations of individual members of the Regency, that they cannot control the populace; that there are at least seventy thousand armed inhabitants in Lisbon; that the Regency dare not let them parade (their exercise has been at an end for some time, and the Regency, at this moment, say they cannot look upon themselves as responsible,) it appears impossible that I should depart from the reasoning of my own mind, to meet a sensation of *I do not know whom*, and lessen the proper military appearance of our only guard. We are now beyond the power of surprise or insult, and I cannot, as my own individual act, alter the state of things. However, I never am devoted to my own way of thinking, and if you recommend the measure (the political reasoning, when the enemy is at a distance, may always be weighed against military regulation), or see any good consequences, I will immediately *order back the guns* to their former station in the artillery barracks."

Marshal Beresford to Sir J. Cradock, April 7, Santarem.

" I, this morning, met no less than *three expresses*, communicating to me the *horrible state of mutiny, for I can call it no less, in which the troops everywhere are, and the inhabitants are in equal insubordination, and they encourage each other. I find two or three regiments have marched away (to what they call to oppose the enemy)* where they pleased, in despite of their officers and generals, who are entirely commanded by them. This you will say is a pleasing state to be in; however, we must face it, and I hope for the best result, and I am sanguine enough to look for such. Colonel Trant will shortly have a pretty strong corps, if the regiments continue thus to volunteer for him."

Mr. Villiers to Sir J. Cradock, February 15.

" I should almost doubt whether the British subjects *could be left in safety in Lisbon*."

Section VII.—False Intelligence.

Sir J. Cradock to Colonel Donkin.

" I believe it is certain that we cannot depend upon the activity of the Portuguese government upon this head," (intelligence,) " either as to promptitude or security."

Colonel Donkin to Sir J. Cradock, January 1, Lisbon.

" Experience has *shown how utterly impossible it is to get correct intelligence here;* an enemy may be within four or five days' march of this city before it is known, unless he attacks on the very line our troops occupy."

Sir J. Cradock to Mr. Frere, March 29.

" It is singular how imperfectly all intelligence, though of such important events, reaches this, and we have not had, for two days, any account from Oporto."

Sir J. Cradock to Lord Castlereagh, March 26.

" Yesterday the Chevalier de Castro stated, from authority, a movement on the part of the French, quite different from a *direct report* from the Junta of Badajos."

No. XXXIII.

Section I.—Extracts from Sir John Cradock's Instructions.

Lord Castlereagh to Sir J. Cradock, December 24, 1808.

" Upon the actual approach of the enemy towards Lisbon in such strength as may render further resistance ineffectual, you will take care that measures may be taken in due time for withdrawing both the British army and *such Portuguese as may be desirous of accompanying it.*"—" The British Admiral will be directed to take effectual measures, with your assistance, for depriving the enemy of all the resources, more especially those of a naval description, which the Tagus contains. Everything of a naval and military description, that cannot be brought away, must, in the last extremity, be destroyed."

Lord Castlereagh to Sir J. Cradock, November 25, 1808.

" I am to signify His Majesty's pleasure that, in the event of any application being made to you from the Regency of Portugal, on the subject of the occupation of the fortresses with His Majesty's troops, you do *refer the subject to Mr. Villiers,* who has received instructions, &c., and you will not make any alteration as to the mode prescribed for garrisoning the fortresses *without directions from Mr. Villiers.*"

Extracts from certain queries put to Lord Castlereagh by Sir J. Cradock, with the answers thereto.

Query.	Answer.
" What may be the situation of my command?"	" The relations with the government of Portugal will be arranged when Mr. Villiers arrives."
" In what light is the force under my command to be considered?" &c., &c.	" Ditto."
" May any Portuguese battalions be levied for English pay?"	" The taking Portuguese battalions into English pay will, if adopted, be managed *through Mr. Villiers.*"
" If any want of provisions should appear in Portugal, may I be allowed to adopt measures in conjunction with the Regency, for obtaining a supply?"	" The general measures of supplying Portugal with provisions will be *referred to Mr. Villiers.*"
" If any Portuguese corps can be got into such forwardness as to be fit to enter Spain, and they should be willing to join Sir John Moore, are they to be put on British pay?"	" *Mr. Villiers will be authorized* to enter upon the discussion of this subject with the Regency, availing himself of your assistance," &c.

END OF VOL. I.

folio 6a

WAB LIBRARY